# MELODY BOBER
# Just for Fun
## BOOK 1

### Notes from the Publisher

*Composers In Focus* is a series of original piano collections celebrating the creative artistry of contemporary composers. It is through the work of these composers that the piano teaching repertoire is enlarged and enhanced.

It is my hope that students, teachers, and all others who experience this music will be enriched and inspired.

*Frank J Hackinson*

Frank Hackinson, Publisher

### Notes from the Composer

As teachers, we know how excited our students are when at times we pull out pieces simply for enjoyment—selections that are not too difficult or demanding, can be learned (and even memorized) quickly and easily and with exciting motives and patterns . . . pieces that are "just for fun."

Introducing *Just for Fun*—a late elementary/early intermediate collection to be used specifically for that purpose, while at the same time serving to review and reinforce concepts from any lesson.

I hope your students will enjoy these pieces as a special treat during those times they want to play . . . just for fun.

*Melody Bober*

Melody Bober

# Contents

# Spirit of the West

Melody Bober

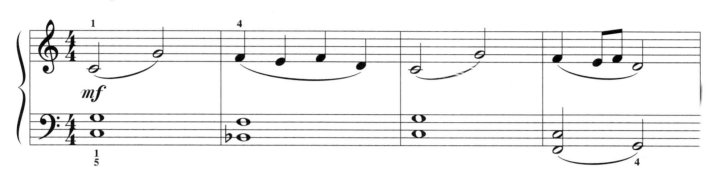

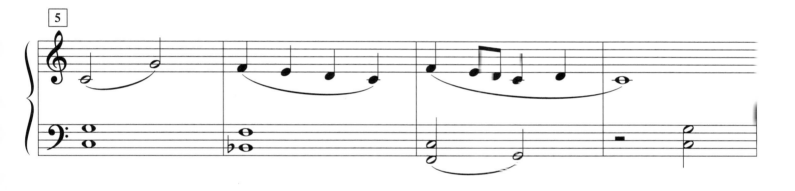

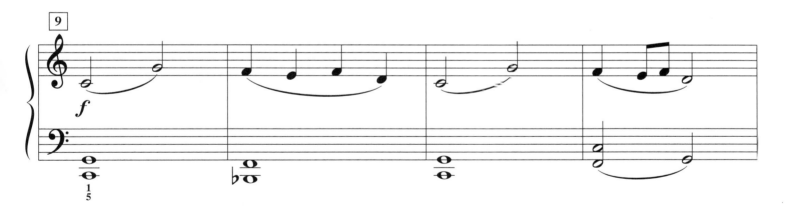

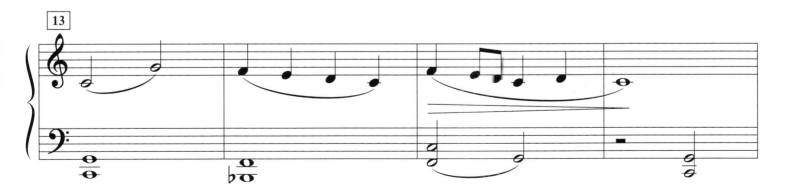

FF1337

4

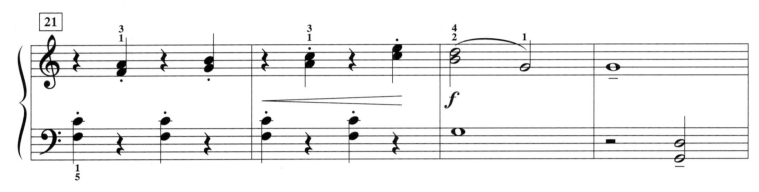

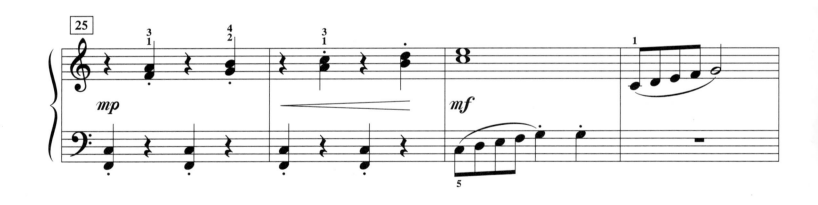

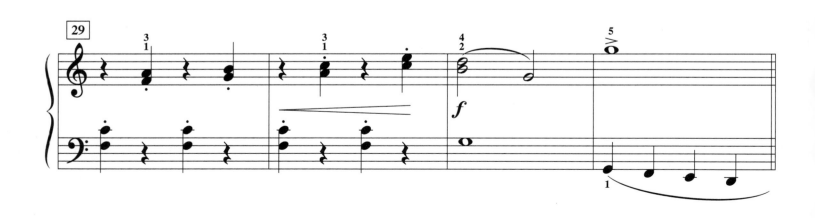

FF1337

# The Night Horseman

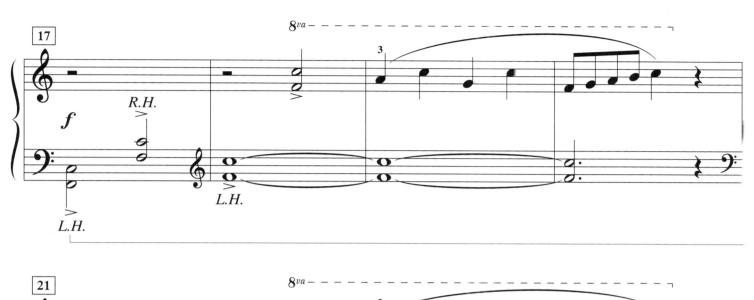

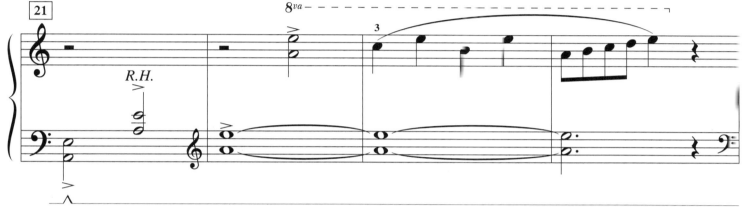

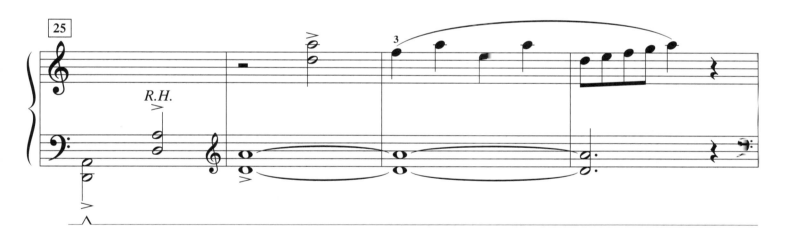

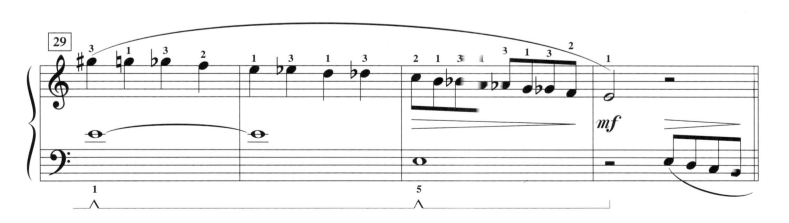

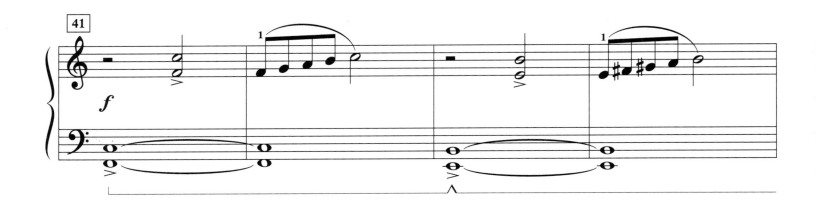

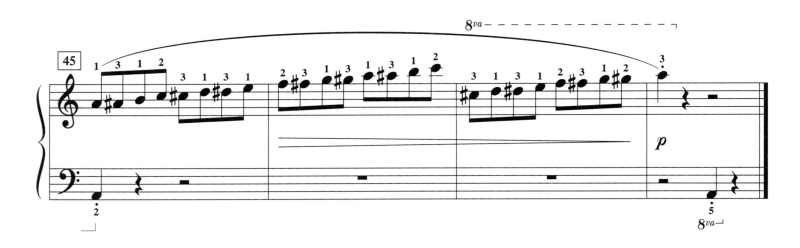

# Fun in the Sun

10

FF1337

11

# Warrior Brave

FF1337

12

# Creepy Cat

**Mysteriously** (♩ = ca. 168)

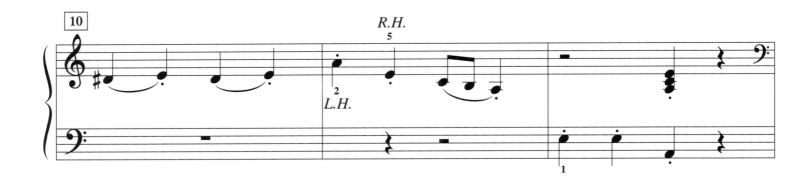

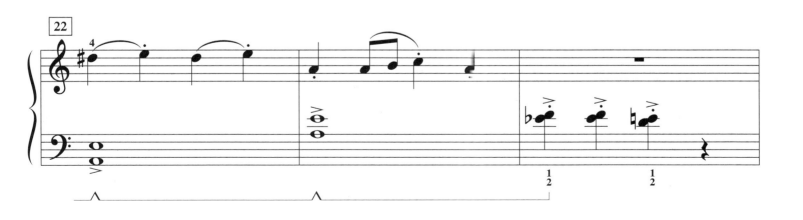

# Just a Little Waltz

# Heading Out to Sea

# Just Jazzin'

**Playfully** (♩ = ca. 116) (even ♫s)

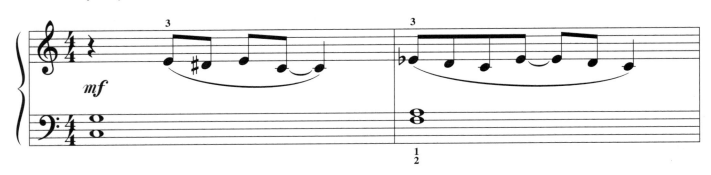

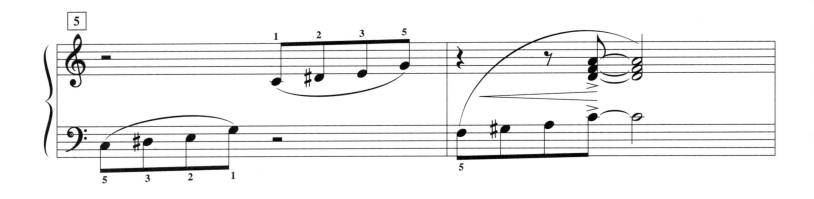

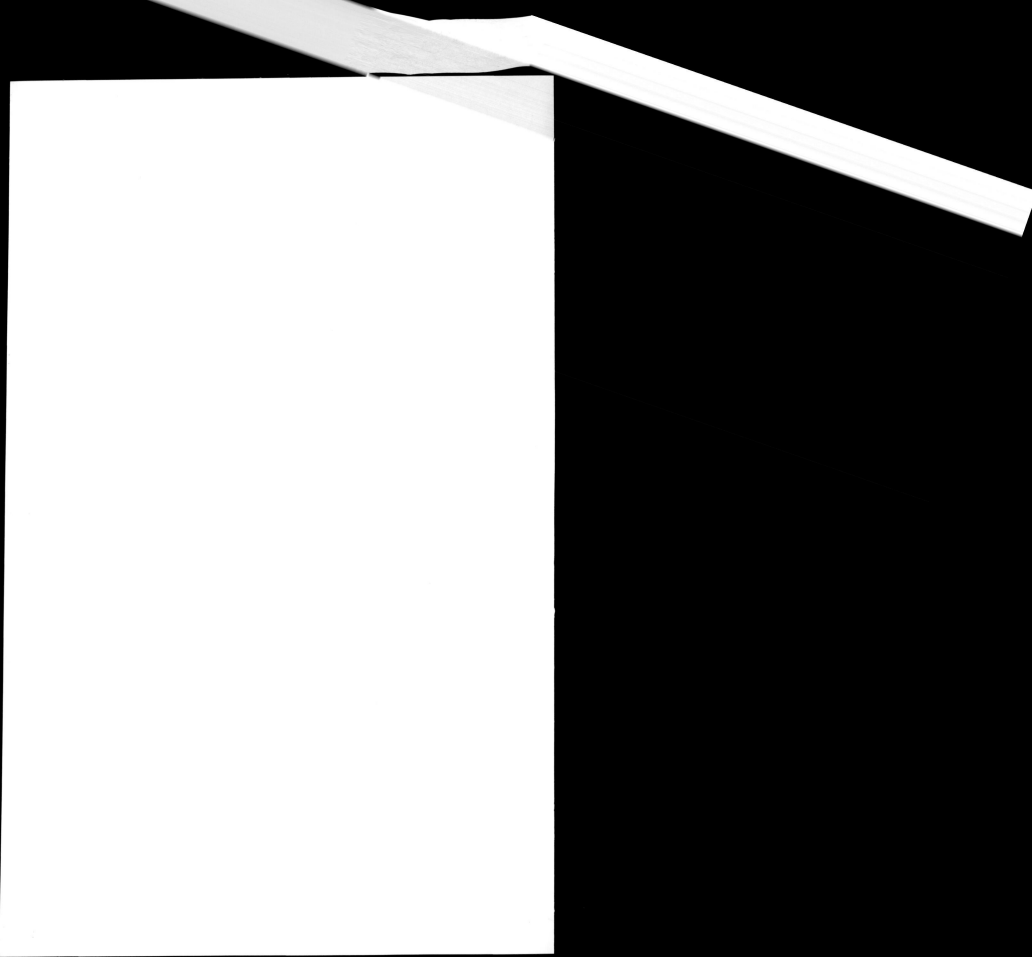

# CULTURE IN PIECES

# OXFORD
### UNIVERSITY PRESS

Great Clarendon Street, Oxford OX2 6DP

Oxford University Press is a department of the University of Oxford.
It furthers the University's objective of excellence in research, scholarship,
and education by publishing worldwide in

Oxford New York

Auckland Cape Town Dar es Salaam Hong Kong Karachi
Kuala Lumpur Madrid Melbourne Mexico City Nairobi
New Delhi Shanghai Taipei Toronto

With offices in

Argentina Austria Brazil Chile Czech Republic France Greece
Guatemala Hungary Italy Japan Poland Portugal Singapore
South Korea Switzerland Thailand Turkey Ukraine Vietnam

Oxford is a registered trade mark of Oxford University Press
in the UK and in certain other countries

Published in the United States
by Oxford University Press Inc., New York

British Library Cataloguing in Publication Data
Data available

Library of Congress Cataloging in Publication Data
Data available

Library of Congress Control Number: 2011923760

Typeset by RefineCatch Limited, Bungay, Suffolk
Printed in Great Britain
on acid-free paper by
MPG Books Group, Bodmin and King's Lynn

ISBN 978–0–19–929201–1

1 3 5 7 9 10 8 6 4 2

"ὡς κομψὸς χαρίεις τ᾽ ἀνήρ"
ἀλλήλοις ὁμοθυμαδὸν
"κἀγχίνους" ψιθυρίζομεν.
σοὶ δ᾽ ὦ τᾶν ἀπὸ καρδίας
    ᾄσομαι μέλος ἡδύ·

"χαῖρε, φίλτατε φιλτάτων,
σὺν θεοῖς γεγονὼς πάλαι
τῶν παπυρολόγων πρόμος
κἀν βροτοῖς κλέος ἀξίως
    ἔξων οὐρανόμηκες.

σωτὴρ γὰρ κατὰ τὴν ἐμὴν
εἶ σὺ τῶν προτέρων μέγας·
μάρτυς Στησίχορός τε χὠ
κλεινὸς Βαττιάδης, θροῶν
    νίκην τὴν Βερενίκης."

                        †C.A.

# *Preface*

This volume originated in a conference with the same title which the editors organized in Christ Church, Oxford, between 20 and 23 September 2006 in honour of Professor Peter Parsons's seventieth birthday, which fell on 24 September. We are grateful to the Delegates of the Oxford University Press for accepting a proposal for a book based on the proceedings, and especially to Hilary O'Shea, who took an interest in the project from its inception.

The conference assembled an international team of scholars who are either former pupils or colleagues of Peter Parsons, and who all share a deep respect for his work. The title of the conference, 'Culture in Pieces' (a quotation from the structuralist critic Roland Barthes), alluded to the problems of reconstitution of tattered papyri and reconstruction of historical and cultural contexts from fragmentary evidence: other implications are discussed in Dirk Obbink's essay. Many though not all contributors tackled specifically papyrological topics, but the general aim was more broadly conceived: to consider how the discovery of new evidence, especially new literary texts, has fertilized or enlarged the study of older evidence, either by setting the old in new light, or by enabling us to ask new questions. Many members of the Classics faculty attended, as did scholars and graduate students from Oxford and elsewhere. Some of the papers were attended by as many as eighty listeners. Time for discussion was allowed after each paper; Professor Parsons himself took an active part.

It was obvious from the start that we could not invite all those who might wish to pay tribute to Peter Parsons, and no disrespect is intended to those whom we did not include in the original invitation. Some scholars whom we approached were unable to accept the invitation to speak, but joined us in person for the event or communicated their good wishes by post and email. One name deserves special mention. We had hoped that Sir Hugh Lloyd-Jones, Peter Parsons's predecessor and long-term collaborator, might be able to play a part in celebrating his successor, but his state of health made this impossible. He was, however, aware of our plans and warmly approved of them. His death in October 2009 is a sad loss to scholarship. We must also record with deep regret the death of one of our contributors, Professor Colin Austin, who was responsible not only for his own chapter but for the dedicatory poem prefaced to the collection.

For the delay in publication the editors must accept the responsibility. Our sluggishness has however meant that our contributors were in a position to cite texts published in P.Oxy. LXXIII (2009), a volume dedicated to Peter Parsons and John Rea, which includes editions of several new texts referred to in the present volume. It also makes it possible for us to record with delight the award of not one but two prizes to our honorand for his book *City of the Sharp-Nosed Fish*: it received the John D. Criticos prize from the Hellenic Foundation in 2007 and the Classical Association Prize in 2008.

The Introduction to this volume is new: Part I offers an account of Peter Parsons's career and character, Part II describes the relation of the papers in this volume to his work and to one another, indicating thematic connections and recurring ideas running through the volume. Of the actual contributions to the conference, all but one appear here in revised and sometimes expanded form. The exception is the paper by Nick Gonis, on 'Papyrology and Greek Poetry in Late Antiquity and Beyond'. We regret that due to the pressure of other commitments, Dr Gonis was unable to provide a version of this paper in a form which he felt would be worthy of the honorand. We hope that the results of his researches in this area will be published elsewhere in the near future. The volume also contains a complete bibliography of Peter Parsons's publications to date: items published up to the summer of 2010 have been included.

For financial support for the conference we are deeply grateful to the British Academy, the Society for the Promotion of Hellenic Studies, the Faculty of Classics at Oxford, the Craven Committee, the Jowett Trust, and the Governing Body of Christ Church. For permission to reprint the photograph of Peter Parsons we thank the original photographer, Jane Bown.

Finally, we owe a great debt to the skill and expertise of the Press, and (like so many others) to Dr Leofranc Holford-Strevens, a copy-editor without peer.

D.O.
R.B.R.

# Contents

# List of Illustrations

*Plates*

reproduced in W. Blake, *Songs of Innocence and Experience*, ed. with
introduction and commentary by G. Keynes (Oxford, 1970). Reproduced
by permission of Oxford University Press

15. Eos abducting Cephalus: pinax, Selinus Temple E: inv. nos. S84TE/1009
and 1045; 550–520 BC. Image from M. C. Conti, 'Il mito di Eos e Kephalos
in un pinax da Selinunte', *Boll. di Arch.* 51–2 (1998) 35, fig. 3; reproduced
with permission of the author

16. P.Oxy. LXX 4762 Ass romance. Papyrology Rooms, Sackler Library, Oxford

# Abbreviations and Conventions

Abbreviations for Greek and Latin authors and works normally follow the system set out in *OCD*, pp. xxix–liv. Abbreviations for collections of papyrus texts follow the system recommended in the *Checklist of Editions of Greek, Latin, Demotic, and Coptic Papyri, Ostraca and Tablets* (http://scriptorium.lib. duke.edu/papyrus/texts/clist.html). Abbreviations of periodical titles, where not listed in *OCD*, may be elucidated from *L'Année philologique*.

Fragmentary texts are cited from the editions generally considered standard: Merkelbach–West for Hesiod, Snell–Maehler for Pindar, Pfeiffer for Callimachus unless a better text is available in *SH* or elsewhere, and so forth. Abbreviated titles for collections of fragments and collaborative works are normally again as in *OCD*, but a few of the most common are listed below for convenience.

| | |
|---|---|
| A–B | C. F. L. Austin and G. Bastianini (edd.) *Posidippi Pellaei quae supersunt omnia* (Milan, 2002) |
| *CA* | J. U. Powell (ed.) *Collectanea Alexandrina* (Oxford, 1925) |
| *CAH* | *Cambridge Ancient History* (2nd edn., Cambridge, 1961–2005) |
| *CEG* | P. A. Hansen (ed.) *Carmina Epigraphica Graeca* (Berlin, 1983–9) |
| *FGrH* | F. Jacoby (ed.) *Die Fragmente der griechischen Historiker* (Berlin and Leiden, 1923–58) |
| *LIMC* | *Lexicon Iconographicum Mythologiae Classicae* (Zurich, 1981–99) |
| Mertens–Pack | P. Mertens, R.A. Pack, updated online version of Pack, accessible at http://promethee.philo.ulg.ac.be/cedopal |
| *OCD* | *Oxford Classical Dictionary*, 3rd edn., ed. S. Hornblower and A. J. Spawforth (Oxford, 1996, rev. 2003). |
| Pack | R. A. Pack, *The Greek and Latin Literary Texts from Greco-Roman Egypt*, 2nd edn. (Ann Arbor, MI, 1965) |
| *PCG* | R. Kassel and C. Austin (eds.) *Poetae Comici Graeci* (Berlin, 1983– ) |
| *PMG* | D. L. Page (ed.) *Poetae Melici Graeci* (Oxford, 1962) |
| Powell | see *CA* |
| *SH* | H. Lloyd-Jones and P. J. Parsons (eds.), *Supplementum Hellenisticum* (Berlin, 1983) |

# Notes on Contributors

**Colin Austin** was a Fellow of Trinity Hall, Cambridge from 1965 to 2008, and subsequently an Emeritus Fellow. He published an edition of the papyrus fragments of Euripides (*Nova Fragmenta Euripidea*, 1968), a commentary (with S. D. Olson) on Aristophanes' *Thesmophoriazusae* (2004), and numerous other works, especially on Old and New Comedy. In particular he co-edited with R. Kassel all volumes so far published of *Poetae Comici Graeci*. He died in August 2010.

**Eric Handley** is Emeritus Regius Professor of Greek at the University of Cambridge. He has published extensively both on papyrology and on Greek comedy, above all on Menander. His commentary on Menander's *Dyskolos* (1965) remains standard.

**Annette Harder** is Professor of Ancient Greek Language and Literature at the University of Groningen. She has published an edition with commentary of Euripides' *Kresphontes* and *Archelaus* (1985), as well as organizing and editing the proceedings of the series of Groningen Hellenistic Workshops. Her edition of Callimachus' *Aetia* is forthcoming from Oxford University Press.

**Albert Henrichs** is Eliot Professor of Greek Literature at Harvard University. He has published extensively on Greek literature, religion, and myth, as well as on important texts found in papyri. His major areas of research include the Greek god Dionysus and his modern reception, the representation of ritual in literature and art, the religious self-awareness of the Greeks, and the history of classical scholarship since 1800. He is the author of *Die Phoinikika des Lollianos* (1972), and of many subsequent articles on the ancient novel.

**Adrian Hollis** is an Emeritus Fellow of Keble College, Oxford, where he was Tutor in Classics for much of his career. He is the author of commentaries on Ovid, *Metamorphoses* 8 (1970) and *Ars Amatoria* 1 (1977), on Callimachus' *Hecale* (1990, 2nd edn. 2009), and on *Fragments of Roman Poetry c.60 BC–AD 20* (2007).

**Richard Hunter** is Regius Professor of Greek at Cambridge University. He is the author of monographs and commentaries on (among others) Apollonius and Theocritus. His most recent publications include *The Shadow of Callimachus* (2006) and *Critical Moments in Classical Literature* (2009).

**Gregory Hutchinson** is Professor of Greek and Latin Languages and Literature at Oxford and a Fellow of Exeter College. His recent publications include *Greek Lyric Poetry: A Commentary on Selected Larger Pieces* (2001), a commentary on Propertius' fourth book (2006), and *Talking Books: Readings in Hellenistic and Roman Books of Poetry* (2008).

**Giulio Massimilla** is Professor of Classical Philology at the Università degli Studi di Napoli Federico II, Naples. In 1996 he published the first volume of a major edition of Callimachus' *Aetia*, and the second volume, completing the work, appeared in 2010.

**Heinz-Günther Nesselrath** is Full Professor of Classics (Greek Literature) at the Seminar für Klassische Philologie, Georg-August-Universität, Göttingen. His research interests include Greek literature of the Roman imperial period, classical Greek comedy, and Greek historiography, both classical and Christian. Among his many publications are *Lukians Parasitendialog: Untersuchungen und Kommentar* (1985), *Die attische Mittlere Komödie: Ihre Stellung in der antiken Literaturkritik und Literaturgeschichte* (1990), (as editor) *Einleitung in die griechische Philologie* (1999), *Platon, Kritias: Übersetzung und Kommentar* (2006), and *Plutarch, On the* Daimonion *of Socrates* (2010).

**Dirk Obbink** is University Lecturer in Papyrology and Greek Literature at Oxford and Tutor in Greek at Christ Church, Oxford. He is director and a general editor of *The Oxyrhynchus Papyri* series. He has edited the Herculaneum papyrus roll containing Philodemus' *De pietate*, as well as editing the collections *Magika Hiera, Philodemus and Poetry,* and *The Language of the Papyri.*

**Christoph Riedweg** is Professor of Classics at the University of Zurich and (since 2005) Director of the Swiss Institute in Rome. His publications include *Mysterienterminologie bei Platon, Philon und Klemens von Alexandrien* (1987), *Ps.-Justin (Markell von Ankyra?), Ad Graecos de vera religione* (1994), and *Pythagoras: Leben—Lehre—Nachwirkung. Eine Einführung* (2002, Eng. tr. 2005).

**Richard Rutherford** is Tutor in Greek and Latin Literature at Christ Church, Oxford. His publications include *The Meditations of Marcus Aurelius: A Study* (1989), a commentary on Homer, *Odyssey* 19 and 29 (1992), *The Art of Plato* (1995), and *Classical Literature, a concise history* (2005).

**Susan Stephens** is Professor of Classics at Stanford University. Her special interest is in the political and social dimensions of Hellenistic literature. *Seeing Double: Intercultural Poetics in Ptolemaic Alexandria*, a study that situates Alexandrian poetry in its Greek and Egyptian political context, appeared in 2003. Trained as a papyrologist and taught by Peter Parsons, she has edited (with Jack Winkler) *Ancient Greek Novels: The Fragments* (Princeton 1995). She is also a co-editor of a forthcoming Companion to Callimachus.

**Martin West** was until his retirement in 2004 a Senior Research Fellow of All Souls, and formerly Professor of Greek at Royal Holloway College, London. Amongst his many publications are editions of the *Iliad* (1998–2000) and of Aeschylus (1990, revised 1998), commentaries on Hesiod's *Theogony* (1966) and *Works and Days* (1978), and numerous monographs, including most recently *The East Face of Helicon* (1997), *Indo-European Poetry and Myth* (2007), and *The Making of the* Iliad (2011).

**Stephanie West** is an Emeritus Fellow of Hertford College, Oxford, and author of *The Ptolemaic Papyri of Homer* (1967) and of the commentary on books 1–4 of the *Odyssey* in the complete commentary on the poem published by Mondadori and subsequently in an English version by Oxford. She is currently working on a commentary on book 4 of Herodotus.

**Michael Winterbottom** was Corpus Christi Professor of Latin until his retirement in 2001. He has edited numerous Latin authors, among them Cicero (*de officiis*), Seneca the Elder, Quintilian, Tacitus (minor works), and Gildas, as well as publishing widely on Latin texts of all periods. His most recent works include a major edition (with R. M. Thomson) of some of the writings of William of Malmesbury.

# Introduction*

*Richard Rutherford and Dirk Obbink*

I

A young American classicist, about to move to a position in Oxford some years ago, was told by a London colleague 'Watch out for Peter Parsons—the nicest man in Oxford.' Niceness, however defined, does not automatically entitle a person to a Festschrift, but the warmth of this tribute is reflected in the personal enthusiasm and affection with which the contributors to this volume have responded to our invitation, and in order to account for this, something should be said of Parsons the man as well as the professor and scholar.[1]

Peter John Parsons was born in 1936 and educated at what he described as 'a neoteric grammar school', Raynes Park County Grammar. The founding headmaster was a friend of W. H. Auden, who had composed the school song. An early interest was genealogy, as the future scholar tried to organize on a chart the tangled relationships of the European royal families. More important, his teachers (notably Alan Cholmondeley) introduced him to the ancient languages: Latin was systematically taught but Greek even then was 'more of a broom-cupboard affair'. Already at fifteen he 'became fascinated with the strange symbols of the ancient Greek alphabet, and discovered that, with some grammar and a dictionary, it was possible to make sense of the high poetry encoded in these symbols.'[2] 'I was clearly a scholarly person,

---

* Section I of the introduction is by Rutherford, section II by Obbink. But we have discussed each other's drafts extensively, and the combined version represents a shared view, except where the first person singular in R.B.R's section indicates personal reminiscence.

[1] Apart from the brief entry in *Who's Who*, I have drawn on a short piece (Parsons 2003) that Peter Parsons contributed in the year of his retirement to *Christ Church Matters*, a newsletter sent out to alumni (issue no. 11, Trinity Term 2003); also on the preface to Parsons 2007, and on a text of the unpublished inaugural lecture which he delivered in 1990. Some other details derive from many conversations over the last 25 or so years; quotations not supplied with a footnote usually derive from particular exchanges during the period of drafting of this introduction.

[2] Parsons 2007, p. xxv.

escaping from life into books,' he later remarked. The Parsons family had no
university background, and the recently founded institution was not one of
the traditional public schools, with decades of experience of sending people
to Oxford and Cambridge; with no more concrete basis for planning, it was
decided that Parsons should make Christ Church his first choice because it
was the first college alphabetically in the first of the three groups into which,
then and for a long time after, the colleges were divided for admissions purposes. In December 1953, attired in his first suit, he took the Oxford entrance
examination, which in those days was actually sat in the individual college
halls, from which candidates were summoned for interview with the tutors in
the subject. The college was cold but the rabbit pie was good. Admission as an
undergraduate at Christ Church ensured that the next four years would be
devoted to his chosen subject, under the guidance of scholars of exceptional
distinction: John Gould, a young and innovative tutor with a broader vision
of Classics than most of those in post (offering not just instruction in Greek
and Latin prose composition but comparisons between Greek tragedy and
Noh drama, and a readiness to see Pound's Propertius as more than just
a melange of mistranslations); David Lewis, whose high standards and
precision in the handling of fragmentary evidence set a sometimes daunting
example; and especially Eric Gray, 'who explained Roman frontiers as one
who had walked them', and with whom Parsons later travelled in the Near
East. E. R. Dodds and W. S. Barrett gave influential classes on Greek tragic
texts; on the Latin side, he received much stimulus and encouragement from
J. G. Griffith, expert and entertaining lecturer on Juvenal, and was impelled
to compete for the Chancellor's Prize in Latin Verse with some Juvenalian
hexameters denouncing the immorality and stylistic feebleness of Ovid. This
and other undergraduate prizes were among the early signs of recognition of
his remarkable grasp of Greek and Latin language and style. Another indication that he was recognized by his tutor as no ordinary undergraduate was
John Gould's suggestion that he accompany him to hear a paper on Catullus
at the Oxford Philological Society, in those days a holy of holies attended only
by eminent scholars.

  Christ Church was to remain a base and a home, though after graduation
(1958) there was an interval in lodgings in St Margaret's Road. On the advice
of Dodds, he began to study papyrology.[3] Edgar Lobel (1888–1982), the
titan of the subject, had retired in 1952 but was still working away in Queen's

[3] With the ironic self-deprecation which we shall frequently meet in his work, Parsons writes:
'(Dodds said) that in the Oxford context two areas particularly needed research and the teaching
that might follow from it, Papyrology and Greek Religion. I thought, rightly, that Greek religion
would require more subtlety and imagination than I possessed; papyrology, on the other hand,
depended in the most concrete way on the process of decoding from which I had started'
(Parsons 2007, p. xxv). Any suggestion that Peter Parsons might be incapable of studying
religious belief and practice is sufficiently refuted by the final chapter of the masterly survey
prefaced by these remarks.

College.[4] But Parsons needed less Olympian guides: his mentors in Oxford (J. W. Barns) and in Michigan (H. Youtie) are brilliantly characterized in the preface to *City of the Sharp-Nosed Fish*. After a year in Michigan learning the minutiae of documentary papyrology, he returned to Oxford and discovered that in his absence the university had created a position in this subject and appointed him to it (1960). Later Barns, who had been the specialist in literary papyri, became Professor of Egyptology and Parsons switched tracks, subsequently performing with equal dexterity as interpreter of documentary and literary discoveries. John Rea, a pupil of Eric Turner in London, arrived in Oxford and took over the documents; this arrangement prevailed from 1965 to 1989, and in that period many of the volumes published by the Egypt Exploration Society in the Oxyrhynchus Papyri series bear the names of Parsons and Rea as editors or contributors. During the same period, many undergraduates and graduates came to work with Parsons or Rea, intrigued by the appearance on the termly lecture list of the regular invitation to 'Papyrology: informal instruction'. Meanwhile John Gould, his former tutor, regularly sent some pupils to Parsons for teaching of a more literary kind (Pindar was a longstanding favourite), and eventually Christ Church was induced to offer him first some meal rights in token payment, then a college attachment (as a 'Research Student', a curious category carrying more kudos than the name might suggest) and living accommodation within the college. From 1964 until retirement Peter Parsons could be found in the remarkable second-floor flat in the seventeenth-century Killcanon building, squeezed between a canon's gardens and the western perimeter of the majestic Peckwater quadrangle. Here countless undergraduate pupils, academic visitors, and aspiring scholars came and admired the view, the flourishing papyrus plants in the window-box, the massive collection of books, and the magnifying glass and microscope which in the days before digital imaging provided the essential tools for the decipherment of unpublished papyri.

As a member of the college's Governing Body but not an actual tutor, Peter Parsons occupied the role of an interested observer: he served loyally on committees ('The papers of the Committee on Domestic Comfort deserve a place in the archives'), including those which appointed younger classical tutors, and played a regular part in the teaching of language and literature to undergraduates reading Classics and studying for the examinations long known in Oxford as Mods and Greats. His classes on prose composition were legendary; on a different tack, he recalls teaching the Acts of the Apostles, then a Mods set book, at 8.00 a.m. to an undergraduate desperate to get out on the cricket pitch. But he did not have a rigidly defined role in the college's teaching and administrative structure until the early 1980s, when he took on

---

[4] Parsons, Rea, and Turner 1983, p. v acknowledged the debt of the series to his work: 'With him died the heroic age.'

the increasingly demanding role of Tutor for Graduates, a position he held for six years: characteristically he saw it as an essential part of the job to organize buffet lunches for batches of graduates. In the Faculty, apart from the papyrology classes, he sometimes offered more synthesizing courses, including a series on Roman Egypt which powerfully impressed the abler in the audience. His broad range of interests encouraged the Faculty to use him as an examiner in the first year that the revised syllabus introduced Literature as an option alongside the traditional pairing of Ancient History and Philosophy: among the powerful performers that year were Robert Parker, John Moles, and Charles Martindale.

But all this was in a way marginal to what was during three decades his chief concern, the continuing publication of the massive holdings of the Oxyrhynchus collection. When he was appointed to his position as University Lecturer in Papyrology, the overall management of the Oxyrhynchus collection was coordinated on behalf of the Egypt Exploration Society by E. G. (later Sir Eric) Turner, Professor of Papyrology at University College London, and by E. C. Skeat of the British Museum. For many years Turner assigned the texts to Parsons and Rea, who eventually became joint editors of the series. The magnitude of this task is not to be underrated: either one or both went through all contributions with a fine-tooth comb, checking drafts against the papyrus, removing obscurity, tidying presentation, and imposing consistency. Through Turner's initiative the British Academy adopted the Oxyrhynchus Papyri as one of its Major Research Projects in 1966. Around the same time Revel Coles, another long-term colleague and friend, was appointed as curator of the collection; he also often contributed to the editorial process. 'The systematic conservation, cataloguing, and photography of the papyri began; and their publication became a collaboration, in which the Academy financed the technical work, the Egypt Exploration Society the printing, and the Universities of London (University College) and Oxford (the Ashmolean [subsequently the Sackler] Library and the Faculty of Literae Humaniores [subsequently the Faculty of Classics] provided premises and manpower.'[5]

From 1966 to 2007 Parsons made substantial contributions to 16 volumes of the series, and in 1973 volume 42 was entirely his own work—46 texts, literary, subliterary and documentary, including writings as various as Hesiod, the lubricious Greek novel on Iolaus, martyr-acts from Alexandria, and letters of Augustus and Trajan. There were also supplementary articles in learned journals, often setting out in more detail both the logic of the reconstruction and the literary-historical significance of these finds. One such paper, 'A Greek Satyricon?', has achieved classic status in its redrawing of the

---

[5] Parsons 1987, 696.

map of the development of the Greek and Roman novel.[6] But much of his most significant work ranged further afield than the Oxyrhynchus collection, vast though it is. In collaboration with the Professor of Latin, Robin Nisbet, he published the *editio princeps* of the Gallus papyrus from Qaṣr Ibrîm, following it up with a more light-hearted treatment in which he questioned the poet's merits.[7] Perhaps his most important single article was the 50-page paper on the Lille fragments of Callimachus' *Aetia*, published in 1977, which not only made sense of some extraordinarily difficult and recalcitrant material but rendered all previous discussion of the structure of Callimachus' poem virtually obsolete.[8] The same year, in the very next issue of the same journal, saw an almost equally important paper on the new fragments of Stesichorus.[9] It was fitting that 1977 should be the year in which Parsons was elected a Fellow of the British Academy. Among his later first publications of unpublished texts, special importance attaches to the fundamental edition of Simonides' *Elegies*, which appeared in 1992 (P.Oxy. LIX.3965), and has generated a vast body of secondary literature.[10]

Since 1960 Hugh Lloyd-Jones had been a constant presence and stimulus in Christ Church as Regius Professor of Greek, and his enthusiasm for the new discoveries made through papyrology was a great support to Parsons. Perhaps especially important was Lloyd-Jones's insistence that the basic collection of Hellenistic poetic texts, J. U. Powell's *Collectanea Alexandrina*, originally published in 1925, urgently needed updating. Even the far superior edition of Callimachus' fragments by Rudolf Pfeiffer was now seriously out of date in the light of the new finds. Accordingly, with the blessing of the enlightened publisher H. Wenzel at De Gruyter, the two scholars embarked in 1973 on a volume which was conceived as and continued to be called a 'Supplement' to Powell: it was originally assumed that it could form one of the pocket-sized Kleine Texte series, but the project grew exponentially, and the final outcome, published in 1982, was a volume which dwarfed Powell's compilation in size as much as it surpassed it in scholarly acumen. In a short paper originally presented to the British Triennial Classics conference in 1978, Lloyd-Jones has described the enterprise in some detail and paid handsome tribute to his collaborator:[11]

Mr Parsons can do anything I can do, and also many things which I cannot do. When boys at Westminster used to defend eccentric interpretations criticised by their Head Master, H. G. Liddell, by saying that they had found them in the lexicon of which he was the editor, Liddell used to say 'Scott wrote that part.' Mr Parsons is the Liddell of our partnership, and as a collaborator I would call him what Pfeiffer called Maas, 'unus instar milium'.

---

[6] Parsons 1971.    [7] Anderson, Parsons, and Nisbet 1979; Parsons 1981; Parsons 1980.
[8] Parsons 1977*a*.    [9] Parsons 1977*b*.
[10] See esp. Boedeker and Sider 2001, including Parsons's own contribution at 55–64.
[11] Lloyd-Jones 1984.

How the division of labour between these two scholars worked in detail must remain their secret, but the result of the partnership is a volume of central importance for the study of Hellenistic literature not only for its own sake but for its influence on Roman culture: as Annette Harder discusses in the present volume, the impact of *Supplementum Hellenisticum* has still to be fully assessed.[12]

In 1989 Hugh Lloyd-Jones retired from the Regius chair and Peter Parsons was appointed his successor.[13] Such elections always involve controversy and wild rumours, but there is no dispute that there was formidable competition for this position, arguably the most distinguished professorial chair in Greek in the world. It is an index of Parsons's distinction and popularity that his appointment was almost universally acclaimed as a brilliantly imaginative one. He held the chair from 1989 until his retirement at the age of 67 in 2003. Those who knew him less well might have feared that the post had gone to an outstanding scholar but not one who would take readily to the burdens of faculty administration and wider lecturing duties. Any such doubts were swiftly confuted. Parsons devoted himself wholeheartedly to his duties, serving not only as Director of Graduate Studies in Classics but also as Chairman of the Faculty Board at a time of uncertainty and change, and playing a part on many university and faculty committees, as well as acting as host to many distinguished academic visitors from all over the world. The set of rooms in Killcanon had never been busier, and in the absence of a full-time secretary, the technology too had to change; successive generations of Macintosh computers replaced the old IBM typewriter with Greek golfball.

In Oxford professors are not necessarily free to choose exactly what they wish to lecture on, but are subject to suggestions from a committee. In the course of his time as Regius Professor he lectured with characteristic polish and preparation on Greek lyric poetry, Pindar, Aristophanes, and Hellenistic Poetry, gave undergraduate reading classes on the *Antigone*, and organized graduate classes on the Homeric Hymn to Aphrodite, Euripides' *Iphigenia in Tauris* and *Phoenissae*, book 2 of Apollonius' *Argonautica*, Callimachus' Epigrams (later the subject of another seminal article), the new Posidippus, and the collection of anonymous epigrammatic *incipits*, as well as contributing to important one-day conferences on Callimachus, Simonides,

---

[12] For an important review see Livrea 1985 (the concluding paragraph, p. 601, includes the comment 'La dottrina e l'acume di Hugh Lloyd-Jones e di Peter Parsons appaiono quasi demiurgiche . . .'). Other reviews are listed in Lloyd-Jones 2005, p. xi. In the preface to this volume Lloyd-Jones regrets that Parsons was unable to collaborate with him in this much shorter supplement owing to other commitments.

[13] Cf. Lloyd-Jones's valedictory lecture, the title essay in Lloyd-Jones 1991, at 232: 'No one is more active or more proficient in the presentation of new material than Peter Parsons, and I am proud to be succeeded by a man who knows Greek as well as he does.'

Empedocles, and 'Sub-Literary Texts' among others.[14] What was especially notable in all these contributions was his consummate professionalism: meticulous preparation, handout material to treasure, and witty, urbane, and punchy delivery. In dealing with graduate students he did not adopt a magisterial role, far less an authoritarian tone. His initial handout at graduate seminars was often adorned with a photocopied image of the delightful red-figure cup by the Euergides painter, which shows a dog scratching itself with its hind leg.[15] The use of the image hinted at a quotation from Housman: 'A textual critic engaged upon his business is not at all like Newton investigating the motions of the planets: he is much more like a dog hunting for fleas.'[16] The classes Parsons organized for graduates were not, of course, confined to textual discussion, but he recognized in this and other spheres the need to consider every problem individually, in line with Housman's words in the same passage: 'every problem which presents itself to the textual critic must be regarded as possibly unique.' Engaging modesty about his own ability and achievements is in his work united with a scepticism about hasty or over-schematic conclusions. He is as reluctant to dogmatize as to polemicize, and in the rare cases where his considered judgement is shown to be wrong or questionable, nothing could be more graceful than his concession: 'the doubts that I myself entertained have been shown to be baseless'.[17]

Papyrology inevitably and rightly begins from the particular: the torn fibre, the half-legible letters, the probable dating and provenance of a scribe. But despite his occasional protestations that he is 'only a papyrologist', Peter Parsons has at various times resisted any effort to marginalize this side of the Classics. Papyrology is not a separate subject.[18] As he emphasises, the textual foundations, whether medieval manuscripts or Hellenistic–Roman survivals, must be treated as just that—fundamental, and any scholarship which loses sight of the fact will be building on sand. More positively, papyrological research demands attention because it is constantly shedding light in unexpected places. To quote his own words:

The argument about the results of our work turns easily into an argument about the value of our work. Once upon a time, we papyrologists had a respected place among the pillars of scholarship. Now we are in danger of being dismissed as technicians;

---

[14] Naturally these classes were conceived as a way of conveying instruction in scholarly method through central authors or new discoveries. On occasion he would lament the need to choose potentially popular subjects, as opposed to getting down to the nitty-gritty—'a seminar on the use of γε in Nicander!' Irony again?

[15] Beazley 1963, 96, no. 136, reproduced in Vickers 1978, no. 35.

[16] Housman 1922, 68–9 = 1972, iii. 1058.    [17] Parsons 1984a, 523.

[18] It is interesting to compare the repeated insistence of his Greek history tutor and colleague, David Lewis, that 'epigraphy is not a separate subject' (Lewis 1972; cf. Lewis 1959; 1997, 6). It appears that Lewis was not appointed to the Greek history chair in 1976 because the electors regarded him as an epigraphist rather than a historian, quite wrongly; twelve years later Oxford got it right with Parsons.

employment is for Generalists. That is a false opposition. It is not just, as Professor Haslam hinted, that our activities fit with curious aptness into modernist discourse: in the most literal way, our texts are artefacts, our readings are creative. The construction of a text is itself a critical act; decipherment determines supplement, supplements build up context, contexts combine in form, form interrogates meaning and supplements, and so circularly; eye and understanding provoke each other. Texts combine into literature, slowly but cumulatively: over the last hundred years we have published, on average, one literary papyrus every ten days. . . we should be proud of a century in which our work has given Greek literature its second Renaissance.[19]

As this and other passages show, Parsons has always kept the broader picture in mind, and the present collection reflects these wide interests. Several of his most widely read pieces provide important surveys of how new discoveries illuminate the old literary landscape or subvert old certainties. '[T]he rise of papyrology has accompanied the decline of certainty.'[20] How the literary-historical map may need to be redrawn is outlined in a number of papers: 'Recent Papyrus Finds: Greek Poetry'; 'Facts from Fragments'; and most importantly, the superb overview of the currents of Hellenistic literature, 'Identities in Diversity', in which a kaleidoscopic picture of the literary ferment of the Hellenistic age is allowed to reveal a few trends and patterns, but the author declines to force the generalizations or draw overconfident conclusions: after posing an agenda of potential research questions, his concluding words are 'I have no answers.'[21] It is obvious that Parsons could write a brilliant and somewhat unorthodox history of Greek literature, but that is not the way he prefers to work. It is worth adding that he could also have been a superb translator (the extracts from a variety of poets rendered into English in 'New Texts and Old Theories' offer tantalizing samples).

Throughout this time, despite the often formidable demands of administration and the increasingly regimented timetable of the Oxyrhynchus publications programme, he continued to respond to scholarly enquiries of all kinds. It is no surprise to find his help acknowledged in many important editions of texts where papyrological evidence (often unpublished) is essential: West's texts of Hesiod, Diggle's Euripides, Dilts's Demosthenes, and among younger scholars the studies of Greek lyric by Gregory Hutchinson and of Pindar's *Paeans* by Ian Rutherford. But many other scholars with different concerns have turned to him for advice, and his name appears in the prefaces of books seemingly remote from his own concerns: Dacre Balsdon's *Romans and Aliens*, for example, or the great work of Stefan Weinstock, *Divus Julius*. Graduate students found him a model supervisor, encouraging yet tireless in his attention to detail.[22] Although once elected to the professorship he saw less of the undergraduate body in Christ Church, he still often

---

[19] Parsons 1994, 22–3.     [20] Parsons 2002, 50.
[21] Parsons 1993, 152–70, at 170; cf. the response of Henrichs 1993, 178–9.
[22] See e.g. the prefaces to Kerkhecker 1999 and Nisbet 2003.

attended social events such as post-examination dinners, and even under-graduates who knew nothing of his detailed research were delighted by the warmth of his personality, communicated through his lecturing style as much as in informal discourse.[23] Within the collegiate structure of Oxford there was also much interchange of a more informal kind: a colleague at Christ Church engaged in the long task of editing Macaulay's *Journal* found him an invaluable authority when seeking to identify the many quotations, often anonymous or cited in abbreviated form. At the lunch table visitors were (and are) delighted by the affability and lightly worn learning of the Regius Professor, ready as he is to converse about culinary practices, Italian opera, or contemporary cinema. The connoisseur of Callimachus is also, to the surprise of many, a notable devotee of cinematic science fantasy: I first heard the title 'Mad Max: Beyond Thunderdome' from this source. Although in his inaugural lecture he declared that in his view the high point of European civilization had been reached on Monday, 29 October 1787, in Prague, it is evident that life is not all high seriousness, and Don Giovanni has been found compatible with Don Corleone.

We have already seen that Peter Parsons is not a scholar who is content to publish for a tiny circle of specialists; already in the earlier phase of his career he had begun to review and write articles which brought his subject alive for the wider reading public. 'Facts from Fragments', although providing insights even for the experts, was published in *Greece and Rome*, a journal chiefly directed at schoolteachers and their sixth-form pupils. Parsons included a piece on the Gallus fragments, with photographs and transcription, in the legendary first issue of another magazine, *Omnibus*, and contributed also to later issues.[24] Substantial essays and reviews in the *London Review of Books* began to appear from 1980 onwards.[25] The need to speak for, and work for the survival of, the Classics was still more incumbent on him when he came to occupy the Regius chair. Besides his regular participation in undergraduate

---

[23] I think particularly here of a pupil of my own who had a spectacular failure of nerve in Mods, left a paper having written almost nothing, and was still distressed by this at the time of the dinner which is regularly held by the tutors at the end of the examination. Only years later, when we were planning the conference in Peter's honour, did I discover that he had unburdened himself to his professorial neighbour at the dinner. In reply to an invitation to attend the conference, he wrote that although he was unable to attend, he sent heartfelt congratulations, adding that he would never forget the kindness and tact that Peter Parsons had shown in conversation with him on that occasion.

[24] For Gallus, see n. 7 above; for later contributions, see Parsons 1984*b* and 1990.

[25] The titles are characteristically eye-catching: e.g. 'How do Babylonians boil eggs?', 'Eels tomorrow, but sprats today'; 'Roman Wall Blues' (references can be traced in the Bibliography of Peter Parsons elsewhere in this volume). Even the more austere articles in scholarly vein can admit a mischievous touch, as in the Browningesque subtitle of his contribution to the Youtie Festschrift, 'The Grammarian's Complaint' (Parsons 1976). Or one might cite the handling of Aristides' *Milesian Tales* in Parsons 1971: 'the ancient verdict on the book is unanimous: dirty' (64).

recruitment days and summer schools, his influence might be felt in unexpected ways. In the late 1980s Oliver Taplin brought the poet-playwright Tony Harrison to meet Peter Parsons in his rooms in Christ Church, and Harrison, like so many before him, fell under the spell of his eloquence and realized the fascination of the world of waste-paper.[26] Already intrigued by the possibility of writing a play on the subject of Grenfell and Hunt and their discoveries, Harrison went on to create *The Trackers of Oxyrhynchus*, first performed at Delphi in 1988 and subsequently in London in 1990: the programme notes, unusually informative and lavishly illustrated, were provided by Peter Parsons and the Egypt Exploration Society. Crossing Waterloo Bridge to attend the first performance at the National Theatre, Parsons relished the unusual blazoning of the name Oxyrhynchus against the night sky. The brilliant conception of blending the drama of the Grenfell–Hunt expedition with a creative re-enactment of the Sophoclean satyr-play *Ichneutae*, one of their early finds, appealed to both scholar and poet. On another level, Harrison's witty verses bring home how easily these papyrological treasures might have been lost, how much indeed is already gone and irrecoverable:

> These chaps, our felaheen, can't see what's unique
> about scraps of old papyrus in ancient Greek.
> We ship back old papyri to decipher them at Queen's
> but they'd use them, if we let them, as compost for their greens.
> Bits of Sappho, Sophocles and Plato
> used as compost for the carrot and potato![27]

In quite different contexts Peter Parsons similarly stressed the formidable forces of time and chance: 'Ancient books were always vulnerable: material fragile, editions small, circulation desultory. The library offered a safe haven. . . . Acceptance into a great library marked a work as authentic or politically acceptable; emperors promoted favourite authors. But favour could do nothing against fire; mould and "the worst enemy of the Muses", worm, put paid to many immortalities.'[28]

In 1998 Oxyrhynchus was again in the news, with the celebration in Oxford of the hundredth anniversary of the beginning of Grenfell and Hunt's operations.[29] To mark the occasion, Parsons wrote an essay on the subject which appeared as the lead article in the *Times Literary Supplement* under the jaunty title 'A Wealth of Garbage' (29 May). Readers were delighted,

---

[26] Source: oral account from both Taplin and Parsons. The published version of Harrison's play mentions Taplin and the French scholar of satyr-drama, Professor F. Lissarague, but not Parsons.

[27] Harrison 1990, 10. Grenfell is the speaker. Both he and A. F. Hunt were Fellows of The Queen's College, Oxford.

[28] *OCD* s.v. 'Libraries'.

[29] See the proceedings volume (Bowman *et al.*, 2007).

publishers intrigued. Not long afterwards he signed a contract for a book about the world revealed by the papyri, the world of Graeco-Roman Egypt.[30] With the continuing preoccupations of his final years as professor, progress was slow, but an interim stage was represented by the excellent BBC radio series *City of the Sharp-nosed Fish* (four episodes) broadcast in June 2002 (presented by Michael Kustow and produced by Amanda Hargreaves). The series used material largely supplied by Peter Parsons, and his deep, sagacious, but humorous tones are heard from time to time alongside the presenter's (with younger colleagues such as Dirk Obbink and Dominic Rathbone providing counterpoint). The titles of the individual episodes are quintessential Parsons: 'Rubbish Tips and Riches'; 'Postcards from an Ancient World'; 'Paper Riddles in the Sand'; 'Greek Tragedies and Daily Soaps'. They whetted the appetite, but the actual book under the same title did not appear until early 2007. It has already been acclaimed as a *tour de force*: beautifully produced, wonderfully illustrated, skilfully structured, and presenting a wealth of information in a deceptively light style which conceals consummate learning and careful judgement: the minimalist notes, though providing the essential source-references, give little idea of the complexities of debate and interpretation which underlie every page (in some passages every sentence). Here social, economic, literary, cultural, and religious history are interwoven with the skill of a scholar who is also a literary artist. Moroever, while many passages testify to the intellectual fascination that the author feels for this lost community and its way of life, a few hint at an even deeper motive, a desire to preserve the lost voices of history, those who played only a small and inconspicuous part on the world stage.

Many private letters survive from ancient Greece and especially ancient Rome, but by and large they survive because written by great men and collected after the author's death by his admirers (so with the uncombed correspondence of the orator Cicero), or by the self-admiring writer during his own lifetime (as with the smug, stylish epistles of Pliny the Younger, lawyer and administrator). Greek Egypt offers something uniquely different, a huge random mailbag of letters to and from small people whose names have not otherwise entered history. We possess no portraits of Akulas or Serenos or Didyme or Apollonios and Serapias. Even their gravestones have vanished. Yet through their letters we still hear them speak.[31]

Fergus Millar once remarked that someone should attempt a *Montaillou* for Oxyrhynchus: no one could have been better equipped to do so than Peter Parsons, and it is hard to imagine anyone else doing it so well.[32]

---

[30] This was not a new project. Over a decade earlier Parsons had suggested a book on this theme to the editor of an eminent university press but was told that it did not sound 'quite our sort of thing'.

[31] Parsons 2007, 136.

[32] Peter Parsons referred to his comment in the *TLS* article referred to above (at p. 3), but noted the significant differences in the nature of the material.

The year 2003 brought retirement. Oxford colleges are stern with their senior members, who as they approach the date of retirement are required to vacate the rooms in which they have taught and researched for decades (Cambridge manages these things rather better). In Peter Parsons's case the experience could have been still more traumatic, as he had been living in the Christ Church rooms for the best part of forty years. But for some time he had been putting down roots in West Oxford, acquiring a house near the home of his long-term partner Barbara Macleod, whose untimely death in 2006 was mourned by all friends of both parties. Her support and encouragement was important in all his activities, but not least in the continued enthusiasm with which, even in her final illness, she pressed him to bring the book on Oxyrhynchus to completion. Fittingly, it is dedicated to her memory.

In the house in West Oxford (with some sifting and much double-banking of shelves) his enormous library could be installed. Gardening, previously a side-interest (visible chiefly in the colourful window-boxes of the Killcanon flat), has become a serious passion. At this stage he was able to shed the burden of chairing the Oxyrhynchus project (an increasingly burdensome role in an age where complex applications are required for funding from government resources), but remains a crucial member of the editorial team. One of the most recent volumes includes his edition of a new novelistic text possibly by Antonius Diogenes; another adds a new element to the conflicting evidence concerning the date of the historian Clitarchus; and there is much more in the pipeline. Other projects also beckon: there are rumours of a plan to compose a practical guide to the papyrologist for Cambridge University Press. The distinguished new Classics Faculty Centre in Oxford, opened in 2007, has provided him with a room in which his editorial work can continue, and so Peter Parsons, now in his eighth decade but still sporting extravagant ties and thick woolly pullovers according to the season, can be spotted in transit between Botley Road and St Giles, usually carrying a battered hold-all which may contain an assortment of fresh offprints, detective stories, goodies from Marks and Spencer's food-hall, and photographs of an unpublished text which has not yet revealed all its secrets. In celebrating his achievement over 70 years we have no intention of suggesting that the Parsons files are closed. We wish him many more years of pleasurable and productive retirement.

## II

This part of the introduction describes the relation of the papers in this volume to one another and to Peter Parsons's interests in the subject of fragmentary texts more generally, indicating thematic connections and recurring ideas running through the volume. The reader is referred to the Bibliography of Peter Parsons for a record of his many and varied publications, a number of which venture well beyond the confines of the topics treated in the following chapters.

Roland Barthes described the delight with which many critics of literature revel in finding culture in pieces.[33] What do the novel and ancient Greek documentary letters have in common? Fact and fiction, parts and wholes, manners and misbehaviour, irony and stylometry: a list of oblique contrasts sums up the themes of the chapters of this book, as it reflects Peter Parsons's varied interests and achievements. Their authors chart a circuitous course that traces ancient literature, above all Greek, and to a lesser extent Latin, literature from their earliest period through their constitution in a fixed textual form in the Hellenistic and Imperial periods to the acme of their stylization under the High Empire. In this literary tradition, where imitators are raised to the status of inventors, lost works are as often the object of attention as preserved ones, and little-known authors often vie with the famous. The principle that no work or author who managed to survive only in tatters should be allowed to be eclipsed by those that enjoyed centuries of untroubled transmission is assumed in the pages that follow. The lability of the textual past, the shifting of artistic fashion, and the loss of cultural memory conspire to render culture in pieces. A resulting demand for new methodologies for filling the gaps, as much focussed on isolating holes in our knowledge as on filling them, is paramount. Methodology, for the authors of the following chapters, is to some extent purpose-built for each genre, period, and problem. Borrowing and analogies from method in archaeology and the social sciences in one chapter, and from the humanistic pursuits of literary criticism, historiography, and biography in another: a variety of approaches is present in eclectic and novel combinations in the essays that follow as it suits the effort at hand in making culture from pieces.

After an early interest in documentary texts, Peter Parsons's career quickly turned toward a specialization in the recovery of the works of lost authors from our surviving evidence of papyri from Graeco-Roman Egypt—in many cases made possible by the accession of newly identified and published texts hiding in the repository of world papyrus collections. Dirk Obbink's essay 'Vanishing Conjecture: The Recovery of Lost Books from Aristotle to Eco' charts the history of this effort, including its influence on postmodern attitudes to literature, from the Renaissance to the present day. Although the aesthetics of the fragment that has emerged in poetry and art since the Romantic period could not have existed in antiquity, he argues for the importance of the fragment as a formal element, in literature as in

[33] Barthes 1973, 82: 'Le plaisir en pièces; la langue en pièces; la culture en pièces.'

archaeology, as containing some of the essential ingredients of the whole in each of its parts.

The world of Early Greek Lyric poetry, reconstructed as it has been in this way from predominantly fragmentary remains, may be seen in the background of Martin West's chapter 'Pindar as a Man of Letters', dealing as it does mainly with the complete poems. West surveys Pindar's reflections in his poetry on his literary predecessors and forebears (and thereby implicitly on literature and literary history). In the process he challenges a common view of Pindar among historians of literature as having at least one foot in the performative and predominantly oral world of his predecessors. West argues that Pindar moved in a world where he not only utilized writing and written works in his own compositions, but also saw to his legacy in the form of a written, autograph corpus of texts, known later in Hellenistic and (in the case of the *Epinikia*) medieval editions.

Such a theory connects easily with the contemporary world of the earliest written prose history, similarly instantiated by a rich papyrological transmission from Hellenistic and (more securely) Roman times. Stephanie West's chapter 'The Papyri of Herodotus' surveys the state of the question on our surviving papyri of Herodotus, including the frequency and extent of the footprint left in the surviving papyrological evidence for individual books of the *Histories*. She intriguingly argues that fewer of the papyrus fragments to witness the *Histories* come from texts of whole books than from drafts, schoolbooks, and private copies of individual passages out of whole books. If this is correct, the Father of History was beginning to become atomized into pieces much earlier than has previously been thought, antedating the transmission of a complete text of the *Histories* to the Middle Ages and Renaissance.

A close sensitivity to refinement of style and attention to the constraints of genre have long characterized Peter Parsons's analyses of literature. An important aspect of the first is the subject of comment in 'The Use and Abuse of Irony', in which Richard Rutherford attempts to circumscribe this elusive but central quality of Greek and Latin literature. Taking Greek drama as a special test case, Rutherford analyses irony as a type of ambiguity present in complex literature, invoked 'when the reader simply cannot believe that a writer can mean what he says'. Arguably, irony can be isolated even in the most fragmentary of texts, and, when known to be present in a given writer (like Euripides) can be enlisted in the process of reconstruction and evaluation from limited or partially preserved evidence.

On the side of genre concerns, Peter Parsons's seminal 1980 treatment of ancient Greek epistolary remains on papyrus ('The Papyrus Letter') showed that some documentary types are as strictly governed by literary conventions (while anchored in down-home, everyday practicalities) as the most literary of genres. Parsons's analysis is borne out and extended by Adrian Hollis's chapter 'Greek Letters from Hellenistic Bactria', showcasing a recently discovered literate letter-writer on the fringes of Greek culture in modern-day Afghanistan, who got his prize-correspondence recorded in stone for preservation to posterity.

What Euripides was to tragedy, Apollonius to epic, and Callimachus to elegy, Menander was to comedy: refined and revolutionary, so much so, in fact, that later ages could claim not to be able to tell the difference between his lifelike portrait of refined urban sophisticates and the reality of life ('O life! O Menander': T83 Kassel–Austin). At the same time, each of the above-named authors tops the lists in the number of surviving papyrus manuscripts for their respective genres. So it is hardly surprising or imbalanced for the present volume to contain a healthy dose of contributions on New Comedy, especially Menander, to whose understanding Peter Parsons has been a longtime contributor. Heinz-Günther Nesselrath's chapter 'Menander and his Rivals: New Light from the Comic Adespota?' expands the repertoire of the poet of New Comedy by adding a plausible candidate to his oeuvre in the form of a fragment presented in current editions of the fragments of Greek Comedy as of uncertain authorship, while maintaining a judicious scepticism as to the level of certainty attainable about Menander's authorship.

Eric Handley's chapter 'The Rediscovery of Menander' surveys the history of the discovery, identification, and editing of the plays of Menander in the last century, built up from literally thousands of individually identified and grouped fragments of papyrus manuscripts. The influence of this gradually shaped composite of an important ancient author (whom Shakespeare, for example, or any author before the twentieth century cannot have read outside of a few proverbs quoted by ancient authors) on the understanding of literary history and the appreciation of literature is also sketched.

In ' "My Daughter and her Dowry"': Smikrines in Menander's *Epitrepontes*', Colin Austin takes as his case-study a single play. With its fragments constituted and ordered into a coherent whole in over a century of painstaking papyrological detective work, it can almost be said to exist as a play in its own right (we have now at least one major fragment from every scene of the play). Austin paints a convincing portrait of one scene of the play in a detailed reconstruction.

Likewise, Hellenistic poetry gets a lion's share of attention. Playing on the title of Peter Parsons's 1982 article on the mining of literary history from fragmentary papyri and texts in the secondary tradition, Annette Harder in her chapter 'More Facts from Fragments' surveys the editorial accomplishment of *Supplementum Hellenisticum*, a long-term editorial effort undertaken by Peter Parsons in collaboration with the then Regius Professor of Greek at Oxford, Sir Hugh Lloyd-Jones. In spite of the overshadowing contributions to the fragments of Callimachus' *Aetia* that anchor the volume, she argues that some of its most important contributions and contents have gone overlooked, in particular the wealth of didactic poetry, and of small poems.

Susan Stephens's chapter 'Remapping the Mediterranean: The Argo Adventure in Apollonius and Callimachus' shows how the remaking of a genre could constitute the remaking and mental remapping of the entire Greek world, over and against the shifts in centres of intellectual and political power brought about by the rise of Ptolemaic Alexandria and the Ptolemies' refashioning of themselves as dynasts in Hellenistic Egypt. Parallels between landscape and literature become especially important in aetiological literature, where the boundary between homeland and hinterland, frontier and the foreign, is charted in both conceptual and geographical terms.

The *Kreuzung* of genres for which Hellenistic poetry became famous finds its instantiation in the melding of historiography and elegy under the hand of Callimachus in the *Aitia* discussed in Giulio Massimilla's 'Theudotus of Lipara'. In the background is glimpsed Peter Parsons's laying of the groundwork for a sound text of the *Victoria Berenices* in the third book of that Callimachean poem. Massimilla also offers a new text that opens the way to understanding of the obscure figure Theudotus and Callimachus' interest in his sacrifice in battle to Apollo and its West-Greek and Etruscan setting.

The afterlife of Callimachus' poetry and his reception among literary critics of Roman antiquity form the subject of Richard Hunter's chapter 'The Reputation of Callimachus'. Hunter surveys the later fortunes of Callimachus, 'that most paradoxical of creatures, a third-century "classic"', a case-study in the ironic turns of fortune in esteem when the renegade neoteric comes to be regarded as canonical and classic by literary critics, grammarians, and learned if not general readers.

The subject of the following chapters shifts to the Roman side of things, without relinquishing their Greek background and underpinnings. The foregrounding of poetry and mythography in Ovid's *Metamorphoses* is established by Gregory Hutchinson in his chapter 'Telling Tales: Ovid's *Metamorphoses* and Callimachus'. Hutchinson imaginatively sees Ovid's *Metamorphoses* as constructing two 'worlds', one of the stories, one of the writer's and reader's activity. These worlds are contrasted but can come close; the inspiration is Callimachus.

On the level of close stylistic analysis, the acute ear for rhythm of the ancient Latin literary critic is brought out in Michael Winterbottom's chapter 'On Ancient Prose Rhythm: The Story of the Dichoreus'. It is clear that ancient readers were at once aware of such refined judgements of style and capable of appreciating them in certain authors. The combination and subtle effects of prose in poetry has been an interest of Peter Parsons since his 1971 article 'A Greek Satyricon', which focussed on a newly discovered fragmentary novel written in prosimetrum. Winterbottom's study proceeds along similar lines, since the Dichoreus and its use as a clausula in Latin prose rhythm are seen to have a basis in Greek practice. At the same time, Winter-bottom argues that Cicero's influential use of the rhythm was dictated not by his Greek teachers in the first instance but by his imitation of Greek and Latin rhetors in both Asia and Rome.

An exercise in complex matters of editing, including bilingual transmission of a source tradition, is offered by Christoph Riedweg's 'Alexander of Aphro-disias, *De prouidentia*: Greek Fragments and Arabic Versions'. Riedweg illustrates the complexity introduced into the editing process by a multi-layered and multilingual source tradition resulting from a work's being preserved only in fragments in the language of its original composition, but more completely in translation into another. At issue is not only how much of the original can be reconstructed using the surviving passages as a control in trying to reconstruct the rest, but how much of the editor's judgement in this regard can be usefully documented in an apparatus criticus. The treatment of editorial problems becomes an exercise in the methodology of linguistic analysis.

The complex intersection of editorial practice with the disentanglement of generic definition leads thematically into a consideration of that cross-cultural and international literary hybrid 'prose-fiction'. No tribute to Peter Parsons would be complete without a major treatment of the ancient novel, with a sideways glance at the representation of the extant novels on papyrus, and the blueprint provided by papyrus fragments for those examples of novels, romance, and mime that failed to survive as wholes in manuscript transmission. In his chapter 'Missing Pages: Papyrology, Genre, and the Greek Novel' Albert Henrichs surveys the attempts to define the genre of the novel, poorly theorized as it was by ancient criticism though hardly without its admirers. Papyrological evidence and sociological models of readership and representation combine to produce a coherent portrait of a genre capable of representing the less than respectable side of Greek life, at times with sophis-tication and urbanity, at others with outrageous breaking of normal literary conventions. The fact that so much of ancient fiction has perished, or sur-vived only in fragmentary form, may have as much to do with uncertainties of definition of the type of literature as with critical strictures on the appropriateness of its subject matter and plot. In many cases its preservation in fragmentary form serves further to obscure what characteristics of a com-mon form may have originally constituted the genre of the novel for ancient readers. For us, it is as Peter Parsons said of Oxyrhynchus: 'even the ruins have perished' (Parsons 1990, 1).

# BIBLIOGRAPHY

Anderson, R. D., Nisbet, R. G. M., and Parsons, P. J. 1979, 'Elegiacs by Gallus from Qaṣr Ibrîm', *JRS* 69, 125–55.

Barthes, R. 1973, *Le Plaisir du texte* (Paris).

Beazley, J. D. 1963, *Attic Red-Figure Vase-Painters*, 2nd edn. (Oxford).

Boedeker, D., and Sider, D. (eds.) 2001, *The New Simonides* (Baltimore and Oxford).

Bowman, A. K., Coles, R. A., Gonis, N., and Obbink, D. (eds.) 2007, *Oxyrhynchus: A City and its Texts* (Egypt Exploration Society, Graeco-Roman Memoirs; London).

Bulloch, A. W., *et al.* (eds.) 1993, *Images and Ideologies: Self-Definition in the Hellenistic World* (Berkeley, Los Angeles, and London).

Harrison, Tony 1990, *The Trackers of Oxyrhynchus* (London).

Henrichs, A. 1993, 'Response', in Bulloch *et al.* 1993, 171–95.

Housman, A. E. 1922, 'The Application of Thought to Textual Criticism', *PCA* 18, 67–84 = *The Classical Papers of A. E. Housman*, ed. J. Diggle and F. R. D. Goodyear, 3 vols. (Cambridge, 1972), iii. 1058–69.

Kerkhecker, A. 1999, *Callimachus' Book of Iambi* (Oxford)

Lewis, D. M. 1959, 'The Testimony of Stones', review of Woodhead, *The Study of Greek Inscriptions: The Listener* (20 August), 281–4.

—— 1972, review of Pleket, *Epigraphica*, ii: *CR*² 22, 130.

—— 1997, *Selected Papers on Greek and Near Eastern History*, ed. P. J. Rhodes (Cambridge).

Livrea, E. 1985, review of *SH*, *Gnomon* 57, 592–601 = id., *Studia Hellenistica*, i (Florence, 1991), 289–303.

Lloyd-Jones, H. 1984, 'A Hellenistic Miscellany', *SIFC*³ 2, 52–71 = id., *Greek Comedy, Hellenistic Literature, Greek Religion and Miscellanea: The Academic Papers of Sir Hugh Lloyd-Jones* (Oxford, 1990), 231–49 .

—— 1991, *Greek in a Cold Climate* (London).

—— 2005, *Supplementum supplementi Hellenistici* (Berlin).

—— and Parsons, P. J. 1983, *Supplementum Hellenisticum* (Berlin).

Nisbet, G. 1993, *Greek Epigram in the Roman Empire: Martial's Forgotten Rivals* (Oxford).

Parsons, P. J. 1971, 'A Greek Satyricon?', *BICS* 18, 53–68.

—— 1976, 'Petitions and a Letter: The Grammarian's Complaint', in A. E. Hanson (ed.) *Collectanea Papyrologica: Texts Published in Honour of H. C. Youtie* (Bonn), 409–46.

—— 1977a, 'Callimachus: Victoria Berenices', *ZPE* 25, 1–50.

—— 1977b, 'The Lille "Stesichorus"', *ZPE* 26, 7–36.

—— 1980, 'Cornelius Gallus Lives', *London Review of Books* (7 February), 9–10.

—— 1981, 'The Oldest Roman Book Ever Found', *Omnibus*, 1, 1–4.

—— 1984a, 'Recent Papyrus Finds: Greek Poetry', *Actes du VIIᵉ Congrès de la FIEC* (Budapest), 517–31.

—— 1984b, 'First Catch Your Text: Latin Manuscripts Old and New', *Omnibus*, 7, 21–3.

—— 1987, 'Eric Gardner Turner', *PBA* 73, 685–704.

—— 1990, 'Oxyrhynchus: Waste-Paper City', *Omnibus*, 19, 1–4.

—— 1993, 'Identities in Diversity', in Bulloch *et al.* 1993, 152–70.

—— 1994, 'Summing up', in *Proc. XX Int. Congr. Pap.* (Copenhagen), 118–23.

—— 2002, 'New Texts and Old Theories', in T. P. Wiseman (ed.), *Classics in Progress: Essays on Ancient Greece and Rome* (Oxford), 39–57.

—— 2003, 'One Foot in the Quad', *Christ Church Matters*, 11 (Trinity Term), 5.

—— 2007, *City of the Sharp-Nosed Fish* (London).

—— Rea, J. R., and Turner, E. G. 1983, *The Oxyrhynchus Papyri*, L (London).

Vickers, M. 1978, *Greek Vases* (Ashmolean Museum, Oxford).

# 1

## Vanishing Conjecture: Lost Books and their Recovery from Aristotle to Eco

*Dirk Obbink*

Let us suppose that many fragments of texts are unearthed by excavators. A team of experts is set to reconstruct them, but they are puzzled by the disparity of topics and treatment. Some fragments, written in Greek, appear to quote known ancient authors, others writers who are complete ciphers; others to discuss banquets, or music, or love (some in poetry, some in prose). Some seem to contain continuous narrative, others are broken up into seemingly unrelated verses of different poems. Some have illustrations attached to them, without corresponding in a clear way to their texts. One narrates a series of events in epic metre, but follows the conventions of iambic poetry. Another contains the remnants of Callimachus' long-lost 'Lock of Berenike'. Still others, written in Latin, exude a new, Alexandrian style (an epigram of Gallus, apostrophizing Lycoris?), or wrap early Christian theology like an envelope inside a later century's text. Since the beginnings and ends of each fragment are missing, scholars come to the conclusion that these fragments never formed coherent works, that they are the rambling trials and compositions of students set copying exercises in a late-antique scriptorium, ranging eclectically and capriciously over different areas of learning. But in this case they would be wrong. For the set of texts I have been describing consists of nothing else than—a collection of offprints from the works of Peter Parsons. The range and subjects covered in this diverse medley of particular interests, together with Peter's concern for the diffusion of knowledge about literary works of all sorts and times, may be taken to define his scholarly activity as a late phase of the work of the Renaissance humanists, for his aim has always been to explicate texts and facilitate access to them.

In the reception of literature from Graeco-Roman antiquity to the present, the failure of whole works to survive—i.e. their recovery in fragmentary form —is far more the rule than the other way around. Even whole genres could perish. In the case of authors who do survive, we usually have but a small and selective portion of their entire oeuvre. Readers from antiquity to the present were more sensitive to risks and lapses in transmission than we are: the digital revolution is one modern expression of such anxiety. Realization of the pre-ponderance of partial transmission puts the fragmentary work in a new light. The relation of the part to the whole, the literary microcosm, and the repre-sentative nature of the text preserved as an extract or quotation become central to the process of reading and interpretation, and call into question the viability of raising the fragment to the status of the whole.

In what follows, I illustrate this with a test-set of texts both new and old, which entered the corpus of Graeco-Roman literature for the first time as fragments, in order to set out some of the ways in which we help ourselves to the textual past, using a variety of different types of fragments to recover lost books. In the process, I consider some little known or previously unknown texts: the oldest Greek literary manuscript; a new fragment of a lost Greek novel; two new fragments of Sappho; and a new fragment of the oldest Greek poet. These I shall use to illustrate some of the rules and basic procedures commonly followed in working from fragments. We have manuals for textual criticism[1] and Greek metre, but a comprehensive guide to the editing of fragmentary texts remains a major desideratum. For documentary texts on papyrus, Herbert Youtie's *Textual Criticism of Documentary Papyri*[2] has become something like a Bible; for literary texts, the closest thing for editors of fragmentary literary texts has been Peter Parsons's 'Facts from Fragments', now badly in need of updating as a result subsequent new papyrus finds.[3] But I claim further that these texts are intrinsically interesting, in and of them-selves, and provide an inroad to new knowledge gained through a process of literary detection.

Take, for example, the famous modern recreation of a fragment:[4]

PAPYRUS

Spring . . . . . . .
Too long . . . . . .
Gongula . . . . . .

Ezra Pound's series of dots are not ellipses (with which the poem is often enough erroneously reprinted),[5] but faithful representations of the papyrologist's underdotting to mark traces of uncertainly read letters,[6]

---

[1] West 1973.     [2] Youtie 1974.

[3] Parsons 1982; cf. Harder, below, ch. 9; Camion *et al.* 1997. Parsons 2002 provides a valuable supplement.

[4] Pound 1916.

[5] Compare the first and final verses of Dorothy Parker's 'fragmentary' poem 'From a Letter from Lesbia' (1926): '. . . So, praise the gods, Catullus is away!', and 'The stupid fool! I've always hated birds . . .'.

[6] Youtie 1974 legislates the rationale for placements of such dots: 'when the editor feels doubt . . .'.

as would have been painfully obvious to readers in the early editions of Sappho by A. S. Hunt and Edgar Lobel. Nor is this fragment simply a modern construct: as has been only recently recognized,[7] it translates Sappho fr. 95, as preserved on a sixth-century parchment fragment (Pl. 1), at least as far as l. 4 of the papyrus:

$$
\begin{array}{ll}
& .\,.\quad.\quad.\\
& .ο υ[\\
& \mathring{\eta}\rho α[\\
& \delta\eta\rho α τ\, .[\\
& \Gamma ο\gamma\gamma υ\lambda α\, .[\\
5 & \mathring{\eta}\ \tau\iota\ c\mathring{α}μ'\ \mathring{ε}\theta\epsilon\, .[\\
& π α\iota c\iota\ μ\acute{α}\lambda\iota c τ α\, .[\\
& μ α c\ \gamma'\ ε\mathring{\iota}c\eta\lambda\theta'\ \mathring{ε}π\, .[\\
& ε\mathring{\iota}π ο ν\cdot\ \mathring{ω}\ \delta\acute{ε}c π ο τ',\ \mathring{ε}π\, .[\\
& ο]\mathring{υ}\ μ\grave{α}\ \gamma\grave{α}ρ\ μ\acute{α}κ α\iota ρ α ν\ [\\
10 & ο]\mathring{υ}\delta\grave{ε}ν\ \mathring{α}\delta ομ'\ \mathring{ε}π α ρ\theta'\ \mathring{α}\gamma α[\\
& κ α τ\theta\acute{α}ν\eta ν\ \delta'\ \mathring{\iota}μ\epsilon ρ\acute{ο}c\ τ\iota c\ [\mathring{ε}\chi\epsilon\iota\ μ\epsilon\ κ α\grave{\iota}\\
& \lambda ω τ\acute{\iota}ν ο\iota c\ \delta ρ ο c\acute{ο}\epsilon ν τ α c\ [\mathring{ο}\text{-}\\
& \chi[\theta]ο\iota c\ \mathring{\iota}\delta\eta ν\ \text{'}A\chi\epsilon ρ[\\
& .].\,.\delta\epsilon c α\iota\delta\,.[\\
15 & .].\,ν\delta\epsilon τ ο ν[\\
& μ\eta τ\iota c\epsilon[\\
& .\quad.\quad.\quad.
\end{array}
$$

Ironically, ll. 1–3 are omitted in Campbell's *Greek Lyric* (vol. i) (Campbell 1990), as being too fragmentary to deserve space.[8] Pound's poem comes at a time when people laughed at the woefully mutilated remains of papyrus discoveries coming from Egypt, and the promises which they held out, often disappointingly, to supply complete texts of long lost literature (especially lyric poetry and the original gospels) from Graeco-Roman antiquity. Not without a humorous touch, Pound's poem perhaps illustrates a side of Sappho that can be glimpsed, if fleetingly, even within the most fragmentary of remains—especially as intuited by a minimalist, modernist aesthetic. An even earlier comment on discoveries of literature from fragmentary manuscripts comes in William Wordsworth's poem, 'Upon the Same Occasion' (1819):

> O ye, who patiently explore
> The wreck of Herculanean lore,
> What rapture! Could ye seize
> Some Theban fragment, or unroll

---

[7] Seelbach 1970.

[8] Campbell 1990, 118. He similarly omits vv. 14–16. Verse 11 was supplemented by Blass. Campbell also prints more extensive restorations, by Schubart and Lobel, in vv. 9–13. At the end of 6 and beginning of 7 Blass had restored the name of Hermes, whose epiphany the poem may have related.

> One precious, tender-hearted, scroll
> Of pure Simonides.
>
> That were, indeed, a genuine birth
> Of poesy; a bursting forth
> Of genius from the dust:
> What Horace gloried to behold,
> What Maro loved, shall we enfold?
> Can haughty Time be just!

Wordsworth's poem begins in sombre tones, a light lament on the passing of summer and time in the voice of an old man. Against this is held up the eternal energy of inspired poetry ('For deathless powers to verse belong'), and to this are called to witness Alcaeus, Sappho, and primitive (Welsh? Gaelic?) poetry ('initiatory strains / Committed to the silent plains / In Britain's earliest dawn'). The final two stanzas, set forth above, challenge time's power to obscure even these literary monuments, juxtaposing exuberant hopes for the rediscovery of lost poetic works, for example, of Pindar ('Some Theban fragment') and Simonides.

Today these stanzas are often read ironically and pessimistically, as if to Wordsworth such wistful wishes for rediscovery would have seemed beyond reach and an occasion for lament. But this would not have been the case. Wordsworth was a close friend and companion of Sir Humphrey Davy, whose experiments in unrolling the charred papyrus scrolls excavated in the eighteenth century from Herculaneum, one of the cities on the Bay of Naples buried by the eruption of Vesuvius in AD 79, held out great promise at that time. There is no reason to read the stanzas quoted above as doing anything other than wishing Davy well in his experiments.

Davy's experiments, alas, were not a great success, although he did manage to recover the name of Sophocles from a fragment of one of the rolls he opened. Wordsworth would have had to wait almost three-quarters of a century for the discovery of a major lyric poet, and as it happens, on a papyrus from Egypt.[9] The Herculaneum library has so far produced mainly prose, philosophical works (some of which would have been already known to Wordsworth). Although several of these centre on the philosophical criticism of poetry, and some contain a large number of quotations of the Greek poets, the treatises of Philodemus, Demetrius the Laconian, and Chrysippus, to name a few of the philosophical authors included in the Herculaneum Library, would not have fulfilled Wordsworth's wishes.[10]

---

[9] Bacchylides, ed. Kenyon 1897; a scrap of Sappho containing fr. 3 had already been published in 1880.

[10] Recent discoveries in our own time at Herculaneum of copies of Ennius' *Annales*, together with the *Faenerator* ('Οβολοςτάτης) of Plautus' successor Caecilius Statius, and very likely Lucretius' *De rerum natura*, would have come closer to Wordsworth's desiderated lyric poetry. On the finds, see http://www.herculaneum.ox.ac.uk/books.html; for Lucretius, see Obbink 2007. Cf. Bardon 1952–6.

## Literary Detection

That process, by which fragments become texts in their own right, can take a
variety of forms of recovery. One is simple discovery. The plot of Umberto
Eco's novel *The Name of the Rose*[11] turns on the fourteenth-century discovery
of the long-lost second book of Aristotle's *Poetics* in the library of an Italian
monastery. It revolves around the story of a monk who perpetrates a series of
murders in order to conceal its theory of comedy from the world. The outcome of the novel is of course a fiction, but one whose pattern was repeated
over and over again during the Italian Renaissance, when such recoveries
were both fashionable and the books lay waiting in monastic libraries, as has
been treated in a fascinating series of studies by Anthony Grafton.[12] Like Eco,
I view the problem posed for the recovery of lost books from fragmentary
evidence as a process of literary detection, i.e. as a mystery to be solved only
by inference from signs. There is good evidence, for example, that copies
of Sappho could still be read in their entirety in eleventh-century Constanti-
nople,[13] and if the Italian Renaissance had come a few centuries earlier we
should have much more of her to read than has been provided by quotations
and papyrus discoveries. At the same time that Eco became famous for *The
Name of the Rose*, Richard Janko made lavish claims to have discovered the
lost second book of Aristotle's *Poetics*, in a form allegedly summarized
in the tenth-century *Tractatus Coislinianus*. Janko even went so far as to
produce an edition of it by combining the *Tractatus'* late Latin paraphrase,
contaminated as it was by later school-theory, with citations and quotations
from Aristotle's original text surviving in the secondary tradition, which he
printed side by side in the reconstruction in his 1984 edition.[14] Janko's
hypotheses have since been refuted and are now generally derided. The subsequent appearance of the same set of terms and polemic against Peripatetics
in the fourth book of Philodemus' *On Poems* preserved on a Herculaneum
papyrus,[15] seemed to provide new fuel to the debate, and the press took
notice. The *New York Times* ran headlines crediting Janko with the discovery
of the real book featured in Eco's novel. Janko's discoveries were almost as
felicitous as the fictional discovery posited by Eco of the lost second book (on
comedy) of Aristotle's *Poetics* (if not quite as exciting a read as Eco's novel).
For, in addition to providing a reconstruction, if not in every case the original
terminology, of Aristotle's theory of comedy, they provided the added context
of a (hostile) first-century-BC reading by an Epicurean philosopher, and a
late-antique (sympathetic) reading by a Peripetetic scholar. Janko's findings
were controversial at the time, partly as a result of the publicity over Eco's

---

[11] Eco 1980.      [12] Grafton 1991; 2001.      [13] Garzya 1971.
[14] Janko 1984, subsequently revised in Janko 1987.      [15] Janko 1991.

simultaneous fantasy find. They have become less so, but some uncertainty remains. In particular not all of the *Tractatus*' terminology can be Aristotle's, while the hostile report of Philodemus contains an element of distortion: it cannot be trusted to be the whole account. So it should be worth posing the question: what constitutes a legitimate fragment, and when are we justified in reconstructing a lost original? By what criteria will recovery be judged a success? I remember being disheartened when a scholar who I thought understood editorial method told me that an edition of a papyrus I had published was, as he put it, 'all you', rather than the text of the ancient author in question, just because the ends of some of the lines were restored. Before addressing that question, it would be useful to review in the first instance why books get lost.

## How Books Get Lost

The historical record lists numerous accounts of lost books. According to Strabo 13. 1. 54, Aristotle was the first to collect books and taught the kings of Egypt how to put a library together. He tells further of the fate of Aristotle's library: Aristotle left his library, including his own manuscripts, to Theophrastus, who left it to Neleus who took it to Scepsis in the Troad and left it to his successors. They were not philosophers and kept the books locked away and carelessly stored. When they heard that the Attalid kings were collecting books for their library in Pergamum, they hid them underground in a sort of tunnel, perhaps a cellar (ἐν διώρυγί τινι), where they were damaged by mildew and worms. Later the family sold the books to Apellicon of Teos, a bibliophile, who tried to repair the worm-damage by transferring the writings to new manuscripts, but did not complete the job satisfactorily, and published the books full of errors. Strabo's story is as fictional as Eco's *The Name of the Rose*. The story has been exposed as a fiction by Jonathan Barnes:[16] the Peripatetics of Strabo's day are being lampooned because Aristotle's doctrines are so difficult to understand, they are suspected of large-scale corruption of the type the story envisages as being caused by the miscopying of the books: 'Thus it was', says Strabo, 'that the older Peripatetics who came after Theophrastus did not possess the books at all, and so were not able to do any serious philosophy but merely declaimed generalities. Their successors were better philosophers, yet for the most part were obliged to speak haphazardly because of the number of mistakes in the books.' Anyone who has had to deal with the text of the *Poetics* may not so readily doubt Strabo's account. But joking aside, the cause of the damage is made plausible enough. Many books must have met a similar fate. A letter on papyrus from

---

[16] Barnes 1997; the idea also appears in Tarán 1974.

Oxyrhynchus tells how the City's record office had become so infested with mice that all the dockets had to be discarded and the records begun anew. And European papyrus collections are filled with the contents of the rubbish mounds of Graeco-Roman cities. To be sure, people did throw books away when they wore out, often after reusing their backs for occasional writing or private copies. The literary value of some of the magical and astrological texts I have published has been impugned by reviewers who observed sulkily that the texts 'had been thrown away, in any case'. But by and large we can be sure that this is not how the vast majority of books were lost. The accounts of the Alexandrian library's having perished due to a single fire or other disaster have been shown to be urban myths. Rather, the majority of books perished when they failed to be copied any longer, in particular at a time when the codex (first of papyrus, later of vellum) was starting to and eventually did replace the cumbersome papyrus roll as the medium of choice for literary books. The situation bears some resemblance to Nicholson Baker's account of how the British Library, and other libraries similarly, discarded vast portions of its holdings of nineteenth-century newspapers bound in folio volumes after archiving digital images of them.[17] Thus, in antiquity some books perished through disuse due to obscurity of dialect, language, metre, or subject-matter when they failed eventually to be transferred to codex-form, while others were not recopied on account of their popularity, having been fully assimilated to the cultural tradition and absorbed by way of encyclopedias, commentaries, anthologies, and epitomes—for example, the majority of the works of Varro or the commentaries of Didymus. I pause only to observe that the paper trail left behind by both types of works will be entirely different, and more predictable, than works that indifferently perish owing to natural disaster or some other means of purely chance destruction.

## Definition and Principles

It is time to offer a definition of a fragment and the activity of working on them. I define a fragment as 'a situated cultural remnant with some collective significance and capable of extension'. By 'situated' I mean that the fragment has a context that can be used as a clue in reconstructing it. No fragment, no cultural artefact exists in a vacuum, for it is a human product. By collective significance I mean that the fragment is recognizable by more than a single person or several, both ancient and modern. By 'capable of extension' I mean that the fragment is at least in theory able to be filled out by content it can be known or conjectured to have once contained, or ordered among fragments of similar content in a plausible series. Working on fragments is the art of

---

[17] Baker 2001.

being distracted in a certain way; i.e. being careful about getting the seemingly trivial exactly right—putting the right questions so as to be able to draw the correct inferences and conclusions about gaps in our knowledge of a text. I see editing fragments as a kind of site report: a first-hand account, based on autopsy, together with all relevant historical and archaeological sources. Every treatment of a fragment ought to be a kind of 'hands-on' practical in techniques of editing, commentary, and where relevant techniques of transcription and recording. It requires constant attention to the constraints of language, grammar, context, space, and probability in order to draw what Peter Parsons has called the 'circle of inevitability' ever closer, in concentric rings, to certainty (not always achieved). Sometimes the results are conjectural, or a restoration takes you just so far in certainty—and you have to guess the rest.

To some collecting fragments is a necessary evil. To others it is a game: a crossword puzzle-like delight filled with dastardly pitfalls and hair-pin turns of fortune. Last week's restorations can be demolished by next week's new finds, and centuries of editorial conjecture toppled by a single new fragment. Anyone who works on fragments has to be the jack-of-all-trades, prepared to take on any medium—manuscripts (and their copying-errors), papyrus, wooden tablets, ostraca, parchment, vellum, and other skins, inscriptions carved on stone or incised with a sharp stylus on lead, silver, or wax. Fragments can be preserved in quotations, in the secondary tradition, and can be embedded in other fragments. Fragments of lost books can preserve the titles and texts of other lost works. Recovery is painstaking. No single individual can do the job alone. The fragment's state of preservation is not up to us. When the fragment says 'jump', we have to say 'how high?' We deal with texts in Greek and Latin, as well as Aramaic, Nubian, Hebrew, Egyptian hieroglyphs, Hieratic, Demotic, Coptic, Sanskrit, Assyrian, Babylonian. These texts range from the Old Kingdom to the Arab conquest and beyond. Their preservation is fortuitous and dependent upon circumstance: a man on a horse carries a book over a mountain; a grammarian finds a strange poem in a library and summarizes it in a commentary; a lexicographer pens the rare gloss; papyrus in Egypt and the Near East, where the water-table is sufficiently low to prevent damage, is found in huge quantities in garbage tips, houses, tombs, graves, and hoards of Graeco-Roman villages. In mainland Greece and Italy, several chance finds of papyri had been carbonized by fire or the pyroclastic flow of a volcano. In Vindolanda in Northern England thousands of wooden-tablets, the postcards of Roman soldiers, were preserved when the fire on the rubbish pile was extinguished by the inevitable British rain. Thus what destroys fragments in one context can preserve them in another.

## Means of Recovery

(*a*) *Simple discovery*. This can take the form of finding a book in the library of
a monastery, as in the case of Eco's *The Name of the Rose*, or a recent trip I
took to the monastery of St Catherine's to find that there were still manuscripts on the shelf of Proclus' commentary on Plato's *Parmenides* which
appear in no western catalogue. But the means by far more common since the
eighteenth century is by archaeological excavation or the discovery of hoards
or treasure-troves. We are all familiar with the Dead Sea Scrolls, or the Coptic
Nag Hammadi codices, or the new Archimedes palimpsest. And certainly
quotations in the works of other ancient authors have provided a rich harvest
of fragments from the Renaissance on. Pl. 2 shows an example of a new
fragment, preserved on a papyrus from Herculaneum of the oldest Greek
poet, Eumelus of Corinth, from a newly discovered fragment of Philodemus'
critique of the Greek myths in his $\Pi\epsilon\rho\grave{\iota}$ $\epsilon\mathring{v}\epsilon\beta\epsilon\acute{\iota}\alpha\epsilon$ (P.Herc. 1692 fr. 3)
published here for the first time:

```
              .   .   .   .
         .].. φο .[.....
         τὴν Ἥρ[αν....
         θέντα δ[.....
         την πο[......
7260     το πραγ[......                    5
         cαν κατ[......
         _cαι. ὁ δὲ [τὴν Εὐ-
         ρώπειαν γράψα[c
         καὶ αὑτῆc τὸν α[ὐ-
7265     τὸν ἐραcθῆνα[ί                    10
         φηcιν καὶ διὰ τ[ὸ
         μὴ ὑπομεῖνα[ι μι-
         χθῆναι ὡc ταυρ[ὸν
         αὐτὴν [τὸν] Δία [πα-
7270     ρηρῆc[θαι ....                    15
         _ται με .[...... ὁ
         δὲ γ[ράψαc .....
              .   .   .   .
```

(*several words missing*) Hera (*several words missing*) trouble (*infinitive missing*). The
author of the *Europea*[18] says that the same (god)[19] became enamoured of her[20] too,
and that, because she would not endure having intercourse, Zeus seduced her in the
form of a bull, (*some words missing*). The author of the (*several words missing*) . . .

For comparison, a fragmentary relief from the archaic period depicting the
same story, now in the Museo Nazionale in Naples (Pl. 3). That a fragment

---

[18] Eumelus of Corinth, 8th-c.-BC epic and lyric poet.
[19] viz. Zeus.          [20] Europa, the eponymous subject of the poem.

(albeit in prose paraphrase) of one of the oldest attested Greek poets, who worked in the eighth century BC, can be recovered from the oblivion of a buried library seems miraculous and beyond the ken even of William of Baskerville. On the other hand we did already have a narrative version from not much more than a century later in sculptural form, perhaps contemporary with the telling of the story in the Hesiodic *Catalogue of Women*. See also the recently published papyrus fragment of Hellenistic mythography (perhaps by the polymath grammarian Apollodorus of Athens), P.Oxy. LXXVI 5094, which cites the *Cypria*, the *Carmen Naupactium*, Stesichorus, and the *Odyssey*, within the same column (Pl. 4).

(*b*) *Conservation, restoration, and edition.* This is the crucible of editorial constitution where the oddities and discrepancies of textual transmission are put to the grammatical and lexicographical test. Forgeries or false ancient claims for ascription are determined by technical or lexical means. The texts preserved on papyrus fragments, for example, may be supplied according to the constraints of grammar, sense, or overlapping texts quoted by ancient authors in the indirect tradition. But they may also physically be extended by joining them with more of the same, identified by technical or textual means. Edgar Lobel spent 40 years sifting through literally millions of small fragments, grouping them on the basis of palaeography, quality of papyrus, and even fibres of the material. The result was whole successive columns of the books of the Greek lyric, epic, and iambic poets made up in individual cases of a hundred or more fragments. Pl. 5 shows a fragment bearing a final marginal graphic (called a coronis) from a papyrus identified by Lobel as coming from a manuscript of Sappho. In the case of fragments preserved in the secondary tradition, care must be given to why a given author is quoting the passage in question: for this may influence greatly the way he or she quotes it: how fully, how exactly: is he honest? To what kinds of texts did he have access, to what extent depend on memory and reading? Housman distinguished between 'quotation' or 'citation' in general, and 'local' or 'specific' quotations, in which authors are scrupulous about representing verbatim a word or phrase of significant interest to them in the context from another text, while exhibiting relative carelessness with regard to the exactitude of the quotation of the surrounding textual material.[21]

Contextualization is of the utmost importance: recognizing that a fragment belongs to a larger work, which itself may not be preserved or transmitted as a whole, leads to a coherent strategy of reconstruction, beginning from minimal supplementation and arriving at the most economical but persuasive formulation of a coherent text, according to the physical constraints of spacing and layout and the linguistic criteria of diction, grammar, and syntax.

---

[21] Housman 1910, 114 = 1972, ii. 801.

This may be illustrated by the following restoration of the text of a new fragment of Lollianos' *Phoinikika*, a text that appears in a very much more bare-bones, conservatively diplomatic version in the *editio princeps* (P.Oxy. LXXIII 4945, iii AD papyrus roll; Pl. 6):

```
                  ].. [..]....[
                  ].ωρ.....[..].[
         .. ἀνές]τραπται·" ἡ δὲ γραῦς ἡ τ[αῦτα ἀ-
         κούουσα] εἶπεν· "ὡς δὴ ἐπισταμέ[νως εἴ-
      5  ρηκας", το]ῦ μυελοῦ ἀναστραφέν[τος
         πάλιν, "σὺ] δὲ ἴδε" μυρρίνης ὕδατ[ι μεμι-
         γμένη οἶν]ον· καὶ οἱ μὲν ἐξήεσα[ν, ἐκεῖνος
         δὲ ἐλυπεῖτο] τὴν κεφαλὴν καλ[υψάμενος.
         καὶ γὰρ ἐ]ώκει ἡ παιδίσκη ἀποθ[νήσκειν· ἐν
     10  δὲ τούτ]ῳ ὁ μυελὸς ἀποστραφεὶς ἀ[λ]λ[ὸ
         ἐπόησε]ν· τῷ δὲ Ἄργιννα ἐξέκαε τὸ σ[τῆθος.
         πάνυ] γὰρ ὠχρὰ καὶ ἀποθνήσκειν δο[κοῦσα
         ἐραστ]ῇ ὅμως αὐτῷ ἐφαίνετο· ἐπεὶ κα[ὶ αὐ-
         τὸ]ν ἔρωτος ὑπέκκαυμα προσελάβε[το. ἐ-
     15  κεῖνος] μὲν οὖν ἀγρυπνῶν τῆς νυκτ[ὸς ἐκεί-
         νης ἔ]λεγ[ε πρὸς] τινα τῶν ἑαυτοῦ ἑτα[ίρων·
         "φίλε ἥ]δύ[τ]ατε, ἐμοὶ αὕτη ἡ γυνὴ οἶ[στρεῖ. εἴ-
         η δὲ αὐτ]ῇ μὴ καὶ οὕτως ἐχούςῃ πλ[εῖον ἔρω-
         τος. ἐὰν γ]ὰρ συγγένωμαι, ῥᾶιον δοκῶ [τοῦ-
     20  το πυθέσθ]αι· ἀλλὰ ἄπιθι καὶ ἀπάγγελ[ε δὴ
         πρὸς τὸν] Γλαυκέτην, ὅπως ἡ ὁ[μιλία γένη-
         ται περὶ] τὴν ἑσπέραν ἐρημία[ς παρούσης.
         δεῖ δὲ θύει]ν καὶ αὐτὸν, εἰ τούτου.[
                  ] οὐχ ἧττον ἢ εἰ ζω..[
     25           ]." ὁ μὲν δὴ ταῦτα πρὸς τ[ὸν Γλαυ-
         κέτην προ]σήγγελλεν· ὁ δὲ πρὸς [αὐτὸν ἀπο-
         πέμψας ὡ]μολόγησεν οὕτω ποή[σειν καὶ
         μέλλειν προτ]είνειν τὴν ε..[
                  ] κατασφαττ[
     30  ὁ δὲ πρὸς τὸν Γλαυκ]έτην ἀπο[στείλας
                  ]ν καὶ τελ[
                  ].πει τη.[
                  ].σθατ.[
                  ]..ηνικ[
     35           ].υτης ἀγ[γελ
                  ].ὑποτο[
                  ]ε καὶ κ[
                  ].υτοιν[
                  ]εας· ευ.[
     40           ]σετ..[
                  ]...[
         .   .   .   .   .
```

at their word: the dating of Hesiod himself depends on his own claim in his
*Works and Days* to have sung at Chalcis in the funeral games of Amphidamas
(who died in the Lelantine War): that poem is taken by modern scholars to be
Hesiod's *Theogony*, not as an imaginary construction. As for self-reference
and quotation of a preceding (complete) poem we have only to look to
Stesichorus' 'Palinode' which alluded to his 'Helen', the existence of which no
one doubts. While it is true that we know little about the organization of
Hellenistic poetry books (so few have survived), the recovery of a collection
of Posidippus' epigrams on a papyrus in Milan shows that by the end of the
third century BC it was typical for poems to be thematically linked or
grouped.[31] Elsewhere in Sappho's corpus, for example, we know that the
names of Sappho's companions recur in linked poems describing related
social settings. In some of these poems, Sappho was given to the representation of dramatic dialogue in a 'she said,' 'he said' form. In the dialogue with
Aphrodite in fr. 1, Sappho recounts a similar invocation in hymnic form of
Aphrodite on another occasion. That occasion may be as fictional as they
come, i.e. constructed for articulating the irony of Sappho in the present
poem having to invoke Aphrodite's aid 'yet again'—nevertheless, Sappho
constructs herself by making her song seem so pervasive that even Aphrodite
can quote a hymn of Sappho's that Sappho sang on another occasion. Given
the formal properties of hymnic and incantatory, magical discourse inherent
in Sappho 1,[32] it seems reasonable to suppose that an ancient reader would
have thought of the address Aphrodite alludes to as existing as a text. The
effect of Sappho 1 depends upon her having been the type of woman who had
previously (and not only once) found herself in a position of having formally
to invoke Aphrodite. That Sappho skilfully reworked earlier material of hers
(or gave the impression of doing so) would heighten and not detract from
readers' or audiences' appreciation of the ironies in the text of fr. 1.

It therefore would be convenient if there existed a preceding text (its
existence postulated by the argument above) that would show her in the
position of having done so, and in the absence of a continuously preserved
text, we can get some way forward through a reconstruction of what a fragment of the hymn preceding fr. 1 would have looked like—a poem that would
have been foundational for Sappho's erotic appeal to Aphrodite. Some details
can be culled directly from the text of Sappho 1, with minor alteration to
adjust person and time. It will have been in Sapphic strophes (as her entire
first book is thought to have been), and have consisted (like the extant text)
of an invocation of Aphrodite. We do not have to look very hard for one of

---

[31]  Bastianini and Gallazzi 2001; Austin and Bastianini 2002.

[32]  In particular, the style has often been noted to be reminiscent of a 'spell of attraction'
(ἀγωγή), such as that given in PGM IV 1511 εἰ κάθηται, μὴ καθήςθω, εἰ λαλεῖ πρός τινα, μὴ
λαλείτω ('if she is sitting, may she not sit, if she is talking with someone, may she not talk'). For
further examples see Winkler 1990, 172–5, cf. 162–9; Mace 1993; Petropoulos 1994; Segal 1996.

those, they are not in short supply among the extant fragments, e.g. fr. 33 *αἴθ᾽ ἔγω, χρυσοστέφαν᾽ Ἀφρόδιτα,* but any one will do to illustrate: the Michigan list of titles, for example, contains several, and there is already one in v. 13: *cὺ δ᾽ ὦ μάκαιρα* may quote the invocation of a hymn that began, like fr. 1, asyndetically, then identified Aphrodite by specific and descriptive epithets, before formally asking her to come. Perhaps it too already 'called upon her a second time' (*δηῦτε κάλημμι*) a familiar motif for an already familiar plight in an infinite regress, giving way to the expression of 'wanting something badly in my raging heart' (17–18 *μάλιcτα θέλω γένεcθαι / μαινόλαι θύμωι*). Next it will have included a request proper: presumably 'yet again to persuade' someone 18 *τινα* (= NN) *δηῦτε πείθε*):

$$... δηῦτε πείθε$$
$$[ἄ]ψ μ᾽ ἄγην ἐc Fὰν φιλότατα. <NN> μ᾽, ὦ$$
$$[20] \qquad Κύπρ᾽, ἀδίκηcι.$$
$$καὶ γὰρ αἰ φεύγει, ταχέωc διώξει·$$
$$αἰ δὲ δῶρα μὴ δέκετ᾽, ἀλλὰ δώcει·$$
$$αἰ δὲ μὴ φίλει, ταχέωc φιλήcει$$
$$κωὐκ ἐθέλοιcα.$$

The penultimate strophe is thus all but quoted in direct speech by Aphrodite in fr. 1 (21–4). Thus fr. 1 can be seen to script the performance of a prior (although not necessarily foundational or primary) hymn, which is recycled in fr. 1 for a subsequent erotic predicament. This strophe has long been lauded for its style, so reminiscent of Greek magical texts, of a curse. But what does Aphrodite have to do with curses? That she is the agency who fulfils them, not makes them, shows that we have Sappho represented as speaking on the prior occasion here. The same stylistic register shows that it is not necessary to change, in the reconstruction, the future indicatives with which Aphrodite mimics Sappho's insistent repetition of the request in the new context provided by fr. 1, for these will have been performative futures in the original hymn, in keeping with the insistent, incantatory tone suggested for it by the text of fr. 1.

## Types of Fragments

The examples afforded by the foregoing analysis permit a fundamental division of literary fragments into types based on means of preservation, as set out in the schematic diagram (Fig. 1.3) opposite.

With the final category, unattested works, one must proceed with extreme caution, providing only inevitable supplements, in order to lead to other, conjectural ones, thus drawing the 'circle of inevitability' ever closer. This helps to resolve a tension (never quite resolved) in the editing process over

Derivation of literary fragments:

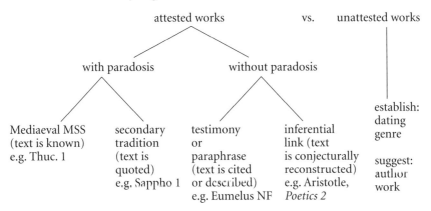

**Fig. 1.3.** Derivation of literary fragments.

whether the goal of the study is to establish the text, as far as it can be known with certainty, or rather to use the edition as an illustrative, plausible reconstruction of a view of the author or work reached on the basis of a fuller study of evidence outside the fragment in question. This tension can be summarized under the heads: *établir* vs. *refaire*. The proponents of *établir* generally take a conservative approach to textual constitution and presentation; they emphasize technique and insist that editing conventions be strictly observed. The proponents of *refaire* indulge in the luxury of *exempli gratia*: they seek primarily to make the work illustrate characteristics suggested from outside the fragment, and stress *Verstehen* or comprehension of the general problematic surrounding the author and his or her remains. But the dichotomy is functionally false. Clearly the choice of method must be determined by type of text and circumstances of preservation and transmission, not just by personal predilection and temperament.

## Principles for Editing Fragments

Those who collect fragments get used to following certain rules.

1. Don't split up integral fragments into smaller units (i.e. don't atomize the fragmentary tradition further).

2. Distinguish direct quotation from paraphrase or adaptation.

3. Pay close attention to context. Albert Henrichs has said that 'collections of fragments are both a blessing and a curse', the latter because they remove material from its original context, thus obscuring the readerly signs that

signal the way it was intended to be (and obviously was) understood when it is quoted. Therefore one should not make the pericope (the amount of surrounding context to be included with a fragment or quotation being studied) too narrow. To pay attention to and when necessary to reconstruct the original context of a fragment is as important as reconstructing the original work from which it was derived, and may be our only key to it. In addition, it provides an unexpected bonus in the form of a received and in many ways new fragment.

4. You must already in a sense know what the text says before you can read or restore it. New knowledge comes by way of correction and refinement or from the new context gained. It may link to another piece of the puzzle. When William of Baskerville, the Franciscan monk and detective in Eco's *The Name of the Rose*, finally lays hands on the long-lost second book of Aristotle's *Poetics*, he 'smiled as he read it, as if he recognized the things he expected to find'. And when questioned by the murderer Jorge as to how he knew it was the second book of Aristotle, he explains that he pieced it together from facts dropped in conversation with the murderer and knowing that these were mentioned in Aristotle's *Rhetoric* and the first book of the *Poetics*, together with a definition of comedy preserved in Isidore: 'Gradually it took shape in my mind, as it had to be. I could tell you almost all of it, without reading the pages that were meant to poison me'. Another way of putting this is, as Lionel Pearson once told me, 'You have to read the books that don't survive before you can understand the ones that do.'

5. Never emend the text at or in a lacuna (Youtie's first law).

6. Always assume that the text makes sense. Even a corrupt one is easier to correct if you start from this principle, and even a sound text is unreadable if you don't.

## Methodology of Restoration and Reconstruction

One proceeds generally on the assumptions of homology, symmetry, and analogy. Small differences may be perceived and carefully noted, and may be useful. I can now distinguish Glenn Most from Tony Grafton, though I used to confuse them. But in general sameness is the rule: *nihil semel repertum*. An analogy from art history and archaeology may be useful. In order to reconstruct the pot, we must first agree that we have a fragment of one, the potsherd (otherwise we shall have nothing to talk about). The controlling assumption is that the pot will be among the finite number of attested shapes, or a predictable variant thereof; for it would not be possible for us to con-ceptualize a shape totally outside our experience—a vessel with the opening on the bottom, for example, or with no aperture at all—without its ceasing to be a pot. In this way fragmentary pots are reconstructed and sectional drawings reconstructing fragmentary ceramics are made using an adjustable gauge known as a 'profile former' to define the shape of the face of the potsherd, then extrapolating its shape with the aid of a diameter chart. An example of the result can be seen in the drawing in Fig. 1.4. One side of the drawing shows the shape and extent of the fragmentary potsherd as found, while the other, symmetrical side reconstructs the shape according to recognized and catalogued patterns, or assimilates it to the closest attested shape. Note, however, that the original fragment, which suggested the reconstructed shape in the first place, is placed in its would-be position (on the left) after analysis has revealed its original shape (shown on the right). There is a logic to the process which at first seems circular, but upon reflection provides a confirmation of the identification of the type: the right-hand, reconstructed side suggests and directs the reconstruction and placement of the fragment on the left, while the conformity of the fragment on the left to the pattern on the right confirms the identification of the type. This approach to fragments has been functional since at least the Renaissance in the history of art, where it continues to hold sway in the modern and post-modern eras as parallel to the aesthetics of the unfinished or incomplete work of art (along the lines of such sentiments as: 'Quand on ne finit pas son travail, on est pris très au sérieux au Musée d'Art Moderne'). A disembodied work or artefact can thus be held to be a purer representation of a formal whole, implied by the logical or symmetrical or grammatical completion of its form, while instantiated firmly if imperfectly in material evidence.[33]

Another way to think of this is in terms of 'fractal theory'. The textual fragment entails a special relation between the part and the whole: as a 'fractal' part of a whole, it bears a symmetrical, recursive nature, much in the way that a branch from a tree or a frond from a fern is a miniature replica of the whole, not identical, but similar in its structural or spacial nature. Thus partially preserved pieces of a text fragmented in transmission (whether in quotation or copying or on a broken papyrus) by extension imply whole texts or shapes, capable of being reconstituted; fragmented letters imply by extension whole letters, or are capable of being delimited to a manageable series of possible letters, which can be further narrowed down according to constraints of space and grammar as a control. This sort of approach to reconstruction of texts has been termed 'lacunology', and is successfully being employed in more and less computer-automated forms to good effect in current work on fragmentary texts.

For a textual fragment the analogous method of presentation would be the diplomatic transcript presented side-by-side with an articulated and restored one. Or in a text with a manuscript tradition, an upper and lower apparatus

---

[33] Zinn 1959; Wanning Harries 1994.

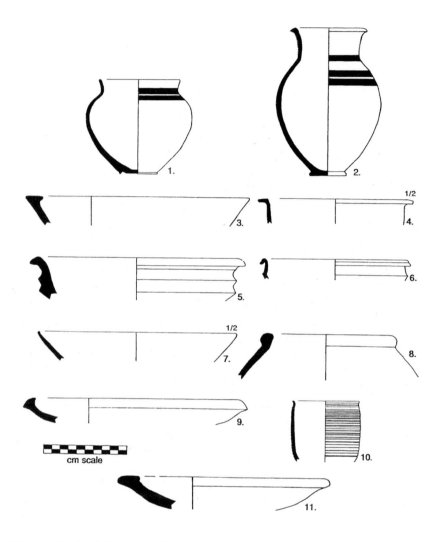

**Fig. 1.4.** Sectional drawings with reconstructions of ceramics.

documenting agreement and disagreement in the text with the primary manuscripts and secondary quotations, or parallels in other ancient authors.

The method works best for well-known types, for which identification depends on the statistical probability of occurrence of known types over aberrant, new ones. When an aberrant shape is discovered, as sometimes happens, reconstruction becomes conjectural and hypothetical, apart from features shared with known types. For there is no preserved example to mimic in reconstruction. It will be necessary to employ imagination, within limits of conceivable variation, and to be satisfied with the suggestion of possible reconstructions. But the method does successfully identify such unique and aberrant cases, and conjectural reconstruction can proceed along the lines of the next closest parallel form, charting predictable developments. Even when a completely aberrant and unexampled shape is discovered, the method is not at a loss: for the new shape is thereby incorporated into the system of shapes that is continually undergoing revision.

In working with fragments no method could be more fundamental: the form of the fragment, once identified, suggests or demands its own completion. It is as effective with papyri and quotations of lost books as it is with potsherds. Literary historians have a lot to learn from reflecting on the common methodology they share with archaeologists when dealing with fragmentary evidence. Last year in a survey I conducted in the Fayum in Egypt we found, for once, an intact, whole pot, buried in the sand. Being of a quite predictable form and whole, it was completely boring, hardly worth a second look. In the end it got left in the back of the van and broken when the theodolite case fell on it. When I was a graduate student at Stanford we were trained in the chronology of Hellenistic pottery shapes by Isabelle and Toni Raubitschek working on Stanford's huge collection of Cypriot vases. We were taught to recognize and visually reconstruct the shapes after the manner of the diagram shown, and also to group and reassemble pieces from the same vase, out of literally hundreds of boxes filled with thousands of sherds. All of these came originally from whole vases that had been broken not in antiquity but during the 1906 earthquake when the art museum collapsed. To this day they provide the material for instruction of graduates in archaeology. Some newly trained modern pot specialists are more concerned with the fabric of pottery than with their shapes and hypothetical chronologies. The latest trend is to cut potsherds, already fragmented pots, with tin-snips so as to reveal a fresh cross-section that might reveal technique or origin of material. Thus even more fragments are created, ensuring on-going archaeological research on the pots into the next millennia.

Not that the task is always a simple one, of course. Analyses of fragmentary evidence certainly admit, like most areas of scholarly endeavour, of different styles of thought. In particular there is a difference between such styles over the point at which quantification of data derived from fragmentary evidence or other specifically analytic methodologies becomes relevant. Simply counting instances of the occurrence of a given author on papyrus, or ranking occurrences by period, produces but crude statistical masses of evidence if undigested, and most scholars find it more informative to assimilate the material bit by bit by reading and studying one papyrus text at a time and then, upon reflection, assimilating it to a larger, reconstructed work or collected corpus.

One conclusion I want to draw from this is that fragments are not fundamentally written, but share avenues of interpretation with other bodies of fragmentary evidence: that is to say, they are not essentially dependent on writing and literacy, but these simply occasion and structure one medium in which fragments survive and are embedded. The methodologies for working on fragments of different media are commutable. Mixed media collections of fragments (e.g. literary texts combined with narratives from visual art) open up many new possibilities. Richard Kannicht's *TGrF* edition of the fragments of Euripides includes vase paintings of scenes from the plays alongside the literary fragments, at least as a version of the play. In theory it ought to be possible to isolate oral fragments, such as formed the basis, for example, for Thucydides' speeches. Or to analyse the oral formulaic system of Homeric composition, as a system that, as Goethe said, 'does your composing for you'—i.e. as built up out of dismembered cola from the last poem heard by the rhapsode, reassembled in another narrative.[34] Compare the epigram for Midas quoted by Plato in which the lines can fall in any order and still say the same thing.[35] Plato faults its composition, for the reason that the order of its parts is not integral to its expression. The point is that fragments are only marginal by their transmission, but they may also be marginal and separate by design, as are marginalia, for example.

Commentaries and scholia, for example, share this fragmentary-by-design character: they have a dismembered existence hovering between the text to which they are referenced and being text in their own right. A common beginning of a line-note in an ancient commentary is ὅτι. A sentence beginning thus is the mark of an ancient commentary, and as such we can identify it in even the smallest scrap of papyrus. ὅτι in such cases means: 'the critical sign is placed in the margin before this line, because . . .' (or sometimes, that 'the poet says this, because . . .'), i.e. introducing an exegetical point. Commentaries can be even more fragmentary and fragmenting still. Franco Montanari has argued[36] that the earliest commentary in its most basic form takes the form of mere spaces between two words (between which, in ancient manuscripts, normally there are no spaces), where alternative articulation is possible and deemed potentially confusing to readers so that disambiguation was needed—i.e. punctuation. An example may be found in P.Oxy. XXI 2288 containing Sappho fr. 1. At vv. 7–9 a mark of punctuation in the papyrus after χρύϲιον shows that it goes with δόμον in 7, not with ἄρμα in 9, thus clarifying a dispute in what has been called the 'most often mistranslated verse in Sappho'.[37] At any rate it shows, given that punctuation in this and literary papyri in general is rarely and selectively provided, the way in which readers in the Roman period were instructed by their teachers, editors, and commentaries to construe the syntax. What can be more fragmentary

---

[34] Cf. Bird 1994.    [35] *Phaedrus* 264 D.    [36] Montanari 1997.
[37] The papyrus' construal of the syntax is argued for on the basis of lyric and epic parallels by Slings 1991, 404.

**Fig. 1.5.** School-Ostrakon (v BC) from Olbia containing *Ilias parua (altera)* fr. 28 Bernabé = 1 Davies (recto on the right, verso on the left).

than blank spaces or (seemingly trivial) marks of punctuation is a question with metaphysical implications addressed, for example, by Eco in *Foucault's Pendulum*.[38] The idea of the margin as the zone of fantasy and banality, imagination and pedantry, drollery and surrealism, into which these fragmentary glosses, signs, and explanations are inscribed goes from Callimachus to Derrida.

My final example comes from the archaic poem of the epic cycle known as the *Ilias parua*. We know its incipit from various sources, and even something about its alleged composition: the pseudo-Herodotean *Vita Homeri* 16, vol. 5 p. 202 Allen says Ὅμηρος ... διατρίβων δὲ παρὰ Θεστορίδῃ ποιεῖ Ἰλιάδα τὴν ἐλάccω ἧς ἐcτιν ἀρχή· Ἴλιον ἀείδω κτλ. A rival tradition in antiquity attributed the poem to Lesches of Lesbos (*Ilias parua* fr. 1 Bernabé = Dubia 2 Davies), and gave different verses as the beginning of the epic:

> Μοῦcα μοι ἔννεπε ἔργα, τὰ μήτ᾽ ἐγένοντο πάροιθε
> μήτ᾽ ἔcται μετόπιcθεν.

However, as recently as the 1970s Russian excavators working at the Greek settlements at Olbia on the Black Sea unearthed an ostrakon (Fig. 1.5) containing the beginning of the *Ilias parua* as given by pseudo-Herodotus.[39]

> Ἴλιον ἀ[ιε]ίδω καὶ Δαρδανίην] ιεὔπω[ιλον
> ἧc πέρι πόλλ᾽ ἔπαθον Δαναοὶ θεράποντεc Ἄρηος]ι

[38] Eco 1988, in many ways a sequel to *The Name of the Rose*; cf. id. 1982; 1998.

[39] Dated to 420–410 BC: see Yu. G. Vinogradov and M. Zolotarev in Lordkipanidze *et al.* 1990, 109 with 119 pl. 10c; *Bull. ép.* (1974), 376 = *SEG* 40. 612 no. 26. Such incipits count against the view of Bowie 1997 that fragments did not circulate as texts in antiquity. Cf. Dionisotti 1997.

Perhaps the letters forming the first verse were scratched into the black-glazed potsherd by a Greek writer who, in learning his letters for the first time, was recording his hearing of the most recently fashionable literature about Troy. And this seems quite remarkable, for its early date, late sixth–early fifth century BC according to the stratigraphy of the find. As far as I know, this is the earliest surviving recorded version of a circulating literary text. As a possible context, one might compare Herodotus' account (4. 79) of Skyles at the festival of Dionysos Bakcheios. (Vinogradov imagines him acting out the Trojan cycle of the ostrakon's text in dramatic festivals.) I myself might have been tempted to regard the ostrakon as a modern forgery, were it not the case that the first verse was subsequently found on another ostrakon, this time from the Chersonese, while another found at Olbia was incised with *Od.* 9. 39:[40]

Ἰλιόθεν με φέρων ἄνεμος Κικόνεccι πέλαccεν.

Given its geographical subject-matter, we might have been tempted to attribute the enduring popularity of this verse in this region in some way to the cult of Achilles in the Troad and on the Hellespont leading to the Black Sea region.[41] But Oliver Taplin suggests to me that, like the incipit of the *Ilias parua* on the other ostrakon mentioned above from Olbia, it might have formed the incipit of a stand-alone recitation or performance of Odysseus' narrative of his wanderings before the Phaeacian court.[42]

The other point that takes on added importance is the role of types. For textual fragments this translates into terms of genre. Identity, homology, analogy, difference, and sameness are perceived by way of recognizable classifications of literary types. Through these types fragments make it possible for past cultures to communicate with us. We relate to fragments, and ultimately reconstruct them, in the same way in which we understand other works of literature, namely by assimilating them to a pattern of possible modes and *topoi* of expression as exampled in extant types, and observing recognizable similarities and expectations, or, when our expectations are disappointed, by assimilating them as new examples to the body of data. Needless to say, if an entirely unexampled type of text suddenly appeared, as has certainly happened since the eighteenth century, we wouldn't know what to do with it, until other examples and parallels appear. The disappointment experienced over the content of the Herculaneum papyri over the past two and a half centuries is a good example. Only recently and very uncertainly have they come into their own, and I maintain that their exact text-types are still not sufficiently recognized.

---

[40] Yailenko 1980, 88 no. 89 = *SEG* 30. 933, dated simply to the 5th c. BC.

[41] As evidenced by the Hymn to Achilles, *VDI* 1990 (3), 49–62 = *SEG* 40. 601.

[42] L.A.H.-S. notes that it remained a well-known quotation from Hellanicus to Epictetus and beyond.

In this sense fragments are essentially no different than whole works. Even in whole works, there is always some information held back, in order to make you seek out more (e.g. Daphnis in pastoral), or to consult a specialist (medical treatises). Thus even whole works are only ostensibly wholes, but functionally they are fragments.

Finally, access to a European museum full of unpublished papyri or an archaeological dig is not necessary in order to reconstruct lost books from fragments: you'll find them in your own back yard, embedded everywhere, as in a speech in Thucydides, for example. Editing fragments is a style of thought and a strategy of reading, applicable even to whole works. Experience itself is discrete and interrupted and fractured and only through reflection reassembled as a continuum. It is the same process of reflection that we apply more systematically and intentionally to recover books from fragments and cultures from artefacts in spite of gaps and interstices that will never be closed.

Working in Naples, and seeing Vesuvius smoking from time to time, I reflect that one day the papyri might be buried by another eruption (it depends only on the way the wind blows) and have to be excavated a second time. I am reminded then that there will come a day when all our books will return to chaos, digital encoding to gibberish, and it will be for a later age to pick up the pieces and see what we had to say.

# BIBLIOGRAPHY

Ansse de Villoison, J. B. G. d', 1783, *Epistolae Vinarienses, in quibus multa Graecorum scriptorum loca emendantur ope librorum Ducalis Bibliothecae* (Zurich).

Austin, C., and Bastianini, G. 2002, *Posidippi Pellaei quae supersunt omnia* (Milan).

Baker, N. 2001, *Double Fold: Libraries and the Assault on Paper* (New York).

Bardon, H. 1952–6, *La Littérature latine inconnue*, 2 vols. (Paris).

Barnes, J. 1997, 'Roman Aristotle', in J. Barnes and M. Griffin (eds.), *Philosophia Togata II: Plato and Aristotle at Rome* (Oxford), 1–69.

Bastianini, G., and Gallazzi, C. (with C. Austin) 2001, *Posidippo di Pella. epigrammi* (Milan).

Bird, G. D. 1994, 'The Textual Criticism of an Oral Homer', in V. J. Gray (ed.), *Nile, Ilissos and Tiber. Essays in Honour of Walter Kirkpatrick Lacey* (Prudentia, 26; Auckland), 36–52.

Bowie, E. L. 1997, 'The Theognidea: A Step Towards a Collection of Fragments', in Most 1997, 53–66.

Burkert, W., *et al.* 1998, *Fragmentsammlungen philosophischer Texte der Antike / Le raccolte dei frammenti di filosofi antichi* (Aporemata, 3; Göttingen).

Cameron, A. 1995, *Callimachus and his Critics* (Princeton).

Camion, A., *et al.* (eds.) 1999, *Über das Fragment — Du fragment* (Heidelberg).

Campbell, D. A. (ed. and transl.) 1990, *Greek Lyric I: Sappho and Alcaeus*, 2nd edn. (Cambridge, MA).

Dionisotti, A. C. 1997, 'On Fragments in Classical Scholarship', in Most 1997, 1–33.

Eco, U. 1980, *Il nome della rosa* (Milan); trans. W. Weaver, *The Name of the Rose* (London, 1983).

—— 1982, *The Aesthetics of Chaosmos: The Middle Ages of James Joyce*, transl. E. Esrock (Cambridge, MA).

—— 1988, *Il pendulo di Foucault* (Milan); trans. W. Weaver, *Foucault's Pendulum* (London, 1989).

—— 1998, *Serendipities: Language and Lunacy*, trans. W. Weaver (New York).

Garzya, A. 1971, 'Per la fortuna di Saffo a Bisanzio', *JÖB* 20, 1–5.

Gow, A. S., and Page, D. L. 1965, *The Greek Anthology: Hellenistic Epigrams* (Cambridge).

Grafton, A. 1991, *Defenders of the Text: The Traditions of Scholarship in an Age of Science, 1450–1800* (Cambridge, MA).

—— 2001, *Bring Out Your Dead: The Past as Revelation* (Cambridge, MA).

Housman, A. E. 1910, 'On the *Aetia* of Callimachus', *CQ* 4, 114–20; repr. in *The Classical Papers of A. E. Housman*, ed. J. Diggle and F. R. D. Goodyear, 3 vols. (Cambridge, 1972), ii. 801–8.

Janko, R. 1984, *Aristotle on Comedy: Towards a Reconstruction of Poetics II.* (London).

—— 1987, *Aristotle, Poetics I; with the Tractatus Coislinianus: A Hypothetical Reconstruction of Poetics II; The Fragments of the On Poets* (Indianapolis).

—— 1991, 'Philodemus' *On Poems* and Aristotle's *On Poets*', *CErc* 21, 5–64.

Kaibel, G. 1894, 'Aratea', *Hermes*, 29, 82–123.

Kenyon, F. G. 1897, *The Poems of Bacchylides, from a Papyrus in the British Museum* (London).

Lehnus, L. 2000, *Nuova bibliografia callimachea (1489–1998)* (Alessandria).

Lordkipanidze, O., Lévêque, P., Geny, É., and Khartchilava, T. 1990, *Le Pont-Euxin vu par les Grecs* (Centre de Recherches d'Histoire Ancienne 100, Ann. Besançon no. 427; Besançon).

Mace, S. 1993, 'Amour, Encore! The Development of δηὖτε in Archaic Lyric', *GRBS* 34, 335–64.

Mair, G. R. 1921, *Callimachus, Hymns and Epigrams* (London).

Merkelbach, R., and West, M. L. 1967, *Fragmenta Hesiodea* (Oxford).

Montanari, F. 1997, 'Fragments of Hellenistic Scholarship', in Most 1997, 273–88.

Most G. W. (ed.) 1997, *Collecting Fragments – Fragmente sammeln* (Aporemata, 1; Göttingen).

Obbink, D. 2007, 'Lucretius and the Herculaneum Library', in S. Gillespie and Ph. Hardie (eds.), *The Cambridge Companion to Lucretius* (Cambridge), 33–40.

Parca, M. 1982, 'Sappho 1.18–19', *ZPE* 46, 47–50.

Parsons, P. J. 1982, 'Facts from Fragments', *G&R*, NS 29, 184–95.

—— 2002, 'New Texts and Old Theories', in T. P. Wiseman (ed.), *Classics in Progress: Essays on Greece and Rome* (Oxford), 39–57.

Petropoulos, J. B. 1994, 'Sappho the Sorceress—Another Look at fr. 1 (LP)', *ZPE* 97, 43–56.

Pound, E. 1916, *Lustra* (New York).

Scaliger, J. J. 1579, 'Commentarius et castigationes in primum isagogicum M. Manilii', in *Castigationes et notae in M. Manilii Astronomicon (Paris), 67.*

Seelbach, W. 1970, 'Ezra Pound und Sappho fr. 95 L.–P.', *A&A* 16, 83–4.

Segal, C. 1996, 'Eros and Incantation: Sappho and Oral Poetry', in E. Green (ed.), *Reading Sappho* (Berkeley), 58–75; revised version of *Arethusa*, 7 (1974), 139–60.

Slings, S. 1991, 'Sappho Fr. 1,8 V.: Golden House or Golden Chariot?', *Mnem.*[4] 44, 404–10.

Tarán, L. 1974, review of P. Moraux, *Aristote: Du Ciel* (Paris, 1965), in *Gnomon*, 46, 121–42; repr. in id., *Collected Papers (1962–1999)* (Leiden, 2001), 372–403.

Turner, E. G. 1973, *The Papyrologist at Work* (*GRBS* Monograph 6. Durham, NC).

Wanning Harries, E. 1994, *The Unfinished Manner: Essays on the Fragment in the Later Eighteenth Century* (Charlottesville and London).

West, M. L. 1973, *Textual Criticism and Editorial Technique* (Stuttgart).

—— 2005, 'The New Sappho', *ZPE* 151, 1–9.

Wilamowitz-Moellendorff, U. von, 1924, *Hellenistische Dichtung in der Zeit des Kallimachos*, 2 vols. (Berlin).

Winkler, J. 1990, 'Double Consciousness in Sappho's Lyrics', in id., *The Constraints of Desire* (New York), 162–87.

Yailenko, V. P. (Яйленко В. П.) 1980, Граффити Левки, Березани и Ольвии) ('Graffiti from Leuce, Berezan', and Olbia'), *VDI* 1980/3 (109), 75–116.

Yatromanolakis, D. 1998, 'Selected Fragments of Sappho: Introductory Studies and Commentary' (D.Phil. thesis, Oxford).

—— 1999, 'Alexandrian Sappho Revisited', *HSCP* 99, 179–95.

—— 2008, *Sappho in the Making: The Early Reception* (Cambridge, MA).

Youtie, H. C. 1974, *The Textual Criticism of Documentary Papyri: Prolegomena*, 2nd edn. (*BICS* Suppl. 33. London).

Zinn, E. 1959, 'Fragment über Fragmente', in J. A. Schmoll gen. Eisenwerth (ed.), *Das Unvollendete als künstlerische Form* (Bern), 161–6.

# 2

## Pindar as a Man of Letters

*Martin West*

Pindar was, I imagine, a difficult man to live with. Certainly he is a difficult poet to translate, and a difficult one to place in literary history. He is not very like any earlier poet that we can point to; Simonides comes closest. Beside him there is Bacchylides, whom we tend to think of as Pindar and water. So from one point of view Pindar appears as an original genius, a great innovator, even an erratic block. On the other hand there appear in his poetry tropes and imagery which find their best parallels in the Rigveda and which seem to be elements of ancient poetic tradition that have come down to Pindar by a line of transmission not represented in what else we have of early Greek poetry.[1] This makes it advisable to be cautious on the subject of his originality. He was evidently heir to lines of tradition independent of the Ionian epic. It is not so strange that it should be so. Pindar is, after all, the only one of the lyric poets to have survived in such quantity, and the only one from Boeotia.[2]

On the other hand we cannot regard him as an aborigine faithfully carrying on an archaic provincial tradition. He is a man of the fifth century, well travelled, with friends and patrons in many parts of Greece, from Rhodes in the east to Sicily in the west, from Thessaly in the north to Cyrene in the south: a man of Panhellenic culture. It is his relationship to that culture, and especially to earlier poetry, that forms the subject of my paper.

If we talk about Aeschylus' or Euripides' attitude towards Homer, it is a matter of inference. They cannot name Homer outright or make an explicit quotation—though Euripides at least can refer unspecifically to 'poets' tales'.[3] The lyric poet, like the elegist, has the freedom to refer to poets, musicians, or other historical persons by name. Already in the seventh century Callinus of

---

[1] See West 2007, esp. chs. 1 and 2.
[2] I do not count Corinna, whom I regard as Hellenistic; cf. West 1970; 1990.
[3] e.g. *Hipp.* 451, *HF* 1315, 1346, *Hyps.* fr. 752g. 18; cf. *IA* 798.

Ephesus appears to have mentioned the name of Homer—I believe as the legendary ancestor whom the Homeridai claimed to be the author of their traditional epic. In the late sixth or early fifth century Simonides refers to Homer and Stesichorus, and Xenophanes refers to Homer and Hesiod. Bacchylides quotes a saying of Hesiod's, and elsewhere he spoke of Homer as a native of Ios.[4]

Pindar indulges this freedom more extensively. If we put together all the passages where he refers to poets or musicians of the past, we get the impression that he had in his head the materials for a history of early Greek poetry and music. It would have been, had he written it, an idiosyncratic history, containing legendary elements and outspoken personal judgements. But here in Pindar we have someone who looks back and surveys his predecessors with a critical and reflective eye.

Homer is for him the poet who propagated the glory of the heroes who fought at Troy: *Φρυγίας κοςμήτορα μάχας*, he calls him (if the anonymous fragment 347 is rightly assigned), 'adorner of the Phrygian war'. It is through Homer that we know of those heroes; this observation underlines the importance of the poet to his patron, of Pindar to Hiero (*Pyth.* 3. 112–15):

Νέςτορα καὶ Λύκιον Cαρπηδόν᾽, ἀνθρώπων φάτῑc,
ἐξ ἐπέων κελαδεννῶν, τέκτονες οἷα cοφοί
ἅρμοcαν, γινώcκομεν. ἁ δ᾽ ἀρετὰ κλεινaῖc ἀοιδaῖc
χρονία τελέθει· παύροιc δὲ πράξαcθ᾽ εὐμαρέc.

Nestor and Lycian Sarpedon, who are the talk of mankind,
we know from resounding verses such as skilled craftsmen
have fitted together. It is through famous songs
that excellence endures, something that few find it easy to achieve.

This is almost to identify myths with poetic sources.

To a degree, Pindar sees himself in the same job as Homer, that of perpetuating fame.[5] For him the Homeric heroes, like his patrons, were real men; no question of their being fictitious characters. But he does not trust Homer to give an accurate account of them. Like Thucydides (1. 10. 3), he sees Homer as being liable, *qua* poet, to exaggerate and embellish the facts. As a devotee of the Aeacidae he invokes the unreliability of Homer in a thoroughly partisan way in the face of Odysseus' infamous defeat of Ajax in the contest over Achilles' armour and Ajax's suicide (*Nem.* 7. 20–8):

ἐγὼ δὲ πλέον᾽ ἔλπομαι
λόγον Ὀδυccέοc ἢ πάθαν διὰ τὸν ἁδυεπῆ γενέcθ᾽ Ὅμηρον,
ἐπεὶ ψεύδεcί οἱ ποτανᾶι <τε> μαχανᾶι

---

[4] Callin. fr. 6 W., cf. West 1999, 377; Simon. *PMG* 564. 4, Xenoph. DK 21 B 10–11, Bacch. 5. 192, fr. 48.
[5] A very Indo-European conception: West 2007, ch. 10.

cεμνὸν ἔπεcτί τι· coφία
  δὲ κλέπτει παράγοιcα μύθοιc. τυφλὸν δ' ἔχει
ἦτορ ὅμιλοc ἀνδρῶν ὁ πλεῖcτοc· εἰ γὰρ ἦν
ἓ τὰν ἀλάθειαν ἰδέμεν, οὔ κεν ὅπλων χολωθείc
ὁ καρτερὸc Αἴαc ἔπαξε διὰ φρενῶν
λευρὸν ξίφοc.

I reckon that Odysseus is held in higher account
than his experience warrants, thanks to that sweet-versing Homer,
for on his falsehoods and his winging artifice
a certain grandeur sits: skilled craft
beguiles and deceives with its tales. The generality
of mankind has an unseeing disposition;
for if it could descry the truth, the stalwart Ajax
would not in anger over arms have driven
a slick sword through his heart.

Pindar is not denying and cannot deny that Ajax committed suicide; he is claiming that the Achaeans were wrong to award the arms to Odysseus, because Odysseus was not really the more deserving and it is only Homer's art that makes it seem plausible that he was. This 'Homer' is evidently the poet of the *Aethiopis* or the *Little Iliad*. (The story of the suicide was told in both epics.) In the Eighth Nemean again (23–7) Pindar insists that Ajax was the worthier hero but that Odysseus' suspect eloquence defrauded him of his prize. Here there is no reference to Homer, and it is unequivocally Odysseus' way with words, not the poet's, that is in question. Pindar brings up the story also in the Fourth Isthmian (35–42), and this time Homer is commended without reserve. You know, he says, of the valour of Ajax, which he cleft on his own sword in the darkness of night, leaving him aggrieved against the sons of the Greeks who went to Troy.

ἀλλ' Ὅμηρός τοι τετίμακεν δι' ἀνθρώπων, ὃc αὐτοῦ
πᾶcαν ὀρθώcαιc ἀρετὰν κατὰ ῥάβδον ἔφραcεν
θεcπεcίων ἐπέων λοιποῖc ἀθύρειν·
τοῦτο γὰρ ἀθάνατον φωνᾶεν ἕρπει,
εἴ τιc εὖ εἴπηι τι· καὶ πάγκαρπον ἐπὶ χθόνα καὶ διὰ πόντον βέβακεν
ἐργμάτων ἀκτὶc καλῶν ἄcβεcτοc αἰεί.

But Homer has done him honour among men,
who set straight all his prowess and told of it on the rod
of his wondrous verses to entertain posterity;
for it travels on immortal in voice,
if someone says something well: across the fruitful land and over the sea
goes the bright beam of fine deeds, unquenched for ever.

No suggestion that Ajax's merits might have been exaggerated by the poet.

 Addressing Arcesilas in the Fourth Pythian (277) Pindar cites Homer as a source of wisdom:

τῶν δ᾽ Ὁμήρου καὶ τόδε cυνθέμενος
ῥῆμα πόρcυν᾽· ἄγγελον ἐcλὸν ἔφα
τιμὰν μεγίcταν πράγματι παντὶ φέρειν.

From the sayings of Homer take this one too to heart
and tend it: he said that a good messenger
confers the greatest dignity on every matter.

This technique of quoting a maxim and prefacing it with a source-reference is one that we can trace back as far as Alcaeus, who refers (fr. 360) to what Aristodemus once said in Sparta, by no means a gormless remark, οὐκ ἀπάλαμνον λόγον, namely "χρήματ᾽ ἀνήρ", 'property makes the man'. Pindar, as it happens, also quotes this apophthegm, though he attributes it to an unnamed Argive (*Isth.* 2. 9–11). There are other passages where he is still less specific. The saying "μηδὲν ἄγαν", 'Nothing in excess', he ascribes to cοφοί, sages or poets (fr. 35b). In another place (*Nem.* 9. 6) he uses the formula ἔcτι δέ τιc λόγοc ἀνθρώπων, 'there is a saying among men'.

In others again a mythical personage is cited as the source. In the Ninth Pythian (94) it is the Old Man of the Sea: he said one should give one's enemy full credit for his good deeds. Was there some collection of precepts ascribed to the Old Man of the Sea? There is no other trace of it. More likely Pindar is alluding to some narrative poem in which a hero met and conversed with the Old Man, as Menelaus did with Proteus in the *Odyssey*, and Heracles with Nereus in the *Geryoneis*.[6] The Stesichorean poem seems a possible source.

A clearer case is the Sixth Olympian (12–17), where Pindar applies to the Syracusan victor Hagesias the praise that Adrastus justly spoke over Amphiaraus in Thebes at the funeral of the Seven: ἀμφότερον μάντίν τ᾽ ἀγαθὸν καὶ δουρὶ μάρναcθαι, 'both a good seer and a good warrior'. Here we would guess that Pindar had the epic *Thebaid* in mind, even if the scholiast did not tell us so on the authority of Asclepiades of Myrlea. It is easy to restore the original hexameter:

ἀμφότερον μάντίν τ᾽ ἀγαθὸν καὶ δουρὶ μάχεcθαι.[7]

Pindar has simply replaced μάχεcθαι with μάρναcθαι. In the Eighth Pythian (39–55) he quotes a prophecy by Amphiaraus about the outcome of the war of the Epigoni: it is not convertible into hexameters but it may well represent the substance of a prophecy given in the Cyclic *Epigoni*.

There is what looks like a comparable case in Bacchylides, who in his third ode (78–84) cites a piece of wisdom that Apollo imparted to Admetus:

---

[6] *Od.* 4. 460–569; Stes. *PMGF* S 16a, cf. Pherec. 16a Fowler.

[7] *Thebais* fr. 8 B. = 6 W., already restored by Leutsch; disputed by Wilamowitz 1901, 1285 n. 1 = 247 n. 3, cf. 1886, 163 n. 4; 1922, 310 n. 3. The verse is borrowed in the epitaph for Aeschines' uncle, the seer Cleobulus (*CEG* 519. 2), and echoed in Soph. *OC* 1314.

θνατὸν ἐὖντα χρὴ διδύμους ἀέξειν
γνώμας, ὅτι τ' αὔριον ὄψεαι μοῦνον ἁλίου φάος,
χὥτι πεντήκοντ' ἔτεα ζωὰν βαθύπλουτον τελεῖς.

Being mortal, you need to nurture
two mindsets: that tomorrow's sunlight is the only one you will see,
and that for fifty years you will live out a life of deep wealth.

Excellent advice, one of the best precepts to have come to us from antiquity. But what was Bacchylides' source? Presumably some ample account of Apollo's servitude to Admetus.

Now, the point I want to make about the passage in the Fourth Pythian, 'From the sayings of Homer take this one too to heart', is that to name a literary source is to go a step further than naming the mythical or historical personage supposed to have uttered the dictum. Pindar is not the only poet of his time to take this step, but it seems to be something fairly new. Simonides uses quotations in three of his melic fragments. In two of them the sources are famous sages, Pittacus and Cleobulus (*PMG* 542. 11, 581). In the third (579) he uses the formula that Pindar also uses, ἔςτι τις λόγος, and here we recognize a paraphrase of some lines from the *Works and Days* (289–92). But in one of his elegies (19. 1–2 W.[2]) he famously quotes a line of the *Iliad* verbatim, and quotes it as Homer's:

ἓν δὲ τὸ κάλλιστον Χῖος ἔειπεν ἀνήρ·
"οἵη περ φύλλων γενεή, τοίη δὲ καὶ ἀνδρῶν".

This finest single thing the Chian said:
'As the breed of leaves, e'en so is that of man.'

The actual name Ὅμηρος appears in a papyrus fragment of what may well be the same poem and may, as Peter Parsons has suggested, belong just before the lines about the man of Chios.[8] The significant thing for my present purpose is that he does not introduce the Homeric verse as 'that fine observation that Glaucus made to Diomedes' (which would be parallel to the quotation of what Adrastus said about Amphiaraus), but as 'that finest of things that the man of Chios said'. This betokens a new attitude towards the poetry of the past.

It belongs in a context that I have sketched elsewhere.[9] In the second half of the sixth century there appears for the first time a lively interest in Homer as a poet and as a man, distinct from his works, and more generally an interest in literary history, in defining and assessing the achievements of past poets and musicians and contrasting the old with the new. The epics begin to be treated no longer as free-standing records of the past but as the artistic creations of

---

[8] P.Oxy. LIX 3965 fr. 26. 14 = eleg. 20. 14 W.[2]; Parsons 1992, 43; cf. West 1993, 10, Sider 1996, 271.

[9] West 1999, 377–80.

an individual, to be praised or criticized. Cynaethus, the poet of the Delian hymn to Apollo, impersonates the blind poet of Chios who wandered from city to city and whose songs constitute a matchless legacy (*Hymn. Ap.* 172–5). Theagenes of Rhegium at the same period is said to have written the first book about Homer (DK 8. 1). Xenophanes criticizes Homer and Hesiod for spreading false and pernicious ideas about the gods (DK 21 B 11). Heraclitus too criticizes Homer, saying that he deserves to be driven out of the ἀγῶνεϲ and whipped. He refers to Homer's reputation as the wisest of men, and cites verses from the *Iliad* as evidence that Homer was an ἀϲτρολόγοϲ (DK 22 B 42, 56, 105). Simonides expresses warm admiration for Homer's achievement. In the proem of his Plataea elegy he writes of the Danaans who fought at Troy (fr. 11. 15–18 W.²),

> οἷϲιν ἐπ' ἀθά]νατον κέχυται κλέοϲ ἀν[δρὸϲ] ἕκητι
> ὃϲ παρ' ἰοπ]λοκάμων δέξατο Πιερίδ[ων
> πᾶϲαν ἀλη]θείην, καὶ ἐπώνυμον ὀπ[λοτέρ]οιϲιν
> ποίηϲ' ἡμ]ιθέων ὠκύμορον γενεή[ν.

> [And they] are bathed in fame that cannot die, by grace
>   [of one who from the dark-]tressed Muses had
> the tru[th entire,] and made the heroes' short-lived race
>   a theme familiar to younger men.

In an epigram inscribed on a Herm in the Athenian Agora following the capture of Eïon in 475[10] it is recalled that the Atridae were accompanied to Troy by an Athenian leader, Menestheus,

> ὅν ποθ' Ὅμηροϲ ἔφη Δαναῶν πύκα θωρηκτάων
> κοϲμητῆρα μάχηϲ ἔξοχον ὄντα μολεῖν.

> Whom Homer once pronounced, of all the cuirassed Danaans,
>   the outstanding arrayer of the battle-line.

Stories began to circulate at the same period about Homer's life. Different cities began to claim him as their own: Cynaethus and Simonides make him a Chiot, Bacchylides said he came from Ios, Pindar is said to have called him (presumably in different poems) both a Chiot and a Smyrnaean.[11] Heraclitus (B 56) adverts to the tale of how this supposedly wisest of men was defeated by a boys' riddle. Debate about the authorship of the various epics was under way. Pindar is cited (fr. 265) as having endorsed the story that Homer, wanting to marry off his daughter and being too poor to afford a dowry, gave away the *Cypria* in lieu of one. The point of the story was that this epic that went under the name of Stasinus of Cyprus was really by Homer. We have

---

[10] Aeschin. *Ctes.* 183; Plut. *Cimon* 7. 6; Page, *FGE* 257 ll. 841–2 (cf. Hdt. 7. 161. 3).
[11] *Hymn. Ap.* 172, Simon. eleg. 19. 1, Bacch. fr. 48, Pind. fr. 264.

seen that at least one of the other Cyclic epics was also, in Pindar's eyes, by Homer, though we do not know whether he was aware of alternative claimants in that case.

Other poets too were the subject of interest. It seems that Stesichorus had already mentioned certain older poets by name, the shadowy Xanthus and the famous Hesiod (*PMGF* 229, 269). Simonides, referring to Meleager's victory with the javelin at the funeral games for Pelias, adds the names of his poetic sources as a warranty of truth: οὕτω γὰρ Ὅμηρος ἠδὲ Cτασίχορος ἄεισε λαοῖς, 'for so Homer and Stesichorus have sung to the peoples' (*PMG* 564). They have been awarded classic status. Hesiod of course also had it. Simonides is said to have defined the relationship of Hesiod's poetry to Homer's by calling Hesiod the gardener who planted the myths of gods and heroes, and Homer the garland-maker who wove the myths into epic structures.[12] For Xenophanes, as later for Herodotus, Hesiod and Homer are jointly responsible for the conventional poetic picture of the gods, and he condemns them for it. Heraclitus criticized a whole series of poets, prose writers, and sages: Homer, Hesiod, Archilochus, Xenophanes, Thales, Bias of Priene, Pythagoras, Hecataeus (B 38–40, 42, 56–7, 81, 105–6, 129).

Both Pindar and Bacchylides cite Hesiod by name. Bacchylides, in the manner of his uncle's citation of the Χῖος ἀνήρ, says (5. 191–3): Βοιωτὸς ἀνὴρ τάδε φών[ηсεν, γλυκειᾶν] Ἡсίοδος πρόπολος Μουсᾶν ('A Boeotian man spoke thus, Hesiod the [sweet] Muses' servant'); Pindar in the Sixth Isthmian (67) just says 'Hesiod'. Again it is clear that Hesiod is one of the principal classics. Pindar's reference is to a line in the *Works and Days* (412); Bacchylides' seems to be to another gnomic poem such as the *Precepts of Chiron*.

Of the non-hexameter poets of the Archaic age, the one who first emerges as a classic is Archilochus. When Heraclitus (B 42) writes that Homer deserves to be whipped out of the ἀγῶνες, he adds 'and Archilochus likewise'. Pindar twice refers to him. The Ninth Olympian begins with the striking allusion to 'Archilochus' song that finds voice at Olympia, the *Kallinikos* triply resounding',

> τὸ μὲν Ἀρχιλόχου μέλος
> φωνᾶεν Ὀλυμπίαι, καλλίνικος ὁ τριπλόος κεχλαδώς.

This is the traditional acclamation τήνελλα καλλίνικε, which so far as we can tell had little to do with Archilochus. The other passage is much more interesting. It comes in the Second Pythian (54–6). Pindar says he must avoid the sting of slander, δάκος ἀδινὸν κακαγοριᾶν, because 'I see from afar cavilling Archilochus, mostly in dire straits, growing fat on abusive enmities':

---

[12] *Gnomol. Vat.* 1144 = *FGrH* 8 F 6; Campbell 1982–93, iii. 366.

εἶδον γὰρ ἑκὰς ἐὼν τὰ πόλλ' ἐν ἀμαχανίαι
ψογερὸν Ἀρχίλοχον βαρυλόγοις ἔχθεσιν
πιαινόμενον.

Here is a fifth-century poet looking back at a seventh-century poet and constructing a picture of his life-style and character from his poems—not just
quoting something from one poem, as in most of the passages we have been
considering. 'I see him from afar': Pindar is conscious of the time-gulf that
separates him from Archilochus, but he gazes across it to contemplate a fellow
poet and fellow mortal, albeit not one with whom he can feel complete sympathy.

At the beginning of the Second Isthmian Pindar looks back at those earlier
poets who composed amatory lyrics:

οἱ μὲν πάλαι ὦ Θρασύβουλε φῶτες, οἳ χρυσαμπύκων
ἐς δίφρον Μοιςᾶν ἔβαινον κλυτᾶι φόρμιγγι cυναντόμεναι,
ῥίμφα παιδείους ἐτόξευον μελιγάρυας ὕμνους,
ὅςτις ἐὼν καλὸς εἶχεν Ἀφροδίτας
εὐθρόνου μνάςτειραν ἁδίςταν ὀπώραν.

Those men of old, Thrasybulus, who stepped into
the gold-headband Muses' car in company with the resounding lyre,
readily discharged their honey-voiced songs for lads,
whoever was comely and had that sweetest ripeness
that solicits fair-throned Aphrodite.

We cannot identify the particular poets he had in mind—Ibycus,
Anacreon?—but here again we see him taking a corpus of older poetry as his
point of departure.

In a papyrus commentary on Alcman a lyric poet is quoted in support of
the opinion that Alcman was a native Laconian (P.Oxy. XXIV 2389 fr. 9).
The poet spoke of some rival to Alcman the 'Laconian builder of skilful
Partheneia', ἀντίφαριν Λάκωνι τέ[κτονι πα]ρθενίων ςοφῶν Ἀλκμᾶ[νι.
Pindar seems the likeliest author of the fragment. The rival to Alcman,
whoever he is—perhaps Pindar himself—is presumably also a composer of
Partheneia. The presupposition is that there is a genre of Maiden Songs, and
that in this genre Alcman is the acknowledged master, the yardstick by which
others are to be judged.

It is in Pindar, in fact, that we first find a theory of genres. His Third Dirge
(fr. 128c) begins:

ἔν τι μὲν χρυcαλακάτου τεκέων Λατοῦc ἀοιδαί
ὥριαι παιανίδες· ἔντι [δὲ] καὶ
θάλλοντος ἐκ κιccοῦ cτέφανον Διο[νύ]cου
ο[    ] †βρομιπαιόμεναι†.

There are, for the children of gold-distaff Leto, songs
of seasonal paean type; there are also
ones that weave(?) a garland from the springing ivy of Dionysus.

The text here becomes very corrupt, but next came evidently a reference to three types of song established in commemoration of deceased sons of Calliope:

> †τὸ δὲ κοίμισαν†
> τρεῖς [      ] *Καλλιόπας, ὧς οἱ cταθῇι μνάμα<τ>' ἀποφθιμένων·*
> ἃ μὲν εὐχαίταν Λίνον αἴλινον ὕμνει,
> ἃ δ' Ὑμέναιον, <ὃν> ἐν γάμοιcι χροϊζόμενον
> νυκτὶ cὺν πρώται λάβεν ἔcχατοc ὕπνοc,[13]
> ἃ δὲ <          > Ἰάλεμον ὠμοβόλωι
> νούcωι πεδαθέντα cθένοc.

One of them sang of Linos (Ailinos) of the fair locks;
one of Hymenaeus, who as he lay with his bride
on the first night was taken by his last sleep;
and one of Ialemos, whose vital force
was fettered by cruel blow of sickness.

Then something was said about Orpheus, but the survey of lyric genres appears to be complete. It is of course not comprehensive—nothing about Epinicia, Hymns, or Partheneia—but so far as it goes it is remarkable enough: Paean, Dithyramb, Linos, Hymenaeus, Ialemos, the last perhaps representing the type of dirge that Pindar is writing at the moment. He speaks of these genres not as constructs of human convention but as givens: *there are* songs of paean type, *there are also* ones that weave a garland of ivy. With the songs for the sons of Calliope the text is too corrupt for us to follow what was said about their genesis, but we can understand the attached final clause, ὧc οἱ cταθῇι μνάμα<τ>' ἀποφθιμένων, 'so that memorials should be set up for her of those who had died'. The inference is that these three types of song were established by the Muse herself, or by another divinity on her behalf.

The theory that we extract from that poem may have been an impromptu creation for the nonce; it does not necessarily represent a firm doctrine of Pindar's. Regarding the dithyramb he gave different accounts in different poems. In the Thirteenth Olympian (18–19), in a short list of Corinth's contributions to Greek culture, the first item that comes to Pindar's mind is the dithyramb.

> ταὶ Διωνύcου πόθεν ἐξέφανεν
> cὺν βοηλάται χάριτεc διθυράμβωι;

From where did Dionysus' delights appear
with the ox-driving dithyramb?

He is no doubt alluding to the legend about Arion of Methymna, that celebrated citharode who according to Herodotus (1. 23) was 'the first we know of who composed dithyramb and named it and produced it at Corinth'.

---

[13] I quote the text as brilliantly restored by W. B. Henry, *ZPE* 128 (1999), 14.

A scholiast on the ode, however, informs us that in his Hyporchemata (fr. 115) Pindar said that the dithyramb was invented in Naxos, and in his First Dithyramb (fr. 71) that it was invented in Thebes. Without having his own words we cannot tell how explicitly he made these claims. The presupposition is anyway that the dithyramb had a πρῶτος εὑρετής.

We get the impression that Pindar has the concept of an evolutionary history in which a succession of innovators in different parts of Greece created and modified the various poetic and musical forms. This is confirmed by a series of fragments in which he makes mention of various early musicians, some of them semi-legendary. He related the encounter between Olympus and Silenus (fr. 157). He referred to Terpander as the inventor of the skolion and of the barbitos (fr. 125); having mentioned or perhaps apostrophized the barbitos, probably in an Enkomion, he goes on:

> τόν ῥα Τέρπανδρός ποθ᾿ ὁ Λέσβιος εὗρεν
> πρῶτος, ἐν δείπνοισι Λυδῶν
> ψαλμὸν ἀντίφθογγον ὑψηλᾶς ἀκούων πακτίδος.

> Which Terpander once, the Lesbian, first invented,
> as he heard at the Lydians' banquets
> the answering plucked note of the tall harp.

Here we have not just a tradition about who invented the barbitos, but a theory of how he came to have the idea: Terpander wanted to make a lyre that would produce the softer, deeper tones of the Lydian harp with its octave-doubling. This is not necessarily Pindar's own original theory; he might have had it from Lasus of Hermione, reputedly his teacher and the author of the first book about music.

Somewhere else (fr. 188) he referred to another famous seventh-century poet and musician, Polymnestus of Colophon. Polymnestus was an aulete whom the musicological writers credit with having invented new enharmonic intervals, new *nomoi*, and new forms of scale and rhythm, and he was also remembered as a poet of elegiac and hexameter verse. He is said to have been already mentioned by Alcman (*PMGF* 145). Pindar's reference is to a well-known saying of his (φθέγγμα πάγκοινον), perhaps a poetic quotation, perhaps anecdotal—the saying itself is not preserved. Another such poet-aulete was Sacadas of Argos, who won victories at the Pythian Games in 586, 582, and 578. He too was somewhere mentioned by Pindar (fr. 269).

In a lyric poem of uncertain genre (fr. 140b = Paean G9 Rutherford) Pindar begins with some verses about the invention of a certain *harmonia* for the auloi, presumably one he is himself using or developing. He says it was invented by someone from Locri, Λοκρῶν τις. It is usually assumed that the *harmonia* in question is the Locrian, although the first line said something about Ionian. The Locrian *harmonia* was later associated with Xenocritus, a

composer of heroic narrative songs in the manner of Stesichorus,[14] but if this
is the *harmonia* that Pindar has in mind, he either does not know of that
attribution or is for some reason being coy about naming Xenocritus. In any
case he is airing his musical science and giving it a historical dimension.

We have seen that Pindar has an extensive familiarity with the poetry of the
past. This poetry was the main source of his mythological knowledge, though
he sometimes felt entitled to make changes. He himself has told us that 'we
know Nestor and Sarpedon from resounding verses such as skilled craftsmen
have fitted together'. In the majestic opening strophe of the Delian Paean
VIIb Sn.–M. (= C2 Rutherford) he indicates that he will not follow Homer's
well-worn track; he probably means that he is going to give an account of the
birth of Apollo that departs from that in the Homeric Hymn.[15] The Homeric
Hymn, of course, had a special status for the Delians. It, or at least the Delian
portion of it, was composed for performance at Delos, and according to the
*Certamen Homeri et Hesiodi* (18) its text was displayed there on a painted
panel. Pindar may therefore have felt that he ought to warn the Delians that
he was going to tell a divergent story. But it is significant that he knows the
Hymn and regards it as the primary source for the myth of Apollo's birth.

It is quite likely that there were already books in circulation in which a
number of 'the Hymns of Homer' had been gathered together, though not yet
the particular collection that was current in Roman times and that we have.
Somewhere Pindar referred to the story of how Hera was trapped fast in the
throne made for her by Hephaestus (fr. 283). The tale had been told by
Alcaeus (frr. 349a–e Voigt), but the *locus classicus* for it was certainly the
fragmentarily preserved Homeric Hymn to Dionysus (no. 1 in our editions),
and this was likely enough Pindar's source.[16]

We have seen that he makes reference to Cyclic epics. I have referred to his
quotations of the *Thebaid* in the Sixth Olympian and probably of the *Epigoni*
in the Eighth Pythian, and to his several allusions to the suicide of Ajax, in
connection with which he names Homer. That is not all. In the Third
Nemean, for example, where again the Aeacidae claim their meed of praise, he
recalls a series of exploits of Peleus, Telamon, and especially Achilles, from his
childhood in Chiron's tutelage to his successes at Troy. He introduces them
with an appeal to older tradition (52): λεγόμενον δὲ τοῦτο προτέρων ἔπος
ἔχω ('I have this as an earlier men's tale that is told'). We cannot identify all
his sources, but towards the end of the passage there is particular emphasis
on Achilles' victory over Memnon, and this must be based on the *Aethiopis*.
Chiron nurtured the young hero and fortified his spirit by every means,

---

[14] Sch. *Ol.* 10. 18b, who quotes Call. fr. 669; in Poll. 4. 65 Φιλοξένου must be an error for
Ξενοκρίτου (Westphal).

[15] Cf. Rutherford 2001, 247–9.

[16] On the Homeric hymn see West 2001*b*; 2003, 26–31; on the history of the collection, West
2003, 20–2.

ὄφρα θαλασσίαις ἀνέμων ῥιπαῖσι πεμφθείς
ὑπὸ Τροΐαν δορίκτυπον ἀλαλὰν Λυκίων τε προσμένοι καὶ Φρυγῶν
Δαρδάνων τε, καὶ ἐγχεςφόροις ἐπιμείξαις
Αἰθιόπεςςι χεῖρας ἐν φραςὶ πάξαιθ', ὅπως ςφίςι μὴ κοίρανος ὀπίςω
πάλιν οἴκαδ' ἀνεψιὸς ζαμενὴς Ἑλένοιο Μέμνων μόλοι.

So that sent by the winds' sea-blasts to Troy
he might withstand the war-cries of Lycians and Phrygians and Dardanians,
and joining battle with the Aethiop spearmen
determine in his heart that their king should not return home,
that furious cousin of Helenus, Memnon (59–63).

The designation of Memnon as the cousin of Helenus shows a meticulous
interest in genealogy; Memnon's father Tithonus was the brother of Helenus'
father Priam. In the Sixth Nemean (49–54) Pindar again uses Achilles'
triumph over Memnon as a prime example of Aeacid prowess and fame, and
he alludes to the older poetry in which this had been related:

καὶ ταῦτα μὲν παλαιότεροι
ὁδὸν ἁμαξιτὸν εὗρον· ἕπομαι δὲ καὶ αὐτὸς ἔχων μελέταν.

And as for this, men of older time
found it for a highway; and I follow it myself studiously.

In two other odes, the Second Olympian (79–83) and the Fifth Isthmian
(39–42), he groups together the three outstanding heroes that Achilles
killed: Cycnus, Hector, and Memnon, spanning the *Cypria*, *Iliad*, and *Aethiopis*. In
the Isthmian he adds a fourth major victim, also from the *Cypria*, Telephus,
not killed but famously wounded. In the Olympian he refers also to Thetis'
having taken her son following his death, after begging Zeus' permission, to
the Isles of the Blest; this does not agree exactly with the *Aethiopis*, where
Achilles was transported to his own island of Leuke in the Black Sea, but it is
easily derived from it. Pindar does refer to the Black Sea island in another ode
(*Nem.* 4. 49).

There is a similar summary celebration of Achilles' career from birth to
death in the Eighth Isthmian (36–7, 46–60). Again Pindar picks out the
wounding of Telephus and the killing of Hector and Memnon, which left Troy
emasculated and secured victory for the Atridae and the recovery of Helen.
But this time he adds some lines about Achilles' funeral (56a–60):

τὸν μὲν οὐδὲ θανόντ' ἀοιδαὶ <ἐπ>έλιπον,
ἀλλά οἱ παρά τε πυρὰν τάφον θ' Ἑλικώνιαι παρθένοι
στάν, ἐπὶ θρῆνόν τε πολύφαμον ἔχεαν.
ἔδοξ' ἦρα καὶ ἀθανάτοις
ἐςλόν γε φῶτα καὶ φθίμενον ὕμνοις θεᾶν διδόμεν.

Not even in death did songs forsake him,
but by his pyre and tomb the Heliconian maidens

> took stand and poured forth their celebrated lament.
> So even immortals saw fit
> to commend a fine man even in death to the goddesses' hymns.

Again Pindar has the *Aethiopis* in view, where it was related how the Muses joined the Nereids in lamenting Achilles.[17] He alludes to Achilles' funeral also in the Sixth Paean (D6 Rutherford), line 99.

I am not aiming to give a thorough account of Pindar's use of the Epic Cycle. There are other clear examples, but the ones I have given are, I think, the most telling. I turn now to the Hesiodic corpus. I have mentioned the place in the Sixth Isthmian where Pindar cites Hesiod by name, referring to a line in the *Works and Days*. It is pretty clear that he also knew the *Theogony*. There is evidence that he was acquainted with at least some of the other poetry that went under Hesiod's name in antiquity, whether or not he knew it as Hesiod's—it is likely enough that he did. In the Sixth Pythian (19–27) Thrasybulus, who has won a chariot victory for his father Xenocrates, is praised for observing the advice that they say Chiron once gave Achilles in the mountains: above all to revere Zeus, but never to withhold due honour from one's parents. We would guess that this came from the well-known poem containing the centaur's precepts to Achilles, namely the Hesiodic *Precepts of Chiron*, and in fact the scholiast says 'the *Precepts of Chiron* they ascribe to Hesiod; they begin . . .' (and then he quotes the first three lines, = Hes. fr. 283). The currency of the poem in the fifth century is confirmed by parodies in Old Comedy.[18] Pindar then proceeds (28–42) to illustrate the rule of honouring one's parents with a story from the *Aethiopis*, that of Antilochus' giving his life for his father Nestor.

Scholiasts identify Hesiodic sources in two other odes. In the Sixth Isthmian (35–56), well before the reference to the *Works and Days*, Pindar relates how Heracles visited Telamon to enlist him as a companion in his expedition against Troy and found a banquet in progress. Telamon called upon him to stand on his lion-skin and pour a libation. Heracles did so, raised his arms to heaven, and prayed to Zeus that Telamon might father a heroic son with a skin as impenetrable as the lion's, whereupon Zeus sent an eagle as an omen. Heracles rejoiced and prophesied that the desired son would be born, and told Telamon to call him Αἴας after the αἰετός. The scholiast reports that the story is taken from the *Megalai Ehoiai* (fr. 250), with the minor difference that there Heracles stepped on the lion-skin on his own initiative, not Telamon's. The prayer, the eagle omen, and the aition of Ajax's name were all there. This nexus of literary motifs is persuasive evidence that Pindar was indeed following the hexameter source.

---

[17] Proclus; reflected in *Od.* 24. 58–61.
[18] Pindar himself actually uses the phrase 'the precepts of Chiron', ταὶ δὲ Χείρωνος ἐντολαί, in fr. 177(c), but we have no idea of the context.

In the Ninth Pythian he tells the story of the Lapith princess Cyrene, a feisty girl who preferred wrestling with lions to weaving. Apollo, following Chiron's guidance, carried her off from the vales of Pelion and set her down in Libya. There she gave birth to Aristaeus, who is also Apollon Nomios, and there the city named after her grew up. At the beginning of the recital the scholiast notes, 'Pindar took the story from the *Ehoie* of Hesiod that begins ...' (and he quotes the first two lines, = Hes. fr. 215). We also have it on Servius' authority that Hesiod gave Aristaeus, the son of Apollo and Cyrene, the name of *Apollo pastoralis*, that is, Ἀπόλλων Νόμιος (= fr. 216). Apart from that we cannot tell how closely the Pindaric narrative matched the Hesiodic, but we may accept that this was his main source, perhaps his only one; there cannot have been much choice.

We do not know how to fit the Cyrene *Ehoie* into the structure of the *Catalogue of Women*, and Giovan Battista D'Alessio has recently argued that it belonged rather in the *Megalai Ehoiai*, the same poem as supplied Pindar with the story about Heracles and Telamon.[19] The relationship between the *Ehoiai* (= the *Catalogue*) and the *Megalai Ehoiai* remains obscure, though there is a consensus that they were separate poems.

The Third Pythian also contains a narrative, the story of Coronis, that has often been thought to reflect a Hesiodic *Ehoie*. The scholiast does not say as much in this case, though he does at two points quote Hesiodic fragments (60, 61) that favour the hypothesis. However, there are problems about reconciling it with other evidence for 'Hesiod', which I will not go into.[20] The question does not affect the big picture.

In the Fourth and Fifth Nemeans (4. 54–67, 5. 26–34) Pindar recalls the story of Peleus, whom Acastus' wife tried unsuccessfully to seduce and then denounced to her husband in the traditional manner. Acastus tried to kill him in the mountains, but he was saved by Chiron. He then attacked and took Iolcus, and married Thetis. The scholiast quotes some Hesiodic lines (fr. 209) about Acastus' attempt on Peleus' life, and we have other Hesiodic evidence for the failed seduction and the taking of Iolcus. There seem to have been some differences of detail in the Pindaric version, but we need not doubt that here again he is following a Hesiodic model.

He did not treat this catalogue poetry just as a fund of mythical narratives. He apprehended from it whole genealogical structures. In the Fourth Pythian, when Jason comes to Iolcus to claim his rightful patrimony from the usurper Pelias, he has a sound grasp of his pedigree. He says he has come to regain the honour that Zeus granted to Aeolus (107). One heifer, he reminds Pelias, was mother both to Cretheus and to Salmoneus, and we are sprung from them in the third generation (142–5):

---

[19] G. B. D'Alessio in Hunter 2005, 206–7.
[20] See the recent discussions by Hirschberger 2004, 334–5, and D'Alessio (as n. 19), 208–10.

μία βοῦς Κρηθεῖ τε μάτηρ
καὶ θρασυμήδεϊ Cαλμωνεῖ· τρίταισιν δ' ἐν γοναῖc
ἄμμεc αὖ κείνων φυτευθέντεc cθένοc ἀελίου χρύceον
λεύccομεν.

Cretheus and Salmoneus were two of Aeolus' sons. Salmoneus was Pelias'
mortal father (his genetic father being Poseidon); Cretheus was the father of
Aeson, the father of Jason. Pindar has internalized the Hesiodic genealogy and
used it to set the story of Jason in a larger perspective. Many other examples
might be cited.

Another hexameter poem that Pindar may have encountered is the
*Arimaspea* of Aristeas, which we know about mainly from Herodotus
(4. 13–15). The Platonist Celsus spoke of Aristeas' mysterious disappearance
and of his reappearance much later with a remarkable tale to tell, and Origen
says that Celsus appeared to have got the story from Pindar and Herodotus.[21]
Perhaps Pindar just knew the legend about Aristeas and not the poem; but
the two are intimately linked in Herodotus' account, and he implies that
the poem was well known: 4. 14. 3 τὰ ἔπεα ταῦτα τὰ νῦν ὑπ' Ἑλλήνων
Ἀριμάcπεα καλεῖται.

On the other hand it is not chronologically impossible that what Pindar
knew of Aristeas came directly from Herodotus, who, after all, claims to have
put the legend together on the basis of his inquiries in Cyzicus, Proconnesus,
and Metapontum.[22] Pindar's interests were primarily poetic, but there is no
reason why he should not have been acquainted also with prose authors
whose subject-matter attracted him. He might well have read an author such
as Hecataeus, for example. In the First Pythian (92–4) he advises Deinomenes
that it is men's posthumous repute alone that provides information about
their lives καὶ λογίοιc καὶ ἀοιδοῖc, 'to storytellers and poets': it seems natural
to take λόγιοι in this coupling as referring to prose writers.[23] He proceeds
to name Croesus and Phalaris as paradigms of men whose good and bad
characters are kept alive in story.

At this point we must confront the question whether Pindar was a 'man
of letters' in the literal sense, a man who read and wrote and operated with
books.

Early Greek poetry, we know, lived in performance. In Pindar's time it was
still probably the case that most Greeks knew their Homer from hearing
recitations rather than from reading. Those who did not have the opportunity
or the stamina to sit through the complete performances of the *Iliad* and

---

[21] Origen, *C. Cels.* 3. 26 = Pind. fr. 271; cf. Bolton 1962, 127, 211–12.
[22] For a searching critique of Herodotus' argument see Stephanie West in Tuplin 2004, 43–67.
[23] Cf. *Nem.* 6. 29–30 παροιχομένων γὰρ ἀνέρων ἀοιδαὶ καὶ λόγοι (λόγιοι codd.,
unmetrically) τὰ καλά cφιν ἔργ' ἐκόμιcαν ('for when men have passed away, it is songs and
stories that preserve their fine deeds for them').

*Odyssey* at the Great Panathenaea at Athens may have been familiar only with the more popular episodes that the rhapsodes favoured.

On the other hand the upper class had been to school and learned to read and write, studying selections from Homer and other poets. After the Persian Wars we find an increasing number of literary and artistic references to reading and writing, clearly reflecting the growth of literacy. Among the cultural benefits he has conferred on mankind Pseudo-Aeschylus' Prometheus includes γραμμάτων cυνθέcεις, μνήμην ἁπάντων, μουcομήτορ' ἐργάνην, 'combinings of letters (to preserve) the memory of everything, handmaid mother of Muses' (*PV* 460–1). By the end of the century it appears from various pieces of evidence that it was not uncommon for individuals, at least at Athens, to own books on subjects that interested them and to use them for private edification.[24]

Poetry had been current in written form for two hundred years before Pindar, and prose works too since the mid sixth century. There must have been a certain number of people, however small, who read books and copied them and built up little collections of them. Pythagoras may have been one such man. Heraclitus (B 129) says of him that he 'practised inquiry most of all men, and selecting these writings he took to himself expertise, learning, knavery':

Πυθαγόρης Μνηcάρχου ἱcτορίην ἤcκηcεν ἀνθρώπων μάλιcτα πάντων, καὶ ἐκλεξάμενοc ταύταc τὰc cυγγραφὰc ἐποιήcατο ἑωυτοῦ cοφίην, πολυμαθίην, κακοτεχνίην.

Heraclitus himself, as I mentioned earlier, refers to a whole series of poets, prose writers, and sages besides Pythagoras: Homer, Hesiod, Archilochus, Xenophanes, Thales, Bias of Priene, Hecataeus. With Thales and Bias it was presumably a matter of reported sayings, but for at least some of the others I suspect that written texts were in question.

The question arises more acutely with Pindar. How would he have known Alcman's Partheneia, if not from a book? They must after all have been current in written transmission throughout the sixth and fifth centuries, or they would not have survived to Alexandria. How would he have known Archilochus' Iambi? There are a couple of isolated references to performance of Archilochus' poetry,[25] but is it likely that Pindar heard enough of it performed to generalize about his life? He might know the *Iliad* from hearing the rhapsodes, but how often did they recite the *Cypria*, the *Aethiopis*, the *Nostoi*, the *Thebaid*, the *Epigoni*? The *Works and Days*? The *Catalogue of Women*, or the *Megalai Ehoiai*? In the case of these Hesiodic works, I am doubtful whether they were ever to be heard in oral performance at all. The

[24] See Pfeiffer 1968, 25–32; West 2001a, 20–1.
[25] Heraclitus B 42; Clearchus fr. 92 Wehrli.

*Catalogue of Women* is in my view a sixth-century attempt at a grand syn-
thesis of mythical genealogies, an undertaking similar to those of the fifth-
century logographers. Its author may himself have used written as well as oral
sources. I see it, in short, as an essentially literary entity.

Pindar must have been accustomed to handling books. His own poems
were composed for performance in the first instance, but he must have kept
copies of them all. The large corpus of his works that was preserved must go
back to his own personal collection: it is not credible that it was formed by
someone going round Greece and Sicily and collecting copies from all the
customers.[26] Perhaps Pindar dictated his texts to a copyist; he need not have
written them out in his own hand. But he was surely fully literate. His
mind turns readily to metaphorical use of the verb 'to write'. In the Third
Olympian (30) he uses it of the nymph Taygete's dedicating a hind and
'writing it sacred to Artemis', ἅν ποτε Ταϋγέτα ἀντιθεῖσ' Ὀρθωσίας ἔγραψεν
ἱράν, as if a dedicatory inscription were involved. He opens the Tenth
Olympian with the striking command 'Read out to me the Olympic victor
son of Archestratus, where he is inscribed on my mind':

> τὸν Ὀλυμπιονίκαν ἀνάγνωτέ μοι
> Ἀρχεστράτου παῖδα, πόθι φρενός
> ἐμᾶς γέγραπται.

The term *poeta doctus* is usually reserved for Hellenistic and Roman poets.
I submit that it is not inappropriate to Pindar. With his wide knowledge of the
poetry of the past and of numerous mythical stories that cannot have been
universally familiar, and with his ability to see the myths as parts of a grand
structure and the poets as figures in a landscape, he must count as one of the
best-educated men that we can identify in his time or before it, a man imbued
with literary culture to the highest degree. He does not use his learning like
Callimachus, to tease, to collude with the reader and exploit the reader's
knowledge, though he is aware that the understanding of his poetry calls for
discernment. But like Callimachus he can set himself in dialogue with past
poetry, take issue with it, assert the right not just to carry on the tradition but

---

[26] Wilamowitz 1900, 40, thinks primarily in terms of the 'house archives' of Pindar's and
Bacchylides' honorands, but adds that the poets' own archives could also be relevant. Pöhlmann
1994, 16, writes 'Sammlungen von Chorlyrik bei den einzelnen Bestellern mag es gegeben
haben. Doch werden diese in allen denkbaren Fällen Gedichte gleicher Gattung, aber von
verschiedenen Verfassern erhalten haben: Apollonhymnen in Delphi, Epinikien für die sport-
lichen Siege der Deinomeniden in Syrakus von Simonides, Pindar, Bakchylides und anderen.
Daß aus solchen disparaten Quellen die alexandrinische Pindarausgabe von 17 Büchern
enstanden sein soll, ist schwer vorstellbar. Man wird daher . . . damit rechnen, daß die
Chorlyriker selbst Abschriften ihrer Werke sammelten und daß diese tradiert wurden.' He goes
on to surmise that Pindar's works could have been preserved in the Aegeids' family house in
Thebes, which Alexander is supposed to have spared when he destroyed the city (*Vita Pindari
Thomana*, p. 5. 15 Dr., cf. Plut. *Alex.* 11), and the ruins of which were visited by Pausanias
(9. 25. 3).

on occasion to denounce it as erroneous and proclaim a new version. And
when he does so, he does it in a scholarly way. The most notorious instance is
his modification of the Pelops story in the First Olympian. He does not
pretend to have authority for his version: 'I will contradict my predecessors',
he says, ἀντία προτέρων φθέγξομαι (36). He rejects their tale that Tantalus
put his son in the stewpot and served him up to his divine dinner guests. He
cannot bring himself to ascribe such undiscriminating gourmandise to the
blessed ones. That horrific myth was too much for the civilized tastes of the
fifth century: they preferred to credit their gods with a gentlemanly paedo-
philia. But Pindar does not simply create a new story, he provides at the same
time an explanation of how the false story got into circulation: Poseidon had
carried Pelops off for love, and because the boy vanished on the day of the
gods' visit the neighbours started to speculate and gossip and spread the ugly
rumour that he had been eaten. What Pindar does here is like a textual critic
giving his story of how a postulated corruption came about. The critic rejects
the manuscripts' reading but accepts that he must take account of it. In the
same way Pindar acknowledges that his poetic sources have an authority that
he cannot simply ignore but must re-evaluate by insight into the nature of the
tradition.

# BIBLIOGRAPHY

Bolton, J. D. P. 1962, *Aristeas of Proconnesus* (Oxford).
Campbell, D. A. 1982–93, *Greek Lyric*, 5 vols. (Cambridge, MA).
Hirschberger, M. 2004, *Gynaikōn Katalogos und Megalai Ēhoiai* (Munich and Leipzig).
Hunter, R. (ed.) 2005, *The Hesiodic Catalogue of Women* (Cambridge).
Parsons, P. J. 1992, 'Simonides, *Elegies*' in *The Oxyrhynchus Papyri*, LIX (London), 4–50.
Pfeiffer, R. 1968, *History of Classical Scholarship*, i (Oxford).
Pöhlmann, E. 1994, *Einführung in die Überlieferungsgeschichte und in die Textkritik der antiken Literatur*, i (Darmstadt).
Rutherford, I. 2001, *Pindar's Paeans* (Oxford).
Sider, D. 1996, 'As is the Generation of Leaves in Homer, Simonides, Horace, and Stobaios', *Arethusa*, 29, 263–82; revised in D. Boedeker and D. Sider (eds), *The New Simonides* (Oxford and New York, 2001), 272–88.
Tuplin, C. J. (ed.) 2004, *Pontus and the Outside World* (Colloquia Pontica, 9; Leiden and Boston).
West, M. L. 1970, 'Corinna', *CQ*[2] 20, 277–87.
—— 1990, 'Dating Corinna', *CQ*[2] 40, 553–7.
—— 1993, 'Simonides Redivivus', *ZPE* 98, 1–14.
—— 1999, 'The Invention of Homer', *CQ*[2] 49, 364–82.
—— 2001a, *Studies in the Text and Transmission of the Iliad* (Munich and Leipzig).
—— 2001b, 'The Fragmentary Homeric Hymn to Dionysus', *ZPE* 134, 1–11.

West, M. L. 2003, *Homeric Hymns. Homeric Apocrypha. Lives of Homer* (Cambridge, MA, and London).

—— 2007, *Indo-European Poetry and Myth* (Oxford).

Wilamowitz-Moellendorff, U. von, 1886, *Isyllos von Epidauros* (Berlin).

—— 1900, *Die Textgeschichte der griechischen Lyriker* (Berlin).

—— 1901, 'Hieron und Pindaros.', *Sitz. Preuß. Akad.*, 1273–318 = *Kl. Schr.* vi (Berlin, 1972), 234–85.

—— 1922, *Pindaros* (Berlin).

# 3

# The Papyri of Herodotus

*Stephanie R. West*

I was lucky enough to be half of Peter Parsons's first papyrology class in 1960/1, so I have a particularly longstanding intellectual debt to acknowledge. Such occasions as the conference from which this paper originated stimulate reminiscence and retrospection, and reflecting on the difference between then and now I am struck by the way in which papyrology in Oxford has moved from the periphery to the centre, where it exercises an ever more powerful attraction for graduate students (and even some undergraduates). To calculate how far this change is to be attributed to our honorand must be left to the accounting system operated by Dike on high, as described in P.Oxy. XX 2256 (Aeschylus F 281a); but on any reckoning his has been a major force behind this development.

It is the possibility of reading literature that failed to make it through the Middle Ages that above all lends glamour to the decipherment of broken and abraded letters. If literary papyrology dealt only with the remains of extant authors, as this paper does, it would attract little interest. But, apart from occasional slight improvements to the text, such material reveals something about the tastes of ancient readers, it has some bearing on literary history, and it is very relevant to the increasing interest in both the reception of classical authors and the history of the book. 'Leider fehlt uns noch immer eine Geschichte der Herodot-Lektüre im Altertum', observed Jacoby almost a century ago;[1] that want remains to be supplied, but the evidence of papyri is an important element in that history.

A fragment preserving a couple of columns may not by itself get us very far, but there are enough papyri of Herodotus to allow some general observations.[2] Mertens–Pack's online database (updated to June 2006) gives 46

---

[1] Jacoby 1913, 504–5.
[2] This study of course builds on earlier surveys: see Paap 1948; Chambers *et al.* 1981, 22–9; Alberti 1983; Rosén 1987, pp. xliii f.; Saerens 1990; Mertens and Strauss 1992; Bandiera 1997.

entries for Herodotus. Four of these are not actually texts of Herodotus: two are commentaries, one is an epitome, or a history which followed Herodotus very closely, and one consists of allusions to Herodotus in a private letter. But we can safely claim over forty Herodotus papyri. A. S. Hunt in 1927 observed that Herodotus had 'occurred rather less frequently in the papyri than might have been anticipated'.[3] This relative shortfall has persisted; contrast Thucydides' score of 95 entries in Mertens–Pack. It is, at first sight, surprising that Thucydides was so much more popular.

Apart from one piece from Dura-Europus, all our Herodotus papyri come from Egypt, the majority from Oxyrhynchus. Most are dated, as might be expected, to the second and third centuries, the long period of peace and prosperity. Apart from one doubtful example, none is Ptolemaic.[4] Given the out-of-the-way authors who were being read in provincial towns during the Ptolemaic period, this negative point is worth thinking about: we might have expected Herodotus' account of Egypt, at least, to attract interest then.[5] But the historians—Herodotus, Thucydides, and Xenophon—enjoyed much greater diffusion under Roman rule.

We see from the papyri of Herodotus that already in the early Imperial period the text was infested with epicisms, hyperionicisms, and Atticisms; it suffered from tendencies both to import *koine* forms and to restore what was supposed to be Ionic. Already in 1919 Grenfell and Hunt noted that the convenient and conventional division of the medieval MSS into two families, Florentine and Roman, was not observable in the papyri;[6] this has remained true. Occasionally the papyri support modern conjectures,[7] but on the whole they confirm the general impression that our texts had already suffered significant corruption before the Hellenistic period brought a greater concern for accuracy and a general rise in standards of book production, an advance affecting Hebrew texts[8] as well as Greek. I see little chance of fulfilment, at any rate from Roman Egypt, of Jacoby's prediction that a substantial discovery

---

[3] Hunt 1927, 135.

[4] A further fragment of the papyrus represented by P.Duke inv. 756 (Mertens–Pack 474.11; Hatzilambrou 2002), preserving parts of 4. 147. 4–5, has been published by Soldati 2005, who prefers a date in the late 2nd or early 1st c. BC to Hatzilambrou's dating to the late 1st or early 2nd c. AD.

[5] Particularly if we accept the arguments advanced by Stephens 2003 that under Ptolemaic rule a greater effort than has generally been supposed was made to bridge the gap between Greek and Egyptian culture.

[6] Grenfell and Hunt 1919, 182 on P.Oxy. XIII 1619.

[7] Theoretically such agreement might merely signify that a modern conjecture was anticipated by an ancient reader. But in practice these coincidences are judged to confirm the soundness of the emendation proposed.

[8] For a brief account see Talmon 1970, esp. 165–70.

of papyri might be expected to bring significant surprises and cure editors of their optimism.[9]

Almost half our papyri (19) come from Book 1; Books 2 and 5 achieve quite a respectable score (six each). Book 8 has four; Book 7 three; Books 3 and 4 two each. Book 6 is not attested at all. There was nothing from Book 9 until the publication in 2004 of P.Oslo inv. 1487,[10] preserving parts of 9. 74–5, now in the library of the University of Oslo—just too late to get into Flower and Marincola's edition (2002).[11] In antiquity, as now, only a small proportion of those who started to read long books actually finished them. Notwithstanding the Herodotean Solon's sage counsel to look to the end (1. 32. 9) comparatively few can have pressed on to see how Herodotus presented the conclusion of the intercontinental conflict whose origins he outlines at the start of his work. If the last chapter contains a message of profound significance for the interpretation of the *Histories* as a whole, the majority of readers in Roman Egypt missed it. The relative popularity of individual books is consistent with the impression we get from citations in ancient authors, both pagan and Christian; Book 1 comes top by a long way.[12] It is of course particularly rich in memorable *novelle*. In principle I regret a tendency of Herodotean scholarship to focus on the first book, but papyrologically the most interesting material so far published comes from there, and the rest of this paper will largely concern papyri from that book.

The first papyrus of Herodotus to be published appeared in the first volume of *Oxyrhynchus Papyri*, in 1898. P.Oxy. I 18 (Pack[2] 466), of the third century, preserves parts of 1. 105–6, from Herodotus' account of the Scythian invasion of Palestine in the seventh century, in the course of which, says Herodotus, a small group of Scythians robbed the temple of Celestial Aphrodite at Ascalon. As is demonstrated by the politically unfortunate consequences for Pericles of his Alcmaeonid descent (on his mother's side) and the chilling tale of the Locrian maiden tribute, the guilt and consequent punishment for sacrilege were deemed in antiquity to be hereditable, and the descendants of these impious Scythians therefore, says Herodotus, suffer from a mysterious 'female sickness' of which he tells us more in his account of

[9] 'Ein größerer Papyrusfund würde vermutlich recht wesentliche Überraschungen bringen und die Herausgeber von dem Optimismus ... heilen, als ob unsere H.-Überlieferung besonders gut sei' (Jacoby 1913, 515 16). While few are likely to find immediately persuasive Benedetto Bravo's argument that the text has suffered serious interpolation (Bravo 2000), his careful scrutiny of passages concerning Scythia and Thrace has exposed a lengthy catalogue of linguistic and stylistic oddities which must make us uneasy about the general soundness of the paradosis.

[10] Maravela-Solbakk 2004.

[11] While precise statistics relating to published papyri are subject to rapid obsolescence, the substantial group of Oxyrhynchus papyri in the pipeline confirms the general proportions, enhancing the lead of Book 1; I am very grateful to Dirk Obbink for letting me see this material.

[12] Of the 27 passages from Herodotus most frequently cited by pagan and Christian writers, eleven come from Book 1: see Ehrhardt 1988, 858.

Scythia (4. 67; cf. Hippoc. *Aer.* 22). The medieval MSS give τοῖϲι τούτων αἰεὶ ἐκγόνοιϲι ἐνέϲκηψε ὁ θεὸϲ θήλειαν νοῦϲον ('On their descendants the god inflicted in perpetuity female sickness'). ὁ θεόϲ must be taken as a generalizing masculine. Our papyrus is more precise about the gender, and gives ἡ θεόϲ. So too do the MSS of [Longinus] *Subl.* 28, where the quotation is introduced with the memorable phrase καὶ τὸ ἀμίμητον ἐκεῖνο τοῦ Ἡροδότου ('and that inimitable sentence of Herodotus'); there ἐνέβαλεν instead of the more unusual ἐνέϲκηψεν suggests that the writer was quoting from memory, and the papyrus provides welcome evidence that the feminine definite article was not simply the product of inaccurate recollection. Even better, P.Oxy. X 1244 (Pack[2] 467), of the early second century, agrees. Subsequent editors (Hude, Legrand, Asheri, Rosén) adopt the feminine. ἡ θεόϲ here raises a further question about some other passages where our MSS agree in the masculine definite article for θεόϲ, but the divinity concerned is female: thus with Hera in the story of Cleobis and Biton (1. 31. 3), with Leto's Egyptian counterpart (2. 133. 2), and again with Hera (6. 82. 1).[13] P.Oxy. X 1244 also confirms Schaefer's palmary conjecture ὑπερθέμενοϲ ('communicating') for ὑποθέμενοϲ ('advising, suggesting') at 107. 1.

However, our papyri offer no help with the following sentence, which has seemed to many to be corrupt: ὥϲτε ἅμα λέγουϲί τε οἱ Ϲκύθαι διὰ τοῦτό ϲφεαϲ νοϲέειν, καὶ ὁρᾶν παρ' ἑωυτοῖϲι τοὺϲ ἀπικνεομένουϲ ἐϲ τὴν Ϲκυθικὴν χώρην ὡϲ διακέαται τοὺϲ καλέουϲι ἐνάρεαϲ οἱ Ϲκύθαι.[14] ('So the Scythians say that it is for this reason that they suffer from this sickness and that those who come to Scythia see among them the condition of those whom the Scythians call "enarees".') The infinitives νοϲέειν and ὁρᾶν both depend on λέγουϲι, but we should expect what the Scythians say to be balanced by what can be observed: the Scythians can explain the cause of the hereditary infirmity, while visitors can observe its effects. Richards 1905, 291, improving on a suggestion of Madvig's, proposed καὶ ὁρᾶν πάρα (or πάρεϲτιν or παρέχει) αὐτοῖϲι τοῖϲι ἀπικνεομένοιϲι κτλ. ('and it is possible for those who come to see for themselves, etc.'). Our papyri simply agree with the paradosis.

Though I have emphasized the popularity of Book 1, a caution is needed. Of the 19 papyri from this book most are quite brief, covering, as these two do, no more than a few chapters. In only one case, P.Oxy. XVII 2096 + XLVIII 3374 (Pack 463), have we clearly got a roll which once contained the whole book. For Book 2 there are two such items, P.Oxy. VIII 1092 (Pack 473)[15] and XLVIII 3376 (Mertens–Pack 468. 2), and one for Book 3, P.Oxy. XIII 1619 (Pack 474). Sometimes an editor can calculate the length of the roll from

---

[13]  See further Harrison 2000, 171–5.

[14]  P.Oxy. X 1244 appears to have omitted ϲφεαϲ.

[15]  In the same hand as four other pieces: see Johnson 2004, 20–1, who notes that the column-width is almost exactly the same as that of P.Oxy. LII 3676 (Plato, *Phaedo*), though the script of the latter is substantially larger (might a customer have specified a 'large print' copy?).

which his papyrus comes, on the assumption that it contained a complete book. Thus Mortimer Chambers, the editor of P.Oxy. XLVIII 3374, reckoned that the complete roll ran to 16 m of papyrus. The editor of some of the unpublished Oxyrhynchus fragments of Book 1 has calculated that two of his putative rolls would measure each *c*.18 m, a third 41 m. Even the first of these does not sound very convenient (though of course it is possible that a long book might be divided between two rolls).[16] We ought to consider the possibility that some of our texts represent excerpts or selections.

Bearing these points in mind, let us look at another section where we have more than one papyrus witness, Herodotus' account of Babylonian marriage customs. The earliest, PSI 1170 (Pack[2] 470), thriftily written on the verso of tax records and dated to the second century, contains 196. 4–199. 3; it presents no particular problems. P.Ross.Georg.15 (Pack[2] 469), of the third century and the most extensive, contains a good part of 196, 202, 203, and probably 200 and 201; the papyrus is written on both sides, but cannot be a page from a codex. From Barcelona, P.Lit.Palau Rib. 10 (Mertens–Pack 469.1), a piece of parchment written on both sides, dated to the fifth century, preserves part of 196, Herodotus' famous description of the Babylonian marriage-market.

A slip in the *editio princeps* of P.Ross.Georg. 15 generated meretricious excitement, as at first glance it appears to be dated to the third century BC,[17] but the truth rapidly becomes clear. The papyrus is written on both sides, the last sentence of 195 and about half of 196 on the recto in one broad column (28–34 letters, an unusually long line for a prose text[18]), then two columns on the verso; the first of these offers only the ends of lines, but the editor, Tsereteli (Zereteli in German), appears to have had no doubt that the end of 199, 200, 201, and the start of 202 stood here; the neighbouring column certainly held the latter part of 202 and 203. It would be natural at first sight to suppose that we have a page from a codex. But the missing text is too much for the space hypothetically available. Tsereteli accordingly concluded that our fragment comes from an opisthograph roll, specifically, from near to the point where the scribe turned over to the back of his roll.

This postulates a very odd format if we are thinking of a roll containing a whole book, as seems to have been generally assumed by those who have discussed this text. 'Opisthograph', like 'paraklausithyron', is a word far more familiar to modern scholars than it can ever have been in antiquity; it was not a regular format for literature. The currency of the term is due to the younger Pliny (*Ep*. 3. 5. 17), who uses it with reference to his uncle's 160 notebooks in very small handwriting; his point is his uncle's zeal in making excerpts from his reading. Presumably the elder Pliny wanted to save space in his book

---

[16] See further Johnson 2004, 146–7.
[17] *a.C.n.* by mistake for *p.C.n.*
[18] See Johnson 2004, 114–15; the 'normal' range is roughly 13 to 24 letters per line.

boxes.[19] In general the use of the verso of a roll to complete what was started on the recto implies that the writer underestimated the amount of space he would need and was too impatient or short of cash to buy further sheets and glue them on—as with those aspirant poets whose recitations Juvenal found so depressing (1. 4–6). For parallels we should look among the documentary papyri. As a literary format this is very unusual, and the editor's description of the hand 'zwischen Unziale und Kursive . . . eine Art Unzialkursive' does not suggest an impoverished enthusiast making his private copy on whatever was available and miscalculating the extent of the text.

In a rather unlikely context our much-lamented colleague Don Fowler questioned Tsereteli's description of the format: 'Is it certain this fragment is not from a codex?' he asked.[20] This led me to consider whether a reasonable codex page would result on the assumption that ch. 199, the notorious account of sacred prostitution, might have been omitted, as it is in the bowdlerizing Roman family, but this hypothesis does not produce a satisfactory result either. So I think we should rather envisage a single sheet containing a long excerpt, allowing some uncertainty as to whether it held all that stands in our texts beween 196 and 202.[21] This papyrus supports two fine conjectures, Eltz's οἶδε for ὧδε (1. 196. 1) and Bergler's διεξέλθοι for οἱ ἐξέλθοι (1.196. 3).

The Barcelona fragment is no less interesting. Its editor took it for granted that it is a page from a codex, a rare format among our Herodotus papyri.[22] But we should bear in mind Sir Eric Turner's warning against assuming that writing on both sides of the material by the same scribe must indicate a codex.[23] The example with which he supports this caution is an *Iliad* papyrus dated to the fifth century (P.Princ. III 109: Pack 592) which has on the one side 1. 216–37, on the other 1. 574–97, the first from Achilles' altercation with Agamemnon, the second from Hephaestus' attempt to make peace between Zeus and Hera. The editor did his sums, and deduced that the piece came from a codex with 50 to 54 lines to a column, and 4 columns to a page: a bizarre format. It is significant that the subject-matter of the two passages is related—quarrels on earth and in heaven: 'the sheet', Turner concluded, 'must have held not a continuous text but selected passages'. So too in the case of the Barcelona fragment we should bear in mind the possibility that here too we have a single sheet containing an interesting excerpt. I need not

---

[19] Cf. Lucian, *Vit. auct.* 9. The 'book sealed with seven seals' of Rev. 5: 1 is written ἔcωθεν καὶ ὄπιcθεν.

[20] Fowler 1989, 89 n. 59 (= 2000, 252 n. 59).

[21] I am very grateful to Dr Buba Kudava, Director of the National Centre of Manuscripts, Tbilisi, who allowed me to see this papyrus during a visit to Tbilisi in October 2007.

[22] P.Lit.Lond. 104 (Pack[2] 476: late 3rd or early 4th c.) is at present the only certain example. P.Oxy. VI 857 (Pack 484: 4th c.; *FGrH* 105 F 3)), from an epitome or a history closely following Herodotus, should also be mentioned.

[23] Turner 1977, 9–10.

dwell on the subject's fascination. It is memorably illustrated by Edwin Long's famous painting (1875), which made the artist's reputation and is one of the highlights of the marvellous collection of Victorian art at Royal Holloway College, amassed by the eponymous Thomas Holloway with the profits from his patent medicine business.[24]

Given the brevity of nearly all our fragments, it is remarkable that we have three witnesses for the Babylonian marriage-market. Similarly two papyri give the story of Darius' avaricious investigation of the tomb of the Babylonian queen Nitocris (1. 187), a much-quoted episode.[25] These are P.Oxy. 3376 (Mertens–Pack 468.2) and P.Mil.Vogl. inv.1212 (Mertens–Pack 468.1). The first of these, dated to the second century, is very probably in the same hand as a large number of fragments of Book 2.[26] The Milan papyrus, dated to the third century, offers just this chapter, in a single column of which the top is missing.

If our papyri represented a random sample from what were once rolls containing complete books (or even half-books, since Book 1 is quite long) we should not expect to get as much duplication as we have seen. It is thus a reasonable inference that several of our shorter fragments are likely to represent extracts.[27] We should thus be cautious about extrapolating book-length rolls from fragments preserving a few chapters, though Herodotus is not the only author to whom such a warning is relevant. If taken seriously, this consideration tends to undermine the usefulness of bibliological statistics. We may compare P.Oxy. 1016 (Pack[2] 1400), which preserves the proem of Plato's *Phaedrus* (227 A–230 E), on the verso of a register of landowners (P.Oxy. 1044). A forked paragraphos at the end, together with a wide right-hand margin, strongly suggests that the rest of the dialogue was not copied.[28] We should be a little more positive and consider what we may infer about reading habits.

Papyri offer the best evidence we have for the mainstream of education in the ancient world. There have recently been published two excellent, complementary, studies of this topic, Teresa Morgan's *Literate Education in the Hellenistic and Roman Worlds* (1998) and Raffaella Cribiore, *Gymnastics of the Mind: Greek Education in Hellenistic and Roman Egypt* (2001). Alan

---

[24] See further Jenkyns 1991, 122–5. It is reproduced on the cover of Kurke 1999; her stimulating discussion of this chapter and 199 offers several useful insights (227–46).

[25] Cf. Greg. Naz. *Epigr.* 84 (with Cyrus instead of Darius); Max. Tyr. *Diss.* 20. 9, Julian, *Or.* 3 (2). 27 (Bidez), Apostol. 11. 41 (*Paroem. Gr.* ii. 526–7: μὴ νεκρῶν θήκας κίνει).

[26] See further Johnson 2004, 32.

[27] There is a similar clustering around a relatively short stretch of text with the three papyri from Book 7.

[28] See further Turner and Parsons 1987, 142–3. I am indebted to Eric Handley, who drew my attention to this text and to the implications of the papyrus containing excerpts from Menander's *Kolax* (P.Oxy. III 409 + XXXIII 2655), on which see Turner in Parsons, Rea, and Turner 1968, 9.

Cameron's latest book, *Greek Mythography in the Roman World* (2004) usefully supplements these. It is clear that boys who continued to get some schooling after the primary stage were introduced to the major authors at what we might call secondary school; but it is difficult to identify school texts. Our boys are past the stage when something like the Ptolemaic teacher's manual published by O. Guéraud and P. Jouguet (1938) would be useful. Herodotus offered much of value to the aspirant rhetorician, or indeed to anyone who aimed at a smattering of Hellenic culture.[29] But an 18-m roll is not what is wanted in the classroom: the teacher needs attractive, easily handled passages, which can be passed round, and replaced without vast expense when they suffer from rough treatment. Teenagers can be introduced to the Ionic dialect and a few famous episodes; they are thus prepared for more extensive independent reading. But the focus of instruction was purely literary, and those who emerged from a thorough training in grammar and rhetoric might have a good store of edifying Herodotean vignettes but little appreciation of the wider historical setting.

Those who had thus been introduced might wish to read more, but not want complete texts. A collection of extracts of well-known passages, to be developed over the years at modest expense—rather as we might photocopy passages for a commonplace book—might have better suited many. We need not think simply in terms of solitary readers. Xenophon's Socrates conjures up an appealing vignette of a reading circle (*Mem.* 1. 6. 14): τοὺς θησαυροὺς τῶν πάλαι coφῶν ἀνδρῶν, οὓc ἐκεῖνοι κατέλιπον ἐν βιβλίοιc γράψαντεc, ἀνελίττων κοινῆι cὺν τοῖc φίλοιc διέρχομαι, καὶ ἄν τι ὁρῶμεν ἀγαθὸν ἐκλεγόμεθα ('Together with my friends I go through the treasures of the sages of old, unrolling the books in which they left them, and we pick out for ourselves whatever good thing we see'). It is tempting to set this activity in the context of the symposium. Under the early empire the reading of literary texts by the educated elite was much more of a social event than we might have expected, and certainly featured among the possibilities for after-dinner entertainment.[30] Antiquarianism, paradoxography, and piquant anecdotes hold a wider appeal than strictly historical narrative.[31] But such extracts tend to enhance the impression that entertainment was more important for Herodotus than accuracy. Certainly such a practice would have fostered a tendency to associate Herodotus with *innumerabiles fabulae* (Cic. *Leg.* 1. 5) and to view the historical record as the framework for a corpus of rhetorical

---

[29] See Cribiore 2001, 144–5.

[30] See further Johnson 2000, 606–25. It is tempting to speculate about Didymus' *Miscellany of Party-Pieces* (*Symmikta Symposiaka*).

[31] During the Second World War a handy Penguin selection from Herodotus appeared not in the dark blue covers appropriate to history but in the orange covers characterizing general fiction (*The Penguin Herodotus*, edited by A. J. Evans, Penguin Fiction No. 330; Harmondsworth. 1941).

exempla, to the neglect of those parts of his work more characteristic of the serious historian.

Here, I suspect, we have the explanation (or at any rate, part of the explanation) why Thucydides is so much better attested in our papyri.[32] Taken in picturesque excerpts Herodotus looks easy; his dialect should have posed no difficulty to readers familiar with Homer. But his range, both in time and space, is daunting. 'One must needs be not merely grammarian and historian, but archaeologist, anthropologist, philosopher and something more to boot, in order adequately to explain and illustrate "the Father of History"' wrote Macan in 1895;[33] in part he was troubled by 'the increase of materials and the rising standard of method', but the Victorian reader could at least take for granted decent maps and an agreed era for events BC. In Roman Egypt the thoughtful reader who started at the beginning of the *Histories* and continued systematically would have found much that was perplexing, and doubts about Herodotus' reliability must undermine perseverance; Lucian's mockery is instructive. 'A history of reception . . . must deal with interpretive frames as well as individual texts . . . Herodotus' *Histories* changed when their readers had also read Thucydides.'[34] The papyri confirm the impression we get from citations, that those who read Herodotus tended to do so in an unhistorical way. We should certainly not assume that a reference to a well-known passage implies that the writer has read the whole work, or indeed even the whole of the book in which it occurs. The thorough, detailed, knowledge which Plutarch displays in the *de malignitate* is likely to have been unusual in his day even among the well-educated.

The most remarkable of the Herodotean papyri is not itself a text of Herodotus but purports to come, according to its unambiguous colophon, from Aristarchus' commentary (*hypomnema*) on Book 1. This is P.Amherst 12 (Pack[2] 483: Paap No. 10, third century; Pl. 7), from Ashmunen/ Hermopolis, published by Grenfell and Hunt in 1901 and now in the Pierpont Morgan library. It is written on the verso of accounts, in a fluent literary hand in an 'informal "severe" style'. A new edition would be most welcome.[35]

---

[32] Not just quantitatively; though the first two books were the most studied, later books are well represented. Not counting fragments from codices, which might be expected to hold several books. Mertens–Pack give 11 entries for Book 7 and 8 for Book 8. (Book 6, which scores only 2 fragments from rolls and one from a codex, was the least popular.) Of course many of these papyri might represent extracts rather than rolls containing complete books; P.Oxy. XIII 1621 (Mertens–Pack 1515, preserving Book 2. 11. 5–9, 35.1), from a collection of speeches, is suggestive.

[33] Macan 1895, p. i.

[34] Humphreys 2004, 26. For a succinct overview of the reception of Herodotus in antiquity see Hornblower 2006.

[35] There are significant differences between Paap's text and the *ed. pr.*, while a version based on Hemmerdinger's attempt at restoration is included among the testimonia in Rosén's edition. How far divergences from the *ed. pr.* represent a real advance is not clear.

We have the remains of two columns, but it is hard to make much of the first. The second starts with notes on Herodotus' account of Babylonian river traffic (194), which he highlights as τὸ ... ἁπάντων θῶμα μέγιστον ... τῶν ταύτηι μετά γε αὐτὴν τὴν πόλιν ('the most amazing thing of all there after the city itself'). (No doubt the neat balance involved in the reciprocal conveyance of boat and donkey appealed to him.) It probably begins with an explanation of διφθέρας cτεγαcτρίδαc (watertight hides) (194. 2). A note on ὄνος ζώς ἐcτιν ('there is a live donkey') (194. 3) evidently turned on the need to distinguish the literal use of ὄνος from its common meaning of 'windlass'. But then we jump from halfway through 194, ignoring the rest of Herodotus' account of Babylonian customs and Cyrus' fatal campaign against the Massagetae, to 215, on the military practices of that people; nothing in 216, the last chapter, receives annotation.

This is very puzzling. We might have expected some comment on the first sentence of 215: Μαccαγέται δὲ ἐcθῆτά τε ὁμοίην τῆι Cκυθικῆι φορέουcι καὶ δίαιταν ἔχουcι ('the Massagetae wear clothing like the Scythian and have a similar way of life'). Full as Herodotus' description of Scythian customs is, he does not actually tell us what they wear, and though we all know that the answer is 'trousers', probably for both sexes, the omission is interesting and might have been expected to attract comment from Aristarchus. But in the note on ἱππόται δέ εἰcι καὶ ἄνιπποι ('they are horsemen and without horses', i.e. they fight both on horseback and on foot) we are alerted to an addendum for the *apparatus criticus*. ἅμιπποι for ἄνιπποι of the paradosis. In our historical sources the term, very often corrupted to ἄνιπποι, is used of light infantry, but for our commentator it evidently means paired riders, a chariot team on horseback: ἵ]πποι δ[ύο εὐ]άγωγοι ἱμᾶcι δεδεμένοι καὶ [ἐπ'] αὐτῶν τινεc ὀχούμενοι ('two docile horses fastened together with thongs and men riding on them').[36] As the editors saw, this can be connected with a passage in Bekker's first rhetorical lexicon (1814, 205. 5) discussing ἅμιππος: ἐὰν διὰ τοῦ ῡ γράφηται ἡ cυλλαβή, ἄνιππος, cημαίνει τοὺς ἵππους μὴ ἔχονταc ἀλλὰ πεζούc. ἐὰν δὲ διὰ τοῦ μ̄, ἅμιππος, ὅπερ καὶ μᾶλλον, cημαίνει τοὺς δύο ἔχονταc ἐζευγμένουc ἵππουc ἱμᾶcι χωρὶc ζυγοῦ καὶ τὸν μὲν ἡνιοχοῦντα, τὸν δὲ μαχόμενον ('If the syllable is written with *nu, anhippos*, the word means those who do not have horses, footsoldiers. But if with *mu, hamippos*, as is actually better (?), it means those who have two horses harnessed with thongs without a yoke and one man driving them while the other fights').[37] We can see how this works in the reliefs in the British Museum from Ashurnasirpal's palace at Nimrud:[38] one of the pair of riders controls both horses while the other concentrates on archery. The technique did not fully

---

[36] δ[ύο εὐ]άγωγοι Radermacher 1902, 139. I have omitted dots under broken letters, since the restoration seems certain.
[37] See further Jacoby on *FGrH* 328 (Philochorus) F 71.
[38] For illustrations see Yadin 1963, 382–5. See further Littauer and Crouwel 1979, 134–9.

exploit the advantages of riding over driving and did not long remain part of Assyrian military practice. I suspect that ἄμιπποι is offered as a conjecture, Herodotus' ἀμφοτέρων γὰρ μετέχουσι ('they make use of both') being deemed to imply something more interesting than 'they fight both on horseback and on foot'. It certainly is not compelling; Herodotus could simply mean that the Massagetai, otherwise resembling the Scythians, differed from them in fighting on foot as well as on horseback. What follows seems hardly relevant to Herodotus: οἱ ἥρωες τοῖς ἅρμασι προσήλαυνον καὶ οὕτως ἀπέβα[ι]νον· οἱ δὲ πρ[ὸς] ἐλάσσ[ω]`ο'cιν,[39] ὁ μὲν ἀπέβαινεν, ὁ δὲ [μ]ένων παρείχετο τὴν τοῦ ἡνιόχου χρείαν ('The heroes used to drive to battle in their chariots and then get down to fight; but against fewer adversaries, one got down while the other stayed to function as a charioteer'). It is quite obscure how this bears on ἄνιπποι versus ἄμιπποι. The use of chariots in the *Iliad* certainly offers plenty of scope for discussion, but Aristarchus' interest in the topic appears only in his insistence that a pair of horses was the heroic norm, a four-horse chariot un-Homeric (Sch. *Il.* 8. 185; Lehrs 1882, 193–4), and what remains of his work on Homer, so far as I can see, throws no light on this passage.[40]

There follows a brief note on cαγάρις: πέλεκυς Cκυθικ[ός, οἷ]ον [a]ἱ Ἀμαζόνες φ[ορ]οῦcιν ('*sagaris*: Scythian axe, such as the Amazons carry'). One might wish that the commentator had thought it worth mentioning that this is one of the celestial golden objects specified in the legend about the origins of Scythian rule which Herodotus later relates (4. 5. 3), where we might have expected to find the bow, as being more obviously characteristic of the Scythian way of life. This is followed by a sentence in which ὀρθῶς seems secure, but little else. The following lemma cιδήρωι δὲ οὐδ' ἀργύρωι χρέωνται ('they use neither iron nor silver') implies a text from which the final οὐδέν was absent; this must be a mistake. The relevance of the quotation from Sophocles' *Poimenes* (F 500), οὐ χάλκος, οὐ cίδηρος ἅπτεται χροός ('neither bronze nor iron affects his flesh'), probably referring to Cycnus, is obscure,[41] but makes a good ending. It looks as if this note has suffered from unintelligent abbreviation: the quotation was kept, but not the argument which it was meant to support or illustrate.

This is a very peculiar text, and we should not cherish the idea that it points to an Alexandrian edition of our author (whatever we think that

[39] 'The supposed ο above ω erased in ἐλαccωcιν is itself more like ω, but there is no reason for the alteration unless the reading was changed, and πρὸς ἐλάccοcιν is in any case required' (eds.).

[40] The strange item of antiquarian information preserved in Bekker's *Anecdota* would have been appropriate in a note on *Il.* 10. 498–502, where Odysseus rides one horse while controlling another, an interesting exception to the general principle that Homeric heroes do not ride, though riding features in the similes (*Il.* 15. 679–84; *Od.* 5. 371).

[41] Paap's suggestion that the commentator wanted to show that Sophocles here drew on Herodotus is not persuasive; cf. Radt ad loc.

would mean). Before it was published there was no reason to suppose that
Aristarchus had composed a commentary on any prose writer, and his
apparent lack of interest in history or geography[42] made it the more surprising that he should have turned his attention to Herodotus. The model of
Homeric criticism, concentrating on grammatical and textual questions,
was not well suited to the analysis of prose texts, especially when geographical
and historical questions had to be faced.

The papyrus does nothing for Aristarchus' reputation.[43] We can play with
the idea that the text we have originated in informal notes which someone
had taken at his lectures—we might compare the records of some of the
seminars which Eduard Fraenkel gave in Italy in the 1960s, which convey a
very strong sense of what interested *him*, rather than of systematic exegesis.[44]
But this analogy is probably misleading, as there is no reason to think that
anything like that style of instruction had a place in the Museum.

The lack of any notes on 195–204 or 206, must indicate that someone
excerpted for his own purposes from a much longer text, taking over citations
mechanically, as appears to have been all too common in the ancient handbooks and commentaries which provided shortcuts to Hellenic culture.[45]
The excerptor appears to have been interested primarily in *Realien*. I would
guess that behind the note on Homeric chariot tactics lies, at several removes,
some discussion by Aristarchus, and that, misunderstood and garbled,
this association has generated a pseudepigraphical attribution to the great
Homerist.[46] Again, I would look to classroom needs, or rather, those of the
schoolteacher keen to add the jam of scholarship to the bread and butter of
familiar texts. 194 and 205 are perfectly suitable as reading matter for
teenagers, while the chapters on the Babylonian marriage-market and sacred
prostitution, on Cyrus' last, problematic, campaign and unedifying death,

---

[42] 'Die vollkommene anistoresie, die für seine philologie charakteristisch ist' (Wilamowitz
1889, 155).

[43] Pfeiffer's discussion (1968, 224–5) is perhaps too kindly. Didymus' choice of material
for comment in dealing with Demosthenes' *Philippics* caused considerable surprise when
the papyrus was first published; see further Harding 2006, 13–20, 31–41. Theon on Pindar's
*Pythians* (P.Oxy. XXXI 2536) proved similarly disappointing; in the latter case unsystematic
excerpting seems certain, see Turner ad loc. From a somewhat later period the commentary
on Terence which passes under Donatus' name bears only a very loose relationship to that
scholar, having suffered from abridgement and reconstitution; the same might be said of
Servius' commentary on Vergil.

[44] See Rossi 1977, Roncali 1994.

[45] See further Cameron 2004 *passim* for a fascinating, or horrifying, survey of specious
scholarship and bogus documentation.

[46] Francesca Schironi (Schironi 2004, 11) implies similar scepticism, though she does not
explicitly mention this text: 'Di Aristarco, come per la maggior parte dei grammatici e filologi
antichi, nulla è conservato per la tradizione diretta. La letteratura erudita, sopratutto quella
esegetica e grammaticale, è infatti caratterizzata da un continuo riutilizzo del materiale a dis-
pozione, che viene variamente elaborato ed epitomato, così da determinare la perdita delle
opere originali in quanto ritenute ormai non più necessarie.'

and the final chapter, dealing with sexual promiscuity and funerary cannibal-ism, might be judged somewhat too sensational for schoolboys and therefore better omitted. It was reassuring to get a fragment of a less perplexing Hero-dotus commentary with the publication of P.Oxy. 4455 (Mertens–Pack 484.01), likewise of the third century. It deals with 5. 52–5, and discusses discrepancies from Xenophon in the account of the Royal Road from Ephesus to Sardis, internal inconsistencies, and lexical points.

We see a rare, and welcome, interest in textual criticism in P.Oxy. 1092 (Pack 473; Paap 12; late second century), which preserves substantial amounts of Book 2, 154–75. A significantly different, and certainly accept-able, version of 162. 5 has been added in the upper margin by a second hand, apparently resulting from collation with another copy. In the body of the text the papyrus supports Abresch's conjecture, οἷα for οἱ, at 175. 1.

Such confirmation is very welcome. Few of the new readings offered by papyri have offered anything surprising; orthographic variants and deviations in word order must of course be carefully considered, but very little of signifi-cant difference has appeared. P.Oxy. 3381 (Mertens–Pack 480.1; second cen-tury), preserving parts of 7. 169–70, brings an interesting novelty at 7. 169. 2. The context is the Pythia's response to a Cretan embassy to Delphi, sent to ask whether they should assist Hellenic resistance to Persia. The Pythia says that they did quite enough in the Trojan war, in helping to avenge Helen's abduc-tion, τὴν ἐκ Cπάρτηc ἁρπαχθεῖcαν ὑπ᾽ ἀνδρὸc βαρβάρου γυναῖκα ('the woman who was abducted from Sparta by a barbarian'). Instead of βαρβάρου the papyrus has δαρδα[ν]ου, i.e. Dardanian; as an ethnic, equivalent to 'Tro-jan', this has poetic resonances. The Pythia's speech is rather high-flown, and whether or not we find persuasive the suggestion that Herodotus was here following a poetic source,[47] this variant, more specific than the traditional reading, has much to recommend it. Short as it is, this papyrus thus contrib-utes significantly to what might be regarded as the papyrologist's primary mission, to inject into our studies regular doses of the unexpected.[48]

# BIBLIOGRAPHY

Alberti, G. B. 1983, 'I papiri e l'archetipo di Erodoto', *Prometheus*, 9. 193–6.
Bandiera, A. 1997, 'Per un bilancio della tradizione papiracea delle *Storie* di Erodoto', *Akten des 21. Internationalen Papyrologenkongresses Berlin, 1995* (Stuttgart and Leipzig), 49–56.
Bekker, I. 1814, *Anecdota Graeca*, i (Berlin).

---

[47] See Macan 1908 ad loc.
[48] This paper has benefited greatly from the comments of other participants in the con-ference; I am particularly grateful to Eric Handley, Dirk Obbink, and Nigel Wilson.

Bravo, B. 2000, 'Pseudo-Herodotus and Pseudo-Thucydides on Scythia, Thrace and the Regions "Beyond"', *ASNP*[4] 5, 21–112.

Cameron, A. D. E. 2004, *Greek Mythography in the Roman World* (New York).

Chambers, M., *et al.* 1981, *The Oxyrhynchus Papyri*, XLVIII (Egypt Exploration Society, Graeco-Roman Memoirs, no. 67; London).

Cribiore, R. 2001, *Gymnastics of the Mind: Greek Education in Hellenistic and Roman Egypt* (Princeton).

Ehrhardt, C. 1988, 'Herodot', *RAC* xiv. 849–61.

Flower, M. A., and Marincola, J. 2002, *Herodotus, Histories Book IX* (Cambridge).

Fowler, D. P. 1989, 'First Thoughts on Closure', *MD* 22, 75–122 = *Roman Constructions* (Oxford, 2000), 239–83.

Grenfell, B. P., and Hunt, A. S. 1919, *The Oxyrhynchus Papyri*, XIII (London).

Guéraud, O., and Jouguet, P. 1938, *Un livre d'écolier du IIIᵉ siècle avant J.-C.* (Cairo).

Harding, P. 2006, *Didymos on Demosthenes* (Oxford).

Harrison, T. 2000, *Divinity and History: The Religion of Herodotus* (Oxford).

Hatzilambrou, R. G. 2002, 'A Duke Papyrus of Herodotus iv 144.2–145.1', *BASP* 39, 41–5.

Hornblower, S. 2006, 'Herodotus' Influence in Antiquity' in C. Dewald and J. Marincola (eds.), *The Cambridge Companion to Herodotus* (Cambridge), 306–18.

Humphreys, S. C. 2004, *The Strangeness of Gods: Historical Perspectives on the Interpretation of Athenian Religion* (Oxford).

Hunt, A. S. 1927, *The Oxyrhynchus Papyri*, XVII (London).

Jacoby, F. 1913, 'Herodot', *RE* Suppl. ii. 205–520.

Jenkyns, R. 1991, *Dignity and Decadence: Victorian Art and the Classical Inheritance* (London).

Johnson, W. A. 2000, 'Toward a Sociology of Reading in Classical Antiquity', *AJPh* 121, 593–627.

—— 2004, *Bookrolls and Scribes in Oxyrhynchus* (Toronto).

Kurke, L. 1999, *Coins, Bodies, Games, and Gold: The Politics of Meaning in Archaic Greece* (Princeton).

Lehrs, K. 1882, *De Aristarchi studiis Homericis*, 3rd edn (Leipzig).

Littauer, M. A., and Crouwel, J. H. 1979, *Wheeled Vehicles and Ridden Animals in the Ancient Near East* (Leiden).

Macan, R. W. 1895, *Herodotus: The Fourth, Fifth, and Sixth Books* (London).

—— 1908, *Herodotus: The Seventh, Eighth, and Ninth Books* (London).

Maravela-Solbakk, A. 2004, 'Fragments of Literary Papyri from the Collection of the Oslo University Library, I: Herodotus 9.74–75', *SO* 79, 102–8.

Mertens, P., and Strauss, J. A. 1992, 'Les papyrus d'Hérodote', *ASNP*[3] 22, 969–78.

Morgan, T. 1998, *Literate Education in the Hellenistic and Roman Worlds* (Cambridge).

Paap, A. H. R. 1948, *De Herodoti reliquiis in papyris et membranis Aegyptiis servatis* (Leiden).

Parsons, P. J., Rea, J. R., and Turner, E. G. 1968, *The Oxyrhynchus Papyri*, XXXIII (London).

Pfeiffer, R. 1968, *History of Classical Scholarship*, i (Oxford).

Radermacher, L. 1902, 'Aus dem zweiten Bande der Amherst Papyri', *RhM*[2] 57, 137–51.

Richards, H. 1905, 'Notes on Herodotus, Books I–III', *CR* 19, 290–6.

Rosén, H. B. 1987, *Herodoti Historiae*, i (Leipzig).

Roncali, R. 1994 (ed.), *Pindaro, Sofocle, Terenzio, Catullo, Petronio: corsi seminariali di Eduard Fraenkel, Bari 1965–69* (Rome).

Rossi, L. E. 1977, *Due seminari romani di Eduard Fraenkel: Aiace e Filottete di Sophocle* (Rome).

Saerens, C. 1990, 'Papyrus d'Hérodote et tradition manuscrite', *Studia Varia Bruxellensia*, 2 (Leuven), 177–92.

Schironi, F. 2004, *I frammenti di Aristarco di Samotracia negli etimologici bizantini* (Göttingen).

Soldati, A. 2005, 'Due frammenti di un unico rotolo? P.Duke inv. 756 e P.Mil.Vogl. inv. 1358 (Herodotus IV 144.2–145.1 e 147.4–5)', *BASP* 42, 101–6.

Stephens, S. A. 2003, *Seeing Double: Intercultural Poetics in Ptolemaic Alexandria* (Berkeley and Los Angeles).

Talmon, S. 1970, 'The Old Testament Text', in P. R. Ackroyd and C. F. Evans (eds.), *The Cambridge History of the Bible*, i: *From the Beginnings to Jerome* (Cambridge), 159–99.

Turner, E. G. 1968, *The Oxyrhynchus Papyri*, XXXIII (London).

—— (Sir Eric) 1977, *The Typology of the Early Codex* (Philadelphia, PA).

—— rev. Parsons, P. J. 1987, *Greek Manuscripts of the Ancient World* (*BICS* Supplement 46; London).

Wilamowitz-Moellendorff, U. von, 1889, *Einleitung in die attische Tragödie* (Berlin).

Yadin, Y. 1963, *The Art of Warfare in Biblical Lands* (London).

# 4

## The Use and Abuse of Irony

*Richard Rutherford*

'"Irony" last resort of commentators' (E. Fraenkel)[1]

A fellow connoisseur of fragments and a one-time colleague of Peter Parsons at Christ Church has recently published an excellent *Companion to Petronius* (2001). In his discussions of this difficult author Ted Courtney offers sense and subtle illumination on every page. But some remarks in the opening pages may give us pause and prompt reflection. There he comments on a type of interpretation which assumes that the author is undermining rather than supporting or endorsing the values of his era. Courtney admits the possibility but his scepticism is evident. He writes: '. . . my own experience is that authors have usually left enough indications to testify to their irony, and that when scholars assume irony in the absence of plain signals, they are generally wrong to do so.'[2] If only it were always that simple!

In this paper I shall consider a number of texts in which irony has been detected, with or without what Courtney calls plain signals, and try to clarify the methodological moves involved in diagnosing irony in a text as a whole. It is important to distinguish what I call local irony, restricted to a specific situation or speaker or scene, from the ironic reading of a whole text. The latter is hard to detect and harder to feel sure of. In practice we commonly use context as a control—in cases involving local irony, the rest of the text provides the crucial context, but we may also look further to other texts by the same author or in the same genre, and still more widely to the cultural and historical milieu. There are potential interpretative problems at each level—we cannot assume that authors never vary or genres never develop or individuals never speak with a different voice from their society. Still greater

---

[1] Fraenkel 1950, 837; cf. 719 (on 1523f) 'the magic wand of irony, by which the commentator converts the sense of a sentence into the exact opposite of what, to the ordinary man, it seems to say.' Cf. Fraenkel 1957, 456 col. 1.
[2] Courtney 2001, 2.

are the problems when dealing with an undateable or anonymous or fragmentary text, where some or all context is lost. Is a fragmentary utterance
typical or unique, sober moralising or pompous pontification? Out of context, even good scholars may be uncertain of tone or genre. A delicious case in
point is Eur. F 930

> οἴμοι, δράκων μου γίγνεται τὸ ἥμισυ·
> τέκνον, περιπλάκηθι τῷ λοιπῷ πατρί.

Oh woe, half of me is becoming a snake; my child, embrace what is left of your father!

Who can be speaking here: Cecrops, Erechtheus, Cadmus (the last is perhaps
most probable)? And what are we to think of this unplaced fragment—is
Euripides seeking to arouse intense pathos or delighted amusement? Such a
metamorphosis could hardly have been enacted on stage; possibly the *oratio
recta* derives from a messenger speech. At the end of the *Bacchae* Cadmus'
dracontification is prophesied, but despite this parallel many have doubted
that this can be from a tragedy: Elmsley declared it a satyric fragment,
Webster thought it must come from comedy; Wilamowitz apparently judged
it spurious.[3] Peter Parsons has confronted such problems often throughout
his career, and his own keen sense of the ironic has given spice to his
scholarship.

I must now give rather more definition to my subject. Irony is of course
a many-faceted term. Discussion of its history and of the theoretical or
ironographical background would more than fill this paper. Let me briefly
survey a few key points, ancient and modern, before turning as swiftly as
may be to practical examples.[4] We see from the earliest instances that an
εἴρων is a dissembler, often a hypocrite: instruction at the Reflectory will
make Strepsiades an εἴρων among other things (*Clouds* 445 ff.—the list also
includes θρασύς, εὔγλωττος, τολμηρός ... ἀλαζών ['brash, glib-tongued,
bold... fraudulent']); Philocleon produces a neat excuse ὡς εἰρωνικῶς
('like a practised dissembler') (*Wasps* 174). In Plato, the concept is applied
to Socrates because his opponents think (with some justification) that he is
feigning ignorance and dullness of wit. But the term can also be used in

---

[3] See Kannicht ad loc. for fuller details. The context of the quotation is interesting, as often.
The lines are quoted by Hermogenes, περὶ εὑρέσεως (4, 12) in his discussion of ' ....... (εγβ.....
('........') ... regards the first line as a clear example of this fault occurring in ...... of
'cheap' or 'base' material; but the second line seems to redeem it with its nobility (ἡ σεμνότης
διορθοῦται). Lines of ambiguous tone evoke a contradictory response.

[4] See further, on the classical background, Diggle 2004, 166–7 on Theophrastus, and bibli-
ography cited there (especially Ribbeck 1876). For modern studies see J. A. K. Thomson 1926,
Sedgewick 1935, Muecke 1969 and 1982, Booth 1974 (reviewed by Empson 1987, 178–83);
Colebrook 2004. Rosenmeyer 1996 is a valuable survey (with the reply by Lowe in the same
volume); he has also addressed related questions elsewhere (see Rosenmeyer 1977 and 1993).
More recent still is the anthology edited by Perkins (2001), with essays focused on irony in
Socrates and Aristophanes' *Clouds,* and on Kierkegaard.

affectionate admiration (as by Alcibiades in the *Symposium*), and Platonic
practice generally has a deep influence on the expanding scope of *eironeia*,
which subsequent rhetorical definitions are not altogether able to contain.[5]

Modern extensions of the concept have ranged far and wide: in 'cosmic
irony', the reality of the world mocks the petty human players; in 'Romantic
irony' the author, or the text, makes fun of itself (as in *Tristram Shandy*).[6] The
'New Criticism' represented by Cleanth Brooks and others came close to the
view that a work *must* involve irony, self-contradiction, or paradox if it is to
be any good, and this notion has continued to have a kind of subterranean
influence on many studies.[7] This does not exhaust the possibilities. Empson
defined seven types of ambiguity;[8] among classicists, Rosenmeyer has sought
to distinguish four main categories of irony: forensic irony, 'blind' irony
(which is what most of us call dramatic irony), structural irony, and *Fiktions-
ironie*; and in a bewildering catalogue he lists no fewer than 79 subtypes;
but when he declares that 'the list . . . is necessarily selective, approximate, and
eminently revisable, begging for subtler and broader entries', we can guess
that he has his tongue firmly in his cheek.[9] I shall attempt a more moderate
approach. What seems fundamental to irony as I see it is the gap between
what is said and what is meant, between *uerba* and *res*. Sometimes a speaker/
author is saying something he does not mean—either in a specific utterance,
or in a whole speech, or even in a work as a whole. At other times there may
be a gap between the author and the narrator or persona within the text
(Ovid the poet is distinct from Ovid the lover). Especially complex is the case
of drama: here, in the absence of the authorial voice, it is not the poet who
speaks but his characters. To claim that the dramatist is presenting a character
ironically is to claim that he does not agree with the opinions expressed,
the attitudes revealed, or at least that the character's perspective is seen as
inadequate (Oedipus, Pentheus). This type of irony is especially difficult to
diagnose or control, as we shall see when I turn to Euripides. But first some
shorter and perhaps simpler examples.

Catullus 49 is a short poem complimenting and expressing thanks to
Cicero.[10] Here is a case where we know quite a lot about both parties and
about the social or cultural milieu, but where we find it difficult to assess the
poem's tone—essentially because the specific context is lacking. Cicero never
mentions Catullus, Catullus names Cicero nowhere but here. We do not know
the date of the poem, we have no idea what service Catullus is thanking the

[5] *Grg.* 489 E, *Rep.* 1. 337 A, etc.; positive use by Alcibiades at *Smp.* 216 E. Cf. Rutherford 1995, 77–8. For rhetorical developments of the concept see Quint. *Inst.* 8. 6. 54–6, 9. 2. 44–53, Lausberg 1963, §§902–4.
[6] Muecke 1969, ch. 5; Fowler 1994.
[7] e.g. Brooks 1951; Heilman 1956; *contra*, Crane 1952, 83–107.
[8] Empson 1930.    [9] Rosenmeyer 1996, 510.
[10] For bibliography see D. F. S. Thomson 1997, 323–4, e.g. Laughton 1970, Tatum 1988.

ex-consul for (a complimentary copy of the *de consulatu suo*?!). 'Some see irony here, but I do not', comments one biographer, referring to Fordyce's discussion (itself somewhat schizophrenic).[11]

The argument runs along two tracks: first, what we might call a gut feeling on the part of the critics that Cicero cannot have been Catullus' type of person. This is dodgy ground—Cicero managed to sustain friendly and witty relations with many lively young men (Caelius is the most obvious); Cicero and Catullus had friends in common (Cornelius Nepos was one); Cicero's own poetic interests were not confined to the tragedies of Ennius,[12] and his digs at the *poetae noui* or the *cantores Euphorionis* come from a significantly later date (closest is the passage in Cic. *Att.* 7. 2. 1 of 50 BC).

The other line of argument is internal, based on the language of the poem. The wording is grandiloquent, the structure extravagant. Of a seven-line poem three lines salute the addressee, three offer an emphatic depreciation of the poet's own status, and the message itself is virtually squeezed out in between. After the superlative, the double vocative, the allusion to the founder of Rome, the three *quot* clauses spanning the whole of time, the fourth line, containing the core of the message, may seem a little bathetic (simply 'Thanks a lot. Yours, Catullus'). The poem seems to pack a tiny amount of meat in the middle of a rather doughy sandwich. All the superlatives: *disertissime, maximas, pessimus* twice, *optimus,* seem to pile on the flattery in a way which hardly rings true for Catullus but savours quite strongly of Cicero's own highly superlative-heavy style. A further point, though it needs caution, is that Catullus patently cannot really believe that he is the *pessimus omnium poeta*: certainly he did not when writing poem 36, where he sidestepped and transferred that title to Volusius; so can he by the logic of *tanto/quanto* seriously assert that Cicero is the *optimus omnium patronus*? I doubt it. But I am less convinced by the argument that has gained currency in recent years,[13] that there is a double meaning in the phrase 'best of all advocates' and also 'best advocate for everybody'— that is, an insinuation that Cicero offers his services to all comers out of an eagerness for fees. It can be objected that *optimus* and *omnium* are closely bound up together. We cannot make sense of the corresponding phrase in the preceding line as 'best poet of everybody'. But setting that detail aside, I think here there is a pretty strong case for reading the poem ironically.

What about another Catullan poem, where not only have we no external evidence but we can, I assume, be fairly confident there was none—that is, that the poem dramatizes a fictitious situation involving (probably) fictional

---

[11]  Stockton 1971, 41 n. 1, referring to Fordyce 1961, 214.
[12]  See Townend 1964.
[13]  e.g. Goold 1983, 245, Morgan 2000, 358. Sceptical too is Syndikus 1984, 249 n. 10.

characters? I refer to poem 45, Acme and Septimius.[14] 'Acme' is evidently a
*nom parlant*, expressing perfection. These lovers seem to belong to a romantic
world of lovers' fantasies rather than to contemporary Rome: here at least the
robust realism of Jasper Griffin does not wholly convince.[15] Here again interpretation rests partly on internal evidence, partly on the reader's assumptions
about what kind of poet Catullus is, what kind of lovers he will find sympathetic. That lands us pretty firmly in a tail-chasing hermeneutic circle.
How far is it legitimate to argue from one poem to another, to demand that
Catullus give us a coherent and consistent picture of his own tastes and
attitudes? Put that way, the fallacies are plain; on the other hand, Catullus
clearly did organize a book of his own poems, whatever it looked like,[16] and
there are evidently cross-references and recurring themes within his work, so
that there is at least some inducement to view one poem in the light of others.
In that case Acme and Septimius certainly come across as starry-eyed and
naïve, lovesick youngsters drooling glutinous protestations worthy only of the
Greek novel, as memorably characterized by Peter Parsons in an entertaining
essay.[17] At most, I would wish to see the poet's compliments in the closing
part of the poem as amused and patronizing.[18] The promises to tackle lions
in Libya, the sickly-sweet diminutive 'Septimille', reminiscent of comedy
(cf. Plaut. *Pseud.* 66 ff.), the ornamental accompaniment of Cupid's kindly
sneezing, create an effect which may well seem irresistibly comical and remote
from the presentation of the erotic, whether committed or hedonistic, elsewhere in the poet's work. But I admit that other views are possible, and this
may be a case where the irony, even if present, is combined with a degree of
affectionate sympathy for the poet's creations.

We have begun to see that the diagnosis of irony or its absence can be based
on one's reading of the text in question, but can also be shaped or directed by
one's knowledge of other works by the author, or by—perhaps misguided—
ideas of the character of the writer. Other considerations may also enter into
play: literary inheritance, generic expectations, and political or ideological
constraints. My next example combines most if not all of these. The proem to
Lucan's *De bello ciuili*, with its grandiloquent praise of Nero, has stimulated
endless controversy.[19] The problem is obvious: Lucan praises Nero as the
source of his inspiration and treats him in the same extravagant style that
Virgil had employed in the opening of the first book of the *Georgics*; yet

[14] For bibliography again see D. F. S. Thomson 1997, 318–19, e.g. Edwards 1928 'ironical without being bitter', Baker 1958, Singleton 1971. Nisbet and Rudd 2004, 134, discussing Hor. *Odes* 3. 9, see no reason not to take Catullus' poem at face value.
[15] J. Griffin 1976 = 1984, 1–31: but in his view Acme is 'no doubt' a freedwoman (1984, 16)
[16] On all this see Hutchinson 2003, with extensive bibliography.
[17] Parsons 1981.
[18] Cf. Lyne 1975, 50–5.
[19] See Dilke 1972; Lebek 1976, 74–107; M. T. Griffin 1984, 156–60; Feeney 1991, 275–6, 298–301; Dewar 1994; Leigh 1997, 23–6 (developed at Leigh 2000, 474–5).

elsewhere in the poem he is not only viciously anti-Caesarian, anti-imperial rule, but also aggressively hostile towards ruler cult (esp. 6. 807–9, 7. 445–59, 9. 601–4). I assume, though not all would agree, that Virgil's praise of Octavian, though high-flown in its Alexandrian manner, is not meant to seem absurd or to be ironically reversed. But despite the obvious literary *imitatio*, this does not dictate how we should interpret Lucan (if only because another imitation of Virgil, Ovid's at the close of *Met.* 15, has interposed). One strategy is to declare the proem an early and unmodified part of the text, to recall the mood of ill-advised optimism which began Nero's reign[20] and to assume a subequent change of heart, appealing to the biographical tradition of a rift between Nero and Lucan. Vacca tells us that *ediderat . . . tres libros quales uidemus*, and critics deduce that this means that the first three books were earlier and are less vigorous in their critique of Caesar and the principate, whereas the rest of the poem postdates the quarrel and shows Lucan on the offensive.[21] Of course, Lucan's early death left the poem not only unrevised but unfinished, so this scenario cannot be ruled out of court; but classicists nowadays are less content with the 'layered look' approach to texts, and it is perhaps implausible that so important a section as the main proem should have been left untouched. More concretely, the argument that Lucan pulls his punches in regard to the empire and its founder in books 1–3 is not easily sustained. Nigidius Figulus in book 1 prophesies civil war and tyrannical rule (1. 669–73).[22]

So the other strategy is to assume a coherence in Lucan's text and thought, and to detect irony in the proem. We may dispense with the more far-fetched versions of this reading, which detect in the proem allusions to Nero's alleged obesity and see *obliquo sidere* at line 55 as a dig at Nero's supposed squint: these have been effectively disposed of in a valuable paper by Michael Dewar. But can we really read the apotheosis, and the declaration that Nero's installation on the throne justifies all the sufferings of the civil wars, as straightforward panegyric? Sometimes it is argued that this must be the case, because any subversive implication would be too dangerous in an imperial court: how could Lucan have ventured any such insult? Hence a variation on the irony theme: according to Stephen Hinds, the proem is not so much ironic as ambiguous.[23] This type of reading has gained much support, though it

---

[20] Cf. Tacitus 1.3.1, 13. in AD 60 the twenty-two year old Nero had not yet the marks of vice written on his features.

[21] Vacca, *Vita M. Annaei Lucani*, l. 43 in Rostagni 1964, 183. See also Tac. *Ann.* 15.49, Suet. *Lucan* 11–22 (Rostagni 1964, 146–7).

[22] M. T. Griffin 1984, 158 notes also 1. 670–2, 2. 62–3 as effectively reversing the thought of 1. 33–45 (cited below in the text).

[23] Hinds 1988, at 23–9. Dewar 1994, 210–11 does not agree with Hinds, but treats his approach with cautious respect. Comparable ideas are developed by Ahl 1984, who introduced the concept of the 'figured style', drawing on ancient rhetorical theory (especially Demetrius 287–95, Quintil. 9. 2. 66, ps.-Dion. Hal. *Ars Rhetorica* 8–9); see also Bartsch 1994.

needs very careful handling: why assume Nero is stupider than Seneca and Burrus? Even if he was, we may not be altogether happy with the picture of Nero lapping up the flattery while courtiers and senators snigger up their toga sleeves—or are we meant to think that Nero did see the irony but declined to acknowledge it?.[24]

Let us look again at the most notorious section of the proem, the opening.

> quod si non aliam uenturo fata Neroni
> inuenere uiam magnoque aeterna parantur
> regna deis caelumque suo seruire Tonanti
> non nisi saeuorum potuit post bella gigantum,
> iam nihil, o superi, querimur; scelera ipsa nefasque
> hac mercede placent. diros Pharsalia campos
> inpleat et Poeni saturentur sanguine manes,
>
> . . .
>
> multum Roma tamen debet ciuilibus armis
> quod tibi res acta est.

Still, if Fate could find no other way for the advent of Nero; if an everlasting kingdom costs the gods dear and heaven could not be ruled by its sovereign, the Thunderer, before the battle with the fierce Giants;—then we complain no more against the gods; even such crimes and such guilt are not too high a price to pay. Let Pharsalia heap her awful plains with dead; let the shade of the Carthaginian be glutted with carnage . . . yet Rome owes much to civil war, because what was done was done for you. (1. 33–45; tr. Duff.)

Irony does not seem to me the most appropriate tool for the reader of this passage. I see this rather as a prize example of Lucan's devotion both to paradox and to carrying an idea to its ultimate extremes. Any page of his epic testifies to his love of hyperbole. Here, it is not so much that he declares 'Nero is great' and we are meant to detect a whispered 'no, he isn't'; rather, the potentially rational position 'civil war was bad, but we now have something better' is pushed to extremes that border on the irrational: Lucan's fervid rhetorical ingenuity extends the idea to its limits, just as elsewhere, in apocalyptic and anti-imperial vein, he declares that Pharsalia marked 'the death of the world' and that the Roman race is enslaved for all time (7. 617, 640). The ideological slant is different, the imaginative perversity follows the same tendency.

We begin, I think, to see a pattern in these ironic readings. Irony is invoked when the reader simply cannot believe that a writer can mean what he says. Catullus (as we imagine him) *cannot* have really admired Cicero (as we construct him) without reservation; he *surely didn't* think that a love-affair like that of Acme and Septimius represented amorous perfection. Similarly historical hindsight makes us incredulous that *Nero* could be praised, even in

---

[24] Cf. Dewar 1994, 209.

a panegyrical passage, with the same high hopes and optimism as the young Octavian, and by *Lucan* of all poets. We have seen in each case that counter-arguments are possible; these examples are not clear-cut. Perhaps they never are: in any instance, different readers will find different arguments more persuasive. But we can formulate a few general principles. First, the paucity of ancient biographical evidence is such that it will seldom be prudent to rest our arguments on the supposed character or career of an individual writer. (There are exceptions, especially involving well-documented authors: for instance, we can be confident that the praise of Caesar in the *Pro Marcello* is not a 'figured speech' because of the supporting evidence for Cicero's enthusiastic response to Caesar's action in a private letter.[25]) Second, we need to justify our analyses from the text itself, and only secondarily from external evidence: authors must be allowed to do different things in different texts, and to be creative in ways which can go beyond the models they imitate or the genres in which they are working. Third, when different parts of a text seem to be contradictory, there is scope for different critical strategies: a compositional approach in terms of chronological layers (as in the argument about Lucan's first three books, or in traditional Homeric analysis), or an acceptance and even celebration of the contradictions, or a movement beyond superficial contradiction to discern a kind of unity on another level (as I attempted above with the case of Lucan). Finally, there is the matter of larger cultural context. Often we know much less about the life of the author than about the times: with due caution, we may be able to use other texts and contexts as controls, at least in terms of confirming that certain things could be said, even if controversially, at a given period. I am thinking here of the debates about what can and cannot be said under an imperial ruler. We should beware of imposing our own assumptions in this matter—emperors differ, even different stages of a given ruler's reign differ. Propertius could declare that no son of his would be a soldier and write in darkly negative terms about the victory of Actium (2. 7. 13–14, 15. 44). Lucan's praise of Cato reflects the hagiographic tradition about the martyr of Utica, a dominant strand in first-century literature.[26] Seneca could be the mentor of Nero yet shower constant praise on the antagonist of Julius Caesar. But it remains the case that the text under discussion must be the central focus: after all, there must always be some text that goes further, says more extreme or extravagant things than any others.

I have spoken of cultural background and period ideology. We might also ask whether there are more absolute, period-free constraints, intrinsic to the human situation, which will assist us in the detection of irony in a text.

---

[25] *Ad fam.* 4. 4: see the arguments of Winterbottom 2002 against the 'figured' interpretation advanced by Dyer 1990.

[26] MacMullen 1966, chs. 1–2.

It is clear that interpreters have at least sometimes adopted this kind of premiss, perhaps unconsciously, in the past. Praise of tyrannical rulers, celebration of Spartan armed-camp ideology, acclamation of war and martial prowess, arguments for the persistent subordination of women, are hard for us liberal pacificist feminist moderns to take straight.[27] Edward Hussey has expressed his distaste and distrust of the Periclean funeral speech with notable firmness:

2. 43 ... ends in a welter of florid rhetoric about death in battle. ... from Pericles' original point of view (the moral primacy of private enjoyment in life) the death of a young man in battle is a tragedy for which there can be no justification. For the sake of the continuance, or expansion, of an empire, such a death is inexcusable. Something is rotten in the thought here, which explains Pericles' evasive words and distracting sound-effects.[28]

Thus Hussey wants to see Thucydides as undercutting Pericles; yet both men were generals and knew that death in war was inevitable. More extreme measures are possible. In a moment of bold determination to allow a great poet to get it right, Robin Nisbet once suggested that in Horace's 'dulce et decorum est pro patria mori' the first two words be emended to 'dulci' (agreeing with 'patria'), but he has since retracted the suggestion.[29] A third example involves the still more controversial battleground of biblical interpretation. In his last years Geoffrey de Ste. Croix, who described himself as 'an atheist, politely militant', decided that he had a duty to speak out against the Judaeo-Christian deity. 'He discovered an ally in an unexpected place; he had long been disgusted by Yahweh's maltreatment of Job, undertaken merely as part of a trial of strength with Satan, and he came to believe that such a reaction of disgust was the effect intended by the final editor of Job'[30]—in other words, that the Book of Job is an ironic text. If a scholar of de Ste. Croix's formidable intellect can arrive at such a radically implausible view, it is yet another proof that we must beware of assuming that ancient writers shared our own attitudes.[31]

In the rest of this paper I want to tackle broader questions, skirting the dangerous shores of Euripidean interpretation. Here we move firmly from cases of 'local irony' to those which involve an ironic reading of a complete

---

[27] Compare also the readings of Virgil associated with the so-called 'Harvard' school. An important survey of the precedents for such interpretations which is also simultaneously a defence of the approach is provided by Thomas 2001; see also Kallendorf 2007.

[28] Hussey 1985, 125.

[29] *Odes* 3. 2. 13, see Nisbet 1988, 16–17, retracted in Nisbet 1995, 433 and now in Nisbet–Rudd 2004 ad loc.

[30] Parker 2001, 451, 475.

[31] If these examples seem unduly Oxonocentric, it is sufficient to invoke the shade of Verrall: for an illuminating essay on his oeuvre see Lowe 2005.

text (see the distinction drawn in my opening discussion above, p. 84). Perhaps nowhere in the classical canon, not even excepting the dialogues of Plato, has irony been invoked so frequently as in the debates on Euripidean drama, whether to defend the poet's artistic originality, to assert his claims as a religious (or atheistic) thinker, or to vindicate a supposedly dull play. There can be no question of tackling the whole of his oeuvre, but I shall address one particular group of plays, those involving self-sacrifice or quasi-voluntary sacrifice, a story pattern of which the dramatist is especially fond.[32] The earliest extant case is the scene in the *Heraclidae* in which the daughter of Heracles agrees to die in order that Athens, which has given refuge to herself and her brothers, may be saved from Argive assault. Her heroism is greeted with universal admiration and gratitude. The parallel story in the *Erechtheus* involves the necessary sacrifice of one of the daughters of the royal house, again to save Athens in time of war; I shall come back to this play later. In the *Phoenissae* the young Menoeceus, son of Creon, learns that his death is necessary to purify the city, appease the anger of Ares, and save Thebes from being sacked. Here the situation is more complex—his father rejects the command of Tiresias and tries to persuade his son to flee into exile and save his life. Menoeceus appears to agree, but when his father has left the stage, declares to the chorus his full intention to die (991 ff.). He does so, and the city is indeed saved, though at a price. (This is the only case where the victim is male, but his youth and virginity are emphasized.) Then there is the *Hecuba*: here, the situation is darker, as the sacrifice is required by the resentful ghost of Achilles: the sympathetic figure of Polyxena must die in order to satisfy the dead Greek warrior. Her virtue and courage bring credit on herself and are admired even by the Greek soldiers, but cause only grief for Hecabe and the other Trojan women; although nobly accepted, her self-sacrifice seems futile.[33] Still more problematic is the *Iphigenia at Aulis*. In the light of the parallel episodes we can readily detect certain story-patterns and motifs which the dramatist skilfully deploys to fresh ends. In almost all cases the necessity of sacrifice is at first resisted by someone—Iolaus in the *Heraclidae* (539 ff.), Hecabe in the case of Polyxena, Creon in the *Phoenissae*, probably Erechtheus in the play of that name. In the *IA* everyone on stage, including the victim, at one point or another resists the terrible demand; but we can be in little doubt, whether in terms of the mythical tradition or the standard plot pattern, that the sacrifice of Iphigenia will go ahead in the end (whatever its outcome): the Trojan war must take place. Sure enough, after at first naturally recoiling from the prospect of death, she in the end rises to the occasion and accepts her heroic duty in a great cause.

[32] See Schmitt 1921; O'Connor-Visser 1987; Kearns 1989, ch. 3; Wilkins 1990.
[33] For more detailed discussion see Mossman 1994, ch. 5.

κἀπ' ἐκεῖν' ἔλθωμεν· οὐ δεῖ τόνδε διὰ μάχης μολεῖν
πᾶσιν Ἀργείοις γυναικὸς οὕνεκ' οὐδὲ κατθανεῖν.
εἷς γ' ἀνὴρ κρείσσων γυναικῶν μυρίων ὁρᾶν φάος.
εἰ † δ' ἐβουλήθη † cῶμα τοὐμὸν Ἄρτεμις λαβεῖν,                    1395
ἐμποδὼν γενήcομαι 'γὼ θνητὸς οὖcα τῆι θεῶι;
ἀλλ' ἀμήχανον· δίδωμι cῶμα τοὐμὸν Ἑλλάδι.
θύετ', ἐκπορθεῖτε Τροίαν· ταῦτα γὰρ μνημεῖά μου
διὰ μακροῦ καὶ παῖδες οὗτοι καὶ γάμοι καὶ δόξ' ἐμή.
βαρβάρων δ' Ἕλληνας ἄρχειν εἰκός, ἀλλ' οὐ βαρβάρους,          1400
μῆτερ, Ἑλλήνων· τὸ μὲν γὰρ δοῦλον, οἱ δ' ἐλεύθεροι.

Consider this point as well: it is not right that this man should have to fight with all
the Greeks and be killed for a woman's sake. One man has greater claim to live and see
the sunlight than ten thousand women! If it is Artemis's will to take this life of mine,
shall I, a mortal, oppose the goddess? Impossible. I give my body to Greece. Sacrifice
me; sack Troy! This will be my memorial for many an age; this my children, my
marriage, my renown! It is natural that Greeks should rule barbarians, mother, not
barbarians Greeks; the one is a race of slaves, the other free men. (1387–1401.)

But is the cause in fact so great? We may accept that most Athenians would
feel that Greek interests should be preferred to barbarians' (Persia's involvement in the latter part of the Peloponnesian war is hardly irrelevant), and that
the language of pan-Hellenic unity might strike a chord in some of those who
sympathized with the sentiments expressed by Lysistrata a few years earlier in
Aristophanes. Talk of alliance among Greeks, aggression towards 'barbarians'
played a significant part in the rhetoric of the period. Gorgias in an oration at
the Olympic games (probably of 408) had called for 'unanimity' among the
warring Greeks; Lysias echoed these sentiments in 388.[34] But in Euripides'
drama the Greeks are not resolving on unity but bent on retribution; they are
in the grip of a heaven-sent affliction (411), a god-inspired passion (δεινόc
ἐμπέπτωκ' ἔρωc 808, cf. 1264). Moreover, both the killing of Iphigenia and
the Trojan war as a whole are dark and disturbing undertakings in the literary
tradition, above all in Aeschylus' influential trilogy. Within the IA itself, the
pan-Hellenic enterprise of the Trojan war has been shown in such a poor light
earlier in the play (Agamemnon's careerism, Menelaus' lustfulness), and the
potential danger of further foreign wife-stealing seems so implausible, that
the heroine's speech must, I believe, be read as noble but deluded. If Iphigenia
had to die, it should have been for a better cause.

A subsidiary problem concerns the strident generalizations, offensive to
modern taste, in the extract quoted above: 'One man has greater claim to live
and see the sunlight than ten thousand women! . . . It is natural that Greeks
should rule barbarians, mother, not barbarians Greeks' (1394, 1400). We

[34] Ar. *Lys.* 1123–56, especially 1128–34: Thucydides 4. 20. 4, 5. 29. 3, Xenophon, *Hellenica*
1. 6. 7, and later 6. 5. 33 ff. For Gorgias' Olympic oration see T1 Diels–Kranz ii. 272. 4–7.

naturally prefer to read such passages in an ironic sense, as overstated or absurd (and the forcefulness with which the views are put forward, without either qualification or argument, reinforces our doubts). Before moving too swiftly to an ironic reading we should bear in mind how many people might have found such statements perfectly reasonable even a century ago. However, it is perhaps possible to draw a distinction between the views of Iphigenia (young, enthusiastic, idealistic) and those of Euripides. The playwright's own opinions are of course irrecoverable, but we can at least note that many women and some foreigners are painted in positive or at least sympathetic lights elsewhere in his work.[35] On a number of grounds, then, an ironic reading of the *IA* does seem justified.[36] That judgement, however, is founded not on modern prejudice or anti-war sentiment, but on the text and characterization of the play itself.

What follows for the other plays which use these motifs? It is a cardinal principle that particular texts must be interpreted individually, not schematically. No amount of demonstration that Jews were commonly presented as out-and-out villains in Elizabethan drama can be allowed to defuse the fascinating ambiguity of Shakespeare's Shylock. Historical contextualizing can in any case only take us so far. We are dealing with mythological situations: it has been well shown by Albert Henrichs that no valid evidence exists for human sacrifice in Greece of the historical period. The theme is, however, a potent one in myth.[37] Hence it is hard to apply the kind of test we might apply with Jonathan Swift's *Modest Proposal*:[38] whereas Swift was pretending to advocate a practical measure in a contemporary social-political situation, Euripides is dramatizing events of the mythical past, and myth typically exaggerates or presents extremes of horror and danger which are happily remote from contemporary life.

In looking at the sacrificial plays of Euripides we can, however, draw a clear distinction between those which involve saving a city and those which seek a different goal. The slaughter of Polyxena is clearly barbaric, by Greek standards as well as our own. The death of Iphigenia is more debatable, but at

[35]  e.g. Hall 1989, ch. 5; also Hall 1997, 118–24.
[36]  For a valuable statement of the contrary position, see Knox 1979, 343–52, especially 348–9. On ideas of pan-Hellenism see further Walbank 1951 = 1985, 1–19; also Dover 1974, 83–5, 279 ff.; Hall 1989, 160–5, 190–200.
[37]  See Henrichs 1981. On the myths and cultic aspects see Kearns 1989, 113–15, 160, 201–2; Parker 1987.
[38]  See further Booth 1974, 105–20. The argument here too might be launched on internal grounds, by examination of the self-subverting rhetoric of Swift's argumentation (on which Booth has helpful comments); an alternative strategy would be to rely on arguments from the sanctity of life and supposedly universal values enshrined in the parent–child relationship. (Cf. p. 92 on Hussey, Nisbet, de Ste. Croix.) No-one but a lunatic, we might wish to argue, would put forward so monstrous a programme. But the discussion by Rawson 2001, especially 69–91, 239–54, gives some reason for reduced confidence in this assumption.

least problematic. We may take a cue from Euripides' own *Electra*, in which Clytemnestra contrasts the hypothetical need for a child to die for the sake of the city with the actual situation facing Agamemnon (1020–9, a passage often neglected in discussion of the *IA*). On this argument, saving the city is intrinsically a worthy motive for the death of a virginal young man or woman (cf. above on the Periclean funeral speech); other goals do not justify this slaughter, even in the remote world of myth.[39]

Nevertheless, some critics of Euripides wish to go further, and darken even the cases I am provisionally treating as 'noble' sacrifices. Helene Foley generalizes: 'Even the uplifting voluntary sacrifices of Euripidean youth are made to seem deceptive and wasteful in the shabby world in which they are performed' and 'the cause for which the victim dies is frequently dubious and the consequences of the ritual death are often ambiguous.'[40] A. N. Michelini goes further, and specifically refers to the *Erechtheus*: discussing Euripidean devices of 'ironic sabotage', she claims that these devices 'work in these plays to undermine and qualify the lofty and idiosyncratic notions of the protagonists. A good example, and another exhibition of Euripidean malignant humor, is *Erechtheus*, where the complacent patriotism of Praxithea's often-quoted speech devolves into a horrific denouement in which she is bereft of all her children, and her husband as well.'[41]

In the remainder of this paper I want to look at the *Erechtheus*, partly with a view to considering whether this ironic or deflating interpretation seems at all justified, partly to reflect on how the newer evidence from the papyrus fragments has altered our picture of the drama.[42] Here again we have an Athenian play, and one concerned with fundamental features of the Athenian mythic tradition: the dispute between Athena and Poseidon for patronage of the land, the defence of Athens against foreign invasion, the establishment of the priestess of Athena Polias. In Euripides' version the war with Eumolpus is given a Greek–barbarian dimension, as Eumolpus (a son of Poseidon) leads a horde of Thracians. The community must be preserved, a royal child must die. The longest fragment surviving through quotation is Praxithea's famous speech declaring that she will submit to her daughter's being sacrificed and presenting arguments for this decision: there is some similarity to Iphigenia's

---

[39] So essentially Wilkins 1990.

[40] Foley 1985, 60, cf. 65; 62 rather vaguely comments that 'ritual here mediates in complex and often ironic ways. . .', ibid. 64 claims that the book will show ways in which 'Euripides, in his involvement with ritual, is simultaneously ironic, theologically iconoclastic, and intensely religious.' For a further survey of opinions see Harder 2006, 148.

[41] Michelini 1987, 90. Cropp in Collard, Cropp, and Lee 1995, 154–5 is suitably cautious.

[42] Editions which precede that of Austin 1968 are now outdated: thereafter see Collard, Cropp, and Lee 1995, 148–94, and Diggle 1998, 106 ff. (the latter includes only a selection other than F 370). The authoritative text and commentary is now Kannicht, *TrGF* v. 391–418 (F 349–70). For a recent discussion see Harder 2006, who, while also rejecting 'ironic' interpretations, is prepared to see a tension between civic self-sacrifice and its personal cost.

speech, but the situation is one which more naturally calls forth such patriotic fervour (F 360, from Lycurgus, *In Leocr.* 100–2). Still, it is striking that the daughter does not speak herself: did she have only a mute part to play, and would this diminish the pathos? (That would be paralleled in none of the other cases, though Menoeceus is silent at first.)

Praxithea's speech is well known and has been much studied. The other substantial fragment among those long known from literary sources is F362, in which Erechtheus gives instructions to his prospective heir before entering battle—probably an adopted son (Ion and Cecrops have been suggested). Austin has compared Act I scene iii of *Hamlet* (1968, 28: 'Polonius senex loquax filio Laertae praecepta dat ultima'). Many (not all) have found Polonius ridiculous, but I am not sure whether the amiable sententiousness of Erechtheus' advice should be seen as absurd. If so, however, this would be a case of 'local irony', a touch of comedy which does not necessarily affect the wider picture. Rather, indeed, any light-hearted element is purged by later events, since Erechtheus dies heroically in battle and will be honoured in cult. We might compare the scene involving the aged Iolaus and his attendant in the *Heraclidae* (vv. 720–47): the old man's determination to participate in the battle seems foolish, but in the end the messenger describes his rejuvenation and spectacular deeds of heroism (vv. 845–66).[43]

The fragments preserved in quotations amount to 120 lines plus a few odd phrases or half-lines. F 370, the Sorbonne papyrus first published by Colin Austin in 1967[44] contains portions of 119 lines as printed in *TrGF*, but this does not take account of the lost sections, especially of the messenger speech, totalling some 108 verses. The most substantial gain is the speech of Athena *ex machina*. Probably only a very few lines followed before the play closed. Consequently we have a reasonably clear framework (and in places much more) for reconstruction of about the last 230 lines of the play. No complete play of Euripides before the 410s exceeds 1600 lines and most are one to two hundred lines shorter. We thus have a fair knowledge of about one-fifth of the play, quite apart from parallel accounts of the myth elsewhere. Interpretation must be cautious, but need not despair.

The papyrus made clear that besides the daughter whom Praxithea offered up, two others had joined her in voluntary death; moreover, King Erechtheus himself has perished. The royal family has been wiped out, and it seems that the king had no son (F360 36f) An adopted heir will ascend the throne of Athens. Praxithea's distress comes through in the very fragmentary lines 370. 23 ff. and esp. 35 ff. But this personal grief should not be seen as negating or undercutting her dedication to the cause of Athens' survival earlier. For one

---

[43] Cf. the commentary of Allan 2001, 183–5.
[44] P. Sorb. 2328: see Austin 1967, revised in Austin 1968, 33–40 (his F 65), with contributions by Peter Parsons and others.

thing, it is short-lived; Athena appears and not only turns away the wrath of Poseidon, but probably bids her cease to grieve (115–16). The most important gain from the papyrus, however, is the cultic aspect. Athena devotes over thirty lines to the religious rites that will commemorate the events of the play (370. 63–97): no other aetiological exposition by a Euripidean deity lasts as long. The speech covers the honours for the daughters, glorified for their nobility (69 γενναιότητος), and stresses that they have not died: 'I myself have lodged their spirits in the heaven, and shall establish a renowned name, "divine Hyacinthids"'; as with Oedipus in the *OC*, the keeping secret of these maidens' sanctuary will ensure that no enemies can make sacrifice to them and win their favour against Athens in future. Athena names honours also for their father, who is to be named Poseidon Erechtheus; Praxithea herself, 'you who have restored this city's foundations', is to become a priestess, the first priestess of Athena Polias. Athena frequently appears at the close of plays with an Athenian dimension (*Suppl., Ion, IT*), and we might expect aetiology to play a part; but the extent of the delineation of state mythology, and its connection with the patriotic ideology asserted in Praxithea's speech, must inform our understanding of the whole mood of the play.

To sum up: the famous speech of Praxithea corresponds with other documents of Athenian ideology in numerous respects (the extended quotation of the passage by the orator Lycurgus offers ample confirmation of this[45]); the sacrifice is justified by the salvation of the city and the repulse of a barbarian horde; those who brought it about are given divine honours and commemorated in ritual enduring down to the dramatist's own time (contrast the futile suicide of Evadne in the *Suppliants*, rooted in personal grief and fruitless for the city); the deity who proclaims these future rituals is not the ambiguous Dionysus or the enigmatic Apollo but Athena herself. Mythological tales may sometimes be treated with reserve, even with humour, in Euripides (Helen, for instance, finds it hard to accept that she was born of a swan's egg); but established cults and rituals of the Athenian polis are not. Furthermore, those who argue for irony in this play fail to show what alternative path should have been followed by the beleaguered Athenians: it cannot be claimed that things would have been better if Athens had been sacked— would the daughters of Erechtheus have survived then?[46] None of this *proves* that an ironic reading of the *Erechtheus* is not the right reading; but it does, I submit, establish an almost overwhelming case for the contrary view.

I have adopted an approach in this paper which depends on assumptions which some may view as archaic: that the poet's intentions, while ultimately

---

[45] Lycurgus, *In Leocr.*100 ff.; cf. Wilson 1996, 312–14 (note his implied adherence to the ironic reading on p. 314).

[46] As Emily Kearns reminds me, this very point is made by the daughter of Heracles as she confronts her death in order to save Athens in *Hcld.* 511–14. More generally, see Mills 1997, ch. 3, especially 89 against ironic readings of the Theseus of *Supplices*.

inaccessible, cannot be irrelevant to interpretation, and that the reception of a work by its primary audience, whether known by direct testimony or deduced from comparable texts or contemporary evidence, should impose some guidelines and constraints for the modern reader. I would not deny that, if we place more emphasis on the role of the reader, then irony may be considered not a quality present in the text but a glint in the eye of the beholder. It still seems to me desirable that we should put our cards on the table, explain our initial assumptions, and consider the strength or weakness of the case for irony in each given case. There is much to be said for reading against the grain as a critical exercise, but that itself presupposes that there is a way of reading with the grain that deserves attention, even priority.

Perhaps we can even go further. In literary criticism as in papyrological decipherment, there are readings which are simply wrong.[47] Nabokov's *Pale Fire* (1962) is a hilarious yet terrifying parable for the commentator: in that book, as we compare the poem by John Slade with the commentary thereon by Kinbote, we swiftly become aware that the commentator's account bears no visible relation to the work on which he is commenting. Less well known, but a work which I think Peter Parsons will relish, is the delightful essay by Douglas Bush in which one of the most famous novels in the English language is analysed in terms of archetypal myths viewed through the lens of Frazer's *Golden Bough* and its inheritors.

Who or what is Bingley, the mysterious, ebullient stranger from the north who descends with his band of followers . . . upon a sleepy, conventional society and whom young people at once look to for providing dances? Clearly he is Dionysus, the disturbing visitor from northern Thrace. . . . It is hardly less clear that Pentheus is Mr. Bennet, the king of his small domain who is resentful of strangers and professedly unwilling to call on Bingley (his lack of tragic integrity is betrayed by his actually calling. . . .) (pp. 20, 21)

[The author's] stories of young love are set against a dark mythic background of death . . . hints of mortality appear . . . in such place names as Longbourn ("man goeth to his long home"; "The undiscovered country from whose bourne No traveller returns") and Netherfield (the nether or lower world) . . . (25)

The novel under discussion is of course *Pride and Prejudice*; the title of the essay, 'Mrs Bennet and the Dark Gods'.[48] This *jeu d'esprit* lacks any framing introduction; in the reprinted version it appears without comment alongside more sober-sided titles such as 'The Humanist Critic' and 'Literature and

---

[47] In practice even hard-liners admit this by their processes of argument: e.g. Fowler 2000, p. vii boldly claims that 'we do what we want with texts'; but he himself criticizes the interpretations of others and clearly finds deficient or misguided the views of (e.g.) Horsfall and White, which he discusses on pp. 79 and 270 respectively.

[48] Bush 1956 = 1966, 20–6 (from which I cite).

Science in the 17th century'. If through some unthinkable cataclysm the bulk of twentieth-century literary criticism were lost but this little piece survived, might it be read one day as a serious account of Jane Austen? In short, irony must always have an important place in the interpreter's toolbag; but if used too freely it may turn in the enthusiastic user's hand, and then, as they say, the joke's on you.[49]

# BIBLIOGRAPHY

Ahl, F. 1984, 'The Art of Safe Criticism in Greece and Rome', *AJP* 105, 174–208.

Allan, W. 2001, *Euripides: Children of Heracles* (Warminster).

Austin, C. 1967, 'De nouveaux fragments de l'Érechthée d'Euripide', *Recherches de papyrologie*, 4, 11–67.

—— 1968, *Nova Fragmenta Euripidea* (Kleine Texte, 187; Berlin).

Baker, S. 1958, 'The Irony of Catullus' Septimius and Acme', *CPh* 60, 256–9.

Bartsch, S. 1994, *Actors in the Audience: Theatricality and Doublespeak from Nero to Hadrian.* (Cambridge, MA, and London).

Booth, Wayne C. 1974, *A Rhetoric of Irony* (Chicago).

Brooks, C. 1951, 'Irony as a Principle of Structure', in M. Zabel (ed.), *Literary Opinion in America* (New York), 729–41.

Bush, D. 1956, 'Mrs Bennet and the Dark Gods', *Sewanee Review*, 64, 591–6, repr. in id., *Engaged and Disengaged* (Cambridge, MA, 1966), 20–6, and C. Kaplan, *The Overwrought Urn* (New York, 1969), 102–7.

Colebrook, C. 2004, *Irony* (London).

Collard, C., Cropp, M., and Lee, K. H. 1995, *Euripides: Selected Fragmentary Plays I* (Warminster).

Courtney, E. 2001, *A Companion to Petronius* (Oxford).

Crane, R. S. 1952, 'The Critical Monism of Cleanth Brooks', in id. (ed.), *Critics and Criticism: Ancient and Modern* (New York and Toronto), 83–107.

Dewar, M. J. 1994, 'Laying it On with a Trowel: The Proem to Lucan and Related Texts', *CQ*[2] 44, 199–211.

Diggle, J. 1998, *Tragicorum Graecorum Fragmenta Selecta* (Oxford).

—— 2004, *Theophrastus: Characters* (Cambridge).

Dilke, O. A. W. 1972, 'Lucan's Political Views and the Caesars', in D. R. Dudley (ed.), *Neronians and Flavians* (London) 62–82.

Dover, K. J. 1974, *Greek Popular Morality in the Time of Plato and Aristotle* (Oxford).

Dyer, R. R. 1990, 'Rhetoric and Intention in Cicero's *Pro Marcello*', *JRS* 80, 17–30.

Edwards, J. B. 1928, 'The Irony of Catullus 45', *TAPA* 59, pp. xxiii f.

Empson, W. 1930 (3rd edn. 1953), *Seven Types of Ambiguity* (London).

—— 1987, *Argufying: Essays on Literature and Culture* (London).

[49] I am very grateful for comments on a draft of this chapter from Matthew Leigh and Robert Parker, and especially to Dirk Obbink for his detailed work on the penultimate version.

Fantham, E. 1992, *Lucan: De Bello Civili II* (Cambridge).

Feeney, D. C. 1991, *The Gods in Epic* (Oxford).

Foley, H. 1985, *Ritual Irony: Poetry and Sacrifice in Euripides* (Ithaca and London).

Fordyce, C. J. 1961, *Catullus: A Commentary* (Oxford).

Fowler, D. 1994, 'Postmodernism, Romantic Irony, and Classical Closure', in I. J. F. de Jong and J. P. Sullivan (eds.), *Modern Critical Theory and Classical Literature* (Leiden), 231–56; repr, in Fowler, 2000, 5–33.

—— 2000, *Roman Constructions* (Oxford).

Fraenkel, E. 1950, *Aeschylus, Agamemnon*, 3 vols. (Oxford).

—— 1957, *Horace* (Oxford).

Goold, G. P. 1983, *Catullus* (London).

Griffin, J. 1976, 'Augustan Poetry and the Life of Luxury', *JRS* 66, 87–105; repr. in id., *Poets and Roman Life* (London, 1984), 1–31

Griffin, M. T. 1984, *Nero: The End of a Dynasty* (London).

Hall, E. 1989, *Inventing the Barbarian* (Oxford).

—— 1997, 'The Sociology of Greek Tragedy', in *The Cambridge Companion to Greek Tragedy*, ed. P. E. Easterling (Cambridge), 93–126.

Harder, A. 2006, 'Praxithea: A Perfect Mother?', in A. Lardinois, M. van der Poel, and V. Hunink (eds.), *Land of Dreams: Greek and Latin Studies in Honour of A. H. M. Kessels* (Leiden and Boston), 146–59.

Heilman, R. B. 1956, *Magic in the Web* (Lexington, KY).

Henrichs, A. 1981, 'Human Sacrifice in Greek Religion: Three Case Studies', in *Le Sacrifice dans l'antiquité* (Fondation Hardt, Entretiens, 27; Vandœuvres-Geneva), 195–242.

Hinds, S. 1988, 'Generalising about Ovid', in A. J. Boyle (ed.), *The Imperial Muse: Ramus Essays on Roman Literature of the Empire* (Berwick, Victoria, Australia) 4–31.

Hussey, E. L. 1985, 'Thucydidean History and Democritean Theory', in P. A. Cartledge and F. D. Harvey (eds.), *Crux. Essays in Greek History presented to G. E.M. de Ste. Croix* (London), 118–38.

Hutchinson, G. O. 2003, 'The Catullan Corpus, Greek Epigram, and the Poetry of Objects', $CQ^3$ 53, 206–21.

Kallendorf, C. 2007, *The Other Virgil: 'Pessimistic' Readings of the Aeneid in Early Modern Culture* (Oxford).

Kearns, E. 1989, *The Heroes of Attica* (*BICS* Supplement 57; London).

Knox, B. 1979, *Word and Action: Essays on the Ancient Theater* (Baltimore).

Laughton, E. 1970, 'Disertissime Romuli nepotum', *CPh* 65, 1–7.

Lausberg, H. 1963, *Handbuch der literarischen Rhetorik* (Munich; Eng. tr. Leiden, 1998).

Lebek, W. D. 1976, *Lucans Pharsalia: Dichtungsstruktur und Zeitbezug* (Hypomnemata, 44; Gottingen).

Leigh, M. 1997, *Lucan: Spectacle and Engagement* (Oxford).

—— 2000, 'Oblique Politics: Epic of the Imperial Period', in Taplin 2000, 468–91.

Lowe, N. J. 1996, 'Tragic and Homeric Ironies: Response to Rosenmeyer', in Silk 1996, 520–33.

—— 2005, 'Problematic Verrall: The Sceptic at Law', in C. Stray (ed.), *The Owl of Minerva: The Cambridge Praelections of 1906* (*PCPS* Suppl. 28), 143–60.

Lyne, R. O. A. M. 1975, *Selections from Catullus: Handbook* (Cambridge).

MacMullen, R. 1966, *Enemies of the Roman Order* (Cambridge, MA, and London).

Michelini, A. N. 1987, *Euripides and the Tragic Tradition* (Madison, WI).

Mills, S. 1997, *Theseus, Tragedy and the Athenian Empire* (Oxford).

Morgan, L. 2000, 'Escapes from Orthodoxy: Poetry of the late Republic', in Taplin 2000, 336–58.

Mossman, J. 1994, *Wild Justice: A Study of Euripides' Hecuba* (Oxford).

Muecke, D. C. 1969, *The Compass of Irony* (London).

—— 1982, *Irony and the Ironic* (London; orig. edn. entitled *Irony*, 1970).

Nisbet, R. G. M. 1988, 'The Old Lie: Dulce et Decorum Est', *Omnibus* 15, 16–17.

—— 1995, *Collected Papers on Latin Literature* (Oxford).

—— and Rudd, N. 2004, *A Commentary on Horace, Odes III* (Oxford).

O'Connor-Visser, E. A. M. E. 1987, *Aspects of Human Sacrifice in the Tragedies of Euripides* (Amsterdam).

Parker, R. 1987, 'Myths of Early Attica', in J. Bremmer (ed.), *Interpretations of Greek Mythology* (London and Sydney), 187–214.

—— 2001, 'Geoffrey Ernest Maurice de Sainte Croix', *PBA* 111, 447–88.

Parsons, P. J. 1981, 'Ancient Greek Romances', *London Review of Books*, 3/15 (20 August), 13–14.

Perkins, R. L. (ed.) 2001, *The Concept of Irony* (International Kierkegaard Commentary, 2; Macon, GA).

Rawson, C. 2001, *God, Gulliver and Genocide: Barbarism and the European Imagination 1492–1945* (Oxford).

Ribbeck, O. 1876, 'Über den Begriff des εἴρων', *RhM*² 21, 381–400.

Rosenmeyer, T. G. 1977, 'Irony and Tragic Choruses', in *Ancient and Modern: Essays in Honour of Gerald F. Else* (Ann Arbor), 31–44.

—— 1993, 'Elusory Voices: Thoughts on the Sophoclean Chorus', in R. M. Rosen and J. Farrell (eds.), *Nomodeiktes: Essays . . . Martin Ostwald* (Ann Arbor), 557–71.

—— 1996, 'Ironies in Serious Drama', in Silk 1996, 497–519.

Rostagni, A. 1964, *Suetonii De Poetis e biografi minori* (Turin).

Rutherford, R. B. 1995, *The Art of Plato: Ten Studies in Platonic Interpretation* (London).

Schmitt, J. 1921, *Freiwilliger Opfertod bei Euripides* (Giessen).

Sedgewick, G. G. 1935, *Of Irony—Especially in Drama* (Toronto).

Silk, M. (ed.) 1996, *Tragedy and the Tragic* (Oxford).

Singleton, D. 1971, 'Catullus 45: What Sort of Irony?', *G&R* 18, 181–7.

Stockton, D. 1971, *Cicero: A Political Biography* (Oxford).

Syndikus, H. P. 1984, *Catull: Eine Interpretation, Teil 1: Einleitung. Die kleinen Gedichte (1–60)* (Stuttgart).

Taplin, O. (ed.) 2000, *Literature in the Greek and Roman Worlds* (Oxford).

Tatum, W. J. 1988, 'Catullus' Criticism of Cicero in Poem 49', *TAPA* 118, 179–84.

Thomas, R. F. 2001, *Virgil and the Augustan Reception* (Cambridge).

Thomson, J. A. K. 1926, *Irony: An Historical Introduction* (London).

Thomson, D. F. S. 1997, *Catullus, Edited with a Textual and Interpretative Commentary* (Toronto).

Townend, G. B. 1964, 'The Poems', in T. A. Dorey (ed.), *Cicero* (London), 109–34.

Walbank, F. W. 1951, 'The Problem of Greek Nationality', *Phoenix* 5, 41–60; repr. in id., *Selected Papers: Studies in Greek and Roman History and Historiography* (Cambridge, 1985), 1–19.

Wilkins, J. 1990, 'The State and the Individual: Euripides' Plays of Voluntary Self-Sacrifice', in A. Powell (ed.), *Euripides, Women, and Sexuality* (London), 177–94.

Wilson, P. J. 1996, 'Tragic Rhetoric: The Use of Tragedy and the Tragic in the Fourth Century', in Silk 1996, 310–31.

Winterbottom, M. 2002, 'Believing the *Pro Marcello*', in J. Miller, C. Damon, and K. S. Myers (eds.), *Vertis in Usum: Studies in Honor of Edward Courtney* (Munich and Leipzig, 2000), 24–38.

# 5

---

# Greek Letters from Hellenistic Bactria

*Adrian Hollis*

Perhaps I should start by mentioning certain kinds of document which I do not intend to discuss at any length under this heading. Least of all (through inability rather than lack of space) the texts in the Bactrian language but the Greek alphabet, from the early centuries AD.[1] Nor indeed—fascinating though they are—the legal and financial documents in Greek alone which have started to emerge in recent years. The first of these[2] provides varied new information: a tax receipt written at Asangorna in the reign of Antimachus Theos, Eumenes,[3] and another Antimachus. It is pleasing to hear that two more such documents await publication in *ZPE*.[4] One of these produces a Bactrian Amphipolis and almost certainly mentions a king Antimachus.[5]

Among the cultural achievements of Hellenistic Bactria (corresponding to modern Afghanistan, Tajikistan, and part of Uzbekistan) one naturally thinks first and foremost of the Bactrian and Indo-Greek coinage[6] with its superb

---

[1] These are the province of Professor Nicholas Sims-Williams. Examples can be found in Canali de Rossi 2004, section X, Bactria and Sogdiana.

[2] Rea, Senior, and Hollis 1994, 261–80. I confess to having laid this before the eyes of our honorand at a Faculty Board meeting.

[3] An addition to the Bactrian king-list. Perhaps an elder son of Antimachus Theos who did not survive long enough to issue coins in his own name, whereas the second Antimachus is plausibly identified with Antimachus II Nikephoros, who struck plentiful drachmae.

[4] Since this was drafted the documents have been published: see Clarysse and Thompson 2007.

[5] Without the title Theos, perhaps therefore Antimachus II. 'Year 30' is puzzling, since on numismatic grounds one would not have credited either Antimachus with so long a reign. A possible solution might be to refer the year to an era rather than the reign of a single king. Recently historians and numismatists have postulated a Graeco-Bactrian era founded (probably by Demetrius I) *c*.185 BC. See Salomon 2005, 364 ff. Year 30 of that era would take us to *c*.155 BC, a reasonable estimate for the *floruit* of Antimachus II Nikephoros. An obstacle, however, is that technical expertise (based on comparison with Ptolemaic Egypt) would date the hand-writing of the new document to the period 220–180 BC (and probably to the earlier part). I am most grateful to Professor Dorothy Thompson of Cambridge for providing information on this text, which should be published before the present book.

[6] Almost always I refer the coins to their BN series, that is to Bopearachchi 1991, a catalogue of the Bibliothèque nationale collection), which includes types not to be found there.

**Fig. 5.1.** (*a*) Eucratides I, gold 20-stater coin (*c*.165 BC), obverse. (*b*) Eucratides I, reverse.

artistry, far surpassing that of any other Hellenistic monarchy. In the precious metals Bactria produced two of the most spectacular of all Greek coins; the gold twenty-stater piece of Eucratides I (Fig. 5.1) and the silver double decadrachm of Amyntas (Fig. 5.2).[7] Clearly both were special issues: the former perhaps to celebrate Eucratides' assumption of the title 'Great King' (see below), the latter to commemorate victories however ephemeral. While Eucratides' magnificent reverse type (charging Dioscuri) has a *terminus ante quem*, since it was imitated by the rebellious Seleucid satrap Timarchus in 162 BC,[8] much later, perhaps about 80 BC, Indo-Greek die-cutters could still rise to an occasion, as for the double decadrachm of Amyntas. The period of

[7] Eucratides series 1 BN (actually in Paris) and Amyntas series 1, found with two others of the same denomination in the Qunduz hoard (Curiel and Fussman 1965), present whereabouts unknown.

[8] One of the very few tetradrachms of Timarchus to escape overstriking was illustrated in the catalogue of Sotheby's Zürich sale, 26 Oct. 1993, no. 68.

**Fig. 5.2.** (*a*) Amyntas, silver double decadrachm, obverse. (*b*) Amyntas, reverse.

highest Bactrian numismatic art stretches approximately from 200 to 150 BC, starting with the final issues of Euthydemus I (whose early and middle-period coinage had been nothing special)[9] and the formidable elephant-scalp portrait of Demetrius I,[10] whose headdress may already lay claim to Alexander-like exploits south of the Hindu Kush. This half-century also produced the tetradrachms of Agathocles and Antimachus Theos,[11] which commemorate earlier rulers of Bactria back to Alexander himself. A notable feature is the sequence of middle-aged or elderly portraits: Euthydemus I, Antimachus I, Apollodotus I.[12] The last two wear causia with diadem, head-gear favoured by six Bactrian or Indo-Greek rulers.[13] Eucratides I honoured

---

[9] Euthydemus I seems to have been the only Bactrian or Indo-Greek king who reigned long enough (? 40 years) to have distinctively young, middle-aged, and elderly coin-portraits.

[10] Series 1 etc.

[11] Agathocles, series 12–18; Antimachus Theos, series 9–10.

[12] Apollodotus I, series 1. Until quite recently no portrait of Apollodotus was known; some scholars even conflated him with Apollodotus II nearly a century later.

[13] See Bopearachchi 1991, 382.

his parents Heliocles and Laodice;[14] one can just make out from their con-
jugate busts that she wears a diadem—a Seleucid princess?[15]—but he does
not.

From time to time I shall return to the coins, but my main concern is with
the traces of Greek literature to be found in this area. It is quite surprising
how extensive these are. The most promising literary category is that of
inscribed verse-epigram (we shall discuss two specimens), but there is also
evidence of a lively interest in philosophy, and the library at Ai Khanoum
contained an unidentifiable Greek tragedy. At the documentary level John
Rea[16] commented on the tax receipt (above), 'I would not have been able to
tell from the writing alone that it did not come from Egypt', and Claude
Rapin[17] received a similar impression from inscriptions in ink on storage
jars found at Ai Khanoum. The same thought might be applied at a higher
cultural level: despite the geographical remoteness of Bactria, it was not cut
off intellectually from Egyptian Alexandria. There was someone at Alexandria
in Arachosia (Kandahar in Afghanistan) who, perhaps in the mid-second
century BC, had read Callimachus as well as Homer.

The two items to be discussed next both come from the royal palace at Ai
Khanoum on the banks of the Oxus, in a room apparently used as a library.
Their nature is remarkable: an unknown tragedy and a philosophical dialogue
on the Platonic theory of forms which some have considered attributing
to the young Aristotle.[18] We are lucky to have anything at all of these texts.
As Jeffrey Lerner[19] explains, 'The work was originally written in ink, which
transferred onto fine earth formed from decomposed unbaked bricks.' I have
nothing to add on the content of the dialogue (see Lerner's discussion),
but should like to say something about the other item, published by Claude
Rapin (text 2a, col. ii).[20]

$$].[.$$
$$[\pm 5]\,.\upsilon\,\theta\epsilon\varrho\,.[ \qquad\qquad ]..[$$
$$....\delta\iota o\varsigma\,\mu.[ \qquad ] \quad .[.$$
$$........[.]\theta\epsilon\dot{\alpha}\gamma\,\gamma a\mu\epsilon\hat{\iota}...[$$
$$........\eta\tau o\upsilon\sigma\iota\upsilon\,\mathring{\eta}\,\tau a\kappa\epsilon\iota.[ \qquad\qquad 5$$

---

[14] Osmus 13 15.

[15] In Hollis 1996, 161–11 made a very speculative attempt to identify this Laodice.

[16] Réd. Seniors and Hollis 1994, 262.

[17] Rapin 1983, 349–51.

[18] Lerner 2003, 45–51. For a good photograph see *CAH Plates to Volume VII.1* (1984), pl. 27.
In February 1990 Jonathan Barnes read to the Oxford Philological Society a paper entitled 'Plato
in Afghanistan'. He tells me that he has not taken it any further; my memory is that he reached
conclusions similar to those of Lerner. David Sedley remarks that the dialogue is clearly the
work of a Platonist, but he sees no particular reason to privilege Aristotle. See now Canali de
Rossi 2004, no. 457.

[19] Rapin 1983, 45.

[20] Rapin 1987, with text at 253. See now Canali de Rossi 2004, no. 458.

```
...... γενοίμην μυρ[
τεκμηρίωι δὲ τῶι...[
    5–8
[±3]........ἡμὶν ἐc χεῖραc[
 2–3
... ου. [            ]            [.
        ].[      ].[.].[.].. [
        ].[      ]..[      ].[              10
    ].[        ]θε[ι]ραc[ ].[
[±3]α[±2].. ν νομίζειν κ...[
[±3].... πε.. ουν ταῦτα [±2].[±2].[
[±3].[.]...[.]. χαωcα..[ 4–5 ]..ν[          15
        ].[                ].[
                            ]α.[

    ].[
[  ±9   ]. ου Διονυc[   ]..[
    4–5
[±3].[2–3].... [±3]του δοκοῦντ..[          20
    ]..[].. [    ]μεθ....[
```

We have here a verse text in regular tragic trimeters.[21] The very fact that Ai Khanoum supplies remnants of an otherwise unknown tragedy is remarkable enough. As far as I know, the contents have not been further discussed; one may put this down to prudence, since too little has been preserved. Nonetheless I cannot resist hazarding a suggestion, which starts from the apparent mention of Dionysus' name in l. 19.[22] Could the matter at issue be Dionysus' claim to divinity as a son of Zeus, and the speaker be a recurring figure—one such as Pentheus, Lycurgus, or Deriades[23]—who furiously rejects that claim? Certain groups of letters, though susceptible to other interpretations, might be made to fit that hypothesis. Particularly l. 20 τοῦ δοκοῦντος (Rapin 1987, 255), perhaps δοκέω as in LSJ I. 4 'seem', 'pretend' [sc. to be a son of Zeus], l. 13 νομίζειν (LSJ II, 'own', 'acknowledge', often of gods or religious practices). If Rapin was on the right track with his ἡμὶν ἐc χεῖραc[, and then μολεῖν,[24] violence is seemingly threatened (LSJ s.v. χεῖρ 6d, ἐc χεῖραc ἐλθεῖν + dative, 'to come to blows or close quarters with'). This might cohere with l. 7 τεκμηρίωι δέ: if the speaker could get his hands on Dionysus, the latter's defeat would give 'proof' that he was no divine son of Zeus.

---

[21] Rapin 1987, 254 provides a metrical scheme, but (according to Martin West) 'he has not paid enough attention to the distance of the words from the left margin and consequently put one or two of them—e.g. in l. 13, where νομίζειν must go before the caesura—in the wrong metrical *sedes*'.

[22] 'I suppose × – ∪]ου Διόνυc[οc (or -ον, -ε) if the theonym is rightly read' (Martin West).

[23] The last-named in the *Bassarica* of Dionysius and the *Dionysiaca* of Nonnus.

[24] ἡμὶν with short iota is something of a Sophoclean mannerism (see Jebb on OC 25). West (cf. n. 20 above) feels that we must have here × – ∪ ἡμὶν ἐc χέ{ι}ραc.

Other groups of letters which (with even less confidence) could be fitted to the above scheme are line 2 θεο, 3 διος, 4 γαμει,[25] 12 ]θε[ι]ρας.[26] Have we here a neglected play by one of the great masters, a product of fourth-century or Hellenistic Athens, or even a local creation?[27] It is worth remembering that this theme would be of particular interest in Bactria, since (according to Euripides, *Bacchae* 15) the god had travelled as far afield as Βάκτρια ... τείχη. Dionysiac motifs are very much to the fore on nickel coins of the Bactrian kings Pantaleon and Agathocles *c.*180–175 BC,[28] some forty years before the destruction of Ai Khanoum.

Staying in Ai Khanoum, but turning now to inscriptions on stone, let us consider the elegiac epigram found in the pronaos of the heroon of Kineas— otherwise unknown but presumably the οἰκιστής of the city:[29]

> Ἀνδρῶν τοὶ σοφὰ ταῦτα παλαιοτέρων ἀνάκειται
>   ῥήματ' ἀριγνώτων Πυθοῖ ἐν ἠγαθέαι·
> ἔνθεν ταῦτα Κλέαρχος ἐπιφραδέως ἀναγράψας
>   εἵσατο τηλαυγῆ Κινέου ἐν τεμένει.

These wise sayings of famous men of old are set up in sacred Delphi, whence Clearchus carefully inscribed and dedicated them to be seen from afar in the precinct of Cineas.

The versification is competent, the vocabulary quite poetic: Πυθοῖ ἐν ἠγαθέαι = *Od.* 8. 80 (-έηι). ἀρίγνωτος is Homeric, τηλαυγής a favourite of Pindar. ἐπιφραδέως occurs three times in Apollonius Rhodius—but if Robert 1973, 225–35 was right in identifying Clearchus with Clearchus of Soli, Peripatetic—he will have earned the appellation!—and pupil of Aristotle, and ascribing the epigram to him personally, this would predate the *Argonautica*, leaving only Parmenides (fr. 1. 16 Diels), whom Clearchus might have read, as a known earlier user of the adverb. The Delphic precepts to which the epigram refers were inscribed on the right-hand side of the base (Robert 1973, 213):

> Παῖς ὢν κόσμιος γίνου,
> ἡβῶν ἐγκρατής,
> μέσος δίκαιος,
> πρεσβύτης εὔβουλος,
> τελευτῶν ἄλυπος.

---

[25] The fiery nuptials of Semele? In column I (which I have not reproduced) the only legible letters are ]γαμου[.

[26] The long hair of Dionysus draws adverse comment in Euripides, *Bacchae* 455–6.

[27] For a survey of tragedies on the πάθη of Dionysus, see Dodds 1960, pp. xxviii–xxxiii.

[28] Pantaleon series 4–5 and Agathocles series 5–7 BN.

[29] Robert 1973, 217–22 discusses in great detail the diffusion of the name Kineas. See now Canali de Rossi 2004, nos. 382, 384.

As a boy, be orderly; in bloom of youth, self-controlled; in middle age, just; as an old man, of good counsel; in death, without pain.

Robert 1973, 214 made the piquant observation that in two Bactrian cities one could read eulogies of ἐγκράτεια: to the north in Ai Khanoum, and to the south in Kandahar (Arachosian Alexandria) from the Greek version of the ethical precepts set up a generation later by the Mauryan emperor Aśoka.[30]

From Ai Khanoum we must travel some 100 km north-eastwards, to the region of Kuliab in Tajikistan. A Russian traveller in 1909 reported the discovery of many Bactrian coins in the area.[31] Recently more than 800 silver coins[32] from Alexander to Eucratides I came to light; a feature of the latter hoard was nearly 50 small silver obols of Demetrius I, otherwise distinctly rare. Almost certainly Kuliab was the origin of a verse inscription honouring Demetrius and his father King Euthydemus I:[33]

Τόνδε coι βωμὸν θυώδη, πρέcβα κυδίcτη θεῶν
Ἑcτία, Διὸc κ(α)τ᾽ ἄλcοc καλλίδενδρον ἔκτιcεν
καὶ κλυταῖc ἤcκηcε λοιβαῖc ἐμπύροιc Ἡλιόδοτοc,
ὄφρα τὸμ πάντων μέγιcτον Εὐθύδημον βαcιλέων
τοῦ τε παῖδα καλλίνικον ἐκπρεπῆ Δημήτριον                5
πρευμενὴc cώιζηιc ἀκηδεῖ(c) cὺν τύχαι θεόφρον[ι].

This fragrant altar to you, Hestia, most honoured among the gods, Heliodotus established in the grove of Zeus with its fair trees, furnishing it with libations and burnt-offerings, so that you may graciously preserve free from care, together with divine good fortune, Euthydemus, greatest of all kings, and his outstanding son Demetrius, renowned for fine victories.

The metre is trochaic—of course a king called Euthydemus could not be named in dactylic verse.

One of the few episodes in Bactrian history of which we have a detailed prose narrative is the three-year siege of Bactra by the Seleucid Antiochus III, which concluded in 206–5 BC (Polybius 11. 39. 8–9):

Finally Euthydemus sent his son Demetrius to ratify the agreement. Antiochus, on receiving the young man and judging him from his appearance, conversation, and dignity of bearing to be worthy of royal rank, in the first place promised to give him

---

[30] *SEG* 20 (1964), pp. 99–101, no. 326, Canali de Rossi 2004, IX Drangiana and Arachosia, no. 290.

[31] See Bernard, Pinault, and Rougemont 2004, 227–356 at 340–1.

[32] Of which Bopearachchi was able to examine more than 200.

[33] Bernard 1973, 341 notes that Kuliab should be interpreted in a broad sense; the valley of the Yakh-su would be an appropriate setting for the ἄλcοc καλλίδενδρον of our inscription (l. 2). The editors in *Journal des Savants* 2004/2 saw only a photograph (see p. 334 of their paper), but had no real difficulty in reading the text.

one of his daughters in marriage[34] and next gave his father permission to style himself King.

We may wonder why Euthydemus I sent his son Demetrius, a mere νεανίσκος (perhaps 18–20 years old), to negotiate with Antiochus, rather than coming in person. Age and infirmity? A desire to avoid direct confrontation between the two principals? A guess (correct as it turned out) that the young prince would make a favourable impression?

It is interesting to compare the titulature of both Euthydemus and Demetrius on the documents available to us. Polybius reflects the position in 205 BC: Euthydemus is allowed to be a 'king', and has already trusted his son with important negotiations. I would date the Kuliab inscription some ten years later, *c.*195 BC. Euthydemus is still alive; Demetrius has not been made joint ruler (a practice common enough among the Bactrian and Indo-Greek royal families), but has won military victories deserving the appellation καλλίνικος.[35] Probably Demetrius had—first in the name of his father— begun the extension of Graeco-Bactrian power south of the Hindu Kush, for which he himself later became famous.[36] Despite these successes Demetrius is not yet styled 'king'. Euthydemus, on the other hand, is not merely 'king' in the Kuliab inscription, but 'greatest of all kings'—by implication greater than anyone else who might have called himself 'great king'. It is hard not to see here a calculated insult to Antiochus III, who took the epithet μέγας *c.*204 BC after his eastern campaign (Appian, *Syr.* 1), and the title βασιλεὺς μέγας in 200 BC.[37]

Another recent discovery, of a unique tetradrachm,[38] takes us probably to the decade 190–180 BC (Fig. 5.3). On the obverse, a bust of Euthydemus I; on the reverse, his familiar 'seated Heracles' type. The legend, however, is a surprise: *ΕΥΘΥΔΗΜΟΥ ΜΕΓΑΛΟΥ*. Beyond doubt this is 'Euthydemus the Great'. Why no *ΒΑΣΙΛΕΩΣ*? Almost certainly because this is a commemorative piece, struck after Euthydemus' death by his son Demetrius. Strong support for that interpretation comes from the control-mark on the reverse, which does not appear on the coins of Euthydemus but was introduced by Demetrius.[39] A more subjective point: Euthydemus I was the only

---

[34] An impulsive gesture? As far as I am aware Antiochus had no legitimate daughter of marriageable age at that date. Certainly there is no hint that such a marriage ever took place.

[35] The epithet perhaps borrowed from Seleucus II Kallinikos (243–226 BC).

[36] Thus MacDowall 2005. The Bactrians might also have viewed their long resistance to Antiochus III as a definite military success.

[37] Ma 2002, Appendix IV, subtly discriminates between the epithet and the title (the latter assumed by the Bactrian king Eucratides I *c.*165 BC).

[38] I have seen only a photograph, from which the reproduction in Senior and Hollis 1999, 11 derives.

[39] Demetrius I, BN series 1E (tetradrachm) and other denominations.

**Fig. 5.3.** Euthydemus I, commemorative tetradrachm.

Bactrian king to have young, middle-aged, and elderly portraits on his coins (reflecting a reign of perhaps forty years). On the new coin, however, he seems of indeterminate age—and is there not a hint of a benign smile upon his face?[40]

A final sweep southwards to Kandahar—whether or not the name is a corruption of 'Alexandria', there seems little doubt that Old Kandahar represents Alexandria in Arachosia. From here is said to come the most remarkable of our items, a twenty-line acrostich[41] elegy containing the autobiography of a merchant, Sōphytos son of Narātos (or Narātes), first published by the same French scholars who gave us the Kuliab inscription:[42]

[40] The same point has been made about some of the tetradrachms commemorating Euthydemus, issued in the next generation by Agathocles and Antimachus Theos. The latter pair hit upon a neater way of designating both the honorand and the issuing monarch. On the obverse, the portrait and name of the king commemorated, with the addition of a title or epithet—in all cases one *not* used by the original king during his lifetime (Agathocles calls Demetrius *ANIKHTOC*, an epithet adopted for himself by the much later Demetrius III). The issuing king is named on the reverse by a genitive absolute, e.g. *BACIΛEYONTOC ΘEOY ANTIMAXOY*, 'during the reign of Antimachus Theos'. About 165 BC Eucratides I (BN series 13), wishing to honour his parents, puts them on the obverse (see Bopearachchi 1991, 209 n. 48) in the genitive case (*HΛIOKΛEOYC KAI ΛAOΔIKHC*) with himself on the reverse in the nominative (*BACIΛEYC MEΓAC EYKPATIΔHC*). The effect is to stress the parent–child relationship ('King Eucratides the Great, son of Heliocles and Laodice').

[41] For the type in general, see Courtney 1990, 3–13.

[42] Bernard, Pinault, and Rougemont 2004, 227–332; for a photograph of the inscribed elegy see ibid. p. 230. The version in Bopearachichi and Boussac 2005, though dated later, represents an earlier stage of the work.

*Ϲωφύτου ϲτήλη*

*Δ* Δηρὸν ἐμῶγ κοκυῶν ἐριθηλέα δώματ᾽ ἐόντα

*Ι* ἲϲ ἄμαχοϲ Μοιρῶν ἐξόλεϲεν τριάδοϲ·

*Α* αὐτὰρ ἐγώ, τυννὸϲ κομιδῆι βιότοιό τε πατρῶν

*Ϲ* Ϲώφυτοϲ εὖνιϲ ἐὼν οἰκτρὰ Ναρατιάδηϲ,

*Ω* ὡϲ ἀρετὴν Ἑκάτου Μουϲέων τ᾽ ἤϲ(κ)ηκα ϲὺν ἐϲθλῆι          5

*Φ* φυρτὴν ϲωφροϲύνηι, (τ)ῆμοϲ ἐπεφραϲάμην

*Υ* ὑψώϲαιμί κε πῶϲ μέγαρον πατρώιον αὖθιϲ·

*Τ* τεκνοφόρον δὲ λαβὼν ἄλλοθεν ἀργύριον,

*Ο* οἴκοθεν ἐξέμολον μεμαὼϲ οὐ πρόϲθ᾽ ἐπανελθεῖν

*Υ* ὕψιϲτον κτᾶϲθαι πρὶμ μ᾽ ἀγαθῶν ἄφενοϲ·          10

*Τ* τοὔνεκ᾽ ἐπ᾽ ἐμπορίηιϲιν ἰὼν εἰϲ ἄϲτεα πολλὰ

*Ο* ὄλβον ἀλωβήτωϲ εὐρὺν ἐληϊϲάμην.

*Υ* Ὑμνητὸϲ δὲ πέλων πάτρην ἐτέεϲϲιν ἐϲίγμαι

*Ν* νηρίθμοιϲ τερπνόϲ τ᾽ εὐμενέταιϲ ἐφάνην·

*Α* ἀμφοτέρουϲ δ᾽ οἶκόν τε ϲεϲηπότα πάτριον εἶθαρ          15

*Ρ* ῥέξαϲ ἐκ καινῆϲ κρέϲϲονα ϲυντέλεϲα

*Α* αἶάν τ᾽ ἐϲ τύμβου πεπτωκότοϲ ἄλλον ἔτευξα,

*Τ* †τὴν καὶ ζῶν ϲτήλην ἐν ὁδῶι ἐπέθηκα λάλον.†

*Ο* Οὕτωϲ οὖν ζηλωτὰ τάδ᾽ ἔργματα ϲυντελέϲαντοϲ

*Υ* υἱέεϲ υἱωνοί τ᾽ οἶκον ἔχοιεν ἐμοῦ.          20

The irresistible force of the trio of Fates destroyed the house of my forefathers, which had flourished greatly for many years. But I, Sophytos son of Naratos, pitiably bereft when quite small of my ancestral livelihood, (5) after I had acquired the virtue of Hekatos [Apollo] and the Muses, mixed with noble prudence, then did consider how I might raise up again my family house. Obtaining interest-bearing money from another source, I left home, keen not to return (10) before I possessed wealth, the supreme good. Thus, by travelling to many cities for commerce, I acquired ample riches without reproach. Becoming celebrated, I returned to my homeland after countless years, and showed myself, bringing pleasure to well-wishers. (15) Straightway I built afresh my paternal home, which was riddled with rot, making it better than before, and also, since the tomb had collapsed to the ground, I constructed another one and, during my lifetime, set upon it by the roadside this loquacious plaque. (19–20) Thus may the sons and grandsons of myself, who completed this enviable work, possess my house.

The editors suggest (pp. 234–5) a date in the second century BC; that seems to fit well with an impression of Greek culture on the increase which the poem conveys, but a later date cannot be ruled out. The elegy is put into the mouth of its subject, Sophytos, who is also the purported composer—perhaps truly, in view of the speaker's pride in his Greek education, but a competent local professional[43] seems rather more likely. Its tone is strongly personal. The parallel closest in spirit (though far inferior in technique) which I have found

---

[43] That too would say something about Greek culture in Arachosia. Occasionally such a one will reveal his name, like the Herodes responsible for nos. 1150–2 in Peek 1955.

is an epitaph from Eumeneia in Phrygia, *c*.AD 200.[44] The Christian Gaius erects during his lifetime a tomb for his family, inscribed with an elegy of just over twenty lines, playing isopsephic games with his name in ll. 1–2. Originally not rich, Gaius had worked hard to obtain a moderately good education, and became a πραγματικός (? attorney or minor government official). Now he uses his expertise and money to help others. There follow religious and moral reflections.

The name Sōphytos is interesting. It certainly has a Greek air: for the first element compare e.g. Socrates, and for the second Amphytos, Aphytos, Diophytos, Neophytos. Perhaps this suggestion of Greek was cherished by the name's philhellene bearer. But Professor Pinault in the first publication (254–9) argues strongly that the names of both Sophytos and his father Naratos were Indian. This view is supported by the fact that the only other known Sophytos came from these same parts. He struck small silver coins— and we now have a tetradrachm (op. cit. 284)—perhaps *c*.310 BC.[45] On the other hand Naratos is more clearly not Greek, even though our Sophytos of the verse-inscription dignifies himself with a Greek-style patronymic, Ναρατιάδης (l. 4).

The first line of the poem astonished me: having long been interested in Hellenistic Bactria, and also in Callimachus' *Hecale*, I never dreamed that the two would converge. But the noun κοκύαι = 'ancestors' (l. 1) is fabulously rare, cited in the *Suda* with a corrupt (and inexplicable) hexameter, almost certainly from Callimachus' *Hecale*.[46] Unless the dating of the inscribed poem to the second century BC (above) is far astray, it must precede the only other surviving occurrence of κοκύαι, in Zonas,[47] an epigrammatist who probably flourished about the turn of the era. Just two lines later we find another Callimachean speciality, τυννός = 'tiny', also in the *Hecale*.[48] Catullus (95. 5) prophesied that Helvius Cinna's *Smyrna* would travel from Rome to Cyprus; now it seems that Callimachus' *Hecale* accomplished no less remarkable a journey, from Egyptian Alexandria to Alexandria in Arachosia.

In the inscribed poem we expect to find a strong influence from Homer, and we are not disappointed, e.g. l. 20 υἱέες υἱωνοί τε (= *Iliad* 2. 666), ἐριθηλής (1), ἕκατος (5, as a title of Apollo rather than an epithet), εὖνις (4) + genitive = 'bereft of'. Also Homeric is the placing of ἐς after its noun (17 αἶαν ... ἐς).[49] But (as well as κοκύαι) νήριθμος[50] breathes the world of learned third-century poetry (Lycophron, *Alex.* 415 and Theocritus 25. 57).[51]

---

[44] Peek 1955, no. 1905.          [45] Mitchiner 1976, i. 23.

[46] Hollis 1990, fr. 137 = fr. 340 Pfeiffer.

[47] *Anth. Pal.* 9. 312 (= Gow–Page, *Garland of Philip*, Zonas 7), 5.

[48] See my note (Hollis 2004, 115–16). τυννός recurs in Call. fr. 471 Pfeiffer (incertae sedis).

[49] Compare *Il.* 15. 59 μάχην ἐς, *Od.* 3. 137 ἀγορὴν ἐς.

[50] Much later the word is favoured by Nonnus.

[51] Although not wishing to deny Theocritean authorship to poem 25, I single it out because its lexical range is rather different from that of Theocritus' other poems.

And where did our poet find φυρτός, 'mixed' (l. 6), otherwise attested only in Hesychius? Even when a form is Homeric, it may also have attracted the learned Hellenistic poets and become strongly associated with them: εἶθαρ (15) was patronized by Antimachus of Colophon, Callimachus, Apollonius Rhodius, Theocritus, and Nicander. The *docti* might argue whether ἄφενος, 'wealth' (l. 10), should be masculine or neuter—on this point Callimachus vacillated.[52] More generally, Sophytos' closing prayer that his descendants may inherit his house (20) recalls that of Posidippus, who hopes to die λείπων τέκνοις δῶμα καὶ ὄλβον ἐμόν (*Suppl. Hell.* 705. 25). We may associate acrostics with learned poets such as Aratus, Nicander, and Dionysius Periegetes, but they also occur in sepulchral epigrams, carrying the name of the deceased; the earliest example known to Courtney[53] came from Palestine, perhaps second century BC—if so, probably not so far removed in time from the Sophytos elegy.

On l. 18 (which the French editors leave unaltered, not indicating any corruption) I must part company from my French colleagues. It seems to me inconceivable that a poet otherwise competent and even refined should suddenly forget how to scan a pentameter (or that, in an elegiac couplet, pentameter must follow hexameter).[54] The text can be rectified quite simply. How might such an error have arisen? Perhaps from the stone-cutter, perhaps from an intermediary between the poet and the inscriber—someone who understood the sense but not the metre. One way to put things right would be to substitute τ' for καί and make a modest change of word-order: τήν τ' ἐν ὁδῶι στήλην ζῶν ἐπέθηκα λάλον. The participle stresses that Sophytos has already, during his lifetime,[55] made provision for his tomb, not leaving it to heirs who might prove negligent or mean. λάλον adds a touch of humour. The word can mean 'loquacious', 'talking too much';[56] the dead from their tomb often implore the living to stop long enough to read their inscription, and—with twenty lines—Sophytos is detaining the passer-by for longer than usual. That is not the only sign of humour: proud though he is of his education in Greek philosophy and literature (5–6) Sophytos decided—when it came to the crunch—that his *summum bonum* (10 ὕψιστον . . . ἀγαθῶν) was Wealth. Could there be a play between ὑψώcαιμι (7) and ὕψιcτον (10)?

---

[52] See West on Hesiod, *Theogony* 112–13.

[53] Peek 1955, no. 662; Courtney 1990, 6.

[54] Bernard, Pinault, and Rougemont 2004, 233 record equal incredulity on the part of Professor F. Chamoux. On the other hand Professor Colin Austin (*per litteras*, after conversation at the conference) feels that to make any alteration would be unjustified improvement of an incompetent poet. This view seems to imply a lower overall estimate than mine of the poet's knowledge and technical skill.

[55] This motif may be followed via Citti *et al.* 1995–2002, s.v. ζάω; it recurs in Latin with 'vivus'.

[56] The adjective also conveys a notion of telling a story without uttering a word, as in Nonnus, *Dionysiaca* 4. 321 λάλον εἷμα (the textile of Philomela).

The poet does not lack verbal ingenuity, e.g. using $\tau\epsilon\kappa\nu o\phi\acute{o}\rho o\nu$ (8) in the new sense of 'interest-bearing'.[57]

In travelling to 'many cities' (11), Sophytos recalls Odysseus.[58] The poem gives no hint whether or not his loss of family property and departure from home were connected with any change of political and military control. Supposing that Sophytos flourished about 150 BC, the shifts of power in the Kandahar region which might have affected him were probably as summarized by Peter Fraser:[59]

> From that time [sc. the 250s BC when Aśoka set up his bilingual edict on the ridge above Kandahar] the region probably remained in Maurya hands for some forty years, until the anabasis of Antiochus III in 206 BC briefly restored it to Seleucid rule, which in its turn lasted for another generation or so, until the area passed, in the early second century BC, into the hands of the Bactrian rulers from the north.

These last left at least one sign of their presence in the name of a city, Demetrias in Arachosia, no doubt called after the son of Euthydemus I.

Traces of Greek poetry in Bactria may be found in the oddest places. Queen Agathocleia, perhaps regent for her son Strato I, added a new word to the Greek lexicon when she described herself on her coins as *BACIΛICCHC ΘEOTPOΠOY*.[60] The compound epithet $\theta\epsilon\acute{o}\tau\rho o\pi o\varsigma$,[61] 'of god-like ways', has a distinctly poetic air—could it have figured in a panegyric of the queen? And Ptolemy (*Geog.* 7. 1. 46) mentions in a list of cities $\mathit{T\acute{\omega}\mu o\upsilon\sigma a}$. Was that really the city's official name? Perhaps rather an invocation of the Muse in a poem celebrating the city, as Tarn suggested?[62]

Though the situation varied somewhat as between the small individual kingdoms, the later Indo-Greek coinage gives a picture of declining Greek culture and language from about 80 BC. In places the standard remains quite high—we have mentioned the double decadrachms of Amyntas. Elsewhere deterioration is rapid. King Apollophanes' die-cutter thinks that his master's genitive case is *AΠOΛΛOΦANOY*.[63] Coins had been bilingual Greek and Prakrit; increasingly the Greek is blundered or omitted altogether. The previous variety of Greek types is almost wholly reduced to Pallas (progressively distorted) on the silver, and Apollo with his tripod on the bronze.

---

[57] Sophytos borrowed money on which he had to pay interest. $\tau\acute{o}\kappa o\varsigma$ covers both childbirth and payable interest.

[58] His vicissitudes (in a different order) are faintly reminiscent of the Prodigal Son: financial ruin, departure for a far country, restoration, and a joyful homecoming.

[59] Fraser 1979–80, 12, in connection with a fragmentary elegiac epigram now republished in Canali de Rossi 2004, pp. 191–2, no. 293.

[60] Bopearachchi 1991, 251–2, series 2–4.

[61] Borrowed, perhaps one generation later, by the Indo-Scythian queen Machene (Mitchiner 1976, v. 480).

[62] Tarn 1951, 246–7.

[63] Exactly the same mistake (more surprisingly) in an inscription from the time of Antiochus III (Ma 2002, 358).

A recent discovery throws interesting light on the balance between cultures and languages. The name, portrait, types, and obverse legend of King Artemidorus' coins seem as Greek as usual, but on one very rare bronze[64] the Prakrit reverse legend (unlike the Greek obverse) proclaims Artemidorus to be 'son of Moa', the powerful Indo-Scythian ruler whom the Greeks called Maues. Apparently this relationship would be reckoned to the king's credit among his Indian subjects, but was not worth advertising in a Greek context.[65]

# BIBLIOGRAPHY

Bernard, P. 1973, *Fouilles d'Aï Khanoum I* (Paris).
—— Pinault, G. and Rougemont, G. 2004, 'Deux nouvelles inscriptions de l'Asie Centrale', *Journal des Savants*, 2004/2, 227–356.
Bopearachchi, O. 1991, *Monnaies gréco-bactriennes et indo-grecques* (Paris).
—— and Boussac, M.-F. (eds.) 2005, *Afghanistan: ancien carrefour entre l'Est et l'Ouest* (Turnhout).
Canali de Rossi, P. 2004, *Iscrizioni dello* [sic] *Estremo Oriente greco* (Bonn).
Citti, V., Degani, E. Giangrande, G., and Scarpa, G. 1995–2002, *An Index to the Griechische Vers-Inschriften* (Amsterdam).
Clarysse, W., and Thompson, D. J. 2007, 'Two Greek Texts on Skin from Hellenistic Bactria', *ZPE* 159, 273–80.
Courtney, E. 1990, 'Greek and Latin Acrostichs', *Philologus*, 134, 3–13.
Curiel, R. and Fussman, G. 1965, *Le Trésor monétaire de Qunduz* (Paris).
Dodds, E. R. (ed.) 1960, *Euripides, Bacchae*, 2nd edn. (Oxford).
Fraser, P. M. 1979–80, 'The Son of Aristonax at Kandahar', *Afghan Studies*, 2, 9–21.
Hollis, A. (ed.) 1990, *Callimachus, Hecale* (Oxford; 2nd edn. 2009).
—— 1996, 'Laodice, Mother of Eucratides of Bactria', *ZPE* 110, 164.
—— 2004, 'Hecale's Babies', *ZPE* 148, 115–16.
Lerner, J. 2003, 'The Aï Khanoum Philosophical Papyrus', *ZPE* 142, 45–51.
Ma, J. 2002, *Antiochus III and the Cities of Western Asia Minor* (Oxford).
MacDowall, D. W. 2005, 'The Role of Demetrius in Arachosia and the Kabul Valley', in Bopearachchi and Boussac 2005, 197–206.
Mitchiner, M. 1976, *Indo-Greek and Indo-Scythian Coinage*, 9 vols. (London).
Peek, W. 1955, *Griechische Vers-Inschriften*, i (Berlin).
Rapin, C. 1983, 'Les inscriptions de la trésorerie d'Aï Khanoum', *BCH* 107, 349–51
—— 1987, 'Les textes littéraires grecs d'Aï Khanoum', *BCH* 111, 225 66.

---

[64] Senior and MacDonald 1998, 55–6. A finer specimen has now turned up.
[65] My thanks are due above all to Paul Bernard, Georges-Jean Pinault, and Georges Rougemont; to the first and third for amicable correspondence, and to all three for allowing me to discuss the Kuliab and Kandahar inscriptions in a preliminary way at the University of Leeds in May 2004, and sending me an offprint of their *Journal des Savants* article. I have also been helped in various ways by Colin Austin, Claude Rapin, Bob Senior, Dorothy Thompson, and Martin West. Rachel Chapman kindly typed my manuscript.

Rea, J., Senior, R., and Hollis, A. 1994, 'A Tax Receipt from Hellenistic Bactria', *ZPE* 104, 261–80.

Robert, L. 1973, 'Les inscriptions', in Bernard 1973, 207–37.

Salomon, R. 2005, 'The Indo-Greek Era of 186–5 in a Buddhist Reliquary Inscription', in Bopearachchi and Boussac 2005, 359–401.

Senior, R. and Hollis, A. 1999, 'Two New Bactrian Tetradrachms', *Oriental Numismatic Society*, Newsletter 159, 11–12.

—— and MacDonald, D. 1998. *The Decline of the Indo-Greeks* (Athens).

Tarn, W. 1951, *The Greeks in Bactria and India* (Cambridge).

# 6

## Menander and his Rivals: New Light from the Comic Adespota?

*Heinz-Günther Nesselrath*

### 1. Comedy's Big Three[1] Around 300 BC

It is well known that during his lifetime Menander—the later 'lone star' of Attic New Comedy—was not the only prominent comic poet and not even the most successful one. Several testimonia[2] tell us that his somewhat older rival Philemon gained more victories in the dramatic contests than Menander did, and as there are eight victories in all attested for Menander, we should have to reckon with more—maybe even considerably more—than that number for Philemon to prove the testimonia right.

The other serious rival of Menander was Diphilus; though we have no reports about his successes on the stage as compared to Menander's, he probably at least did not come far behind (securely attested are three victories in dramatic contests), and in some testimonia[3] he is named together with Menander and Philemon so as to form something like a triad of New Comic Poets (similar to Tragedy's Aeschylus, Sophocles, and Euripides, and to Old Comedy's Cratinus, Eupolis, and Aristophanes). Diphilus is explicitly put on a par with Menander by Athenaeus (6. 258 E), who tells us that the parasite

---

[1] One may wonder whether to these three should be added poets like Timocles and Alexis, who were eminent comic playwrights in their own day; these two (and others) are, however, never named as members of a group of select authors, as Menander, Diphilus, and Philemon are (see below, n. 3).

[2] Philem. test. 7. 23. 24, in Kassel and Austin 1989, 222, 226. The testimonia and citation-fragments of Menander are cited from Kassel and Austin 1998; those of Diphilus from Kassel and Austin 1986; the Comic Adespota from Kassel and Austin 1995.

[3] Men. test. 93 K.–A. (= Philem. test. 27 = Diph. test. 14), 144 (= Philem. test. 29 = Diph. test. 16), 148 (= Philem. test. 28 = Diph. test. 15).

whom Diphilus put on stage in his play *Telesias* matched the memorable *kolax* that Menander created in the play of the same name.

Furthermore, the number of plays those three poets produced are remarkably similar, too: Menander is reported to have written 105 (test. 46), 108 (test. 1, 3, 63) or 109 (test. 46) plays; for Diphilus, 100 plays are attested, and for Philemon 97. All of them treated similar topics and themes and employed more or less the same set of characters undergoing similar delusions and disappointments, errors, and exaltations. Thus one may well feel entitled to ask the question: would—or could—an Athenian spectator of about 300 BC, who was accustomed to see Philemon triumph on the stage much more often than Menander, have guessed that 2300 years later the plays not of Philemon, but of Menander could again be read and sometimes even seen on the stage?

## 2.  The Balance Shifts: The Slow but Sure Posthumous Ascendancy of Menander

After New Comedy's Big Three had gone from this earth, what happened to them was something remarkably similar to the fate of Attic Tragedy's Big Three a bit more than one hundred years earlier: just as Euripides eclipsed Aeschylus and Sophocles during the subsequent history of theatre, so now Menander began to outshine Philemon and Diphilus and finally became even more the sole representative for his genre than Euripides ever would for tragedy.

This development did not come about quickly, and there is comparatively little evidence to show us exactly how it happened; but there is at least some evidence that it did happen. One telling indicator for it may be the phenomenon of Roman adaptation of Greek Comedy: we can see that Plautus—the pre-eminent comic playwright of Rome's budding literary scene in the last decades of the third and the first decades of the second century BC—still drew his plays apparently in about equal numbers from New Comedy's Greek masters: among his surviving plays he adapted four of Menander, four of Diphilus, and three of Philemon. Just a few decades later this practice had changed considerably: Plautus' slightly younger rival Caecilius was the first Roman comic poet to draw massively on Menandrean models at the expense of other Greek poets; at least eight or possibly even thirteen (if not more, of which we do not know) of his plays were adapted from Menander's plays, while we have no information whether he also used Diphilus' or Philemon's comedies. Of Terence's six plays, four are adapted from Menander and two from the very much Menander-like Apollodorus of Carystus, and we know that his lamentably early death overcame him while he was returning from a journey to Greece in search of yet more Menandrean plays to adapt[4]—apparently those available in Italy had already all been used by other Roman poets (notably Caecilius; but there were other Roman comic writers who drew their inspiration from Menander as well: Terence's nemesis Luscius Lanuvinus, Atilius, Turpilius, and Afranius). All in all, we know for certain that a fourth or even a third (24 at a minimum, 32 at a maximum) of all Menandrean plays were adapted by Roman poets, and the actual number may have been considerably higher. Thus, it is hardly an exaggeration to say that by the middle of the second century BC, the Roman comic stage had become thoroughly 'Menanderized': its poets seem almost exclusively to have been interested in adapting Menander (and some Menander-like plays of the following generation). Terence is in fact the last for whom the use of at least a scene from Diphilus (within the otherwise Menander-derived *Adelphoe*) is securely attested; apart from that, Diphilus and Philemon already then had apparently all but vanished from the adaptation process.

What about the presence of the three poets' plays as reading material for an educated public? In this area we have a rather interesting testimonium that at least to some extent may seem to contradict the tendencies we thought to discern while looking at the development of the Roman adaptations. This testimonium is provided by the treatise 'On style' by an author called Demetrius, who is most probably to be situated in the first century BC: Demetrius tells us (ch. 193)—in the context of a discussion about the respective merits of the 'disjointed style' (λέξις διαλελυμένη) and the 'written style' (λέξις γραφική)—that the former 'is also called the actor's style since the asyndeton stimulates dramatic delivery, while the written style is easy to read', and he remarkably associates the first with Menander, 'while Philemon is read' (translations by D. Innes): not Menander but Philemon provides people with more readable comedies, while Menander seems better suited for being acted on stage. On the grounds of this testimonium we should actually expect that at least in Demetrius' time there were still many texts of Philemon's comedies in circulation, and perhaps we might also expect that at least some of them should have made it—in the form of more or less mutilated papyri—into the present times.

Well, if they did, we at least cannot tell; so far, remains of Philemon's comedies on papyrus have only been identified in two short entries in a gnomologium of the second century AD (frr. 128–9 K.–A. in vol. VII). There may and actually there should be Philemoniana among the Comic Adespota, and I shall offer further suggestions about that possibility below,[5] after some

---

[4] The Suetonian *Vita Terenti* that Donatus placed in front of his commentary on Terence's plays gives as reasons for this journey *animi causa et uitandae opinionis qua uidebatur aliena pro suis edere* (Donat. *Vit. Ter.* 5, p. 7. 9–10 W.), which implies that Terence was looking for new Greek originals to counter the opinion that he was simply recycling earlier Roman adaptations; it adds explicitly that he was returning *cum centum et octo fabulis conuersis a Menandro* (*Vit. Ter.* 5 p. 7. 17 W. = Men. Test. 63 K.–A.).

[5] See below, pp. 134, 136.

remarks on the fate of the three poets up until the end of antiquity that are pertinent to our question.

Ultimately, of course, none of the three did make it beyond the so-called 'Dark Centuries'[6] before the re-emergence of a real interest in ancient Greek literature in eighth- and ninth-century Byzantium. Still, even though Menander, too, did not come through the bottle-neck of *metacharakterismos* and thus survive into the age of the medieval codex, he had retained far better chances of being rediscovered one thousand years later than his rivals Diphilus and Philemon: not only had he obviously been much more copied on papyri, which then gradually came to light from the end of the nineteenth century, but he had also been much more quoted by other authors in antiquity itself: for Philemon we have only 196 citation-fragments (plus the two aforementioned entries in a papyrus gnomologium), and even less remains of Diphilus (only 132–4 citation-fragments and a mutilated three-line quote in a grammatical commentary on papyrus), while for Menander there are 894 citation-fragments in the *PCG* volume VI 2, and there were even more—namely 951—in the preceding Körte edition. The smaller number in the more recent edition is mostly to be explained by the fact that rather a lot of quotations could in the meantime be integrated into the ever-increasing remains of Menander on papyrus. In fact the very possibility of integrating such quotations into papyrus finds (and thus ascertaining that those papyri can be attributed to a definite author) is very much enhanced by the high number of quotation fragments in Menander's case, and it shows us in comparison once again how badly Menander's two great rivals have fared: as the number of ancient quotations from Menander is almost five times as high as that from Philemon and even seven times as high as that from Diphilus, likewise the chances are proportionately much greater that we can detect Menandrean texts among papyri which have not preserved an explicit author attribution. This largely explains the astonishing success of rediscovery Menander enjoyed after the large-scale publication of papyri set in: thanks to these papyri large parts (in a few cases almost the whole) of eight Menandrean plays (*Aspis, Dyskolos, Epitrepontes, Kolax, Misoumenos, Perikeiromene, Samia, Sikyonios/-oi*) have been restored to us, as well as substantial scenes of ten others (*Georgos, Dis Exapaton, Heros, Theophoroumene, Karchedonios, Kitharistes, Koneiazomenoi, Leukadia, Perinthia, Phasma*). No other ancient dramatic author has profited so much from the labours of papyrology.

[6] For the label 'Dark Centuries' (for the period between 600 and 800 AD) see (e.g.) Wilson 1997, 104–5, Kambylis 1997, 327–8.

## 3. New Comedy's 'X-Files': The Adespota

However, even with such a stunning success-story as Menander has had since
the end of the nineteenth century, there remain a considerable number of
papyrus fragments of comic plays which—up to now, at least—could not
securely be attributed to their original writer(s) and thus remain in a semi-
obscure state of authorless limbo, being called adespota. In *PCG* VIII, which
is exclusively devoted to Comic Adespota, 156 (nos. 1000–1155) are texts on
papyrus of very variable size (ranging from a few lines up to almost 400). Of
these 156, thirty[7] are more substantial and worth being scrutinized more
closely (though many of them are in a poor state of preservation).

In the sixteen years since the appearance of the *PCG* Adespota volume,
substantial further work on comic adespota on papyrus has mainly been done
by one of the most eminent English experts on Menander, namely Geoffrey
Arnott, in connection with his immensely useful three-volume Loeb edition
of Menander.[8] In vol. iii of that edition, Arnott also deals with a number of
the just-mentioned papyrus adespota, claiming seven of them for Menander
(namely nos. 1001, 1006, 1027, 1084, 1089, 1096, 1147), while rejecting eight
others (namely nos. 1000, 1008, 1014, 1017, 1032, 1073, 1091, 1093). In at
least some of these cases, however, one may well ask whether Arnott uses
sufficiently sound criteria for his judgement. For example:

(1) No. 1000 is rejected, because its words are severely taken to task for
their 'poverty-stricken flatness' and because they 'nowhere show one glint of
Menandrean imagination'.

(2) On the other hand, no. 1001 is accepted (and presented by Arnott as
Menander's 'Fabula incerta 2'), because 'the quality of imagination and
expression . . . seems higher than that achieved in the remains of any of his
[= Menander's] comic rivals' (of whom, alas, we know so very little).

(3) Likewise, no. 1006 is declared Menandrean (and edited by Arnott as his
'Fabula incerta 3'), because 'the lively imagination which it reveals strongly
favours its attribution to Menander'. Imagination again . . .

(4) No. 1008, on the contrary, is rejected (after being tentatively attributed
to Menander's Ἀνεψιοί by Christina Dedoussi), because (in Arnott's words)
'the papyrus yields no hard evidence in support of Dedoussi's theory, and

[7] Adesp. 1000 (2nd c. BC), 1001 (2nd c. BC), 1006 (2nd/3rd c. AD), 1007 (1st/2nd c. AD), 1008
(1st or 2nd c. AD), 1014 (3rd c. BC), 1017 (3rd c. BC), 1018 (1st c. BC), 1027 (2nd/1st c. BC),
1032 (3rd c. BC), 1047f. (2nd c. AD), 1063 (1st c. AD), 1064 (3rd c. BC), 1073 (3rd c. BC), 1084
(3rd /4th c. AD), 1089 (3rd c. BC), 1091 (2nd /3rd c. AD), 1092 (3rd c. BC), 1093 (3rd c. BC), 1094
(3rd c. BC), 1096 (4th c. AD), 1097 (1st c. AD), 1103 (2nd c. AD), 1112 (2nd c. AD), 1129 (2nd c.
AD), 1132 (1st c. AD), 1141 (3rd c. AD), 1146 (3rd / 2nd c. BC), 1147 (3rd c. BC), 1152 (2nd/3rd c.
AD). For the possible significance of the division into BC and AD, see below.
[8] Arnott 1979–2000.

there is one factor that speaks against Menandrean authorship. The narrative part of this ... prologue begins by naming the two brothers (...), but Menander's extant prologues ... either avoid naming any character or restrict such naming to one main person.' To me, this does not seem to be a particularly strong argument, especially in view of the fact that—up to now at least—we have sufficient evidence from just five prologues from over a hundred Menandrean plays, so that any newly found prologue could prove this argument wrong.

(5) No. 1014 is rejected on the basis of rather weak arguments as well, namely because 'there are neither links with any known fragments of Menander nor any other clues to its author' and because 'the writing ... lacks distinction and imagination'.

(6) Things do not get better with no. 1017, which is condemned because of 'serious weaknesses in the writing—a lack of verbal distinction, with an unimaginative repetition of words and phrases—[which] were first noted by Wilamowitz ... and demonstrated at greater length by Körte ...; these effectively demolish any attribution to Menander and suggest rather authorship by some inferior comic dramatist of Menander's time or the succeeding generation'.[9]

(7) Admittedly, some better reasons—better because Menander enjoyed a considerably greater popularity than his two rivals in Lucian's day—are given for presenting no. 1027 as Menander's 'Fabula incerta 4': 'The attribution to Menander ... is reinforced by the fact that Lucian ... purloins three of its first four lines at the start of his *Juppiter tragoedus*'.

(8) No. 1032, however, again is rejected. Arnott himself originally wanted to ascribe this papyrus to Menander's *Perinthia*, but recanted when he edited the remains of *Perinthia* in his second Loeb volume (pp. 477f.) Apparently he then even did not find it worthy of Menander at all, because he did not include it as one of the 'Fabulae incertae' in vol. III, but he has supplied no explicit reasons for that.[10]

(9) No. 1073 is rejected because it seems to be a rather common type of cook-speech (and that is quite a good reason, not least because Menander—as far as we can tell—in fact seems to have avoided this type of set speech for cooks).

(10) As for no. 1084, which Arnott presents as Menander's 'Fabula incerta 6', 'there is [in Arnott's words] nothing in the style and language ... that conflicts with, but much that suggests, Menandrean authorship'.

(11) Similar reasons are given for the presentation of no. 1089 as 'Fabula incerta 5': 'there is nothing in the metre or diction ... that is unmenandrean,

---

[9] One might, however, come to different (and more favourable) conclusions about this fragment; see below, pp. 133–4.

[10] Again, a more favourable view is possible; see below, pp. 135–6.

while the writing has a liveliness, wit and imagination not unworthy of that dramatist'. This time, however, even Menander—if he really was the author— does not wholly escape the criticism of his modern English editor, who admonishes him in one respect quite severely: 'the staging of the exits in vv. 15–21 seems rather pedestrian'. And this prompts me to deviate into a brief excursus. If, then, even Menander may at times have relaxed a little and indulged in some 'pedestrian' writing, could not other pieces condemned by modern critics as 'pedestrian' have been written by him as well? And could not—on the other hand—other authors whom critics rate as more pedestrian than Menander at least from time to time have soared to greater stylistic and imaginative heights? But if these pieces of writing happened to turn up on one of our papyri without any indication of author, arguments like those presented by Arnott would almost inevitably lead us to regard these texts as Menandrean while their real authors would continue to be condemned as incapable of having written such gems. These are the consequences of trying to determine authorship more or less exclusively on stylistic grounds. End of excursus; back to our list, where four more items await us.

(12) Comic adespoton no. 1091 (twenty-nine partly mutilated lines) was tentatively attributed by Webster to Menander's *Phasma*; Arnott, however, excluded it from his Menander edition, because 'none of the character names preserved in this fragment . . . reappear in *Phasma*' (p. 371).

(13) Comic adespoton no. 1093 (the longest text, with 395 mostly heavily mutilated lines) is rejected by Arnott, because he detects 'a general lack of imaginative ideas and wording, and a style that has no distinction . . .', though he has to concede: 'The fact that the play was considered to be worth copying in two different papyri suggests that it was the work of an established comic dramatist, but probably not one of the first order.' This last remark induces me to wonder what comic writers Arnott would consider to belong to this 'first order'—only Menander or a few others (Diphilus? Philemon?) as well?

(14) No. 1096 is claimed for Menander by Arnott (and presented as his 'Fabula incerta 7'), because 'although these fragments do not contain any ties with previously known quotations from Menander, their language, style, metrics, and imaginative quality combine to indicate a common source in one of his plays.' We had that kind of reasoning before . . .

(15) The last item on this list is no. 1147 (again a rather long piece, with remains of 244 verses), which is edited by Arnott as 'Fabula incerta 8', and this time his reasoning is to be commended at least for its candour: 'nothing in the preserved portions of text ties in with any known quotation from Menander or any other comic poet, but there is a general—if subjective—feeling that the style of the comic trimeters, particularly in its imaginative use of language, brings Menander to mind more than anyone else.'

It should be made clear that I did not give this survey of Arnott's opinions regarding the 'Menandrean' or 'un-Menandrean' quality of a number of interesting comic adespota to make him look foolish or totally unfounded in his ascriptions. I would rather hope that something else—and indeed much more serious—might have emerged from this list, namely how subjective and (in the last resort) speculative the game of trying to rescue comic adespota out of their authorless limbo can be: As we have seen, in many (and probably too many) cases Arnott's ascriptions and rejections rest more or less solely (or at least mainly) on criteria like 'imagination' and 'style' on which it is very hard to get a firm grasp; one man's imagination may be another man's dullness (and yet another's eccentricity).

All in all, this leaves us with a big problem: If even such a scholar as Arnott (who surely had a better grasp on Menander's qualities than most other classicists, myself certainly included) cannot—in very many cases at least—find better criteria than 'liveliness', 'imagination', and 'style' for distinguishing Menandrean from un-Menandrean comic writing, can there be any really 'hard' indicators at all—apart, of course, from explicit ascription pure and simple (which has, however, not yet come to light on any New Comedy papyrus texts for any authors except Menander) to help us separate Menander from his rivals? I am afraid I cannot give you a reassuring and affirmative answer to this question; instead, in the remaining parts of my paper, I shall try to do two things: first, I shall try to point out one possible criterion that is certainly not totally foolproof, but seems to me to be at least less subjective than those employed by Arnott and other scholars; secondly, having pointed out so much rather subjective reasoning before, I shall feel free cheerfully to indulge in some subjective reasoning myself and present to you two comic adespota which I personally find very appealing ('lively' and 'imaginative' in Arnott's words) and which—in my opinion—could well have been written by either Diphilus or Philemon (though I will not stick my neck so far out and actually claim that they really were). Thus I should like to show that there really *is* good comic writing to be found among the adespota, but that it need not necessarily—or inexorably—be connected with Menander.

## 4. Were Earlier Times Better Times for Menander's Rivals? The Criterion of Age

From the totality of 156 comic adespota on papyrus edited in *PCG* VIII, I singled out thirty more substantial fragments that I called worthy of being looked at more closely. Now, if one does so, one can make an interesting observation regarding the time of their being written down: of these thirty items, fifteen (or half of them) were written in the third to first centuries BC: ten in the third, one in the third or second, two in the second, one in the second or first, and one in the first century BC. Again, of those ten of third-century origin, six have in the past been tentatively attributed to poets other than Menander and two to him (the rest being more or less undecided); of the five of second- or first-century date, non-Menandrean authorship has been suggested for three, the other two being attributed to Menander. These numbers change perceptibly for the fifteen papyri of AD dates: five of them have been claimed for Menander, one for Philemon[11] (with not very convincing reasons,[12] one should add), two or three have had both Menandrean and non-Menandrean ascriptions, while the rest (six) have more or less been left undecided.

These numbers convey the impression that the rate of non-Menandrean papyri of New Comedy diminishes progressively the further down we get in Antiquity. This would, of course, tie in very handsomely with other observations we have already made regarding the slowly but surely increasing pervasiveness of Menander in our record: not only did the later Roman comic poets turn much more to Menander as provider of models for their plays than their predecessor Plautus, but also the rhetorician Demetrius still regarded Philemon (and not Menander) as the more readable (as opposed to performable) of the great writers of Attic New Comedy. Thus we may have reason to believe that the possibility of non-Menandrean adespota increases with the age of the papyri.[13] As I already said, this is—unfortunately—not a foolproof or failproof criterion, but at least some kind of guideline to help us narrow down the prime suspects for non-Menandrean comedy in our papyrus evidence: in fact, papyri of the third century BC may be the most promising candidates to find comic writing by Diphilus or Philemon, and to two of them I shall now turn.

## 5. Of Quarrelling Friends and Fleeing Pimps: Two Specimens of Possibly Non-Menandrean Greek New Comedy

The first of these specimens to be considered here is Com. Adesp. 1017 K.–A., condemned as we have seen (above, p. 124) as unworthy of Menander. It contains 109 verses in all (a substantial number complete, but also a sizable number of more or less mutilated lines), apparently all written in iambic trimeters.

> ] ητι υν, ὦ δέσποινα, σὲ
> ]ε τὸμ πατέρα δὲ τουτονὶ
> ]οντα τὸν τῶν γεγονότων

[11] Adesp. 1047–8 (actually two short fragments, possibly from different plays).
[12] See Kassel and Austin ad loc.
[13] The occurrence of non-Menandrean fragments in gnomologia on papyri, mentioned earlier (above, p. 121), may be considered as exceptions to this rule.

]ν, ὡς ἔοικε, πραγμάτων

]γος ἐστὶν ἢ μάτην                                         5

]τουτονὶ μὲν οὖν ὁρῶ

]ν χαῖρε πολλά, Φαίδιμε

]. γ᾽ ἀκούσας ὅτι πάρει·

ε]ὐθύς. (ΦΑ.) οὐ μή μοι πρόσει

::] διὰ τί; (ΦΑ.) τοῦτ᾽ ἤρου με καὶ               10

]κως με προσβλέπειν; :: ἐγώ.

(ΦΑ.)    ]σαυτὸν εἶδες ο . . . η τύχη

τ]οῖς θεοῖς δέ. :: μανθάνων

*desunt uersus fere 14*

τίνος κελεύσαντ[ος; :: . . . . . . . . . .] αὐτὸς ἂν

ἠνάγκασας τοιαῦτα ποιῶν. :: Ἡράκλεις,          15

τί με πεποίηκας, θύγατερ; ἄρτι μανθάνω

τὸ πρᾶγμ᾽· ἐκεῖ νῦν ἐστιν, ὡς ἔοικ᾽. :: ἐκεῖ. <::>

οἷον πεποίηκας, θύγατερ. οὐκ ἂν ᾠόμην,

θύγατερ· τί ταῦτα, θύγατερ; ἆρ᾽ ἀφίσταται;

(ΝΙ.) ὡς οὐκ ἀπήντων οὐδαμοῦ τῶι Φαιδίμωι,    20

αὐτὸς †μεμενηκον† δεῦρ᾽ ἀναστρέψας πάλιν.

μὴ πολὺ διημάρτηκα τὸν Χαιρέστρατον

εἰς λιμένα πέμψας. ἡμέτερος οὗτος φίλος

διαδ[ . . . . . ]τ . . .   (ΦΑ.) μετὰ τὸν οἰκεῖον πάλιν

.[              ]τα καὶ τίνα δεῖ τρόπον             25

(ΝΙ.) χ]αῖρ᾽, [ἑ]ταῖρε φίλτατε,

περίβαλέ <μ᾽>, ἱκετεύω. (ΦΑ.) τί χρὴ νυνὶ ποιεῖν;

ἡ μὲν συνήθει᾽, ἡ φιλία, τὸ διὰ χρόνου

. . . . . . ]ἠγάπηκε κα[ὶ . . . ] . . . .[

*desunt uersus 2*

τε[                                                     30

]τιμήν γε δὴ

ἑτ]αιρείαν ἁπλῶς

] . τε τῶι

]τοτε

]γὰρ ἀπόδειξις φίλου                  35

γε]γονέναι

]ν. (ΦΑ.) ὑπερηκόντικας

]τοῖς πεπραγμένοις

ὑπερεπιτηδείως διάκεισαι. (ΝΙ.) τί σὺ λέγεις;

(ΦΑ.) ἐμοῦ πρόνοιαν εἶχες; (ΝΙ.) οἴομαί γε δή.       40

(ΦΑ.) ἀνδρειοτέρους, νὴ τὴν Ἀθηνᾶν, νενόμικα

ὅσοι δύνανται τοῖς φίλοις ἀντιβλέπειν

ἀδικοῦντες ἢ τοὺς τοῖς πολεμίοις μαχομένους.

τοῖς μέν γε κοινὸς ὁ φόβος ἐστί, καὶ καλὸν

ὑπολαμβάνουσι πρᾶγμα ποιεῖν ἑκάτεροι,           45

τούτοις δ᾽ ὅπως ποτ᾽ ἐπιτρέπει <τὸ> συνειδέναι

αὑτοῖσι θαρρεῖν πολλάκις τεθαύμακα.

(ΝΙ.) πρὸς δὴ τί τοῦτ᾽ εἴρηκας; (ΦΑ.) ὦ τάλας ἐγώ·

ὅσον διημάρτηκα τοῦ ζῆν· τοῦ βίου
τί γάρ ἐστιν ἡμῖν τῶν φίλων μεῖζον ἀγαθόν;　　　　50
εἰ τοῦτο μήτ᾽ ἔγνωκα μ[ήτ᾽ ἐπίστ]αμαι
ὡς δεῖ θεωρεῖν ἀλλὰ λα[νθάνουσί] με
οἱ μὲν ἐπιβουλεύοντ[ες, οἱ δ᾽ ἄλλ]ως φίλοι
ὄντες, τί τὸ ζῆν ὄφελός [ἐστι; (ΝΙ.) πῶς λέγε]ις;
τί δ᾽ ἐστὶν ὃ λελύπηκέ ς᾽; [ (ΦΑ.) ἤρου τοῦ]τό με;　　　　55
(ΝΙ.) ἔγωγε, καὶ τεθαύμακ᾽ οὐ μετ[ρίως ς᾽ ὁρ]ῶν
ςυντεινόμενον πρὸς ἐμαυτόν. [ (ΦΑ.) . . . . . εἰ]πέ μοι,
ἐρῶντα τῆς γυναικὸς ἀνακο[ινοῦν . . . . . ]ν
πρὸς ςαυτόν, οὐθὲν τῶν ἐμα[υτοῦ πρ]αγμάτων
κρύπτοντα; (ΝΙ.) πάντ᾽ οὐκ [. . . . . . . . . . ] περίμενε.　　　　60
(ΦΑ.) περίμενε; ταύτην τοῦ πατρός μ᾽ ἀ[πο]ςτερεῖν
μέλλοντος ἠξίω[κας,] οἶδ᾽, αὐτὴν [γ]αμεῖν.
(ΝΙ.) διαμαρτάνεις. (ΦΑ.) πῶς; οὐκ ἔμελλ[ε]ς λαμβάνειν
αὐτήν; <ΝΙ.> ἄκουςον, ὦ [μ]ακάρι᾽— (ΦΑ.) ἀκήκοα.
(ΝΙ.) οὐκ οἶςθας— (ΦΑ.) οἶδα πάντα. (ΝΙ.) πρὶν [μ]αθεῖν; τίνα　　　　65
τρόπον; (ΦΑ.) κατηγόρηκέ μοι τὰ πράγματα
ἀλλότριον ἡμῖν ὄντα ς᾽. (ΝΙ.) ὦ τᾶν, Φαίδιμε,
ἐπ᾽ ἀριςτέρ᾽ εἴληφας τὸ πρᾶγμα· μανθάνω
ςχεδὸν γὰρ ἐξ ὧν πρός με τὴν ὑποψίαν
ἔχεις· διὰ τὸ δ᾽ ἐρᾶν ςε ςυγγνώμην τινὰ　　　　70
ὅμως δίδωμι καίπερ ἀγνοούμενος.
(ΦΑ.) πείθεις μ᾽ ἀκοῦςαι τὸ παράδοξον τί ποτ᾽ ἐρεῖ[ς.
(ΧΑ.) οὐκ ᾠχόμην εἰς λιμέν᾽· ἀπαντήςας με γὰρ
ςύμπλους ἀνέςτρεψέν τις εἰπὼν ὅτι πάλαι
ἀπελήλυθεν δεῦρ᾽. ∷ αποσαω . . . . . . . . .　　　　75
(ΧΑ.) τίς οὗτος; ὤ, Νική[ρ]ατ[ος] <καὶ> Φαίδιμος
αὐτός γ᾽ ἔοικε. χαῖρε πολλά, Φαίδιμε.
(ΦΑ.) νὴ καὶ ςύ γ᾽, ὦ Χαιρέςτρατ[᾽.]ι[. .]ςεις φιλεῖν.
(ΝΙ.) χειμάζομαι γὰρ οὐ μετρίως ὑπὸ τοῦδ᾽ ἐγώ.
(ΧΑ.) τί δ᾽ ἐςτίν; οὐ δήπουθεν ἠγνόηχ᾽ ὅτι—　　　　80
(ΦΑ.) οὐκ ἠξίουν, Χαιρέςτρατ᾽, ὄντα μοι φίλον
ὥς φηςι— (ΧΑ.) παῦςαι, μηθὲν εἴπῃς, πρὸς θεῶν,
Φαίδιμε. (ΦΑ.) τί δ᾽ ἐςτί; (ΧΑ.) μεταμ[ελήςει ςοι τάχα.
(ΦΑ.) εὖ ἴςθι, βουλοίμην ἄν· ἐμὲ μὲν ῥάιδιον
ἔςται μεταθέςθαι γὰρ μαθόντ᾽, ἀλλ᾽ οὑτοςί^　　　　85
(ΧΑ.) οὐκ ἂν ἐπιτρέψαιμ᾽ οὐθὲν εἰπεῖν ςοι παρὼν
ἄτοπον, ςυνειδὼς τὰ περὶ τοῦτον πράγματα.
εἰ γὰρ τοιοῦτοι . . . . . . . . . . . . . . ψιλοι,
οὐκ ἔςθ᾽ ὅ τι οὐ πράξαις ἂν ἕνεκα πίςτεως.
ἀλλ᾽ ἐκποδὼν ἡμῖν γενοῦ, Νικήρατε,　　　　90
ἵνα μὴ παρόντος ςου ποιῶμαι τοὺς λόγ[ο]υ[ς.
(ΝΙ.) εἰςέρχομαι καὶ ςὺ μετ᾽ ἐμοῦ γ[. .]αρ . . . . ι
[. . .]

In each of the first thirteen lines, the first five or six syllables are missing, so that we cannot always be sure where changes of speaker occurred. In v. 7 someone apparently newly arrived on the stage cordially (χαῖρε πολλά) greets a young man called Phaidimos. This Phaidimos, however, reacts in a very unfriendly way, telling the new arrival to stay clear of him (9 οὐ μή μοι πρόϲει). As the following lines show, Phaidimos is obviously very upset (10–11 τοῦτ᾽ ἤρου με καὶ / ]κωϲ με προϲβλέπειν;) about something for which he holds the newly arrived person responsible (or guilty); already Sandbach[14] compared the famous scene in Menander's *Dis Exapatôn* (reproduced and expanded in Plautus' *Bacchides*), where one friend feels betrayed by another. Unfortunately we cannot observe how this quarrel unfolded after v. 13, because at this point there is a gap of about 14 lines.

When the text resumes, we get sixteen lines, of which nine are complete and most of the others fairly substantially preserved. In the first of these lines (v. 14) someone (probably the father, whom we can identify in vv. 16 and 18–19) asks in what seems to be a very upset mood (as the following lines prove): 'Who ordered (him/her/you to do) this?' (τίνοϲ κελεύϲαντ[οϲ;), and when he is told 'You yourself would have made him/her/me by doing such things' (14–15: .........] αὐτὸϲ ἂν / ἠνάγκαϲαϲ τοιαῦτα ποιῶν), he really explodes (v. 15–6): Ἡράκλειϲ, / τί με πεποίηκαϲ, θύγατερ; The daughter is addressed three more times in vv. 18–19 (οἷον πεποίηκαϲ, θύγατερ. οὐκ ἂν ᾠόμην, / θύγατερ· τί ταῦτα, θύγατερ;), and this unusual repetition clearly shows how very upset her father is. Despite these four vocatives, it is not totally certain that the girl addressed is actually present on the stage (except perhaps at 14–15); in his distraught state, her father might very well address her, as if she were present; this might be confirmed by the end of v. 19, where the father apparently speaks of his daughter in the third person: ἆρ᾽ ἀφίϲταται;[15]

Possibly after these exclamations the distraught father stormed off the stage (into his house), because in v. 20 a new character with the name of Nikeratos—a name which in other plays indicates an elderly man, but probably not here—is speaking who has just come in from one of the side entrances, as his first words show, and who at first is alone on the stage. Nikeratos tells us that his search for Phaidimos (from which he apparently just now returns) has been in vain, and he asks himself whether he may in fact have committed a grave error by sending one Chairestratos to the harbour (vv. 20–3).

Next, in v. 24 Phaidimos (whom we had last seen fuming at another person in vv. 9–13) seems to come out of a house and to be talking back into it (vv. 24–6); in vv. 26–7 Nikeratos apparently sees him while he is coming out and

---

[14]   In Gomme and Sandbach 1973, 731.
[15]   Sandbach wanted to change this to ἀφίϲταϲαι, but Kassel and Austin retain what seems to them to be the papyrus reading; see also Austin 1973, 282, no. 257, ad loc.

cordially greets him (χ]αῖρ', [ἑ]ταῖρε φίλτατε, / περίβαλέ <μ'>, ἱκετεύω). Phaidimos, however, again (as in the earlier scene) does not respond in kind; rather, he seems to freeze and wonder how he should react (vv. 27–9: τί χρὴ νυνὶ ποιεῖν; / ἡ μὲν συνήθει', ἡ φιλία, τὸ διὰ χρόνου / . . . . . . . ]ἠγάπηκε κα[ὶ . . . ] . . ῳ[). These words make it quite clear that in former times Phaidimos was connected with Nikeratos in a long and intimate friendship; but now he apparently feels betrayed by him.

Though there are now two lines missing and the following seven verses in a very mutilated state (only the last few words are preserved), the scene continues, and an uneasy conversation must have started between those two people. In vv. 37–9 Phaidimos seems to comment on his friend's doings in a very sarcastic way (ὑπερηκόντικας /        ]τοῖς πεπραγμένοις / ὑπερεπιτηδείως διάκεισαι). In reaction to this, in v. 39 Nikeratos bewilderedly asks what Phaidimos is driving at (39 τί cὺ λέγεις;). To this, Phaidimos responds with a peremptory question of his own: 'Did you care for *my* interests?' (40 ἐμοῦ πρόνοιαν εἶχες;), to which Nikeratos answers cautiously, but affirmatively (οἴομαί γε δή). Phaidimos, however, totally disregards this answer and immediately launches into a sarcastic declaration of his own (in vv. 41–7): in his opinion those who still dare to look their friends in the eyes while wronging them must really be braver than those who fight the enemy (41–3 ἀνδρειοτέρους, νὴ τὴν Ἀθηνᾶν, νενόμικα / ὅcοι δύνανται τοῖς φίλοις ἀντιβλέπειν / ἀδικοῦντες ἢ τοὺς τοῖς πολεμίοις μαχομένους); for enemies on both sides of a battlefield know what they have to fear, and each of them believe that they are doing the right thing, but in the case of those who have wronged their friends he has often wondered how their bad conscience still lets them be confident of themselves (44–7 τοῖς μέν γε κοινὸς ὁ φόβος ἐcτί, καὶ καλὸν / ὑπολαμβάνουcι πρᾶγμα ποιεῖν ἑκάτεροι, / τούτοιc δ' ὅπωc ποτ' ἐπιτρέπει <τὸ> cυνειδέναι / αὑτοῖcι θαρρεῖν πολλάκιc τεθαύμακα).

Nikeratos, however, still does not understand what all this is supposed to be about (v. 48 πρὸc δὴ τί τοῦτ' εἴρηκας;). Nevertheless, Phaidimos continues speaking in riddles (one is reminded of Theseus in Euripides' *Hippolytos* confronting his son, whom he believes to have raped his stepmother, Theseus' wife Phaidra). Now he pathetically declares that he really must have missed the very essence of life itself; for if there is no greater asset in life than friends and if he has not been able to choose them carefully an that lit supposed friends have turned out to be something totally different—namely sinister schemers and hypocrites—what use is life? (48–54 ὦ τάλαc ἐγώ· / ὅcον διημάρτηκα τοῦ ζῆν· τοῦ βίου / τί γάρ ἐcτιν ἡμῖν τῶν φίλων μεῖζον ἀγαθόν; / εἰ τοῦτο μήτ' ἔγνωκα μ[ήτ' ἐπίcτ]αμαι / ὡc δεῖ θεωρεῖν ἀλλὰ λα[νθάνουcί] με / οἱ μὲν ἐπιβουλεύοντ[εc, οἱ δ' ἄλλ]ωc φίλοι / ὄντεc, τί τὸ ζῆν ὄφελόc [ἐcτι;—'Poor wretch that I am! How far have I gone astray in life! For what greater good in life is there for us than our friends? If I have not recognized this and do not know how one has to observe it, but am still in the dark regarding those who scheme against me or those who are no real friends—what use is life?')

Despite all these wordy statements, Nikeratos still does not know what Phaidimos is talking about and has to ask once more, why his friend is so upset (54–5 πῶς λέγε]ις; / τί δ᾿ ἐστὶν ὃ λελύπηκέ ς;), but when Phaidimos only responds with another harsh question (55 ἤρου τοῦ]τό με;), he at last begins to understand that Phaidimos is angry with him (56–7 τεθαύμακ᾿ οὐ μετ[ρίως ς᾿ ὁρ]ῶν / ςυντεινόμενον πρὸς ἐμαυτόν). Now Phaidimos finally becomes more explicit: has he not told Nikeratos everything about the woman he fell in love with (this is certainly the meaning of vv. 57–60, even though these lines have some gaps the exact wording of which cannot be restored with total confidence)? Nikeratos' answer to this is even less restorable (because of a substantial gap), but he now seems to grasp what Phaidimos is driving at and implores him to wait (περίμενε) and hear him out.

'Wait?' Phaidimos scornfully repeats and now he at last pours out the accusation he has so long held back behind riddling sentences: when his (Phaidimos') father intended to deprive him (Phaidimos) of the woman he loved, his glorious friend Nikeratos planned to marry her himself! (61–2 ταύτην τοῦ πατρός μ᾿ ἀ[πο]ςτερεῖν / μέλλοντος ἠξίω[κας,] οἶδ᾿, αὐτὴν [γ]αμεῖν). With this, an excited altercation begins: 'You are mistaken!' 'How? Didn't you intend to take her?' 'Now listen, my friend . . .' 'I've heard enough!' 'You don't understand . . .' 'I understand everything!' 'Before learning it? How can you?'—'The facts themselves have plainly told me that you are my enemy!' (63–7 *(NI.)* διαμαρτάνεις. *(ΦΑ.)* πῶς; οὐκ ἔμελλ[ε]ς λαμβάνειν / αὐτήν; <*NI.*> ἄκουςον, ὦ [μ]ακάρι᾿— *(ΦΑ.)* ἀκήκοα. / *(NI.)* οὐκ οἶςθας— *(ΦΑ.)* οἶδα πάντα. *(NI.)* πρὶν [μ]αθεῖν; τίνα / τρόπον; *(ΦΑ.)* κατηγόρηκέ μοι τὰ πράγματα / ἀλλότριον ἡμῖν ὄντα ς᾿.)

After this rapid and violent exchange, Nikeratos at last gets a chance to start an explanation: 'Please, Phaidimos! You've got the thing all backwards! I begin to see for what reasons you now hold me in suspicion. But because you are in love, I am willing to forgive you, even though you judge me wrong' (67–71 ὦ τᾶν, Φαίδιμε, / ἐπ᾿ ἀριςτέρ᾿ εἴληφας τὸ πρᾶγμα· μανθάνω / ςχεδὸν γὰρ ἐξ ὧν πρός με τὴν ὑποψίαν / ἔχεις· διὰ τὸ δ᾿ ἐρᾶν ςε ςυγγνώμην τινὰ / ὅμως δίδωμι καίπερ ἀγνοούμενος). These words get Phaidimos to listen to him (72 πείθεις μ᾿ ἀκοῦςαι τὸ παράδοξον τί ποτ᾿ ἐρεῖ[ς—'you persuade me to listen to what unexpected thing you are going to tell').

At this very moment a new character comes on stage: Chairestratos, whom Nikeratos in v. 20 declared he had sent to the harbour to meet Phaidimos. Chairestratos comes back without having gone all the way to the harbour, because he had in the meantime met someone who told him that Phaidimos had already come hither, and now, of course, he sees Nikeratos and Phaidimos together. He greets Phaidimos, whom he obviously sees for the first time (77 χαῖρε πολλά, Φαίδιμε), and Phaidimos, still in a bad mood, somewhat morosely returns the greeting (78). What he says in the second half of v. 78 cannot be recovered with certainty, but it seems to prompt Nikeratos to turn to Chairestratos for help: 'I'm quite buffeted about by this man!' (79: χειμάζομαι γὰρ οὐ μετρίως ὑπὸ τοῦδ' ἐγώ).

Chairestratos starts to speak: 'What is it? I am, of course, well aware . . .' (80: τί δ' ἐcτίν; οὐ δήπουθεν ἠγνόηχ' ὅτι—), but he doesn't get to complete his sentence, as Phaidimos cuts him short: 'I did not think it right that he, being my friend, as he claims . . .' (80–1 οὐκ ἠξίουν, Χαιρέcτρατ', ὄντα μοι φίλον / ὥc φηcι—), whereupon it is now Chairestratos' turn to interrupt him: 'Stop! Don't say anything, for the gods' sake, Phaidimos!' (82–3 παῦcαι, μηθὲν εἴπηιc, πρὸc θεῶν, / Φαίδιμε.). Now Phaidimos is the one to ask what the other means (an ironic reversal of Nikeratos' former role), whereupon Chairestratos warns him that he might have to repent any rash words (ΦΑ.) τί δ' ἐcτί; (ΧΑ.) μεταμ[ελήcει cοι τάχα). Phaidimos tries again to state his position: 'Know it well that I would very much like to do so; for me it will be easy to come around, once I've learnt things; but this one here . . .' (84–5 εὖ ἴcθι, βουλοίμην ἄν· ἐμὲ μὲν ῥάιδιον / ἔcται μεταθέcθαι γὰρ μαθόντ', ἀλλ' οὑτοcί—), and again he is cut short by Chairestratos: 'As long as I am present, I will not allow you to say anything out of place, because I well know how things stand with this man' (86–7 οὐκ ἂν ἐπιτρέψαιμ' οὐθὲν εἰπεῖν cοι παρὼν / ἄτοπον, cυνειδὼc τὰ περὶ τούτου πράγματα), and then he extols Nikeratos as a real friend: 'if you had only three friends like him, there is nothing you might not achieve, as far as trustfulness is concerned' (88–9 εἰ γὰρ τοιοῦτοι τρεῖc γένοιντό cοι φίλοι, / οὐκ ἔcθ' ὅ τι οὐ πράξαιc ἂν ἕνεκα πίcτεωc). After this ringing endorsement he turns to Nikeratos and asks him to stand aside so that he may talk with Phaidimos in private (90–1), and Nikeratos obliges by announcing that he will go into the house (92 εἰcέρχομαι καὶ cὺ μετ' ἐμοῦ γ[. .]αρ....ι).

With v. 93, a new column begins, and it is not clear how much is missing between this new column and the preceding verses. In 93 someone (Phaidimos?) addresses Chairestratos, but already after 95 the act ends with the rubric *ΧΟΡΟΥ*. After that there are beginnings of fourteen further verses, but neither does it become clear who is speaking them nor do they yield anything that might be connected with the preceding scene.

That scene, however, which I have taken some pains to comment upon here, seems to me a vivid and alluringly written piece of dramatic acting. Earlier classicists (I have already quoted Arnott in this regard) found much to criticize in these verses: 'serious weaknesses in the writing', 'lack of verbal distinction', 'unimaginative repetition of words and phrases'. I have to confess that I cannot share these judgements: if there is repetition, it is very intentionally employed to convey a speaker's emotion; and what is meant by 'lack of verbal distinction', I am quite unable to discern. I have already noted that the riddling remarks of Phaidimos in vv. 41–7 and 48–54 may have been modelled after the angry Theseus in Euripides' *Hippolytos*; they might also be good examples of the γραφικὴ λέξις that Demetrius *On Style* attributes more to Philemon than to Menander. Furthermore, I already noted that the scene has justifiably been compared to the famous quarrel between friends in Menander's *Dis Exapatôn*; set against Menander's scene, the wording of this quarrel seems much more extravagant (almost baroque) and aiming at dramatic effects, and comparing this with Menander's elegant simplicity, one might be tempted to call this an 'un-Menandrean' style of presenting a quarrel on stage. So we may in effect have quite some, I will not say hard evidence, but at least some grounds for suspecting that this lively scene is not owed to Menander but to one of his great rivals.

My second example will take us from quarrelling friends to a probably much more unsavoury character, but not immediately: Com. Adesp. 1032 K.–A., again rejected by Arnott (above, p. 124), comprises all in all remains of 78 verses, of which, however, only 26 (written in iambic trimeters) are well-nigh completely preserved and thus legible and intelligible.

> (Α) τὸ δ]αιμόνιον τὰ τοιαῦτα το[ῖс] φ[ρονοῦсιν] ἐ[ῦ]
> παρα]δείγματ᾽ ἐκτίθεсιν, ἀλλοτρίαν ὅτι
> ζωὴ]ν ἔχομεν ἅπαντες, ἣν ὅταν δοκῇ
> πάλ]ιν παρ᾽ ἑκάστου ῥαιδίως ἀφείλετο.
> ἀλλ᾽] εἰсιὼν μετὰ τῆс ἱερείας βούλομαι                                5
> τὴν ἐπιμέλειαν τῶν προсηκόντων λαβεῖν.
> (Β) ἄνα]γ᾽, εὐλάβει, βέλτιστε· πρὸс θεῶν πάρες.
> διώ]κομαι γάρ, κατὰ κράτος διώκομαι
> ὑπὸ] τοῦ καταράτου κληρονόμου· ληφθήсομαι.
> (Γ) . . . . ] δίωκε, Cωсία, сυνάρπαсον                                    10
> τὸ]ν ἀνδραποδιстήν, λαβέ, λάβ᾽ αὐτόν. οὐ μενεῖς;
> (Β) ὦ φιλτάτη Δήμητερ, ἀνατίθημί сοι
> ἐμαυτόν, ἀξιῶ τε сώιζειν. (Γ) ποῖ сύ, ποῖ;
> (Β) ἤρου με; πρὸс τὴν ἀсφάλειαν ἐνθαδὶ
> ει . . . κ᾽ ἐμαυτὸν ἀντεταξάμην τέ сοι.                                15
> (Γ) οὐκ] ἔст[ι]ν ἀсφάλειά που πεποιηκότι
> τοιαῦτ᾽·] ἀκολ[ο]ύθει θᾶττον. (Β) ἃ ἃ μαρτύρομαι
> μαρ]τύρομ᾽ ὑμᾶс, ἄνδρες· ἂν τὴν χεῖρά μοι
> πα]ρ[ὰ] τῆι θεῶι τιс προсφέρηι, πεπλήξεται
> παραχρῆμά τ᾽ εὐθὺс τἀπίχειρα λήψεται.                              20
> (Γ) τί] φῄιс; ὑπὸ сοῦ, μαстιγία; (Β) νὴ τὸν Δία
> τὸ]ν Ὀλύμπιον καὶ τὴν Ἀθηνᾶν, εὖ γε καὶ
> πα]λαιстρικῶс· πεῖραν δ᾽ ἐὰν βούληι λαβέ.
> (?) ἅπ]αντες ἡμεῖс γ᾽ οἱ παρόντες ἐνθάδε
> . . . . . ]ομέν сε παρανομεῖν εἰс τὴν θεόν.                          25
> (Γ) . . . . . ]ό γ᾽, ἄνδρες, εὖ γε· προсπαίζειν δοκεῖ
> *(end of column)*

Our text starts at a quiet pace and on a rather sombre note: In vv. 1–4 a speaker pronounces consoling words—to someone else or to himself?—about a (real or alleged) loss of a human life: 'God puts such things before the eyes of sensible people to show them that we all have our lives not as a firm possession, but as something which he can easily take away again from each of us whenever it suits him (τὸ δ]αιμόνιον τὰ τοιαῦτα το[ῖc] φ[ρονοῦcιν] ἐ[ῦ] / παρα]δείγματ' ἐκτίθηcιν, ἀλλοτρίαν ὅτι / ζωὴ]ν ἔχομεν ἅπαντες, ἣν ὅταν δοκῆι / πάλ]ιν παρ' ἑκάστου ῥαιδίωc ἀφείλετο). In vv. 5–6 the same speaker continues and announces that he will now go inside 'with the priestess' and see to it that the necessary things are done (ἀλλ'] εἰcιὼν μετὰ τῆc ἱερείαc βούλομαι / τὴν ἐπιμέλειαν τῶν προcηκόντων λαβεῖν). Fulfilling this announcement, he then apparently goes into a building (a temple?), and this scene ends.

The stage, however, does not seem totally empty: apparently someone remains, who is then almost knocked over by a new character who literally bursts onto the stage from one of the side entrances in vv. 7–9 and shouts: 'Get out of the way! Take care, my friend! For the gods' sake, let me through! I'm being pursued, mightily pursued by the damned heir! He will catch me!' (ἄνα]γ', εὐλάβει, βέλτιcτε· πρὸc θεῶν πάρεc. / διώ]κομαι γάρ, κατὰ κράτοc διώκομαι / ὑπὸ] τοῦ καταράτου κληρονόμου· ληφθήcομαι). Thus opens a lively scene which apparently is very different from the preceding one; obviously the poet fully intended this glaring contrast.

The fugitive's anxieties are immediately shown to be well-founded, for already in the next line the pursuer appears, together with a slave as his helper: 'Come on, pursue him, Sosias, grab the kidnapper, take him, take him—[*to the fugitive*] will you stop?' (10–11: ἕπου,] δίωκε, Cωcία, cυνάρπαcον / τὸ]ν ἀνδραποδιcτήν, λαβέ, λάβ' αὐτόν. οὐ μενεῖc;). The fugitive, of course, does no such thing, but takes sanctuary at what seems to be an altar of the goddess Demeter in front of the temple which the person of the earlier scene had entered: 'Oh dearest Demeter, I render myself unto your protection and beg you to save me (12–13 ὦ φιλτάτη Δήμητερ, ἀνατίθημί cοι / ἐμαυτόν, ἀξιῶ τε cώιζειν). His pursuer tries to prevent this ('Where do you want to go, where?'), but the fugitive seems to have reached the safety-providing altar and now even behaves as if he were bracing himself to fight back: 'You ask? I've placed myself in this spot of safety and now take position against you!' (13–15 ποῖ cύ, ποῖ / (B) ἤμμι με; πρὸc τὴν θεφιλὴ ινι ἐνθαδὶ / ει . . κ' ἐμαυτὸν ἀντεταξάμην τέ cοι). Nevertheless the pursuer tries to drag him away: 'There is no safety for you anywhere, after you have done such things! Come on and follow me!' (16–17 οὐκ] ἔcτ[ι]ν ἀcφάλειά που πεποιηκότι / τοιαῦτ'·] ἀκολ[ο]ύθει θᾶττον), but the fugitive protests at the top of his voice and threatens even more to defend himself: 'Ah! Ah! I call you, men, as my witnesses, as my witnesses: if someone lays his hand on me, while I'm here at the side of the goddess, he will be hit and get the reward for his behaviour immediately' (17–20: ἃ ἃ μαρτύρομαι / μαρ]τύρομ' ὑμᾶς, ἄνδρες· ἂν τὴν χεῖρά μοι / πα]ρ[ὰ] τῆι θεῶι τις προσφέρηι, πεπλήξεται / παραχρῆμά τ' εὐθὺς τἀπίχειρα λήψεται). The pursuer reacts scornfully to this blustering: 'What? A hit from you, scoundrel?' (21: τί] φήις; ὑπὸ coῦ, μαςτιγία;), while the fugitive tries to keep up his threats: 'Oh yes, by Olympian Zeus and Athena, a nice and palaestra-like hit! Try it out, if you want to!' (21–3: νὴ τὸν Δία / τὸ]ν Ὀλύμπιον καὶ τὴν Ἀθηνᾶν, εὖ γε καὶ / πα]λαιστρικῶς· πεῖραν δ' ἐὰν βούληι λαβέ).

It is not totally clear who now replies with the following words: 'We all, who are present here, believe that you commit a sacrilege against the goddess' (vv. 24–5 ἅπ]αντες ἡμεῖς γ' οἱ παρόντες ἐνθάδε / νομίζ]ομέν ce παρανομεῖν εἰς τὴν θεόν). Could the speaker be the person whom the fugitive almost ran into at the beginning of the scene? A less likely possibility is the person who entered the temple at the end of the earlier scene, because on coming out he would surely have asked first what this commotion was all about. The last almost fully preserved line (26) seems then to be spoken again by the pursuer: 'Well spoken, friends! He thinks he can joke with us' (26 . . . .]ό γ', ἄνδρες, εὖ γε· προσπαίζειν δοκεῖ). One would have liked to see how this showdown developed further, but after the words just cited the column ends; of the remaining forty-nine verses too little is preserved to give us more information about the play to which the scene just described belongs.

We are certainly rather lucky to have just this scene preserved, because at least to my knowledge it is practically unique within the surviving (or up to now rediscovered) remains of Greek New Comedy. Up to a point, there is one scene preserved on papyrus from Menander's *Perinthia* which exhibits something similar, namely a terrified slave sitting as a refugee on an altar while preparations are being made to light a fire around him and thus drive him from his sanctuary. The man who flees to the altar in our fragment is a totally different person, trying to put on a brazen face vis-à-vis his pursuers and even to strike a self-righteous pose; and this man was no slave but probably—as the word μαςτιγία by which he is addressed in v. 21 seems to show—a pimp or brothel-keeper. We have no brothel-keeper acting similarly in the extant remains of Menander, but we know that Philemon presented a flamboyant πορνοβοσκός in his *Adelphoi* (fr. 3 K.–A.) praising great old Solon for his far-sighted founding of brothels. And again, we might have another good example for the γραφικὴ λέξις attributed to Philemon by Demetrius *On Style*. Of course, these are far from clinching arguments, but they may at least help us to keep an open mind regarding the attribution of this lively and interesting fragment.

## 6. Is The Rest Silence? Some Sober Summing-up

Even if the two preceding specimens of Greek New Comedy of the early third (and possibly even late fourth) century BC were really not written by Menander (which cannot be proved), the fact remains that our search for viable criteria to ascertain this has so far been in vain, and in the present state of our knowledge nothing is left to us to rely on but cautious and self-conscious subjectivity. Already tomorrow, one newly published scrap of papyrus may confirm my feeling that one of the pieces presented above really was written by someone else than Menander—or it may just as well totally confound this opinion. Whichever of these possibilities may happen, we simply must hope that more papyri from New Comedy will come to light and not only show us that attractive non-Menandrean plays were enjoyed both on the stage and by reading for at least some time after their authors had died, but also provide us with a better grasp of what made Menander stand out so much that he survived the others much longer and does so even today.

## BIBLIOGRAPHY

Arnott, W. G. 1979–2000, *Menander*, 3 vols. (Cambridge, MA, and London).

Austin, C. 1973, *Comicorum Graecorum fragmenta in papyris reperta* (Berlin and New York).

Gomme, A. W., and Sandbach, F. H. 1973, *Menander. A Commentary* (Oxford).

Kambylis, A. 1997, 'Abriß der byzantinischen Literatur', in Nesselrath 1997, 327–8.

Kassel, R. and Austin, C. (eds.) 1986, *Poetae Comici Graeci V: Damoxenus–Magnes* (Berlin and New York).

—— 1989, *Poetae Comici Graeci VII: Menecrates–Xenophon* (Berlin and New York).

—— 1995, *Poetae Comici Graeci VIII: Adespota* (Berlin and New York).

—— 1998, *Poetae Comici Graeci VI 2: Menandri Testimonia et Fragmenta apud scriptores servata* (Berlin and New York).

Nesselrath, H.-G. (ed.), 1997, *Einleitung in die griechische Philologie* (Stuttgart and Leipzig).

Wilson, N. G. 1997, 'Griechische Philologie in Byzanz', in Nesselrath 1997, 104–5.

# 7

## The Rediscovery of Menander

*Eric Handley*

### Introduction

The story I have to tell is twofold. It is about the recovery of text from papyri, beginning in the nineteenth century, advancing spectacularly in the twentieth, and continuing in the twenty-first. We wonder how long it will go on. It is not just about quantity. The new texts change our perspectives. We can ask more questions of them, and questions of new kinds. The parallel development is that of the recovery and study of visual material relating to these texts. It ranges from scenes depicted in paint or mosaic to statuettes of actors and images of the masks that they wore. Each of these objects, whether painted, paved, carved, or however made, is something to be interpreted in its own right. But these theatrical souvenirs also let us ask new questions about Menander; and together with the texts, they reflect the reception of Menander in the Western world over a period of about a millennium after his death in or about 291 BC. It follows that what I have to say will be highly selective, but I hope not inappropriately so.

Papyrus, made from the pith of reeds, includes, for our purposes, vellum, made from animal skins. While planning this survey, I was asked to look at an unpublished scrap of a vellum codex from Oxyrhynchus. Between the two sides, it has some eighteen words that can be made out, including a proper name; there is another abbreviated name in the margin, and a further word or two can be reasonably guessed. It is now in a volume of *The Oxyrhynchus Papyri*, the series that Peter Parsons has done so much to promote, both before and during his tenure of the Regius Chair of Greek, and still now. It is a small offering, but new; and I am grateful for the chance to present it here. It will be referred to later on. The text is set out at p. 156 below.

This scrap may do to illustrate the backroom side of work on new frag- ments. Many more await study and publication. They come, as a rule, without any predetermined identity. As a rule—this applies also to everything else I say here—as a rule, the style of the handwriting distinguishes a literary text from a document; metre distinguishes verse from prose; dialogue, part-marking and style, where there is enough to tell, distinguish drama from other verse and tragedy from comedy; possibly Old Comedy from New. By these tests, our vellum scrap is a scrap of New Comedy. What it contributes, and whether it is Menander or not, we shall consider later. For now, we should look at the bigger picture, in which this piece might be an interesting coloured dot.

## Survival and Recovery

Books rarely survive from Antiquity, even more rarely whole books or sub-stantial parts of them. An exception is the Cairo Codex of Menander.[1] Once he had done with it, its owner, a senior civil servant, Dioskoros of Aphro-ditopolis, used its leaves as protective topping for a jar in which he kept documents. It was then about a hundred years old, like my disintegrating Oxford Text of Aristophanes, replaced at last by Nigel Wilson's new edition (2007). So the Cairo Menander was found when Dioskoros' house was excavated. Another exception is the Bodmer Codex,[2] found buried in the sands in an abandoned monastery library; it was much used, and had had to be resewn twice. These two are epoch-making in the rediscovery of Menander—early-twentieth-century and post-mid-century.

For other whole books surviving *in situ*, one thinks of Herculaneum. Among the carbonized book-rolls found there is a copy of a play of New Comedy in Latin, with the recognizable title *Obolostates siue Faenerator*, 'The Moneylender', of Caecilius Statius;[3] but, it seems, no Menander yet. Techniques of reading this very difficult material are still being developed; they are applicable to some of the Menander papyri. Caecilius' play, first identified in the 1990s, is the first text, apart from quotations, of any Latin writer of New Comedy other than Plautus and Terence to survive to the present day. Perhaps there is more to come.[4]

---

[1] Cairo, Egyptian Museum, P.Cair JE43227, 2nd half of 5th c. AD, Aphroditopolis. H. 30.1 cm × 18 cm; 33–8 lines (usually 35), Menander (*Heros, Epitr., Perik., Samia*, etc. [C]. Ed. pr. Lefebvre 1907, 1911; new facs. Koenen 1978; Cavallo and Machler 1987, pl. 16b; Turner 1977, no. 227.

[2] Geneva, Bibliothèque Bodmer, P.Bodmer 25+4+26, and other minor frr., 1st half of 4th c. AD, provenance not stated: Panopolis (?). H. 27.5 cm × 13 cm; 45–54 lines (fol. 19ʳ only 38). Menander, *Samia, Dysk., Aspis*. [B]. Ed. pr. (4), Martin 1958, (25–6) Kasser and Austin 1969*a*; 1969*b*, with plates; Cavallo and Maehler 1987, pl. 5b; Turner 1977, no. 225.

[3] Naples, P.Herc. 78. Research progresses: see Kleve 1996; 2001.

[4] I am grateful to the First Naples Conference of the Friends of Herculaneum Society, June/July 2006, for up-to-date reports of the excavations and a sight of P.Herc. 78 and other papyri.

You could say that the Cairo Menander was recycled, being used not as a book but as packaging. Another mode of recycling is when old books were cut up as core material for plaster mummy cases, which were then surfaced and painted. Such is the Milan Posidippus Papyrus, with its hundred-odd previously unknown epigrams, first fully published in 2001.[5] Written material from mummy cartonnage was being obtained very much earlier, admittedly at first by rather primitive methods. From the later third century BC we have the papyrus roll of Menander's *Sikyonioi* in Paris. Parts of it were extracted and published (though not then identified) in 1906, the rest in 1965.[6] There is scope for more recoveries of this kind.[7]

Writing material was often reused. The back of a roll, perhaps an out-of-date account, is less good for writing than the carefully prepared front side; but sound sheets can be used to make a practicable copy of a play or other text, like the Oxyrhynchus *Dis Exapaton*, with its tall columns of 51 lines.[8] Oxyrhynchus offers other comparable examples.[9]

Otherwise—I am thinking especially of vellum, but also of papyrus—the ink could be scrubbed or scraped off, and the sheets refashioned to take a new text. There is great interest currently in palimpsested manuscripts of this kind, and in advanced techniques of image intensification for deciphering them. A recent discovery is a twice-palimpsested manuscript in the Vatican that includes two leaves with nearly 200 lines each from *Dyskolos* and another play of Menander.[10] This codex is represented in the bottom script, dated to the fourth century AD. Its remains await comprehensive decipherment. It may one day be thought to mark another epoch of rediscovery, along with the Cairo Codex and the Bodmer Codex. Even now, it has its value. With so economical a format, at five or six leaves a play, it must have contained a

---

[5]   Milan, P.Mil.Vogl. VIII 309. *Ed. pr.* Bastianini and Gallazzi 2001.

[6]   Paris, Inst. de Papyrologie de Paris, P.Sorb inv. 2272–3 + 72, later 3rd c. BC, Ghoran. H. 16 cm; 21–4 lines per column. Menander, *Sikyonioi* (*-os*). [S]. *Ed. pr.* (2272–3, with 72 re-edited), Blanchard and Bataille 1965, with facs. Turner and Parsons 1987, no. 40; Handley 1997, 186–7.

[7]   The advantage of this source of supply is that once you have extracted the papyrus by chemical (or preferably biochemical) means, it is (or should be: it isn't always) in a stable and relatively easy-to-read state. The disadvantage is that you destroy the painted surface, unless you take great care to remount it on a model of what you propose to undo. I am grateful here to personal contacts over the years with André Bataille, Knut Kleve, and W. H. Willis. See Handley 1988 for an account of early experiments in London and elsewhere.

[8]   Egypt Exploration Society, P.Oxy. 4407, 3rd/4th c. AD (on the back of a document with date AD 241/2), Oxyrhynchus. H. 32 cm; 51 lines per column. Menander, *Dis Exapaton*. [O13]. Ed.pr. (in part) in Handley 1968; (in full), P.Oxy. LXIV (1997) 4407, with pl. iii; Sandbach 1990; Arnott 2004, 37–8.

[9]   On the range of sizes and styles of Oxyrhynchus rolls, see Johnson 2004.

[10]   Vatican, BAV, sir. 623, ff. 212 + 217 and 211 + 218, 1st half of 4th c. AD, provenance not certain, twice later palimpsested. H. *c.*27.5 cm × 24.5, two columns, each of 49 lines. Menander, *Dyskolos* [305]–402 + 403–[500] (196 lines). A leaf of a vellum codex, and another leaf with a different play (?*Titthe*). Description and discussion in D'Aiuto 2003, 266–83 with tavv. 13–14 and fig. 1.

collection of plays by Menander; for what it is worth, the play still to have its identity confirmed was not, as might have been expected, one of the two companions of *Dyskolos* in the Bodmer Codex. It looks as if one should be more and more cautious in drawing up a canon of survivors. Our small scrap represents one more codex, and it too must have had more than one play.

The most numerous survivors, like our small scrap, are pieces of books that were just thrown away, sometimes roughly cut up or torn before they were. Sometimes a clutch of broken pieces can be expertly reassembled, as with the roll of *Dis Exapaton,* or the leaf from a codex containing *Aspis*[11]—both of these indebted to Dr Walter Cockle—or there is Sir Eric Turner's reconstruction of the fragmentary Oxyrhynchus codex of *Misoumenos,*[12] a play which, since then, has acquired more text still. Next to pieces that are certainly identified (as when they overlap with a text already known) there is a throng of ghosts waiting to drink blood, so that they can speak to us. All told, we can think of a good thousand years of copies, of which we have our thin, small, valuable, essentially random scatter.

'Overlap with a text already known' usually means coincidence with a reliably attested quotation. Quotations (and similar reminiscences) were all there was of Menander until the first stirrings of rediscovery in the nineteenth century. The stock is large—say about a thousand items—and very varied. There are single word citations in lexica and grammars; single lines or short extracts quoted for their antiquarian interest or their improving sentiments; and among all this, passages with intellectual impact or literary appeal. All are the product of selection, for whatever purpose, whether now obvious or not; they are not random survivals, as papyrus fragments essentially are. With hindsight, we can recognize some limitations of this quoted material. It barely reflects the niceties of Menander's stage dialogue; it necessarily falls short on dramatic movement or plot, and on the depiction of character. To test this, look at a play of Shakespeare's in the *Oxford Dictionary of Quotations,* and throw in a few entries culled from the *OED* or elsewhere. Here too work is not static. That is plain from volume VI 2 of Kassel–Austin, *Poetae Comici Graeci* (1998), as well as from studies by these editors and others of other comic poets. Menander is still particularly important because of the comparisons we can make between the direct transmission of the text represented by papyri and the indirect transmission from quotations.[13]

---

[11] Egypt Exploration Society, P.Oxy. 4094, later 6th c. AD, Oxyrhynchus. H. 31.5 cm × [18–19], 29 and 33 lines. Menander, *Aspis,* remains of vv. 170–98 and 199–231. One leaf, with page numbers ρμβ (142) and ρμγ (143). *Ed. pr.,* Handley, P.Oxy. LXI (1995), 4094, with pls. i–iv; see also Handley and Hurst 1990, 143–8; Jacques 1998, pp. cvi–cix.

[12] Egypt Exploration Society, P.Oxy. 2656, 4th c. AD, Oxyrhynchus. H. 30+ × 14 cm, 35–40 lines. Menander, *Misoumenos.* Four reconstructed leaves from a single-quire codex [O10]. *Ed. pr.* Turner 1965, with facs.; id. 1977, no. 234a.

[13] A few examples with discussion: Handley and Hurst 1990, 125–9.

# Then and Now: Gilbert Murray's Menander

Gilbert Murray was born in 1866. It was some years after he had moved from Oxford to succeed Jebb in Glasgow (that was in 1889) that the first whole leaf of a codex of Menander was published, the leaf of *Georgos* in Geneva.[14] When the Cairo Codex was published in 1907, he was back in Oxford again; the next year, he was Regius Professor. Though there were other accessions in his lifetime, Murray's Menander is essentially that of the Cairo plays: he died in 1957, before *Dyskolos* became generally available. Murray's translations from Greek Tragedy sold in their tens of thousands. As well as Aristophanes' *Frogs,* he translated *Perikeiromene* (*The Rape of the Locks,* 1942), and *Epitrepontes* (*The Arbitration,* 1945; 2nd edn. 1949), restoring and reconstructing freely as he went.[15] There are lucid essays by him on Menander in J. U. Powell and E. A. Barber's *New Chapters in Greek Literature* (1929) and as a final chapter of his own *Aristophanes: A Study* (1933). As a measure of what has happened since that time, F. G. Allinson's Loeb edition of Menander, published in 1921, makes one volume of 540 pages; Geoffrey Arnott's Loeb Menander—true, with more commentary—makes three volumes, published between 1979 and 2000, with a total of 1674 pages. Even so, when volume I is replaced, there will be more of *Epitrepontes* to add, some of it first edited by Peter Parsons;[16] some more recently identified material from this play is published in volume LXXIII (2009) of *Oxyrhynchus Papyri.*

In his essay in *New Chapters,* Gilbert Murray began by regretting that 'even after the great discoveries in papyri . . . we have no single comedy complete'. Like many in earlier generations, including Goethe,[17] he admired the quotations for their elegance and human sympathy. One can sense how strongly they would have appealed to his fine sensitivity to the Greek language and to the liberal temperament that inspired his work for the United Nations. From there, it was a congenial step to his sympathetic treatment of (as he puts it, making a paradox) 'plays in which the heroines are generally either prostitutes or girls who have illegitimate children and the heroes worthless

---

[14] Geneva, PGenève inv. 155, 5th–6th c. AD, acquired in Egypt, provenance unknown. H. [30] × [18] cm, written area 27 × 12 cm, 44/43 lines. Menander, *Georgos* 1–87. [G]. Single leaf, numbered ϛ′(6) and ζ′(7). *Ed. pr.* Nicole 1897–8; facs. *New Pal. Soc.* 1, Pt 4 (1906), 74–5; Turner 1977, no. 230; Austin 2004.

[15] Though they made much less theatrical mileage than the translations from tragedy, the two Menander translations have sometimes been produced on stage, and were broadcast by the BBC: Wilson 1987, 395. For some other productions of Menander, see Blume 1998, 44–5 and nn.

[16] P.Oxy. LX (1994), 4020–3, with other Menander. See now Furley 2009.

[17] See Blume 1988, 35 with n. 55; ch. 2 of this book, pp. 16–45, is cordially recommended for a fuller account of the loss and recovery of Menander than that given above. See now also Blanchard 2007, 9–27.

young rakes'. The wars and upheavals of the later fourth century, as seen from Athens, enter little into the world of Menander's characters. Their lives are in some sense an escape from reality; but servitude, statelessness, the break-up of families, exile, and other misfortunes are in the background to make situations that can call into question the demands of black-and-white moral rules. Against this background, with special reference to *Epitrepontes* and *Perikeiromene*, Murray's essay makes his case in the dramatist's favour. Given the state of some societies today, with still more experience of global turmoil and disturbed values, one can go a long way in sympathy with this approach.

For all that, as Murray well knew, the response of Menander to the world about him is more complex than might seem. We see this when quotations that have meant so much for the appreciation of the writer are viewed in a perspective supplied by their context. 'Whom the gods love die young', from the *Dis Exapaton*, is the first of the quotations admired by Murray in the essay of 1929 that we are quoting. It has another colour when we consider the context given by Plautus' adaptation in the *Bacchides*, where it is a slave's sarcastic remark to his elderly master (816–17). Similarly, a passage several times quoted, and once put together as Fragment 117, is now *Dyskolos* 447–53. Elaborate sacrifices, it says, are performed to please those who make them, not the gods; true piety comes with the simplest offerings. This, we now know, is part of a protest by the misanthrope Knemon about disturbances at the shrine next to his house. The context gives an edge, or an ironic twist, which the excerpt itself lacks: the flower in the vase looks different from the flower on the plant.[18]

Examples can be multiplied. They show that context in Menander is vitally important. It is not just a matter of giving a familiar topic a fresh impact. The same principle applies on a much larger scale, in regard to scene-setting, structure, and characterization; and it has been much easier to recognize as we have more continuous text. Knemon's denunciation of extravagant sacrifices, apart from its immediate effect, has a function in the character-portrait that the play provides. Alongside the anger and the hostility to his fellow men, there appears a core of principled attitude with which we are invited to identify. It is sometimes said that characters in New Comedy do not develop. What does develop is the impression we form of them from different contexts—that is, not only from their words and actions as they are presented directly, but from what other characters say to them and do to them and say about them. We are enabled, indeed tacitly invited, to evaluate these words and actions in accordance with their sources. Knemon does not appear in the play until v. 153. The build-up to his appearance is not unlike that given to two other extraordinary characters: Philoctetes in Sophocles' tragedy and the

---

[18] And sometimes *is* different: see n. 13 above; but I am here concerned with context, not textual variation.

Cyclops in Euripides' satyr-play. We see all three first though other eyes; our first view of Knemon comes from Pan in the prologue speech. We go on through the play's pattern of incidents, with Knemon at the core of them, until his long speech that brings the dramatic climax (708–47). Now had the whole work survived only as this one speech, much of what has been written about Knemon could still have been written. But in a narrative description of character, we lose the dramatic interest of the presentation. I take Knemon as an example to show how conspicuously, in this kind of drama, a whole play, or large parts of one, scores over short or incomplete sequences, never mind the briefer kind of excerpt.

Fortune's lesser gifts are not to be despised. Following on the *Dyskolos*, the 1960s saw the recovery of large parts of *Sikyonios* and *Misoumenos*, as well as the much-tattered lines of *Dis Exapaton* with their special interest from Plautus' adaptation in *Bacchides*.[19] None of this, of course, was known to Murray. An example of what he could appreciate, and help others to appreciate, is the short scene in *Perikeiromene* between Polemon and Pataikos, which (like Knemon's speech in *Dyskolos*) is at the heart of the play. Glykera left Polemon, we recall, because he had cut off her hair with his sword in a rage brought on by the belief, in fact false, that she was being unfaithful. Here, from the 1929 essay, is an extract from Murray's treatment of it:

> (*Pataikos*) Of course, if she had been your wife. . . .
> (*Polemon*) What a thing to say! If!
> (*Pataikos*) Well, there is a difference.
> (*Polemon*) I regard Glykera as my wife.
> (*Pataikos*) Who gave her in marriage to you?
> (*Polemon*) She herself.

'Very good,' says Pataecus, 'No doubt she liked you then, and now she has left you because you have not treated her properly . . .'. 'Not treated her properly!', cries the poor soldier, 'That hurts me . . .'.

The translation is not literal, but admirably catches the pace of Menander's dialogue: less happy is the narrative interjection 'cries the poor soldier': he is better speaking for himself.

As a tailpiece to this: *The Times* of 18 January 2006 reports a case in which a Mr Smith (we are not told with what motives of anger or jealousy) cut off his ex-girlfriend's ponytail with the kitchen scissors. She sued, and lost her case before the magistrates, who held that the removal of hair did not constitute an assault occasioning actual bodily harm. The High Court rejected this view on appeal, holding that Mr Smith had a case to answer. Is modern truth, I wonder, stranger than ancient fiction? And in ancient fiction, is there still food for thought?

---

[19] See above, nn. 6, 12, and 8.

## The Shock of the New

How far do the newer discoveries match Murray's passage of *Perikeiromene*? I could make choices, but that would be anthologizing all over again, and it seems preferable to consider some of the overall gains that more text brings us.

With more text, the grammar of dramatic composition is clearer. We now have three plays, *Misoumenos* and *Epitrepontes*, as well as *Dyskolos*, that are verifiably divided into five acts; the other survivals are consistent with this pattern, and it is reflected in the Mytilene mosaics; it would now be rash to suppose that it was not standard in Menander's time. With more examples available, something can also be said about a characteristic pattern of act-endings. Quite often, the high moments of action are brought down, and a new development initiated, by the entry, for a short appearance at the end of the act, of a new character or characters who will open up a theme that is to be prominent in the next act, thus at once leading to the break between acts and bridging it. This is not simply a mechanical phenomenon; it is one of the ways of keeping the higher moments of high comedy in control.[20]

Much attention has been given to theatrical conventions in the last generation of 30-plus years, with (for example) a book-length study of structural patterns in Menander by Alain Blanchard.[21] While the longer pieces allow us to discern recurrent patterns of composition and their variations, the shorter pieces may then fall recognizably into place and in return fill out the picture. Recurrent formulae let us recognize fragments for what they are, even from a coincidence of a few letters, as with the introduction of the chorus and at the end of plays.[22] The formal language of an Athenian betrothal appears repeatedly.[23] Its appearance in our new fragment, even to the extent of 'dowry' and 'take your sister', shows us what is happening; the fact that the incident is spread over two sides of a leaf suggests that this time the proceedings are more developed than some. It is satisfying to see a norm established; but we are dealing with a creative situation, not a legislative one: we should allow, with due caution, that the dramatist sometimes overrides his

[20] The integral role of minor characters is important here: see e.g. three case studies by Hurst 2004; or the discussion of cook-scenes by Handley 1970, 3–17. See also next n.

[21] Blanchard 1983; Blume 1998, 32–6, Handley 1987, on acts and scenes; Bain 1977, on actors and audience; Frost 1988, on exits and entrances.

[22] Introduction of the Chorus: for the formula 'I'm off: there are people coming', with some variants, see on *Dyskolos* 230–2 and Handley and Hurst 1990, 130–1, with *PCG* VIII 1153; for play-endings, see on *Dyskolos* 968–9, with Handley and Hurst, 131–2, and *PCG* VI 2 *903, 908, *910.

[23] For betrothal formulae, see on *Dyskolos* 842–4, with Gomme and Sandbach 1973 on *Perik.* 1010–1, and P.Oxy. LXVIII 4646, noting also P.Oxy. XV 1824 in *PCG* VIII 1045, where in 12 λα]μβάν[ω δέ]χομα[ι seems to be recognizable.

own rules. It is good, if we guess that he did so, also to guess why; and to remember what a small sample of our author we have: perhaps 5%, even now, as opposed to about a quarter of Aristophanes.[24] I shall not remark here on the many ingenious and instructive attempts that have been made to recover Menander from Plautus and Terence; if I did, I should want to stress the improved understanding of all three authors that comes as we rediscover more of one of them.

From the Testimonia in editions of Menander, one can readily see something of the division between admirers of his language, like Plutarch and Quintilian, and his detractors, notably the Atticists Phrynichus and Pollux.[25] Their canons of purism may well have contributed to a reduced circulation of the plays in circles aspiring to correct literary usage. Among the first studies to exploit the new text from the Bodmer Codex was a paper by Sandbach in 1970.[26] Currently, interest in the language of Greek comedy is well shown in a book of essays edited by Andreas Willi with a valuable introduction by him.[27] The references to Menander in recent commentaries on Aristophanes also demonstrate the impact that the new texts have had. Menander's innovation is not in vocabulary, for his range is limited, compared with Aristophanes, and he is much less colourful: special situations apart,[28] he deploys a relatively confined choice of words to convey, in delicate informal versification, an impression of the live spoken discourse of personal relationships.

One idiom may serve as a case-study: 'Speech within Speech'. This is the current term for what happens when characters quote words directly, often without such explanatory phrases as 'he asked', 'she said', and so on.[29] The device is not unique to Menander, but was well developed by him, and he is followed by Terence. It must have called for a refined style of acting. When the text is damaged, it certainly calls for, and sometimes defeats, skilled editing; and it is not always easy to translate. One of the nicest examples, though not new, is in *Samia*, Act III at 252–61. Demeas, in soliloquy, tells what he overheard the women saying as they prepare Moschion's wedding feast in the kitchen:

---

[24] Blume 1998, 16; cf. 44.

[25] See e,g, *PCG* VI 2 Test. 101 and 103–4 as against 119 and 120 (= 38, 41–2, 46 and 47 KT).

[26] Sandbach 1970, 'Menander's manipulation of language for dramatic purposes'.

[27] Willi 2002.

[28] Special situations: for instance the bogus doctor with his Doric dialect at *Aspis* 431–64; and occasional passages where tragic or other poetic idiom raises the tone above the norm of colloquial style, as in recognition scenes like *Perik.* 779–827, where we have also stricter, tragic-style metre and single-line exchanges of dialogue in the tragic manner. See further *Dysk.* 946–53 and commentators there; *Theophoroumene* 31–57 Arnott; *Leukadia* 11–16 Arnott.

[29] Survey and discussion: Nünlist 2002; for background, Bers 1997. See also Arnott 1979–2000, ii. 252 on *Misoumenos*; Lamagna 1998, 289–302; Handley 2002, 178–87, from which, with minor alterations, the following quotation and discussion derive.

"λούϲατ᾽, ὦ τάλαν,
τὸ παιδίον" φηϲίν, "τί τοῦτ᾽; ἐν τοῖϲ γάμοιϲ
τοῖϲ τοῦ πατρὸϲ τὸν μικρὸν οὐ θεραπεύετε;"
εὐθὺϲ δ᾽ ἐκείνη "δύϲμορ᾽, ἡλίκον λαλεῖϲ"      255
φήϲ᾽· "ἔνδον ἐϲτὶν αὐτόϲ." "οὐ δήπου γε· ποῦ;"
"ἐν τῶι ταμιείωι", καὶ παρεξήλλαξέ τι·
"αὐτὴ καλεῖ, τίτθη, ϲε" καὶ "βάδιζε καὶ
ϲπεῦδ᾽· οὐκ ἀκήκο᾽ οὐδέν· εὐτυχέϲτατα."
εἰποῦϲ᾽ ἐκείνη δ᾽ "ὦ τάλαινα τῆϲ ἐμῆϲ      260
λαλιᾶϲ", ἀπῆιξεν ἐκποδών, οὐκ οἶδ᾽ ὅποι.

'Oh dear, do bath the baby, girls,' says she, 'How can you neglect the little one on his father's wedding day?' Quick as quick, 'Oh, you do talk loud,' says the girl, 'Master's in there' 'No, surely not. Where?' 'In the pantry'—and then she raised her voice a bit, 'Mistress wants you, Nurse: off you go, hurry. (He's heard nothing, by great good luck)'. 'Oh dear, I do talk so,' says she, and away she goes somewhere or other.

It is typical of Menander that there is more to the seemingly trivial exchange than this short quotation shows. In its context, it has the double irony of the unintended (and therefore credible) revelation to Demeas of the baby's parentage, together with that of the young girl's misplaced confidence that he had heard nothing. It is for the actor to do what he can with that. He may be good at playing women's parts; but here he has to speak as an old man quoting women, and in a situation typical of women's lives, without losing his own dramatic identity. For Quintilian, in a well-known passage (*Inst.* 11. 3. 90–1), the young orator should not overdo the effect of mimicry when he quotes people, as some actors do in Menander, as when a young man in quoting an old man makes his voice tremble, or switches to a treble when playing a woman.[30]

## Images of New Comedy

The first facsimile of the Cairo Codex was published by Gustave Lefebvre in Cairo in 1911; so, in Halle, was Carl Robert's *Die Masken der neueren attischen Komödie*. Of the editors and critics of Menander, Alfred Koerte and T. B. L. Webster were especially familiar with the visual representations of comedy.[31] The terracottas of Lipari come from excavations of 1948 onwards;[32] the

---

[30] '. . . cum mihi comoedi quoque pessime facere uideantur quod, etiam si iuuenem agant, cum tamen in expositione aut senis sermo, ut in Hydriae prologo, aut mulieris, ut in Georgo, incidit, tremula uel effeminata uoce pronuntiant . . .'.

[31] They met in the late 1920s in Leipzig, where Webster attended seminars after graduation from Oxford, and became a family friend (D. J. Allan, pers. comm., 1975).

[32] See especially Bernabò Brea 1981; 2001.

mosaics of Mytilene were known from the late 1960s;[33] continuing surveys by Richard Green in *Lustrum* show how active this field of work now is.[34] Not everyone is equally entranced; nor was Gilbert Murray in his time. He writes, in the 1929 essay quoted above (p. 142), of 'the grotesque comic masks found on vases and frescoes', dismissing in the same sentence the Latin plays as 'the rather coarse-grained and dissolute imitations of Plautus and Terence' (p. 11); he is there pointing up an argument; he has a little more to say on masks at pp. 22–3; and on New Comedy in Latin at p. 33: 'the Roman adaptations of Plautus and Terence, the former much rougher, coarser and more boisterous in form, the latter showing much delicacy of style, but somewhat flattened and enfeebled'.

It can be asked (though here I shall do no more than ask) how far such aesthetic considerations are still valid after nearly half a century of new discoveries and of changes of perception. What is clear is that the tradition represented by the visual representations of New Comedy has its own contributions to make to the study of the plays and fragments as well as to the reception of Menander and his contemporaries in later centuries. A few examples may serve adequately to illustrate this, and also to ask speculatively if there are any representations that relate specifically to plays other than Menander's.

Menander himself first. The Lipari image, dating from before 252 BC, is the oldest surviving portrait (Fig. 7.1).[35] The St Petersburg head is a good specimen of the many later examples.[36] New discoveries and fresh study in the last thirty years have helped to distinguish portraits of Menander from portraits of Virgil; they can be very like each other.[37]

In the Mytilene *Samia*, at the moment we see, Demeas believes (wrongly) that his partner has had a child by his adopted son. He throws her out: οὔκουν ἀκούεις; ἄπιθι (369). The cook/caterer comments from the background (Pl. 8(a)).[38] That adds a dimension to the audience's viewpoint. It also keeps the emotional temperature within bounds proper to Comedy. Chrysis has the baby with her. Neither text nor picture tells us for sure if she also had with

---

[33] The basic publication is Charitonidis, Kahil, and Ginouvès 1970.

[34] Green 1989; 1995 [1998]; 2008. The increasing volume of the work surveyed, including discussions of theatres, is evident from the number of pages, and still more clearly from the number of items in each survey, respectively 670, 1083, and 1612.

[35] Terracotta portrait mask of Menander, Lipari, before 252 BC. Bernabò Brea 1981, frontispiece, cf. 245–6 with fig. 415; id. 2001, 167 with fig. 230.

[36] Marble portrait head of Menander in St Petersburg, Hermitage inv. 850, 1st/2nd c. AD or later. Richter 1965, ii, Menander no. 37.

[37] On portraits of Menander, see further Charitonidis, Kahil, and Ginouvès 1970, 27–31; Fittschen 1991; Ashmole 1973; Webster 1995, under 3AS 5.

[38] Mosaic floor panel with scene from Menander, *Samia*, Act III (369 ff.), Chorapha, Mytilene, AD 350 or later. Charitonidis, Kahil, and Ginouvès 1970, T 5; Webster 1995, XZ 31 (6DM 2.5); Ferrari 2004, 128–9; Dedoussi 2006.

**Fig. 7.1.** Portrait-mask of Menander, Lipari.

her the old nurse and her attendant women: they are referred to, but were they taken for granted by both producer and artist? Commentators differ: the latest, Christina Dedoussi, in her recent edition, thinks that they were on stage. If so, the picture simplifies the staging.

We can guess that the scene in the lost *Plokion* (Pl. 8(*b*)) was similar (we do know that the old man there quarrelled with his wife). It would just be a guess, perhaps worthwhile. The composition may have been derivative, even if the situation was broadly parallel.[39]

*Theophoroumene* is more complicated. The Mytilene mosaic recalls a lively spectacle with music (Pl. 9(*a*)).[40] Two young men appear as votaries of Cybele, with musical instruments typical of her cult; they perform a cult-tune to test if the girl's possession by the goddess is genuine. That much we get, in the first instance, from a combination of the labelled mosaic scene with the fragment

[39] Mosaic floor panel with scene from Menander, *Plokion*, Act II, Mytilene. Charitonidis, Kahil, and Ginouvès 1970, T 2; Webster 1995, XZ 29 (6DM 2.1); the fragments in Sandbach 1990, 311 ff., *PCG* VI. 2.

[40] Mosaic floor panel with scene from Menander, *Theophoroumene*, Act II, Mytilene. Charitonidis, Kahil, and Ginouvès 1970, T 8; Webster 1995, XZ 39–40 (6DM 2.5); Handley 1969; Csapo 1997 with Handley 1997, 197; Ferrari 2004, 130–3. For the fragments, see Sandbach 1990, 143 ff., Arnott 1979–2000, ii. 49 ff., and further Bastianini in Bastianini and Casanova 2004, 205–14 with tavv. ii iii, on PSI 1480, 1st c. BC/1st AD, provenance unknown, ascribed by Handley 1969 to this play (vv. 31–57 Arnott). See further Nervegna 2010.

of an elegant papyrus roll that was thereby confirmed in its identity.[41] The Mytilene representation differs, however, from the scene as given by two mosaics found at Pompeii, one entire (Pl. 9(*b*)), one fragmentary,[42] as well as a wall-painting from neighbouring Stabiae (Pl. 10(*a*));[43] these also relate to terracottas from Myrina (Pl. 10(*b*)) and Lyon (Fig. 10(*c*)) with replicas of the two main figures.[44] The Mytilene version substitutes the slave Parmenon for the piper, and switches the small boy from left to right. Excited by the new discovery, I and others more expert than myself thought that the Mytilene version gave a different point in the action. Eric Csapo applies a radical corrective.[45] He argues that in their context the scenes are dominated by artistic and compositional considerations and not by recollections of staging. It is easier to disagree with some of the answers obtained by this approach than to disagree with the admirable basic question. It is best addressed together with the depictions of *Synaristosai*, to which we turn.

Compared with the Dioskourides version (Pl. 11(*a*)),[46] the Mytilene scene of *Synaristosai* is again out of step. It transposes right to left; at the left is the old woman making the speaking gesture, with the small attendant tucked behind her (Pl. 11(*b*)).[47] The Zeugma version of the scene, a recent discovery, is composed in a rectangle, not in a square (like the Stabiae version of

---

[41] Florence, Bibl. Medicea Laurenziana, PSI 1280, late 1st/2nd c. AD, Oxyrhynchus. H. 15cm; 15 lines per column. Menander, *Theophoroumene* [F2]. *Ed. pr.* Norsa and Vitelli 1935; facs. Norsa 1939, tav. 9D. For its text, see Sandbach and Arnott, as in previous n.

[42] (i) Floor-mosaic (illustrated) signed by Dioskourides of Samos, Naples, Mus. Nazionale 9985, from Pompeii, late 2nd c. BC after original of *c*.300 BC. Menander, *Theophoroumene*. Webster 1995, 3DM 2; Trendall and Webster 1971, frontispiece (with the Mytilene version, above, n. 40), see under V. 3–4. (ii) Floor-mosaic, fragmentary, Pompeii, Ufficio scavi, inv. 17735. Stefani 1999 [2000], 279–80 with fig. 4. Menander, *Theophoroumene*, composition as in (i) above and the Stabiae painting, n. 43 below, confirming small figure at left, two young men (cymbalist and tambourine-player) with music girl; discussion by Green 2008, 231.

[43] Wall-painting, Naples, Mus. Naz. 9034, from a villa in Campo Verano, Stabiae, 1st c. AD. Menander, *Theophoroumene*, after the same archetype as (i)–(ii) in n. 42. Webster 1995, 5NP 1; Andreae 2003, Abb. 226.

[44] (i) Terracotta statuette in Athens, NM 5060, from Myrina, 2nd c. BC. Cymbalist (= Lysias in *Theophoroumene*). Trendall and Webster 1971, V. 10; Bieber 1961, fig. 342; (ii) Terracotta statuette in Lyon, E–272–43, from Myrina, 2nd c. BC. The lower arms broken—but recognizable as Kleinias, the tambourine-player of *Theophoroumene*. Trendall and Webster 1971, V. 9; Bieber 1961, fig. 341 is similar.

[45] Csapo 1997.

[46] Floor-mosaic signed by Dioskourides of Samos, Naples NM 9987, from Pompeii, late 2nd c. BC, a pair with that of n. 42 (i) above. Menander, *Synaristosai*. Webster 1995, under XZ 37 (3DM 1); Bieber 1961, fig. 347; Green and Handley 1995, fig. 50.

[47] Mosaic floor panel, Mytilene; Charitonidis, Kahil, and Ginouvès 1970, T 6; Green and Handley 1995, fig. 51; Webster 1995, under XZ37 (6DM 2.3), with the mosaic of n. 46 above. Trendall and Webster 1971, V. 1 and colour plate facing p. 8, again with the mosaic of n. 46. Opening scene of Menander, *Synaristosai*, Act I (= Plautus, *Cistellaria* 1 ff.); fragments, Arnott 1979–2000, iii, including P.Heid. 175 and P.Oxy. 4305 (*PCG* VIII, adesp. 1074, 1155), both ascribed; Arnott 2004, 49–53.

*Theophoroumene*); it has a second small attendant on the left (Pl. 12(*a*)).[48] If an inspired guess by Thierfelder is correct, an unattributed line of comedy was the first line of this play. What the old woman said was 'On my oath by Artemis, I really have enjoyed my lunch.' Plautus in his version doubles up the remark, once for each guest.[49] More than one force may be at work; my present view is that in the Mytilene dining room the traditional stage scenes were modified to reflect recitations from the plays, not productions. Hence the interest, not only in the titles, but in giving the act and the characters' names. In *Theophoroumene*, Parmenon the slave replaces the pipe-player because he has a speaking part and the piper hasn't. In *Synaristosai*, the old woman Philainis is on the left because she speaks first. One reads the picture left-to-right like a scene-heading. So, in the *Samia* scene, the cook, on the left, speaks first because his movement into the background marks the start of the sequence.[50]

Notably, the Zeugma mosaic moves away from comedy towards the life it depicts. The figures have naturalistic faces, with hardly any, if any, recollection of masks. This departs from the convention, well formulated by Richard Green,[51] by which comic scenes depict their performers in costume with masks, while tragic scenes look beyond the performers' stage costume to depict what the scene represents. There are Lipari terracottas that match well-known dramatic types, but do not have the open mouths characteristic of actors' masks. They may be deliberate naturalistic variations. Two examples follow.

The Mature Hetaira is a woman who has supported herself by taking a lover, or lovers (Pl. 12(*b*)).[52] The False Maiden is a younger woman with a secret side to her life, such as a young man by whom she is pregnant (Pl. 12(*c*)).[53] Plangon in *Synaristosai* is a credible example of a False Maiden; Chrysis in the *Samia* will do nicely as a Mature Hetaira. We can recall her exchange with young Moschion in 80–3: 'Father'll be furious,' says he. 'And he'll get over it again. You see, he's in love, badly so, just like yourself. That pacifies the angriest man very quickly.' Need one hear more?

---

[48] Floor-mosaic from Zeugma, Syria, early decades of 3rd c. AD, signed by Zosimos of Samosata. Abadie-Reynal, Darmon, and Manière-Lévêque 2003, 79–99 with fig. 23 (colour). Menander, *Synaristosai*: composition similar to the Dioskourides version, but with second small figure extreme left Handley, 2002, 171 n. 21; Arnott 2004, 49–53.

[49] Fr. 11 Arnott, *PCG* VIII, adesp. 479; Plautus, *Cistellaria* 10–11, 15.

[50] More argument is needed, but a similar consideration may have affected the Mytilene *Epitrepontes*, with its muddled representation of the characters and their names. See Handley 1997, 197; 2002, 269–73, with reference to symposium performances, and Furley 2009, 148.

[51] Green 1991.

[52] Terracotta mask of the Mature Hetaira, Lipari, inv. 9768, before 252 BC, with naturalistic features. Bernabò Brea 1981, 387/xxxix.

[53] Terracotta mask of the False Maiden, Lipari, inv. 9762, before 252 BC, with naturalistic features. Bernabò Brea 1981, 364/xxxvii.

The scene with revellers on the glass beaker in Los Angeles has been dis-qualified by some as comedy because the figures seem to be maskless.[54] The Zeugma mosaic weakens the argument. I have suggested elsewhere that the original may have been Philemon's *Phasma*, the likely model for Plautus' *Mostellaria*, which was also known by its Greek title, *Phasma*. It was not Menander's *Phasma*: we know that too well. The key points are that Plautus makes great play with the revellers' arrival; that it is not a conventional *komos*, but a special one—a scene with a drunken young man supported by his girl; they arrive at a house door closed in broad daylight, with two slaves who will later, if *Mostellaria* is any guide, be speaking characters material to the plot. To borrow words I once heard from Richmond Lattimore, this suggestion has been met with almost universal dissatisfaction, and I shall say no more.

More promising, perhaps, is a well-known Pompeian wall-painting (Pl. 13(*a*)).[55] The slave strikes the attitude of a messenger of classical tragedy as he tells the two lovers some news that upsets them; there is a fair parallel in a classic scene from Sophocles with Oedipus and Jocasta reacting to the messenger's revelations (Pl. 13(*b*)).[56] I like to think that the message in our scene was 'Your father's here'. Plautus makes a great show of it, in elevated emotional style: *Most.* 348–51.

> Iuppiter supremus summis opibus atque industriis
> me perisse et Philolachetem cupit erilem filium.
> occidit spes nostra, nusquam stabulum est confidentiae.
> nec Salus nobis saluti iam esse, si cupiat, potest.

One can quote many representations of comic masks or figures that are essentially decorative, not specific, like the slave on an altar taking refuge from punishment. Borderline may be the mask of the Flatterer as seen among the gems related to comedy in the British Museum,[57] or the seal impressions of

---

[54] Glass beaker in Los Angeles, County Mus. of Art, M. 87. 113 (ex Cohn), 1st c. BC/1st c. AD. Webster 1995, under XZ 47 (4XG 1). Young man supported by a girl, with two slaves, approaches a closed house-door; Greek text above the painting. Possibly a scene from Philemon, *Phasma*: cf. Plautus, *Mostellaria* 313 ff. See Handley 1997, 192–3 with nn. 20–4.

[55] Wall-painting with a scene from Comedy, Pompeii I.vi.11, 3rd quarter of 1st c. AD. Webster 1995, 5NP 5a; Bieber 1961, fig. 395; Green and Handley 1995, fig. 67. Possibly after Philemon, *Phasma,* the sequel to the scene of n. 54 above, Plautus, *Most.* 348 ff. Cf. Handley (n. 54) and Green 1997, 141 with n. 29.

[56] Sicilian calyx-krater, Syracuse, Museo Archeologico P. Orsi, 66557, attributed to the Capodarso painter, *c.*350/325 BC. Trendall and Webster 1971, III. 2, 8; Green and Handley 1995, fig. 20. Messenger, Oedipus, Jocasta, *et al.*: Sophocles, *OT* 924 ff. Cf. Handley (n. 54), with fig. 60.

[57] A group of gems, London, BM, 1st c. BC to 1st c. AD: Green and Handley 1995, figs. 63–6, including (63) the mask of the Flatterer, as in Menander, *Kolax* (Terence, *Eunuchus*) and elsewhere. Webster 1995, 4XJ 66. Plutarch recalls the play in his essay on the Flatterer, *Moralia* 57 A.

**Fig. 7.2.** Seal-impression, Delos.

Delos (Fig. 7.2).[58] Even though Menander's play *Kolax* had a considerable literary life, one's girl friend, when given a ring with a kolax mask, would perhaps not instantly close her eyes and think of Menander, but rather more vaguely of the appealing side of this popular rogue.

Another gem, now apparently lost, has in contrast an image that is highly idiosyncratic (Fig. 7.3).[59] There are two bound figures either side of a single

[58] Seal-impressions, Delos, mid and to mid-1st c. BC, representing masks and whole figures. See Boussac 1997, with 33 illustrations and further references: the Flatterer (Kolax) in figs. 44–5; catalogue, Pr 639 and Pr 642: the latter is illustrated here. Large numbers of these seal impressions survive and are interesting not least in view of their relatively early date; when fully studied, they may add significantly to the iconography of New Comedy.

[59] Red jasper gem, once Florence, Grand-Ducal collection, 1st c. AD or later. Old man at doorway, flanked by two figures with arms bound at wrist; young man in long clothes (or woman?) to his right, and slave to his left. Wieseler 1851, pl. XII, 16; Webster 1995, 4XJ 2. Perhaps a representation of the opening tableau of the Greek original of Plautus' *Captiui*: see 1 ff., 37 ff., 110 ff., 195 ff., with Handley 1997, 193–4.

**Fig. 7.3.** Red jasper gem, once in Florence.

doorway, and an old man (or his overseer) dominates them in front of it. The left-hand figure has an overly long robe if male; but we might recall Demosthenes' contemptuous description of Aeschines in *False Embassy* (19). 314 'progressing through the Agora with his clothes down to his ankles'. Was the play the Greek original of what we know as Plautus' *Captiui*? In *Captiui*, the young man and the slave change roles. A bogus young man has to look exaggeratedly so; for no comic disguise must be perfect. How the matter of the masks was managed I do not know. The *Captiui* is in any case unusual. Plautus' treatment of it has been much discussed; but it does not in any case look like a derivative of Menander: Philemon, Diphilus, and A. N. Other have all been thought of as possibilities. Again, I shall not pursue here what is no more than a speculative conjecture. What we gain from unidentified scenes of this kind is much like the gain from unidentified fragments—an encouragement to keep the mind open—open to the thought that Menander's rivals, like Menander himself, may yet have survived longer than one might think, and may yet be able, like Menander, to surprise us.

## Another Particle of Menander?

From a selection of examples, we have seen something of the progress of the rediscovery of Menander, with some suggestions in passing of ways in which that progress might continue. Over the last hundred years, Menander has been transformed from a lost author who lived largely on his reputation into a dramatist with qualities of plot structure, character portrayal, and language capable of appreciation at first hand. Gilbert Murray was taken as a landmark in the recognition that beyond academic study and reconstruction there are also ways for the new texts to live on in modern times in sympathetic translation and sometimes in performance. The representations from the ancient world of scenes and actors from the New Comedy of Menander and his contemporaries have benefited similarly from important accessions and increased sophistication in their interpretation. In their growing quantity, they can be seen not simply as theatrical stills or some kind of visual aid to the texts, but documents of popular interest in the genre of comedy at various levels of society and in different parts of the Graeco-Roman world. In that way, their survival complements the survival of copies of the plays.

Against this broad background it is time in conclusion to consider in more detail the scrap of new text that was mentioned at the beginning of this survey. The enquiring reader may already have turned to it as set out with its notes below. Might it, one asks, be a fragment of anyone's play? Hardly. Even if it is impossible to say with precision when Menander's rivals ceased to be read and copied, these lines from a codex of the sixth/seventh century, to which, from its handwriting, this manuscript should be assigned, can hardly represent anything else but a relic of a collection of plays by Menander.[60]

Why might the play be *Georgos*? I see six arguments. (i) We have the name Gorgias. Gorgias, the country boy, is a character in *Georgos* (but so he is in *Dyskolos*—one of several points of likeness between these two plays); (ii) In particular, riches and poverty are an issue in *Georgos* (so again in *Dyskolos*); (iii) we lack a name in *Georgos* for the leading young man: Chaireas, the other name we have, would do nicely (but so might some other); (iv) the betrothal seems to have involved a major reconciliation: in *Georgos*, the leading young man had promised to marry Gorgias' sister, who was already pregnant by him: the apparently inescapable obstacles were another marriage arranged for him in his absence and a plan by the rich old man Kleainetos to marry the girl; (v) Gorgias and Chaireas are known as two friends from Achilles Tatius, *Leucippe and Clitophon* (4. 25; but the novelist need not have been thinking of this or any other play); and (vi) the play *Georgos* is known to be a survivor from fragments of four copies including the Geneva leaf.[61] This does not add up to proof. It does, I suggest, make a case for conjecture.[62] From new texts to come, or perhaps known texts overlooked, it may attract confirmation. It stands here as a small sample of the way in which rediscovery proceeds.

---

[60] It belongs, with the papyrus codex of *Aspis* (above, n. 11) among the latest surviving texts of Menander, and is to be added to the list of vellum codices given by D'Aiuto 2003, 278–82.

[61] Above, n. 14.

[62] The remains of the play leave many obscurities. Austin 2004 gives a new text of 1–98 (= G + B4 + F); for discussion, see Arnott 1979–2000, i. 97, and Webster 1974, 141–4.

## A FRAGMENT OF A COMEDY FROM OXYRHYNCHUS

(*Oxyrhynchus Papyri*, vol. LXXIII no. 4937)
(See above pp. **138, 141, 145–6, with n. 23 and 154–5**)

POxy inv. 58 A(21)b        7.6 × 2.6 cm        Vellum, saec. vi/vii;

Sloping majuscule

Side A (hair side)

| | |
|---|---|
| 1 | .....].:ευπορ. [ |
| 2 | .ερωμεταπροικο[ |
| 3 | ακηκοαςμου·ταυθ'. [ |
| 4 | cφοδρ'εcτινευδο.[ |
| 5 | καμοιδοκω...[ |

| | |
|---|---|
| 1 | .....]ς· εὐπορε[ι |
| 2 | φέρω μετὰ προικό [ς |
| 3 | ἀκήκοάς μου· ταῦθ' ἃ̣ [ |
| 4 | cφοδρ' ἐcτὶν εὖ δοχ[θέντα |
| 5 | κἀμοὶ δοκῶ...[ |

Side B (flesh side)

| | |
|---|---|
| 1 | ]..ιδικ.[ |
| 2 | ]μειςηκετε: |
| 3 | ]νοεις:ουδεεν |
| 4 | ]δελφηνλαμβανειν **χαιρ** |
| 5 | ]...ςγοργια· |

| | |
|---|---|
| 1 | π]ερὶ δίκη[ς |
| 2 | ὑ]μεῖς: ἥκετε: |
| 3 | ]νοεῖς· οὐδὲ ἕν |
| 4 | **Xα.** ἀ]δελφὴ λαμβάνειν |
| 5 | ]...ς, Γοργία. |

A1. Possibly εὐπορε[ῖc; the verb is in any case certain. For the reference to wealth, compare Menander, *Dyskolos* 284–6 μήτ' αὐτός, εἰ cφόδρ' εὐπορεῖς, πίcτευε τούτωι, μήτε τῶν πτωχῶν πάλιν ἡμῶν καταφρόνει, said by Gorgias to the rich man's son Sostratos; and, again on wealth and poverty, *Georgos* 1KT/2 Arnott, with εἰ καὶ cφόδρ' εὐπορεῖ γάρ in v. 4.

A4. Aorist ἐδόχθην is first quoted by LSJ from Polybius; δοκ[οῦντα is discounted by the trace of an oblique stroke after δο.

B3. Metre demands a short syllable before νοεῖc, e.g. ἃ νοεῖc, μετανοεῖc.

B4. The *nota personae* to the right of the column refers to a mid-line speaker change.

B3–5. e.g. (**Γο.**) οὐδὲ ἕν | ἔcτ' ἐμποδών, continuing with **Xα.** τὴν cὴν ἀ]δελφὴν λαμβάνειν | ἔτοιμός εἰμι πίcτιν ἐπι]θεὶς, Γοργία, that is: (**Go.**) 'Nothing [stands in the way]' Ch. [I am ready, on my oath] to take [your] sister in marriage'; for πίcτιν ἐπιθεὶς, see *Dysk.* 308.

## BIBLIOGRAPHY

Abadie-Reynal, C., Darmon, J.-P., and Manière-Lévêque, A.-M. 2003, 'La maison et la mosaïque des *Synaristosai* (*Les femmes au déjeuner* de Ménandre'), in AA.VV. *Zeugma. Interim Reports* (*J. Roman Archaeology*, Suppl. 51; Portsmouth, RI), 79–99.

Allinson, F. G. 1921, *Menander: The Principal Fragments* (Cambridge, MA, and London).

Andreae, B. 2003, *Antike Bildmosaiken* (Mainz).

Arnott, W. G. 1979–2000, *Menander*, 3 vols. (Cambridge, MA, and London).

—— 2004, 'New Menander from the 1990's', in Bastianini and Casanova 2004, 35–53.

Ashmole, B. 1973, 'Menander: An Inscribed Bust', *AJA* 77, 61, with pls. 11–12.

Austin, C. 2004, 'Le papyrus de Genève du Campagnard', in Bastianini and Casanova 2004, 79–94.

Bain, D. 1977, *Actors and Audience: A Study of Asides and Related Conventions in Greek Drama* (Oxford).

Bastianini, G. and Casanova, A. (eds.) 2004, *Menandro: cent'anni di papiri. Atti del convegno internazionale di studi, Firenze, 12–13 giugno 2003* (Florence).

—— and Gallazzi, C. 2001, *Posidippo di Pella, Epigrammi. (PMilVogl VIII. 309)* (Milan) [in collaboration with C. Austin].

Bernabò Brea, L. 1981, *Menandro e il teatro greco nelle terracotte liparesi* (Genoa).

—— 2001, *Maschere e personaggi del teatro Greco nelle terracotte liparesi* (Rome).

Bers, V. 1997, *Speech in Speech: Studies in Incorporated* Oratio Recta *in Attic Drama and Oratory* (Lanham, MD, and London).

Bieber, M. (1961), *The History of the Greek and Roman Theater*, 2nd edn. (Princeton).

Blanchard, A. 1983, *Essai sur la composition des comédies de Ménandre* (Paris).

—— 2007, *La Comédie de Ménandre* (Paris).

—— and Bataille, A. 1965, 'Fragments sur papyrus du *ΣΙΚΥΩΝΙΟΣ* de Ménandre', *Recherches de Papyrologie*, 3, 103–76, pls. vi–xiii (Paris).

Blume, H.-D. 1990, 'Der Codex Bodmer und unsere Kenntnis der griechischen Komödie', in Handley and Hurst 1990, 13–36.

—— 1998, *Menander* (Erträge der Forschung, 293; Darmstadt).

Boussac, M.-F. 1997, 'Masques et acteurs de théâtre sur les sceaux de Délos', in Le Guen 1997, 145–64.

Cavallo, G., and Maehler, H. (1987), *Greek Bookhands of the Early Byzantine Period, AD 300–800* (*BICS* Suppl. 47; London).

†Charitonidis, S., Kahil, L., and Ginouvès, R. 1970, *Les Mosaïques de la maison du Ménandre à Mytilène* (Basel).

Csapo, E. 1997, 'Mise en scène théâtrale, scene de théâtre artisanale: les mosaïques de Ménandre à Mytilène, leur contexte social et leur tradition iconographique', in Le Guen 1997, 165–82.

D'Aiuto, F. 2003, '*Graeca* in codici orientali della Biblioteca Vaticana' in L. Perria (ed.), *Tra Oriente e Occidente: Scritture e libri greci fra le regioni orientali di Bisanzio e l'Italia* (Testi e studi bizantino-neoellenici, 14; Rome), 227–96.

Dedoussi, C. 2006, Μενάνδρου Cαμία. Εἰcαγωγή, κείμενο, μετάφραcη, ὑπόμνημα (Athens).

Ferrari, F. 2004, 'Papiri e mosaici: tradizione testuale e iconografia in alcune scene di Menandro', in Bastianini and Casanova 2004, 127–49.

Fittschen, K. 1991, 'Zur Rekonstruktion griechischer Dichterstatuen. 1. Teil: Die Statue des Menander', *Ath. Mitt.* 106, 243–79, Abb. 52–78.

Frost, K. B. 1988, *Exits and Entrances in Menander* (Oxford).

Furley, W. D. 2009, *Menander*, Epitrepontes (*BICS* Suppl. 106; London).

Gomme, A. W., and Sandbach, F. H. 1973, *Menander: A Commentary* (Oxford).

Green, J. R. 1989, 'Theatre Production: 1971–1986', *Lustrum*, 31, 7–95, index 273–8.

—— 1991, 'On Seeing and Depicting the Theatre in Classical Athens', *GRBS* 32, 15–30.

Green, J. R. 1995 [1998], 'Theatre Production: 1987–1995', *Lustrum*, 37, 7–202, index 309–18.

—— 1997, 'Deportment, Costume and Naturalism in Comedy', in Le Guen (1997), 131–43.

—— 2008, 'Theatre Production: 1996–2003'. *Lustrum*, 50, 7–302, index 367–90.

—— and Handley, E. W. 1995, *Images of the Greek Theatre* (repr. 2001; London and Austin, TX).

Handley, E. W. 1968, *Menander and Plautus: A Study in Comparison* (inaugural lecture, University College London).

—— 1969, 'Notes on the *Theophoroumene* of Menander', *BICS* 16, 88–101.

—— 1970, 'The Conventions of the Comic Stage and their Exploitation by Menander', in Turner 1970, 3–42.

—— 1987, 'Acts and Scenes in the Comedy of Menander', *Dioniso*, 47, 299–312.

—— 1988, 'A Particle of Greek Comedy', in J. H. Betts, J. T. Hooker, and J. R. Green (eds.), *Studies in Honour of T. B. L. Webster*, 2 vols. (Bristol, 1986–8), ii. 51–5.

—— 1997, 'Some Thoughts on New Comedy and its Public', in Le Guen 1997, 185–200.

—— 2002, 'Acting, Action and Words in New Comedy', in P. E. Easterling and E. Hall (eds.), *Greek and Roman Actors: Aspects of an Ancient Profession* (Cambridge), 165–88.

—— and Hurst, A. (eds.) 1990, *Relire Ménandre* (Recherches et Rencontres, 2; Geneva).

Hurst, A. 2004, 'Ménandre en ses recoins', in Bastianini and Casanova (2004), 55–70.

Jacques, J.-M. 1998, *Ménandre, tome I. 3: Le Bouclier* (Paris).

Johnson, W. A. 2004, *Bookrolls and Scribes in Oxyrhynchus* (Toronto and London).

Kasser, R., and Austin, C. 1969*a*, *Papyrus Bodmer XXV: Ménandre, La Samienne* (Geneva).

—— ——1969*b*, *Papyrus Bodmer XXVI: Ménandre, Le Bouclier* (Geneva)

Kleve, K. 1996, 'How to Read an Illegible Papyrus: Towards an Edition of PHerc. 78, Caecilius, Obolostates sive Faenerator', *Cronache Ercolanesi*, 26, 5–14.

—— 2001, 'Caecilius Statius, The Moneylender (PHerc 78)', *Atti del XI Congresso Internazionale di Papirologia*, ii. 725 (Florence).

Koenen, L. 1978, *The Cairo Codex of Menander: A Photographic Edition . . . with a Preface by L. K.* (Institute of Classical Studies, London).

Lamagna, M. 1998, 'Dialogo riportato in Menandro', in E. García Novo and I. Rodríguez Alfageme (eds.), *Dramaturgía y puesta en escena en el teatro griego* (Madrid), 289–302.

Lefebvre, G. 1907, *Fragments d'un manuscrit de Ménandre* (Cairo).

—— 1911, *Catalogue général des antiquités égyptiennes du Musée du Caire. No. 43227. Papyrus de Ménandre* (Cairo) [revised text, with facsimile].

Le Guen, B. 1997 (ed.), *De la scène aux gradins: Théâtre et representations dramatiques après Alexandre le Grand* (Pallas 47; Toulouse).

Martin, V. 1958, *Papyrus Bodmer IV: Ménandre, Le Dyscolos* (Geneva).

Murray, G. 1929, 'Menander', in J. U. Powell and E. A. Barber, *New Chapters in Greek Literature, Second Series* (Oxford; repr. New York, 1974), 9–34.

—— 1933, *Aristophanes: A Study* (Oxford) [see ch. X, 'Menander and the Transformation of Comedy', 221–63].

—— 1942, *The Rape of the Locks: The* Perikeiromene *of Menander* (London).

—— 1945, *The Arbitration: The* Epitrepontes *of Menander* (London; 2nd edn. 1949).

Nervegna, S. 2010, 'Menander's *Theophoroumene* between Greece and Rome', *AJP* 131, 23–68. [See Appendix, 60–3, listing paintings and mosaics reproducing New Comedy scenes].

Nicole, J. 1897–8, *Le Laboureur de Ménandre* (Basel and Geneva).

Norsa, M. 1939, *La scrittura letteraria greca dal secolo IV a. C. all'VIII d. C.* (Florence).

—— and Vitelli, G. 1935, 'Dai papiri della Società italiana, I: Frammento di commedia', *ASNP* 4: 1–3.

Nünlist, R. 2002, 'Speech within Speech in Menander', in Willi (2002), 219–59.

Richter, G. M. A. 1965, *The Portraits of the Greeks*, 3 vols. (London).

Robert, C. 1911, *Die Masken der neueren attischen Komödie* (Halle).

Sandbach, F. H 1970, 'Menander's manipulation of language for dramatic purposes', in Turner 1970, 113–43.

—— 1990, *Menandri reliquiae selectae*, 2nd edn. (Oxford).

Stefani, G. 1999 [2000], 'Mosaici sconosciuti dall'area vesuviana', *Atti del VI Colloquio dell'Associazione Italiana per lo Studio e la Conservazione del Mosaico* [= *AISCOM* 6], 279–90 (Venice).

Trendall, A. D., and Webster, T. B. L. 1971, *Illustrations of Greek Drama* (London).

Turner, E. G. 1965, *New Fragments of the* Misoumenos *of Menander* (*BICS* Suppl. 17; London).

—— (ed.) 1970, *Ménandre* (Entretiens Hardt, 16; Geneva).

—— 1977, *The Typology of the Early Codex* (Philadelphia).

—— rev. Parsons P. J. 1987, *Greek Manuscripts of the Ancient World* (*BICS* Suppl. 46; London).

Webster, T. B. L. 1974, *An Introduction to Menander* (Manchester).

—— 1995, *Monuments Illustrating New Comedy*, 3rd edn. rev. and enlarged by J. R. Green and A. Seeberg (*BICS* Suppl. 50; London).

Wieseler, F. 1851, *Theatergebaüde und Denkmäler des Bühnenwesens bei den Griechen und Römern* (Göttingen).

Willi, A. (ed.) 2002, *The Language of Greek Comedy* (Oxford).

Wilson, D. 1987, *Gilbert Murray, OM, 1866–1957* (Oxford).

# 8

## 'My Daughter and her Dowry': Smikrines in Menander's *Epitrepontes*

### Colin Austin

Peter taught me Papyrology. That was over four decades ago. After graduating in Cambridge in the summer of 1962 I had started research on Aristophanes and was concentrating on *Thesmophoriazusae*.[1] Hugh Lloyd-Jones was my supervisor. We were in the middle of the apocalyptic Cuban Missile Crisis, when Khrushchev thought he could checkmate Kennedy by installing Soviet nuclear warheads in America's backyard. After those sizzling and scary days I arrived in Oxford in January 1963 to face the coldest and longest winter in living memory. I eventually ended up in the freezing little attic at the top of Killcanon, just above Peter's rooms. Killcanon may have killed the canons but it didn't kill me. Aristophanes kept me alive, and so did Menander, and so did Peter with his unique friendship and wonderful teaching. When the *Sicyonios* miraculously arrived from Paris shortly afterwards,[2] I was already in my element, in a dream world of my own, and ever since I've felt at home and at ease with early Ptolemaic papyri recovered from mummy cartonnage, provided they are written in verse.[3] My love affair with Menander is not over yet. How could it be, when at this very moment we await with eager anticipation what novelties lurk under several layers in a Vatican palimpsest?[4] And it is no secret that further snippets from the beginning of *Epitrepontes* will soon enrich our knowledge of the play, thanks to the expertise of Eric Handley. In April 2000, in a lecture at the Vitelli institute in Florence,[5] I talked about the welcome little P.Oxy. 4020 (published by Peter Parsons in 1994), which contains a prose *hypothesis* of the play and a colourful description of the main characters, including the γέροντα φιλάργυρον Smikrines, who is always counting his pennies. And putting together, in a complicated jigsaw, overlapping scraps from Cairo, Florence, Michigan, and Oxford, I did my best

---

[1] Austin and Olson 2004, pp. vii–ix.  [2] Blanchard and Bataille 1964.
[3] Austin 1967; Austin and Bastianini 2002.  [4] D'Aiuto 2003, 271.  [5] Austin 2001.

to reconstruct in detail the end of Act III and the beginning of Act IV. Here I propose to roam more freely across the board and present the results of new progress on various passages. My warmest thanks go to Eftychia Bathrellou, a Ph.D. student from Greece, who very kindly allowed me to mention some of her bright ideas and readings, and to William Furley of Heidelberg, for generously showing me a draft of his forthcoming edition of the play. The three of us have sometimes independently come up with the same suggestion. I can only hope we are not suffering from collective delusion. Papyrology, as you all know, is a slippery business and forced U-turns are part of the game, as will become clear at the end of my talk.

The fourth-century *Membrana Petropolitana* was originally discovered by Tischendorf, way back in 1844, in the monastery of St Catherine on Sinai.[6] Cobet published the recto in 1876[7] and Jernstedt the verso in 1891,[8] but it was only after the publication of the Cairo codex in 1907[9] that people realized it contained an early scene of *Epitrepontes*.[10] In 1994 Peter Parsons brought into the picture the tattered and tantalizing scraps of P.Oxy. 4021.[11] Here, to begin with, is Arnott's version of the recto page:[12]

(Cμ.)    ... ἄνθρωπος οἶνον. αὐτὸ τοῦτ' ἐκπλήτ[τομαι
ἔγωγ'. ὑπὲρ δὲ τοῦ μεθύσκεσθ' οὐ λέγω.
ἀπιστίαι γάρ ἐσθ' ὅμοιον τοῦτό γε,
εἰ καὶ βιάζεται κοτύλην τις τοὐβολ[οῦ           130
ὠνούμενος πίνειν ἑαυτόν.
(Χαιρ.)                    τοῦτ' ἐγ[ὼ
προσέμενον· οὗτος ἐμπεσὼν διασκ[εδᾶι
τὸν ἔρωτα. τί δέ μοι τοῦτο; πάλιν οἰμω[ζέτω.
(Cμ.)  προῖκα δὲ λαβὼν τάλαντα τέτταρ' ἀργύρ[ου   135
οὐ τῆς γυναικὸς νενόμιχ' αὐτὸν οἰκέτ[ην.
ἀπόκοιτός ἐστι. πορνοβοσκῶι δώδεκα
τῆς ἡμέρας δραχμὰς δίδωσι.
(Χαιρ.)                    δώδεκα·
πέπυς]τ' ἀκριβῶς οὑτοσὶ τὰ πράγματα.
(Cμ.)  μηνὸ]ς δια[τ]ροφὴν ἀνδρὶ καὶ πρὸς ἡμερῶν
ἕξ.]                                           140
(Χαιρ.) εὖ] λελ[όγ]ισται· δύ' ὀβολοὺς τῆς ἡμέρας,
ἱκανό]ν τι τῶι πεινῶντι πρὸς πτις[άνη]ν ποτέ.
(Ἀβρ.)  Χαρίσι]ός σ[ε] προσμένει, Χαιρέ[στρατε.
τίς ὅδ' ἐς]τὶ δ[ή] γ[λυκύτατ'];
(Χαιρ.)                    ὁ τῆς [νύμφης πα]τήρ.

---

[6] Koerte 1938, pp. xvi f.      [7] Cobet 1876.

[8] Jernstedt 1891, 204–18, with a handwritten facsimile. A photograph appears as frontispiece in Capps 1910.

[9] Lefebvre 1907.      [10] Van Leeuwen 1908, 16–17; Capps 1910, 34–5.

[11] P.Oxy. 4021 (saec. III[P]) ed. P. J. Parsons (vol. LX, 1994) with pl. IV.

[12] Arnott 1979, 396–8.

(Ἀβρ.)   ἀλλὰ τί παθ]ὼν ὡς ἄθλιός τις [φιλόσοφος
βλέπει σκύθρωφ' ὁ] τρισκακοδ[αίμων;]
(Χαιρ., or possibly *Cμ.*)                    [ψάλ]τριαν                    145
                                      ]cαν γυναῖκα [. . . . . . . .]ι

We are plunged at once *in medias res*. 'I am not talking about his drunken-
ness', says Smikrines, recriminating against his son-in-law Charisios. 'What
borders on the incredible is that he insists on drinking wine he buys at one
obol the half-pint', κοτύλην τις τοὖβολοῦ, obviously an exorbitant price,
something like fifteen pounds a glass for a top claret. Smikrines then brings
up the subject of the all-important dowry, four silver talents, twice the going
rate, if you compare the dowries in *Aspis* (135) and *Misoumenos* (976).
Even the millionaire Kallippides in *Dyskolos* (844) draws the line at three
talents for his daughter. Charisios, however, sleeps away from home and
pays a pimp twelve drachmas every day—enough to feed a man for a month
and six more days besides. Smikrines' arithmetic is quite correct: with
6 obols to a drachma, it all adds up to 72 obols, or 2 obols a day for 36 days.
Habrotonon now comes out of the house. 'Who is this, then, sweety?' she asks
Chairestratos, who replies 'The father of the bride.' Editors have always
printed with approval Wilamowitz's imaginative supplements in 144–5:[13] 'But
what's the matter with him? Why is the poor man looking glum like some sad
philosopher?' To fill the space at the beginning Koerte had substituted ἀλλὰ
τί for τί δή, as there is room for two extra letters.[14] He would also have been
wise, I think, to replace παθών with μαθών to make it clear we are dealing
with a mental, not a physical, condition.[15] Habrotonon's question remains
unanswered and, as Smikrines is obviously the speaker in what follows,
I would much prefer Chairestratos to elaborate with e.g.

δριμὺ βλέπ]ων ὡς ἄθλιός τις φ[ιλόσοφος
ἀκριβολογεῖθ'.

'Scowling like some sad philosopher, he's pedantically adding up his sums.'
The round left side of the *phi* is still clearly visible on the photograph.[16]
Smikrines, for his part, pays no attention but continues as before:

(*Cμ.*)               ὁ] τρισκακοδ[αίμων ψάλ]τριαν
πρὸς τὴν ἐνοικοῦ]caν γυναῖκ' [ἐπεισάγε]ι

'The scoundrel brings in a harp-girl in addition to his wife who lives inside.'[17]

---

[13]  Ap. Koerte 1910, 209–11.        [14]  Koerte 1938, 11.        [15]  See Kühner–Gerth ii. 519.
[16]  For δριμὺ βλέπειν cf. Ar. *Ran.* 562 and Plat. *Rep.* 7. 519 A, for ἀκριβολογεῖcθαι ibid. 3. 403 D
and Wankel on Dem. 18. 240 (pp. 1060–1). Gow on Theoc. 14. 6 collects references on ascetics.
[17]  For ἐπεισάγει cf. 695. For γυναῖκα in *scriptio plena* cf. ἔγωγε at 128 and γλυκύτατε at 143
(before the change of speakers).

The verso takes us to the end of Act I. I now switch to Martina's more recent text, which incorporates the latest scraps from P.Oxy. 4021:[18]

```
                    ...[ ].[                                         150
    προϲε[
    ......[
    ἀποδου.δ[
    Ἀβρ.  τη..ρ.ικ..[ ]..[
    ϲ..
    ογερω..ε..τω[.]..[                                               155
    α..ο.[.].κα.ον[.]..[ ]..[
            χ[
    τηϲ γ.[.].οϲ.ε.[..]..[ Ἁ]βρο[του
Ἀβρ.    ἀλλ'οὐκ ἐκαλ.[              ].ων[..].[
(?Ἀβρ.)   οὕτωϲ ἀγαθόν τί ϲοι γένοιτο, μὴ λέγε
    ἀεί πο[τε]—                                                      160
Χαι.         οὐκ ἐϲ κόρακαϲ; οἰμώξει μακρά.
Ϲμ.    εἴϲ<ε>ιμι δ' οὖν εἴϲω, ϲαφῶϲ τε πυθόμενοϲ
    ἅ]παντα τ[αῦ]τα τῆϲ θυγατρόϲ, βουλεύϲομαι
    ὄντινα τ]ρόπον πρὸϲ τοῦτον ἤδη προϲβαλῶ.
(?Χαι.)  φράϲω[μ]εν αὐτῶι τοῦτον ἥκοντ' ἐνθάδε;
(?Ἀβρ.)  φράϲωμ]εν.                                                 165
(Χαι.)         οἷον κίναδοϲ, οἰκίαν ποεῖ
    ἀνάϲτα]τον.
(Ἀβρ.)        πολλὰϲ ἐβουλόμην ἅμα.
(Χαι.)  πολλάϲ;]
(Ἀβρ.)        μίαν μὲν τὴν ἐφεξῆϲ.
(Χαι.)                    τὴν ἐμήν;
(Ἀβρ.)  τὴν ϲ]ήν γ'. ἴωμεν δεῦρο πρὸϲ Χαρίϲιον.
(Χαι.)  ἴωμ]εν· ὡϲ καὶ μειρακυλλίων ὄχλοϲ
    εἰϲ τ]ὸν τόπον τιϲ ἔρχεθ' ὑποβεβρεγμέν[ων,                        170
    οἷϲ] μ[ὴ]'νοχλεῖν εὔκαιρον εἶν[α]ί μο[ι δοκεῖ.
```

A few key words can be extracted from the ruins of vv. 150–8. First of all, ἀποδούϲ in 153, spoken by Smikrines. He clearly wants Charisios to return the dowry, ἀποδοὺϲ δ[ὲ τὴν προῖκ', with τὴν προῖκα picked up by Habrotonon in the next line. This theme runs through the play like a leitmotif: ἀποδιδότω τὴν προῖκα, 'let him give back the dowry', he shouts at Chairestratos at 688 and when he finally returns in Act V Onesimos greets him as 'the grumpy chap, who has come for his dowry and his daughter', ὁ χαλεπόϲ, ἐπὶ τὴν προῖκα καὶ τὴν θυγατέρα / ἥκων (1079–80). In 155 an apostrophe after the gamma makes one hesitate between ὅ γε ἐρῶν, 'the lover', and ὁ γέρων, 'the old man'. As Habrotonon is the speaker, a reference to old Smikrines is perhaps more appropriate. There is, in fact,

---

[18] Martina 1997, 16–18.

another intrusive apostrophe after gamma in this papyrus (fr. 3, l. 8 γ'ενοιτ[ο). Smikrines carries on with the imperative ἐράτω, 'let him love', or even the present ἐρᾶι τῶ[ν, 'he loves the . . .', and the mention, in the next line, of 'a hundred wineskins', ἀσκού[c] ἑκατόν, both readings plausibly deciphered by Bathrellou. We should like to know more about this nightly orgy (τῆc νυ[κ]τόc in 157) but the gaps in the text leave us in the lurch. Was Smikrines saying 'Let him love a tart and let him drink . . .', ἐράτω [πορνιδίου καὶ πινέτω? The reading ἀεί πο[τε] in 160 is extremely problematic. In three successive articles Geoffrey Arnott has recently claimed that it is 'inescapable' and even provides us with 'one little treasure'.[19] Habrotonon, according to him, tells Chairestratos μὴ λέγε / "ἀεί ποτ'", 'Don't keep on saying "for ever".' 'This implies', Arnott maintains, 'that Chairestratos had not only used that expression in his last remark, but also used it once or more than once earlier in the scene—thus providing a further instance of Menander's desire to individualize characters by giving them a fondness for particular expressions.' Unfortunately, ποτε is a pseudo-reading and was rightly rejected by Parsons. The papyrus clearly has αειπον followed by an upwards sloping dash. We could reasonably postulate that in uncial script a delta has dropped out after alpha and read ἃ <δ'> εἶπον. There is no reason why μὴ λέγε at the end of 159 should not be used absolutely, as at *Misum.* 792, Ar. *Vesp.* 37, *Pax* 648, in the sense 'don't say so', i.e. 'keep quiet'. Habrotonon is here begging Chairestratos to keep his mouth shut. But when she proceeds with ἃ <δ'> εἶπον—'But what I said . . .', Chairestratos cuts her short with the curse οὐκ ἐc κόρακας; οἰμώξει μακρά, 'Oh, go to hell. You'll pay for this, you will', addressed to Smikrines, as an aside. The rest of the scene is unproblematic, so we may now move on to the beginning of Act II, where we have another splendid soliloquy by Smikrines. This is P.Oxy. 4641, and I give the text as republished three years ago by René Nünlist, after he presented it to the Papyrus Congress in Florence.[20]

```
(Cμ.?)   . . . . ] . ουτ . ν θυγατέρ[α
  . . . τὸ] δὴ λεγόμενον η[
  . . . . . ] . ε πείcηι καρτερηc[-
  . . . . ] . ν τὸ μὴ παρὰ τοῦ τοι[ούτου
  . . . . . ]ν πεπόηκε μυρίου[c                          5
  . . . ]ον γε τὸ κακόν, εἰ δεήc[ει
  . . . . ] . λέγοντ' "ἄcωτόc εἰμ', ου[
  . . . . ]ϲτα, μεθύω, κραιπαλῶ, [
  . . ] . [ . . ] . δουν αὐτῶι φράcω ν[
π]εῖραν προcάγειν, ὡc νῦν α[                            10
  ]θειc λέγει τούτῳ γάρ· ε[
```

[19]  Arnott 2000, 154; 2004*a*, 280; 2004*b*, 46.
[20]  P.Oxy. 4641 (saec. II/III) ed. R. Nünlist (vol. LXVIII, 2003) with plate III; Nünlist 2004.

ἐ]ργάζετ'· ἐρρῶϲθαι γάρ ἐϲτ.[
ἀ₁ργὸϲ δ' ὑγιαίνων τοῦ πυρ₁έττοντοϲ πολύ        = Men. *Ep.* fr. 6
ἐ₁ϲτ' ἀθλιώτεροϲ· διπλάϲιά γ' ₁ἐϲθίει
μ₁άτην· ἰδεῖν βουλήϲομ' αὐ[τὸν                              15
(Δ.)   π]ροϲμείνατ', ὦ δείληϲ μετα[
(Cυ.)  ἔρ]ρωϲο καὶ τὸ κατὰ ϲὲ πρόϲμ[εινον μόνον.
       π]αρ' ἕνα γάρ ἐϲθ' ἕκαϲτον ἡ ϲω[τηρία.
(Δ.)   ο]ὐθὲν λέγειϲ δίκαιον. CΥPICK(OC) οὐ μα[
       . . . .]ϲ πρὸϲ τὸν δεϲπότην [                       20
       . . . . .]ον. κατοικεῖ δ' ἐνθα[δ
       . . . . . . .].[.]μεν οἰκε..ου[

The precious daughter appears in l. 1 but the accusative has to be elided, θυγατέρ[', to fit the metrical pattern. The lack of article before the noun shows that it was perhaps used generally, 'a daughter'. Before it τούτων looks plausible and could well refer again to the dowry, and the subject of the sentence is likely to be Charisios, 'this fellow here thus deprives a daughter of these things', e.g.

ὁδὶ δὲ] τούτων θυγατέρ[' ὧδ' ἀποϲτερεῖ,

'being always, as the saying goes, the slave of his desires',

ἀεὶ τὸ] δὴ λεγόμενον ἥ[ττων ὢν πόθων.

At 668–9 Smikrines describes Charisios in very similar terms: τοῦτο δὴ τὸ λεγόμενον/ ἥττων ἑαυτοῦ, 'to quote the usual phrase, lacking in self-control'. Smikrines then addresses himself, much like Demeas in *Samia* (356): 'Don't listen to him at all, hold out, Smikrines',

μηδὲν] ϲὲ πείϲηι, καρτέρηϲ[ον, Cμικρίνη,

as Nünlist well supplemented l. 3. 'It's best not to stand any nonsense from such a character',

λῶιϲτ]ον τὸ μὴ παρὰ τοῦ τοι[ούτου πράγματα
λαβεῖ]ν

4 ἀγαθ]ὸν Nünlist        5 Nünlist

Xenophon has the phrase πράγματα λαμβάνει.[21] Nünlist then prints πεπόηκε μυρίου[ϲ, but it is difficult to see what Charisios could have done to ten thousand people! I suggest we articulate the Greek differently and read πεπόηκε μυρί' οὗ[τοϲ ἔκτοπα, 'this fellow has done ten thousand abnormal things'. Smikrines goes on: 'And what a fine disgrace if I'll have to put up with him saying "I'm good for nothing"—isn't this ridiculous?—"I'm drunk. I've got a hangover"—disgusting, rather'.

[21] Xen. *Lac.* 2. 7.

καλ]όν γε τὸ κακόν, εἰ δεῆc[ει μ' ὑπομένειν
αὐτὸ]ν λέγοντ' "ἄcωτόc εἰμ'"—οὐ [γὰρ τάδε
γελα]cτά;—"μεθύω κραιπαλῶ"—[βδελυρὰ μὲν οὖν.

6 init. Nünlist, fin. Handley    7 init. Nünlist, fin. Austin    8 Austin

In the papyrus there are high dots before and after ἄcωτόc εἰμ' and μεθύω κραιπαλῶ, which make it clear that these are the actual words Smikrines imagines Charisios will use. All the rest is comment by Smikrines. So rather than Nünlist's attractive πόρνηc ἐρῶ, 'I'm in love with a prostitute' at the end of 8, I would prefer a remark like βδελυρὰ μὲν οὖν as the climax to Smikrines' indignation. 'So I'll tell him to his face to try a new tactic, because just now he's simply "good for nothing"',

πα]ρ[όντ]ι δ' οὖν αὐτῶι φράcω ν[έαν τινὰ
π]εῖραν προcάγειν, ὡc νῦν ἄ[cωτόc ἐcτι δή.

9 init. Nünlist, fin Austin    10 fin. Austin

The phrase πεῖραν προcάγειν need not have any sexual overtones here, as Nünlist imagines, 'to make another pass'. Smikrines will tell Charisios to try again, to make a fresh start, and he pointedly throws back at him his own chosen word ἄcωτοc. 'Because nobody is telling him: "a sensible man works hard." It's fine to be healthy, but a healthy idler is far worse off than one in bed with fever: he eats twice as much and all for nothing'.

ο]ὐθεὶc λέγει τούτωι γάρ· "ε[ὔβουλόc τιc ὢν
ἐ]ργάζετ'." ἐρρῶcθαι γάρ ἐcτι [μὲν καλόν,
ἀργὸc δ' ὑγιαίνων τοῦ πυρέττοντοc πολύ
ἐcτ' ἀθλιώτεροc· διπλάcιά γ' ἐcθίει
μάτην.

11 εὔβουλοc Austin, τιc ὢν Handley    12 fin. Nünlist

In v. 14 Stobaeus, who quotes the line,[22] has an unmetrical γοῦν for γε and most editors had wrongly accepted Wilamowitz's transposition of the two words διπλάcια and μάτην to read μάτην γοῦν ἐcθίει / διπλάcια.[23] Kock in 1888 had already thought of changing γοῦν to γε[24] and Leo in 1908 was the first to print the text as here.[25] Smikrines now ends his monologue by saying he will be seeing Charisios later on:

ἰδεῖν βουλήcομ' αὐ[τὸν ὕcτερον.

15 ὕcτερον Austin, P. Brown

Before he can depart, the charcoal-burner Syriskos, with his wife and the baby, arrives on stage, hotly pursued by the shepherd Daos: 'Wait!',

[22] *Ecl.* 3. 30, 7 (p. 665 Hense).    [23] Wilamowitz 1908, 53 n. 1.
[24] *CAF* iii (Leipzig, 1888), 51 (Men. fr. 175).
[25] Leo 1907, 133, followed by Robert 1908, 88.

προcμείνατ'. 'What an afternoon!' And the line may be completed either with Handley's ὦ δείληc μετα[τρόπου, μείνατε, 'what a changing afternoon, wait', or my own ὦ δείληc μετα[πιπτούcηc κακῶc, 'The afternoon is turning out the wrong way'. Syriskos' answer to this is: 'Goodbye and as far as you are concerned, you wait by *yourself*. Everyone is responsible for his own safety'.

> ἔρ]ρωcο καὶ τὸ κατὰ cὲ πρόcμ[εινον μόνοc·
> π]αρ' ἕνα γάρ ἐcθ' ἕκαcτον ἡ cω[τηρία.

Nünlist had supplemented πρόcμεινον μόνον, 'You *just* wait', but both Bathrellou and Furley have seen that μόνοc, 'on your own', is far more pointed and appropriate, as shown by the general comment in the next line.[26] 'That's not just', οὐθὲν λέγειc δίκαιον, retorts Daos, sheepishly. Syriskos holds all the cards in his hand at this point, as he intends to bring the case before his master Chairestratos, to restore the jewels to the baby. That is why Daos is desperately chasing after him. 'You don't deter me', says Syriskos. 'I'll turn to my master. Chairestratos lives here,

> οὐ μ' ἀ[ποcτρέφειc.
> ἐγὼ δ]ὲ πρὸc τὸν δεcπότην [τραπήcομαι
> τὸν ἐμ]όν. κατοικεῖ δ' ἐνθα[δὶ Χαιρέcτρατοc.

He then proposes to go in, ἀλλ' εἰc]ί[ω]μεν, if Nünlist's supplement is correct at the beginning of v. 22. But the scene that immediately follows in the Cairo codex makes it clear that he does not enter Chairestratos' house at this point—just as Smikrines does not leave the stage at v. 15 but remains throughout until his departure at v. 370 after the arbitration scene. So Daos must have said something in the next few lines to make Syriskos stay back. Before ου[ at the end of 22 there is a clear trace of an upright, most probably nu. We may imagine Syriskos justifying his intention to his wife with something like 'But let's go in. Those who throw empty words at us do not deserve our company',

> ἀλλ' εἰc]ί[ω]μεν. οἱ κενοὺ[c ἡμῖν λόγουc
> [ῥίπτοντεc οὔκ εἰc' ἄξιοι κοινωνίαc.]

Not more than three lines are missing before the start of the Cairo codex, where Daos and Syriskos are still seen exchanging insults, before Syriskos finally climbs down from his high horse and offers arbitration as a compromise (219–20).

Let us now look at some passages in the Cairo codex. The first is v. 284. Daos is arguing 'If he'd been walking with me when I found these things, a

---

[26] I am happy to withdraw the suggestions I tentatively made ap. Nünlist 2004, 103 and in Austin 2004*a*, 136.

windfall shared by both of us (a "joint Hermes"), then he'd have taken half and I the rest.' All editors print

$$\epsilon i\ \kappa a i\ \beta a\delta i\zeta\omega\nu\ \epsilon\hat{v}\rho\epsilon\nu\ \mathring{a}\mu'\ \mathring{\epsilon}\mu o i\ \tau a\hat{v}\tau a\ \kappa a i$$
$$\mathring{\eta}\nu\ \kappa o\iota\nu\grave{o}\varsigma\ \mathring{E}\rho\mu\hat{\eta}\varsigma,\ \tau\grave{o}\ \mu\grave{\epsilon}\nu\ \mathring{a}\nu\ o\mathring{v}\tau o\varsigma\ \mathring{\epsilon}\lambda a\beta[\epsilon\nu\ \mathring{a}\nu,$$
$$\tau\grave{o}\ \delta'\ \mathring{\epsilon}\gamma\acute{\omega},$$

with a second ἄν at the end of 284, a supplement first suggested by Leo in 1907 and others independently.[27] In 1990 Slings showed that this was certainly wrong as Menander, in line with fourth-century usage, would not have repeated ἄν in such a short and simple sentence.[28] Sling's own solution ἔλαβ[έ τι, 'he would have got some part of it', is weak and artificial (Daos is here referring to the baby) and I submit to your judgement what Furley and I had both come up with before we met: τὸ μὲν ἂν οὗτος ἔλαβ[έ που, 'he'd have taken half, I *suppose*.' ἄν followed by που is well attested.[29]

At 521 Sandbach adopts 'with due reserve' (*Comm.* p. 338) Arnott's bold transposition of δέ to seventh place in the sentence, ἐὰν οἰκεῖον ᾖ / αὐτῶι τὸ πρᾶγμ<α δ'>, the only exact parallel being fr. com. adesp. 1000, 33.[30] Would it not be easier to postulate a simple omission?

$$\mathring{\epsilon}\grave{a}\nu\ \delta'\ o\mathring{\iota}\kappa\epsilon\hat{\iota}o\nu\ \mathring{\eta}$$
$$a\mathring{v}\tau\hat{\omega}\iota\ \tau\grave{o}\ \pi\rho\hat{a}\gamma\mu',\ <o\mathring{v}\kappa>\ \epsilon\mathring{v}\theta\grave{v}\varsigma\ \mathring{\eta}\xi\epsilon\iota\ \phi\epsilon\rho\acute{o}\mu\epsilon\nu o\varsigma$$
$$\mathring{\epsilon}\pi\grave{\iota}\ \tau\grave{o}\nu\ \mathring{\epsilon}\lambda\epsilon\gamma\chi o\nu\ \kappa a\grave{\iota}\ \mu\epsilon\theta\acute{v}\omega\nu\ \gamma\epsilon\ \nu\hat{v}\nu\ \mathring{\epsilon}\rho\epsilon\hat{\iota}$$
$$\pi\rho\acute{o}\tau\epsilon\rho o\varsigma\ \mathring{a}\pi a\nu\tau a\ \kappa a\grave{\iota}\ \pi\rho o\pi\epsilon\tau\hat{\omega}\varsigma;$$

'But if he is involved in the affair, will he *not* fall head over heels to convict himself and, drunk as he is now, blurt everything out before I say a word?' For the two clauses closely linked by καί after the negative compare Eur. *Andr.* 1066–8

$$o\mathring{v}\chi\ \mathring{o}\sigma o\nu\ \tau\acute{a}\chi o\varsigma$$
$$\chi\omega\rho\acute{\eta}\sigma\epsilon\tau a\acute{\iota}\ \tau\iota\varsigma\ \Pi\upsilon\theta\iota\kappa\grave{\eta}\nu\ \pi\rho\grave{o}\varsigma\ \mathring{\epsilon}\sigma\tau\acute{\iota}a\nu$$
$$\kappa a\grave{\iota}\ \tau\mathring{a}\nu\theta\acute{a}\delta'\ \mathring{o}\nu\tau a\ \tau o\hat{\iota}\varsigma\ \mathring{\epsilon}\kappa\epsilon\hat{\iota}\ \lambda\acute{\epsilon}\xi\epsilon\iota\ \phi\acute{\iota}\lambda o\iota\varsigma;$$

A scribe may well have failed to see that the sentence is interrogative and instinctively left out what appeared to him as a meaningless οὐκ. Omissions are not uncommon in our Menander papyri. A good example is at 270, where the reply has dropped out after ἐδέου Cυρίcκ'; The supplement <ἔγωγε>, proposed by both Hense[31] and van Leeuwen in his second edition,[32] is very attractive, but palaeographically neater would be <ᾤμην> dropping out

---

[27] Leo 1907, 319. See also Headlam 1908, 6; Richards 1908, 48 = 1909, 101; Wilamowitz 1908, 51 n. 2.

[28] Slings 1990, 11–12.

[29] Soph. *OT* 1116 τάχ' ἂν που, Plat. *Apol.* 38 в ἴcωc δ' ἂν δυναίμην ἐκτεῖcαι ὑμῖν που μνᾶν ἀργυρίου, etc.

[30] Arnott 1968, 231.      [31] Hense 1908, 156.      [32] Van Leeuwen 1908, 23.

before ὅλην and used in the ironical sense 'I thought I did', i.e. 'Of course I did'.[33]

Now the notorious hypermetric crux at 576. I reproduce here Rudolf Kassel's recent note (Kassel 1996):

Epitr. 398–401 [573–577], Onesimos spricht.

> ἂν δέ τις λάβηι μ[έ] τ[ι
> περιεργαcάμενον ἢ λαλήcαντ᾽, ἐκτεμεῖν
> δίδωμ᾽ ἐμαυτοῦ τοὺς †ὀδόνταc†. ἀλλ᾽ οὑτοcὶ
> τίc ἐcθ᾽ ὁ προcιών;

'A notorious puzzle' (Gomme-Sandbach); selbst das verzweifelte Auskunftsmittel, ein durch Stottern des aufgeregten Sklaven entstandenes unmetrisches Monstrum anzuerkennnen, ist schon empfohlen worden. Durch Änderungen des Versschlusses wie {ἀλλ᾽} οὑτοcί oder ἀλλ᾽ ὁδί ließ sich zwar das Versmaß herstellen, aber die Zähne blieben erhalten, und da gilt nach wie vor 'teeth are knocked or pulled out, not cut out' (Gomme-Sandbach).[34] Am meisten hat immer noch der Gedanke von Capps und Robert für sich, daß dem Sklaven eigentlich τοὺς ὄρχεις vorschwebt, deren Nennung dann ausbleibt. Dies könnte so ausgedrückt gewesen sein: ἐκτεμεῖν/δίδωμ᾽ ἐμαυτοῦ τούc, τὸ δεῖν, –ἀλλ᾽ οὑτοcί κτλ. Vgl. Sam. 547 τὸ δεῖνα· μικρόν, ὦ τᾶν –οἴχεται, wo Sandbach anmerkt: 'Demeas may here simply be playing for time, hoping that something *will* come into his head'. Eup. fr. 261 wird eine πορδή, im Stil der megarischen Posse, von der Frage τὸ δεῖν᾽, ἀκούεις; begleitet (δεῖν᾽ von Meineke aus δεινῆc hergestellt). Treffend geben bei Aristophanes Pac. 879 und Lys. 1168 van Leeuwen an der ersten, Wilamowitz an der zweiten Stelle den Sinn wieder: 'verba quaerens', 'τὸ δεῖνα schiebt er vor, weil er sich noch besinnt'. Die Obszönitäten werden hier nicht unterdrückt, sondern nur ein wenig aufgeschoben. Hier ist überall τὸ δεῖνα als eine Art Interjektion verwendet. Als Objekt steht ein euphemistisches 'Dingsda' Ach. 1149, ἀνατριβομένωι τὸ δεῖνα.

In 1907 Wilamowitz had noted: 'Den Vers durch Tilgung von ἀλλά einzurenken, mißfällt, aber οὑτοcί in ὁδί zu ändern auch.'[35] We clearly expect the meaning:

> If anybody finds that I
> Have interfered or gossiped, I will let
> Him cut my—balls off. But who's coming here?

to quote Maurice Balme's recent verse translation.[36] In the same way Euclio tells the old servant Staphyla in the *Aulularia*: 'By heaven, if I don't have your tongue torn out by the very roots, I give you orders, I give you full authority, to hand me over to anyone you please to have me castrated',

---

[33] As illustrated by Stevens 1976, 23–4. See also Austin and Olson 2004 on Ar. *Thesm.* 27.

[34] Eric Handley quotes, however, from Craig Taylor's *Return to Akenfield* (London, 2006, p. 202): 'They started up a pig company that supplied pigs every month, so they asked me if I would go work outside with these little pigs. You had to *cut the teeth out* and look after them. Then . . . I was castrating these pigs and I worked there I suppose eight or nine years.'

[35] Wilamowitz 1907, 864.     [36] Balme 2001, 99.

> si hercle ego te non elinguandam dedero usque ab radicibus,                    250
> impero auctorque <ego> sum, ut tu me cuivis castrandum loces.
>
>     251 <ego> *Guyet*

Kassel's solution τούς, τὸ δεῖν' for τοὺς ὀδόντας is very ingenious, but the corruption remains unaccounted for and one would expect a down-to-earth slave like Onesimos to call a spade a spade, not use, like the chorus at *Acharnians* 1149, a colloquial euphemism, 'to cut out my you-know-what'. That is why I have come up with an alternative proposal, 'to cut out my—what am I saying?', τούς—, for two reasons. The first is that Onesimos may have had an amusing last-minute change of mind. He realizes in the nick of time that he has no real desire to let himself be castrated, so he stops in mid-sentence: 'What am I talking about?' Now τί φημ'; in the text could easily have induced an inquisitive or cheeky schoolboy to enquire from a blushing teacher: 'what does this τί φημ' refer to?' The latter, at a loss, would have prudishly bleated out 'teeth' instead of 'testicles' and this would explain how, in the course of transmission, a clumsy and unmetrical 'explanatory gloss', ousted the original reading.[37]

To conclude, I reproduce here the beginning of Act IV as preserved in P.Mich.inv. 4807 fr. 1 and 2 of the second century BC, first made public by Koenen in a Seminar-Tischvorlage in 1992, and I also append the critical apparatus I provided at the end of my Florence lecture.[38] I welcome this chance to make amends for a papyrological *faux pas*.

> (Cμ.) οὐκ οἶδα τούτων [
> ἀλλ' ἀπιέναι δε[ῖ
> μ῀ ἐςτὶν ἁ₁ρ₁ετή, ₁τὸν ἄτοπον φεύγειν ἀεί.
> (Πα.) παπαῖ, τί τοῦτ' ἐςτ[                                                    705
> ἀεὶ ςὺ γίνηι κύριο[ς   (Cμ.)
> †οκιαι† ςχολὴ γὰρ ἐ[
> (Πα.) τἀμφίβ[ο]λα δεῖ[
> (Cμ.) πάλαι προτει[
> (Πα.) ὑπέρ <γ'> ἐμ[α]υτοῦ θ[                                                  710

702 marg. [Ζ]μι῀ M [τῶν κακῶν ἄλλην λύςιν Gronewald       703 Παμφίλη, τοῖς ἔμφροςιν (vel τῶν ἐμφρόνων) e.g. Austin (vid. ad 704)       704 Orion anthol. 7, 6 (περὶ ἀρετῆς) ἐκ τοῦ Ἡνιόχου Μενάνδρου· (fr. 157). sequitur μ῀ — ἀεί = Monost. 464 J. An. Gr. III p. 467, 4 Boiss. ἀρετή ἐςτι τὸ — ἀεί. Floril. ἄριςτον καὶ πρῶτον μάθημα ed. Schenkl, WSt 11 (1889) 11 (nr. 13) ἀρετῆς ἴδιόν ἐςτι τὸ φεύγειν ἀεὶ πᾶν ἄτοπον. [Liban.] char. epist. 73 (IX p. 41, 4 F.; codd. VUPaBADPH) ὑβριςτική· εἰ καλὸς ἦςθα, πολλοὺς ἂν εἶχες φίλους γνηςίους. ἐπειδὴ φαῦλος ἔφυς, εἰκότως οὐδένα κέκτηςαι φίλον. ἕκαςτος γὰρ τῶν ἐμφρόνων ἀνδρῶν ςπουδὴν ποιεῖται τὸν ἄτοπον — ἀεί (τὸ φεύγειν ἀεὶ τὸν ἄτ. B) τὸν ἄτοπον Orion, [Liban.] VUPaBA: τὴν ἄτ- [Liban.] PH: τὸ ἄτ- (id est τᾶτ-) Monost., An. Gr., [Liban.] D (Floril.): τό <γ'> ἄτ- Desrousseaux, Mél. Navarre (1935) p. 152       705 marg. [Πα]μ M παπαῖ Koenen:

---

[37] A bowdlerizing explanation had already been put forward by Schmid 1943, 157. He aptly compared Ar. *Au*. 443 for an obscenity omitted just after the article.

[38] Austin 2001, 23.

παπα M [οὐκ ἂν ᾠόμην, πάτερ e.g. Austin           706 αιεισυγεινη M μου. (Cμ.) ταῦτ' ὄνου
Gronewald coll. Ἔγχ. fr. 6 (= fr. 141 Koe.)        707 οκιαι M: cκιά Gronewald: ὅ καὶ Koenen[1]
ἐ[πιμένειν οὐκ ἔcτι νῷιν e.g. Austin              708 marg. [Πα]ᵘ M δεῖ[ται Gronewald, tum
νῦν, πάτερ, e.g. Austin, tum πολλῆς cχολῆς Gronewald   709 marg. [Ζμι]ᵏ M προτεί[νω
coι Gronewald, tum τὰ λῷιcτα, Παμφίλη e.g. Austin   710 marg. [Πα]ᵘ M γ' add.
Stoevesandt θ[αυμάcαιμ' ἂν εἰ λέγοιc e.g. Austin

Smikrines and Pamphile come out of the house together. 'I don't know any other solution to this grievous problem', says Smikrines, 'but we must go away, Pamphile. For sensible people, there is only one virtuous course, always to shun an abnormal person',

οὐκ οἶδα τούτων [τῶν κακῶν ἄλλην λύcιν,
ἀλλ' ἀπιέναι δε[ῖ, Παμφίλη. τοῖc ἔμφροcιν
μῖ' ἐcτὶν ἀ[ ρ] ετή, [ τὸν ἄτοπον φεύγειν ἀεί.

My supplement at the end of 703, τοῖc ἔμφροcιν, derives from the comment in an anonymous work sometimes attributed to Libanius and entitled Ἐπιcτολιμαῖοι χαρακτῆρεc or *Characteres epistolici*. Under the heading ὑβριcτική, 'insolence', we read 'If you were beautiful, you would have many good friends. Since you were born ugly, it's not surprising you haven't got any. Every sensible person takes care always to avoid someone who is not normal', ἕκαcτοc γὰρ τῶν ἐμφρόνων ἀνδρῶν cπουδὴν ποιεῖται τὸν ἄτοπον φεύγειν ἀεί. Pamphile replies: 'Good heavens! What's this? I wouldn't have thought it, father. You always try to be my lord and master',

παπαῖ, τί τοῦτ' ἐcτ['; οὐκ ἂν ᾠόμην, πάτερ·[39]
ἀεὶ cὺ γίνηι κύριό[c μου.

'That's of no importance', answers Smikrines—literally 'the shadow of a donkey', a proverbial phrase used elsewhere by Menander—'The two of us simply haven't the leisure to stay here any longer,'

ταῦτ' ὄνου
cκιά· cχολὴ γὰρ ἐ[πιμένειν οὐκ ἔcτι νῷιν.

'Ambiguous situations require plenty of leisure, father—at this very moment',

τἀμφίβολα δεῖ[ται νῦν, πάτερ, πολλῆc cχολῆc.

'For some time now I've been offering you the very best advice, Pamphile',

πάλαι προτεί[νω coι τὰ λῷιcτα, Παμφίλη.

In 710, as I hinted, something is not quite right. Wrong division of words—the nightmare of papyrologists—has caused havoc and led more than one

---

[39] Cf. fr. com. adesp. 1017, 18 οἷον πεποίηκαc, θύγατερ. οὐκ ἂν ᾠόμην.

astray.[40] How can Pamphile use of herself a masculine pronoun, ἐμαυτοῦ for ἐμαυτῆϲ? We should read of course

$$\text{ὑπέρ } <\gamma'> \text{ ἐμ[ο]ῦ τοῦθ᾽ [ὥϲ τιϲ ἀλλότριοϲ λέγειϲ,}$$

'When you say this on *my* behalf, you are talking like a stranger'. The γε is heavily sarcastic and for ὑπὲρ ἐμοῦ compare *Dysk.* 742.[41]

Pamphile is a noble young lady, full of dignity. She forgave her husband and I hope she will forgive me for treading on her toes. I shall try not to repeat the mistake. *Humanum est errare, diabolicum perseuerare.*


## BIBLIOGRAPHY

Arnott, W. G. 1968, 'Some Textual Reassessments in the Teubner Menander', *CQ²* 18, 224–40.

—— 1979, *Menander,* i (Cambridge, MA).

—— 2000, 'Notes on Some New Papyri of Menander's *Epitrepontes*', in E. Stärk und G. Vogt-Spira (eds.), *Dramatische Wäldchen: Festschrift für Eckard Lefèvre zum 65. Geburtstag* (Hildesheim), 153–63.

—— 2004a,'Menander's *Epitrepontes* in the Light of the New Papyri', in D. L. Cairns and R. Knox (eds.), *Law, Rhetoric and Comedy in Classical Athens (Essays in Honour of D. M. MacDowell)* (Swansea), 269–92.

—— 2004b, 'New Menander from the 1990's', in Bastianini and Casanova 2004, 35–53.

Austin, C. 1967, 'De nouveaux fragments de *l'Erechthée* d'Euripide', *Recherches de papyrologie,* 4, 11–67 with pls. i–ii.

—— 2001, 'L'Arbitrage de Ménandre', *Comunicazioni dell'Istituto Papirologico 'G. Vitelli',* 4, 9–23.

—— 2004a, 'Black Holes and Hallucinations: Notes on the Text of Menander', *Eikasmos,* 15, 125–38.

—— 2004b, 'More Black Holes in Menander: Notes on the *Dyskolos*', *Sem. Rom.* 7/2, 207–19.

—— and Bastianini, G. 2002, *Posidippi Pellaei quae supersunt omnia* (Milan).

—— and Olson, S. D. 2004, *Aristophanes: Thesmophoriazusae* (Oxford).

Balme, M. 2001, *Menander: The Plays and Fragments* (Oxford).

Bastianini, G., and Casanova, A. (eds.) 2004, *Menandro: cent'anni di papiri. Atti del convegno internazionale di studi, Firenze, 12–13 giugno 2003* (Florence).

Blanchard, A., and Bataille, A. 1964, 'Fragments sur papyrus du ϹΙΚΥΩΝΙΟϹ de Ménandre', *Recherches de papyrologie,* 3, 103–76 with pls. vi–xiii).

Capps, E. 1910, *Four Plays of Menander* (Boston).

---

[40] Cf. Arnott 2004a, 286: '710 (*Πα.*) ὑπὲρ <δ'> ἐμ[α]υτοῦ θ[ (<δ'> suppl. Stoevesandt).'

[41] As in P.Oxy. 4019 (saec. III^p), ed. P. J. Parsons (vol. LX, 1993) p. 26. In Austin 2004b, 217, περὶ ἐμοῦ should be corrected to ὑπὲρ ἐμοῦ. I note with pleasure that William Furley had also thought of ἐμ[ο]ῦ τοῦθ᾽ [ at *Epitr.* 710.

Cobet, C. G. 1876, 'Menandri fragmenta inedita', *Mnem.*[2] 4, 285–8 = id., *Miscellanea critica* (Leiden, 1876), 438–41.

D'Aiuto, F. 2003, '*Graeca* in codici orientali della Biblioteca Vaticana', in L. Perria (ed.), *Tra Oriente e Occidente: Scritture e libri greci fra le regioni orientali di Bisanzio e l'Italia* (Testi e studi bizantino-neoellenici, 14; Rome), 227–96

Headlam, W. 1908, *Restorations in Menander* (Cambridge).

Hense, O. 1908, 'Zum Menanderfund', *BPhW* 28, 737–50.

Jernstedt, V. (Ернштедтъ В.) 1891, Порфиріевскіе отрывки изъ Аттической комедии. Палеографическіе и филологическіе зтюды ('Porphyrian Fragments from Attic Comedy: Palaeographical and Philological Studies'), (Записки Историко-филологическаго факультета Императорскаго С.-Петербургскаго Университета, 26; St Petersburg, 1891).

Kassel, R. 1996, 'Aus der Arbeit an den Poetae Comici Graeci', *ZPE* 114, 57–9.

Koerte, A. 1910, *Menandrea* (Leipzig).

—— 1938, *Menandri quae supersunt*, 3rd edn., i (Leipzig).

Kühner, R. 1989–1904, *Ausführliche Grammatik der griechischen Sprache. Zweiter Teil: Satzlehre*, 2nd edn. rev. B. Gerth (Hanover and Leipzig).

Lefebvre, G. 1907, *Fragments d'un manuscrit de Ménandre* (Cairo).

Leeuwen, J. van, 1908. *Menander*[2] (Leiden).

Leo, F. 1907, 'Bemerkungen zu den neuen Bruchstücken Menanders', *NGG* 1907, 315–41.

—— 1908, 'Der neue Menander', *Herm.* 43, 120–67.

Martina, A. 1997, *Menandri Epitrepontes*, i (Rome).

Nünlist, R. 2004, 'The Beginning of *Epitrepontes* Act II', in Bastianini and Casanova 2004, 95–106.

Richards, H. 1908, 'Emendations of the New Menander Fragments', *CR* 22, 48; repr. id., *Aristophanes and Others* (London, 1909), 101.

Robert, C. 1908, *Der neue Menander* (Berlin).

Schmid, W. 1943, 'Menandreum', *Phil.* 96 (1943), 157–8.

Slings, S. R. 1990, 'Menander's *Epitrepontes* 284', *ZPE* 80, 11–12.

Stevens, P. T. 1976, *Colloquial Expressions in Euripides* (Wiesbaden).

Wilamowitz-Moellendorf, U. von, 1907, 'Zum Menander von Kairo', *SB Bln* 1907, 860–72.

—— 1908, 'Der Menander von Kairo', *NJA* 21, 34–62; repr. id., *Kleine Schriften*, i (Berlin 1935), 249–70.

# 9

## More Facts from Fragments?

*Annette Harder*

### 1. Introduction

The title of this chapter is, of course, inspired by Peter Parsons's own article 'Facts from Fragments',[1] in which he showed the impact on our understanding of Greek poetry of a variety of often small papyrus fragments. Going through the various literary genres one by one he reached interesting conclusions both about details and about larger issues such as, for example, the storylines of many plays of Euripides—thanks to the papyrus fragments of the *hypotheses*—or the existence of poetic scholarship in the fourth century BC (well before Alexandrian scholarship on Greek poetry was flourishing) in the papyrus commentary on an archaic cosmogonic poem found at Derveni.[2]

What follows focuses on *Supplementum Hellenisticum*, the joint effort of Peter Parsons and Hugh Lloyd-Jones,[3] and addresses the question whether more 'facts' can be found there. *Supplementum Hellenisticum* is an impressive work of scholarship, collecting as it does all the material of Hellenistic poetry found in Greek papyri and in other sources in addition to the material collected earlier in works like Meineke's *Analecta Alexandrina* (1843), Powell's *Collectanea Alexandrina* (1925), and Pfeiffer's edition of the fragments of Callimachus (1949).[4] The work first appeared in 1983 and it is interesting to

---

[1] Parsons 1982.    [2] Parsons 1982, 188, 189.
[3] See Lloyd-Jones and Parsons 1983 and the additions in Lloyd-Jones 2005.
[4] These three works were very useful tools for earlier scholars: Meineke collected the testimonia and the fragments from Hellenistic poetry quoted by ancient authors; Powell also included a number of papyri, published before 1925. Both left out Callimachus, whose fragments were collected in a complete and authoritative edition by Pfeiffer. As the amount of papyri of Hellenistic poetry in general as well as of Callimachus' poems had increased further after 1925 and 1949 and scholars saw that Powell's collection of quoted fragments was by no means complete, *Supplementum Hellenisticum* filled a distinct need in 1983 (see Lloyd-Jones 1984, 55–7). Even so, it does not contain all poetic fragments of the Hellenistic period, as it leaves out, e.g., some lyric fragments, fragments of drama, and the many poems inscribed on stone in that period (see Lloyd-Jones and Parsons 1983, p. ix). As *Supplementum Hellenisticum*

1. P.Berol. 9722 fo. 4r (= BKT 5.2, pp. 14–15) containing Sappho fr. 95. Parchment (vi AD). See p. 22.

2 P.Herc. 1672 fr. 3 containing Philodemus, *On Piety* citing Eumelus' *Europia*. Papyrus (i BC). See pp. 28–9.

3. Limestone funerary relief, Tarentum (vi BC). See p. 28.

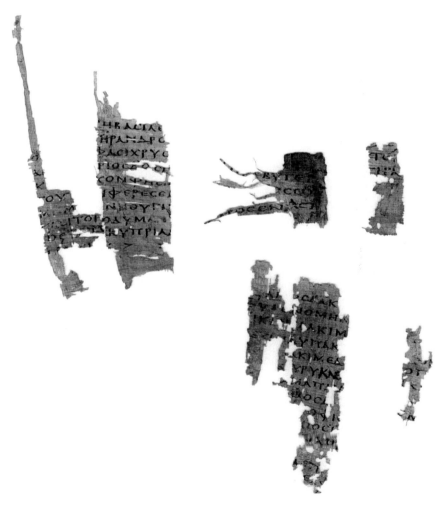

4. P. Oxy. LXXVI 5094 Mythography (Apollodorus of Athens?). See p. 29.

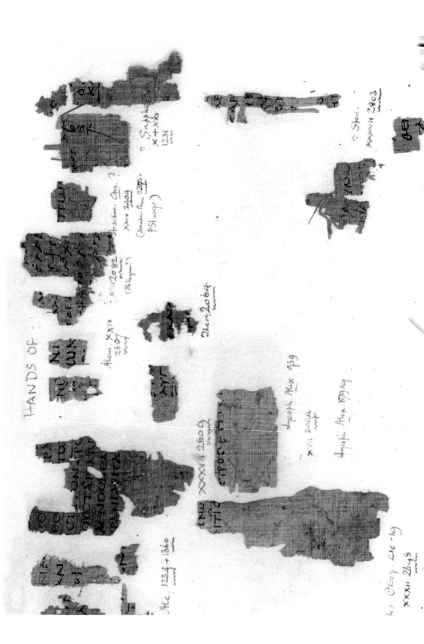

5  P.Oxy. X 1231 + XXI 2289 (Sappho bk. 1) additional fragment with coronis identified by E. Lobel. See pp. 33–8.

**6.** P. Oxy. LXXIII 4945 Lollianos, *Phoinikika*. See pp. 30–1 and 316–18.

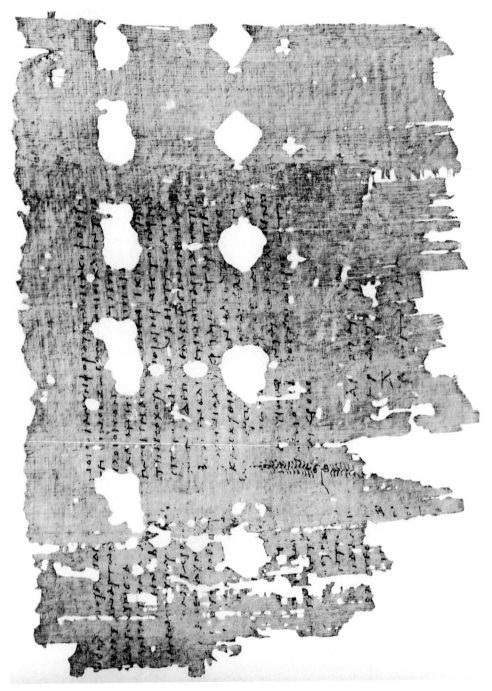

7. P.Amh. II 12, purportedly Aristarchus' commentary on Herodotus. See pp. 77–80.

**8 (a)–(b).** Mosaic scenes from Chorapha, Mytilene: Menander, *(a) Samia, (b) Plokion*. See pp. 148–9.

**9** *(a).* Mosaic scene from Chorapha, Mytilene: Menander,
*Theophoroumene.* See p. 149 n. 40.

**9** *(b).* Mosaic scene from Pompeii: Menander,
*Theophoroumene.* See p. 150 n. 42.

10 (a). Wall-painting in Naples, from Stabiae: Menander, *Theophoroumene*. See p. 150 n. 43.

10 *(b)–(c)*.   Terracotta statuettes from Myrina: *(b)* in Athens, *(c)* in Lyon. See p. 150 n. 44.

11 *(a)*. Mosaic scene from Pompeii: Menander, *Synaristosai*. See p. 150 n. 46.

11 *(b)*. Mosaic scene from Chorapha, Mytilene: Menander, *Synaristosai*. See p. 150 n. 47.

12 (*a*). Floor-mosaic by Zosimos of Samosata: Menander, *Synaristosai*. See p. 151 n. 48.

12 *(b)–(c)*.  Terracotta masks, Lipari. See p. 151.

13 *(a)*.  Wall-painting with a scene of comedy, Pompeii. See p. 152.

13 *(b)*.  Sicilian calyx-krater, Syracuse: Sophocles, *Oedipus Tyrannus*? See p. 152.

**14.** Sunflower: W. Blake, *Songs of Innocence and Experience* (1794), p. 43.
See p. 248 n. 20.

15. Eos abducting Cephalus: pinax, Selinus
Temple E. See p. 254 n. 31.

16. P. Oxy. LXX 4762 Ass romance. See pp. 317–18.

look back at the 26 years since then and to ask: 'What happened once we had this big collection of material? What impact has *Supplementum Hellenisticum* had on subsequent scholarship? Have scholars made the most of the opportunities offered by this collection? Are there further possibilities to profit from it?' Like most answers, the answers to these questions are complex.

On the one hand we have several examples of the work's impact. The collection of those papyrus fragments of Callimachus' *Aetia* which had been published after Pfeiffer's edition of 1949 has greatly enhanced our knowledge of that poem. It is very useful to have the fragments, which had been published in various series and journals, now collected in one volume. In particular the fragments of the *Victoria Berenices* have been of great importance and the fact that they were now easily accessible in *Supplementum Hellenisticum* (*SH* 254 68C) has certainly helped to make them an object of a great deal of profitable scholarly attention. In 1988 Peter Bing discussed two anonymous hexameter fragments, *SH* 946 and 947, in order to form a picture of conventional Hellenistic epic poetry and to compare it with the work of 'modern' Hellenistic poets like Callimachus.[5] By means of a careful analysis of these fragments and a comparison with Homer he was able to show their conventional and somewhat clumsy character and to relate them to the muddy Assyrian river of Callimachus' second *Hymn*.[6] He inferred that apparently there was an ongoing tradition of this kind of poetry and that there continued to be audiences who were pleased by it. Another group of fragments which received attention was the small collection consisting of *SH* 958 and 969, two fragments of Hellenistic encomiastic elegy with military subjects discussed in great detail by Silvia Barbantani in her book Φάτις νικηφόρος in 2001.[7] She suggested that this kind of elegy was the object of criticism in Callimachus' prologue to the *Aetia*. Each of these contributions is valuable on its own, but taken together they help to increase our insight in several important aspects of Hellenistic poetry and may be discussed in connection with the views of Alan Cameron.[8] He denied the existence of long Hellenistic epics and regarded the hexameter fragments in *Supplementum Hellenisticum* rather as remains of shorter encomiastic poems; he further argued that the style of elegy was the main issue in the *Aetia* prologue. It would be worth exploring whether further systematic investigation of the relevant epic and elegiac fragments in *Supplementum Hellenisticum* could shed fresh light on these issues.

---

covers the last three centuries BC, a sequel containing a modern edition of the Greek poetic fragments of the subsequent Roman period would also be very welcome.

[5] See Bing 1988, 50 ff.

[7] The title of the book is based on a supplement of *SH* 969. 1 by Terzaghi, which, somewhat ironically, the editors of *Supplementum Hellenisticum* mention only in their apparatus.

[8] See Cameron 1995.

On the other hand, one gets the impression that in spite of these promising and interesting results the great bulk of *Supplementum Hellenisticum* has not yet been incorporated into the scholarly discourse on Hellenistic poetry as much as it could or should have been and that further investigation of what it has to offer possibly could lead to more interesting results, also concerning the so-called book-fragments. Many of these fragments were of course known before 1983, but they had not yet been brought together in a systematic way in a modern edition, so that it was very hard to acquire an overview of what they had to offer.

We are entitled, then, to ask which fragments or issues could be further explored on the basis of *Supplementum Hellenisticum* and whether one may expect to find new 'facts' (i.e. anything that impacts on our understanding of Greek poetry) or insights from exploring these fragments or issues. This paper will focus on the genre of didactic poetry as a case study and show what an analysis of all the material in *Supplementum Hellenisticum* has to offer (though no exhaustive treatment is intended). At the end a few other groups of texts will be mentioned and some further possibilities for profiting from the wealth of material in *Supplementum Hellenisticum* will be indicated.

## 2. Didactic Poetry in *Supplementum Hellenisticum*

In Hellenistic poetry the genre of didactic poetry is represented by a few works which have been preserved and much discussed, such as Aratus' *Phaenomena* and Nicander's *Theriaca* and *Alexipharmaca*, and presumably also works like Callimachus' *Aetia* should be regarded as part of the tradition of didactic poetry.[9] The genre as a whole has been the object of scholarly interest in various monographs, articles, and collections of essays,[10] but in this discussion the fragments have been largely ignored and the contribution which could be made by *Supplementum Hellenisticum* has not yet been explored systematically.[11]

If, however, we search through *Supplementum Hellenisticum* for fragments of didactic poetry, it becomes manifest what a useful tool this work is, because it enables us to gather much additional information, which may help to form a better picture of this genre in Hellenistic poetry.

In the first place we acquire information about the kinds of subjects that were of interest to writers of didactic poetry. Thus we are able to extend the picture that was created by focusing only on the astronomical and medical

---

[9] See e.g. Kaesser 2005; Harder 2007.

[10] See e.g. Effe 1977; 2005; Dalzell 1996; Fakas 2001; Volk 2002.

[11] In Effe's monograph on didactic poetry (1977) the fragmentary poems were still left out. Parsons 1982, 185–6, however, briefly indicates the importance of fragments of didactic poetry and discusses some examples.

work of Aratus and Nicander. The fragments show a great variety of subjects, which may be divided into three categories, although the boundaries are not always very strict: (i) scientific subjects, probably with a certain emphasis on instruction and the practical use for the reader; (ii) scholarly subjects, in which the emphasis is more on the transmission of (often antiquarian) knowledge; (iii) practical instruction in various areas of the readers' daily life. As to the first category, quite a number of fragments are from didactic poetry about astronomy,[12] medical subjects,[13] or geography,[14] and some are about stones,[15] while Archimedes *SH* 201 is an elegiac poem about the mathematical problem of the number of the cattle of Helios. The second category contains works on philosophy,[16] aetiology,[17] various kinds of catalogues,[18] stories from Attica (?),[19] metamorphoses,[20] the labours of Heracles,[21] and perhaps a theogony.[22] In the third category we find works on the catching of fish[23] and hunting,[24] and cookery,[25] while *SH* 207 suggests that at some stage a certain Arrianus made a Greek version of Virgil's *Georgics* in hexameters.[26]

[12] Alexander Ephesius *SH* 19–22; Aratus *SH* 86–91; Artemidorus *SH* 213; Hegesianax *SH* 465 (and 466–70); Hermippus *SH* 485 (and 486–90); Sminthes *SH* 729; and perhaps adesp. *SH* 922.

[13] Aglaias *SH* 18 (elegiac); Aratus *SH* 92–8; Eudemus *SH* 412A (elegiac); Heliodorus *SH* 471 (and 472?); Numenius, *Theriaca SH* 589 (and 590–4) and perhaps *SH* 595 from another medical work; Philo *SH* 690 (elegiac).

[14] Alexander Aetolus *SH* 20; Alexander Ephesius *SH* 19 and 23–38; Callimachus Iunior, Περὶ νήcων *SH* 309; Zenothemis, Περίπλουc *SH* 855 (and 856–8); and perhaps Pancrates, Θαλάccια Ἔργα *SH* 598–600 and Philostephanus *SH* 691, which may be from a work about unusual harbours.

[15] Satyrus *SH* 717–19 (which might be poetry or prose); Zenothemis *SH* 859–62 (perhaps from a work about stones, but the fragments could also be part of his geographical work).

[16] Timon, *Indalmoi, SH* 841–4 (elegiac) and *Silloi, SH* 775–840. Because these works have received considerable scholarly attention elsewhere (see e.g. Long 1978) I shall not go into them very much in this chapter.

[17] Butas, *Aetia Romana, SH* 234–5 (elegiac); Dionysius, *Aetia, SH* 387–8. Cf. also Simias fr. 8 Powell on the origins of the names of months (elegiac?).

[18] Thus we find a catalogue of *erotes* in Artemidorus *SH* 214 (an elegiac fragment, which may be part of his *Phaenomena*; cf. the elegiac fragments in Phanocles frr. 1–6 Powell); of men in Sostratus *SH* 732–4 (elegiac). Cf. the catalogue of women in Nicaenetus fr. 2 Powell (also mentioned in *SH* 732), obviously part of the tradition of the Hesiodic *Catalogues*.

[19] Perhaps in Euphorion *SH* 417; cf. also frr. 34–6 Powell and see Pfeiffer 1968, 122, 150; Krevans 1984, 177.

[20] Antigonus Carystius, Ἀλλοιώcειc *SH* 50; Didymarchus *SH* 378A; Parthenius, Μεταμορφώcειc *SH* 636–7 (where, however, 637 might be poetry or prose); Theodorus Μεταμορφώcειc *SH* 749 (and 750?); adesp. *SH* 938 (which, however, could also be part of a *Theogony*). Cf. also the fragments of Nicander's *Heteroioumena* (on which see Gow and Scholfield 1953, 205–6).

[21] Diotimus *SH* 393–4.

[22] Adesp. *SH* 938 (which, however, could also be part of a *Metamorphoses*).

[23] Caecalus *SH* 237; Numenius *SH* 568–82 (and 583–8); Pancrates *SH* 601 (and 598–600); Posidonius *SH* 709.

[24] Perhaps Sostratus *SH* 735.

[25] Archestratus *SH* 132–92; Euthydemus, Περὶ ταρίχων *SH* 455.

[26] For other *Georgica* see the fragments of Nicander (and the introduction in Gow and Scholfield 1953, 209) and the anonymous fragment in Page 1942, 506–8, which according to the editor might be Hellenistic.

Many of these works of didactic poetry are attributed to specific authors and, although most of them are little more than names, some stand out a little more and allow us to form a picture of their work and interests, like Archestratus and Timon, but also some of the poets of whom we have less material. On the whole we have just a substantial list of names,[27] which shows that authors like Callimachus, Aratus, and Nicander, and in later Greek poetry authors like Dionysius Periegetes, Oppianus, and Ps.-Orpheus (in his *Lithica*) were no exceptions in writing didactic poetry and in choosing the themes listed above. Several fragments, however, help us to form at least some idea of what kind of people these authors were.

Some of them apparently played a more or less prominent role in society. Thus we may infer from *SH* 19 that Alexander Ephesius, apart from his poems about astronomy and geography, also wrote a historical work (perhaps about the *Bellum Marsicum*; see *SH* 39) and was politically active. Strabo, to whom we owe this information, calls him a ῥήτωρ and tells us that he was also referred to as ὁ Λύχνος.[28] *SH* 236 informs us that Butas, the author of an *Aetia Romana*, was a slave who had been given his freedom and acted as a political adviser for Cato. Aglaias of Byzantium, who wrote a poem in elegiacs about the cure of eye-diseases for his friend, the poet Demetrius in the first century AD, was a doctor according to *SH* 18. 2.

Other fragments indicate that some poets also were working within the framework of a royal court. Thus *SH* 464 contains an anecdote about Hegesianax, who, when asked to perform a dance for Antiochus III, let him choose between a bad dance and a good performance of poetry. Antiochus chose the second and was so pleased with it that Hegesianax was invited to join him for dinner and became a 'friend' of the king. In *SH* 412A we read that the *Theriaca* of Eudemus were approved of by Antiochus IV and in *SH* 752 we are informed that Theodorus, who wrote a *Metamorphoses* and various epic poems, also wrote a poem in hexameters for Cleopatra.

Some indications of the intellectual affinities of the poets may be found in *SH* 485, which tells us that Hermippus of Smyrna, who wrote a *Phaenomena*, was a Peripatetic philosopher,[29] and in *SH* 605, where we find evidence of contacts between Parthenius and poets like Virgil and Gallus.

Sometimes the material also allows further conclusions about the function and nature of the didactic works, as poets may refer to addressees, intended readers, and the origin and purpose of their work. Thus in the prooemium of

---

[27] An alphabetical list of names derived from the fragments in *Supplementum Hellenisticum* includes Aglaias, Alexander Ephesius, Antigonus Carystius, Aratus, Archimedes, Arrianus, Artemidorus, Butas, Caecalus, Callimachus Iunior, Didymarchus, Dionysius, Diotimus, Eudemus, Euthydemus, Hegesianax, Hermippus, Numenius, Pancrates, Parthenius, Philostephanus, Posidonius, Ptolemaeus, Satyrus, Sminthes, Sostratus, Theodorus, Timon, Zenothemis.

[28] See further C. Selzer in *Der Neue Pauly*, i. 478 s.v. Alexandros [22, aus Ephesos].

[29] See Fraser 1972, ii. 656 n. 52, 1090 n. 459; Bollausée 1999.

Archestratus' Ἡδυπάθεια in *SH* 132 ἱcτορίηc ἐπίδειγμα ποιούμενος
Ἑλλάδι πάcηι ('making a display of the results of his research for the whole
of Greece') and 133 ὅπου ἐcτὶν ἕκαcτον | κάλλιcτον βρωτόν τε ('where
every kind of food and . . . is the best') the author claims to be writing for the
whole of Greece and to inform his readers where the best food (and drink?) is
to be found. He based his work on his travels and investigations and
addressed it to his friends Moschus and Cleandrus, according to Athenaeus,
who quotes *SH* 133. Also Aglaias of Byzantium gives a clear indication of the
lasting and universal usefulness of his work on eye-diseases in *SH* 18. 5–6 καὶ
coὶ (sc. Demetrius) δ' ἔξοχον ἔcται ἐc ἄχθεα, παντί τ' ὄνειαρ | παρμόνιμον,
κάμψηιc ἄχρι κεν ἐc πλέοναc ('and for you it is an excellent means against
suffering and for everyone it is a lasting advantage, until you will join the
majority of people in death').

As to the nature of the didactic poems, one may find evidence about the
use of mythic material, about metre and about the presentation of the poems.
In Hegesianax *SH* 468–70, preserved in three passages of Hyginus' *Astronomica*, we see that his astronomical work, the *Phaenomena* (presumably
written in the late third or early second century BC), apparently contained a
certain amount of mythical material: in this respect it may be compared
with the *Phaenomena* of Aratus and the work of Nicander. The myths of
which we find evidence in the fragments of Hegesianax are of the kind that
were told by other Hellenistic poets as well and perhaps suggest a certain
focus on heroes and episodes that were related to human history and the
progress of civilization.[30] Thus in *SH* 468 we see that he included a story
about Theseus, who had to lift a rock in Troezen and bring the sword which
was hidden below it to his father Aegeus in Athens, an episode which was also
dealt with in Callimachus' *Hecale*.[31] In *SH* 469 we find a story about the
benefits of Demeter, who sends Triptolemus to far-away regions like Thrace,
in order to teach people to live by means of agriculture and to abandon
the wild means of feeding themselves which they used before. This
issue reminds us of the interest in Demeter in the Hellenistic period, evidence
of which is also found in works of Callimachus, like the sixth *Hymn* and
fr. 63 of the *Aetia*, and somewhat earlier in Philitas' *Demeter* (praised by
Callimachus in *Aetia* fr. 1. 9–10). *SH* 470 shows that Hegesianax also referred
to the story of Deucalion and the flood, which later was treated at length in
Ov. *Met.* 1. 381 ff. and obviously played an important part in the history
of mankind. Although the fragments may represent only a very small part of
Hegesianax's work, it should be noticed that their contents recall the attention
given to human 'progress' in Callimachus' *Aetia*.[32] The way in which this

---

[30] One should of course bear in mind that the amount of material is very small, so that these
conclusions are somewhat speculative and must be treated with caution.
[31] Cf. frr. 7–11 Hollis.     [32] See Harder 2003, 299 ff.

subject-matter seems to be well tuned to the moods of the times could fit in with the anecdote in *SH* 464 about the pleasure Antiochus III derived from the poem and the praise of Hegesianax in *SH* 712.

The fragments also show that didactic texts could be both in hexameters and in elegiac distichs. As to the question whether there is a difference between elegiac and hexameter didactic in the sense that the elegiac didactic was more playful and personal—as is suggested by Callimachus' *Aetia* and for Latin poetry by the work of Ovid[33]—the fragments offer no clear indications, because generally the material is too scanty. In fact the cookery book by Archestratus, which has been considered as a kind of parody of didactic epic,[34] is in hexameters.

Concerning the presentation of didactic poetry one may observe that the dialogue format, known from the first two books of Callimachus' *Aetia*, in Latin poetry from Ovid's *Fasti*, and in later Greek poetry from Ps.-Orpheus' *Lithica*, was employed by other poets too. Timon used it in his *Indalmoi* (*SH* 841–4) and *Silloi* (*SH* 775–840). In *SH* 495, an intriguing fragment attributed to Herodicus, we find part of a dialogue about love between Aspasia and Socrates, told by the latter. One may wonder how much the poem owed to Plato's *Symposium* and in what ways it developed the notion of Socrates being taught by a wise woman as found in the episode with Diotima. In Philo of Tarsus *SH* 690 a multifunctional painkiller introduces and describes itself in an elegiac fragment of twenty-six lines in a way which recalls the speaking objects in Callimachus' *Aetia*, like the lock of Berenice in fr.110. Philo's fragment begins as follows:

> Ταρϲέος ἰητροῖο μέγα θνητοῖϲι Φίλωνος
> εὔρεμα πρὸϲ πολλάϲ εἰμι παθῶν ὀδύναϲ

> I am the great invention for mortals by Philo, the doctor from Tarsus,
>      against the pains of many kinds of suffering.

Adesp. *SH* 938 shows that the Muses appeared in a didactic work (which may have been a *Theogony* or a *Metamorphoses*), the prooemium of which owes a great deal to that of Hesiod's *Theogony*. The date of this poem, however, is disputed as it has been attributed to the third century AD as well as to the third century BC.

Collecting the fragments of didactic poetry in *Supplementum Hellenisticum* also leads to an interesting collection of contexts from the authors who quoted the poems. Generally the work of the didactic poets is used by later prose authors, such as Strabo, Athenaeus, Pliny, Hyginus, Diogenes Laertius, as a source without further reflection. However, the fact that these authors quoted this poetry shows that they found it of (some) importance. Besides,

---

[33] See further Effe 1977, 104–5 n. 5; Fantuzzi and Hunter 2004, 34; Kaesser 2005, 97.
[34] See Effe 1977, 234 ff.

the authors who quote from the text of the poems sometimes add remarks about those fragments, and taken together these passages provide some insight into the way in which these works were regarded in later periods and thus into the reception of the genre.

We find several indications that the work of the Hellenistic didactic poets was regarded as a serious source of knowledge by later writers who possess a certain amount of authority in the same field. This applies for authors like Aratus and Nicander, the reception of whom gives ample evidence of serious treatment by later authors, as in e.g. the commentaries on Aratus by astronomers like Attalus and Hipparchus.[35] The material in *Supplementum Hellenisticum* provides evidence of a similar attitude towards the authors of whom only fragments were preserved and may thus shed some additional light on one of the much-debated questions concerning didactic poetry: 'Why write didactic poetry if the knowledge thus transmitted is also available in prose sources?'[36] The serious treatment of the didactic poems which we find in the authors who quote from them may make us wonder whether for most people in antiquity this was a valid distinction. Even Galen, who is the only author who addresses this issue in a critical manner, still treats a poetic source of knowledge quite seriously in another context, as will be shown below.

We see that Archestratus is appreciated as an important and knowledgeable source of information and as a poet in the tradition of Hesiod and Theognis by Athenaeus, from whom almost all the fragments of this poet are derived. In the context of *SH* 154 Athenaeus calls him ὁ τῶν ὀψοφάγων Ἡcίοδος ἢ Θέογνιc ('the Hesiod or Theognis among the gourmets') and an author ὃν ἀντὶ τοῦ Ὁμήρου προcκυνεῖc ('whom you worship on a plane with Homer'), and in the context of *SH* 192 he elaborates on this theme by stating:

θαυμάζειν δ᾽ ἐcτὶν ἄξιον τοῦ τὰc καλὰc ὑποθήκαc παραδιδόντοc ἡμῖν Ἀρχεcτρ- άτου, ὡc Ἐπικούρωι τῶι cοφῶι τῆc ἡδονῆc καθηγεμὼν γενόμενοc κατὰ τὸν Ἀcκραῖον ποιητὴν γνωμικῶc καὶ ἡμῖν cυμβουλεύει τιcὶ μὴ πείθεcθαι, αὐτῶι δὲ προcέχειν τὸν νοῦν, καὶ ἐcθίειν παρακελεύεται τὰ καὶ τά.

It is appropriate to admire Archestratus, who gave us these wonderful precepts, because having become a guide in pleasure for the wise Epicurus, in a didactic way like the poet from Ascra, he advises us too not to believe certain people, but to pay attention to himself, and he urges us to eat this and that.

When quoting other fragments he calls him e.g. ὁ ... πολυΐcτωρ Ἀρχέcτρατοc ('the very learned Archestratus') (*SH* 173) and ὁ ... cοφὸc

---

[35] See the contributions by Mike Tueller and Roger MacFarlane (on Aratus) and by Myrto Hatzimichali (on Nicander) in Harder, Regtuit, and Wakker 2009.

[36] See on this question in general the literature mentioned in n.10; the discussion on Aratus and didactic poetry in Fantuzzi and Hunter 2004, 224–38; and the discussion of Callimachus' *Aetia*, read as a work in the tradition of didactic poetry, in Harder 2007.

Ἀρχέϲτρατοϲ ('the wise Archestratus') (*SH* 176) and even more exuberantly ὁ ϲοφώτατοϲ Ἀρχέϲτρατοϲ ('the most wise Archestratus') (*SH* 178) and ὁ ... πολυμαθέϲτατοϲ Ἀρχέϲτρατοϲ ('the most learned Archestratus') (*SH* 186). Although all this may be a little tongue-in-cheek, the overall impression in combination with the sheer quantity of quotations is still that Athenaeus found Archestratus quite useful for his own purposes.

Elsewhere too we find evidence that didactic poetry was taken quite seriously as a source of information. Thus we find evidence of a serious treatment of the astronomical and geographical work of Alexander Ephesius by various authors. *SH* 21, a fragment on the harmony of the spheres from his astronomical work, was quoted at length by Theon of Smyrna and partly translated into Latin by Calcidius, and *SH* 22 perhaps is an indication of his use by Hyginus in his *Astronomica*. In *SH* 24 we read in Cicero's letters to Atticus how he borrowed Alexander's geographical work when he was planning to write a geographical work himself, and then returned it, finding it unhelpful, after all, because though not useless, it was bad poetry written by a careless man who knew nothing: *a Vibio libros accepi; poeta ineptus tamen et scit nihil, sed non est inutilis* ('I received the books from Vibius; the poet, however, is not very good and he knows nothing, but still he is not useless') and *libros Alexandri, neglegentis hominis et non boni poetae sed tamen non inutilis, tibi remisi* ('I have returned to you the books by Alexander, a careless man and not a good poet, but even so not useless'). In spite of Cicero's rather severe judgement, the fact that he took pains to borrow and consult the work suggests that it was considered reasonably important. This fits in with the fact that we see in *SH* 25–32 and 34–7 how Alexander was frequently used as a source by Stephanus of Byzantium and in *SH* 33 we find clear evidence of a passage of Alexander being imitated by Dionysius Periegetes. Altogether the evidence seems sufficient to assume that Alexander's work was firmly embedded in the tradition of geographical knowledge.

Concerning other authors too we see that they are often quoted by serious later prose authorities in their field, so that again one gets the impression that they were considered as relatively important. Thus *SH* 466–70 show that Plutarch and Hyginus probably used Hegesianax's *Phaenomena* and Plutarch even comments οὐ φαύλωϲ ὑπογράφων ὁ Ἁγηϲιάναξ εἴρηκε ('Hegesianax, writing not badly, has said . . .') (*SH* 466). In a similar way *SH* 486–90 show that the *Phaenomena* of Hermippus found their way into Hyginus' *Astronomica* and the scholia on Aratus. The impression of their relative importance created by the number and nature of the quotations seems to be confirmed by an epigram, attributed to one of the Ptolemies,[37] in *SH* 712:

---

[37] Probably Ptolemy IV Philopator according to Fraser 1972, ii. 1090 n. 459.

πάνθ' Ἡγησιάναξ τε καὶ Ἕρμιππος <τὰ> κατ' αἴθρην
  τείρεα καὶ πολλοὶ ταῦτα τὰ φαινόμενα
βίβλιοις ἐγκατέθεντο, †ἀπὸ σκοποῦ δ' ἀφάμαρτον†
  ἀλλ' ὅ γε λεπτολόγος σκῆπτρον Ἄρατος ἔχει.

Hegesianax and Hermippus and many others put all the stars
  in the sky and all those celestial phenomena
into books † . . . †,
  but the subtly speaking Aratus holds the sceptre.

In this epigram we see that Hegesianax and Hermippus, though surpassed by Aratus, are still the only other poets of *Phaenomena* mentioned by name. As we have seen above, the contents of Hegesianax's work may suggest some reasons for this praise.

Many fragments show that Timon was regarded as an author who took part in the scholarly discourse and hence as a serious source by authors like Diogenes Laertius; and in *SH* 412A we see how Eudemus' *Theriaca* had been transcribed by Heras and Asclepiades and thus found its way to the work of Galen.[38]

On the other hand there is evidence of a more critical attitude too. We see in *SH* 690 that Galen comments seriously on an elegiac poem by Philo of Tarsus, in which a multi-functional painkiller describes itself, but twice remarks that Philo, who to a large extent relies on mythological periphrasis, writes αἰνιγματωδῶς ('in riddling words') (on 17–18 and 20). Elsewhere Galen was even more sceptical and, in his judgement about the medical works of Aratus and others in *SH* 98 and 471, thought that the treatment of antidotes and medicine in general was not really a subject for poets. In his view the treatment of such subjects at poets' hands was dangerous and the poets themselves showed a certain awareness of this by beginning their poems with a strong assertion that they meant no harm:

καὶ περὶ μὲν τῶν ἁπλῶν θανασίμων ἐπὶ τοσοῦτον εἰρήσθω, περὶ δὲ τῶν συνθέτων
(sc. φαρμάκων τῶν θανασίμων) λεχθήσεται. ἐκτίθεσθαι δὲ τὰς τούτων σκευασίας
μοχθηρόν μοι δοκεῖ, καίπερ πολλῶν ἐπιχειρησάντων ταῖς τούτων συγγραφαῖς,
ὧν ἐστιν Ὀρφεὺς ὁ ἐπικληθεὶς Θεολόγος καὶ Ὧρος ὁ Μενδήσιος ὁ νεώτερος
καὶ Ἡλιόδωρος ὁ Ἀθηναῖος τραγωιδιῶν ποιητὴς καὶ Ἄρατος (*SH* 98) καὶ ἄλλοι
τινὲς τῶν τοιούτων συγγραφεῖς. τούτους μὲν οὖν ἄν τις θαυμάσειεν ἐμμέτρως
ἐπιχειρήσαντας ταῖς περὶ τούτων πραγματείαις, μέμψαιτο δ' ἂν εὐλόγως διὰ
τὰ πράγματα. διδάσκειν γὰρ μᾶλλόν ἐστι καὶ προσάγειν τοὺς βουλομένους ἐπὶ
κακωι, τὸ πλησίον ἐπιχειρεῖν ταῖς τούτων σκευασίαις. οἱ γοῦν τῶν καλῶν τούτων

---

[38] Other examples include *SH* 466 and 470, where Hegesianax is praised as a serious source for Hyginus' work on astronomy; 487–90, where Hermippus is regarded in a similar way as a source for works on astronomy; 593, where Numenius is regarded as a serious source in the area of *theriaca*; 598, where Athenaeus is giving a lengthy summary of the work of Pancrates; 858, where Zenothemis is praised by Aelian in his *Natura Animalium*; and 859–62, where the same author is used as a source by Pliny in his *Naturalis Historia*.

ποιημάτων συγγραφεῖς, τὴν παρὰ τοῖς πολλοῖς εὐλαβούμενοι καταδρομήν, ἐναρχόμενοι τῆς τούτων παραδόσεως τοὺς ἐντευξομένους πείθειν ἐπιχειροῦσιν ὡς οὐκ ἂν εἴησαν φαῦλοι τὸ ἦθος οὐδὲ τῶν τοιούτων φθοροποιῶν διδάσκαλοι, ὥσπερ καὶ Ἡλιόδωρον ἐν τοῖς πρὸς Νικόμαχον ἀπολυτικοῖς ἐναρχόμενόν ἐστιν εὑρεῖν οὕτω γράφοντα . . . (SH 471 = De antidotis 2. 7. 908–9 [xiv. 144 Kühn].)

And this should be enough said about the simple poisons, but now I shall speak about the compound poisons. Setting out the recipes for those seems difficult to me, although many people attempt writing them down, among them Orpheus, also called the Theologian, and the younger Orus of Mendes and Heliodorus of Athens, the tragic poet, and Aratus and some other writers on such subjects. One could perhaps admire them because they attempted the treatment of those subjects in metre, but one could also with good reason reproach them for what they are doing. For closely meddling with such recipes means rather that one is teaching and leading to evil those who are willing. In any case, the authors of those beautiful poems want to avoid the unfavourable judgement of the majority and, when they embark upon the transmission of this material, they try to convince their future readers that they are not bad in character and no teachers of such things as cause destruction, just as we can find Heliodorus in his *Apolytica* for Nicomachus writing thus at the beginning . . .

This passage by Galen is followed by a fragment of Heliodorus of seven lines in which he first invokes a series of gods and then asserts that he was not led astray by bribes or forced or led by a desire to please to undertake bringing evil on somebody, but that his hands are pure and his reasoning is undefiled by evil. We may deduce from this claim that not only Galen, but also readers of this kind of medical poetry were sceptical. This may seem to contradict the evidence of the serious treatment of didactic poetry listed above, but it seems conceivable that different attitudes coexisted and that, perhaps, in the matters of life and death with which medical science was concerned, there was a stronger tendency towards a more critical attitude.

Besides, the later didactic poets may also be compared unfavourably with older poets. In the context of quoting *SH* 237, 568, 601, and 709 Athenaeus comments that Homer was more accurate on halieutics (the art of fishing) than didactic poets like Caecalus of Argos (*SH* 237), Numenius of Heraclea (*SH* 568), Pancrates of Arcadia (*SH* 601), Posidonius of Corinth (*SH* 709), and Oppianus. Behind this view we seem to find the notion that Homer, because he is the best poet, is also the greatest authority on a variety of technical subjects. In *SH* 455 Athenaeus criticizes the Athenian poet Euthydemus, who pretends to quote what Hesiod wrote:

Εὐθύδημος ὁ Ἀθηναῖος, ἄνδρες φίλοι, ἐν τῶι περὶ ταρίχων Ἡσίοδόν φησι περὶ πάντων τῶν ταριχευομένων τάδ᾽ εἰρηκέναι· . . . (SH 455). ταῦτα τὰ ἔπη ἐμοὶ μὲν δοκεῖ τινος μαγείρου εἶναι μᾶλλον ἢ τοῦ μουσικωτάτου Ἡσιόδου. πόθεν γὰρ εἰδέναι δύναται Πάριον ἢ Βυζάντιον, ἔτι δὲ Τάραντα καὶ Βρεττίους καὶ Καμπανοὺς πολλοῖς ἔτεσι τούτων πρεσβύτερος ὤν; δοκεῖ οὖν μοι αὐτοῦ τοῦ Εὐθυδήμου εἶναι τὰ ποιήματα.

Euthydemus of Athens, my friends, says in his work about preserved fishes that Hesiod spoke as follows about all the goods that are preserved . . . To me these words seem to be spoken by a butcher rather than by the most poetical Hesiod. For how could he know about Parium or Byzantium and even more about Tarentum and the Brettians and the Campanians, being many years older than they? To me therefore it seems that these poems are by Euthydemus himself.

Here we see criticism on several points: the poetry is apparently found inferior to that of Hesiod, who is praised by a strong superlative; the poet is also found lacking in historical awareness as he does not seem to realize that he mentions places and peoples who were as yet unknown to Hesiod; and finally he is unmasked as a cheat.

Careful analysis of all these contexts in which the fragments are quoted may lead to further refinements in our view of the function and reception of didactic poetry and on the much disputed question why poets chose to write about subjects which were also dealt with in prose handbooks. In several instances one may rightly suspect hidden agendas and assume that the poets wanted to convey topical messages in the poems,[39] so that the transmission of knowledge was not the works' primary purpose. Even so, the ancient readers of didactic poetry on the whole apparently did not share the modern view that knowledge and instruction presented in poetic form should not be taken as seriously as when it was offered in a prose work (even though some authors were not quite satisfied with the work of those poets).

We also get some hints of the impact of the genre in small poems which also deal with subjects associated with didactic poetry (or with scientific or scholarly prose). The fact that Ptolemy *SH* 712 is an epigram dealing with poets on astronomy also gives an indication of the importance of that kind of poetry and offers some information about the way in which the genre of didactic poetry became a source of inspiration for poets who were writing in another genre.

## 3. Conclusion

In summary, one may say that the material collected in *Supplementum Hellenisticum* shows that the genre of didactic poetry must have flourished throughout the Hellenistic period and covered a wide range of subjects. There is evidence that the poets were well integrated into their social and political environment and the fragments give indications that they also shared the literary concerns of their times. The material also helps us to get a some-what clearer picture of several issues related to the genre of didactic poetry,

---

[39] As in e.g. Callimachus' *Aetia*, Virgil's *Georgics*, Ovid's *Metamorphoses* and *Fasti*; see in general Effe 1977 and on the *Aetia* Harder 2003.

particularly concerning the appreciation and reception of this poetry in later antiquity, where the evidence suggests that the works were taken more seriously than we may be inclined to assume. In this respect the results derived from the texts in *Supplementum Hellenisticum* suggest that it may be worth reinvestigating the whole indirect tradition and reception of didactic poetry, i.e. also those of the authors who are preserved in medieval manuscripts or whose fragments are not in *Supplementum Hellenisticum* (like e.g. most of the fragments of Nicander). It is quite conceivable that this kind of research would lead to a better view of the way in which didactic poetry functioned in antiquity.

As was done in the case of didactic poetry, one could also assemble fragments from other genres in *Supplementum Hellenisticum*. Thus one could collect and study the fragments about historical subjects, such as Theodotus' Περὶ Ἰουδαίων *SH* 757–64, or about Roman themes, such as Butas' *Aetia Romana* (*SH* 234–5), Melinno's *To Rome* (*SH* 541), and Simylus' *Tarpeia* (*SH* 724). Another interesting group would be the remains of court-poetry, such as Arcesilaus Pitanaeus *SH* 121 (for Attalus), Archimelus *SH* 202 (for Hiero), and Hermodotus *SH* 491–2 (for Antigonus Monophthalmus) and the hexameter poems about the deeds of kings listed in *SH* p.XVII. Also the subject of the poetic style of the fragments could be further pursued along the lines set out by Peter Bing in 1988.

At the end of this chapter I return to the beginning of Peter Parsons's article about 'facts from fragments'. There he quotes the description of a classicist given by John Earle in 1632, who states that a critic is 'the surgeon of old authors, and heals the wounds of dust and ignorance',[40] and he adds that this applies particularly to the papyrologist. We may add that this applies even more particularly to Peter Parsons himself, whose work may be considered as a major act of surgery. It is now the task of his successors in the field to continue his work and help the authors and texts he saved to live on and play their part in the classical heritage.

## BIBLIOGRAPHY

Barbantani, S. 2001, Φάτις νικηφόρος (Milan).
Bing, P. 1988, *The Well-Read Muse: Present and Past in Callimachus and Hellenistic Poets* (Hypomnemata, 90; Göttingen).
Bollausée, J. 1999, *Hermippus of Smyrna and his Biographical Writings. A Reappraisal* (Leuven).
Cameron, A. 1995, *Callimachus and his Critics* (Princeton).

---

[40] Parsons 1982, 184.

Dalzell, A. 1996, *The Criticism of Didactic Poetry: Essays on Lucretius, Virgil and Ovid* (Toronto, Buffalo, and London).

Effe, B. 1977, *Dichtung und Lehre: Untersuchungen zur Typologie des antiken Lehrgedichts* (Zetemata, 69; Munich).

—— 2005. 'Typologie und literarhistorischer Kontext: Zur Gattungsgeschichte des griechischen Lehrgedichts', in Horster and Reitz (2005), 27–44.

Fakas, C. 2001, *Der hellenistische Hesiod: Arats Phainomena und die Tradition der antiken Lehrepik* (Wiesbaden).

Fantuzzi, M., and Hunter, R. 2004, *Tradition and Innovation in Hellenistic Poetry* (Cambridge).

Fraser, P. M. 1972, *Ptolemaic Alexandria*, 3 vols. (Oxford).

Gow, A. S. F., and Scholfield, A. J. 1953, *Nicander* (Cambridge).

Harder, M. A. 2003, 'The Invention of Past, Present and Future in Callimachus' *Aetia*', *Hermes*, 131, 290–306.

—— 2007, 'To Teach or Not to Teach . . .? Some Aspects of the Genre of Didactic Poetry in Antiquity', in M. A. Harder, A. A. MacDonald, and G. J. Reinink (eds.), *Calliope's Classroom* (Leuven, Paris, and Dudley, MA), 23–48.

—— Regtuit, R. F., and Wakker, G. C. (eds.), 2009, *Nature and Science in Hellenistic Poetry* (Hellenistica Groningana, 15; Leuven).

Hollis, A. S. 1990, *Callimachus: Hecale* (Oxford).

Horster, M., and Reitz, C. (eds.), *Wissensvermittlung in dichterischer Gestalt* (Stuttgart, 2005).

Kaesser, C. 2005. 'The Poet and the "Polis": The *Aetia* as Didactic Poem', in Horster and Reitz 2005, 95–114.

Krevans, N. 1984, 'The Poet as editor' (diss. Princeton).

Lloyd-Jones, H. 1984, 'A Hellenistic Miscellany', *SIFC* 77, 52–72; repr. in id., *Greek Comedy, Hellenistic Literature, Greek Religion, and Miscellaneous: The Academic Papers of Sir Hugh Lloyd-Jones* (Oxford, 1990), 231–49.

—— 2005, *Supplementum Supplementi Hellenistici* (Berlin).

—— and Parsons, P. J. 1983, *Supplementum Hellenisticum* (Berlin and New York).

Long, A. A. 1978, 'Timon of Phlius: Pyrrhonist and Satirist', *PCPhS* 204, 68–90.

Meineke, A. 1843, *Analecta Alexandrina* (Berlin).

Page, D. L. 1942, *Greek Literary Papyri* (Cambridge, MA, and London); subsequently reissued as *Select Papyri*, iii.

Parsons, P. J. 1982, 'Facts from Fragments', *G&R* 29, 184–95.

Pfeiffer, R. 1949, *Callimachus*, i (Oxford).

—— 1968, *History of Classical Scholarship*, i (Oxford).

Powell, J. U. 1925, *Collectanea Alexandrina* (Oxford).

Volk, K. 2002, *The Poetics of Latin Didactic* (Oxford).

# 10

## Remapping the Mediterranean: The Argo Adventure in Apollonius and Callimachus

*Susan Stephens*

Recent studies have taught us the importance of landscape in the construction of the Greek imagination. Place is an intricate blend of the real and the imagined, composed of a location's natural phenomena, like mountains and rivers, the divine associations these phenomena inspire, expressed in stories and rituals, and the boundaries imposed by culture that generate categories of inclusion or exclusion.[1] Consider, for example, the immensely potent myth of Athenian autochthony and how it is articulated in the funeral oration embedded in Plato's *Menexenus*. Autochthony breeds virtue in contrast to the familiar migrating (and foreign) ancestors claimed by other Greeks:

οὕτω δή τοι τό γε τῆς πόλεως γενναῖον καὶ ἐλεύθερον βέβαιόν τε καὶ ὑγιές ἐστιν καὶ φύσει μισοβάρβαρον, διὰ τὸ εἰλικρινῶς εἶναι Ἕλληνας καὶ ἀμιγεῖς βαρβάρων. οὐ γὰρ Πέλοπες οὐδὲ Κάδμοι οὐδὲ Αἴγυπτοί τε καὶ Δαναοὶ οὐδὲ ἄλλοι πολλοὶ φύσει μὲν βάρβαροι ὄντες, νόμωι δὲ Ἕλληνες, συνοικοῦσιν ἡμῖν.

So strong and healthy is the nobility and freedom of the city (sc. Athens), and so averse to foreigners in its nature, because we are pure Hellenes and unmixed with foreigners. For no descendants of Pelops or Cadmus or Aegyptus or Danaus or any others who are foreign in nature, but Hellene in culture, live among us. (245 C–D.)[2]

If who you were and how you thought of yourself was to a large extent formed by where you lived and the accreted mythologies of that place, some of the earliest surviving Greek poetry provides testimony to the importance of arranging and remembering the stories that delimited local identities.

---

[1] Leontis 1995, 17–25; Cole 2004, 7–29.
[2] Hall 2002, 214 discusses this passage at some length in the context of 'Hellenic' identity.

Much of Hesiod, for example, provided a conceptual organization of space and boundaries in the forms of catalogues that linked a specific human group to a place and to its divinities via genealogical (usually matrilineal) descent.[3] Foreigners like Cadmus or Aegyptus or Danaus held pride of place in many of these genealogies—a constant reminder that the boundaries between Greek and non-Greek were permeable and often subject to revision.

In contrast to the places populated by heroes who predated or returned from the Trojan war, or colonies that might boast of a venerable mother city, Alexandria was new, a space that Greeks had only begun to inhabit after 332 BC. It had no defining narratives of place, no indigenous or founding families, no gods. We can document that the earliest settlers, who were mostly from Cyrene and the Cyrenaica, Macedon and Thessaly, Ionia and islands of the southern Mediterranean, continued to identify not with their new home but with their places of origin.[4] They styled themselves, for example, Cyrenaean or Samian or Thessalian. Callimachus offers us some insight into this world in an unplaced fragment from the *Aetia* when an Athenian resident in the city is found celebrating not a local festival, but the *Anthesteria* from his home city of Athens (fr. 178. 1–2 Pfeiffer). Alexandria specifically lacked origin myths, and we can see this deficiency being remedied in the opening sections of the *Alexander Romance*, with its narratives of Alexander as the city's *oikist* (1. 31–3).

The first poets of the city—Callimachus, Theocritus, and Apollonius—made important links with earlier Greek poetry by emphasizing the connections of Menelaus and Helen with the local landscape: the opening of the *Victoria Berenices*, for example, designates the Pharos as Helen's island, alluding to an alternative version of her elopement to Troy with Paris (fr. 383 Pfeiffer + *SH* 254. 5–6). This Helen was detained in Egypt and returned chaste to her husband while Paris made off only with her *eidolon*.[5] Similarly, Apollonius in a now almost non-existent poem identified Canopus (or Canobus) as the helmsman of Menelaus who fell asleep on the Egyptian shore, where he suffered a fatal snakebite.[6] 'Canopus' occurs in the *Prometheus Bound* (846) as the name of the coastal region of the westernmost branch of the Nile. This Greek form was probably derived from an Egyptian designation for the region, but by the Hellenistic period, Apollonius and others translated the landscape from the alien to the familiar by incorporating

---

[3] West 1985, 1–11, and see the discussion in Hall 1997, 83–8 on 'decoding the genealogical grammar'.

[4] Mueller 2005, 42.

[5] Stesichorus apparently recounted this version of the Helen myth, which now survives in Herodotus 2. 113–20 and in Euripides' *Helen*. See now Kelly 2007, 1–21.

[6] Fr. 3 Powell, and see Krevans 2000, 80–4. She notes that P. B. Schmid in his 1947 study of Apollonius' *ktisis*-poems already claimed that Apollonius was connecting 'Egyptian locales with the earliest cycles of Greek saga' (78 and n. 32).

the region (via the story of the helmsman) into the cycle of *nostoi*, or adventures of Greek heroes returning from the Trojan war.[7]

These examples, however, also illustrate the limits of this sort of mythic remapping: Alexandria lacked a past, and attempts to link it with Homer or the heroes of the Trojan war simultaneously reinforce the marginality of its own landscape in relation to that of old Greece. What Alexandria needed was a myth celebrating its own space that might reverse the inherited hierarchies of place: a myth that allowed Greeks to claim Egypt by right of ancestry. The argument of this paper is that Callimachus and Apollonius both turned to the legend of the Argonauts with its implicit and explicit links to Libya and *de facto* to Egypt to craft a legitimating myth for Greek occupation of an older, richer culture. It is essential to remember that 'Libya' included the whole stretch of North Africa from the Kinyps (the river that separated Carthaginian territory from Greek) to the shrine of Zeus Ammon, and for most ancient geographers it stretched as far as the west bank of the Nile. Strabo, for example, has a long discussion in his first book about the consequences of using the Nile to divide Asia from Libya (1. 2. 25 end, p. 32). When the world is thus divided, Alexandria, which lies some 25 miles west of the Nile, falls within the ancient Libyan territory that the gods gave to Greeks to settle.[8] In considering how these two early Ptolemaic poets appropriated and shaped the Argo adventure to conform to new circumstances, we can gain some insight into the processes of cultural formation taking place in the early city. This undertaking is complicated by the fact that Callimachus' Argonauts represent for us truly 'culture in pieces'—only a handful of fragments from the first book of the *Aetia* survive. For that reason, I shall begin with one earlier poem, Pindar's *Pythian* 4, then turn to Apollonius' *Argonautica*, before considering Callimachus.

The story of the Argonauts and their expedition to recover the Golden Fleece was extremely old.[9] Homer in the *Odyssey* was familiar with a venture that already had many of the features of the later epic: in book 12, Circe remarks about the *Planctae*:

> οἴη δὴ κείνηι γε παρέπλω ποντοπόρος νηῦς
> Ἀργὼ πασιμέλουσα, παρ᾽ Αἰήταο πλέουσα·
> καί νύ κε τὴν ἔνθ᾽ ὦκα βάλεν μεγάλας ποτὶ πέτρας,
> ἀλλ᾽ Ἥρη παρέπεμψεν, ἐπεὶ φίλος ἦεν Ἰήσων.

---

[7] Canopus, of course, does not occur in the *Odyssey*, and if he figured in pre-Hellenistic versions of Menelaus and Helen in Egypt, the sources are now lost. Narratives of return were immensely useful in forging genealogical links to the heroic past; each hero might stop in several places before finally reaching his home city. Menelaus and Helen's post-Trojan war adventures in North Africa were especially prominent in the Hellenistic period (Malkin 1994, 48–66).

[8] This is set out in much greater detail below.

[9] For the intersection of the *Odyssey* and the *Argonautica*, see West 2005.

The only seafaring ship to pass though that way was the Argo, of interest to all, sailing back from Aeetes. And her too would it have cast immediately upon the great rocks but Hera sent her through, since Jason was dear. (*Od.* 12. 70–3.)

References to Jason or his crew surface in a wide variety of genres ranging from the genealogically shaped poems of Hesiod,[10] to Mimnermus' elegies, to Greek tragedy (Euripides' *Medea* is the best known), to lost epics, to mythographers like Dionysius Scytobrachion, who was a near contemporary of Callimachus and Apollonius.[11] However, the sole surviving intact treatment of the story of the Argonauts before Apollonius comes not from epic, but from Pindar: *Pythian* 4, one of several victory odes written for the Battiad kings of Cyrene. At 299 lines long, it is often described as Pindar's most 'epic' poem, and would surely have felt at home in the Hellenistic period. It is a dense narrative that tells its story more through allusion to or ellipse of seemingly well-known events than by recounting them in any detail. Scholars have certainly noted the many overlaps between Pindar's epinician and Apollonius' epic, but usually they belong to a general tally of which writer included which events from some notional whole story. Yet if *Pythian* 4 is read as a more central intertext for Apollonius and for Callimachus, in the sense of an earlier work whose meanings form an essential part of the subsequent texts' signification, we can begin to see how the distinctive elements of one particular colonization myth was adapted to accommodate early Alexandria.

Pindar's narrative was written for Arcesilaus IV, the king of Cyrene, to commemorate his victory in the chariot-race at the Pythian games in 462 BC.[12] At the time of writing Arcesilaus' Battiad rule was being seriously threatened by political unrest, and the strategy of *Pythian* 4 is to present a case for the reinstatement of an exiled member of the aristocracy, Demophilus, as an integral part of the poet's argument. The adventures of the Argonauts are framed by a brief tribute to the victor and a rather longer closing plea for the return of Demophilus. The link between this contemporary political frame and the myth is the figure of Euphemus. He was a member of the crew of the Argo, but also the ancestor of the Battiads of Cyrene. The logic of the juxtaposed parts is that even though Euphemus forgot the instruction of the oracle, the divine will in time was fulfilled. Just so, we may infer, it is the divine plan that Demophilus be reinstated. Arcesilaus can comply or obstruct, but in the latter case can only delay its inevitability.

*Pythian* 4 begins at the end of the adventure, where the Argonauts have broken their return journey on Thera. Callimachus begins his Argonaut

---

[10] The Libyan adventures seem to have featured in the *Megalai Ehoiai* (F 253), on which see D'Alessio 2005, 195–9.

[11] For a detailed survey consult Dräger 1993.

[12] It was the second of two odes that celebrated that victory: the other (*Pythian* 5) was more typical in length and style.

sequence close by: at 'Anaphe, neighbour to Laconian Thera' (fr. 7. 23 Pf. = 9. 23 Massimilla) while Apollonius ends his poem on Anaphe (4. 1717). On Thera, Medea foretells the founding of the royal house of Cyrene.

$$καὶ τὸ Μηδείας ἔπος ἀγκομίσαι$$
$$ἑβδόμαι καὶ σὺν δεκάται γενεᾶι Θή-$$ 10
$$ραιον, Αἰήτα τό ποτε ζαμενής$$
$$παῖς ἀπέπνευσ' ἀθανάτου στόματος, δέσ-$$
$$ποινα Κόλχων. εἶπε δ' οὕτως$$
$$ἡμιθέοισιν Ἰάσονος αἰχματᾶο ναύταις·$$
$$"Κέκλυτε, παῖδες ὑπερθύμων τε φωτῶν καὶ θεῶν·$$
$$φαμὶ γὰρ τᾶσδ' ἐξ ἁλιπλά-$$
$$κτου ποτὲ γᾶς Ἐπάφοιο κόραν$$
$$ἀστέων ῥίζαν φυτεύσεσθαι μελησιμβρότων$$ 15
$$Διὸς ἐν Ἄμμωνος θεμέθλοις·$$

[Battus was destined] to fulfil the words of Medea in the seventeenth generation on Thera, words that the mighty daughter of Aeetes, the mistress of the Colchians, once breathed from her immortal mouth. She spoke as follows to the demigod crew of spear-carrying Jason. 'Harken, sons of high-spirited mortals and gods. I say that from this sea-beaten land (sc. Thera) the daughter of Epaphus (sc. Libya) will one day be planted with a root of famous cities amid the foundations of Zeus Ammon.' (*P. 4. 9–16.*)

She explains that a clod of Libyan earth (βώλακα δαιμονίαν, 4. 37) that had been previously given to Euphemus by a son of Poseidon was destined, when washed into the sea, to come to rest on the island of Thera; and from there in the fullness of time, Battus, one of Euphemus' descendants, would come to colonize Libya. Through its instrumentality, Euphemus would become the ancestor of the Cyrenaean royal house: over seventeen generations, his descendants would migrate from Lemnos to Sparta to Thera and thence to Libya—the land of Zeus Ammon.

The clod of Libyan earth given as a gift that comes to rest on Thera, that is, on Greek soil, confers by its migration an autochthonous claim to Libya, which subsequently becomes Greek in fulfilment of the prophecy.[13] Pindar imaginatively links the lengthy process to a fecund sexuality—Libya is first described as a white breast (ἀργινόεντι μαστῶι, v. 8), and as a feminine space to be ploughed. Jason's ploughing of the barbarian soil of Colchis—when he undertakes the tests set by Aeetes—anticipates the actions of the descendants of Euphemus, who in the fullness of time come to plough the fertile soil of Libya. The Argonauts' coupling with the Lemnian women is again likened to ploughing. And the resulting 'seed of Greek heroes' in their turn are the destined 'ploughmen' of Libya. As Pindar puts it, now reverting to his own voice:

[13] See Calame 2003, 109 for the logic of this 'marine' autochthony.

καὶ ἐν ἀλλοδαπαῖς
σπέρμ' ἀρούραις τουτάκις ὑμετέρας ἀ-            255
κτῖνος ὄλβου δέξατο μοιρίδιον
ἆμαρ ἢ νύκτες· τόθι γὰρ γένος Εὐφά-
μου φυτευθὲν λοιπὸν αἰεί
τέλλετο· καὶ Λακεδαιμονίων μιχθέντες ἀνδρῶν
ἤθεσιν ἔν ποτε Καλλίσταν ἀπώικησαν χρόνωι
νᾶσον· ἔνθεν δ' ὕμμι Λατοί-
δας ἔπορεν Λιβύας πεδίον
σὺν θεῶν τιμαῖς ὀφέλλειν, ἄστυ χρυσοθρόνου,            260
διανέμειν θεῖον Κύρανας.

And then in foreign fields (sc. the beds of Lemnian women) did the allotted days or nights receive the seed of your splendid prosperity. For there the race of Euphemus was planted and came into existence for ever after. Sharing in the customs of men of Lacedaemon eventually they settled on an island once called *Kalliste*. From there, Leto's son granted you the plain of Libya to make rich with the favour of the gods, to govern the divine city of golden-throned Cyrene. (*P.* 4. 254–61.)

In Pindar's account, therefore, the entire adventure of the Argonauts unfolds as an *aition*, and one with ramifications for the contemporary world of the victor. The specific rhetoric of the *aition* is the manifest destiny of that Libyan clod, even when, or especially when, the human instruments do not understand the process. The Pindaric dynamic is a movement from a moment shrouded in the mists of the past (the time of the guest-gift of the clod) to the island of *Kalliste*/Thera (the place where Medea prophesies and from which Battus sets out for Libya), and from Thera to the cultivated fields of North Africa. The juxtaposition of the disparate prophecies from successive time-periods reinforces the inevitability of the events—as if the god were constantly sending reminders.[14] And as a result, in Pindar the expedition of the Argonauts assumes cosmic importance, a necessary step in the divinely prompted colonization of North Africa. To take this a bit further, and employ the structuralist arguments of Claude Calame: within Pindar's scheme the union of Jason and Medea serves as a precursor of the reunion of Greece and Libya in the properly submissive hierarchy in which barbarian female—whether woman or land—is tamed and ploughed and rendered fertile by Greek male conquest. Thus Jason sleeping with Colchian Medea, Euphemus sleeping with the Lemnian woman, who bears the ancestor of Battus, and ultimately Battus and his colonizers sleeping with Libyan women are all linked by divine plan. And in another Cyrenaean poem, *Pythian* 9, divinity actually establishes the paradigm—the whole colonizing chain

---

[14] Calame points to five distinctive temporal planes (2003, 47).

is begun by Apollo himself taming by conquest and inseminating the eponymous nymph, Cyrene.[15]

In his *Hymn to Apollo* Callimachus employs these same tropes of colonization, the conquest of local women, though a bit more discreetly: Apollo sleeping with his 'bride' Cyrene and the Spartan/Theran colonists joining in the dance with the local Libyan women:

> Cπάρτη τοι, Καρνεῖε, †τόδε† πρώτιστον ἔδεθλον,
> δεύτερον αὖ Θήρη, τρίτατόν γε μὲν ἄcτυ Κυρήνης.
> ἐκ μέν cε Cπάρτης ἕκτον γένος Οἰδιπόδαο
> ἤγαγε Θηραίην ἐς ἀπόκτιcιν ...
> ἦ ῥ' ἐχάρη μέγα Φοῖβος, ὅτε ζωcτῆρες Ἐννοῦς                      85
> ἀνέρες ὠρχήcαντο μετὰ ξανθῆιcι Λιβύccηιc,
> τέθμιαι εὖτε cφιν Καρνειάδες ἤλυθον ὧραι.
> οἱ δ' οὔπω πηγῆιcι Κύρης ἐδύναντο πελάccαι
> Δωριέες, πυκινὴν δὲ νάπηιc' Ἄζηλιν ἔναιον.
> τοὺς μὲν ἄναξ ἴδεν αὐτός, ἑῆι δ' ἐπεδείξατο νύμφηι              90
> cτὰς ἐπὶ Μυρτούccης κερατώδεος, ἧχι λέοντα
> Ὑψηὶc κατέπεφνε βοῶν cίνιν Εὐρυπύλοιο.

Sparta, O Carneian, was your first foundation, and then Thera, and third was the city of Cyrene. From Sparta the sixth generation of Oedipus led you out to their colony at Thera ... Indeed Phoebus rejoiced greatly when the belted warriors danced with the yellow-haired Libyan women, when the due season for the Carneia came. The Dorians were not yet able to approach the springs of Cyre, but lived in thickly wooded Azelis. These did Phoebus himself see, and showed to his bride, standing on horned Myrtussa, where the daughter of Hypseus killed the lion that was a bane to Eurypylus' cattle. (*hAp.* 72–5, 85–92.)

In this poem, however, Callimachus omits the clod of earth given to Euphemus. Rather his focus is on the latter part of the long history: Apollo's prophecy to Battus. He marks the transition from Sparta to Thera to Cyrene and identifies the Cyrenaean royal house as having descended in six generations from Oedipus.[16] For Cyrenaean Callimachus these genealogies are not bits of lore gleaned from lucubrations over obscure writers of local histories; rather they constitute the defining myths of his own polis, important elements in his construction of self: these are promises made about 'my city' to 'my kings' and 'my ancestors' (*hAp.* 65–71).[17] Despite the omission of earlier events we

---

[15] Calame discusses these texts and their 'isotopies' in a number of places: see especially 1990, 287–92; 1993, 38–40 and nn., as well as 2003, 54–5.

[16] *Pyth.* 4. 283; for fuller genealogical details see Hdt. 4. 145–9. Dräger 1993, 228–6 discusses the Battiad genealogies as they occur in Hesiod, Pindar, and Herodotus; see his very useful schematic presentation on p. 276. See Calame 2003, 86–101 for the transformation of Pindar's 'fractured narrative' into 'political' time in Herodotus.

[17] See West 1985, 87 for the fascinating conjecture that Eugammon of Cyrene had previously incorporated elements from local Cyrenaean mythology into his *Telegonia*.

can be sure that Callimachus is operating within the same frames of reference as *Pythian* 4. The story of the clod Irad Malkin describes as follows:

The fundamental Greek charter myth of Libya includes Sparta, Thera, and Cyrene . . . [s]pecifically, this charter myth articulates a colonial right of possession. It is the story of the original clod of earth—a piece of Libyan soil, *pars pro toto*—granted to the mythic ancestor of the real founder of Cyrene, Battos. This ancestor was the Minyan Euphemos, one of the Argonauts.[18]

Callimachus' emphasis on the proximate cause of the Cyrene foundation, namely, Apollo's Delphic prophecy to Battus, within a hymn to Apollo for the well-being of the city makes excellent sense, especially since Callimachus claimed the Battiads as ancestors. The Argonauts and the gift of Libyan soil belong to a prehistory of events in the Apollo hymn and even when omitted from the narrative they cannot be far from the surface.

Callimachus layered time in his Apollo hymn in an analogous way to Pindar: the narrative moves between Callimachus in present time, Apollo and Cyrene as the mythological founders, and the first colonists celebrating the rite of the Carneia on Libyan soil. Apollonius too experiments with a layering of time in his epic, most obviously when he constructs an adventure that takes place in the pre-Homeric world, and creates opportunities for the Homeric world to intrude into his own text. This is particularly visible in book 4, when the adventurers reach the Odyssean landscape of the western Mediterranean, stopping at Circe's island, and later at the court of Alcinous and Arete on Phaeacia, where Jason and Medea are married. Apollonius has his Argonauts also encounter the Sirens, and much is made of their passage through the *Planctae*—a subject (as we saw above) that was already present in the *Odyssey*. In Apollonius' version, Thetis and the sea-nymphs carry the Argo through these treacherous waters. Her presence and that of Peleus, who is a member of the Argo's crew and Thetis' estranged husband, remind us that they are the parents of Achilles, who is as yet a child. The adventures of Heracles present an even more complex temporal picture: since Heracles was for a brief time a member of the expedition, he appears in the present as well as in the future and the immediate past. After he leaves the expedition in search of Hylas, much of the area that the heroes traverse provides an opportunity to allude to Heracles' recent presence. In book 4, for example, the Argonauts evidently catch sight of him just after he has stolen the apples of the Hesperides as he passes on his way to the under world for his final adventure. In Apollonius, thus, heroic events seem always already to have happened, whatever their actual temporal relationship to the events of the poem. I suggest that this layering of heroic events through the allusive as well as actual presence of both Homeric heroes and Heracles in the text is a deliberate construct to create the impression of narrative inevitability similar to that of

[18] Malkin 1994, 174: see also 179–80 on other 'right to land' motifs in Greek foundation myth.

Pindar, where the simultaneous presence of several generations linked in prophecy restricts the potential for heroic action.[19]

But unlike Pindar, Apollonius tells the events of his story in chronological order, but in such a way that his poem appears framed Pindarically. Allusions to the Pindaric texts are prominent at the beginning but especially at the end of the *Argonautica*,[20] where Apollonius concludes his narrative with this same clod of Libyan earth. In place of Medea's vatic outpouring, Apollonius sets out the gift exchange as a lengthy incident at book 4. 1550–90, and lest we fail to take the point the event is reprised at the very end where the connection between the clod and the white breast of Libya (Pindar's ἀργινόεντι μαστῷ) is worked out in a rather baroque dream sent to Euphemus.

> Ἀλλ' ὅτε δὴ κἀκεῖθεν ὑπεύδια πείςματ' ἔλυςαν,
> μνήςατ' ἔπειτ' Εὔφημος ὀνείρατος ἐννυχίοιο,
> ἁζόμενος Μαίης υἷα κλυτόν· εἴςατο γάρ οἱ
> δαιμονίη βῶλαξ ἐπιμάςτιος ᾧ ἐν ἀγοςτῷ
> ἄρδεςθαι λευκῇςιν ὑπὸ λιβάδεςςι γάλακτος,                         1735
> ἐκ δὲ γυνὴ βώλοιο πέλειν ὀλίγης περ ἐούςης
> παρθενικῇ ἰκέλη· μίχθη δέ οἱ ἐν φιλότητι
> ἄςχετον ἱμερθείς· ὀλοφύρετο δ' ἠΰτε κούρην
> ζευξάμενος, τὴν αὐτὸς ἑῷ ἀτίταλλε γάλακτι·
> ἡ δέ ἑ μειλιχίοιςι παρηγορέεςκεν ἔπεςςι·                            1740
> "Τρίτωνος γένος εἰμί, τεῶν τροφός, ὦ φίλε, παίδων,
> οὐ κούρη· Τρίτων γὰρ ἐμοὶ Λιβύη τε τοκῆες.
> ἀλλά με Νηρῆος παρακάτθεο παρθενικῇςιν
> ἂμ πέλαγος ναίειν Ἀνάφης ςχεδόν· εἶμι δ' ἐς αὐγὰς
> ἠελίου μετόπιςθε, τεοῖς νεπόδεςςιν ἑτοίμη."                        1745

But when they had loosed their ship's cables in calm weather, Euphemus then recalled a dream he had had at night, when he was honouring the glorious son of Maia. The divine clod seemed to him to be at his breast, held in his arms and suckled by white drops of milk, and from the clod, small though it was, came a woman like a young virgin. Overcome by strong desire he lay with her, but lamented as though he had coupled with his own daughter whom he had nourished with his own milk. But she soothed him with gentle words: 'I am of the race of Triton, my friend, your children's nurse, not your daughter, for Triton and Libya are my parents. Entrust me to the maiden daughters of Nereus so that I may dwell in the sea near Anaphe. I shall return again to the sun's rays, when I am ready for your descendants.' (4. 1731–45.)

Apollonius employs the same colonizing trope—sexual conquest (though here nicely tinged with incest averted) and Pindar's term—δαιμονίη βῶλαξ—for the clod of earth.[21] But Pindar's δαιμονίη βῶλαξ was forgotten (*Pyth.* 4. 41) and destiny's plan delayed when it was inadvertently washed into the sea. In Apollonius Euphemus recounts his dream to Jason, whose

---

[19] For a fuller discussion see Stephens 2003, 183–96.     [20] Hunter 1993, 152–3.
[21] See Calame 2003, 61–3 on the clod as nurturer of the *genos* of Euphemus.

behaviour vis-à-vis divinities has been prescient throughout the poem. Jason understands the significance of the clod and thoughtfully explains its importance for the reader:

> "βώλακα γὰρ τεύξουϲι θεοὶ πόντονδε βαλόντι
> νῆϲον, ἵν' ὁπλότεροι παίδων ϲέθεν ἐννάϲϲονται
> παῖδεϲ, ἐπεὶ Τρίτων ξεινήιον ἐγγυάλιξε
> τήνδε τοι ἠπείροιο Λιβυϲτίδοϲ· οὔ νύ τιϲ ἄλλοϲ
> ἀθανάτων ἢ κεῖνοϲ, ὅ μιν πόρεν ἀντιβολήϲαϲ."
> ὣϲ ἔφατ'· οὐδ' ἁλίωϲεν ὑπόκριϲιν Αἰϲονίδαο      1755
> Εὔφημοϲ, βῶλον δὲ θεοπροπίηιϲιν ἰανθεὶϲ
> ἧκεν ὑποβρυχίην. τῆϲ δ' ἔκτοθι νῆϲοϲ ἀέρθη
> Καλλίϲτη, παίδων ἱρὴ τροφὸϲ Εὐφήμοιο·

'When you have cast the clod into the sea, the gods will make an island, where the future sons of your sons shall dwell, since Triton gave you this piece of the Libyan land as a guest gift. It was no other immortal than he who gave it to you when he met you.' So he (sc. Jason) spoke, and Euphemus did not ignore the answer of the son of Aeson, but rejoicing at this prophecy he cast the clod into the deep. From it arose an island, Kalliste (= Thera), the holy nurse of the sons of Euphemus. (4. 1750–8.)

Let me now attempt to position this within its contemporary context. Libya had more than one colonial settlement, and the clod of earth 'granted to the mythic ancestor' could be invoked to justify more than one foundation. Since Libya included the whole of North Africa from the territory of Carthage to the west of the Cyrenaica as far as the west bank of the Nile, Alexandria, as I said above, also fell within the clod's entitlement. If this seems to be a geographic stretch for us, it was uncontroversial for the Hellenistic audience: Posidippus locates Alexandria in Libya in his Pharos epigram (116. 3 A–B), as does Callimachus in the *Apotheosis of Arsinoe*, where the deified Philotera exclaims, upon seeing the smoke from her sister Arsinoe II's funeral pyre, 'Is it that my Libya is being harmed?'[22]

I suggest that the effect of the Pindaric framing is to add a dimension of foundation narrative to Apollonius' epic that implicitly extended the range of Pindar's prophecy to include the new Libyan foundation of Ptolemaic Alexandria. It is even possible that when Apollonius wrote his poem, Cyrene was once again under Ptolemaic control. This would have happened after the union of Euergetes and Berenice II, the daughter of Magas, the ruler of Cyrene, in 246 BC.[23] But in fact Apollonius strips his version of the colonization myth

---

[22] ἦρά τι μοι Λιβύα κα[κοῦται; (fr. 228. 51 Pf.). I am grateful to Alessandro Barchiesi and G.-B. D'Alessio for calling this passage to my attention.

[23] Bagnall 1976, 25–7. It should be remembered that Ptolemy I was instrumental in setting up the Cyrenaean *politeuma*, and that in the early Ptolemaic period Cyrenaeans were the largest Greek population group within Egypt. Clarysse 1998, 3–4 points out that Jason was a popular Cyrenaean name in this period, and it occurs in documents and inscriptions within Egypt. This increases the likelihood that a contemporary audience regarded Alexandria and Cyrene as a cultural continuum.

of any Cyrenaean particularity. Jason speaks only of a piece of Libya. Because
epic necessarily falls in the heroic past, it may be that explicit references to
contemporary Alexandria contravened generic sensibilities (though clearly
references to contemporary circumstances were acceptable to Virgil). I believe
there may be another reason for Apollonius' temporal positioning of his
poem that I will return to at the end of this paper. At this point let me
mention an obvious feature of Apollonius' story that nudges the reader
towards Greek claims not just to Libya, but explicitly to Egypt. At least from
the time of Herodotus Colchis was associated with Egypt. Herodotus informs
us in book 2 of his *Histories* that the Colchians seemed to him to be Egyptian,
namely, the descendants of soldiers from the army of the Egyptian pharaoh,
Sesostris, who supposedly ranged as far as the Black Sea in his conquests
(2. 103–4). Sesostris' exploits occur as well in the *Alexander Romance* and in
Apollonius' near contemporary, Hecataeus of Abdera.[24] Apollonius himself
(although he does not name the king) identifies Colchis as a foundation of
Sesostris (4. 272–9). Thus if we may extend the logic of foundation myth that
we found above in *Pythian* 4, in which women and land are conflated, Jason's
ploughing of Colchian soil and his sexual conquest of Egyptian-descended
Colchian Medea anticipates and confers legitimacy on the Argonauts'
descendants, who in the fullness of time will return to the region from which
the Colchians themselves originally came.

If the Colchians are implicitly identified as Egyptian in the *Argonautica*, in
the tale of the Argonauts embedded in Callimachus' *Aetia* it is the Colchian
colonization of the west that is emphasized. But discussion of these fragments
requires that they first be placed within the broader narrative frame of the
*Aetia.* The *Aetia* now consists of four books. Consensus has it that the first
two were composed no later than the 270s, then at a later time a third and
fourth book added. The last two books are now framed by poems on topical
events: the victory of Berenice in the Nemean games and the marriage of
Berenice II to Ptolemy III (which places this arrangement at least after 245).[25]
The *Aetia* as we have it opens with a prologue in which Apollo appears to the
schoolboy Callimachus to instruct him on how to write poetry. This is
immediately followed by a dream sequence in which Callimachus encounters
the Muses, and according to a poem from the *Palatine Anthology* is transported from Libya to Helicon.[26] We might infer that in the time of his dream
he is in Cyrene, though later at the beginning of book 3 and the end of book 4

[24] See my discussion, 2003, 32–6, 177–8.
[25] It is not clear whether the *Aetia* (in whole or in part) predated the *Argonautica*. See e.g.
Cameron's discussion (1995, 249–62) on the relative chronologies and potential interaction of
Callimachus and Apollonius. See also the discussion below of the internal poetic chronologies
of the two.
[26] *AP* 7. 42. 5 εὖτέ μιν ἐκ Λιβύης ἀναείρας εἰς Ἑλικῶνα.

Callimachus is securely located in Alexandria.[27] Within the *Aetia* as a whole the temporal frame oscillates between a Callimachus who locates his persona in the 'real time' and space of Libya (Alexandria and probably Cyrene) and the hyperspace of his conversation with the Muses. Within these spaces he narrates events that range from the pre-Homeric to the very recent, the consequences of which are manifested by rituals, objects, or foundations in locations throughout the Mediterranean. Book 1, for example, begins with allusion to Minos, who controlled the Mediterranean with the kind of sea power that the Ptolemies aspired to; he then introduces Jason and his companions, who undertook a sea voyage to the edges of the known world that in many respects resembled the expedition of Alexander. Heracles figures in slightly later fragments: he was cultivated as an ancestor of the Ptolemies. Within these earlier *aitia* we often find foundation stories and geographical references that appear to remap or decentre the Mediterranean world, moving away from Athens and Sparta and Corinth and Thebes, to Illyria and Epirus, South Italy, Sicily, North Africa, the islands controlled by the Ptolemies— Samos, Paros, Thera—and the areas of the Ionian coast of the most interest in Ptolemaic expansion.

The framework for the first two books of the *Aetia* is a conversation between Callimachus and the Muses that constantly makes hearers aware of the role of memory in preserving and transmitting the discrete pieces of regional cultures that form the subject of the individual stories.[28] Callimachus begins by asking the Muses about the Graces. The next *aition* introduces the Argonauts. Why, Callimachus asks the Muses, do they celebrate the rites of Anaphe with abuse? The Argonauts return at the end of book 4; the last *aition* but one (frr. 106–8 Pfeiffer) tells of the Argonauts' abandoning an anchor at Cyzicus.[29] Thus we have a rudimentary ring-composition in which the Cyzicene anchor focuses our attention back to the events of the earlier sequence. The final *aition* in the collection is the *Coma Berenices*, which brings us to the world of contemporary Alexandria, and also Cyrene. The marriage of Ptolemy III and Berenice II is the proximate cause for the dedication of a lock of hair, the event that occasioned the poem, and also for reunification of Egypt and Cyrene. The fourth book ends with the creation of a new star: after Berenice II dedicates a lock of her hair for the safe return of her husband, Euergetes, from the Syrian war, Conon, the court astronomer,

---

[27] See Parsons 1977 for the construction of these two books framed by an epinician for Berenice's victory at the Nemean games at the beginning of book 3 and the dedication of the lock of her hair as the final poem of book 4. Both poems locate themselves in Alexandria.

[28] For the temporal layers of the poem see Harder 2003.

[29] The object itself is anonymous, but derives its significance by attachment to a heroic story; thus the local rock could be seen, from a later period's perspective, as an anchor of the Argonauts. An anecdote from Appian's *Syriake* (63) provides a valuable perspective on these relics: Seleucus was killed by Ptolemy Ceraunus while bending over a local altar as he tried to discover whether it was left by the Argonauts or on one of the *Nostoi*.

discovers the hair has become a new 'star among the old' (fr. 110. 64 Pf.). With this final *aition* mythological events from the past converge to end in Alexandria, a city that now controls Cyrene and, as a result of Ptolemy III's Syrian campaign, has extended its influence much further in the eastern Mediterranean and Aegean.[30] In the lock, become star, the city now has its own distinctive, place-marking object that other ages and other peoples will remember when they look up in the night sky.[31] Or rather the city now has the power to invest an adventitious object with its own symbolism for future peoples to acknowledge.

Callimachus' Argo adventure now consists of six papyrus fragments that certainly belong to the same *aition,* a number of notices from the scholia to Apollonius' poem that convey information about it, and a handful of fragments that might belong, because they are similar to material found in Apollonius.[32] The fragments that have been located in this *aition* already number at least 100 lines.[33] Even if what we have of the *aition* represents less than half of the original, the extreme degree of narrative compression resembles *Pythian* 4 more closely than other available models. Ostensibly, Callimachus does not set out to tell the entire story of the Argonauts but only to account for the ritual abuse in Apollo's worship on Anaphe. Thus the sequence has a natural end that seems to fall around frr. 17–19 Pfeiffer = 19–21 Massimilla,[34] which relate how Medea's serving women innocently precipitate the events that the rite subsequently commemorates. Callimachus' tale is told as a flashback, and like Pindar's *Pythian* it begins toward the end of the adventure—at Thera's neighbour, Anaphe. The Muse Calliope seems to be the principal speaker. Calliope, like Medea, begins by relating the details of colonial enterprise: in her own voice she tells Callimachus about the Colchian settlements in the west, noting that: 'these things would come to fulfilment in the future' (fr. 12. 6 Pf. = 17. 6 Massimilla). In a later fragment, when the Argonauts have been caught up in oppressive darkness, she gives us Jason's prayer as he beseeches Apollo. Jason has only mentioned the point where the adventure begins when the text breaks off:

ἀλλ' ὅγ' ἀνι]άζων ὃν κέαρ Αἰσονίδης
coὶ χέρας ἠέρ]ταζεν, Ἰήιε, πολλὰ δ' ἀπείλει
    ἐς Πυθὼ πέ]μψειν, πολλὰ δ' ἐς Ὀρτυγίην,
εἴ κεν ἀμιχιθαλόεccεν ἀπ' ἠέρα νηὸς ἐλάccηιˌcˑ

---

[30] Hölbl 2001, 46–51.
[31] See Harder's discussion of the end of the *Aetia* as 'the Present as the Past of the Future' (2003, 303–6).
[32] Frr. 37, 484, 584, 602, 617, 673, 706, 716 Pf.
[33] In comparison, the episode of Acontius and Cydippe has at least 120 lines, the *Coma Berenices* 95 lines, and the *Victoria Berenices* (if we accept all the fragments that D'Alessio 2007 would include) was over 170 lines.
[34] In what follows I use Massimilla 1996 for the Argo fragments.

], ὅτι σήν, Φοῖβε, κατ᾽ αἰςιμίην
πείςματ᾽] ἔλυςαν ἐκ[λ]ηρώςαντό τ᾽ ἐρετμά          10
], πικρὸν ἔκοψαν ὕδωρ·
]...ἐπώνυμον Ἐμβαςίοιο
]...ἐν„ Παγα̣ιϲ̣αῖϲ·

But the son of Aeson, grieving in his heart, raised his hands to you, *Hieios*, and promised to send many gifts to Pytho, many to Ortygia, if you would drive away the inauspicious (?) cloud from the ship . . . because, Phoebus, at your instruction, they loosed the hawsers and filled out the oar banks, . . . struck the bitter waters; . . . name of Apollo the Embarker . . . at Pagasae. (Frr. 18. 5–13 Pf. = 20. 5–13 Massimilla.)

Given its purpose—to remind Apollo that they have been acting in response to his directives—Jason's prayer need only recall a few interactions with the god, and we might infer from the fact that the adjective ἀμιχθαλόεccαν is used elsewhere only in describing Lemnos that much of the Argo adventure was conveyed allusively.[35] The last three surviving fragments (frr. 19–21 Pf = 21–3 Massimilla) are probably spoken by Calliope in her own voice. They tell of Apollo breaking up the gloom, and of Medea's servants, whose behaviour initiates the rites.[36]

Callimachus' narrative of the Argo adventure begins with a question to the Muses about an episode very near the end of their return journey to Colchis:

κῶc δέ, θεαί, ι . [ . . . ] μ̣ὲν ἀνὴρ Ἀναφαῖοc ἐπ᾽ αἰc[χροῖc,
ἡ δ᾽ ἐπὶ δυ[cφήμοιc] Λίνδοc ἄγει θυcίην,          20
η . . τηνε.[ . . . . τ]ὸν Ἡρακλῆα cεβίζηι;
ι . . επικ.[ι . . . ]ωc ἤρχετο Καλλιόπη·
Αἰ̣γλήτην ̣Ἀνά̣φην τε, Λακωνίδι γείτονα Θ̣ήρηι,
π]ρῶτ[ον ἐνὶ μ]νήμηι κάτθεο καὶ Μινύαc,
ἀ̣ρχμενοc ὡc̣ ἥρωεc ἀπ᾽ Αἰήταο Κυταίου          25
αὖτιc ἐc ἀρχαίην̣ ἔπλεον Αἱμονίην
]εν, ὁ δ᾽ ὡc ἴδεν ἔργα θυγατρ[όc
] ἔλεξε τάδε·
ι]κα̣[ι . . ] ἔθ̣νοc̣ Ἰ̣ηονεc αλλα μενε . ι..[ι
ι] πάντα δ᾽ ἀνατρά̣ιπελα·          30
ιcοὖc̣θ[ε          ἐ̣ιποιήcαντό με φόρτον,
ιcοῦ[cθε          νή̣ι]ον ὅ cφε̣ι φέρει
ιαὔτανδ̣[ρον          ]̣ Ἥλιοc ἴcτω
καὶ Φ̣ᾶcιc [ποταμῶν ἡμε]τέρων β̣α̣ιc̣ι̣λεύc·

---

[35] Homer, *Iliad*. 24. 753, *hAp*. 36, and see the very helpful discussion in Massimilla on fr. 20. 8. It is possible, since Lemnos contained a volcano, that the adjective refers to the smoke that precedes eruption and the birth of a new island. But Bettarini's suggestion that the adjective means 'inauspicious' and refers to the Lemnian women is equally attractive (2003, 82–3).

[36] The story is related in Conon (8) as well, though there is considerable debate about how much of Conon is an accurate reflection of Callimachus. See Pfeiffer's long note (i. 17) and Livrea 2006, 96.

Why, goddesses, does a man of Anaphe with insults and Lindos with blasphemies perform a sacrifice, . . . honour Heracles? . . . Calliope began: Apollo the Radiant and Anaphe, neighbour to Thera, first fix in your memory and the Minyans, beginning from when the heroes sailed back from Cytaean Aeetes towards ancient Haemonia . . . and when he saw his daughter's deeds . . . he spoke thus: 'Ionian race . . . everything is overturned . . . hasten? They have betrayed me . . . hasten . . . the ship that carries him men and all . . . Helios and Phasis, king of rivers, stand by me . . . (Fr. 7. 19–34 Pf. + *SH* 249A = 9. 19–34 Massimilla.)

Even in its fragmentary state we can see the emphasis placed on landscape and its constituent peoples: Thera is identified as Laconian, an obvious reference to the myth of Libyan colonization (discussed above) since Euphemus would move from Laconia to Thera to Libya. Argonauts are the genealogically potent 'Minyans'. Thessaly is given its older name of Haemonia.[37] Aeetes is Cytaean. Cytaea is identified as the name of the town where Medea was born, and it is usually taken as a generic alternative for Colchian (especially in Latin poets).[38] However, Cytaea is not near the Phasis, but at the southern entrance to the Bosporus, so the name is more likely to particularize the Colchian landscape, which by the third century was studded with Greek settlements: one town (Nymphaion) seems even to have commemorated an embassy or visit from an early Ptolemy in a wall depicting sailing ships, one of which was called Isis with its name enclosed in a cartouche.[39] Calliope's use of ancient names serves to remind us that place is a palimpsest of past inhabitants, current descendants, or their replacements, and of the ever-present possibility of change.

Calliope's remarks seem to insist that much of the Adriatic had Colchian settlements: she first mentions Polai, on the coast of northern Illyria, then Orician Amantine, which was, according to Stephanus of Byzantium, near Corcyra and Oricus. Calliope tells us that when the Colchians were unable to catch the Argonauts:

> οἱ ₁μὲν ἐπ'Ἰλλυρικοῖο πόρου cχάccαντεc ἐρετμά
> λâ₁α πάρα ξανθῆc Ἁρμονίηc ὄφιοc
> ἄc₁τυρον ἐκτίccαντο, τό κεν "Φυγάδων" τιc ἐνίcποι
> Γρ₁αικόc, ἀτὰρ κείνων γλῶcc' ὀνόμηνε "Πόλαc"

some of the Colchians, dropping their oars by the Illyrian strait, by the stone of blonde Harmonia, the snake, established a small town, which a *Graikos* would call 'of the Exiles' but their tongue named 'Polai' . . . (Fr. 11 Pf. = fr. 13 Massimilla).

---

[37] The scholium on Ap. Rh. 3. 1090 quotes Rhianus as saying: 'Once the older generation called it Pyrrhaia, from Pyrrha, the ancient wife of Deucalion, but then Haemonia from Haemon, who was a stalwart son of Pelasgus, and Haemon sired Thessalus from whom the people have taken the name Thessalian' (= Rhianus 25 Powell).

[38] Mayer 1986, 50.

[39] Hind 1992–3, 99–100. It also may implicitly distinguish Aeetes' Colchian period from the time when (according to Eumelus) he was king of Corinth (see e.g. Pausanias 2. 3. 10).

And in the next fragment we are told:

> Φαιήκων ἐγένον[τ]ο ..[
> ἑϲμὸν ἄγων ἑτέροιϲ ι .[.]ι ... [
> ἔκτιϲε Κερκ[υ]ραῖον ἐδέθλιον, ἔνθ[εν ἀν’ αὖτιϲ
> ϲτάντεϲ Ἀμιαιρτίνην ὄικιιϲαν Ὠρικίην.
> καὶ τὰ μὲν ὧιϲ ἤμελλε μετὰ χρόνον ἐκτελέεϲθαι

... of the Phaiacians they were ... leading a band by others? ... established a Corcyraean settlement, and migrating from there they settled Orician Amantine. And these things would come to fulfilment in the future. (Fr. 12.2–6 Pf. = fr.17.2–6 Massimilla.)

There seems to have been a strong tradition of Colchian settlement in the Adriatic, which is recorded in Roman as well as Hellenistic and later Greek sources. Local islands were even called the Apsyrtides.[40] Calliope’s account continues to acknowledge these competing cultural layers. The two names for one space, *Pola* and *Phugadon*, imply non-Greek and Greek cultures living in close proximity, while *Graikos,* which was not the standard name for Hellenes but for north-western Greek peoples around Epirus and Dodona later incorporated into the broader category of Hellene, reminds us that even the seemingly stable identity of ‘Greek’ was always under construction and revision.[41] Orician Amantine[42] suggests an even more complex cultural layering: the Colchians in question had first settled in Corcyra, and when expelled, they moved into this new area. According to pseudo-Scymnus, for example, it was originally founded by the Euboeans returning from Troy (442–3), and was also a region where Cadmus had exercised power.[43] But why does Callimachus devote so large a portion (relatively speaking) of the extant remains to Colchian settlements? One reason, surely, is that these areas were particularly familiar in contemporary events. For example, Pyrrhus, who was related to Ptolemy Soter by marriage, when he was king of Epirus added southern Illyria to his territory.[44] Then, as a result of a subsequent marriage to Agathocles’ daughter, Pyrrhus gained control of Corcyra (her dowry) and Oricum. Also, Illyrian tribes were causing constant disruption to the delicate political balance in Epirus and Macedon during this period, a circumstance which regional dynasts could ill afford to ignore when plotting their campaigns of territorial expansion.

[40] Ps.-Scymnus 373, Str. 6. 5. 5 (315 C).
[41] West 1985, 52–6, Malkin 1998 148–50 *Graikos* becomes the standard name for Greeks used by the Romans and other peoples of the west, but Aeetes, looking from the east (in the passage quoted above), speaks of ‘Ionians’ (Ἰήονεϲ), a regional designation for Greeks in the East that outsiders came to apply to Greeks generally. See Massimilla’s commentary on fr. 9. 29.
[42] See Malkin 1998, 78–9.
[43] See Massimilla’s commentary on fr. 14. 4.
[44] While Pyrrhus was on his Italian campaign it is possible that Ptolemy II provided a military presence to protect his Epirote kingdom (so Hölbl 2001, 73 n. 105).

But there may have been another explicitly genealogical connection. Philip and Alexander had maternal ancestors from these regions: Eurydice, Alexander's grandmother, was Illyrian, Alexander's mother, Olympias, came from Molossian Epirus. In fr. 11 Pf. = 13 Massimilla, quoted above, a local rock formation is described as the 'stone of the blonde Harmonia, the snake', an allusion to Cadmus and Harmonia. Cadmus, of course, was a key figure in Greek genealogical mapping: a Phoenician, he migrated to Greece and settled in Thebes, but at the end of his life, in accordance with Apollo's instructions he and his wife went to Illyria, where they were turned into the snakes that the monument commemorates. Cadmus is a tangible reminder of the central (one might even say normative) role the outside colonizer played in Greek myth, and his kin included Illyrius, the eponymous ancestor of Illyria, and Membliarus, the colonizer of Anaphe. Cadmus was also an ancestor of the Battiads of Cyrene, who traced descent from Oedipus (as we saw in Callimachus' *Hymn to Apollo*). It is distinctly possible, as Enrico Livrea observes, that Eurydice, Alexander's Illyrian grandmother, who was the wife of Amyntas III, traced her descent from Harmonia.[45] Thus the reference to the story of Cadmus might reasonably be understood as a compliment to the ancestors of Alexander, or even the Ptolemies, who tried to link their own lineage to Alexander. If this is right, then Colchian migrations complete the circle: Egyptians settling in Colchis, Colchians settling in Illyria and Epirus, the territory from which Philip's maternal ancestors came, and finally Alexander, with his Illyrian blood, and the Ptolemies, who claimed descent from Macedonian kings, conquering and settling Egypt, complement and extend the Sparta–Thera charter myth, and reinforce the inevitability of Greek migration back to Ptolemaic Alexandria.

In the opening of this paper I suggested that Apollonius' tale was in part setting the scene for the Ptolemaic colonization of Egypt, an event far in the future that necessarily fell outside his epic. Callimachus' poem engages with the charter myth of North Africa as well, though both Alexandria and Cyrene are present in his text. His version begins: Αἰγλήτην Ἀνάφην τε, Λακωνίδι γείτονα Θήρῃ. Apollo is Callimachus' patron deity, Thera the mother city of his city, Cyrene. He begins the *aition* then not far from where he left off in the prologue—Apollo and Cyrene. We cannot know what further details of the myth Callimachus included—Euphemus and the clod? the clod becoming Thera? In a slightly later fragment (17 Pf. + *SH* 250 = 19 Massimilla, at vv. 9–10), when the Argonauts are disoriented by the enclosing darkness, the reference to Nonacrine Kallisto (the Great Bear), whom they can no longer see, is surely a pun on *Kalliste*, the earlier name for Thera (as we saw in the passage of Pindar quoted above). Like the Great Bear (Kallisto) *Kalliste* is also invisible, either until Apollo and his prophecy makes its future clear or until it

---

[45] 2006, 98 and n. 29.

rises from the sea.[46] But this is speculative. What we do know is that Ἀιγλήτην Ἀνάφην τε, Λακωνίδι γείτονα Θήρηι, is where Callimachus begins. It is also where Apollonius ends.

It is well known that more than a few lines in these six fragments of Callimachus' compressed tale have close parallels in Apollonius, not clustered in one place, but scattered throughout the longer text. This cannot be accidental. The two texts, by virtue of careful appropriation, are designed to call attention to their interrelationship. There is no obvious way to decide which version is prior, though many scholars have assumed that the first two books of the *Aetia* would have predated the *Argonautica*.[47] But an argument may also be made in the other direction: namely, that Callimachus deliberately borrowed from and compressed Apollonius' tale in such a way that readers of both would be aware that Callimachus begins where Apollonius ends.[48]

Apart from questions of *imitatio* or *aemulatio* or simple plagiarism, what might be the point of this kind of what one might call extreme intertextuality? Of deliberately constructing one poem in such a way that the other becomes a *de facto* allusion to and in some cases almost quotation of the notionally prior text? The key is Thera. Thera has no independent poetic life. When it does occur in Pindar and in Callimachus' *Hymn to Apollo*, it inevitably signals Greek claims to North Africa. If Apollonius ends the *Argonautica* by leaving the fulfilment of those claims to a later time, Callimachus' *Aetia* takes up that narrative and extends it to the Ptolemaic present. By embedding elements of one poet's version in the other's in such a way that they form an apparent temporal sequence, the promise in the one comes to be fulfilled by the trajectory of the other.[49] If in Apollonius Thera does not yet exist (Euphemus' clod will become the island), in what we now have of Callimachus, Thera[50] is already present as part of the triptych of our charter myth—Sparta—Thera—[ ]. We are left to fill in the brackets. But Thera is

---

[46] As in Apollonius' version.

[47] In support of Callimachean priority, Albis 1995 makes the clever suggestion that at 1. 418–19 Apollonius imitates Jason's prayer to Apollo in Callimachus (fr. 18. 6–7: πολλὰ δ' ἀπείλει ἐς Πυθὼ πέμψειν, πολλὰ δ' ἐς Ὀρτυγίην), placing in Jason's mouth the remark that 'you are responsible for my labours' (αὐτὸς γὰρ ἐπαίτιος ἔπλευ ἀέλθων). He argues that ἐπαίτιος was a punning reference to the *Aetia*. See also Hunter's comments, 1993, 123.

[48] Writing into another poet's poetic chronology is not unfamiliar in the Alexandrian environment: Theocritus' *Idyll* 17 takes up the chronology of Callimachus' *Hymn to Delos* at the point where Callimachus leaves off: the birth of Ptolemy II in Cos. See Stephens 2003, 164–5.

[49] The phenomenon of one historian taking up where his predecessor left off is quite familiar (see e.g. the discussion in Marincola 1997, 237–40), and the poetic behaviour I am focusing on could be related, as a way of enhancing one's authority by 'continuing' an earlier work. However, historians do not usually write prequels to their predecessors' narratives, or work out chronological sequences simultaneously with their contemporaries. These latter two scenarios are much more likely to have been the conditions under which these poems were created.

[50] Thera continued to be a strategically important Ptolemaic possession for centuries, Bagnall 1976, 123–34.

now embedded within Callimachus' larger temporal unit, which—wherever the poet and his Muses wander in their narratives—has not just been anchored in contemporary Cyrene but comes to its end in Libyan Alexandria. In fact, the *Aetia* ends with one final *aition* in which Cyrene and Alexandria have been reunited by virtue of the marriage of Berenice and Ptolemy Euergetes.[51] At the end of Callimachus' poem Alexandria is a place no longer on the margins but central, both to its own mythology, and to the Mediterranean. Even the heavens, thanks to the catasterized lock, have been enlisted to proclaim the arrival and centrality of the Ptolemies.[52]

## BIBLIOGRAPHY

Albis, R. 1995, 'Jason's Prayers to Apollo in Aetia 1 and the Argonautica', *Phoenix*, 49, 104–9.

Bagnall, R. S. 1976, *The Administration of Ptolemaic Possessions outside Egypt* (Leiden).

Bettarini, L. 2003, 'Λῆμνος ἀμιχθαλόεccα (*Il.* 24, 753)', *QUCC* 74, 69–88.

Calame, C. 1990, 'Narrating the Foundation of a City: The Symbolic Birth of Cyrene', in L. Edmunds (ed.), *Approaches to Greek Myth* (Baltimore and London), 277–341.

—— 1993, 'Legendary Narration and Poetic Procedure in Callimachus' Hymn to Apollo', *Hellenistica Groningana*, 1, 37–55.

—— 2003, *Myth and History in Ancient Greece: The Symbolic Creation of a Colony* (Princeton).

Cameron, A. 1995. *Callimachus and his Critics* (Princeton).

Clarysse, W. 1998, 'Ethnic Diversity and Dialect', in A. M. F. W. Verhoogt and S. P. Vleeming (eds.), *Two Faces of Graeco-Roman Egypt: Greek and Demotic and Greek–Demotic Texts and Studies Presented to P. W. Pestman* (= *P.Ludg.Bat.* XXX). 2–13.

Cole, S. G. 2004, *Landscapes, Gender, and Ritual Space* (Berkeley, Los Angeles, and London).

D'Alessio, G. B. 2005, 'The *Megalai Ehoiai*: A Survey of the Fragments', in R. Hunter (ed.), *The Hesiodic Catalogue of Women: Constructions and Reconstructions* (Cambridge), 176–216.

—— 2007, *Callimaco: inni, epigrammi, frammenti* (Milan).

Dräger, P. 1993, *Argo Pasimelousa: Der Argonautenmythos in der griechischen und römischen Literatur* (Stuttgart).

Hall, J. 1997, *Ethnic Identity in Greek Antiquity* (Cambridge).

—— 2002, *Hellenicity: Between Ethnicity and Culture* (Chicago).

---

[51] It is possible that the union of Acontius and Cydippe in book 3 prefigures the royal marriage as healing a political rupture. The two are descended respectively from Codrus (Athens) and Minos (Crete). Callimachus' first *aition* features Minos mourning the death of his son, who was killed by the Athenians, the reason for the long-term enmity between the two powers.

[52] This paper is dedicated with admiration and affection to Peter Parsons, whose customary scepticism has always made me think.

Harder, A. 2003, 'The Invention of Past, Present, and Future in Callimachus' *Aetia*', *Hermes*, 131, 290–306.

Hind, J. G. F. 1992–3, 'Archaeology of the Greeks and Barbarian Peoples around the Black Sea (1982–92)', *Archaeological Reports*, 39, 82–112.

Hölbl, G. 2001, *A History of the Ptolemaic Empire* (London and New York).

Hunter, R. 1993, *The* Argonautica *of Apollonius* (Cambridge).

Kelly, A. 2007, 'Stesikhoros and Helen', *MH* 64, 1–21.

Krevans, N. 2000, 'On the Margins of Epic: the Foundation-Poems of Apollonius', *Hellenistica Groningana*, 4, 69–84.

Leontis, A. 1995, *Topographies of Hellenism* (Ithaca, NY).

Livrea, E. 2006, 'Il mito argonautico in Callimaco: l'episodio de Anafe', in G. Bastianini and A. Casanova (eds.), *Callimaco: cent'anni di papiri. Atti del convegno internazionale di studi. Firenze, 9–10 giugno 2005* (Florence), 89–99.

Malkin, I. 1994, *Myth and Territory in the Spartan Mediterranean* (Berkeley, Los Angeles, and London).

—— 1998, *The Returns of Odysseus: Colonization and Ethnicity* (Berkeley, Los Angeles, and London).

Marincola, J. 1997, *Authority and Tradition in Ancient Historiography* (Cambridge).

Massimilla, G. 1996, *Aitia: Libri primo e secondo* (Pisa).

Mayer, R. 1986, 'Geography in the Latin Poets', *Greece & Rome*, 33, 47–54.

Mueller, K. 2005, 'Geographical Information Systems in Papyrology', *Bulletin of the American Society of Papyrologists*, 42, 63–92.

Parsons, P. J. 1977, 'Callimachus: Victoria Berenices', *ZPE* 25, 1–50.

Stephens, S. A. 2003, *Seeing Double: Intercultural Poetics in Ptolemaic Alexandria* (Berkeley and Los Angeles).

West, M. L. 1985, *The Hesiodic Catalogue of Women* (Oxford).

—— 2005, 'Odyssey and Argonautica', *CQ*[2] 55, 39–64.

# 11

## Theudotus of Lipara
## (Callimachus, fr. 93 Pf.)

*Giulio Massimilla*

This paper deals with the textual constitution and the interpretation of a fragment from the fourth book of Callimachus' *Aetia*, entitled *Theudotus Liparensis* in Pfeiffer's edition (fr. 93).[1] With the exception of the *Coma Berenices* (fr. 110 Pf.), *Theudotus Liparensis* is the longest fragment in the whole of the fourth book. But, although some research has been done on the historical and religious issues connected with fr. 93 Pf., so far scholars have not taken great interest in the study of its actual text. A closer examination of the fragment is therefore still missing, and that is what I intend to offer here.

It will be seen that this kind of approach, besides shedding more light on the fragment as a whole, has led to some progress, regarding both textual constitution and interpretation: on the one hand, it has produced a couple of new readings in the text of the papyrus preserving the fragment; on the other hand, it has suggested a way of reconstructing the contents of a part of the fragment (vv. 6–18), for which no overall explanations had been so far proposed. I hope that this research (*si parua licet!*) is suited to a volume of essays in honour of Professor Peter Parsons, whose masterly achievements in the study of literary papyri and Hellenistic poetry are very well known.

To begin with, I offer a newly constituted text of the fragment and of the relevant *Diegesis Mediolanensis*, based on the direct inspection of the papyri. Greek texts are accompanied by apparatuses of my own making. I call attention to the new readings at the end of v. 5 and in v. 16: it will be seen that they have an influence on the interpretation of those two passages.

---

[1] Cf. Pfeiffer 1949, 99–100.

Νέκτα₁ρος α[......]₁ν」 γλύκιον γένος ηραπ₁εδο[
    κ[.] δονηδυ[.......]ς ἀμβροσίης
ὑμέας γαῖ ἀνέδ[ωκε, τ]ὰ καὶ τερπνίστατα πά[ντων
    νεῖςθε διὰ γλῶς[ςαν γλεύ]κεος ὄσσα πέρα.
δείλαιοι, τυ[τθόν] μιν ἐπὶ πλ<έ>ον ἢ ὅσον αὖ[ον            5
    χεῖλος ἀναγλ[......]π̣.ρ ἀναινομένου
ἀνδρὸς ανουν[.........]ς ἐπέταςςεν[.].[
        ω.[.] μίαν νης.[          . . .
    οἰκήςας Λιπά[ρ-
τῃς ω.. Τυ[ρςην-                                            10
ἤλυθ᾽ ἄγων π[
    πολλά, τὸ δ᾽ ἐκ.[
φη[.]αρ ἀποτρ[
    ἱερὸς εἰ Φοίβου [
δημόθεν ως.[                                                15
    τουτο.επει[
.]ςτ᾽ ἐπὶ τὴν ν[
    .]ηςαιον προτ[
                            . . .

1–18 ad hoc fragmentum spectat Schol. (CFD; cf. BabG; 'Galli' mentionem om. Pm₃ZC₁
Conr.) Ou. *Ib.* 465, 125 La Penna *Tyrrheni, obsidentes Liparium castrum, promiserunt Apollini
quod, si faceret eos uictores, fortissimum Liparensium ei sacrificarent. habita autem uictoria,
promissum reddiderunt, inmolantes ei quendam nomine Theodotum* [hic desinunt Pm₃]. *unde
Gallus: 'Theodotus captus Phoebo datur hostia, quamuis / nequaquam sit homo uictima grata deo'*
(Schol. ad Callimachi *Aetia* redire iam coniecerat Zipfel 1910, 32; vd. etiam Rostagni 1920,
71, 90)

1–7 P.Oxy. XVIII 2170 fr. 1. 4–10 (*init. uu.*) + *PSI* XI 1218 fr. c,4–10 (*fin. uu.*)

1 P.Mil.Vogl. I 18 (= *Diegeseis Mediolanenses*) col. iii 12–13: lemma    fort. Hesych. s.v. ψύθιον,
ψ 257, IV 314 Schmidt ὀλιγοχρόνιον

8–18 P.Oxy. XVIII 2170 fr. 1. 11–21

pap. coniunxit Lobel    1 suppl. Lobel    .[: in P.Oxy. potius α quam o, in *Dieg.* pars laeva litt.
rotundae (potius o quam α)    ]γλυκιον *PSI*: ]ν̣.θιον *Dieg.*, prob. ]ν ψύθιον, v.l.?    ad fin. π₁έδο[ιο Körte
1935, 234: εςο[ Lobel ap. Pintaudi 2006, 201, ap. Lehnus 2006, 214    Θεύδοτος Liparensis in hoc carmine
prob. commemoratus est (cf. Schol. Ou. supra allata)    2 init. κ vel χ    3–5 omnia e.g. suppl.
Lobel, praeter v. 5 αὖ[ον, quod ipse suppleui (Lobel proposuerat ἄκ[ρον, quod cum ultimo uestigio non
congruit)    3 υμεας vel υμερς    5 τὺ pap.    επιπλον pap.: corr. Maas ap. Vogliano 1937b,
172 (cf. fr. inc. sed. 636 Pf.*)    ad fin. pars superior sinistra litt. υ vel τ vel χ    6 γλ[ vel γκ[
καί]περ dubitanter Vitelli    7 ταςε pap., altera litt. ς suprascripta    ].[: apex hastae ad laeuam flexus
8 ωρ vel ως    prob. νῆςο[ν    9–10 suppl. Lobel (cf. *Dieg.* iii 13–14)    9 οἰκήςας vel οἰκί[ς]ςας
Lobel    10 ω.. ego (priore loco hasta uerticalis; altero apex hastae uerticalis): ω. Pfeiffer    13 φῆ
[γ]ὰρ ἀποτρ[έψειν Maas (cf. Hom. *Il.* 2. 37 φῆ γὰρ ὅ γ᾽ αἱρήσειν*): ἀποτρ[οπίη dubitanter Livrea 1973,
421 (comm. ad Ap. Rh. 4. 1504)    15 .[: fort. α    16 potius γε quam τε    τε ego: γ Pfeiffer
τουτο] γ᾽ ἐπει proposuerim    18 ν]ηςαιον? Pfeiffer: ]θιςδ̣ vel ]ηςδ̣ Lobel, at post ς potius α, ut v. 13
in απο

*Diegesis Mediolanensis*
(col.  iii)  Νέκταρος   .[......]ν υθιον   γένος   η]ραπεδο[——    ——]
Λιπαραιο[......]ο  |   Τυρςην[——]ιας[——|¹⁵...]ετης[——]δο[——|——]..[——|
[ll. 17–23 desunt] |——].τε[——|

P.Mil.Vogl. 18 col. iii 12–16 et 24      12–13 lemma = fr. 93,1 Pf. (de singulis litt. vd. app. ad loc.)
13 λιπαρ in pap. disp. Pfeiffer 1934*a*, 384; 1934*b*, 12 (νπαρ Norsa–Vitelli), mox αιο, ut videtur, potius quam
αιω (αιο Vogliano, vd. etiam Lobel locc. citt.)      13–14 ὑπ]ὸ Ι Τυρϲην[ῶν prop. Lobel ibid.      in lacuna
ll. 17–23 novam enarrationem incipere potuisse non omnino est negandum

A part of fr. 93 Pf. came first to light in 1934, when Girolamo Vitelli
published a papyrus,[2] later to become *PSI* XI 1218,[3] a fragment of which
preserves the ends of our vv. 1–7.[4] That year he and Medea Norsa also published the *Diegeseis Mediolanenses.*[5] Edgar Lobel immediately noticed that
our v. 1 in *PSI* 1218 and one of the lemmata in the *Diegeseis*[6] are in fact the
same hexameter,[7] although the two sources differ in the text of one word.[8]
It followed that this verse was the beginning of a poem. According to the
*Diegeseis*, the poem itself was the fifth one (or, less probably, the fourth one)
in the fourth book of the *Aetia.*[9]

Unfortunately the *Diegesis* of the elegy is very much damaged as regards the
lemma and especially the summary, seven lines of which are completely lost.[10]
Scanty as the evidence was, Rudolf Pfeiffer managed to reconstruct the overall
contents of the poem in the same year 1934.[11] He based his interpretation on
the two only words that can still be recognized in the summary of the *Diegesis*,
namely the ethnic Τυρϲηνός (already spotted by Vitelli) and the ethnic
Λιπαραῖος (detected by Pfeiffer himself). He connected these two words with
a piece of information that we find in the scholia to a passage of Ovid's *Ibis*
(465–6). Here are Ovid's verses:

[2] Vitelli 1934.      [3] Vitelli 1935.
[4] Fr. c. Cf. Vitelli 1934, 9, 11; Vitelli 1935, 134–6, 139.
[5] Norsa and Vitelli 1934.
[6] *Dieg.* iii 12–13 (Norsa and Vitelli 1934, 19, 36).
[7] Lobel's identification was reported by Maas 1934, 439 (cf. also Vitelli 1935, 134). It was later
accepted by Vogliano 1937*a*, 90–1, 121; 1937*b*.
[8] *PSI* γλύκιον, *Dieg.* ψύθιον (see *infra*).
[9] It is likely that the elegies at the beginning of book 4 (designated after the titles assigned to
them by Pfeiffer) were arranged as follows: (i) a poem dealing with an unknown subject (fr. 86
Pf. = lemma in *Dieg.* ii 10); (ii) *Daphnephoria Delphica* (frr. 87–89 Pf.), the lemma of which was
lost somewhere in the missing lines 14–20 of *Dieg.* ii; (iii) *Abdera* (fr. 90 Pf. = lemma in *Dieg.* ii
29–30); (iv) *Melicertes* (fr. 91 Pf. = lemma in *Dieg.* ii 41 + *SH* 275 + fr. 92 Pf.); (v) *Theudotus
Liparensis* (fr. 93 Pf.; fr. 93, 1 Pf. = lemma in *Dieg.* iii 12–13). But if we assume that the lines
11–28 of *Dieg.* ii summarized only one elegy (which is less likely, because the average length of
each *Diegesis* for the *Aetia* is ten lines), we get the following series: (i) *Daphnephoria Delphica*
(frr. 86–9 Pf.; fr. 86 Pf. = lemma in *Dieg.* ii 10); (ii) *Abdera*; (iii) *Melicertes*; (iv) *Theudotus
Liparensis.*
[10] *Dieg.* iii 17–23. It cannot be ruled out that within this gap the summary of
*Theudotus Liparensis* finished and the lemma and the summary of another poem followed. If so,
since the lemma of a new *aition* appears in *Dieg.* iii 25–6 (*Leimonis*, fr. 94 Pf.), we should assume
that the thirteen lines of *Dieg.* iii 12–24 regarded two different elegies, i.e. *Theudotus* and
another unknown poem. But the average length of each *Diegesis* for the *Aetia* (see n. 9) does not
favour this hypothesis. Cf. Norsa and Vitelli 1934, 13; Vogliano 1937*a*, 121.
[11] Pfeiffer 1934*a*, 384; 1934*b*, 12–14.

uictima vel Phoebo sacras macteris ad aras,
  quam tulit a saeuo Theudotus hoste necem.

Or may you be sacrificed a victim at the altar of Phoebus, the death that Theudotus suffered from his cruel enemy.

And here is what we read in the scholia:[12]

The Etruscans, besieging the Liparian citadel, vowed that they would sacrifice to Apollo the bravest of the Liparensians if the god made them victorious. And when they gained the victory, they fulfilled their promise, sacrificing to him a certain man by the name of Theudotus.[13] Therefore Gallus wrote: 'Theudotus is captured and sacrificed to Phoebus, although a human victim is by no means welcome to the god.'

As Zipfel and Rostagni pointed out long ago, here the name *Gallus* is a corruption of *Callimachus*, as in other scholia to the *Ibis*:[14] therefore, although the following Latin distich (*Theodotus captus* etc.) is clearly fictitious, the scholia prove that Callimachus told the sad story of Theudotus. Now Pfeiffer, connecting this fact with the two residual words in the *Diegesis*, brilliantly inferred that the episode was in the fourth book of the *Aetia*.[15]

Pfeiffer's inference was confirmed in 1941, when Lobel published P.Oxy. XVIII 2170,[16] a papyrus by the same hand as *PSI* 1218. He combined a fragment of the former[17] with the fragment of the latter mentioned above, realizing that the two fragments were parts of the same papyrus. He founded this join on the lemma of the *Diegesis* and reinforced it by remarking that in P.Oxy. 2170 a paragraphos is written above the verse which he considered the incipit of the elegy. In this way Lobel brought to light the beginnings of our vv. 2–18.

The expanded text of the poem resulting from the join of the two papyri confirms that its subject is in fact the story of Theudotus, as Pfeiffer had guessed:[18] firstly the strings of letters λιπα[ and τυ[ (vv. 9 and 10) favour the supplements Λιπά[ρ- and Τυ[ρσην-; secondly μίαν νης.[ (v. 8) and ]ησαιον (v. 18) suggest μίαν νῆσο[ν and ν]ησαῖον, both referring to the island of Lipara; thirdly the mention of Apollo (v. 14) suits the outline of the episode, as we read it in the scholia to the *Ibis*.

---

[12] For the Latin text, see the apparatus of sources above.
[13] Up to this point the translation of the scholia is by Nisetich 2001, 155.
[14] See Pfeiffer's note on (Call.) fr. inc. auct. 789.
[15] Zipfel and Rostagni had already surmised that the evidence on Theudotus in the scholia on Ovid's *Ibis* is referred to the *Aetia*.
[16] Lobel 1941.   [17] Fr. 1.
[18] Callimachus surely accommodated the name Θεόδοτος to the elegiac couplet by using the form Θεύδοτος, which corresponds to the Ovidian *Theudotus*. Cf. also Call. *Aet.* fr. 178. 21 Pf. = 89. 21 M. Θεύγενες (instead of Θεόγενες). The form θεύς (instead of θεός) is used by Callimachus at *Cer.* 57 and perhaps in another passage (fr. inc. auct. 731 Pf. = 139 M.). It occurs in several inscriptions in the Doric κοινά and is said to be 'Doric' and 'Ionic' by grammarians: cf. Hopkinson 1984, 131; Massimilla 1996, 465–6.

In his edition of P.Oxy. 2170, Lobel also printed the first seven lines of the
elegy as they result from the combination of the two papyri, but confined
himself to proposing the acute supplements of vv. 3–5 reported above, without further discussion. He did not offer any comments on the following
verses and remarked that 'our fr. 1 preserves too little for it to be possible to
say that this story [i.e. Theudotus' story] is recorded there', although he
admitted that 'the occurrence of λιπα[ and τυ[ . . . and . . . ιεροϲειφοιβου[
. . . is consistent with it'.[19] Lobel's caution about the contents of the expanded
text was dismissed by Pfeiffer, who definitely assigned the title *Theudotus
Liparensis* to it, when he published it as fragment 93 in his 1949 edition of
Callimachus' fragments.[20] Nevertheless Pfeiffer himself was quite laconic in
his notes on this passage (which are, to be sure, precious as usual): he only
offered a brief discussion of vv. 1–4, made a couple of morphological
remarks, and quoted some verbal parallels.

As I said at the outset, I now intend to engage in a closer reading of the
fragment, by which I will try to reconstruct its various narrative stages.

But first some information must be provided about the historical background of the text. In this regard, although the exact chronology and development of the wars between Etruscans and Liparensians are somewhat
controversial, it seems safe to say that they loomed up already during the first
half of the sixth century and exploded during the first quarter of the fifth
(before the Etruscans' defeat at Cumae in 474).[21] These wars were related by
Timaeus[22] and Antiochus of Syracuse;[23] either or both of them may well be
Callimachus' source for Theudotus' story.[24]

The most remarkable feature of the elegy is the human sacrifice. Within the
fourth book of the *Aetia*, the same topic appeared in the previous poem
(*Melicertes*),[25] where Callimachus said that the Leleges residing in Tenedos,
whenever threatened with grave danger, used to immolate babies at the
altar of Melicertes. The contiguity of the two elegies does not seem to be
fortuitous: as Pfeiffer suggested long ago,[26] Callimachus probably wishes to
emphasize the cruelty of that custom and to make clear, at the same time, that

[19] Lobel 1941, 54.
[20] Pfeiffer 1949, 99–100. Pfeiffer notes that fr. inc. sed. 481 οἱ δὲ τὸν αἰνοτάλαντα
κατέϲτεψαν ('they crowned the most miserable man'), perhaps referring to a human victim
at the point of death, could regard Theudotus and therefore belong to our elegy.
[21] Cf. Secci 1959, 100; Colonna 1984 = 2005; Pallottino 1985; Gras 1985, 514–22; Cristofani
1987, 74–6.
[22] Tim. *FGrH* 566 F 164 ap. Diod. 5. 9. 4–5.
[23] Antioch. Syr. *FGrH* 555 F 1 ap. Paus. 10. 11. 3–4. Cf. further Strabo 6. 275; Paus. 10.
16. 7.
[24] Colonna 1984, 574 = 2005, 229 is inclined to think that Callimachus read about Theudotus
in Theophrastus' Περὶ Θυρρηνῶν (cf. Schol. Pind. *Pyth.* 2. 2).
[25] Fr. 91 Pf. + *SH* 275 + fr. 92 Pf.
[26] Pfeiffer 1934*b*, 13–14.

it did not pertain to the Greeks, but to barbarous peoples such as the Leleges and the Etruscans.[27]

As Pfeiffer himself pointed out,[28] the Etruscan practice of sacrificing their enemies was also known to Livy (7. 15. 10), who relates that the people of Tarquinia once immolated 307 Roman soldiers.

Another very interesting reference to the Etruscan sacrifices of human beings was detected by Giovanni Colonna[29] in Tzetzes' *Chiliads* (8. 884–5):

βίαιοι γὰρ οἱ Τυρρηνοὶ καὶ θηριώδεις ἄγαν,
ὡς μέχρι καὶ Ἱέρωνος ἱερουργεῖν ἀνθρώπους.

The Etruscans were very violent and brutal, so that they sacrificed human beings even until the age of Hieron.

Colonna thinks that Tzetzes refers here to our *aition*: so he dates Theudotus' killing to the span of years 485–480 BC, when Hieron I was about to succeed his brother Gelon in Syracuse.[30] It seems to me that Tzetzes' statement is too vague to be confidently ascribed to Callimachus' elegy: nevertheless a date approximating to the one assigned by Colonna to Theudotus' sacrifice would still fit the overall chronology of the wars between Etruscans and Liparensians.

Let us now turn to our fragment. It is a bit of a paradox that vv. 1–6, although they belong to the best preserved part of the text, seem to be quite intractable, as regards both their specific interpretation and their relevance to Theudotus' story.

Before offering a translation of this passage, I should like to deal with my new reading in the text at the end of v. 5. It seems to me that the final trace in *PSI* 1218 (after alpha), recorded without description by Vitelli and disregarded by Pfeiffer, does not recommend ἄκ[ρον, proposed by Lobel and accepted by Pfeiffer.[31] I would rather read αυ[ and supplement αὖ[ον. The phrase αὖ[ον | χεῖλος ('dry lip') can be compared with Nic. *Ther.* 339 χείλε' . . . αὐαίνεται and Quint. Smyrn. 10. 280 χείλεσιν αὐαλέοισιν, who both refer to thirst, caused by the bite of a snake or by fever. It also recalls a passage of Callimachus' Hymn to Demeter (v. 6), where the fasting women who celebrate the ceremony in honour of the goddess are said to spit ἀφ' αὐαλέων στομάτων ('from dry mouths'), i.e., according to the scholion, ἐκ τῶν αὐαλέων χειλέων τοῦ στόματος.

---

[27] This is also the conclusion of recent scholarship in history of religions, as regards the ancient Greeks' own knowledge of human sacrifice (although, as far as I know, the story of Theudotus has not been noted in that connection): cf. e.g. Henrichs 1981, 233; Hughes 1991, 187–8; Bonnechère 1994, 312. (I owe these references to Dr D. Obbink and Dr R. Rutherford.)
[28] See his note ad loc.
[29] Colonna 1984, 559–60 = 2005, 214–15.
[30] Colonna 1984, 563 = 2005, 217. Cf. also Colonna 1989, 361–5 = 2005, 313–17.
[31] Pfeiffer writes ἄ[κρον. The trace after alpha looks actually like the upper left-hand part of υ or τ or χ.

So here is a tentative translation of our text (down to χεῖλος):

A race sweeter than nectar ... than ambrosia, the earth sent you up, and across the tongue you go, most delightful of all things that are beyond new wine. Poor wretches, him (?) a little more than the dry lip ...

As far as I can see, two or more earthborn creatures—human or animal or vegetable—are addressed (v. 3 ὑμέας) and said to form a race (v. 1 γένος). This race is probably qualified as being sweeter than nectar and ambrosia: here γλύκιον seems to be the normal comparative of γλυκύ rather than the rare adjective γλύκιον (meaning itself 'sweet'),[32] because it is natural to take the genitives νέκτα₁ρος and ἀμβροσίης for two terms of comparison. Instead of γλύκιον, the lemma in the *Diegesis* has ψύθιον, probably a *uaria lectio*. In this form (namely, ψύθιον) the word is an entry in Hesychius' lexicon (ψ 257 Schmidt), perhaps stemming from Callimachus' verse, and its explanation is 'short-lived' (ὀλιγοχρόνιον);[33] but again it would be morphologically possible to consider ψύθιον a comparative, though we do not find it used elsewhere. On the whole, our passage seems to make more sense if we accept the reading γλύκιον ('sweeter'): by writing νέκτα₁ρος ... γλύκιον, Callimachus varies the Homeric phrase γλυκὺ νέκταρ (*Il.* 1. 598).[34]

The extraordinary sweetness of the creatures addressed seems to be re-affirmed in one more comparison: they go across the tongue as the most delightful of all the nourishments which surpass new wine (vv. 3–4). After an exclamation of grief or abhorrence perhaps applying to the same group (v. 5 δείλαιοι), a reference is made to someone or something (μιν) and—again by means of a comparative (τυ[τθόν] ... ἐπὶ πλ<έ>ον ἢ ὅσον, 'a little more than')—a 'dry lip' is possibly mentioned (vv. 5–6 αὖ[ον | χεῖλος): this last phrase seems to concern the act of drinking, which is already implied by nectar (v. 1)[35] and new wine (v. 4).

The subject of these verses and their relevance to the story of Theudotus are a mystery. Before the publication of P.Oxy. 2170, Eric Barber wondered whether Theudotus' blood was somehow compared with nectar.[36] The expanded text of vv. 1–6 puzzled Pfeiffer,[37] who only made a tentative reference to a passage of Euripides' *Hippolytus* (vv. 742–51), describing the gods' western gardens, and to a scholion to v. 748, stating that both ambrosia

---

[32] Cf. Soph. *Phil.* 1461 (*u.l.*), Aristot. *Eth. Eud.* 1238ᵃ28, *SGO* 01/12/01 v. 5 (1st c. BC?).

[33] The word ψύθιος occurs also in a fragment of Nicander (*SH* 562. 3 ψυθί[οιςι, suppl. Lobel), but its meaning there is 'untrue' (cf. Call. *Hec.* fr. 288.1 Pf. = 90. 1 H. ψύθος).

[34] As for the exceptional γλυκύτης of ambrosia, cf. Ibyc. *PMGF* 325.

[35] Nectar and ambrosia are the gods' drink and food respectively: cf. Hom. *Od.* 5. 93, [Hom.] *Hymn.* 2. 49, 3. 10, Plat. *Phaedr.* 247 ε. But some poets regard ambrosia as a drink (Sapph. fr. 141. 1 Voigt, Aristoph. *Eq.* 1095, Anaxandr. *PCG* 58. 1–2) and nectar as a food (Alcm. *PMGF* 42, Anaxandr. loc. cit.).

[36] Barber 1935, 177.

[37] See his note *ad loc.*: 'quomodo disticha de nectare et ambrosia cum fabula Lipar. de victima humana cohaereant, adhuc obscurum est.'

and nectar originate there. Giovan Battista D'Alessio guesses that someone, just after tasting an extremely sweet delicacy, is said to meet with a wretched death.[38] Markus Asper proposes taking δείλαιοι (v. 5) for an address to the Etruscans, who would be urged to grant the condemned man something sweeter than nectar and ambrosia: this could have some connection with life or be the last meal, deferring the execution a little.[39]

It seems to me that none of these astute suggestions accounts for *all* the elements that can be gleaned from the text. I confess that I myself am unable to reconstruct the contents and the point of the passage in a satisfactory way. I am especially baffled by the address ὑμέας γαῖ᾽ ἀνέδ[ωκε ('the earth sent you up', v. 3). Who are these? Prose-writers apply the phrase γῆ ἀναδίδωσι to the earth yielding plants and fruits,[40] but poets use it in a broader sense, which includes also human beings and animals: 'dark earth ... sent up Pelasgos [primordial Arcadian mountain and hero], in order that a race of mortals might exist' (Asius);[41] 'the sky and the earth ... beget and sent up to light everything: the trees, the birds, the animals reared by the sea and the race of mortals' (Euripides);[42] 'Earth herself sent up' the horse Arion (Antimachus).[43] The wider range of the phrase in poetry makes it particularly hard to identify the sweet-tasting creatures of our verses and to understand the relevance of this passage to Theudotus' story.

To sum up, it seems that the mystery of vv. 1–6 has not yet been solved. Nevertheless I admit that I find quite tempting a suggestion put forward by Alessandro Pagliara.[44] He suspects that our passage alludes to the word Μελιγουνίς, which was the ancient name of Lipara, as Callimachus himself says in his hymn to Artemis (v. 47f).[45] Pagliara notices that a plausible etymological meaning of Μελιγουνίς would be 'born from honey' or also 'born in honey' (μέλι + γίγνομαι): such a meaning would refer to the fertility of that volcanic island and so have the same connotation as the etymology of the name Λιπάρα, i.e. 'shiny', 'rich'. If Pagliara's conjecture is right, we may wonder whether Callimachus is opposing here the extraordinary sweetness of the Liparian *race* (v. 1 γένος), implied by the very name (Μελιγουνίς) of the

---

[38] D'Alessio 1996, 506.

[39] Asper 2004, 159.

[40] Cf. e.g. Hippocr. *Aër.* 12. 5, Thuc. 3. 58,4, Plut. *Cam.* 15.3.

[41] Asius fr. 8 129 Bernabé = fr. 8 Davies Πελασγὸν ... | γαῖα μέλαιν᾽ ἀνέδωκεν, ἵνα θνητῶν γένος εἴη,

[42] Eur. fr. 484. 2–6 (Melanippe Sophe) οὐρανός τε γαῖα ... | ... | τίκτουσι πάντα κἀνέδωκαν εἰς φάος· | δένδρη, πετεινά, θῆρας οὕς θ᾽ ἅλμη τρέφει | γένος τε θνητῶν.

[43] Antim. fr. 32. 5 Wyss = 31. 5 Matthews αὐτὴ Γαῖ᾽ ἀνέδωκε. Cf. also Ap. Rh. 2. 1209 ὃν αὐτὴ Γαῖ᾽ ἀνέφυσε (about the snake that guards the golden fleece).

[44] Pagliara 1992, 316–18.

[45] In using this rare word, Callimachus was probably inspired by Philitas (fr. 1 Sbardella = frr. 1 and 1a Spanoudakis). Cf. further Euph. *CA* fr. 51. 8, Strab. 6. 275, Plin. *Nat. hist.* 3. 93, Hesych. *s.u.* Μελιγουνίς.

*earth* that sent them up (v. 3),[46] to the bitterness of the Etruscans, who sacrificed Theudotus without any mercy (vv. 5–6).[47]

Quite unexpectedly I found that a closer reading of the following and worse preserved part of the fragment (vv. 6–18) was more rewarding.

When the word ἀνδρός in v. 7 was still unknown, Lobel had remarked that the verb ἀναινομένου ('refusing', v. 6) could be interpreted in accordance with the purport of the fictitious distich included in the scholia to Ovid's *Ibis*, which has been quoted above ('Theudotus is captured and sacrificed to Phoebus, although a human victim is by no means welcome to the god'): especially if Vitelli was right in reading and supplementing καί]περ ('although') before ἀναινομένου, Callimachus—according to Lobel— perhaps meant that Theudotus was sacrificed to Apollo, although this god refuses human victims.[48] But since the word ἀνδρός came to light, it looks more probable that ἀνδρός and ἀναινομένου stay together and refer to Theu- dotus: perhaps the poet said that Theudotus was an excellent soldier, although on the verge of the execution he understandably became just a man refusing to die.[49] Then the verb ἐπέτασσε(ν) ('enjoined', v. 7) could apply to the chief of the Etruscans, who bade his men kill Theudotus.

I suspect that Callimachus, after briefly anticipating in vv. 6–7 the end of the story, in the following verses went back to its earlier stages, namely the siege of Lipara, Theudotus' bravery and the Etruscans' solemn vow to Apollo.

In v. 8 the easy supplement μίαν νῆϲο[ν suggests itself: it was possibly said that 'only one island', i.e. Lipara (mentioned in v. 9), withstood without any allies the siege laid by the Etruscans (probably mentioned in v. 10). Its bravest defender was Theudotus, who in v. 9 seems to be described as 'inhabiting Lipara' (οἰκήϲας Λιπά[ρ-).[50]

In vv. 11–12 the verbs ἦλυθ' ἄγων and the neuter adjective or pronoun πολλά may be taken together: perhaps the leader of the Etruscans 'went' to

---

[46] A previous reference to the *ground* of Lipara is perhaps to be found at the end of v. 1, if we accept the supplement πιέδο[ιο, proposed by Körte 1935, 234. Note, however, that Lobel read ϲ instead of δ at this point of the *Diegesis*: see Pintaudi 2006, 201; Lehnus 2006, 214.

[47] I do not agree with Pagliara when he argues that in v. 1 νέκταρ means 'honey', as at Eur. *Bacch.* 143 μελισσᾶν νέκταρι (cf. also Antiphil. *Anth. Pal.* 9. 404. 8 = GP 1050, Apollonid. *Anth. Pal.* 6. 239. 6 = GP 1142): as a matter of fact, in our passage the mentions of both nectar and ambrosia—the former at the beginning and the latter at the end of the same couplet—show that the two words refer to the drink and food of the gods. Furthermore, according to Pagliara, Callimachus is not opposing the sweetness of the Liparensians to the bitterness of the Etruscans (as I should be inclined to think), but the sweetness of νέκταρ to the bitterness of Theudotus' blood (see already Pfeiffer's note ad loc.).

[48] Lobel's idea was reported by Vitelli 1935, 135.

[49] Cf. Nisetich 2001, 284: 'a man | refusing: indicates, perhaps, that Theudotus . . ., for all his bravery in battle, was a reluctant victim'.

[50] What we know about the story of Theudotus does not favour the reading and supplement οἰκί[ϲ]ϲας Λιπά[ρ- ('founding' or 'colonizing Lipara'), alternatively proposed by Lobel.

the altar, 'bringing' with him 'many' animal offerings to propitiate Apollo.[51]
It is noteworthy that in a passage from the first book of the *Aetia* (fr. 18. 6–7
Pf. = 20. 6–7 M.) the pronoun πολλά refers to the numerous offerings, which
Jason vows to send to Apollo in Delphi and Delos, if the god will save the
Argonauts from getting lost in the darkness: πολλὰ δ' ἀπείλει | ἐς Πυθὼ
πέ]μψειν, πολλὰ δ' ἐς Ὀρτυγίην ('he promised to send many gifts to Pytho
and many to Ortygia').[52] Furthermore, the verbal identity of the remains of
our v. 11 and the first half of a hexameter by Apollonius Rhodius (2. 491 ἦλυθ'
ἄγων ποίμνηθεν), noted by Pfeiffer, may suggest that here Callimachus is
talking about offerings to Apollo: in the Apollonian passage, as a matter of
fact, the pious youth Parebius 'joins' the seer Phineus and the Argonauts,
'bringing from the flock' two rams, which Jason and the sons of Boreas
sacrifice directly to Apollo.

The supplement φῆ [γ]ὰρ, proposed by Paul Maas in v. 13,[53] would be
suitable to introduce the vow of the Etruscan chief, made by him in the name
of all his army: he 'declared' that they would sacrifice their bravest enemy to
Apollo. In the following verse he perhaps stated that this immolation would
take place 'if Phoebus' holy' *aid* or *benevolence* (or some other word of similar
meaning) brought about the conquest of Lipara.

In v. 15 the word δημόθεν may still be included in the Etruscan leader's
promise to Apollo: conceivably he added that the intended victim would
be no mercenary soldier, but a man taken 'from among the people' of the
Liparensians. Pfeiffer remarks that the extremely rare adverb δημόθεν occurs
in the proem of Apollonius Rhodius' *Argonautica* (1. 7).[54] It seems to me that
this verbal parallel gives extra support to the notion that our vv. 13–15 dealt
with the vow to Apollo. In the passage from the *Argonautica*, as a matter of
fact, the word δημόθεν is part of the famous prophecy in which Apollo
himself predicted that Pelias' death would be caused by the plots of the man
whom he would see coming to him 'from among the people' wearing just one
sandal (of course in reference to Jason).[55]

As regards v. 16, when I first inspected P.Oxy. 2170 (far before I devised
an overall interpretation of our fragment), I noticed that the traces of the

---

[51] The Etruscans' worship of Apollo is proved by their Delphic dedications: cf. Gras 1985,
681–94.

[52] Lobel's supplement in v. 7 is confirmed by Apollonius Rhodius' imitation at *Arg.* 4. 1704–5
πολλὰ δὲ Πυθοῖ ὑπέσχετο, πολλὰ δ' Ἀμύκλαις, | πολλὰ δ' ἐς Ὀρτυγίην ὑπερείσια δῶρα
κομίσσειν. Cf. Massimilla 1996, 275 f.

[53] Cf. Pfeiffer's apparatus ad loc.

[54] δημόθεν is a Homeric *hapax*, meaning 'at the public cost' (*Od.* 19. 197): in Apollonius'
passage the metrical position of the word is the same as in the *Odyssey* (beginning of hexameter,
as in our text), but the sense is different. Cf. further Leonid. Tar. *Anth. Pal.* 9. 316. 2 = *HE* 2128
('from the town', as opposed to ἀπ' ἀγρῶν) and *Anth. Pal.* Append. I 275. 2, iii. 45 Cougny ('by
deme').

[55] For the precise meaning of δημόθεν in the Apollonian passage, cf. Vian 1976, 50.

antepenultimate letter[56] suggest π rather than ν and thought of the articulation τοῦτό γ' ἐπεί. Now it seems to me that these words would be appropriate for the end of the Etruscan chief's concise speech: 'after'[57] he said 'this much', he resumed the siege of Lipara. The words ἐπὶ τὴν in v. 17 and the very probable adjective ν]ηϲαῖον ('insular'), supplemented by Pfeiffer in v. 18, would both fit a quick description of this return to war.

I am of course aware that the remains of vv. 6–18 are too scanty for one to be sure of the reconstruction I have suggested here, let alone of every detail in it. Nevertheless I find that an interpretation along these lines would be consistent with the extant text, while keeping close to the outline of Theudotus' story, as we read it in the scholia to the *Ibis*.

It seems to me that this investigation into the particularly thorny problems of fr. 93 Pf. may provide two lessons for the students of Callimachus' fragments. On the one hand, it shows that a thorough examination of the texts and an endeavour to take a multiplicity of issues into account (such as literary connections, historical background, religious custom, etc.) are very much needed when we deal with the fragmentary works of that difficult and versatile poet. On the other hand, it suggests that we should not confine ourselves to treating the more celebrated fragments of Callimachus (such as, within the *Aetia*, the *Prologue*, or the *Lock of Berenice*), since there are many others that may offer a wider field to profitable speculation and sometimes to new acquisitions. In both respects, as in many others, we can by good fortune look up to the example set by Professor Parsons.

## BIBLIOGRAPHY

Asper, M. 2004, *Kallimachos: Werke* (Darmstadt).

Barber, E. A. 1935, review of Pfeiffer 1934*b*, *CR* 49, 176–7.

Bonnechère, P. 1994, *Le Sacrifice humain en Grèce ancienne* (*Kernos* suppl. 3, Athens and Liège).

Colonna, G. 1984, 'Apollon, les Étrusques et Lipara', *MEFRA* 96, 557–78; repr. in id. 2005, i/1. 213–29.

—— 1989, 'Nuove prospettive sulla storia etrusca tra Alalia e Cuma', in *Atti del Secondo Congresso Internazionale Etrusco*, i (Rome), 361–74; repr. in id. 2005, i/2. 313–25.

—— 2005, *Italia ante Romanum imperium: scritti di antichità etrusche, italiche e romane (1958–1998)*, 6 vols. (Pisa and Rome).

Cristofani, M. 1987, *Saggi di storia etrusca arcaica* (Rome).

[56] The foot of an upright followed by the right-hand part of a high curved horizontal joining an upright.

[57] The postponement of ἐπεί is not unusual in Callimachus' poems: cf. Massimilla 1996, 295 (n. on fr. 26. 1 ϲκῶλοϲ ἐπεί μιν).

D'Alessio, G. B. 1996, *Callimaco*, ii: *Aitia, Giambi, Frammenti elegiaci minori, Frammenti di sede incerta* (Milan).

Gras, M. 1985, *Trafics tyrrhéniens archaïques* (Rome).

Henrichs, A. 1981, 'Human Sacrifice in Greek Religion: Three Case Studies', in J. Rudhardt and O. Reverdin (eds.), *Le Sacrifice dans l'antiquité* (Entretiens sur l'antiquité classique, 27, Vandœuvres-Geneva), 195–242.

Hopkinson, N. 1984, *Callimachus: Hymn to Demeter* (Cambridge).

Hughes, D. D. 1991, *Human Sacrifice in Ancient Greece* (London and New York).

Körte, A. 1935, 'Literarische Texte mit Ausschluß der christlichen', *APF* 11, 220–83.

Lehnus, L. 2006, 'Nota sulle osservazioni di Lobel a Vitelli a proposito delle *Diegeseis*', *QS* 63, 213–19.

Livrea, E. 1973, *Apollonii Rhodii Argonauticon liber quartus* (Florence).

Lobel, E. 1941, 'Callimachus, Αἰτίων δ΄', in E. Lobel, C. H. Roberts, and E. P. Wegener (eds.), *The Oxyrhynchus Papyri*, XVIII, 51 6.

Maas, P. 1934, review of Norsa and Vitelli 1934, *Gnomon*, 10, 436–9.

Massimilla, G. 1996, *Callimaco: Aitia, libri primo e secondo* (Pisa).

Nisetich, F. 2001, *The Poems of Callimachus* (Oxford).

Norsa, M., and Vitelli, G. 1934, Διηγήϲειϲ *di poemi di Callimaco* (Florence).

Pagliara, A. 1992, 'Μελιγουνὶϲ-Λιπάρα: note di toponomastica eoliana', *Kokalos*, 38, 303–18.

Pallottino, M. 1985, 'Proposte, miraggi, perplessità nella ricostruzione della storia etrusca', *SE*[3] 53, 3–16.

Pfeiffer, R. 1934*a*, 'Zum Papyrus Mediolanensis des Kallimachos', *Philologus*, 89 (NF 43), 384–5.

—— 1934*b*, *Die neuen* Διηγήϲειϲ *zu Kallimachosgedichten* (Munich).

—— 1949, *Callimachus*, i: *Fragmenta* (Oxford).

Pintaudi, R. 2006, 'Note di Edgar Lobel alle *Diegeseis* di Callimaco', *QS* 63, 187–211.

Rostagni, A. 1920, *Ibis: storia di un poemetto greco* (Florence).

Secci, E. 1959, 'Tradizioni cultuali tirreniche e pelasgiche nei frammenti di Callimaco', *SMSR* 30, 83–107.

Vian, F. 1976, *Apollonios de Rhodes: Argonautiques*, i: *Chants I–II* (Paris).

Vitelli, G. 1934, 'Nuovi frammenti degli *Aitia* di Callimaco', *ASNP*[2] 3, 1–12.

—— 1935, 'Frammenti degli Αἴτια di Callimaco', in *Papiri della Società Italiana*, XI, 134–9.

Vogliano, A. 1937*a*, 'Διηγήϲειϲ di poemi di Callimaco', in id. (ed.), *Papiri della R. Università di Milano*, i. 66–145.

—— 1937*b*, 'Excursus IV a Callimaco (PSI XI 1218 c)', in id. (ed.), *Papiri della R. Università di Milano*, i. 172–3.

Zipfel, C. 1910, *Quatenus Ovidius in Ibide Callimachum aliosque fontes imprimis defixiones secutus sit* (diss. Leipzig).

# 12

## The Reputation of Callimachus

*Richard Hunter*

This chapter concerns three related moments, stretching (probably) from the early imperial period to late antiquity, in the reception of Callimachus; all attest to the importance attributed to this figure, but also to the very different ways in which that importance was negotiated. Callimachus and his poetry were awkward presences.

I

Cεβηριανόϲ· ... τὰ μὲν οὖν τῶν ἄλλων ποιητῶν ἀπεδέχετο μετρίωϲ, τὸν δὲ Καλλίμαχον εἰϲ χεῖραϲ λαβὼν οὐκ ἔϲτιν ὅτε οὐ κατέϲκωπτε τὸν Λίβυν ποιητήν· ἀνιώμενοϲ δὲ ἐπὶ μᾶλλον, ἤδη πολλαχοῦ καὶ τῶι βιβλίωι προϲέπτυε.

Severianus did not mind the works of other poets, but whenever he took up Callimachus, he only had words of mockery for the Libyan poet. When he was particularly upset, his habit was even to spit on the book. (*Suda* ϲ180 Adler = Callimachus T 85 Pfeiffer.)

Under the lemma of 'Severianus' the *Suda* preserves extracts about this man from Damascius' *Philosophical History*, also known as the *Life of Isidorus* (i.e. the fifth-century Neoplatonist from Alexandria).[1] Severianus came from a distinguished family and was to have a very active, if ultimately unsuccessful career (Damascius' judgement on him is that he never allowed sufficient time for reflection before acting). As happens to many, Severianus wanted to be a philosopher, but his father rather wanted him to make money by being a lawyer. As soon as his father died, however, Severianus seized the chance for a long-hoped-for trip to study with Proclus in Athens; he was on the point of

---

[1] Cf. Athanassiadi 1999; Zintzen 1967 may also be consulted. On the problem of the title and nature of the work cf. Athanassiadi 1999, 39–42, 63–4. The passage discussed here is fr. 108 Athanassiadi.

setting out when he was stopped by a dream. He dreamt that he was seated on
the ridge of a mountain and that he was driving the mountain as though it
were a chariot; something seems to have gone wrong with the text at this
point, but it would seem that fate led him in this curious position up towards
another life, one which 'seemed to be lofty and grand, but was rough
(τραχύc) and impossible to achieve (ἀνήνυτος)'. Severianus thus abandoned
philosophy and, as Damascius says, 'blessed quietness' (ἀπραγμοcύνη
εὐδαίμων), and threw himself instead into political life. He was an ambitious
and stern man, did not like coming second, and (inevitably) ended on the
wrong side; an apparently rather bloody career as a judge came back in
the end to haunt him.

Severianus was, however, also an extremely learned man and supporter of
literary study; Damascius ranks him among the top three κριτικοί of his
lifetime (fr. 106b Athanassiadi = 276 Zintzen). Certainly, his dream has a rich
literary pedigree, befitting a man of wide reading in classical literature. The
trail begins with the Hesiodic path to Arete, which is 'long and steep and
rough (τρηχύc) at first' (WD 290–1), and continues through any number of
'life choices' passages, many descending of course from Prodicus' 'Heracles at
the crossroads', one of the foundational texts of sophistic self-identity.[2] We
may, however, be reminded particularly of Lucian's *Dream* (32 Macleod) in
which our hero has to choose, not between philosophy and politics, but
between Paideia and Sculpture. Paideia takes Lycinus in her chariot for a
bird's eye view of the world and of the fame that he will win; when he returns
from the trip he is dressed in the fine robes of the powerful. Severianus'
dream may have lacked the irony of Lucian's self-presentation, but it
itself may have been a Proclan way of setting Proclus aside. In his *Life of
Proclus* Marinus relates how Athena, the guardian goddess of Byzantium and
goddess of wisdom, appeared to the young Proclus and turned him from the
pursuit of rhetoric to that of philosophy (chs. 6, 9);[3] this is not quite a 'life
choices' dream on the Prodican model, but it is not far away, and Severianus
might have borrowed from it to dignify his choice of the non-contemplative
life.

Severianus, then, was a man whose judgement, in both legal and literary
matters, was to be feared. Why did he spit on Callimachus?[4] Perhaps the most
obvious answer lies in fact in his connections with Neoplatonism, despite
his turning away from the pursuit of wisdom. As we know from Proclus'
commentary on Plato's *Timaeus* (i. 90. 16–20 Diehl), Critias' report in that
dialogue of his like-named grandfather's opinion that if Solon had been given
a chance to fulfil his career as a poet he would have surpassed Hesiod and

[2]  Cf. Philostratus, *Lives of the Sophists* 482–3.      [3]  Cf. Saffey and Segonds 2001, 79.
[4]  Cobet 1873 is worth recording: 'Fastidio et ipse et contemno poesin Callimacheam, sed
nihil ad Severianum'; I imagine that the librarians of Leiden were very relieved.

Homer and all other poets in fame (*Timaeus* 21 c–d) had caused deep worry, but the explanation which literary scholars had offered was that this (manifestly crazy) view had been put in the mouth of an ἰδιώτης; moreover, it had been established long ago by Porphyry's teacher Cassius Longinus, the greatest authority of his day, that Plato had no peer as a judge of poets (Longinus fr. 34 Patillon–Brisson). To Proclus we also owe the perhaps now better known report of Plato's preference for Antimachus (T 4 Matthews) over the fashionable Choirilos: 'Callimachus (fr. 589 Pf.) and Douris (*FGrHist* 76 F83) are thus talking idle rubbish when they claim that Plato was not up to the task of judging poets. The text before us shows that his was the judgement of a philosopher.' Proclus' standard move in distinguishing between literary and philosophical learning need not concern us here; suffice for the present that a criticism, such as Callimachus', of Plato was never to be forgotten or forgiven, and Severianus' spitting may perhaps be traced to this old wound. It is normally assumed,[5] on the basis of this passage of Proclus, that it was Plato's well-attested fondness for Antimachus which led to Callimachus' strictures, but another passage of Proclus refers to criticism of Plato's poetic judgement by some of Proclus' (unnamed) predecessors because of the *Timaeus* passage, and Kroll and Festugière at least saw there a further reference to Callimachus and Douris.[6] The two grounds for grievance probably in any case infected each other: the fondness for Antimachus in later antiquity, and particularly among the Neoplatonists, is well known.[7] If it is true that, in the *Against Praxiphanes*, Callimachus called Aratus πολυμαθῆ καὶ ἄριϲτον ποιητήν (fr. 460 Pf.), then one can readily imagine what later antiquity might have made of that judgement.[8]

It might prove interesting to collect all the extant references to Callimachus in the Neoplatonists and those in their orbit, but I have made no attempt to do this systematically. Porphyry and Proclus both cite Callimachus in support of their views, though it is perhaps worthy of note that Proclus manages on both occasions to avoid naming Callimachus explicitly (he is 'the Cyrenaean poet' or just 'some poet').[9] Of some interest is the long discussion by

[5] Cf. e.g. Pfeiffer 1968, 94; Cameron 1995, 304.

[6] Proclus, *In Platonis Rem publicam commentarii*, i. 43. 9–14 Kroll (cf. Festugière 1970, 61).

[7] Cf. Wyss 1936, pp. lv f.; Matthews 1996, 75.

[8] It has often been guessed that it was in this same work, in which Plato seems to have appeared as a character, that Callimachus (or one of his characters?) criticized Plato's judgement, cf. Immisch 1902, 273; Brink 1946, 25 n. 2; Pfeiffer 1968, 136.

[9] See fr. 588 Pf. and the citations apparatus in Pfeiffer's edition of the *Hymn to Delos* 84–5; for Porphyry cf. frr. 413 (= Porphyry fr. 374 Smith), 427, 588 Pf. This relative infrequency of citation contrasts markedly (if unsurprisingly) with the prominence of citations from Callimachus' poetry in the Homeric scholia; I count some 40 in Erbse's edition of the scholia to the *Iliad*, but no explicit citations from the grammatical works. Among Hellenistic poets, Callimachus is followed in the *Iliad* scholia at some distance by Euphorion (12), Aratus' *Phainomena* (8), Apollonius' *Argonautica* (perhaps 5) and Theocritus (4).

Porphyry of the words ἁματροχιά and ἁρματροχιά.[10] Thanks to Peter Parsons, we know that the former of these appeared in the great elegy for Berenice II which opened the third book of the *Aitia*. Porphyry says that it is no surprise if many contemporary critics of Homer get some things wrong, when even Callimachus, who has the reputation for being ἀκριβέϲτατοϲ καὶ πολυγράμματοϲ, did not know the difference between these words, and he returns to Callimachus' ignorance at the end of a rather laboured note. That most scholars now think that it was Porphyry who could not understand Callimachus, not Callimachus who could not understand Homer, may be left to speak for itself.[11]

Spitting declares allegiances as well as enmities; the world moves in oppositions, and the opposite pole to Callimachus was, of course, Homer. Callimachus T 84 Pf. is taken from Eunapius' account of the rivalries among sophists (i.e. Professors of Rhetoric) to succeed Julian of Cappadocia in fourth-century Athens:[12]

ἡ δὲ αὐτὴ δόξα τῶν ἀνθρώπων Προαιρεϲίωι κἀκεῖνον ἀντήγειρεν, ὡϲεὶ Καλλ-ίμαχον Ὁμήρωι τιϲ ἀναϲτήϲειεν.

The same popular opinion set up Diophantus in opposition to Prohaeresius, which is like setting Callimachus against Homer. (XII 1, p. 494 = Callimachus T 84 Pfeiffer.)[13]

Eunapius' 'Homer' is Prohaeresius the (Christian) sophist and teacher to whom the pagan Eunapius owed unrepayable personal debts;[14] the language in which he describes his rhetoric, teaching, and indeed physical appearance is that of a god—he is ὁ θειότατοϲ Προαιρέϲιοϲ (X 2. 1, p. 486), Eunapius thought of him as ἀγήρων καὶ ἀθάνατον (X 1. 3, p. 485)—and however debased the currency of such language was by this time, there is no doubting the power of the sway which this man, who 'filled the *oikoumene* with his *logoi* and his pupils' (X 8.4, p. 493), held. Eunapius reports that after one of his marvellous performances, built on a prodigious memory, the audience showed their appreciation by licking his chest, as though he were a statue of a god (X 5. 4, p. 489). If, however, Eunapius knew how to praise, he certainly also knew how to stick the knife in: Prohaeresius' enemies are depicted as snakes waiting to attack (X 4. 1, p. 488), and Eunapius' account of Prohaeresius' rival, Diophantus, the 'Callimachus' of the story, is gloriously venomous. According to Eunapius, Diophantus, who in fact delivered a funeral oration for Prohaeresius, only got as far as he did because of the φθόνοϲ of men (a very Callimachean motif) who never like to see one individual, in this case Prohaeresius, as the undisputed master of a field. Here is

---

[10] Porphyry, *Quaest. Hom.* 1. 263–4 Schrader = Sodano 1970, 15–17 = Schlunk 1993, 12–13.
[11] Cf. Luppe 1978.
[12] On these events cf. Kennedy 1983, 137–41; Penella 1990, 85–8.
[13] References to Eunapius follow the dual system of Giangrande's edition (Rome 1956).
[14] On Prohaeresius cf. Penella 1990, 83–94.

part of the close of Eunapius' brief notice about Diophantus: 'The present writer knew Diophantus and often heard him speak in public. It has, however, not seemed appropriate to include in this work anything which the writer has remembered of those speeches, for the present work is a record of important men, not a satire . . . He left two sons who devoted themselves to extravagance and money-making' (XII 4, p. 494).

The opposition which informs Eunapius' contrast between Prohaeresius and all his rivals is, as the opposition between Homer and Callimachus shows, that of the difference between the god-given gifts of inspiration and the petty struggles of ordinary $\tau\acute{\epsilon}\chi\nu\eta$, the $\mu\iota\kappa\rho o\lambda o\gamma\acute{\iota}\alpha$ $\kappa\alpha\grave{\iota}$ $\pi\epsilon\rho\iota\tau\tau\grave{\eta}$ $\mathring{a}\kappa\rho\acute{\iota}\beta\epsilon\iota\alpha$ (X 6. 14, p. 491) of ordinary sophists. Eunapius stresses Prohaeresius' $\mu\acute{\epsilon}\gamma\epsilon\theta o\varsigma$ $\phi\acute{\upsilon}\epsilon\omega\varsigma$; the sophist speaks in a great flood ($\dot{\rho}\acute{\upsilon}\delta\eta\nu$ X 5. 2, p. 489) and $\mathring{\epsilon}\nu\theta o\upsilon\epsilon\iota\hat{\omega}\nu$ (X 5. 3, p. 489), and his enemies are struck by thunderbolts (X 5. 6, p. 490), such as a Zeus or the 'Zeus of poetry' would hurl; he himself is not just a Socrates (X 7. 2–3, p. 492), but also a character from Homer, a Priam or an Odysseus (X 3. 6–4. 2, p. 488). Opposed, as we have seen, to Homer is Callimachus. Consider the case of the hapless Sopolis, another rival of Prohaeresius. Eunapius introduces him as a piece of worthless scum brought in to make up the numbers of professors (X 3. 9, p. 487), and his formal notice of Sopolis is worth reproducing in full:

καὶ Cωπόλιδος ἠκροάσατο πολλάκις ὁ ταῦτα γράφων. καὶ ἦν ἀνὴρ εἰς τὸν ἀρχαῖον χαρακτῆρα τὸν λόγον ἀναφέρειν βιαζόμενος, καὶ τῆς ὑγιαινούςης Μούςης ψαύειν ὀριγνώμενος. ἀλλ' ἔκρουε μὲν τὴν θύραν ἱκανῶς, ἠνοίγετο δὲ οὐ πολλάκις· ἀλλ' εἴ που τι καὶ ψοφήςειεν ἐκεῖθεν, λεπτόν τι καὶ ἀςθενὲς παρωλίςθαινεν ἔςωθεν τοῦ θείου πνεύματος· τὸ δὲ θέατρον ἐμεμήνεςαν, οὐδὲ τὴν πεπιεςμένην ῥανίδα τὴν Καςταλίαν φέροντες. τούτωι παῖς ἐγένετο· καὶ ἐπιβεβηκέναι τοῦ θρόνου τὸν παῖδα φάςκουςιν.

The present writer often heard Sopolis lecture. He was a man who sought to force his style to match that of the ancients and he strove to touch the Muse in sound health. But though he knocked loudly enough at her door, it did not open very often. If ever it did creak open a little, a faint and weak whiff of the divine spirit slipped out from within; the audience, however, went mad, for they could not take even a single drop squeezed out from Castalia. Sopolis had a son, and people say that this son too was elected to a chair. (Eunapius XIII, p. 494.)

Beyond the marvellous barb of the closing $\phi\acute{a}\epsilon\kappa o\upsilon\epsilon\iota\nu$ ('people say . . .') and the presentation of Sopolis' efforts at poetry as a piece of comic door-knocking, it is hard here not to be reminded by 'the Castalian drop' of the small but pure Apolline trickle of the end of Callimachus' *Hymn to Apollo*, particularly when we remember Prohaeresius' contrastingly great flood of words; that Sopolis' inspiration is $\lambda\epsilon\pi\tau\acute{o}\nu$ would seem also to point towards Callimachus. The key to understanding what lies behind Eunapius' intellectual structure here is, of course, his reference to Sopolis knocking on the Muse's door, for this takes us directly to a famous passage of

Plato which was of great importance to Neoplatonists and late antique poetics generally:

ὃς δ' ἄνευ μανίας Μουϲῶν ἐπὶ ποιητικὰϲ θύραϲ ἀφίκηται, πειϲθεὶϲ ὡϲ ἄρα ἐκ τέχνηϲ ἱκανὸϲ ποιητὴϲ ἐϲόμενοϲ, ἀτελὴϲ αὐτόϲ τε καὶ ἡ ποίηϲιϲ ὑπὸ τῆϲ τῶν μαινομένων ἡ τοῦ ϲωφρονοῦντοϲ ἠφανίϲθη.

But whoever comes to the doors of poetry without madness from the Muses, in the belief that craft (*techne*) will make him a good poet, both he and his poetry, the poetry of a sane man, will be incomplete[15] and eclipsed by the poetry of the mad. (*Phaedrus* 245 A.)

Plato's distinction between poets who write under divine inspiration and those who write merely ἐκ τέχνηϲ was to become a principal source of Homer's authority in later antiquity.[16] In his commentary on this passage of the *Phaedrus*, the fifth-century Neoplatonist Hermeias (pp. 98–9 Couvreur) illustrated the distinction from, on the one hand, Homer and Pindar and, on the other, Choirilos—rightly, I think, identified by Adrian Hollis as Choirilos of Samos—and Callimachus.[17] Whereas poets of *techne* 'do not even approach the doors of the Muses', inspired poets—Homer above all—'all but hammer on their doors and are filled from that source.' Eunapius' treatment of sophists stands squarely in these same traditions.


## II

Spitting on Callimachus inevitably calls to mind the infamous and anonymous distich that is Callimachus T 25 Pfeiffer:

Καλλίμαχοϲ τὸ κάθαρμα τὸ παίγνιον ὁ ξύλινοϲ νοῦϲ·
αἴτιοϲ ὁ γράψαϲ Αἴτια Καλλιμάχου. (*Anth. Pal.* 11. 275.)

Text and punctuation are disputed, and the meaning—apart from the fact that it is not flattering to Callimachus—anything but obvious.[18] The emendation Καλλίμαχοϲ in v. 2, a change which Luigi Lehnus has pointed out is not due to Bentley alone,[19] is now regularly adopted without discussion, as for example by Denys Page and by Alan Cameron in the course

---

[15] Commentators rightly note that διελή both means 'uncompleted' and also suggests 'uninitiated'.

[16] Other passages too (e.g. *Laws* 3. 682 A) were, of course, adduced in support; cf. Proclus, *Commentary on Timaeus* i. 64 Diehl; Russell 1989, 326–8.

[17] Cf. Hollis 2000, Hunter 2006, 92–3. For the connection between this observation and 'Longinus', *De subl.* 33 (below, p. 230) cf. already Immisch 1932, 189–90, although Immisch identified Hermeias' 'Choirilos' with the encomiast of Alexander.

[18] For a tentative translation cf. below, p. 228.

[19] Cf. Lehnus 1990, 291–2.

of his helpful treatment of this epigram.[20] The distich is bound to remain mysterious, but a little further ground-clearing may be possible.[21]

It was observed long ago that the form of this distich resembles the description of the presentation copy of a book;[22] we might think of Martial's *apophoreta* on literary texts (14. 183–96), one of which might be rude about the book offered (14. 196), or indeed of Crinagoras' famous poem on Callimachus' own *Hecale* ( = T 28 Pfeiffer):

> Καλλιμάχου τὸ τορευτὸν ἔπος τόδε· δὴ γὰρ ἐπ' αὐτῶι
> ὡνὴρ τοὺς Μουcέων πάντας ἔcειcε κάλωc·
> ἀείδει δ'Ἑκάληc τε φιλοξείνοιο καλιήν
> καὶ Θηcεῖ Μαραθὼν οὓc ἐπέθηκε πόνουc.
> τοῦ cοι καὶ νεαρὸν χειρῶν cθένοc εἴη ἀρέcθαι,
> Μάρκελλε, κλεινοῦ τ' αἶνον ἴcον βιότου.

Callimachus' is this chiselled poem; the man shook out all the Muses' reefs in its composition. He sings of the hut of the hospitable Hecale and of the labours which Marathon set for Theseus. May you too achieve the youthful strength of his hands, Marcellus, and an equal praise for a glorious life. (*Anth. Pal.* 9.545 = XI G–P.)

We might think also of Callimachus' own epigram on Aratus' *Phainomena*:

> Ἡcιόδου τό τ' ἄειcμα καὶ ὁ τρόποc· οὐ τὸν ἀοιδῶν
> ἔcχατον, ἀλλ' ὀκνέω μὴ τὸ μελιχρότατον
> τῶν ἐπέων ὁ Cολεὺc ἀπεμάξατο· χαίρετε λεπταί
> ῥήcιεc, Ἀρήτου cύμβολον ἀγρυπνίηc.

Hesiod's is the subject-matter and the manner: not the ultimate of songs, but it may be that the man from Soli has skimmed off the sweetest of verses. Hail subtle lines, the evidence of Aratus' sleeplessness. (*Anth. Pal.* 9.507 = Epigram XXVII Pfeiffer.)[23]

Callimachus' poem is framed by the name of the source of Aratus' inspiration (Hesiod) and by Aratus himself; for the author of the abusive distich, which is framed rather by the repetition of Callimachus' name, Callimachus can blame (αἴτιοc) no one but himself.[24] We might therefore consider reading Καλλιμάχου in v. 1, a text printed (together with Καλλίμαχοc in v. 2) by Wilhelm Christ, though never, as far as I can ascertain, discussed by him.[25]

---

[20] Page 1981, 17–18, Cameron 1995, 227–8.

[21] For the view that the distich mimics lexical entries, whether offering different definitions listed asyndetically for 'Callimachus' or successive parodic entries from a Callimachean 'glossary', cf. Cairns 1995.

[22] Cf. Susemihl 1891, 350–1, 895.

[23] The translation is intended as an aid to readers of this essay, not as an interpretation of the poem; I discuss this poem further in Hunter 2009, 257–62. For ἀοιδῶν in v. 1 cf. now P.Oxy. LXVIII 4648.

[24] Eustathius (*Hom.* 1422. 30) cites v. 2 of the anonymous epigram to illustrate αἴτιος in what Eustathius claims is the post-Homeric sense 'guilty, deserving punishment'. If Καλλίμαχοc is retained in v. 1 (cf. below), the most likely sense of κάθαρμα will be 'outcast', 'rubbish', φαρμακός.

[25] Cf. Christ 1889, 402 = 1890, 437.

παίγνιον, which commentators have found difficult in its application to Callimachus himself, is not rare as a term to describe a single piece or form of literature (cf. *LSJ* s.v. III 3), and is of course paralleled by the Latin *nugae* (cf. Catullus 1, Martial 14. 183 of the *Batrachomyomachia*). One of Leonides of Alexandria's numerological games uses the term for a presentation epigram:

τήνδε Λεωνίδεω θαλερὴν πάλι δέρκεο Μοῦσαν,
    δίστιχον εὐθίκτου παίγνιον εὐεπίης.
ἔσται δ' ἐν Κρονίοις Μάρκωι περικαλλὲς ἄθυρμα
    τοῦτο καὶ ἐν δείπνοις καὶ παρὰ μουσοπόλοις.

Look once more at this example of Leonides' flourishing Muse, a two-verse plaything of wit and grace. This will be a beautiful toy for Marcus at the Saturnalia, and at dinner-parties, and among those engaged with the Muses. (*Anth. Pal.* 6. 322.)[26]

With *Anth. Pal.* 11. 275 Pfeiffer linked, as Callimachus T 25a, the final two couplets of Martial 10. 4:

qui legis Oedipoden caligantemque Thyesten,
    Colchidas et Scyllas, quid nisi monstra legis?
quid tibi raptus Hylas, quid Parthenopaeus et Attis,
    quid tibi dormitor proderit Endymion,
exutusue puer pinnis labentibus, aut qui                                          5
    odit amatrices Hermaphroditus aquas?
quid te uana iuuant miserae ludibria chartae?
    hoc lege, quod possit dicere uita 'meum est'.
non hic Centauros, non Gorgonas Harpyiasque
    inuenies: hominem pagina nostra sapit.                                       10
sed non uis, Mamurra, tuos cognoscere mores
    nec te scire: legas Aetia Callimachi.

You who read of Oedipus and Thyestes in the gloom and Colchian women and Scyllas, what are you reading about but monstrosities? What use to you will be ravished Hylas or Parthenopaeus and Attis, what use the sleeping Endymion, or the boy who shed his drooping wings or Hermaphroditus, who loathes the waters which love him? What pleasure do you get from the worthless mockery of a wretched sheet? Read this, of which life can say 'It's mine!'. Here you will not find Centaurs or Gorgons or Harpies: my page knows real people. But, Mamurra, you don't want to recognize your own habits or to know yourself; you can read Callimachus' *Aitia*.

Martial's subject is the earthy realism and immediacy of his poems in comparison to the arcane mythology of the *Aitia*. Pfeiffer presumably associated the two testimonia on the grounds of the shared hemistich with which both poems end, but the earlier part of Martial's poem should also attract

---

[26] Cf. Page 1981, 515–16.

attention in the present context. Poem 10. 4 is part of an introductory series to Book 10, and—like the distich against Callimachus—it develops from the form of a 'book advertisement' (*hoc lege . . .*); *ludibria* in v. 7 is clearly not too far away from παίγνιον. As Lindsay and Patricia Watson note in their commentary, 'Since *ludibrium* can also mean a jest, there is an implication that it is elevated poetry which is frivolous rather than the humble genre of epigram.'[27] Martial may in fact have been thinking of the Greek couplet, though I do not know whether that sheds any further light on its provenance.

For what it is worth, confronted with τὸ κάθαρμα τὸ παίγνιον as a description of a poem of Callimachus, my first thought would have been of the *Ibis*, and it is, I suppose, not out of the question that *Anth. Pal.* 11. 275 is intended as a mock 'advertisement' for that poem rather than for the *Aitia*.[28] ὁ ξύλινος νοῦς awaits (in my view) convincing interpretation,[29] but applied to a literary work νοῦς is likely to mean 'intention, meaning' (cf., e.g., Plato, *Symposium* 222a2).[30] A first shot at a translation—reading Καλλιμάχου in v. 1—would therefore be something like: 'Callimachus' is the piece of refuse, the plaything, the wooden (?) meaning; responsible is he who wrote the *Aitia* of Callimachus'; much of course awaits elucidation.[31] A final point. With either nominative or genitive forms at the beginning and end of the distich we have a stylistic trick which is in fact much more common in Latin than in Greek.[32] Here it might just be intended to be itself a parody of Callimachus:[33]

Ἀστακίδην τὸν Κρῆτα τὸν αἰπόλον ἥρπασε νύμφη
ἐξ ὄρεος, καὶ νῦν ἱερὸς Ἀστακίδης.

[27] Cf. also Hutchinson 1993, 24.

[28] Watson 2005, 271 suggests that κάθαρμα picks up Callimachus' own image from the end of the *Hymn to Apollo*. He also suggests (an issue which I had pondered before reading his article) that παίγνιον picks up Callimachus' self-presentation as, in the view of the Telchines, writing παῖς ἄτε.

[29] Lucia Prauscello (private communication) has attractively suggested that the reference may be to the (frequently mocked) 'bookish' character of Callimachus' poetry, notably the *Aitia*; the point would be that the tablet or *pinax*, a mark of the poet (cf. esp. Callimachus fr. 1. 21–2), was made of wood. Other usages which might be relevant are ὑπόξυλος of a poet or sophist who looks good, but is worthless 'inside' (i.e. whose wooden substance is coated with gold or silver, cf. Phrynichus, *Praeparatio Sophistica* 115. 12–15 Borries), and the book-collector's συκίνη γνώμη at Lucian, *Adu. Indoctum* 6 (where, however, the choice of adjective is influenced by the context).

[30] I am inclined to compare τρόπος in Callimachus' epigram for Aratus (above, p. 226), but the matter is clearly not yet resolved.

[31] Martin West notes that, with the genitive in v. 1 and Bentley's nominative in v.2, one could also punctuate after παίγνιον, 'Callimachus' is the piece of refuse, the plaything; the wooden mind is responsible, Callimachus who wrote the *Aitia*.'

[32] Cf. McKeown on Ovid, *Amores* 1. 9. 1–2, Wills 1996, 430–5.

[33] A related, but different, effect is found in Callimachus, *Epigram* 19 Pf. It is very unclear whether such framing is the effect signalled by *Graecula quod recantat echo* at Martial 2. 86. 3, but that poem is another rejection of 'Callimachean' poetry in favour of poetry such as Martial's, which (ironically) is designed for a readership of connoisseurs.

A nymph snatched Astakides the Cretan goatherd from the mountain, and now Astakides is a sacred one. (*Anth. Pal.* 7. 518. 1–2 = XXII. 1–2 Pfeiffer.)

## III

Wondering which poems of Callimachus (or was it a complete edition?) Severianus is most likely to have spat on can help fill an idle minute. One can imagine, for example, that no one with connections to the Neoplatonists would have cared much for the *Hymns*;[34] a glance at the *Hymns* of Proclus will show that we are moving in a very different world, and it is a nice irony that the survival of both texts was to be so intimately linked. Just as the poetic criticism of the Neoplatonists was rooted in various modes of allegorical interpretation, which—as is well known—had found little favour in the Alexandria of Callimachus and Aristarchus,[35] so Neoplatonist poetry was a very different thing from the spare detachment of Callimachean verse. Porphyry tells a self-congratulatory story about one of his own poems:

At the feast in Plato's honour I read a poem entitled 'The sacred marriage'. Much of it was expressed mystically and in the veiled language of divine inspiration, and someone said that Porphyry was crazy; Plotinus, however, said in the hearing of everyone, 'You have shown us the poet, the philosopher, and the expert in mysteries.' (*Life of Plotinus* 15.)

No one would, I think, have said this about Callimachus. Just as he himself was a γραμματικός, so, in the anti-Callimachean tradition, his poetry—like, for example, that of Erinna—was an object of study for pedants and γραμματικοί, whereas Homer was a worthy study for true κριτικοί.[36] Crates of Mallos' famous distinction (fr. 94 Broggiato) between the κριτικός, who must be the master of all λογικὴ ἐπιστήμη, and the γραμματικός, who needs to know only about glosses, prosody, and such matters, is here broadened out (in a quite different philosophical environment) to the kind of poetry which falls into their respective spheres. In many ways Callimachus was (perhaps paradoxically) an Aristotelian; Peter Struck has recently described the revolutionary Aristotelian idea of 'the poet as master craftsman, who produces a finely wrought piece of art marked by clarity and elegance', and that does not seem a bad description of Callimachean ideals.[37] A similar picture emerges from a consideration of poetic *dianoia*. Peter Green has remarked on how surprisingly little trace both allegorization and

---

[34] Lehnus 2002, 27 assumes that it was the *Aitia*, Callimachus' best known and 'signature' work, upon which Severianus vented his impatience.

[35] Cf. e.g. Feeney 1991, 35–40. Lamberton 1986 offers a convenient introduction to the later traditions of allegorical interpretation.

[36] Cf. e.g. Antiphanes, *AP* 11. 322 (= Callimachus T 71 Pf., Erinna T 11 Neri). For the explicit linking of Callimachus and Aristarchus cf. Philip, *AP* 11. 347 ( = LXI G–P); the final two verses are Callimachus T 70 Pf.

[37] Struck 2004, 68.

rationalization have left in the *Argonautica* of Apollonius,[38] and even if he has
overstated the case, the basic point remains, particularly when we compare
Apollonius' epic with Virgil's. As for Callimachus, he did not write an epic as
such, and what he did write neither suggested any real interest in allegorical
interpretation nor offered the 'higher interpreters' any footholds from which
to operate within his text, should they have wished to do so.[39]

The poetry of inspiration and the poetry of pure *techne* differ in much
more than just style. Perhaps the best-known discussion of this subject are the
famous chapters (33–6) of *On the Sublime* about the difference between
'faultless' and 'sublime' writing.[40] 'Longinus' elsewhere acknowledges the
place for allegorical reading of some at least of Homer's sublime poetry,[41]
although he himself does not pursue this (and his remarks on Homer's gods
in 9. 7 are in fact of a decidedly non-allegorical kind) and he lays no stress
upon this style of interpretation in comparing poets of the two kinds.
Rather, he appeals to his own views about 'grandeur' and the relative 'size' of
different literary virtues. More than one modern reader of these chapters
of *On the Sublime* has been deafened by the silent absence of the name of
Callimachus, for everything from the opening reference to the καθαρός τις
cυγγραφεὺc καὶ ἀνέγκλητος (33. 1) to Archilochus' chaotic flood-tide (33.
5) and on to our real admiration for big rivers (35. 4) seems to point to the
language and imagery of the poet of Cyrene; Donald Russell has indeed called
this section of *On the Sublime* 'a manifesto directed against what we may
call the Callimachean ideal'.[42] Callimachus' apparent absence from *On the
Sublime* deserves more attention than it often receives.

The structure of 'Longinus'' discussion seems to be by genre, a term which
is here helpfully vague but in which metre obviously plays an important role:
to Homer are opposed Apollonius of Rhodes and Theocritus, both of whom

---

[38] Green 1997, 25–40; cf. also Feeney 1991, 81–2 on Eros in Book 3.

[39] It is instructive to compare Callimachus' dismissal of the Homeric story (*Iliad* 15. 192–4)
of the cosmic lot-drawing (*Hymn to Zeus* 60–7) with the later allegorical interpretations of the
scholia and 'Heraclitus', *Hom. Probl.* 41; Callimachus' alleged disdain for the Homeric story
sounds not unlike 'Heraclitus' 41. 5, but this attitude then takes them in very different
directions.

[40] I here accept the now most common dating of *On the Sublime* to the 1st c. AD, although
much of the argument would not be affected if the treatise were significantly later; for the claims
of Cassius Longinus (above, p. 222) cf. most recently Heath 1999.

[41] *De subl.* 9. 6–7, concerning the *theomachia* of *Iliad* 20, which seems to have been one of the
earliest passages to be interpreted allegorically, cf. Plato, *Republic* 2. 378 D–E (probably echoed
by 'Longinus' here), Theagenes fr. 2 D–K, cited in the B scholia on *Iliad* 20. 67. It is noteworthy
that both Porphyry (1. 240–1 Schrader from the same scholium) and 'Longinus' observe that
the literal sense of the passage offends against τὸ πρέπον, for this is not a common criterion of
judgement in what survives of *On the Sublime*. There is, incidentally, no trace of such allegorical
readings in the fragments of Cassius Longinus; for him ἀλληγορία is matter of verbal style,
cf. fr. 48. 258–79 Patillon–Brisson.

[42] Russell 1989, 308, cf. Fuhrmann 1992, 199–202. I have discussed some aspects of this
passage in Hunter 2003, 219–25.

wrote *epos*, though of very different kinds; to Pindar 'in the field of μέλη' is opposed Bacchylides, and 'in tragedy' Sophocles is opposed to Ion of Chios. The odd one out seems at first to be the opposition between Archilochus and the *Erigone* of Eratosthenes. The standard explanation, adopted for example by Wilamowitz and Russell,[43] is that iambus, of which Archilochus was the undisputed master, and elegy belong together as differentiated from both hexameters and lyric. There is no doubt that elegy and iambus are often treated together,[44] but there may be more to be said here before we accept this apparent anomaly in 'Longinus'' system.

It is of course no surprise to find Archilochus in a roll-call of sublime poets: throughout antiquity he travels with Homer as one of the two premier expressions of Greek poetic genius.[45] It is, however, iambus, and particularly its aggressive power, with which Archilochus is normally associated: for Theocritus, for example, Archilochus is simply τὸν πάλαι ποιητάν | τὸν τῶν ἰάμβων (*Epigram* 21 Gow). Which iambic poet could have been held up against him to exemplify flawless skill rather than flawed genius? In one sense, of course, this is idle speculation as 'Longinus' could doubtless have found an iambic poet and/or a poem, had he wanted to do so. That said, there were not many options available. One name of course occurs to us immediately—that of Callimachus—but here there were problems. Callimachus' *iamboi* are avowedly imitative of Hipponax, one of the other canonical iambists, and an opposition between Callimachus and Archilochus in the field of iambus might well have looked at least rhetorically unconvincing. More funda-mentally, however, we may well believe that iambic poetry did not fit easily into a work concerned with ὕψος; however we understand the πεζὸς νομός of the epilogue to Callimachus' *Aitia* (fr. 112. 9), *iamboi* were unelevated, and though this certainly did not rule out flashes of 'the sublime', it made iambic less promising territory than, say, epic. Quintilian reports the view that, if Archilochus falls short of the highest place in the poetic hierarchy, it is a fault of his subject-matter, not of his *ingenium* (10. 1. 60).[46] So too, Galen contrasts the iambics of Archilochus and Hipponax with Homer ἐν ἐξαμέτρωι τόνωι ... ὑμνήςοντος and Pindar ἄιςοντος ὑψηλῶς (x. 12 Kühn = Archilochus

[43] Cf. Wilamowitz 1904, 238, Russell 1964, 159. Doreen Innes has suggested to me that we should see the contrast between Archilochus and Eratosthenes not as a contrast within a separ-ate poetic category, but 'as a coda to the epic genre' which 'repeats with *uariatio* the overarching antithesis of the whole section', i.e. between flawed genius and flawless skill. This is an attractive suggestion, inter alia, because it leaves Longinus' operating with just the three 'big' genres—epic, tragedy, and choral lyric—and removes genres which are naturally 'un-sublime', such as iambic and elegy. On the other hand, the rhetoric of the passage and the transitional τί δέ; seem to force us to ask what the link between Archilochus and Eratosthenes is; cf. further below, p. 234.

[44] Cf. e.g. Pfeiffer 1968, 182.

[45] Cf. e.g. Plato, *Ion* 531 A, Dio Chrys. 33. 11; a particularly striking statement is Velleius Paterculus 1. 5.

[46] Juxtaposition to the 'grand' virtues of Pindar (10. 1. 61) reinforces the point.

T 68 Tarditi); the choice of verbs is there very telling. 'Longinus' refers to Archilochus in only two other places. In 10. 7 there is a reference to an obviously sublime passage describing a shipwreck; in his most recent note on the passage, Russell refers this to the storm description in trochaic tetrameters of frr. 105–6 West,[47] but the actual identification of the passage in question (and its metre) must remain uncertain. In 13. 3 Archilochus is listed among the Ὁμηρικώτατοι, and most scholars would, I think, accept that 'Longinus' could there be referring, and referring accurately, to all or any part of Archilochus' output.

The structure of 'Longinus'' analysis of poets in ch. 33 is first hexameter poetry, then Archilochus/Eratosthenes,[48] then lyric, and then finally tragedy; alongside 'Longinus' we may place the organization of what survives of the epitome of Dionysius of Halicarnassus' *On imitation*[49]—hexameters, lyric, tragedy, comedy—and of Quintilian's account of the Greek reading recommended for would-be orators in *Institutio oratoria* 10. 1—hexameters, elegy, iambus, lyric, Old Comedy, tragedy, New Comedy. The similarities between all three structures are obvious, and it has long been accepted that, if Quintilian did not actually use Dionysius himself, those two texts at least draw from a common Hellenistic source.[50] As 'Longinus' is all but certainly taking aim at Caecilius of Caleacte, a contemporary of Dionysius and certainly one sharing many of his literary sympathies,[51] it may be that he also reflects a discussion in Caecilius which drew on similar sources to those of Dionysius and Quintilian. It was not 'Longinus'' purpose to produce a comprehensive and consistent literary survey, but some conclusions may be drawn from the similarities between these three texts.

The absence of comedy from these chapters of 'Longinus' is most easily explained by the fact that comedy, like iambus, was not naturally promising territory for the 'sublime', though even Aristophanes had his moments (*De subl*. 40. 2). Secondly, it is clear that, in both Greek and Latin literature (cf. 10. 1. 93–6), Quintilian treats elegy and iambus quite separately;[52] he may have had a particular reason for wishing to include elegy—the desire to be able subsequently to name the Roman practitioners of a genre in which *Graecos prouocamus* (10. 1. 93)—but it is his choice of elegists which particularly attracts attention:

---

[47] In the 1995 revision of the Loeb edition; some support is lent to this identification by the citation of that poem by 'Heraclitus', *Homeric Problems* 5. 3.

[48] But cf. above, n. 43.

[49] Cf. Aujac 1992, Battisti 1997, Dion. Hal. ii. 202–14 U.–R.

[50] Cf. e.g. Steinmetz 1964. We may note also Horace, *AP* 73–85, where the order of metrically defined 'genres' is epic (Homer), elegy, iambus (Archilochus), drama (as the heir of iambus), lyric; with Horace's *exiguos elegos* (v. 77) compare perhaps 'Longinus'' description of Eratosthenes' *Erigone* as ἀμώμητον ποιημάτιον (33. 5).

[51] Cf. Russell 1964, 58–9.

[52] For this separation cf. also Dio Chrys. 18. 8.

elegiam . . . cuius princeps habetur Callimachus, secundas confessione plurimorum Philetas occupauit.

In elegy Callimachus is considered the leading poet, with Philitas, in the opinion of most judges, taking second prize. (10. 1. 58.)

Whether or not there was a standard Hellenistic list (or canon?) of elegists, as there certainly was later (cf. Callimachus T 87 Pfeiffer), may be doubted,[53] but Quintilian's failure to mention, say, Callinus or Mimnermus remains striking. Callimachus' fame in the Roman world cannot be doubted (cf. e.g. Horace, *Epist.* 2. 2. 100, Ovid, *Amores* 1. 15. 13), but—whatever the identity of the nameless judges to whom Quintilian appeals—elegy is the only poetic genre in his survey in which a Hellenistic poet takes primacy, for Menander and New Comedy represent a special case; elsewhere, Quintilian has, of course, no qualms about naming Hellenistic poets and does so freely in this chapter: beyond Philitas and Callimachus we have Apollonius, Aratus, Theocritus, Nicander, Euphorion.[54] As for Dionysius, he moves directly from *epos* to lyric. This could perhaps be the result of the activity of Dionysius' epitomator, or it could simply be that Dionysius saw no value for would-be orators in elegy, as Quintilian too treats Greek elegy as little more than relaxation after the serious business. Nevertheless, when we see which elegists Quintilian names, whether or not he has taken the names from an earlier (Greek) list, Dionysius' reticence about elegy (at least) seems susceptible of another explanation.[55] In what survives of his critical works Dionysius never directly names a Hellenistic poet *qua* poet (Menander again being a special case);[56] Callimachus is mentioned four times, but only in his capacity as grammarian.[57] If we only had Dionysius' testimony, we should have no idea that Callimachus ever wrote poetry. In this *damnatio memoriae,* we see the full force of Dionysius' classicizing agenda, and we see it perhaps also in the omission of elegy from the *De imitatione.*

What then of 'Longinus'? He too could simply have passed over elegy in silence, but it may be that the temptation to stick the knife into 'the

---

[53] Cf. Kroehnert 1897, 30, *contra* Steinmetz 1964. The choice of the relatively obscure Callinus alongside Mimnermus in later lists could be explained in more than one way. Flashar 1979, 85 seems to accept that Philitas and Callimachus appeared in Hellenistic lists as the latest poets to be included.

[54] Steinmetz 1964 argues that, in taking a view of Greek literary history not marked by unbridgeable epochal distinctions, Quintilian adopts a typically Roman perspective. At the Oxford conference Stephen Harrison suggested that Quintilian has simply borrowed Callimachus and Philitas from Propertius 3. 1. 1; the influence of Roman poetry on Quintilian's lists can hardly be doubted, but although Quintilian explicitly cites Horace, *Odes* 4. 2 in describing Pindar's virtues at 10. 1. 61, it is clear from Dionysius' closely parallel account of Pindar that, there at least, Quintilian was using Greek sources as well as Horace.

[55] Cf. Tavernini 1953, 24–5.

[56] At *De comp. uerb.* 4 he mentions Sotadean verses.

[57] *Isaeus* 6, *Demosthenes* 13, *Dinarchus* 1, 9.

Callimacheans' proved too strong. There were, however, dangers. Callimachus' reputation as an elegist, perhaps indeed *the* elegist (cf. Quintilian
10. 1. 58 above), stood second to none (including Archilochus); if 'Longinus'
had posed the question 'Would you rather be Archilochus or Callimachus in
the field of elegy?', he could not be sure of the answer. Callimachus was, not to
put too fine a point on it, just too big a fish, in both the Greek and Roman
critical traditions,[58] for 'Longinus' to take on: his silent absence from the
firing-line in *On the Sublime* 33 is in fact a most eloquent tribute to his
reputation. Nicholas Richardson suggested that 'Longinus'' silence was owed
to the fact that 'with his great range of invention, variety of style, and constant
ability to take us by surprise, [Callimachus] stands apart from and above the
other poets of his period';[59] that judgement would, I think, be shared by many
moderns, but we should rather seek an explanation within 'Longinus'' own
agenda and ideology. Callimachus was in fact almost that most paradoxical of
creatures, a third-century 'classic', a poet supreme in his own genre, even
when set in competition with the great figures of the past, and 'Longinus'
simply could not allow 'Hellenistic classics'. Eratosthenes, on the other hand,
famously τὸ βῆτα, was never in any danger of carrying off τὸ πρωτεῖον
(*De subl.* 33. 1). Callimachus is the absent presence made manifest through
lesser mortals. Both Apollonius and Eratosthenes were, in the ancient biographical tradition, pupils of Callimachus,[60] and—for what it is worth—
modern scholarship at least sees the poetry of both as imitative of Callimachus: why shoot the organ-grinder when you can kill off his monkeys?
As for the other poets named, Theocritus is said in the biographical
tradition, obviously on the basis of *Idyll* 7, to have been a pupil of Philitas
and Asclepiades and is associated with Aratus, Callimachus, Nicander, and
Ptolemy Philadelphus,[61] and Ion of Chios is a model famously appealed to
by Callimachus himself in *Iambus* 13.[62] Nothing, we might think, would have
suited 'Longinus'' apparent purpose better than an opposition between
Homer and, say, the *Hecale*, Callimachus' τορευτὸν ἔπος (Crinagoras, *Anth.
Pal.* 9. 545. 1, above, p. 226), but Callimachus makes no explicit appearance in
what survives of *On the Sublime*. Such studied neglect, both like and unlike
Severianus' public displays of distaste, speaks volumes.

---

[58] For the imperial period at Rome cf. the remarks of Jaillard 2000 on a letter of Hadrian in
which Callimachus seems to be numbered among 'the most noteworthy (ἐλλογιμώτατοι)
poets of Greece and Rome' (*SEG* 51 (2001), no. 641).

[59] Richardson 1985, 398.

[60] Cf. Callimachus T 11, 12, 13, 15 Pf.

[61] Cf. *Vita Theocriti* A, pp. 1–2 Wendel, 'Anecdoton Estense', p. 9 Wendel.

[62] We have more to learn about the choice of Ion to set against Sophocles; it may be that Ion's
versatility is relevant (cf. Eratosthenes' many-sidedness), and I wonder also whether the fact that
Ion related an anecdote about Sophocles which Athenaeus at least thought worth preserving
(13. 630 E–634 F = Ion fr. 104 Leurini) is relevant here.

Having selected the elegiac *Erigone* as his target, where then was 'Longinus' to go? A poem about the invention of wine and a drunken murder might well, of course, have made a critic think of Archilochus, himself a famous drinker and devotee of the wine-god; if Erigone hanged herself in Eratosthenes' poem, Archilochus' poetry had notoriously made the daughters of Lycambes do the same thing out of shame. Although the number of testimonia for Archilochus' place in the pantheon of elegy is indeed far outweighed by those for iambus, there are enough ancient indications and enough papyri, now of course happily joined by the 'Telephus' of P.Oxy. 4708, to show that this side of his poetic activity was certainly not entirely forgotten within scholarly classifications: he was indeed claimed by some to be the inventor of elegy.[63] Here is not the place to discuss whether the 'Telephus elegy', which by any standards is certainly Ὁμηρικώτατον, can help us with 'Longinus'' description of how Archilochus' flood carries with it πολλὰ καὶ ἀνοικονόμητα, but for the moment we should be content with recognizing that the 'Telephus elegy' has perhaps slightly altered the balance of interpretation for this passage of *On the Sublime*.[64]

One of the poems which appears in *Supplementum Hellenisticum* in a form unrecognizable from that which it had twenty years before is the so-called 'Seal' of Posidippus (*SH* 705 = Posidippus 118 A–B). As suggested by Hugh Lloyd-Jones in 1963, Posidippus here wishes for himself posthumous honours such as those which Archilochus enjoyed, but he also forbids weeping and lamentation at his death, though one may shed tears for the 'Parian nightingale'.[65] Why did Posidippus choose Archilochus as the poet with whom to contrast himself? The standard answer is (rightly) Archilochus' fame and cult and perhaps the new life given to that cult in the middle of the third century, to which the 'Mnesiepes inscription' bears eloquent witness.[66] Does, however, Posidippus also think of Archilochus specifically as a poet of elegiacs, and hence as the great founding figure of his own 'genre'? Does 'nightingale' not just mean 'poet' here, but—particularly in a context of mourning—evoke the

---

[63] Cf. Archilochus T 118, 146 Tarditi, Mimnermus T 21A, 21B Allen (all concerning rival claims to the 'invention' of elegy), Aristotle fr. 937 Gigon. The absence of Archilochus from Hermesianax fr. 7 Powell is open to more than one interpretation. For the characteristics of the Alexandrian edition of Archilochus' elegiacs cf. Obbink 2006, 1–2.

[64] That 'Longinus' was indeed here thinking of Archilochus' narrative elegies was suggested, before the publication of the 'Telephos' by Bowie 2001, 51–2. Bowie pointed both to the general structure of 'Longinus'' *synkrisis* and to the criticism of Archilochus' *abundantia* in a passage (from a poem of unknown metrical genre) about the rape of Deianeira at Dio Chrysostom 60. 1 (= Archilochus fr. 286 West), and suggested that both Dio and 'Longinus' had the same poem in mind, perhaps the only 'mid-length elegiac mythical narrative' of Archilochus to have survived. He further noted that, in describing the *Erigone*, 'Longinus' uses a word, ἀμώμητον, which Archilochus had used (fr. 5 West) of the shield he had abandoned.

[65] Lloyd-Jones 1963, 87–8, 90–2. There is now, of course, a huge bibliography; a good starting-point is still Dickie 1998, 65–76.

[66] Cf. Clay 2004; for Posidippus ibid. 30–1.

nightingale as itself a mourner (cf. Aristophanes, *Birds* 217), itself an 'elegiac' bird?[67] However that may be, Posidippus chose Archilochus, whereas Callimachus, in the 'Reply to the Telchines', apparently chose Mimnermus, one of Archilochus' rivals for the title of 'inventor' of elegy, as his authorizing archaic model.[68] The 'Reply' and the 'Seal' are often thought to be related intertextually—usually not to the credit of Posidippus, who is, of course, among the list of 'Telchines' offered by the Florentine *diegeseis*—but we simply do not know enough about literary debate in the third century to know just how charged these respective choices of authority were. What with hindsight we can say is that the appeal to Archilochus and Mimnermus as models may be seen to evoke a dichotomy which was to inform a great deal of later poetry and criticism.[69] Whereas, however, Callimachus' critical fame came to surpass that of the model he claimed, Posidippus, though his wish for a statue seems to have been fulfilled, has never remotely threatened the μυρίον κλέος of the Parian nightingale.[70]

## BIBLIOGRAPHY

Athanassiadi, P. 1999, *Damascius: The Philosophical History* (Athens).
Aujac, G. 1992, *Denys d'Halicarnasse: Opuscules rhétoriques*, v (Paris).
Battisti, D. G. 1997, *Dionigi di Alicarnasso: Sull'imitazione* (Pisa and Rome).
Bowie, E. L. 1986, 'Early Greek Elegy, Symposium and Public Festival', *JHS* 106, 13–35.
—— 2001, 'Ancestors of Historiography in Early Greek Elegiac and Iambic Poetry?', in N. Luraghi (ed.), *The Historian's Craft in the Age of Herodotus* (Oxford), 45–66.
Brink, C. O. 1946, 'Callimachus and Aristotle: An Enquiry into Callimachus' ΠΡΟΣ ΠΡΑΞΙΦΑΝΗΝ', *CQ* 40, 11–26.

[67] Cf. e.g. Callimachus, *Anth. Pal.* 7.80.5 ( = *Epigram* 2 Pfeiffer), Catullus 65.10–14. How early the elegiac couplet was specifically connected with mourning remains a difficult question, for some relevant considerations cf. Bowie 1986, 22–7; Hunter 1992, 18–22; 2006, 29–30.

[68] I have wondered whether the 'Telephus elegy' might shed light on Callimachus' rejection of long poetry concerning ἥρωας (fr. 1.5).

[69] I do not, of course, mean to imply that Posidippus' choice of Archilochus involved a conscious rejection of Mimnermus (cf. *AP* 12. 168 = Posidippus 140 A–B), any more than we should assume that Callimachus turned his back on Archilochus (too much weight is often placed upon fr. 544 Pfeiffer). When in *Odes* 2. 20 Horace both turns into a swan (cf. Call. fr.1. 39–40) which flies beyond *inuidia* and also forbids mourning at his death, he may be combining the 'Seal' of Posidippus' with Callimachus' 'Reply'; for possible links between the 'Seal' and *Odes* 3.30 cf. Di Benedetto 2003, 14–15.

[70] For this chapter cf. also Hunter 2008, 537–58. I am much indebted to Doreen Innes, Luigi Lehnus, Dirk Obbink, Lucia Prauscello, Richard Rutherford and the audience of the Oxford conference for helpful discussion and corrections; the structure and style of the oral presentation has been preserved as far as the Editors allowed. It is a very great pleasure to be able to offer this chapter to Peter Parsons, as an utterly inadequate return for all that his work has taught me.

Cairns, F. 1995., 'Callimachus the "Woodentop" (*AP* XI 275)', in L. Belloni, G. Milanese, and A. Porro (eds.), *Studia classica Iohanni Tarditi oblata*, i (Milan), 607–15.

Cameron, A. 1995, *Callimachus and his Critics* (Princeton).

Christ, W. 1889, *Geschichte der griechischen Litteratur* (Nördlingen; 2nd edn. Munich, 1890).

Clay, D. 2004, *Archilochos Heros: The Cult of Poets in the Greek Polis* (Washington, DC).

Cobet, C. G. 1873, 'Severianus et Callimachus' *Mnem.*² 1, 204.

Di Benedetto, V. 2003, 'Omero, Saffo e Orazio e il nuovo Posidippo', *Prometheus*, 29, 1–16.

Dickie, M. 1998, 'Poets as Initiates in the Mysteries: Euphorion, Philicus and Posidippus', *A&A* 44, 49–77.

Feeney, D. C. 1991, *The Gods in Epic* (Oxford).

Festugière, A. J. 1970, *Proclus: Commentaire sur la République* (Paris)

Flashar, H. 1979, 'Die klassizistische Theorie der Mimesis' in *Le classicisme à Rome aux Iers siècles avant et après J.-C.*, Entretiens sur l'antiquité classique XXV (Vandœuvres-Geneva), 79–97.

Fuhrmann, M. 1992, *Die Dichtungstheorie der Antike* (Darmstadt).

Green, P. 1997, *The Argonautika by Apollonius Rhodios* (Berkeley).

Heath, M. 1999, 'Longinus, *On Sublimity*', *Proceedings of the Cambridge Philological Society*, 45, 43–74.

Hollis, A. 2000, 'The Reputation and Influence of Choerilus of Samos', *ZPE* 130, 13–15.

Hunter, R. 1992, 'Writing the God: Form and Meaning in Callimachus, *Hymn to Athena*', *MD* 29, 9–34.

—— 2003, 'Reflecting on Writing and Culture: Theocritus and the Style of Cultural Change', in H. Yunis (ed.), *Written Texts and the Rise of Literate Culture in Ancient Greece* (Cambridge), 213–34 (= Hunter 2008, 434–56).

—— 2006, *The Shadow of Callimachus* (Cambridge).

—— 2008, *On Coming After. Studies in Post-Classical Greek Literature and its Reception* (Berlin and New York)

——2009, 'Hesiod's Style: Towards an Ancient Analysis', in F. Montanari, A. Rengakos, and C. Tsagalis (eds.), *Brill's Companion to Hesiod* (Leiden), 253–69.

Hutchinson, G. O. 1993, *Latin Literature from Seneca to Juvenal* (Oxford).

Immisch, O. 1902, 'Beiträge zur Chrestomathie des Proclus und zur Poetik des Altertums', in *Festschrift Theodor Gomperz dargebracht zum siebzigsten Geburtstage* (Vienna), 237–74.

—— 1932, *Horazens Epistel über die Dichtkunst* (*Philologus* Suppl. 24/3; Leipzig).

Jaillard, D. 2000, 'À propos du fragment 35 de Callimaque', *ZPE* 132, 143–4.

Kennedy, G. A. 1983, *Greek Rhetoric under Christian Emperors* (Princeton).

Kroehnert, O. 1897, *Canonesne poetarum scriptorum artificum per antiquitatem fuerunt?* (Königsberg).

Lamberton, R. 1986, *Homer the Theologian* (Berkeley).

Lehnus, L. 1990, 'Notizie callimachee II', *Paideia*, 45, 277–92.

—— 2002, 'Callimaco prima e dopo Pfeiffer', in *Callimaque* (Entretiens sur l'antiquité classique XLVIII; Vandœuvres-Geneva), 1–33.

Lloyd-Jones, H. 1963, 'The Seal of Posidippus', *JHS* 83, 75–99 [ = *Greek Comedy, Hellenistic Literature, Greek Religion, and Miscellanea* (Oxford 1990), 158–95].

Luppe, W. 1978, '*ΟΥΔΕΙC ΕΙΔΕΝ* '*ΑΜΑΤΡΟΧΙΑC* *(Kallimachos fr. 383, 10 Pf.)*', *ZPE* 31, 43–4.

Matthews, V. J. 1996, *Antimachus of Colophon* (Leiden).

Obbink, D. 2006, 'A New Archilochus Poem', *ZPE* 156, 1–9.

Page, D. L. 1981, *Further Greek Epigrams* (Cambridge).

Patillon, M., and Brisson, L. 2001, *Longin, Fragments, Art Rhétorique. Rufus, Art Rhétorique* (Paris).

Penella, R. J. 1990, *Greek Philosophers and Sophists in the Fourth Century* A.D. *Studies in Eunapius of Sardis* (Leeds).

Pfeiffer, R. 1968, *History of Classical Scholarship* (Oxford).

Richardson, N. J. 1985, 'Pindar and Later Literary Criticism in Antiquity', *Papers of the Leeds Latin Seminar*, 5, 383–401.

Russell, D. A. 1964, '*Longinus': On the Sublime* (Oxford).

—— 1989, 'Greek Criticism of the Empire', in G. A. Kennedy (ed.), *The Cambridge History of Literary Criticism* (Cambridge), 297–329.

Saffey, H. D., and Segonds, A.-P. 2001, *Marinus: Proclus ou Sur le Bonheur* (Paris).

Schrader, H. 1880, *Porphyrii quaestionum Homericarum ad Iliadem pertinentium reliquiae* (Leipzig).

Schlunk, R. R. 1993, *Porphyry: The Homeric Questions* (New York).

Sodano, A. R. 1970, *Porphyrii quaestionum Homericarum Liber I* (Naples).

Steinmetz, P. 1964, 'Gattungen und Epochen der griechischen Literatur in der Sicht Quintilians', *Hermes*, 92, 454–66.

Struck, P. T. 2004, *Birth of the Symbol* (Princeton).

Susemihl, F. 1891, *Geschichte der griechischen Litteratur in der Alexandrinerzeit*, i (Leipzig).

Tavernini, N. 1953, *Dal libro decimo dell'Institutio Oratoria alle fonti tecnico-metodologiche di Quintiliano* (Turin).

Watson, L. 2005, 'Catullan Recycling: *cacata carta*', *Mnem.*[4] 58, 270–7.

Wilamowitz-Moellendorff, U. von, 1904, *Griechisches Lesebuch* (Berlin).

Wills, J. 1996, *Repetition in Latin Poetry* (Oxford).

Wyss, B. 1936, *Antimachi Colophonii Reliquiae* (Berlin).

Zintzen, C. 1967, *Damascii Vitae Isidori Reliquiae* (Hildesheim).

# 13

## Telling Tales: Ovid's *Metamorphoses* and Callimachus

*Gregory Hutchinson*

Two chief interests in recent criticism of the *Metamorphoses* have been narratology and intertextuality. But little has been done, except incidentally, to relate these areas to each other. The relation between them is in my view important. It reveals a larger aspect of the *Metamorphoses*, and brings into general and detailed reading of the poem a somewhat new approach.[1]

Two areas of narratology and intertextuality will concern us particularly: the use of secondary narrators, that is of narrative within narrative, and the reworking of sources for myths. Both areas are unusually significant for this poem: *mise en abyme* here reaches extremes of prominence and complexity; as for the use of sources, relatively little Latin hexameter poetry had devoted itself to narrating Greek myths, and especially a plurality of Greek myths. The areas have much to relate them. Each has to do, on different levels, with who tells the story: internally the narrators, externally the poets. Each is aligned with the sectional character of the poem: every new story brings in a different set of sources; most secondary narrators tell one story, and all secondary narrative roughly begins and ends at the boundary of a story if not a section. Each area is characterized by accumulation and complexity: in the simplest cases, a secondary narrative lies inside a primary narrative, and a source is perceived lying behind the narrative being read. Each area has its links to the central figure of the poet, a point which needs expansion.[2]

---

[1] Farrell 1992, 263–7, provides an excellent example of intertextuality and narratology related on a small scale—along quite different lines from those suggested here.

[2] Besides adaptations of Greek poems (Homer, Apollonius), the main known instances of hexameter poetry on Greek myth are Cicero's *Alcyones*, Catullus 64 and the other neoteric mini-epics (Cato's *Diana*?, Calvus' *Io*, Cinna's *Smyrna*, Cornificius' *Glaucus*), and Macer's *Ornithogonia*. Virg. *Ecl.* 6. 72–3 (Gallus) involve many uncertainties. Outside hexameter (and drama), we have Laevius' experimental poems (within *Erotopaignia*?) *Adonis* etc., Cicero's *Pontius Glaucus*, Catullus 63. For a useful table of non-primary narratives in the *Metamorphoses*, see Wheeler 1999, 207–10; cf. further e.g. Nikolopoulos 2004.

*Mise en abyme* involves the primary narrator, a figure who is plainly indicated as a poet (1. 1–4, 15. 871–9). Which poet is clear. The rolls of the text will have had a title, perhaps attached to the outside; prominent overlap with other works of Ovid's, and explicit mentions in the *Tristia*, confirm for the reader the identity of the *nomen . . . nostrum* (15. 876). There is thus a formal connection to the author as conceived by the reader: to the poet who has designed all the levels of the narrative and is not just one of the narrators, and who has produced a given episode from a source or sources, necessarily with erudition and skill. A conspicuous narrator has often been discerned in the *Metamorphoses*: but we should not let the reader's consciousness of the constructed poet end there.[3]

The poet as primary narrator and the poet as designer and researcher involve two different sides of the poem: the world of mythological events and the world of authorial activity. *Mise en abyme* has a place within the poem both as fictional world and as self-consciously literary text; the use of sources has a place within the poem only as literary text. Secondary narrative in particular enables contrasts and connections, sometimes specific and pointed, between these two worlds of the poem, the story world and the writer's world; both narrative and sources are involved. Bringing in contrasts is an essential move. Critics have often seen parallels between secondary narrators and the poet; it is more enlightening to begin from an opposition between the story world and what we may call the writing world: the world in which the writer works and creates and the reader reads. In the story world, stories and speech are commonly fraught with practical consequence or personal involvement; in the writing world, scholarly activity and literary entertainment are separated from practicality. This opposition can be infringed, but the infringements are marked, not unmarked.[4]

Authors may now perhaps be staging a shy resurrection; but the poet in view here is more the reader's construction than the biographical actuality.

---

[3] References to *Metamorphoses*: *Tr.* 1. 1. 117–22 (includes own fate as metamorphosis), 7. 11–40 (*Naso* just before), 2. 83–5 (*maius opus* than *Ars*), 555–52, 3. 14. 19–24 (*last* poem of a book of *Tristia*, cf. 1. 1—emphatic connection with author), 4. 10. 83–4, 129–30 (penultimate couplet of book reworks end of *Metamorphoses*). Cf. Hinds 1985, 20–7. Early references: Sen. *Rh. Con.* 3. 7. 1 *Ouidius . . . in libris Metamorphoseon*), Sen. *Apoc.* 9. 5 (*eamque rem ad Metamorphosis Ouidii adiciendam*).

[4] For 'writing world' I had originally used 'text world', much as in Lowe 2000, 74–5, 268. But this term would be too confusing, now that text-world theory has become more prominent (see Werth 1999, Gavins 2007, Hutchinson forthcoming); the standard use of the term by cognitive psychologists is different again (cf. e.g. Denhière and Baudet 1989). No equivalent of Lowe's 'N-world' is introduced. References below to Callimachus and other writers used by the poet in the writing world do not imply that they appear as characters within that world, as if it were a story world.

The rest of Ovid's oeuvre is relevant to this construction: *Ouidii* in the title gains meaning for the reader principally from the other works. In such a connected corpus earlier works even acquire fresh point from later, like earlier books of a poem: all the works are in a sense part of one work. An external writer relevant to the construction of the poet is Callimachus. Whatever we think about Roman Callimacheanism, Callimachus is the chief Greek poet for Ovid's main genre elegy; and his *Aitia* is the most famous poem where a collection of myths is (notionally) united by their structure and specifically their ending.[5]

The *Aitia* is also a direct model for the *Fasti*, which Ovid was writing at least close in time to the *Metamorphoses*. Neither had been released by Ovid before his exile. In my view, *Fasti* and *Metamorphoses* are to be read together in a vast syncrisis, where elegy and the Roman (predominantly) are set against hexameter and the Greek (predominantly). In any case the reader is, for example, openly invited to compare the telling of Persephone's rape in the two works: *plura recognosces* (F. 4. 418). In the *Fasti* the primary narrator at the start (4. 417–18) indicates the poet's learning and alludes to Callimachus; in the *Metamorphoses* the tertiary narrator at the start plays on her replacement of a mortal poet (5. 344–5 *utinam modo dicere possim | carmina digna dea!*). The *Fasti* makes the reader of the *Metamorphoses* all the more aware of the Callimachus-like scholarly and intellectual work behind both poems, but overtly cloaked in one by epic convention.[6]

Callimachus' use of sources for his works was made clear internally (as at fr. 174. 53–77 Massimilla = 75. 53–77 Pfeiffer). It will have been made clear for readers after his time by commentaries and marginal comments: so on the first *aition* of the *Aitia* (Sch. Flor. on frr. 5–9[18] M. = 3–7[18] Pf., pap. 44. 35–6 van Rossum-Steenbeek). But other Greek poets used sources. Callimachus made his use prominent, in a way which excludes simple immersion in the stories: consciousness of the poet's activity cannot be kept in a separate compartment

[5] Cf. Hutchinson 2008, ch. 2 and 208–9. For fresh aspects of Callimachus' impact see Hunter 2006; but the present piece concerns particular aspects of the *Metamorphoses*, connected with Callimachus, not Callimachus' general influence on the poem.

[6] Cf. direct scholarly references at e.g. F. 3. 857–53, 4. 85–90, 703–808, 5. 167–8, 619–20, and e.g. 1. 101, 3. 177 *uates operose dierum*. The near-confession of fiction at 6. 251–3, after 9–0, is in my view a key moment. 4. 418 *plura recognosces, pauca docendus eris* points to learning; 417 *exigit ipse locus raptus ut uirginis edam* plays on propriety (for *exigit* cf. Hdt. 2. 2. 3, Cic. *Cael.* 32) and on the refusal to tell this story at Call. *H.* 6. 16–23. Cf. also Fantham 1998, 174; Hinds 1987, 37–40, 71, and 122–5 for *Met.* 5. 344–5 (for the text of Gallus fr. 1 Courtney = Hollis 2007, 145 see now Capasso 2003, 41; Hutchinson 2008, 24–5, 31 n.40). On the date of the *Fasti*, cf. Syme 1978, ch. 2; Herbert-Brown 1994, 215–33. Cameron 1995, 353–4, stresses the resemblance between *Aitia* and *Metamorphoses*, without elaborating on the *Fasti*. The teleological role of Rome in the *Metamorphoses* does not annul the contrast with the *Fasti*: it gives meaning to the dialectic of the poems.

of the reader's experience. Callimachus also mingles *mise en abyme* with the use of sources: this encourages Ovid's readers to see these areas belonging together. Callimachus, further, relates and confuses story world and writing world.[7]

Fr. 174 M. = 75 Pf. displays the use of a source at length; this use is shown to underlie the story of Acontius, and is pointedly implied to underlie the *mise en abyme* with the Muses in books 1 and 2 (fr. 174. 76–7 M. = 75. 76–7 Pf.). The risks of *telling* are shown when the constructed poet is about to bring in erudite but improper knowledge (4–9, with much vocal language); this connects and contrasts with Cydippe's innocent but unfortunate use of speech and reading within the story world. In fr. 50 M. = 43 Pf., the poet's actual knowledge of sources (οἶδα 46 . . . οἶδα 50 . . . ) is confronted with his fictional source the Muses; a Muse delivers a secondary narrative (58–83). The scene was probably preceded by an account of a meeting at a party (fr. 89 M. = 178 Pf.); this had pointed to the fictionality of the Muses as source through another (fictional) *mise en abyme*, and had further implied the poet-narrator's knowledge of sources (23–30). In *Hymn* 5, the mysterious speaker launches into a *mise en abyme* by pointing to both writer and writer's source: μῦθος δ᾽ οὐκ ἐμός, ἀλλ᾽ ἑτέρων (56). The rationale for the tale (cf. 51–6) draws various groups together: female worshippers who see with impunity, male Argives who are not present but are warned against seeing, and suggested male readers. The preceding graphic description of the naked Athena (23–8) opposes story world to writing world but brings the worlds teasingly close: the reader figuratively sees Athena. Ovid takes all this further, more strikingly exploiting his two worlds and their opposition.[8]

Finally, on sources: Ovid will have used 'handbooks' and prose treatises in some way, for material and especially structure. Readers will have been conscious of this transformation, so common are summaries and lists on sub-literary papyri and elsewhere. But still more prominent sources in readers' conception of the poet's activity will be famous poets, whose presence will be obvious, and authors of metamorphosis poems, who are Ovid's immediate model. Subliterary works themselves often indicate literary sources. *Pont.* 3. 3.

---

[7] Sch. Flor.: τ(ὴν) δ᾽ ἱστορίαν ἔλαβεν π[(αρὰ) Ἁγίου] κ(αὶ) Δερκύλου (fr. 8 Fowler); Aristotle is seen as not the source. Cf. Ag. and Derc. fr. 4a. 21–2 Fowler (commentary on Antimachus, in Matthews 1996, 441–4), on 'Fontes Argivi', κ[. . . . . . . . ] τῶν Ἁ[γί]ου καὶ Δερκύλου παρέκειτο, [ἀφ᾽] ὧ[ν ἐφα]ίνετο ὁ Κα[λλίμαχος] ἅπαντ[α ε]ἰληφώς.

[8] For play on the reader's not seeing a goddess's body cf. *Met.* 10. 578–9. The view on Call. *H.* 5. 23–8 (cf. ὦ κῶραι 27) would receive a further layer of paradox from Hunter's points (1992, 17–18); but Athena's activity rather than visibility could be thought masculine. On the narrator there, see Morrison 2005; for Callimachus' narrators generally, Harder 2004, and now Morrison 2007, ch. 3. The identity of primary narrator and poet assumed in the *Diegeses* (cf. esp. pap. 43. 233–4, 331–4 van Rossum-Steenbeek) will shape reading by Romans.

45 *nomina neu referam longum collecta per aeuum*, of mythological examples, indicates the erudite impression which the *Metamorphoses* is to make.[9]

Three episodes will now be discussed, to illustrate some of the relationships between events, narrators, and writers, and the interaction between story world and writing world. All involve the telling of incriminating tales, particularly about extra-marital liaisons. After the discussion, points will be drawn together to offer a general picture of the relation between the two worlds.

## 1. Coronis

The story of Coronis (2. 531–632) marks, as regards the writing world, a crucial point in the poem. The use of inset narrative, and perhaps of sources, becomes much more intricate than hitherto. The links with Callimachus are significantly ostentatious, and are reinforced in the ensuing stories; they relate to Callimachus' use of *mise en abyme* and sources. Using Callimachus himself both as a source and as the direct model of *mise en abyme* promotes the entanglement of these aspects. The episode starts with allusion not only to the *Hecale* but to 'Acontius': *lingua fuit damno, lingua faciente loquaci* the crow became white, cf. ἦ πολυιδρείη χαλεπὸν κακόν, ὅστις ἀκαρτεῖ | γλώccηc (fr. 174. 8–9 M. = 75. 8–9 Pf., see above). The *poet* has just taken over (536–40) the abundant comparisons which Callimachus gives to his crow (*Hec.* fr. 74. 15–17 Hollis). The poet's identity is strongly marked by allusions to Rome and the Roman poetic tradition (535–5 *seruaturis . . . Capitolia uoce* | . . . *anseribus*, cf. Lucr. 4. 683 *Romulidarum arcis seruator, candidus anser*), and by a particularly flamboyant transition. Ovid's famous copiousness with words and the abundance of stories in the poem play behind the birds' more damaging loquacity. The poet and Callimachus are highly visible.[10]

[9] Cf. for mythological prose Cameron 2004; Cole 2004; work by Professor J. Farrell will also be relevant. P.Oxy. LXIX 4711 at any rate reminds us of the importance of metamorphosis poems for Ovid's work; cf. Hutchinson 2006a (an updated version in Hutchinson 2008, ch. 9). The literary knowledge of actual readers is no more of a problem in this than in other areas; but even readers who know only famous poets could perceive the general picture suggested here.

[10] Bömer 1969, 372, Feeney 1999, 27, Barchiesi 2005, 282, do not mention the gesture to Lucretius' *Rom-*, unique in his poem. On section, myths, and sources, see, among much else, Powell 1906; Jacoby in *FGrH*, III b i. 600–3; Wimmel 1962; Burkert 1966; Kron 1981; Henrichs 1983; Luppe 1984, 109–18; Parker 1987, 195–7; 2005, 221–2, 433–4; Robbins 1990; Keith 1992, chs. 1–2; Simon 1992, Baudy 1993; Miller 1999, 414–16; Wheeler 1999, 130–2; Burgess 2001; Rosati 2002, 286–8; Cameron 2004, 286–92; Gildenhard and Zissos 2004; S. J. Green 2004, 133–4; Barchiesi 2005, 279–88; Currie 2005, ch. 14; Moscadi 2005; Ciampa 2006, 93–5; Fulkerson 2006; Hollis 2009, 224–52. Callimachus is prominent at another crucial point, 8. 811–884 (cf. Hardie 2004, 169–72). Here the poet's literary power to metamorphose his material (to make a non-Callimachean story like Callimachus and a Callimachean story unlike Callimachus), and the changing of stories themselves through successive sources (cf. 8. 729–40), present from the writing world a contrast with the life-changing transformation by gods and humans discussed within the story world (8. 811–19, 726–40, 879–84). Cf. Sanders 2006, 64, on Ovidian metamorphosis as an image for artistic adaptation in recent fiction.

Within the story world, we have multiple telling. Telling is bound up with practicality: raven and crow tell Minerva and Apollo incriminating news, so causing calamity for themselves and others; Coronis tells Apollo, in direct speech, of her pregnancy (608–9), so causing Aesculapius' rescue; the raven tells his story to warn the crow, while they are both in flight. There can be no such purpose or action for Callimachus' crow; after her speech narrator and narratee fall asleep (fr. 74. 21–2 Hollis). Secondary narrators and characters in the events are joined by practicality as well as identity. The extremity of Apollo's reaction to news within the narrative (600–5) exemplifies the impact of telling within the events. He lets fall his plectrum, forgetting his environs, and takes up his bow to kill his lover. Telling also involves criticism of the gods: the raven's speech emphasizes the harshness of Minerva's treatment, Coronis' the harshness of Apollo's.[11]

Knowledge, and ignorance, are disastrous in the story world. Apollo *scire coactus erat* (615); in acquiring forbidden knowledge the Cecropidae acted sinfully. Seeing, impossible outside the story world, within it encompasses prohibited knowledge (556 *uiderent*, 561 *uident*, 749 *uiderat*, 756 *uidit*), the informer's discoveries (557 *speculabar*, 544 *inobseruata*, 599 *uidisse*), the guilty shame of the victim of tales (*conspectum . . . fugit* 593), and Apollo's terrible experience watching Coronis' funeral (623 *spectante* in simile, cf. 620 *uidit*).[12]

The arrangement of narrators and narrative bridges story world and writing world. The talkative raven's narrative squeezes in three separate stories to interrupt the story in progress (its disgrace by Athena; its original transformation; Nyctimene's transformation). Its animus and gossipiness distinguish it from the poet and his multiple stories: his elegant strategy stands in counterpoint. The assignment of direct speech is another aspect of his handling of tellers. The crow gets no speech. Nor does Apollo: his speech in Pindar, which so powerfully expresses divine humanity, becomes mere narrative. οὐκέτι | τλάσομαι ψυχᾶι γένος ἀμὸν ὀλέσσαι (*Pyth.* 3. 40–1) becomes *non tulit* (628; for *sua . . . semina* cf. σπέρμα θεοῦ καθαρόν *Pyth.* 3. 15). Coronis, who has no speech in Pindar, receives one here. These last two choices assist the writer's criticism of Apollo. Some of the crow's narrative on the raven in Callimachus (fr. 74. 13–20) is given to the primary narrator in Ovid. This happens at the start, as we saw (fr. 74. 15–17, cf. *Met.* 2. 534–41), and at the end (fr. 74. 19–20, cf. *Met.* 2. 596–532). Coronis' story is not now a subordinate part of the bird's narrative; the bird's narrative becomes subordinate to the primary narrator's account of Coronis. Pindar is taken out of Callimachus and developed. The handling of narrators can scarcely be separated from the handling of sources.

[11]  For the commonest view on the crow's speech in Call. fr. 74 Hollis, see Hollis 2009, 225.
[12]  See e.g. Sharrock 2002 and Salzman-Mitchell 2005 for *connections* between looking and reading; the idea of a contrast too is important for this poem.

The use of sources in the writing world is even more complicated than the *mise en abyme*. The story of Apollo's bird probably appeared in Boios' metamorphosis poem (Ant. Lib. 20 inscr., 20. 7); but narrative structure points clearly to Callimachus too, wording to Pindar. Pindar is as significant as Callimachus; a sequence of controversy becomes important. Pindar emphatically writes [Hesiod's] raven (F 60 Merkelbach–West) out of his account: the god's informer was his own omniscient mind (*Pyth.* 3. 27–9). The theological motivation is completely explicit (29–30). Callimachus reverts to the raven; no theological point is clearly made by the reversion. But the *Metamorphoses*, in continuing the reversion, presents an utterly fallible god, who is not omniscient and makes painful mistakes: an undignified lover from the *Amores* (cf. *Amores* 1. 7). The treatment of Apollo, and Coronis, in the *Fasti* deliberately diverges (*F.* 1. 291–2 Coronis a nymph; 2. 247–66 Apollo's omniscience sees through crow; 6. 707–8 less pathos than *Met.* 6. 382–400; 761–2 Apollo not ineffectual on Jupiter). Also contrasted is Apollo's slowness to take vengeance with his bow in Call. fr. 64. 8–17 M. = 114 Pf. (cf. *Met.* 2. 612–13). Criticism of the divine emerges in both story world and writing world of the *Metamorphoses*, and in the handling of both sources and speakers.[13]

The writing-world criticism is less personally based than the raven's or Coronis'. It may gain edge from Augustus' links with Apollo, touched on in the poem (15. 865, cf. 1. 557–55). But the treatment will seem at least as much a play on epic divinities; and there is a long tradition of criticizing Apollo. The connections of criticism in the story world and in the writing world remind us that negation and affirmation of other texts was crucial to Kristeva's original conception of intertextuality, and related to the multiplicity of viewpoints in narrative.[14]

*Scitetur ut omnia* of the avidly curious raven (547–8) perhaps contrasts, through *omnia*, with Callimachus' and his follower's disinterested love of

---

[13] Compare the overlap of characters' and primary narrator's discussion of Diana and Actaeon at 3. 141–2, 251–7, which connects with criticism in the writing world. The work of [Hesiod] from which F60 is quoted was probably not the *Catalogue*: cf. West 1985, 69–72. The treatment of the marriage makes Pindar seem to engage with that text in particular rather than the story in general; commentaries could have suggested either possibility to Ovid, cf. Sch. Pind. 3. 14 and 52b Drachmann, but controversy on some level will have been apparent. Coronis' treatment in the *Fasti* may well be related to her cult: cf. *Inscr. It.* xiii/2, p. 2. 1, and elsewhere Hdas. 4. 3–5, *Inscr. Perg.* 8 (3). 72. 1–4, 122. *Met.* 4. 787, 5. 181 play with Pindar's pious refusal of disbelief at *Pyth.* 10. 48–50, cf. 29–30. Corone and Nyctimene appear in the prose series of metamorphoses at Cameron 2004, 287; they may well have come in a metamorphosis poem. The appearance of Nyctimene in the *Hecale* is not positively indicated by fragments. On Call. fr. 64. 4–17 M. = 114 Pf. cf. D'Alessio 1995; I am grateful to Professor D'Alessio for discussion.

[14] For her earliest conceptions, see Kristeva 1969, 145–53, 194–5, 255–7 (note that 'qui par ailleurs *se présente* comme centré *par un* sens' (255) is misprinted in 1978, 194, as ' . . . contré . . .'). Bloom 1997 has a related approach, though more nuanced, and more authorial in language (cf. p. xxiii); but 'anxiety' would not fit the *Metamorphoses* well. Cf. Hardie 1993, 118. An overview of how the concept of intertextuality has been developed: Allen 2000.

**Fig. 13.1.** Athena and a daughter of Cecrops: Attic red-figure lekythos, Antiken-museum Basel, Inv. BS 404, attributed to the Phiale Painter, 450–400 BC.

knowledge (cf. 4. 790–4, and many Callimachus-like inquiries, e.g. 15. 9–10). The poet, as we saw, has just become prominent and been compared with the raven (2. 534–41; cf. for bird and poet *Hec.* fr. 74. 9 Hollis ἐπιπνείουϲι, *Met.* 2. 550 *meae praesagia linguae*, 15. 879 *uatum praesagia*). The poet's static and scholarly knowledge of other poets' accounts can be seen to contrast impli-citly with characters' dramatic and emotional acquisition of knowledge, on the same events, through other characters' accounts (vv. 540–1 obliquely contrast poetic πολυιδρείη). This comparison of poets' and characters' knowledge will emerge more openly in the story to be discussed next. But on telling we have already observed clearly an antithesis between the story world and the more detached and intellectual writing world.[15]

That antithesis itself is complicated by the evocation of practicalities that belong to the Augustan world of poet and reader. [Hesiod's] γῆμε (cf. ἱερῆϲ ... δαιτόϲ), of Ischys, is polemically opposed by Pindar: that γάμοϲ was an affair, not a wedding (*Pyth.* 3. 12–19). Ovid's poet turns the relationship with Ischys at least figuratively into *adulterium*, punished in anger by the husband. Anger and punishment are envisaged by the *Lex Iulia de adulteriis coercendis*, though only the adulterer may legally be killed by the husband, and under certain conditions. An informer (*index* 546) has reported the adultery to the

---

[15] The crow's reporting to Athena, derived from Amelesag. *FGrH* 330 F 1 by Callimachus, is highly unusual in versions of this story. This delay in Athena's intervention (contrast e.g. Attic red-figure lekythos, Basel, Inv. BS 404, attributed to the Phiale Painter, 450–400 BC: Schmidt 1968, reproduced as Fig. 13.1), makes possible her less grandiose reaction at *Met.* 2. 752–9; cf. Feeney 1991, 245–5.

husband, seeking a reward. *AA* 2. 575 *quam mala, Sol, exempla moues! pete munus ab ipsa* strongly suggests that informers were active under the *Lex Iulia*, motivated by rewards. (Without a link to *mala exempla, munus* would come in too abruptly.) The contemporary resonance, and the evocation of the world of love in Ovid's modern poems, makes the criticism and the idea of telling less detached for constructed poet and readers.[16]

## 2. Leucothoe

In our next story Clytie informs Leucothoe's father that Leucothoe had slept with the Sun (4. 167–273). Callimachus is again a vital figure in the relationship between worlds; but the story world may be considered first. The daughters of Minyas are telling the story as they weave. On one level, they appear to be detached narrators. The stories are to pass the time (40–1, *uacuas . . . ad aures*); the present tale . . . *ceperat aures* (271). The stories are chosen because they are not well known: *quoniam uulgaris fabula non est* (53) is said of the first tale, *uulgatos taceo . . . amores | Daphnidis* (276–7) is said by the third speaker. This story is set, like Pyramus', in the remote east (the capital of 'Persia').[17]

Within the events, telling and knowledge have extreme effects. Vulcan's dismay at the Sun's news of his wife's adultery (173–5) echoes Apollo's own reaction to the news of Coronis' 'adultery' (Ovid has forcefully assimilated Sun and Apollo, 1. 752, 2. 24, 36, 110, 399, 4. 349). In another zeugma his *mens* and what he is holding *excidit* (*et mens et . . . opus . . . | excidit*, cf. 2. 801 *et pariter uultusque deo plectrumque colorque | excidit*; much less close e.g. 14. 350). This response connects with Leucothoe's reaction when she hears that

---

[16] At Luc. *Alex.* 38, Aristid. 47. 73 γάμος evidently indicates an actual marriage-ceremony between Coronis and Apollo; Asclepius' cult is relevant. Serv. *Aen.* 7. 761 *adulterium committere* could be influenced by Ovid, though Servius like Hyg. *Fab.* 202 makes the crow Coronis' *custos*. On the *Lex Iulia* (*RS* (Crawford 1996) no. 60, ii. 781–5) see e.g. Treggiari 1991, 277–98; McGinn 1998, ch. 5; Mette-Dittmann 1991, 34–130; Fayer 2005, esp. 221–55. Material about rewards for *indices* could have been included in the *Lex Iulia* itself (cf. *RS* 2. 90; an *index* under this law Suet. *Ner.* 35. 2); but more likely are private arrangements with prosecutors (including husbands). Cf. Mommsen 1899, 504–5. For Augustus' enforcement of his laws cf. Dio 54. 19. 2. Ovid's uses of *index* and *indicium* have much interest, cf. e.g. *Am.* 3. 13. 7–12, *Met.* 2. 706 (cf. 694), 5. 542, 551, 6. 578, 14. 27, 15. 502.

[17] Ovid has chosen, at least, a version of Pyramus' and Thisbe's story which moves it from the usual Cilicia to Babylon; cf. Knox 1989. The secondary narrator somewhat exaggerates the rarity of Salmacis and Hermaphroditus' tale (cf. 276–87), from the perspective of Roman readers; a recent addition is *SGO* (Merkelbach and Stauber 1998–2004) 01/12/02. 15–22 (different version). On the Minyeides and Leucothoe, see e.g. Dietze 1905, 28; de Luce 1982, 84–5; Barkan 1986, 57; Hutchinson 1988, 331–2; Solodow 1988, 181–2; Janan 1994; Tronchet 1998, 501–3; Fowler 2000, 157–9; Cameron 2004, 44, 286–7, 290–1, 297–8; Fantham 2004, 43, 46–8; Nikolopoulos 2004, 146–7; and now Barchiesi and Rosati 2007, 243–54, 260–83, 293–6.

her interlocutor is not her mother but the enamoured Sun: she too drops what she is holding (228–9; note *et . . . et*). But she becomes a victim, not an agent, of punishment: this is part of Venus' revenge on the Sun. Clytie's *indicium* has a more terrible effect than the Sun's (cf. 14. 25–7): the mortal Leucothoe is buried alive. *uulgat adulterium* (236) contrasts and connects with the more innocent circulation of tales; even that the Minyeides avoid.[18]

But the Minyeides' telling too has consequences. It is part of their resistance to Bacchus' cult: they are staying indoors rather than joining his worship. They will be punished by metamorphosis into bats; a *minimam et pro corpore uocem* (412) will replace their speech. The story of the Sun is partly a celebration of that god (172); the speaker and the two secondary narratees think him a real god (172), unlike Bacchus (273). They are condemned to hate light and to frequent the evening and night (414–15).[19]

They participate in the obvious narrative opposition of inside and outside that marks the characters' fortunes and gender roles within the whole series of stories. Love forces the Sun, quintessentially a god of outside, to assume a woman's form and join Leucothoe weaving indoors: a setting akin to the Minyeides' own. Leucothoe undergoes the most extreme 'inside' when she is buried alive, though she emerges into the air as a flower; her rival suffers outside, *sub Ioue nocte dieque* (260). The Minyeides have chosen an indoor world of restrained femininity and aloofness, rather than the wild and popular cult of Bacchus; they will remain creatures of *tecta . . . , non siluas* (414).[20]

The secondary narrator shares in the theme of looking, by the Sun and at the Sun, which dominates her narrative. She begins with a deixis to the Sun whom she and her sisters can see: *hunc* (169). But later, darkness stops them from knowing (410) in what way they have changed shape (cf. 13. 871–2, 956–9). For all their knowledge of stories (the first speaker *plurima norat*, 43), they are ignorant of the future, like Leucothoe, Clytie, and the Sun, who fails to see as he should (with 195–7 contrast e.g. *F*. 4. 580–4). They are subject to the story world's rules; metamorphosis is their lot. Telling now falls to a sister from another trio, Ino; she tells (*narrat*, 418) of Bacchus' power. While the

---

[18] Other pieces of speech in the story are eminently practical and involve trickery, self-defence, divine power (223–4, 238–9, 251). Cf. and contrast with 232–3 and 238–9 *F*. 2. 178 *quid facis? inuito est pectore passa Iouem*. For Apollo and Sun, cf. Barchiesi 2005, 237–8, with lit.; Apollod. *FGrH* 244 F 95–9.

[19] Cf. Ant. Lib. 10. 4 ἔφυγον δὲ αἱ τρεῖς (metamorphosed) τὴν αὐγὴν τοῦ ἡλίου. For 169–72 cf. 5. 341–5. At 4. 302–15 Salmacis' *sisters* tell her to lead a more normal, less idle life—one of outdoor hunting, *duris uenatibus*. Cf. and contrast 36–9. On 273 *sed non et Bacchus in illis* see Heinsius 1758, 497.

[20] The accusation that Dionysus has escaped the sun's rays (Eur. *Bacch*. 457–9) is ironic for the audience. With *conataeque loqui* (412) cf. the same phrase of the Pierides, 5. 870 (cf. also 13. 569). The sunflower's yearning is given transcendental significance in Blake's *Songs of Innocence and of Experience*; it forms part of a trio of poems on plants as people, all on p. 43 in Blake's original. See Pl. 14 of the present volume.

Minyeides have acquired a new name (415), *uespertiliones*, Bacchus' *nomen* is celebrated all over Thebes (416–17).[21]

Again the arrangement of the narrators makes a bridge between story world and writing world. The primary narrator at first (4. 17–27) blends his voice with those of the Theban women praising Bacchus, like Catullus in poem 63 (*typanum tuum, Cybebe, tua, mater, initia*, 9). But at the end of the narrative on the Minyeides the narrator shows, and could show, no personal anxiety for himself, as at the end of Catullus 63, or Theocritus 26 (on Dionysus): this divergence points to the detached poet. The secondary narrator's harangue to the enamoured character at 192–203 recalls the primary narrator addressing Narcissus at 3. 431–5 *credule, quid frustra . . . ?* and addresses from the primary narrator in other works of Ovid, e.g. to Pasiphae at *AA* 1. 303–10. The harangue at folly is especially striking when addressed to a god: criticism of the divine by constructed poet as well as secondary narrator is involved. The Sun is prominent in Augustus' monuments, and the length of days in the year was marked by the shadow of an obelisk dedicated to the Sun; this adds contemporary and extra-textual impudence to the picture of the Sun getting his times all wrong under the impact of love (197–9).[22]

*Solis referemus amores* (170) at first suggests a series, and recalls the primary narrator's *primus amor Phoebi* (1. 452; cf. *primus* in a different sense 4. 171). The different mode of narration is brought out, all the more as Sun and Apollo have been identified. The frequently evoked story of Phaethon (cf. esp. 204, 245–5) reminds us still more strongly of the shift to secondary narrative. The poem is advancing in complexity.[23]

More important for the writing world in this episode is the use of sources. We have already seen the Minyeides avoiding stories that are *uulgaris, uulgatos*. This conjures up a Callimachean aesthetic, but in the story world is linked to shunning the revelling masses (32 *solae*, cf. Ant. Lib. 10. 1 τὰς ἄλλας γυναῖκας ἐμέμψαντο). They cannot actually remove themselves from the story world. The poet, by contrast, is displaying a literary learning within a separated writing world. The story of the Minyeides themselves comes from one of Ovid's central generic sources, Nicander (fr. 55 Schneider), as well as Corinna (*PMG* 665: an interesting source for the poet of the *Amores*).

[21] The opening reference to the sun may evoke choral performance, cf. Soph. *Ant.* 100–9, and Pind. *Pae.*9. 1–20 (A1 Rutherford), Hor. *Saec.* 1–12 (or 9–12). But the opening turns into that of Propertian elegy *hunc quoque . . . cepi amor Solem*.

[22] Cf. Heslin 2007, correcting Buchner 1982 and 1996; dedication CIL vi. 702. The Sun was depicted on the top of the Palatine temple (Prop. 2. 31. 11). The three sisters singing while weaving recall the narrative strategy of Cat. 64. 305–83; but neither weaving nor song is divine or prophetic. The Minyeides are ignorant as well as knowedgeable.

[23] The suggestion of a list points to lists of gods' loves as in Philodemus, *De Pietate*, there with theological point: see Henrichs 1972, 86–91 for Apollo. Ovid's most important source in this regard is probably Apollodorus' περὶ θεῶν, cf. Obbink 2004, 181–201.

**Fig. 13.2.** Mars and Venus accused: sarcophagus, Grottaferrata, *c.*AD 160.

Leucothoe's highly recherché story comes in a prose series of metamorphoses (for the text see Cameron 2004, 287) and is questionably claimed (*Narr. Ov. Met.* 4. 5) to derive from [Hesiod] (fr. dub. 351 Merkelbach–West); but the myth was not, we can confidently assert, ordinarily familiar to Roman readers.[24]

The point is stressed by the structure: the comic tale of Mars and Venus, from the supremely well-known Homer and from Ovid's own *Ars Amatoria*, precedes the tragic tale, from a much less famous source. This is underlined by the end of the comic tale *haec fuit in toto notissima fabula caelo* (189 itself echoes *AA* 2. 561, which gives *notissima* further point); it is underlined too by the more familiar loves of the Sun at 203–4, with allusion to Homer, Pindar, and the story of Phaethon. This last indicates that the poem itself has now moved into less well-trodden territory. *fertur* at 245, the Sun 'was said' to have

---

[24] Poetry and art make it clear that, say, Parthenius' stories were not part of Roman readers' usual fund. The *Narrationes'* reference to Hesiod (note *indicat*) is unlikely to prove the *Catalogue* the origin for this 'romantic' tale set in Persia (Cameron 2004, 9, 41–5; Ὀρχομένου for Orchamus the father in the Anonymus Florentinus is probably just an intriguing error). The summary in the Anonymus Florentinus might suggest that this and the two obscure stories preceding come from metamorphosis poems (cf. Antoninus' sources). The poet's academic erudition and the secondary narrators' hauteur can perhaps be contrasted with the Sun's practical allegation of a *res arcana* (223–4); for *arcan-* of readings to a few and of difficult literature cf. Cic. *Att.* 16. 3. 1, Stat. *Silv.* 5. 3. 158.

grieved no less than after Phaethon's death, not only points to the constructed poet's source, but makes the notional source within the secondary narrative compare the two stories.[25]

The use of the *Ars Amatoria*, with its narratorial attack on the Sun not for love but for informing on lovers (2. 575–5), increases the complication which allusion to adultery brings. Leucothoe's action as well as Mars' and Venus' is described as *adulterium* (171, 236, cf. 182); the informing in both cases is *indicium* (190, 257, cf. 236). The *Lex Iulia* allows the father, under conditions, to kill his daughter for adultery. Leucothoe's punishment carries connotations of grim Roman attitudes to morality, in the punishment of unchaste Vestals. *Non tristibus* of the joking gods (187) plays on contemporary ethos. To draw in an earlier work of Ovid's, especially the *Ars Amatoria*, makes still less firm the boundary between the writing world and a real world with practical outlooks and actions. Once Ovid is punished for the *Ars Amatoria*, and points to Homer's telling about Mars and Venus as a precedent (*Tr.* 2.

---

[25] Mars' and Venus' affair is among the most popular myths in Pompeian decoration: cf. Pugliese Carratelli and Baldassarre 1990–2003, e.g. iii. 618 (Pompeii V 1. 23, 26), 1016–18 (V 4a), iv. 21–2 (VI 1. 7), 140–2 (VI 2. 4), v. 871–2 (VI 16. 15, 17), viii. 934–5 (IX 1. 20). On Ovid's reworking of Homer in *AA* 2. 561–92 see Holzberg 1990; Janka 1997, 404–20. Eurynome, the mother imitated by the Sun, recalls a Callimachean homonym (fr. 384. 44–5 Pf., cf. fr. 7 M. = 5 Pf.), like the mother Chariclo in the Callimachean section of book 2 (Chiron's wife).

377–8), the separation of safe and unsafe telling acquires further infringe-
ment and irony.[26]

## 3. Cephalus and Procris

The final episode is that of Cephalus and Procris (7. 661–865). There even
within the story world telling is full of contrasts and connections. Within
the events themselves, telling and speaking are attended with terrible consequences; deceit and error, though central themes of the poem, enter even
more than usual. When the unrecognizable Cephalus tests his wife, he at
first stops himself telling the truth (728), tricks her with verbal offers
(739–40), then reveals himself as a *fictus adulter* (741) and *uerus coniunx*, with
disastrous results. Later his own song is misunderstood by an informer, who
narrates what he has misinterpreted to Procris. Repetition of speech only
compounds illusion, rather than dispelling it (contrast *AA* 3. 727–30); this
marks the knowing goddess's revenge. (Not only does *aura* echo *Aurora*, but
the repetition implied through 810–12, cf. 837–9, echoes the repetition of
*Procris* which angered the goddess.) Even inarticulate noises lead to Cephalus'
mistaken killing of his wife. Procris' brief cry (*uox* 843–4) leads to revelation
of Cephalus' error; an erroneous speech of her own (*errorem* 858) leads to
final enlightenment, in Procris' case uncertainly achieved (858–52; cf. the
conjugal death at 12. 423–8). Procris' earlier reaction to the *indicium* provides
an extreme form of emotional reaction to telling (826–30); this is mixed with
uncertainty of its truth.[27]

---

[26] See *Dig.* 48. 5. 5 pr.–1 for the law including both *stuprum* and *adulterium* and using the
words *promiscue*; 48. 5. 23. 2–24. 4 for father killing daughter caught in the act. (The context
gives fewer Roman suggestions at *Met.* 8. 592–4.) For *tristibus* cf. e.g. *AA* 3. 801 *tristis custodia*;
for *non*, Prop. 3. 23. 17 *non stulta puella*, 4. 2. 23 *non dura puella*, Cat. 10. 3–4 *scortillum . . . non
sane illepidum neque inuenustum*. On the punishment of Vestals (*defodere uiuam*, ζώcαc
κατορύττεcθαι DH *Ant.* 1. 78. 5, Plut. *Mor.* 286 F, etc., despite the complications), cf. Mommsen
1899, 928–9; Martini 2004, 96 n. 54. Pliny's account (*Ep.* 4. 11. 7–10) has much in common with
Ovid; with 239–40 cf. Plut. *Num.* 10. 7. See too *F.* 6. 457–50 (with Littlewood 2006, 142). At *Tr.* 2.
337–8, *quis nisi Maeonides . . . narrat . . . ?* points by another meaning to Ovid's own treatment
in *AA* 2. A legal reading of the Sun's action is clear on a sarcophagus from Grottaferrata, *c*.AD
160, Sichtermann 1992, 91 (*LIMC* 'Apollon/Apollo' 428; Fig. 13.2); he is immediately to the right
of the seated Zeus.

[27] Both the version in the *Ars*, where Procris rushes forth to meet Cephalus, and that in the
*Metamorphoses*, where she makes a noise in the bushes, seem to have existed in the tradition:
cf. Sch. Hom. *Od.* 11. 321 (V), Eust. *Od.* 1. 420 (cf. Serv. *Aen.* 6. 445). The repetition and address
to 'Aura' recalls songs from *tragedy*: Eur. *Hec.* 444 αὖρα, ποντιὰc αὖρα, *Phaeth.* fr. 773. 38
Kannicht ] πότνι᾿ αὖρ[α]; 'Aura' may appear in a Greek source, cf. Pherecyd. 34 b. 40 Fowler. On
this episode and myth, see e.g. Heinsius 1758, 583–4 (on 7. 754, 762); Pöschl 1959; Otis 1970,
410–13; Labate 1975; Segal 1978; P. Green 1979–80; Fontenrose 1979–80; Davis 1983, esp. ch. 6;
Hunter 1983, 181; Ahlheid 1986; Anderson 1990; Pechillo 1990–1; Tarrant 1995; Montuschi
1998; Bernsdorff 2000, 33–44; Hardie 2002, 75–7; Gibson 2003, 356–79; Fantham 2004, 83–5;
Rimell 2006, 97–103.

In the events, then, emotion and error are combined; Cephalus' narrative is filled with emotion, but comes much closer to truth. (He errs partly by exaggerating the case against himself.) He stresses his own truth near the start, whether or not truly (703–4). This first-person homodiegetic narrative is a deeply painful act for him; his story is always with him. Tears begin and end his account (689, 864); the tears at the end are shared by the secondary narratees (*flentibus haec lacrimans heros memorabat*, 864). Beginning in emotion is characteristic of many secondary narratives in the poem. The terrible truth of Cephalus' killing Procris is long deferred; the fatal part of the narrative is preceded by more silence (794).[28]

Sight is important within the narrative: the sight of love (703, 727, 860) and of wonder (780, 790–1), but also the criterion of truth (833–4 *nisi uiderit ipsa,* | *damnatura sui non est delicta mariti*), which leads to further error (Cephalus'). In narrating to Phocus, Cephalus has to use Phocus' mind to help Phocus perceive Procris' beauty (732–3), or to conjure up the metamorphosed animals (791: *aspicio* beginning of line; ideal second person *putares* at end). But Phocus' sight of the spear is the vital starting-point for the story (672, 679–82, 756).[29]

The primary level of the narrative and the writing world mix. The primary narrator and narratees are visually more detached from the narrative even than Phocus. They have only words; but they can proceed even further into the truth because of their greater distance from Cephalus. Emotion raises more complex questions. It depends in part on the individual actual reader how near he or she comes to the emotion of secondary narrator and listeners when the story closes; the poet may seem to be pursuing intense involvement. Procris' death ends the book with a striking violation of the poem's rules: there is no metamorphosis but only the slightest alteration of expression; the life brought after the plague contrasts. Readers are left to wonder about the relation between the constructed poet's emotional engagement and his fidelity to the secondary narrator's perspective.[30]

---

[28] For the pain of narrative cf. grief at beginning 7. 517–19 (the pattern of Aeacus' story reverses Cephalus'), 8. 884–9. 5, 9. 327–8, 11. 289–90, (12. 542–4,) 13. 280–2, 643–4, 14. 129 (cf. Virg. *Aen.* 2. 3–13); 9. 324–5 grief at end, 394–5 grief at end shared by secondary narratee (cf. *Pont.* 1. 4. 53). In that pair from book 9, the secondary narrators' emotional structure (cf. 9. 325–8) contrasts with the neat bringing together in the writing world of stories from different books of Nicander (1 and 4). The episode of Dryope especially plays on speech and the roles of narrator and character (328–9, 362, 380, 388, 392). Here, vv. 861–2 add a Callimachean element to the exchange of stories (cf. *Ep.* ? 3 Pfeiffer), as in the last part of the next book.

[29] Cf. for such starting-points, eminently Callimachean, 1. 887–8 (with aetiological query), 8. 573–5, 881–9. 3 (with query on cause), 11. 751–4, 14. 312–23 (aetiological inquiry on statue). In Callimachus cf. esp. frr. 64. 4–17 Massimilla, 103 Pfeiffer, 199 Pfeiffer, and also *Ep.* 15 and 43 Pfeiffer.

[30] For secondary narrators shaping their lives in narrative, cf. Hutchinson 2008, ch. 3. A subordinate metamorphosis, apart from Laelaps' and the fox's, comes into the episode at 722 (contrast Pherecyd. fr. 34a9–10, b 34–5 Fowler; Ant. Lib. 41).

The use of sources brings in further elements. It is again particularly important to the writing world, and hard to separate from the narratology. As conspicuously as possible, at the centre of his poem, in consecutive books and close together, Ovid reworks stories from consecutive books in the *Ars Amatoria* (Daedalus near the beginning and Cephalus near the end of books 2 and 3). This revisiting of the poet's past work can be contrasted with Cephalus' revisiting of his past deeds. Where Cephalus regrets, it seems much more plausible to see the poet as proudly displaying the value of a criticized poem (cf. *Rem.* 361–98); the high ideal of marriage—however imperfectly achieved by the characters—is pointedly *continued* from the earlier account of Cephalus and Procris. There is some metamorphosis of the two stories' tendency (Cephalus, Daedalus): both now manifest human limitations and divine knowledge or power. (Aurora is implicitly criticized.) The narrative from *Ars* 3 is allowed to dominate climactically the account of Cephalus and Procris in the *Metamorphoses*. A story now precedes (694–793) which particularly evokes a source summarized by Ant. Lib. 41; but the metamorphosis of dog and fox which there formed a culmination now becomes a separated story inside Cephalus' main narrative (cf. 757–51).[31]

**Fig. 13.3.** Death of Procris: Attic red-figure column crater, London E 477, *ARV*[2] 1114.15, attributed to the Hephaestus Painter; 475–425 BC.

[31] Antoninus' source is probably a Hellenistic poem, quite likely a metamorphosis poem; a promising candidate is Nicander, who mentioned the dog and perhaps the metamorphosis elsewhere: Nic. fr. 97 Schneider, Poll. 5. 38 (cod. B). The elements of Ovid's tale are mostly familiar: Eos' pursuit of Cephalus is common in Greek art, as is the dog (cf. Weiss 1986, 758–79, Simantoni-Bournia 1992; pinax, Selinus Temple E, inv. nos. S84TE/1009 and 1045, 550–520 BC, Conti 1998; see Pl. 15), and comes at Ov. *Am.* 1. 13. 39–40, *Her.* 4. 93–5, *AA* 3. 84; Paus. 10. 29. 7

The emphasis in the *Ars* on Procris' emotion now changes. The secondary narrator's emotion is the most fully described; Procris' emotions, good and bad, match Cephalus', but in the last part reach him indirectly, through report (827) or conjecture (862). The handling of narrative brings out the difficulties of knowing someone else's feelings; the handling of sources brings out the importance of both sides in marriage. (The narrative in the *Ars* had lacked the form of symmetrical suspicion.) The emphasis on both sides in the *Metamorphoses* connects with the structure of the whole *Ars*, and the antagonism of the sexes that underlay it. But now partnership is the intermittently attained ideal; Procris' rejection of marriage and hatred of men (745–5) is a temporary crisis. That significant event and choice of plot will appear to the reader an evocation of Callimachus (*H.* 3. 209–10).[32]

The use of the *Ars* complicates still further the relation to actual views in the contemporary world. In this regard, *criminis . . . index* (824) and *indicio* (833) again bring into the text the world of Augustan laws (cf. *damnatura* 834; *adulterium* 717). In this episode the error-laden events wildly distort the archetypal scene of husband discovering lovers: the wife thinks she discovers her husband with a lover, but is killed herself. There is more confusion: the husband is abducted (704, cf. 697); the weapon has a *crimen* (794–5); the *adulter* discovered by the husband is the husband (cf. the ironic *uni* at 735–5). All suggests the possibility, on a practical level in the contemporary world, of a penetrating argument against enforcing Augustan laws: it is bad for marriage, which needs trust. The argument rests on an exalted conception of marriage, not on irresponsible hedonism. The narrative form may conjure up from the contemporary world the praise of a woman's life and marriage sometimes delivered after her death by a husband. The narrative possibilities are seen in the *Laudatio Turiae* (*CIL* vi. 41062).[33]

---

τὰ δὲ ἐς τὴν Πρόκριν καὶ οἱ πάντες ἄιδουςιν implies much poetry on Procris, cf. Sophocles' tragedy and Eubulus' comedy, and note Attic red-figure column crater Lond. E 477, *ARV*[2] 1114. 15, attr. Hephaistos P., 475–425 BC (*LIMC* Kephalos 26 = Fig. 13.3); narrative with all these elements: esp. Hyg. *Fab.* 189, cf. Serv. *Aen.* 6. 445. The dog's chasing the fox, and the metamorphosis into stones, are ascribed to the Epic Cycle (*Epig.* fr. 3 West, cf. also Kabirion skyphos, mid 4th c. Athens NM 10429 (*LIMC* Kephalos 34), Wolters and Bruns 1940, 98 and pl. 10; Apollod. 2. 4. 8–7, Paus. 9. 19. 1); but a narrative leading from marital dispute to fox-chase would probably suggest for readers a particular link with Antoninus' source, all the more so if a metamorphosis poem.

[32] He was probably the most familiar source on Procris' period with Artemiot the alternative sojourn with Minos, which greatly alters the tale, comes in Ant. Lib. 41. It is referred to at *Rem.* 453, where Minos' infidelity with Procris is suggested (cf. Apollod. 3. 15. 1).

[33] Cf. Wistrand 1976; Flach 1991; Ramage 1994. *iaculi . . . crimina* perhaps gestures to the Attic ritual condemnation, after trial, of the knife that killed the sacrificial victim (Parker 2005, 187–91). Ovid evades the trial and exile of Cephalus for killing Procris: Hellan. frr. 44, 169 Fowler, Apollod. 3. 15. 1, Paus. 1. 37. 5, cf. pap. 69 fr. 11 van Rossum-Steenbeek (*P.Oxy.* 4306). Cephalus leads an Athenian embassy (7. 490–3, 501–7). The emphasis must fall on the quasi-legal problems of infidelity within the marriage.

The argument, then, has suggested the value of confronting story world and writing world, and exploring the consequences in detail. A broad contrast emerges. Characteristic of the story world are the practical consequences, or emotional pain, of telling and discovering. Error and ignorance are common elements here; so is the vivid and causal impact of actual sight. The writing world is marked by a separation from practicality and physicality, and by a scholarly and intellectual sphere of activity. Seeing is excluded; reading and books are crucial. The area of telling in this world includes both telling by texts and the literary organization of telling. Knowledge of various kinds precludes error.

Secondary narrators often form a striking focus for interrelation between these worlds: they may share, or contrast with, characteristics of the writing world. The opposition of worlds can be complicated by contemporary resonance and the author's earlier works. Argument about the divine often blends intellectual debate in the writing world with the characters' engaged responses; the poet's apparent emotional involvement can sometimes infringe the separation of worlds.

The use of sources needs to be approached, not just as a convenient tool for exhibiting the author's choices, but as an intrinsic part of the text for the reader: it is vital in the formation of the writing world. It has often proved hard to separate in our discussion from narratological design, so important for both story world and writing world.

The forms and procedures of the poem are bound up with its intellectual and argumentative energy. Ovid has advanced Callimachus' experiments to still more vigorous results, and enhanced the critical spirit of his own poem.[34]

## BIBLIOGRAPHY

Ahlheid, F. 1986, 'De liefde van Cephalus en Procris', *Lampas*, 19, 261–71.
Allen, G. 2000, *Intertextuality* (London and New York).
Anderson, W. S. 1990, 'The Example of Procris in the *Ars Amatoria*', in M. Griffith and D. J. Mastronarde (eds.), *Cabinet of the Muses: Essays on Classical and Comparative Literature in Honor of Thomas G. Rosenmeyer* (Atlanta, GA), 131–45.
Barchiesi, A. 2005, *Ovidio*: Metamorfosi, i: *Libri I–II* (Milan).
—— and Rosati, G. 2007. *Ovidio*: Metamorfosi, ii: *Libri III–IV* (Milan)
Barkan, L. 1986, *The Gods Made Flesh: Metamorphosis and the Pursuit of Paganism* (New Haven and London).
Baudy, D. 1993, 'Ein Kultobjekt im Kontext: Der Erichthonios-Korb in Ovids Metamorphosen', *WS* 106, 133–55.

---

[34] Peter's kindness, canniness, and skill with words can scarcely be rivalled. This little piece is offered to him with gratitude and admiration. I owe thanks to the following for their help in obtaining images: Dott.ssa M. C. Conti, Prof. J. Elsner, Prof. Dr G. Koch, Dott.ssa D. Lanzuolo, Dr T. Mannack, and Frau V. Slehofer.

Bernsdorff, H. 2000, *Kunstwerke und Verwandlungen: Vier Studien zu ihrer Darstellung im Werk Ovids* (Studien zur klassischen Philologie, 117; Frankfurt am Main).

Bloom, H. 1997, *The Anxiety of Influence: A Theory of Poetry* (2nd edn., New York).

Bömer, Fr. 1969, *P. Ovidius Naso: Metamorphosen. Kommentar*, i (Heidelberg).

Buchner, E. 1982, *Die Sonnenuhr des Augustus* (Mainz am Rhein).

—— 1996, 'Horologium Augusti', *LTUR* iii. 35–7.

Burgess, J. S. 2001, 'Coronis Aflame: The Gender of Mortality', *CP* 96, 214–27.

Burkert, W. 1966, 'Kekropidensage und Arrhephoria', *Hermes*, 94, 1–25.

Cameron, A. 1995, *Callimachus and his Critics* (Princeton).

—— 2004, *Greek Mythography in the Roman World* (Oxford).

Capasso, M. 2003, *Il ritorno di Cornelio Gallo: il papiro di Qaṣr Ibrîm venticinque anni dopo* (Naples).

Ciampa, S. 2006, 'I poeti ellenistici nei papiri ercolanesi di Filodemo', *CErc* 36, 87–102.

Cole, T. 2004, 'Ovid, Varro, and Castor of Rhodes: The Chronological Architecture of the *Metamorphoses*', *HSCP* 102, 355–422.

Conti, M. C. 1998, 'Il mito di Eos e Kephalos in un pinax da Selinunte', *Boll. di Arch.* 51–2, 33–48.

Courtney, E. 2003, *The Fragmentary Latin Poets* (2nd edn., Oxford).

Crawford, M. H. (ed.) 1996, *Roman Statutes*, 2 vols. (*BICS* Supplement, 64; London).

Currie, B. G. F. 2005, *Pindar and the Cult of Heroes* (Oxford).

D'Alessio, G. B. 1995, 'Apollo Delio, i Cabiri Milesii e le cavalle di Tracia: osservazioni su Callimaco frr. 114–115 Pfeiffer', *ZPE* 106, 5–21.

Davis, G. 1983, *The Death of Procris: 'Amor' and the Hunt in Ovid's* Metamorphoses (Rome).

Denhière, G., and Baudet, S. 1989, 'Cognitive Psychology and Text Processing: From Text Representation to Text-World', *Semiotica*, 77, 271–93.

Dietze, J. 1905, *Komposition und Quellenbenutzung in Ovids Metamorphosen* (Hamburg).

Fantham, E. 1998, *Ovid,* Fasti *Book IV* (Cambridge).

—— 2004, *Ovid's* Metamorphoses (Oxford).

Farrell, J. 1992, 'Dialogue of Genres in Ovid's "Lovesong of Polyphemus" (*Metamorphoses* 13. 719–897)', *AJP* 113, 235–58.

Fayer, C. 2005, *La familia romana*, iii (Rome).

Feeney, D. C. 1991, *The Gods in Epic: Poets and Critics of the Classical Tradition* (Oxford).

—— 1999, '*Mea tempora*: Patterning of Time in the *Metamorphoses*', in P. Hardie, A. Barchiesi, and S. Hinds (eds.), *Ovidian Transformations: Essays on the* Metamorphoses *and its Reception* (*PCPS* Suppl. 23; Cambridge), 13–30.

Flach, D. 1991, *Die sogenannte Laudatio Turiae: Einleitung Text, Übersetzung und Kommentar* (Darmstadt).

Fontenrose, J. 1979–80, 'Ovid's Procris', *CJ* 75, 287–94.

Fowler, D. P. 2000, *Roman Constructions: Readings in Postmodern Latin* (Oxford).

Fulkerson, L. 2006, 'Apollo, *paenitentia*, and Ovid's *Metamorphoses*', *Mnem.*[4] 49, 388–402.

Gavins, J. 2007, *Text World Theory: An Introduction* (Edinburgh).

Gibson, R. K. 2003, *Ovid,* Ars Amatoria *Book 3: Edited with Introduction and Commentary* (Cambridge).

Gildenhard, I., and Zissos, A. 2004, 'Ovid's "Hecale": Deconstructing Athens in the *Metamorphoses*', *JRS* 94, 47–72.

Green, P. 1979–80, 'The Innocence of Procris: Ovid *A.A. 3.* 887–746', *CJ* 75, 15–24.

Green, S. J. 2004, *Ovid,* Fasti *I: A Commentary* (*Mnemosyne* Suppl. 251; Leiden and Boston).

Harder, M. A. 2004, 'Callimachus', in I. de Jong, R. Nünlist, and A. Bowie (eds.), *Narrator, Narratees, and Narratives in Ancient Greek Literature* (*Mnemosyne* Suppl. 257, Leiden and Boston), 63–81.

Hardie, P. R. 1993, *The Epic Successors of Virgil: A Study in the Dynamics of a Tradition* (Cambridge).

—— 2002, *Ovid's Poetics of Illusion* (Cambridge).

—— 2004, 'Ovidian Middles', in S. Kyriakidis and F. De Martino (eds.), *Middles in Latin Poetry* (Bari), 151–82.

Heinsius, N. 1758, *Nic. Heinsii Commentarius in P. Ovidii Nasonis Opera Omnia,* ed. J. F. Fischer (Leipzig).

Henrichs, A. 1972, 'Towards a New Edition of Philodemus' Treatise *On Piety*', *GRBS* 13, 67–98.

—— 1983, 'Die Kekropidensage im PHerc. 243: von Kallimachos zu Ovid', *CErc* 13, 33–43.

Herbert-Brown, G. 1994, *Ovid and the* Fasti: *A Historical Study* (Oxford).

Heslin, P. 2007, 'Augustus, Domitian and the so-called Horologium Augusti', *JRS* 97, 1–20.

Hinds, S. 1985, 'Booking the Return Trip: Ovid and *Tristia* 1', *PCPS* 31, 13–32.

—— 1987, *The Metamorphosis of Persephone: Ovid and the Self-Conscious Muse* (Cambridge).

Hollis, A. S. 2007, *Fragments of Roman Poetry: c.80 BC–AD 20* (Oxford).

—— 2009, *Callimachus,* Hecale: *Edited with Introduction and Commentary* (2nd edn., Oxford).

Holzberg, N. 1990, 'Ovids Version der Ehebruchsnovelle von Ares und Aphrodite (Hom. *Od. θ* 266–366) in der *Ars Amatoria* (II 561–92)', *Würzburger Jahrbücher,* 16, 137–52.

Hunter, R. L. 1983, *Eubulus, the Fragments: Edited with a Commentary* (Cambridge).

—— 1992, 'Writing the God: Form and Meaning in Callimachus, *Hymn to Athena*', *MD* 29, 9–34.

—— 2006, *The Shadow of Callimachus: Studies in the Reception of Hellenistic Poetry at Rome* (Cambridge).

Hutchinson, G. O. 1988, *Hellenistic Poetry* (Oxford).

—— 2003, 'The *Aetia*: Callimachus' Poem of Knowledge', *ZPE* 145, 47–59.

—— 2006a, 'The Metamorphosis of *Metamorphosis*: P. Oxy. 4711 and Ovid', *ZPE* 155, 71–84.

—— 2006b, 'Hellenistic Epic and Homeric form', in M. J. Clarke, B. G. F. Currie, and R. O. A. M. Lyne (eds.), *Epic Interactions: Perspectives on Homer, Virgil, and the Epic Tradition Presented to Jasper Griffin* (Oxford, 2006), 105–29.

—— 2008, *Talking Books: Readings in Hellenistic and Roman Books of Poetry* (Oxford).

—— (forthcoming), 'Space and Text Worlds', in J. Murray and C. Schroeder (eds.), *The Cambridge Companion to Apollonius* (Cambridge).

Janan, M. 1994, '"There beneath the Roman ruin where the purple flowers grow": Ovid's Minyeides and the Feminine Imagination', *AJP* 115, 427–48.

Janka, M. 1997, *Ovid, Ars Amatoria: Buch 2. Kommentar* (Heidelberg).

Keith, A. M. 1992, *The Play of Fictions: Studies in Ovid's* Metamorphoses *Book 2* (Ann Arbor).

Knox, P. E. 1989, 'Pyramus and Thisbe in Cyprus', *HSCP* 92, 315–28.

Kristeva, J. 1969, Σημειωτική. *Recherches pour une sémanalyse* (Paris).

—— 1978, Σημειωτική. *Recherches pour une sémanalyse (Extraits)* (Paris).

Kron, U. 1981, 'Aglauros, Herse, Pandrosos', *LIMC* i/1. 283–98.

Labate, M. 1975, 'Amore coniugale e amore "elegiaco" nell'episodio di Cefalo e Procri (Ov., *Met.*, 7, 661–865)', *ASNP*³ 5, 103–28.

Littlewood, R. J. 2006, *A Commentary on Ovid:* Fasti *Book 6* (Oxford).

Lowe, N. J. 2000, *The Classical Plot and the Invention of Western Narrative* (Cambridge).

Luce, J. de, 1982, 'Metamorphosis as Mourning: Pathological Grief in Ovid's *Metamorphoses*', *Helios*, 9, 77–90.

Luppe, W. 1984, 'Epikureische Mythenkritik bei Philodem — Götterliebschaften', *CErc* 14, 109–24.

Martini, M. C. 2004, *Le Vestali: Un sacerdozio funzionale al "cosmo" romano* (Collection Latomus, 282; Brussels).

Massimilla, G. 1996, *Callimaco. Aitia. Libri primo e secondo. Introduzione, testo critico, traduzione e commento* (Pisa).

Matthews, V. J. 1996, *Antimachus of Colophon: Text and Commentary* (*Mnemosyne* Suppl. 155; Leiden, New York, and Cologne).

McGinn, T. A. J. 1998, *Prostitution, Sexuality, and the Law in Ancient Rome* (Oxford).

Merkelbach, R., and Stauber, J. 1998–2004, *Steinepigramme aus dem griechischen Osten*, 5 vols. (Stuttgart).

Mette-Dittmann, A. 1991, *Die Ehegesetze des Augustus: Eine Untersuchung im Rahmen der Gesellschaftspolitik des Princeps* (Historia Einzelschr. 67; Stuttgart).

Miller, J. F. 1999, 'The Lamentations of Apollo in Ovid's *Metamorphoses*', in W. Schubert (ed.), *Ovid. Werk und Wirkung. Festgabe für Michael von Albrecht zum 65. Geburtstag* (Studien zur klassischen Philologie, 100; Frankfurt am Main), i. 413–21.

Mommsen, Th. 1899, *Römisches Strafrecht* (Leipzig).

Montuschi, Cl. 1998, '*Aurora* nelle Metamorfosi di Ovidio: un topos rinnovato, tra epica ed elegia', *MD* 41, 71–125.

Morrison, A. D. 2005, 'Sexual Ambiguity and the Identity of the Narrator in Callimachus' *Hymn to Athena*', *BICS* 48, 27–46.

—— 2007, *The Narrator in Archaic Greek and Hellenistic Poetry* (Cambridge).

Moscadi, A. 2005, 'L'episodio degli uccelli parlanti nell'*Ecale* di Callimaco', *Comunicazioni*, 5 (2003), 29–43.

Nikolopoulos, A. D. 2004, *Ovidius Polytropos: Metanarrative in Ovid's* Metamorphoses (Spudasmata, 98; Hildesheim, Zurich, and New York).

Obbink, D. 2004, 'Vergil's *De pietate*: From *Ehoiae* to Allegory in Vergil, Philodemus, and Ovid', in D. Armstrong, J. Fish, P. A. Johnston, and M. B. Skinner (eds.), *Vergil, Philodemus, and the Augustans* (Austin, TX), 175–209.

Otis, B. 1970, *Ovid as an Epic Poet* (2nd edn., Cambridge).

Parker, R. C. T. 1987, 'Myths of Early Athens', in J. Bremmer (ed.), *Interpretations of Greek Mythology* (London and Sydney), 187–214.

—— 2005, *Polytheism and Society at Athens* (Oxford).

Pechillo, M. 1990–1, 'Ovid's Framing Technique: the Aeacus and Cephalus Epyllion (*Met.* 7. 490–8. 5)', *CJ* 86, 35–44.

Pöschl, V. 1959, 'Kephalos und Prokris in Ovids Metamorphosen', *Hermes*, 87, 328–43.

Powell, B. 1906, *Erichthonius and the Three Daughters of Cecrops* (Cornell Studies in Classical Philology, 17; New York).

Pugliese Carratelli, G., and Baldassarre, I. (eds.) 1990–2003, *Pompei: Pitture e mosaici*, 11 vols. (Rome).

Ramage, E. S. 1994, 'The So-called *Laudatio Turiae* as Panegyric', *Athenaeum*, 82, 341–70.

Rimell, V. 2006, *Ovid's Lovers: Desire, Difference, and the Poetic Imagination* (Cambridge).

Robbins, E. 1990, 'The Gifts of the Gods: Pindar's Third *Pythian*', *CQ*² 40, 307–18.

Rosati, G. 2002, 'Narrative Techniques and Narrative Structures in the *Metamorphoses*', in B. W. Boyd (ed.), *Brill's Companion to Ovid* (Leiden, Boston, and Cologne), 271–304.

Rossum-Steenbeek, M. van, 1998, *Greek Readers' Digests? Studies on a Selection of Subliterary Papyri* (*Mnemosyne* Suppl. 175; Leiden, New York, and Cologne).

Salzman-Mitchell, P. B. 2005, *A Web of Fantasies: Gaze, Image, and Gender in Ovid's Metamorphoses* (Baltimore).

Sanders, J. 2006, *Adaptation and Appropriation* (London and New York).

Schmidt, M. 1968, 'Die Entdeckung des Erichthonios: Zu einer neuen Lekythos des Phialemalers und einem ungedeuteten Vasenbild', *MDA* 83, 200–12.

Segal, C. 1978, 'Ovid's Cephalus and Procris: Myth and Tragedy', *Gräzer Beiträge*, 7, 175–205.

Sharrock, A. R. 2002, 'Looking at Looking: Can You Resist a Reading?', in D. Fredrick (ed.), *The Roman Gaze: Vision, Power, and the Body* (Baltimore and London), 265–95.

Sichtermann, H. 1992, *Die mythologischen Sarkophage, 2. Teil: H. Apollo bis Grazien* (Die antiken Sarkophagreliefs, 12; Berlin).

Simantoni-Bournia, E. 1992, 'Kephalos', vi/1. 1–5.

Simon, E. 1992, 'Koronis', *LIMC* vi/1. 104–5.

Solodow, J. B. 1988, *The World of Ovid's Metamorphoses* (Chapel Hill and London).

Syme, R. 1978, *History in Ovid* (Oxford).

Tarrant, R. 1995, 'The Silence of Cephalus: Text and Narrative Technique in Ovid, *Metamorphoses* 7. 885ff.', *TAPA* 125, 99–111.

Treggiari, S. 1991, *Roman Marriage: Iusti Coniuges from the Time of Cicero to the Time of Ulpian* (Oxford).

Tronchet, G. 1998, *La Métamorphose à l'œuvre: Recherches sur la poétique d'Ovide dans les Métamorphoses* (Leuven and Paris).

Weiss, C. 1986, 'Eos', *LIMC* iii/1. 747–89.

Werth, P. 1999, *Text Worlds: Representing Conceptual Space in Discourse* (London).

West, M. L. 1985, *The Hesiodic* Catalogue of Women (Oxford).

Wheeler, S. M. 1999, *A Discourse of Wonders: Audience and Performance in Ovid's* Metamorphoses (Philadelphia).

Wimmel, W. 1962, 'Aglauros in Ovids Metamorphosen', *Hermes*, 90, 326–33.

Wistrand, E. 1976, *The So-Called* Laudatio Turiae: *Introduction, Text, Translation, Commentary* (Göteborg).

Wolters, P., and Bruns, G. 1940, *Das Kabirenheiligtum bei Theben*, i (Berlin).

# 14

## On Ancient Prose Rhythm: The Story of the Dichoreus

### *Michael Winterbottom*

On the summit of the Nemrut Dağ in southern Turkey King Antiochus I of Commagene, at some date around the middle of the first century BC, caused to be erected a monumental inscription. In a famous passage, Eduard Norden used it to exemplify the quantitative rhythms of Hellenistic prose.[1] To this notable place our honorand and I paid a pilgrimage during the late seventies; and the present paper was conceived as a reminder of our eastward travels together.

I start by wielding the broad brush. The story of ancient prose rhythm is punctuated by mysterious transitions. *First*, there is the move to the Hellenistic rhythms we see in Antiochus' inscription, marked by a liking for a cretic base. It is my impression, but no more than an impression, that such rhythms may have developed from fainter tendencies in Isocrates. The Hellenistic system itself raises questions. How widely, and over what span of time, was it practised? *Second*, there is the taking over of the system, and arguably its modification, by the Romans. *Third*, in Greek, is the change from the quantitative system to the accentual one that we see taking place some time in the fourth century of our era. What is the relation, if any, between the two systems? Why did Atticizing writers spurn one but embrace the other? Did accent ever play any part in the quantitative system? *Fourth*, the parallel development in Latin from quantitative to accentual clausulae. How are we to date and assess this change? And, here more pressingly, arises the same question I asked of Greek rhythm: what part, if any, did the language's natural word-accent play in the long period before it began to dictate the norms of prose rhythm? In this paper I suggest some slight footnotes to the books that might be written (by others) about the first, second, and fourth of these transitions. The dichoreus, and Cicero, will be my threads through the maze.

---

[1] Norden 1958, 141–5. Diggle 2005, 67 scans one section of the inscription.

There is no reason to suppose that the Greek quantitative system was transplanted into Latin single-handed by Cicero.[2] But Cicero inevitably looms large in our thoughts about this transition, not merely because his writings give us such lavish examples of the application of the system, but because his theoretical works touch explicitly on prose rhythm. Later, we can find no help in the ninth book of Quintilian, where, if I am right, there is hardly a single type of ending to a Latin sentence that is not recommended. Cicero's own prescriptive remarks, both in *De Oratore* and *Orator*, are hardly more helpful. But we cannot but listen carefully when, in *Orator*, he draws our attention to details of rhythmic *practice*. It is the modern habit to think of the system as being cretic-based (I have already used the phrase myself). Cicero talks in terms of verse feet, but he does not here mention cretics. He introduces his account (*Orat.* 212) by singling out the dichoreus, or double trochee, as the ending which 'Asia has most pursued'. Even this foot is praised somewhat faintly ('non . . . uitiosus in clausulis', 213); it was not to be overused. But Cicero points with approval (214) to dichorei in a passage of C. Carbo: *persolutas* and then *comprobauit*, the latter greeted by cries of approval from the Roman audience. On the other hand, he has cited (213) from Carbo a short sentence ending *esse rem publicam* without remarking what sounds to us the insistent double cretic. Similarly, in analysing a passage from Crassus later, he points out (224) another dichoreus, *aestimasti*. In these discussions, he names no other type of foot, except the spondee. We should note that when he talks of dichorei, he each time refers to *a single word* of this metrical shape.[3] An earlier more theoretical and prescriptive discussion (*Orat.* 215–19)—an astonishingly confused and unhelpful discussion, it must be said— adds a further point which will prove to be of interest. A dactyl may come at the end of a sentence when it stands in for a cretic (217; it is not clear how we should know when it does not); similarly Cicero says (218) that a cretic is better than a paeon at the end of a sentence.

It is natural to suppose that these views of Cicero in some way reflected Greek theory and Greek practice. Of the theory, we know nothing. And the evidence of the practice is sadly scanty.

The rhythmical Nemrut Dağ inscription was set up during a reign that lasted from *c.*69 to *c.*36 BC. So too the parallel material from Arsameia.[4] Norden himself[5] found similar rhythms in the fragments of the much earlier orator and historian Hegesias of Magnesia (perhaps of the third century). In

---

[2] For C. Gracchus see Courtney 1999, 132. But the material is scanty, and not always easy to assess.

[3] This is the practice, too, of metrical theorists writing during the Empire. Cf. esp. Diomedes in Keil 1855–80, i. 469, 28 'singulis enim partibus orationis singulos pedes dabimus'.

[4] Dörner and Goell (1963), 36–91. In my discussion of the Greek evidence, I count as 'rhythmical' clausulae of the types found commonly in Cicero (below, p. 265).

[5] Norden 1958, 134–8.

discussing some years ago what I not very ashamedly called the Asian style of Greek declamation,[6] I added to the equation the (often corrupt) fragments of the Greek declaimers cited by the Elder Seneca, who survived into the reign of Gaius. But the net can be cast rather wider and later. Donald Russell has remarked on the appearance of such rhythms in certain of the letters attributed to Phalaris.[7] That gives us no firm date. Nor does James Diggle's striking demonstration (developed from a hint by Spencer Barrett) that the hypotheses to Euripidean tragedies are quantitatively clausulated: he remarks that 'our collection of hypotheses, so far as I can see, may have been compiled at any date between the 2nd century B.C. and the 1st century A.D.'[8] We are on firmer ground if (as Professor Russell has suggested to me) we turn to the works of Philo of Alexandria, who was already an old man in AD 39/40, and of Onasander, who dedicated his treatise on generalship to the consul for AD 49. A definite date can be assigned to a clearly rhythmical speech delivered by Nero in AD 67.[9] Some decades later comes a no less rhythmical communication of the Prefect of Egypt written in the nineteenth year of either Trajan or Hadrian.[10] The inscriptional evidence is (to my knowledge) disappointingly sparse. But, so far as it goes, it does nothing to upset the impression we obtain from other sources, that a system that goes back deep into the Hellenistic age did not long outlast the first century of the Christian era. I suppose that this is a symptom of the way in which Atticism triumphed during the Second Sophistic.

Does this material, such as it is, support Cicero's assertion that Asia especially favoured the dichoreus, or chime in with his apparent approval of final cretics?

To take some soundings: I count eleven sentence ends in Onasander's stylized proem.[11] They muster one double cretic, four cases of cretic + spondee, and two dichorei (one of them forming a complete word). It is striking that of the remaining four sentences, three end with a single cretic.[12] In the (very short) 23rd letter of Phalaris,[13] before nineteen pauses marked by Hercher's punctuation (including commas), I find twelve rhythmical endings. Seven of these are dichorei; three form a single word. At the seven remaining pauses can be found three lone cretics. In a much longer sample from Philo's *Life of Moses*,[14] I find, at the first hundred major breaks, forty clear rhythms;[15]

---

[6] Innes and Winterbottom 1988, 8.      [7] Russell 1988, 97 n. 29, specifying e.g. Letter 23.
[8] Diggle 2005, 67.      [9] Oliver 1989, no. 296 = Smallwood 1967, no. 64.
[10] Tcherikover 1957–64, no. 435 (the continuous part of the text is at ii. 231–2).
[11] Illinois Greek Club 1923, 368–74.
[12] See also Diggle 2005, 39; among 112 endings of sentences, he finds 14 unresolved cretics, only one preceded by another cretic and six forming a single word. For Cicero, see below, p. 265.
[13] Hercher 1872, 413–14.
[14] i. 1–83.
[15] A considerable number of others could be regarded as resolved forms of the main types.

nine of them are unresolved dichorei, three forming a complete word. In addition, eleven sentences end in a single cretic (four forming a complete word). It looks as though Cicero's remarks on final cretics and on dichorei, though they will be based on impression rather than statistics, have some basis in Greek reality.

It is time to turn to Cicero's own practice. I have analysed 100 successive strong pauses (those marked in a modern text by a full stop, an exclamation mark, or a question mark: see the Key below, pp. 274–5) in a long passage in the grand style from towards the end of the speech for Sulla (69–90). I find 28 instances of Type 1 metrical clausulae,[16] seven of Type 1a, and seven of Type 2. 26 dichorei (Type 3) bring the total up to 68.[17] I add that in twelve other places a sentence ends in a lone cretic (i.e. one not preceded by another cretic). No one takes this 'clausula' very seriously, but Zielinski found that it represents over 10% of all the endings in Cicero's speeches.[18]

It is clear, then, that Cicero follows what he regarded as Asian practice so far as dichorei are concerned. Further, he is very ready to place last the ditrochaic words which he admired in Carbo and Crassus: thus *ponderandum, deprecatus, multitudo*, and thirteen more, more than half of the total of Type 3 endings.

I come now to the question of quantity and accent. I shall proceed by comparing the practice of Cicero, as seen in my sample, with that of the Christian writer Arnobius (fl. 300), full details of which were given in a remarkable monograph by H. Hagendahl.[19] That my sample from Cicero is so small is not important for my purposes. I am not conducting a statistical investigation, but proposing a methodology.

Arnobius is one of those writers who have been judged to employ the so-called *cursus mixtus*,[20] 'in which', according to an authoritative handbook, 'the ictus of metrical patterns was made to coincide with word accent'.[21] But serious difficulties attend discussion in these terms. Are we justified in talking of ictus in prose? It may seem natural to moderns to think of a Ciceronian Type 1 clausula, for instance, as carrying a beat on the two initial longs of the cretic and the spondee that make it up. But, as we have seen, Cicero did not talk of cretics at all. And it has been weightily argued that ictus in general is a

---

[16] For the types, see below, p. 266.

[17] These figures correlate well enough with those given by Zielinski (1904), still the only source for complete figures for Cicero's speeches. His end-chart shows 23.3% of Type 1, 4.3% of Type 1a, 11.1% of Type 2, and 27.8% of Type 3.

[18] As for other Latin writers, I note (for example) in a sample of 100 clausulae from Apuleius' *Metamorphoses* (5. 1–14) no fewer than 17 final cretics in endings that by my criteria are not quantitatively rhythmical.

[19] Hagendahl 1937.

[20] Hagendahl himself (1937, 26) talks of 'une prose métrique à tendances rythmiques'; cf. also p. 24.

[21] Tunberg 1996, 114. Cf. Hagendahl 1937, e.g. p. 27: 'dans ces trois types ... l'*ictus* et l'accent se confondent toujours'.

will-o'-the-wisp.[22] In view of all this, I present my argument in a way that does not involve taking a stance on ictus,[23] or, for that matter, on the nature of the Latin word-accent in the times of Cicero and of Arnobius.

The metrical types already identified look forward to accentual counter-parts when the cursus sets in: Type 1 foreshadowing the Planus, 1a the Trispondaicus, 2 the Tardus, and 3 the Velox.

1   $-\cup--\times$ (where $\cup$ represents a short and $\times$ a common syllable): looks forward to the Planus ó o o ó o (where each o is one syllable).

1a  $-\cup\cup\cup-\times$: looks forward to the Trispondaicus ó o o o ó o

2   $-\cup--\cup\times$: looks forward to the Tardus ó o o ó o o

3   $-\cup--\cup-\cup$: looks forward (see below) to the Velox ó o o o o ó o [24]

Now if we look at my list of a hundred endings from the *Pro Sulla* to see which could be regarded as metrical alone, as accentual alone, or as both, we find, *on the assumptions I make*, that 23 endings are metrical only, 11 accentual only, and 45 both metrical and accentual. To put it another way, 68 are metrical, 56 accentual. Those assumptions are as follows.

Metrical clausulae are here defined as those conforming to Types 1, 1a, 2, and 3 *without (further) resolutions*.

Accentual clausulae are here defined as those conforming to the two major types of Planus (pp2, p3p), two types of Tardus (p4pp, pp3pp), one type of Trispondaicus (p4p), and the major type of Velox (pp4p).[25] These are the six types that top the list if one tots up the figures given in the tables in Janson 1975, 109–15. Those tables show how various medieval practice was, and in this paper I only use the general term 'cursus' for convenience.

But, and this is a crucial point, no absolute value can be placed on such figures as I offer above for the passage from *Pro Sulla*. It is not merely that this is a tiny sample. Much more important, the figures are dictated by the assumptions made about what counts as a metrical clausula and what as an accentual. To tighten or relax the criteria for either skews the relative figures. We have seen how Quintilian in effect regarded almost any ending as rhythmical. Modern scholars do not go as far as that. But such a list as

---

[22] Note Stroh 1990, 116 = 2000, 216: 'Wir heutigen Latinisten aber sollten . . . auf alle Fälle daran festhalten, daß . . . lateinische Verse nie mit einem Iktus gesprochen wurden, *neque intra scholarum muros neque extra*.' I am very grateful to Dr Peter Kruschwitz for advising me in these matters.

[23] My conference paper did talk in those terms, and I am not sure that they are necessarily mistaken. There is a very enticing parallel with the interplay of metre and accent in the Virgilian hexameter.

[24] Any further inclusions on either side (and such could be defended) would clearly affect the overall figures. No definition of either metrical or accentual clausulae would be 'correct'.

[25] The notation is that introduced by Janson 1975, 13–14. The first element states whether the penultimate word is paroxytone, p, or proparoxytone, pp. The second states the number of syllables in the final word and the position of the accent, p or pp.

R. G. M. Nisbet's in the introduction to his edition of the *In Pisonem*[26] comes
perilously close to being all-inclusive, if we allow free resolution of long
syllables. Equally, a very large proportion of possible endings to sentences,
where the two final syllables are neither of them monosyllables or longer than
tetrasyllables, will be found to conform to the practice of the cursus.[27] Where
definitions are so fluid, we cannot possibly expect to get absolute results to an
enquiry conducted on these lines. The figures I have given are cited merely to
give a rough idea of the extent of the agreement of accentual and metrical
clausulae in a single (grand) passage from a Ciceronian speech. They do *not*
prove, and are not here cited to prove, that Cicero's prose is metrically clausulated, accentually clausulated, or a mixture of the two.

The fact is that there are no firm criteria for deciding whether a given piece
of prose is metrical or accentual. There is, instead, a spectrum on which
everything from Cicero's speeches to a papal bull from the Middle Ages can
be placed. The existence of this spectrum makes polarization of metrical and
accentual rhythm, and talk, too, of *cursus mixtus*, unprofitable. No Latin prose
could fail to have some proportion of accentual clausulae, and some proportion of clausulae that can be taken metrically. But in any given author the
proportions will vary, and we have no reason to suppose that there is a
smooth and continuous historical development.[28]

To judge the interplay of accent and quantity in Cicero, then, we need to
proceed in a more nuanced method than by merely counting up quantitative
and accentual clausulae. We need to see how far Cicero's practice appears to
be influenced, consciously or unconsciously, by the natural stresses of the
spoken language.

We have seen that a very common quantitative rhythm in my sample from
the *Pro Sulla* is Type 1, where a cretic is followed by a trochee or spondee (i.e.
a long plus an anceps). A helpful table in Hagendahl[29] shows eight subtypes,
distinguished by the different typologies of the individual words. Far the most
frequent in Arnobius is the type *sórte uersári* (on Janson's notation p3p:
74%); some long way behind comes the type *óppidum claúdi* (pp2: 15%).
These types will later be favoured in the cursus as two forms of the Planus.[30]
Conversely, the type (*corpor*)*is minus fausta* musters merely 0.6%. But the

[26] Nisbet 1961, p. xvii. The list is introduced by the words: 'The following are the clausulae
most often used by Cicero.'
[27] If this rule is enforced, the accentual possibilities number ten only. Six of these are the
endings stipulated in the text to n. 25. A seventh is a second type of trispondaicus that I did not
include there (pp3p). The other three are p2, p3pp, and pp4pp.
[28] It may well be that Ammianus, writing before 395, paid more attention to accent than any
other writer before the cursus set in.
[29] Hagendahl 1937, 27.
[30] See the tables in Janson 1975, 109–15. The type pp2 is always well outnumbered by p3p,
and sometimes vanishes altogether.

figures for Cicero tend in the same direction. In my sample, out of 28 cases of Type 1, he employs p3p (*sórte uersári*) 14 times (50%), pp2 (*óppidum claúdi*) three times (11%). Ten of the other eleven deserve attention.[31] One (*fingíque non pósse*) is of the Planus type *facta de pomo*, third in popularity with Arnobius.[32] Three show pentasyllabic endings, a typology very unpopular with Arnobius, and criticized by Quintilian (9. 4. 97) as 'soft': a sign of changing tastes, reflected in hexameter poetry too.[33] The other six raise for the first time a question that will recur later. The clausula *pátriae sit inuéntus* would later be called a subtype of the Velox. The other five all have the shape *nátum putauérunt* (p4p), the accentual (Trispondaic) equivalent of metrical Type 1a (*esse uideatur*), to be discussed below. Just as Stroh has argued that we have no right to thump out the rhythms when reading a hexameter,[34] so, perhaps, it may be felt that such clausulae as these were spoken purely according to the accent. In that case, they should be thought of, not so much as instances of metrical clausula Type 1, but rather as forerunners, unconscious but significant, of cursus endings.

Type 1a is conventionally regarded as a resolved form of Type 1. I distinguish it here because in the typology *esse uideatur* (p4p) it was already noticed in antiquity as a hallmark of Cicero's style, but especially because it played an important role in the development of the cursus. The Type p4p is not of course the only one possible; another would be pp3p (*praéditus honóre*). Both look forward to the later Trispondaicus. But Arnobius (though less keen on Type 1a than Cicero: 2% only) almost always employed p4p (Hagendahl, 56–7), and, in my sample, Cicero always does (7 out of 7).[35]

Similar results follow examination of Type 2 (double cretic). Hagendahl (p. 31) shows that the three subtypes (out of eleven) favoured by Arnobius are of the shapes *uéllet indícere* (p4pp: 52%), *égerint céteri* (pp3pp: 24%) and (*submo*)*uére de saéculis* (16%). The others are nowhere, statistically. All these three foreshadow the Tardus. In the sample from Cicero, there are four cases of p4pp, two of pp3pp. But just as we found cases where Cicero mimicked the metrical rhythm of *esse uideatur* with accentual endings like *natum putauerunt*, so here: there are two cases of the type *ípsi succúmbere*, where there is no cretic base, but where the accents fall into the Tardus rhythm of *uéllet indícere*. It seems just as appropriate to say that here the double cretic is

---

[31] In the eleventh, *ferri oportere*, the elision makes it hard to know how we should treat it accentually.

[32] For the accentuation of prepositions, *non*, etc. see Hagendahl 1937, 14–17.

[33] In 9. 4. 65 Quintilian remarks of this clausula: 'etiam in carminibus est praemolle.' We may, however, think that in prose a subsidiary accent on the first syllable of such words gives something approximating to the Planus rhythm. *incitauerunt* may have satisfied Cicero in the same way as did *Cassiepia* at the end of one of his hexameters (*Arat.* frg. 30 Traglia).

[34] See n. 22.

[35] For the cursus practice, see again the tables in Janson 1975, 109–15. Writers varied a good deal in their preferences between the two types mentioned.

mimicked by its accentual counterpart as to identify a metrical clausula where three longs precede a cretic.[36] It is again very tempting to read according to the accent rather than metrically.

Let us take stock. Cicero employs Types 1, 1a, and 2 in all 42 times. In 35 cases, he falls into what would later be called an accentual rhythm.[37] If his rhythmic practice as a whole is to be markedly differentiated from Arnobius', the difference must lie in their treatment of dichorei.

The position here is more complex, and I shall in the body of this paper only contrast with Cicero's practice two crucial aspects of Arnobius'.

1. In Arnobius, according to Hagendahl (p. 33), out of 458 dichoreic endings, the foot forms a single final word of four syllables on no fewer than 383 occasions (84%); and of these 383, the vast majority (361: 79% of the whole group) are preceded by a proparoxytone, whether a cretic, an anapaest, a dactyl, or a tribrach. The result, accentually, was a Velox.

This is highly significant. In the Planus and the Tardus, the norm was a two-word unit, with two stress accents, separated by two unstressed syllables. The one-word dichoreus by itself, with its one main stress, perhaps came to be felt to be less satisfying than such units. The Velox remedied that, though the stresses were here separated by four rather than two unstressed syllables. (The analogy with Greek accentual practice is patent.)

What of Cicero? Among the 16 clausulae where a dichoreus forms a single word (e.g. *ponderandum*), we find two cases where the final dichoreic word is preceded by an anapaestic word (e.g. *numerum transferetis*), two where it is preceded by a cretic word (e,g, *innocens iudicetur*) and another where it is preceded by a dactylic word (*ordine multitudo*). Relevant also here are the four cases where a final word consists of four long syllables; in each a proparoxytone precedes (e.g. *iudices obtestatur*). Cicero clearly felt that the heavy final word needed to be lightened by what came before.[38] Arnobius was to deal with this differently, by disfavouring an accumulation of longs at the end of the sentence.[39] We gain for Cicero, however, another nine cases that could be taken for a Velox, four of them not metrically rhythmical on my definition.

2. We come now to trisyllable endings, of bacchiac shape ($\cup$ – –), preceded, of course, by a longum. These are comparatively rare in Arnobius, but Hagendahl (pp. 42–3) lists fourteen cases where the bacchius is preceded

---

[36] Nisbet 1961, p. xvii draws attention to it as a variant on the double cretic, Zieliński 1904 found that it formed 7.2% of all the clausulae he counted. See further below, p. 273.

[37] It may further be observed that in Types 1 and 2 he prefers a subtype that has a paroxytone penultimate. This preference will no doubt be the result of natural tendencies in the language; see Orlandi 2005, 400. Intriguingly, this preference also results in avoidance of a cretic penultimate word in these types (in my sample only 1, 86, and 98). It is as though Cicero prefers not to flaunt the cretic (or is not aware that it is a cornerstone of his system).

[38] Cf. Aili 1979, 56, and also 94 (true even of Sallust!).

[39] Hagendahl 1937, 260.

by a paroxytone (*nouerámus redíre*). This, as Hagendahl remarks, is a type of the Planus. In my sample from Cicero, there are three such cases, and it is again tempting to read according to the accent rather than to stress the dichoree (e.g. *tándem iuuábit*). Further, Arnobius displays sixteen cases where the bacchius is preceded by a monosyllable and this group is preceded in turn by a proparoxytone (Hagendahl, 41–2: type *nesciens quod petatur*). This is equivalent to the kind of Velox discussed in the previous paragraph. Cicero, on the other hand, only once in my sample[40] employs a monosyllable before a final bacchius, and there a proparoxytone does not precede. But I notice instances earlier in the *Pro Sulla* (e.g. 37 'Cassio non fuisse').[41]

There are then signs, but only faint ones, of the development that was to harness the dichoreus to the purposes of the Velox. But then his remarks in *Orator* suggest that Cicero felt, as Arnobius obviously did not, that a final dichoreus, especially if formed by a single word, provided a satisfactory clausula in itself.

Even in Cicero, as we have seen, the metrical Types 1, 1a, and 2 closely foreshadow the accentual types (Planus, Trispondaicus, and Velox).[42] A crucial further advance towards the cursus was taken when Cicero's treatment of the dichoreus came to seem unsatisfactory: this, as I have suggested, because its single accent, in contrast to the other types, began to be felt to be insufficient on its own. Arnobius' practice shows us the final dichoreic tetra-syllable being supported by a preceding proparoxytone, a final bacchius being supported by a proparoxytone plus a monosyllable. We have seen that both these moves were to some extent anticipated in Cicero. Cyprian's *Ad Donatum*, written well before Arnobius, displays them in full flower.[43] It would be agreeable if the development of this twin technique for expanding the dichoreus could be used as a chronological marker. But authors after Arnobius do not follow a single system.[44]

On the wider question of the time of the adoption of the accentual system, we have to recall the idea of a spectrum. I have argued that Cicero's *Kunstprosa* is on that spectrum; its rhythms are not *toto caelo* different from what comes later. As for the cursus, that too is on the spectrum. It only differed from the practice of the Christian fathers in an increased readiness to

---

[40]  My no. 72.

[41]  Add 9 'aduerteris me uidebis', 10 'ille me non coegisset'.

[42]  Not always, as we have seen, with neat correspondence between metrical type and accentual type.

[43]  For the pp4p shape, note that Sacerdos (Keil 1855–80, vi. 494–5, of uncertain date; cf. also *Catholica Probi*, ibid. iv. 42–3), both in clausulae of his own composition and in examples from Cicero, lists desirable clausulae ('structuras . . . delectabiles') that always scan accentually. Not all would scan metrically: e.g. *fieri potuisset, omnia placuerunt, lumina deponebant, contemnere persuadenti, decipere contendebat*; then from Cic. *corpore perhorresco, temporis deuitare, composui rationem*.

[44]  But Cassiodorus' *Variae*, for one, does seem to be 'Arnobian' in this respect.

cast away the metrical substructure. But it would not have astonished the Cicero who could find satisfactory closure in *nihil audire, ipsi succumbere*, or *iudices obtestatur*.

It may be objected that this paper has merely shown how often a clausula may be taken both metrically and accentually. But that in itself is significant of the ease with which the transition from quantitative to accentual rhythm could proceed. As to my suggestion that Cicero paid more attention to accent than to quantity in speaking his clausulae, it may, as well as (for me) being plausible in itself, help us to solve a problem that has always worried me: how did Cicero, who seems to have little theoretical awareness of the nature of his final rhythms, produce such markedly rhythmical prose? I suggest that he had not been *taught*, by his Greek masters in Rome and in Rhodes, to speak rhythmically. Rather, by listening to certain orators in Rome and especially to Greek *rhetores* in Asia (and Rome too),[45] he perhaps came to feel (*a*) a conscious preference for a final dichoreic word; (*b*) aside from that, an (unconscious?) preference for clausulae where the two penultimate words were not both dissyllables, and where a monosyllable was only welcome if it cohered closely with an adjacent word; and (*c*) an (unconscious?) preference for clausulae where two unstressed syllables separated the final stressed syllables. From these three preferences might flow much of a rhythmical 'system' that Cicero could observe but not, with any cogency, explain to others.[46]

# APPENDIX

I hive off to this appendix some details about my sample from Cicero's *Pro Sulla* (for the Key to my system of reference, see below, pp. 274–5). In particular, my text does not deal at all fully with the 32 cases that do not fall neatly under the types. For these, see below, pp. 273–4.

| Type 1: | pp2 (*móribus dícam*) [3] | 1* 65 86* |
|---|---|---|
| | p3p (*natúra conuérti*) [14] | 4 7* 9 12* 13 18* 28 29* 54 55 76* 79 82* 83 |
| | p4p (*nátum putauérunt*) [5] | 8 17 43 61 93 |
| | Others: [6] | 35 39 50 56 63 92 |
| | Total 28 | |

---

[45] But of course this is only to push the question further back. How did *they* come to speak thus?

[46] I am very grateful to Gregory Hutchinson for giving his meticulous attention to an early draft of this paper, to Tobias Reinhardt for commenting acutely on the conference version, and to Peter Kruschwitz for asking a vital question after I delivered it. Leofranc Holford-Strevens offered acute comments at a late stage, making objections (which I have attempted to counter) but also raising wider issues which cannot be dealt with here.

Comments: 1. There is only a single elision within the clausula (63). In the eight cases (asterisked above) where the clausula starts with one of a pair of words, elision precedes at 12 and 76.[47]
2. There are three cases where a five-syllable word forms the clausula (39 56 92). Elision precedes the first of these.
3. 50 is in effect a case of p3p. Similarly, 35 might be read as a variation on the Velox (pp4p). See above, p. 268.

**Type 1a:** p4p (*ésse uideátur*) [7]   10* 38* 42 70* 73 94* 99
Total 7

Comment: There is no case of elision within the clausula. Where the clausula starts with one of a pair of words (cases asterisked above), elision precedes at 70 (once out of four instances).

**Type 2:** p4pp (*mentésque conuértere*) [4]   2 15* 23 68
pp3pp (*éxpetas ámplius*) [2]   98* 100
Other [1]:   52
Total 7

Comments: 1. There is never elision within the clausula. Elision does not precede in either of the two cases (asterisked above) where the clausula starts with the first of a pair of words.
2. In 52 there is a very strong pause after *ipsi tacemus*, and one might wish to hear a rhythm in those words (dichoreus, but readable as Planus; cf. above, p. 270). *graue* then follows with isolated emphasis, picking up 'graue est hoc dictu fortasse, iudices, graue' earlier in the structure (for which see Berry ad loc.).

**Type 3** p3p (*tándem iuuábit*) [3]   51 66 91
p4p (*Súlla deprecátus*) [2]   20 41
pp3p (*scéleri fuérunt*) [2]   5 90
pp4p [5]   24 40 53 71 89
Other [14]:

ending with tetrasyllable [9]   3 36E 45E 46E 49E 58 62 75E 88E
with trisyllable [2]   57 72
with two disyllables [3]   21 48E 84
Total 26

Comments: 1. The instances of p3p, p4p and pp4p can be read accentually as well as quantitatively (see above pp. 270, 268, 269).
2. There is a single case of elision *within* the dichoreus (57 *aliquando amico*, at the end of a remarkably fragmented sentence). Where the dichoreus is formed by a single tetrasyllabic word (16 cases), elision (signalled by E) *precedes* six times. This is a high figure compared with the other types (see above), and perhaps confirms that the dichoreus was felt at this period to be a free-standing clausula.

---

[47] The possible relevance of this observation, and of others like it below, will appear later (below, this page).

3. To come to the 14 'others':

(*a*) Nine end with a tetrasyllable, regarded by Cicero as a satisfying end to a sentence (above, p. 265). It may be noted that in only three cases, 3 58 62,[48] does a monosyllable precede: typical of Cicero's instinctive feeling for the accumulation of longer words at the sentence close. In all three the monosyllable coheres closely with the following verb (3 a copulative; 58 and 62 *non*),[49] with longer words preceding.

(*b*) In three cases the dichoreus is split between two disyllables (once preceded by elision). We should, however, note the strong pause after *fecit* in 21, and the overall structure of the sentence ending in 84, 'nihil uideo esse . . . odio dignum, misericordia digna multa'; *multa* is to some extent isolated by its correspondion with *nihil* at the start and by the correspondence of *misericordia digna* with the earlier *odio dignum*.

(*c*) In one of the two remaining instances, 72 *reddo ac remitto*, we may join *ac* with the following verb so closely as to produce in effect a final tetrasyllable (elision precedes: see above).

'Anomalies' I turn now to the remaining 32 endings. My intention is not to force these into pre-conceived moulds, though some in fact may be thought to fit them, but rather, if possible, to throw further light on Cicero's practice.

1. I start with the 9 cases (some already discussed in the body of the paper) where an ending, though not falling under the strictest quantitative categories employed above, is readily seen as accentually rhythmical. These are:

| | |
|---|---|
| pp4p, with four long final syllables (Velox) [4] | 6 67 96 97 |
| pp4p, with final word of the shape $\cup - - \times$ (Velox) [1] | 85[50] |
| p4pp, with spondaic (not trochaic) first word (Tardus) [2] | 14 16 |
| pp2, with the first word ending in a tribrach (Planus) [1] | 25[51] |
| p3p, with the first word formed of two shorts (Planus) [1] | 78 |
| Subtotal 9 | |

2. Then come the 12 cases of final cretic (see above, p. 265). They are: 19 22 27 30*[52] 31*[53] 32* 44* 59 64* 69* 77 80*. Asterisks mark the (seven) cases where the final word ends in a short syllable, making the cretic rhythm less obvious. In 22 64 77 80 three longs precede (see above, n. 36). For 14 (*ipsi succumbere*), see above, p. 268.
Subtotal 12

---

[48] To these may be added 45, where the elided *esse* precedes *audietur*. But it should be observed that a pause follows *esse*, and that *debet* precedes it, giving a dichoreus in its turn at the colon end.

[49] Cf. n. 32.

[50] *turpitudinis inuratur*: this might perhaps be regarded metrically as a resolved Type 1.

[51] *eripuit hora*, which might perhaps be regarded metrically as a resolved Type 3.

[52] *fuisse creditis*: metrically Nisbet's Type 4 (so too 69 *semper oderis*). Berry's note points out the five successive iambi at the end of the sentence (*credatis* Zielinski).

[53] *crimine recognoscite*, which could be taken metrically as a resolved Type 2.

3. A ragbag [11]: 11 *ne sit infinitum*; 33[54]; 34[55]; 26[56]; 37 *scelerum reperietis*; 47[57]; 60[58]; 74[59]; 81[60]; 87 *pristinum recuperabit*; 95.[61]
Subtotal 11

# Key

The text of the *Pro Sulla* employed was that of Berry 1996. I neglected the following short commata (I here cite section numbers): 72 *factum quaero*, 80 *quid uero*, 83 *sed quid ego*, 84 *quid ergo*. The hundred sentence-ends, which I have numbered consecutively, can be identified by the following final words (section numbers are given in brackets); any punctuation of Berry's within the quoted words is recorded.

(**69**) 1 moribus dicam; 2 mentesque conuertere; 3 arguitur est ponderandum; 4 natura [nom.] conuerti; (**70**) 5 sceleri fuerunt; 6 rem publicam coniurauit; 7 caede uersatum; 8 natum putauerunt; 9 sperasse miretur; 10 esse uideatur; (**71**) 11 ne sit infinitum; 12 esse damnatum; 13 natura [nom.] conuicit; 14 ipsi succumbere; 15 uita [nom.] conuinceret; (**72**) 16 uestros proponite; 17 consideratum uideretur; 18 posset effundi; 19 misericordior inuentus est; 20 Sulla [abl.] deprecatus; 21 quod fecit, ipsi; (**73**) 22 splendorem in publicis; 23 incohata compareant; 24 ordine multitudo; 25 eripuit hora; 26 accipere potuisse; 27 grauior quam in ceteris; (**74**) 28 lucemque uitare; 29 paene multauit; 30 fuisse creditis; 31 crimine recognoscite; (**75**) 32 proposita [abl.] degeret; 33 ista suspicio; 34 sceleris exarsit; (**76**) 35 patriae sit inuentus; 36 indutae extiterunt; 37 scelerum reperietis; 38 stare potuisse; 39 quaedam incitauerunt; (**77**) 40 numerum transferetis; 41 nihil adiuuabit; (**78**) 42 tormenta minitatur; 43 loci relinquatur; 44 num quae audacia; 45 esse audietur; (**79**) 46 audisse arbitramur; 47 uestra [nom.] moueat; 48 esse testem; 49 perfugia improborum; 50 fingique non posse; (**80**) 51 tandem iuuabit; 52 ipsi tacemus, graue; 53 liceat dignitatem; (**81**) 54 dignitatis adferre; 55 illumque laudarunt; 56 non insequebantur; 57 aliquando amico; 58 aliquid, non credidisse; 59 adessent ceteri; 60 esse grauior; (**82**) 61 adfuerunt reprendantur; 62 dixerunt non adfuerunt; 63 ferri oportere;

[54] *ista suspicio*, both a resolved form of Type 1 and a Tardus.
[55] *sceleris exarsit*, easily taken metrically as a resolved Type 1. Accentually, it is the type of Trispondaicus rejected above, p. 267 n. 27.
[56] *accipere potuisse*, both a Velox and a resolved form of Type 1a.
[57] *uestra* (short final vowel) *moueat*: not happily to be taken as a resolved dichoreus. The rhythm of the sentence depends more on the word-play ('si nihil uos P. Sullae fortuna moueat, iudices, uestra moueat').
[58] *esse grauior*, take, if you will, as a resolved dichoreus.
[59] 'non defenderem, si coniurasset': words put into his own mouth by Cicero, hardly a considered sentence.
[60] *quam necesse fuit*, an unpromising candidate for a resolved Type 1.
[61] *erepta sunt non repetit*: hardly a resolved Type 2.

64 oppressa est res publica; 65 constantissime sensit; 66 grauitatis fuisse; 67 rem publicam conseruandam; (**83**) 68 uitamque defendere; 69 semper oderis; 70 esse uideantur; (**84**) 71 innocens iudicetur; 72 reddo ac remitto; 73 inuidique patiantur; (**85**) 74 defenderem, si coniurasset; 75 coniurasse arbitrarer; 76 esse delatam; (**86**) 77 defendi ac tegi; 78 nihil audiui; (**87**) 79 naturaeque debentur; 80 quam qui lenissimus; 81 quam necesse fuit; 82 illa [nom.] suscepta; 83 uoluntate deducor; (**88**) 84 misericordia [abl.] digna multa; 85 turpitudinis inuratur; 86 perfrui possit; 87 pristinum recuperabit; 88 calamitate occiderunt; 89 filius nominetur; 90 dedecoris relinquat; (**89**) 91 gratulari sinatis; 92 campi et disciplinarum; 93 eiciatur laboramus; 94 uita [nom.] uideatur; 95 erepta sunt non repetit; 96 iudices, obtestatur; (**90**) 97 inimicitiae deduxerunt; 98 expetas amplius; 99 dolore retinetur; 100 foedissimi criminis.

## Postscript

I remarked (several years ago) that 'the inscriptional evidence is (to my knowledge) disappointingly sparse' (above, p. 264). I can now add a long Aretalogy of Isis from Maroneia, said to be dated *c.*150–100 BC, where the quantitative rhythm is all-pervasive. The text is to be found in *Inscriptiones antiquae partis Thraciae quae ad ora maris Aegaei sita est*, ed. Louisa D. Loukopoulou *et al.* (Athens, 2005), E 205, pp. 383–5. At the 28 major pauses I find 14 cretic + spondee clausulae (some with resolutions), 8 dichorees (three preceded by a cretic), and one final cretic. Similar rhythms are often found at minor pauses, where I note 3 cases of cretic + dichoree. I am very grateful for the help of Angelos Chaniotis, but for whom I should not have known of this inscription.

## BIBLIOGRAPHY

Aili, H. 1979, *The Prose Rhythm of Sallust and Livy* (Stockholm).

Berry, D. H. 1996, *Cicero: Pro P. Sulla Oratio* (Cambridge).

Courtney, E. 1999, *Archaic Latin Prose* (Atlanta).

Diggle, J. 2005, 'Rhythmical Prose in the Euripidean Hypotheses', in G. Bastianini and A. Casanova (eds.), *Euripide e i papiri* (Florence), 27–67.

Dörner, F. K., and Goell, T. 1963, *Arsameia am Nymphaios* (Berlin).

Hagendahl, H. 1937, *La Prose métrique d'Arnobe* (Göteborg).

Hercher, R. 1872, *Epistolographi Graeci* (Paris).

Illinois Greek Club (ed.), 1923, *Aeneas Tacticus, Asclepiodotus, Onasander* (Loeb Classical Library; Cambridge, MA, and London).

Innes, D. C., and Winterbottom, M. 1988, *Sopatros the Rhetor* (*BICS* Supplement 48; London).

Janson, T. 1975, *Prose Rhythm in Medieval Latin from the 9th to the 13th Century* (Stockholm).

Keil (ed.), H. 1855–80. *Grammatici Latini*, 7 vols. and supplement (Leipzig)

Nisbet, R. G. M. (ed.), 1961, *M. Tulli Ciceronis in L. Calpurnium Pisonem oratio* (Oxford).

Norden, E. 1958, *Die antike Kunstprosa*, 5th edn. (Stuttgart).

Oliver, J. H. 1989, *Greek Constitutions of Early Roman Emperors* (Philadelphia).

Orlandi, G. 2005, 'Metrical and Rhythmical Clausulae in Medieval Latin Prose: Some Aspects and Problems' in T. Reinhardt, M. Lapidge, and J. N. Adams (eds.), *Aspects of the Language of Latin Prose* (Proceedings of the British Academy, 129; Oxford), 395–412.

Russell, D. A. 1988, 'The Ass in the Lion's Skin: Thoughts on the *Letters of Phalaris*', *JHS* 108, 94–106.

Smallwood, E. M. 1967, *Documents Illustrating the Principates of Gaius, Claudius and Nero* (Cambridge).

Stroh, W. 1990, 'Arsis und Thesis oder: Wie hat man lateinische Verse gesprochen?', in M. von Albrecht & W. Schubert (eds.), *Musik und Dichtung. Neue Forschungs-beiträge, Viktor Pöschl zum 80. Geburtstag gewidmet* (Frankfurt am Main), 87–116; repr. in id., *Apocrypha: Entlegene Schriften*, ed. J. Leonhardt and G. Ott (Stuttgart, 2000), 193–216.

Tcherikover, V. A. 1957–64, *Corpus Papyrorum Judaicarum* (Cambridge, MA).

Tunberg, T. O. 1996, 'Prose Styles and *Cursus*', in F. A. C. Mantello and A. G. Rigg (eds.), *Medieval Latin: An Introduction and Bibliographical Guide* (Washington, DC), 111–21.

Zielinski, T. 1904, *Das Clauselgesetz in Ciceros Reden* (Leipzig).

# 15

## Alexander of Aphrodisias, *De prouidentia*: Greek Fragments and Arabic Versions

### Christoph Riedweg

The fact that an item of Greek 'philosophy in pieces' can at least partly be restored thanks to Arabic sources may be of more than merely antiquarian interest in the present historical circumstances. It highlights common strands of thinking and of *Logos* in both cultures that are all too often neglected in modern reasoning about a 'clash of civilizations'.

One of the favourite philosophers with Arabic culture was the Aristotelian Alexander of Aphrodisias (*c.* AD 200).[1] It is in fact surprising to see how widely read his treatise Περὶ προνοίας has been in the Arabic world, be it Islamic or Hebrew or Christian, ever since the ninth century.[2] Two translations of a quite different stamp have come down to us.[3] The earlier, anonymous one—D15

---

[1] Cf. Badawi 1968, 94 ff.; D'Ancona and Serra 2002; Rashed 2004. On Alexander's life in general Thillet 1984, pp. vii ff.; Sharples 1987, 1177–8; Goulet and Aouad 1989, 125 ff.; Fazzo in Fazzo and Zonta 1998, 72–3, etc. A recently discovered inscription from Aphrodisias shows that Alexander's father too was a philosopher and that both father and son bore the same name Τίτος Αὐρήλιος Ἀλέξανδρος, see Chaniotis 2004a, 388–9; 2004b, 79 ff. (I owe this reference to Ewen L. Bowie); also Sharples 2005, who, moreover, was kind enough to read and comment on an earlier version of the present paper.

[2] Cf. Ruland 1976, 144 ff.; Thillet 1979, i. 60 ff.; 2003, 64 ff.; Zonta in Fazzo and Zonta 1998, 87 ff, 167 ff. The authenticity of the treatise, whose title figures in Ibn 'Abī 'Uṣaybia's catalogue of works (cf. Thillet 1984, pp. liv n. 3, lxvii), is not to be doubted; cf. Thillet 1960, 322–3; 1979, i. 9 ff., 2003, 13 ff.; Fazzo in Fazzo and Zonta 1998, 35–6 n. 49; Fazzo 2000, *passim*). There are plenty of parallels in other writings by the same author, which witness to the intellectual texture characteristic of this Peripatetic (see also the first apparatus of the edition below). Ruland 1976, 133 suggested that *De prouidentia* may be announced in Alex. Aphr. *Quaest.* 2. 21, p. 70. 33 ff. Bruns (cf. Thillet 1979, i. 12–13; 2003, 14; also Burguière and Évieux 1985, 285 n. 1). However, Sharples 2000, 363–4 now offers a different and even more attractive interpretation of this passage (see below, n. 62).

[3] For their relation cf. Ruland 1976, 107 ff.; Fazzo in Fazzo and Zonta 1998, 70–1. A different view in Thillet 2003, 139 ff., who advances the hypothesis that D15 might be the Arabic translation of an apocryphal Greek rewriting of Alexander's Περὶ προνοίας in Neoplatonic and astrological terms.

according to Dietrich's list of preserved Arabic translations of Alexander's works[4]—is commonly attributed to the circle of the famous Islamic philosopher al-Kindī (*c*.800–*c*.870).[5] It covers only part of the treatise;[6] although based directly on the Greek original,[7] the translation strikes one as a rather free reworking of the text with a clear focus of interest: i.e. the influence of the stars according to the Aristotelian understanding of providence. This emerges already from the author's variation of the title of Alexander's work: 'On the Direction of the Spheres'[8] ('Über die himmlischen Leitungen').[9]

The second translation (D18), which we owe to a Christian Arabic philosopher of the tenth century, 'Abū Bišr Mattā ibn Yūnus al-Qunnā'ī (*c*.870–940),[10] favourably contrasts with D15 in its faithfulness to the Greek text, as has since long been recognized and will become even more evident in the course of the present paper.[11] Experts in Arabic, indeed, stress the author's tendency to translate the text as literally as possible, even at the cost of becoming almost incomprehensible: 'la traduzione è spesso così letterale da risultare intelligibile solo a chi sappia leggere e ricostruire, dietro le righe del testo arabo, il dettato del testo greco', according to Mauro Zonta, who also observes that this may partly be due to the fact that the author explicitly based his translation on a Syriac version (Syriac translations notoriously stick extremely closely to the original wording).[12]

Both D15 and D18 have been transmitted side by side in two manuscripts. The present locations of these manuscripts in a sense again bridge the gap between East and West: the earlier one from the thirteenth century belongs to El Escorial in Spain; the other one, from 1477/8, is now to be found in the Süleymaniye Library in Istanbul.[13] Unfortunately, my own knowledge of

---

[4] Dietrich 1964, 97–8.     [5] Cf. on al-Kindī in general Rudolph 2004, 15 ff.

[6] Roughly the second part, starting from p. 34b in Ruland's synoptical translation.

[7] Cf. Fazzo and Wiesner 1993, 129 n. 29; Zonta in Fazzo and Zonta 1998, 87; Thillet 2003, 146.

[8] Fazzo and Wiesner 1993, 129, 131.

[9] 'Abhandlung des Alexander von Aphrodisias über die himmlischen *Leitungen*' (p. 34b. 3–4 Ruland; literally 'Über die leitenden Einflüsse des *Himmels*' according to Ruland 1976, 137. Cf. in general on D15 and its philosophical orientation Ruland 1976, 137 ff. and Fazzo and Wiesner 1993, 129 ff. 131 'It is then clear that D15, unlike D18, appears to be a treatise mostly concerned with the physical and astrological influence of the stars on the world, rather than with the theoretical and philosophical problems connected with the concept of *pronoia* and its formulation in Aristotelian terms', etc.).

[10] For other translations and works by the same Nestorian author see Thillet 1979, i. 14–15; cf. also Dietrich 1964, 114; Badawi 1968, 190.

[11] Its periphrastic title summarizes the first doxographical section of Alexander's treatise, 'Abhandlung des Alexander von Aphrodisias, in der er die Meinung *Demokrits* und *Epikurs* und die übrigen neuartigen (Ansichten) der sonstigen Philosophen über die *Vorsehung* genau darlegt und erklärt' (p. 2. 3 ff. Ruland).

[12] Zonta in Fazzo and Zonta 1998, 88; on Syriac translations in general cf. Brock 2005.

[13] E = Scorial. arab. Derenbourg 798/Casiri 794; S (C in Ruland) = Constantinopolit. Millet-Carullah 1279; see Ruland 1976, pp. v ff.; Zonta in Fazzo and Zonta 1998, 88; Thillet 2003, 11 ff.

Arabic is still limited to phrases like Inshallah and Alhamdulillah, so that I have to rely on modern translations. The problem is, however, eased by the fact that three highly accurate translations of at least D18 are at our disposal. Two of them have been almost simultaneously produced, both originating in doctoral theses: the German one by Ruland (1976), which includes a translation of D15, distinguishes itself particularly by its constant attempt at retrieving original Greek words from the translation;[14] the French translation of D18 by Thillet 1979, which for the first time fully considered the Greek fragments,[15] was not properly published, with a substantial introduction, till 2003.[16] In the meantime, Mauro Zonta had already printed his Italian translation of D18, in close collaboration, for the Greek texts, with Silvia Fazzo (1998).[17] It is in fact a characteristic, if sometimes problematic feature of this Italian edition that for sections where a Greek text is available, the translation is based on this and not on the (Syro-)Arabic version of D18.[18] To make up for my own lack of knowledge of Arabic, I have been able to draw on the expertise of an eminent scholar and colleague at Zurich University, Ulrich Rudolph, who is particularly well versed in the field of the Arabic reception of Greek philosophy and who was kind enough to discuss critical passages with me at length.

As for the Greek fragments, we owe them exclusively to Cyril of Alexandria. Alexander's treatise may have been known to other Greek writers in Antiquity as well,[19] yet the controversial Patriarch was, as it looks at least to date, the only one who literally quoted from Alexander's Περὶ προνοίας. All quotations are to be found in Cyril's refutation of Julian's forceful attack on the Christians, scathingly called 'Galilaeans' by the Emperor in order to demonstrate that the claim of Christianity to be a world-wide religion and not a locally limited phenomenon was flawed and fraudulent right from the

---

[14] The original impulse to provide a literal translation—cf. Ruland 1976, p. ix 'Sie (sc. die Übersetzung) wollte ursprünglich "wörtlich" sein, einmal um den stilistischen Kontrast von D18 und D15 deutlich werden zu lassen, dann um spürbar Griechisches "transparent" zu machen'—remains recognizable throughout the finally published translation.

[15] Cf. already Thillet 1960, 317. Ruland, who did not know Grant's article, was made aware only shortly before publishing his thesis of at least the existence of fr. 2, which Heiland 1925, 1 refers to (cf. Ruland 1976, 234–5).

[16] Thillet 2003 on the whole rather neglects D15, whose authenticity he questions (79, 107 n. 292, 133–4, 139 ff.; cf. above, n. 3).

[17] D15 is at odd moments considered for the reconstruction of the sense by Zonta 1998, 129 n. 30, 137 n. 34, 165 n. 51.

[18] '. . . la traduzione . . ., nei pochi casi in cui il testo greco è sopravvissuto, è stata condotta direttamente su quest'ultimo, relegando in nota le varianti proprie della traduzione araba' (Zonta in Fazzo and Zonta 1998, 93; cf. Fazzo 2000, 402 n. 12). Such a decision, understandable as it may be on principle, involves the risk of underrating the importance of the Arabic tradition for a reconstruction of the text of the Greek fragments.

[19] See Thillet 1979, i. 54 ff.; 2003, 45 ff., who traces the history of Alexander's treatise in the Greek world.

beginning.[20] In an attempt at beating Julian at his own game, Cyril in his massive counter-attack repeatedly resorts to pagan texts otherwise lost: besides Julian's *Κατὰ Γαλιλαίων*, works by Porphyry and extracts from Aristoxenus, particularly to the *Hermetica* and Alexander's *Περὶ προνοίας*. This is one of many reasons why a new critical edition of Cyril's refutation, for which we are basically still relying on Aubert's edition from the seventeenth century,[21] has since long been overdue. The research presented in this paper actually originates from preparing the edition of books 1–5, which I have taken on as member of a project group including Wolfram Kinzig, Martin Ritter, Gerlinde Huber-Rebenich, Stefan Rebenich, and Markus Vinzent. I am particularly happy to offer this contribution to Peter Parsons, whom I met for the first time during an unforgettable and highly formative year at Oxford in 1988–9. It was at the end of this academic year that the rumour spread that Peter, whose notorious modesty and gentleness are rivalled only by his scholarship, had just been appointed to become the new Regius Professor of Greek. I vividly remember the enthusiasm with which this news was universally welcomed.

In an important article of 1964 R. M. Grant for the first time drew general attention to the Greek fragments of Alexander's *On Providence* in Cyril by quoting the relevant passages in translation and summarily commenting on them. Before this, the fragments had gone virtually unnoticed by scholars.[22] The situation has, of course, considerably improved with the Arabic translations becoming generally accessible, and in particular the Italian Hellenist mentioned above, Silvia Fazzo, has produced very valuable pieces of scholarship on the topic in recent years. Yet still much work remains to be done. This is only partly due to the fact that Fazzo was still obliged to use Migne's deficient edition (the text in Migne's *Patrologia Graeca* is basically the one by Spanheim from 1696, who in turn reprinted Aubert's edition of 1638 almost unchanged).[23] What is more, a painstaking consideration and evaluation of the Arabic versions and in particular of D18 can in more than one place decisively contribute to restoring what was most likely the original wording of Alexander's text, or else allows us, at least, to become aware of lacunae, of single words and phrases left out by Cyril.

---

[20] According to Julian, we are dealing with a local phenomenon of Judaea; had it remained locally restricted, it would look fully acceptable to Julian; yet Paul, the greatest impostor ever, successfully made it all up to expand beyond the geographical and ideological limits of Judaeism (*Contra Galilaeos* frr. 19 ff. Masaracchia).

[21] See below.

[22] An exception is Bruns 1890, 223, 234; cf. also Regazzoni 1928, 95. Moraux 1942, 195 ff. did not yet know about the treatise (still id. 1967*a*), but cf. id. 1967*b*, 169 ff.; 1970, 58, etc.; in general Fazzo 2000, 400–1; also Thillet 2003, 10. Burguière and Évieux 1985, 282 ff. n. 1 still ignore the Arabic tradition, and Bergjan 2002, 231 ff. does not take account of the Greek fragments.

[23] Cf. Riedweg and Oesterheld 2000, 418–19.

In numbering the fragments, Grant followed the order of appearance in Cyril's text. It has, however, since then become evident from the Arabic version that Cyril freely jumps from one place to another picking out passages which would suit his own argument. A new numeration of the fragments seems therefore necessary.[24] Cyril's presentation of the material is also in other respects rather misleading, as Grant already suspected[25] and as has now clearly emerged from the Arabic. Not only did he regularly change the plural 'gods' (preserved in the Christian's Arabic translation, which is another proof of its fidelity) into the singular[26]—a procedure well known also from other texts.[27] What is more bewildering, he sometimes did not hesitate to present as Alexander's own opinion what in the original was unmistakably marked out as the teaching of other philosophers.[28] Alexander indeed had started his treatise with a doxographical section, sketching the view concerning providence held by the Atomists and Epicurus, who would entirely deny that providence should govern anything that happens in nature, and then summarizing the diametrically opposed doctrine, which we may reasonably label Stoic.[29] The quotation from Alexander that Cyril adduces to support his reasoning about the necessity of laws and order in human society as well as in nature (where they witness to God's craftsmanship), is introduced by him as the Peripatetic's own opinion (fr. 1), whereas it is in fact the view held by the second, the Stoic group:

The others' view ['Ansicht'] and opinion on philosophy and providence is diametrically opposed to the one [held] by these philosophers [sc. Leucippus, Democritus, Epicurus]. For they maintain . . .'. (D18, p. 4. 19 ff. Ruland; throughout this paper, if not otherwise stated, I am following the extremely accurate German translation by Ruland, which in the main body of the article I have rendered into English for the convenience of the English-speaking reader, sticking to the German translation as literally as possible.)

Editors always have to make clear whether they are restoring the original wording of the source or the wording of the author quoting from that source. This principle is all too often neglected particularly in editions of later Greek texts, where the temptation to emend a quotation according to its original

---

[24] Already Thillet 1979, i. 58–9; 2003, 54 ff. followed the Arabic version in presenting the fragments.

[25] Cf. Grant 1964, 276 ff.          [26] Cf. Fazzo 2000, 404 with n. 19.

[27] Cf. e.g. Riedweg 1990.

[28] Cf. Fazzo 2000, 405, 416, who suggests the hypothesis that Cyril might be quoting Alexander's Περὶ προνοίας from a second-hand source, which she thinks could explain the changes. Slightly different is her view on p. 418, where a preparatory phase envisaged in which Cyril and/or his collaborator/s made extracts from 'l'eredità più fruibile, da un punto di vista cristiano, dell'antichità classica e della filosofia non cristiana'; the two theories are harmonized at the end of the article on p. 419.

[29] It is characteristic of Alexander of Aphrodisias to avoid mentioning the Stoics; cf. Thillet 2003, 15 regarding also Alexander's Περὶ εἱμαρμένης.

seems hard to resist; yet quotations may always, of course, have been altered on purpose or deviations may be due to a misunderstanding or an error by the author of the source. In the present case, it is perfectly clear that nothing has to be changed in Cyril's text,[30] whereas for Alexander himself the conjecture <φαϲι> after γίνεϲθαι virtually suggests itself (Alexander has a fondness for the expression γίνεϲθαί φαϲι):[31]

For <they maintain> that nothing in the world happens without providence, because everything [they say] is full of the divine and it pervades all that is.

As for the rest of this fragment portraying the Stoic doctrine of divine providence, the Arabic translation D18 clearly brings to the fore two more lacunae in Cyril's quotation. The first one, which is quite substantial, follows after 'Therefore also all that comes into being does so according to the will of the gods': instead of the plural τῶν θεῶν to be restored from the Arabic translation, Cyril offers at this place the singular τοῦ θεοῦ, which may also have triggered off his omission of the phrase that follows in the Arabic version: 'insofar as they care for the things and guide each of them' (or, in Thillet's translation, 'du fait qu'ils sont les garants et les administrateurs de chacune d'elles').[32] As Ulrich Rudolph tells me, the Arabic construction here uses a participle, which can also serve as a noun. I would therefore suggest as an *exempli gratia* supplement <ὡϲ φυλαϲϲόντων τε καὶ διοικούντων ἕκαϲτον αὐτῶν>, the verb διοικεῖν being quite popular particularly in Stoic contexts.[33]

The two manuscripts transmitting the Arabic text offer different readings for the last sentence of this fragment. It emerges clearly, however, that Cyril's

---

[30] For the convenience of the reader, I would however hint at the alterations of the original by introducing ellipsis points . . . before the beginning of the quotation and at the place where Cyril left out Alexander's φαϲι.

[31] The TLG offers five passages.

[32] Cf. 'inquantoché questi ultimi sono i custodi e gli amministratori di ciascuna di esse' (Zonta). Fazzo 2000, 406–7, too, considers this phrase to be original.

[33] Cf. Chrys. frr. 528, 937, 945 (*SVF* ii. 169. 33, 269. 18, 272. 38 ff.) = Alex. Aphr. *De fato* 22, p. 43. 7 ff. Thillet φαϲὶν δὴ τὸν κόϲμον τόνδε, . . . ὑπὸ φύϲεωϲ διοικούμενον ζωτικῆϲ τε καὶ λογικῆϲ καὶ νοερᾶϲ, ἔχειν τὴν τῶν ὄντων διοίκηϲιν ἀΐδιον κατὰ εἱρμόν τινα καὶ τάξιν προιοῦϲαν κτλ.; moreover, Alex. Aphr. *Mant.* 2, p. 113. 11–12 Bruns αὐτὴ δὲ [sc. ἡ φύϲιϲ] τὰ καθέκαϲτα μετὰ τοῦ νοῦ διοικεῖ. See also Ps.-Arist. *De mundo* 6, 398ᵇ4 ff., arguing against the Stoic doctrine, ὥϲτε, εἴπερ ἄϲεμνον ἦν αὐτὸν αὐτῶι δοκεῖν Ξέρξην αὐτουργεῖν ἅπαντα καὶ ἐπιτελεῖν ἃ βούλοιτο καὶ ἐφιϲτάμενον <ἑκαϲταχοῦ> διοικεῖν, πολὺ μᾶλλον ἀπρεπὲϲ ἂν εἴη θεῶι κτλ. For φυλάττειν cf. e.g. Alex. Aphr. *Mant.* 25, p. 181. 22 ff. Bruns ἐν γὰρ τοῖϲ ἐπιτηδείοιϲ ὅϲον ἐπὶ τῆι φυϲικῆι παραϲκευῆι πρὸϲ τὰ ἀντικείμενα τῆϲ εἱμαρμένηϲ ἰϲχὺϲ εἶναι δοκεῖ, ἐν θατέρωι τῶν ἀντικειμένων κατέχουϲα αὐτὰ καὶ φυλάττουϲα κατά τινα τάξεωϲ ἀκολουθίαν. ἃ γὰρ οὐκ ἂν οὕτωϲ ἔχοι ἄνευ τῆϲ εἱμαρμένηϲ, ταῦτα παρὰ τῆϲ εἱμαρμένηϲ ἐν τῆιδε τῆι τάξει φυλάττεϲθαι δοκεῖ· τοιαῦτα δέ ἐϲτιν οὐκ ἄλλα τινὰ τῶν ὄντων ἢ τὰ ἐν γενέϲει καὶ φθορᾶι· ὥϲτε ἐνταῦθά που καὶ τὸ τῆϲ εἱμαρμένηϲ; Ps.-Arist. *De mundo* 2, 391ᵇ10 ff. λέγεται δὲ καὶ ἑτέρωϲ κόϲμοϲ ἡ τῶν ὅλων τάξιϲ τε καὶ διακόϲμηϲιϲ, ὑπὸ θεοῦ τε καὶ διὰ θεὸν φυλαττομένη.

quotation is again incomplete.[34] Adopting the reading of the Constantinopolitanus (S), Thillet translates: 'Car la suite et l'ordre des choses qui existent par nature . . .'. The reading of the El Escorial manuscript (E) also unmistakeably indicates that a second noun must have stood in the original, even if it is in this tradition grammatically linked with τάξις: literally 'For the sticking ['das Anhaften': *luzūm*, from the verb *lazima*, a word that also seems to cover the idea of a logical conclusion] of things, that are by nature, to order . . .' (Ulrich Rudolph; cf. Ruland 'For the *dependence* of natural processes from an eternal and unchangeable order'). I would therefore venture to add <ἀκολουθία καί> in the text. And in fact, the combination of ἀκολουθία and τάξις occurs rather frequently in Alexander, which makes the proposed conjecture look extremely likely. Particularly relevant are two passages, where Alexander describes the Stoic doctrine of providence and fate:

Alex. Aphr. *Mant.* 25, p. 185. 1 ff. Bruns ἀλλὰ μὴν ὁμολογεῖται πάντα τὰ καθ' εἱμαρμένην γιγνόμενα <u>κατὰ τάξιν καὶ ἀκολουθίαν</u> γίγνεσθαί τινα καί τι ἐφεξῆς ἔχειν ἐν αὐτοῖς. οὐ γὰρ δὴ τοῖς ἀπὸ τύχης ὅμοια τὰ τῆς εἱμαρμένης κτλ.

Alex. Aphr. *De fato* 34, p. 65. 21–2 Thillet ταῦτα γὰρ οὕτως ἔχει <u>ἀκολουθίας τε καὶ τάξεως.</u>

Both passages are included in Hans von Arnim's *Stoicorum Veterum Fragmenta* (Chrys. frr. 920, 1002, *SVF* ii. 266. 8 ff., 295. 23–4 respectively). The same should have applied to fr. 1 of Alexander's Περὶ προνοίας, whose textual emendation is therefore of importance not only for Alexander, but also for the history of Stoic (and anti-Stoic) thinking.

The second fragment, and this again is obliterated by Cyril's way of quoting it, still belongs to Alexander's doxographical summary of the Stoic doctrine of providence.[35] It would therefore be another natural candidate for inclusion in a new edition of the *Stoicorum Veterum Fragmenta*. The comparison with the Arabic translation is also in this case for various reasons highly revealing. First of all, it shows that Cyril is not greatly concerned with the thread of the argument, since he omits the first half of a chain of reasoning, by which Alexander's Stoics try to make the conclusion inevitable, that the gods, as a consequence of their specific status, must look after the world, on the analogy of the lord of a house, who would always do the same in his realm. The only theoretical objection that might be proposed would, according to Alexander's Stoics, be that the gods were either lacking in both power and will, or else that,

---

[34] A different view in Fazzo 2000, 407, 'amplificazione esegetica per opera di chi curò la versione araba'.

[35] Cf. also Fazzo 2000, 406, whose interpretation of Πάντα γὰρ εἶναι μεστὰ τοῦ θείου as a Christianization against the Arabic 'Tutte le cose sono piene di dio', however, I would call into question (the difference between the sing. θεός and the abstract τὸ θεῖον should not be overrated).

despite having enough power, they remained unwilling to take care of things on earth.[36] The first of these two possibilities is entirely disregarded by Cyril, with the consequence that it becomes virtually impossible to understand, what ἑκάτερον, ἄμφω, and θάτερον are referring to in the section he quotes. In the Arabic translation, the sentences preceding Cyril's quotation run as follows:

For (the Stoics say) if they do not exert providence over things on earth, they [do not do so] *either* because they do not want to [most likely βούλεσθαι] and also are not capable [δύνασθαι], *or*, because they are, of course, capable, but do not wish to provide for things on earth and therefore leave them without providence. And if one of these sub-possibilities is unworthy of gods, then it is refuted. For that gods are not *able* to provide over things on earth, [sc. they hold] to be a statement completely unworthy of gods (a *contradictio in adiecto*). For according to that statement God is *less* able than human beings, because for the latter it is not too difficult or impossible to administer their houses, yet for the gods [to administer] correspondingly [the universe] is supposedly too difficult and impossible! (p. 6. 22 ff. Ruland.)

At this point, Cyril steps in, replacing again the plural 'gods' by the singular form at the beginning,[37] where an editor of Alexander will therefore have to emend the text into Τὸ δὲ λέγειν μὴ βούλεσθαι τοὺς θεοὺς τῶν ἐνταῦθα προνοεῖν παντελῶς ἀλλότριον θεῶν. In the next sentence I would propose to change Cyril's somewhat odd Φθόνου γάρ τινος into Φθον<ερ>οῦ γάρ τινος, for two reasons: first, that is what the Arabic says: 'the behaviour of someone who is *envious*', and second, the noun φθόνος, unlike φύσις, can hardly stand for the person herself or himself.

This is, of course, a minor change. Yet in the following sentence, which draws the conclusion to the preceding alternatives, Cyril is evidently again quoting the original rather freely, first by again changing the plural 'gods' into the singular and then by skipping not only a further predicate of ἑκάτερον but also the whole second part of the subordinate clause introduced by Ἐπειδὴ δέ:

But if [sc. they say] *each one* of these two properties is incompatible with the gods' nature and at variance [with it], and if also both *together* would not befit God . . . (p. 8. 13 ff. Ruland.)

The word translated by Ruland as 'is at variance ('im Widerspruch stehe')' is derived from a root with the basic meaning 'to part with ['sich trennen von'], be unlike' according to Ulrich Rudolph, and then only 'to be at variance with'. It would seem to me that the Greek διαφέρειν covers more or

[36] Cf. for this type of argument, going back to Plato's *Laws*, Sharples 1995, 6 ff.; 2003, 116 ff.; Thillet 2003, 88–9 n. 243 ad loc.; sim. Alex. Aphr. *De prou.* interp. Arab. D18, p. 24. 16 ff., 26. 22 ff. Ruland.
[37] Cf. Fazzo 2000, 406.

less the various shades of meaning contained in the Arabic word, so that one might risk putting <καὶ διαφέρον> as a supplement into Alexander's text (Alexander is quite fond of participial expressions like διαφέρον or -τα τινός, and at one place he even combines διαφέροντα and ἀλλότρια).[38]

As for the second part of the subordinate clause 'and if also both *together* do not befit God' (which by the way takes up the first reason why the gods according to Alexander's Stoics might possibly not exert any providence),[39] any attempt at supplementing must necessarily remain highly hypothetical. But I should think that something like <καὶ δὴ καὶ ἀμφότερα ἅμα τῶι θείωι οὐχ ὑπάρχει> may not be completely off the mark (the Arabic literally means, according to Ulrich Rudolph, 'and both the properties [sc. are] not for God', i. e. 'do not befit him, belong to him', which could well render the Greek expression ὑπάρχειν τινί; see e.g. Alex. Aphr. *In Arist. Top.* p. 163. 3 ff. Wallies ἀλλὰ καὶ εἰ λέγοι τις τὸν θεὸν ἐμπαθῆ, δεῖ αὐτὸν ἢ ἥδεσθαι ἢ λυπεῖσθαι ἢ φοβεῖσθαι ἢ ἐπιθυμεῖν· εἰ δὲ μηδὲν τούτων εὔλογον τῶι θεῶι ὑπάρχειν, ἀναιροῖτ' ἂν καὶ τὸ εἶναι αὐτὸν ἐμπαθῆ). Considering that Alexander in the preceding phrases seems to have used the plural θεοί and that the neuter τὸ θεῖον is the subject in the subsequent clause, I would assume that already the singular 'God' in the Arabic version stands for the Greek τῶι θείωι, which entails emending περὶ αὐτὸν into περὶ αὐτὸ[ν] (of course only when editing Alexander!). Incidentally, it was thanks to the Arabic translation that scholars finally became aware that the doxographical clause Ταύτης δὲ τῆς δόξης κτλ. still forms part of Alexander's argument and not of Cyril's, as editors of the latter, following manuscripts VM (but not F!),[40] wrongly suggested.[41]

Fragments 3 and 4 are extracted from a later section of Alexander's treatise: Both extreme positions on providence, as sketched at the beginning of the treatise, have in the meantime been refuted, and Alexander is now developing the Aristotelian doctrine.[42] The gains of a careful comparison of the Greek wording with the Arabic one are somewhat less impressive in these cases. The Arabic version of the first clause of fr. 3 runs slightly differently from the Greek text, the equivalent of ἀΐδιον referring to both γένεσιν and διαμονή.[43] Moreover, another adjective seems to have been added to ἀΐδιον (literally 'essential/substantial ['wesentlich/wesensbedingt'] and eternal': Ulrich

[38] *In Arist. Mete.* p. 181. 7 ff. Hayduck τὸ μὲν γὰρ θερμὸν συγκριτικὸν μὲν τῶν ὁμογενῶν φαμεν, διακριτικὸν δὲ τῶν διαφερόντων τε καὶ ἀλλοτρίων.
[39] Cf. p. 6. 23–4 Ruland 'so *entweder*, weil sie es nicht möchten und auch nicht könnten'.
[40] For the textual transmission of Cyril's *Against Julian* cf. Riedweg 2000.
[41] See Fazzo 2000, 404; Thillet 2003, 56 n. 179.
[42] A detailed table of contents of the Arabic version D18 in Ruland 1976, 150 ff. and Fazzo in Fazzo and Zonta 1998, 42 ff.; cf. Thillet 1979, i. 53; 2003, 83.
[43] For once, Ruland seems here to have made a mistake in relating the word to σωτηρίαν ('Die ewige Selbsterhaltung der irdischen Dinge').

Rudolph), for which, however, I cannot see a suitable place in the Greek text.[44] In the following sentence, the Arabic supplies the moon in addition to 'the sun and the other stars'. It must remain open whether this was the original reading or rather an addition by the translator; however, in view of passages like Alex. Aphr. *In Arist. Mete.* p. 143. 32–3 Hayduck ἡ ὄψις περὶ τὸν ἥλιον ἢ τὴν σελήνην ἢ δηλονότι τῶν ἄλλων τι ἄστρων and *De prou.* interp. Arab. D18, p. 52. 7–8 Ruland 'the discussion about sun, moon and all the other stars', I am inclined to put <καὶ τῆς σελήνης> into the text.

In refuting again the Stoic conception of divine providence, which assumes the divine itself to be responsible for and active in the origin and preservation of life on earth, Alexander insists in fr. 4, that the gods' most adequate and best activity is rather θεωρία, which they carry out 'continuously and uninterruptedly'. The Arabic version talks in this context of the 'activities through which God exists and through which he is what he is' (p. 56. 2–3 Ruland). Zonta proposes to interpret this as 'endiadi per il greco τὸ εἶναι αὐτῶι'.[45] However, since ὑπάρχειν and εἶναι are sometimes connected in Alexander,[46] I would rather suggest that we should restore the Greek text according to the Arabic and write <τὸ ὑπάρχειν> καὶ τὸ εἶναι.

Unfortunately, for three more fragments in Cyril no equivalent passages in the Arabic versions have come down to us. There are, however, interesting points of contact in the line of argument, which give us some clue as to the original place of at least two of the fragments. In Cyril's *Against Julian* 3. 9 we read (fr. 5 of Alexander's *On Providence*):

One may see in precisely these examples the favour of the divine nature towards us. For since it was not possible that by nature the virtues should be in us, it gave [sc. us] the power, over which it had the authority [ἧς ἦν αὕτη κυρία], and made the acquisition of the virtues not dependent on some others, but on ourselves, so that what was impossible for us to get from it, we might receive through ourselves as from it. If actually we were able to have the virtues on the ground of nature, no room would have been left for wickedness. But since this is impossible—for nature goes only so far as to make us capable of receiving the virtues—necessarily everything capable of

---

[44] I actually wonder whether the two adjectives may not be considered some kind of periphrasis of ἀΐδιον (cf. also the rendering of ἀτόπου φύσεως in fr. 2 with 'dessen Natur ein Höchstmaß an Verworfenheit, Verdorbenheit und Untätigkeit ... aufweise'; see Fazzo 2000, 404 n. 16 and Thillet 2003, 89 n. 247 ad loc. 'Ces trois mots rendent l'unique ἄτοπος de Cyrille'). Or have we to reckon with the influence of Aristotle's famous passage on the συνεχὴς γένεσις (and φθορά) in GC 2. 10. 336ᵃ15 ff.? For the Arabic translation of this fragment in general see Fazzo 2000, 407–8.

[45] Zonta 1998, 137 n. 34; cf. Thillet 2003, 111 n. 299 'peut être une redondance'.

[46] Cf. in particular Alex. Aphr. *In Arist. Metaph.* p. 431. 10 ff. Hayduck ἀλλ᾽ ἔστιν ἐν πράγμασι ψεῦδος τὸ μὴ εἶναι μηδὲ ὑπάρχειν αὐτό, ὥσπερ καὶ ἀληθὲς ἂν εἴη πάλιν ἐν πράγμασι τὸ ὑπάρχειν αὐτὰ καὶ τὸ εἶναι, οὐχ ὁμοίως τῶι λέγειν αὐτὰ εἶναι; see also 285. 19 ff. and id. *In sens.* 116. 11 ff. Wendland; also Arist. *De caelo* 2. 14. 297ᵇ22 etc.

receiving something to which there is an opposite is capable of receiving the opposite as well. (Transl. by R. M. Grant, modified by Ch. R.).[47]

This is sound Aristotelian teaching, as developed in *Ethica Nicomachea* 2. 1. 1103ᵃ23 ff., 3. 7, 1113ᵇ6 ff. (cf. also Alex. Aphr. *De fato* 27, p. 51. 21 ff.; *Eth. probl.* 29, p. 161. 20 ff. Bruns; *Mant, p.* 121. 26–7 Bruns). As we may gather from the beginning of the fragment, Alexander introduced the human capability of receiving virtues at this point as another example of the many favours which the divine nature has bestowed on human beings: it has equipped us also in the ethical realm with all that is needed to live a good life, even if it seems to have encountered some resistance, which limited its sphere of action.

That is precisely what Alexander has made clear on the last pages of the Arabic translations.[48] Nature, he says, has definitely privileged man as against all other creatures. She not only puts food at our disposal, wherever we go, but also offers us, beyond the essentials, what makes human life perfect: the power (most likely δύναμις in the Greek version) of λόγος and νοῦς, which allows us to compensate for all shortcomings (p. 98. 1 ff. Ruland).[49] But since it is only a power and therefore potential, humans as such are imperfect and feeble. Moreover matter, with its characteristic weakness, cannot always fully oblige the Creator:[50]

Well, *matter* because of its specific weakness, which is inherent in it, cannot in all cases comply with and follow the *Creator*, who coins [or realizes] the form that is [potentially] extant in it, but in some cases it [sc. matter] is far away from it and unable to do it. Because, for the things on earth, which, as is known, draw their existence *out* of matter, it [sc. matter] is not in all respects the cause for their preserving the *continuity* of order: for what is able to be *and* not to be, is only the foundation and *basis* for what comes into being. (p. 104. 3 ff. Ruland.)

The translation by ʾAbū Bišr Mattā ibn Yūnus (D18) abruptly breaks off at this point: 'The treatise is finished, and praise be [given] to God lavishly; as he is, are his [sc. people].' It seems quite plain that this paragraph is not a very suitable end to a treatise on divine providence.[51] And indeed, the less accurate

[47] Cf. for the syllogisms in the second half Fazzo 2000, 411–15 n. 34.

[48] Cf. also Fazzo 2000, 412–13.    [49] Quoted below.

[50] Cf. also Ruland 1976, 136; there are some parallels with Numen. fr. 52 des Places (cf. Thillet 2003, 44–5), who however goes as far as to call matter *causam malorum.*

[51] Cf., however cautiously, already Thillet 1979, i. 59 'Faut-il admettre que notre traduction a été faite sur un texte lacuneux?' etc.; also Zonta in Fazzo and Zonta 1998, 165 n. 51: 'Il testo di D18 si interrompe così. Diamo la traduzione della chiusa di D15 . . ., che continua l'argomentazione e potrebbe essere ispirata ad un testo più completo dell'opera'; Thillet 2003, 59 'L'absence, dans la version arabe, du passage cité par Cyrille [sc. fr. 6 = fr. 4 Grant], pourrait être un motif d'admettre que cette traduction ne donne pas le texte entier de l'ouvrage'; as emerges from the following n. 184, Thillet thought that this fragment should have had its place somewhere within the Arabic translation, 'Ce ne serait donc pas seulement la fin du traité (comme le remarque M. Zonta 1998, 165, n. 51) qui manquerait.' Cf. ibid. 133–4.

rendering from the Kindī circle (D15) carries on at least for a short while, talking about the double nature of matter which is receptive of privation (στέρησις) as well as of form (and therefore at the same time striving and not striving at perfection and eternity). 'And for this reason fault sometimes enters into the earthly world, not on account of the heavenly bodies, but of matter, as we have shown and explained' (p. 106. 3 ff. Ruland). In this version, too, the translation thereafter ends on a negative note (error caused by matter), for the few sentences that still follow in D15 are evidently nothing more than an attempt by the translator at rounding off his work, highlighting again its physical and astrological focus as expressed in the title 'On the Direction of the Spheres'.[52] There can be hardly any doubt that after this clarification as to the problems caused by matter, some positive remarks on the beneficial activity of providence would have followed in the original.

And that is exactly what we get in fr. 5 and also in fr. 6. Both fragments talk about ethical and intellectual potentialities which divine nature or providence has granted to human beings, potential gifts whose realization entirely lies with the individual (virtue, contemplation of the divine realm of being). Fr. 5 has left clear traces in the 18th chapter entitled 'On the Eternal Providence' of the 'Metaphysics' by the Iraqi philosopher ʿAbd-al-Laṭīf al-Baġdādī (1162–1231),[53] where it actually follows a passage which precisely corresponds to the final observations of D18 concerning the potential of the human intellect to make up for all shortcomings and to acquire happiness.[54]

Interestingly enough, the beginning of fr. 6 refers to an earlier passage, where the same topic—i.e. that 'our greatest happiness lies in pious reverence

---

[52] 'Und es ist jetzt klar und offensichtlich, wie die Himmelskörper die irdische Welt *ganzheitlich* leiten. (Was) aber die *Teil*leitung (angeht), so hat der Philosoph in dem Buch, das *Astrologie* heißt, mit überzeugenden, unwiderlegbaren Worten dargelegt, wie diese vor sich geht. Das ist das Ende dessen, was wir von diesem Traktat gefunden haben. Er ist zu Ende, und Preis sei Gott in Fülle für seine reichliche Hilfe. Wie er ist, so sind die Seinen. Die Abhandlung des Alexander über die himmlischen Leitungen ist zu Ende' (p. 106. 5 ff. Ruland). To judge from the wording ('Das ist das Ende dessen, was wir von diesem Traktat gefunden haben'), it seems likely that already the source/s of the two Arabic translators was/were incomplete.

[53] Cf. in general on this philosopher Neuwirth 1976, 1* ff., 263 ff.

[54] Cf. p. 216 of the German translation of this chapter in Rosenthal 1965, 214 ff. 'Dem Menschen ist die intellektuelle Potenz zur Behebung jeder Art von Mängeln gegeben worden. Sie ermöglicht es ihm, die Tätigkeit auszuüben, welche ihn zum Erwerb der ihm und jedem einzelnen Individuum zustehenden Glückseligkeit treibt. Sie ermöglicht es uns, die göttlichen Dinge zu erkennen' etc. (corresponding to Alex. Aphr. *De prou.* p. 100. 1 ff. Ruland) and p. 217 'So ist uns die Potenz zum Erwerb der Tugenden gegeben, und deren Erwerb unserem freien Willen und unserer Erwerbstätigkeit überlassen worden ... Könnten wir die Tugenden von Natur aus ohne diese uns zu ihrem Erwerb gegebene Potenz aufnehmen, würde die Schlechtigkeit nirgendwo mehr Platz finden, und wir würden nicht mehr nach Vornehmheit und Wissen verschieden sein. Da dies jedoch nicht möglich ist, gehen die Bemühungen der Natur dahin, uns zur Aufnahme der Tugenden zu bewegen. Daraus folgt, daß wir auch die Laster aufnehmen. Denn alles, was ein Gegenteil hat, muß notwendigerweise auch dies aufnehmen können, und die Laster sind das Gegenteil der Tugenden' etc. (corresponding almost literally to Alex. Aphr. *De prou.* fr. 5; cf. also Thillet 2003, 59).

towards the divine'—was already briefly mentioned ($o\hat{v}$ $\kappa a\grave{\iota}$ $\delta\iota\grave{a}$ $\tau\hat{\omega}\nu$ $\mathring{\eta}\delta\eta$ $\pi\rho o\epsilon\iota\rho\eta\mu\acute{\epsilon}\nu\omega\nu$ $\mathring{\epsilon}\pi$' $\mathring{o}\lambda\acute{\iota}\gamma o\nu$ $\mathring{\epsilon}\mu\nu\eta\mu o\nu\epsilon\acute{v}\sigma a\mu\epsilon\nu$). And, indeed, we not only read in the last section of D18 about the gifts of the divine, which enable us to live a life that is reputed to be the most perfect, but also about the true happiness that consists in the knowledge of the divine by means of the $\nu o\hat{v}\varsigma$:[55]

*Like* a human being that prefers his favourite children and holds [them] in higher regard, nature not only gives us the *essential goods*, but also does not let us lack or want for any of the *other* goods: as an example one may refer to those that can be provided for a life that is considered to be the *most perfect*. (p. 98. 9 ff. Ruland.)

Out of it [sc. the power of Nûs] he also accomplishes activities that express his desire of possessing the *full happiness* that befits him. For the knowledge of the divine is bestowed on us only from the *Nûs*: the knowledge, which is characteristic of us and through which we *differ* from all other living beings and surpass [them] in rank! (p. 100. 13 ff. Ruland.)

Fr. 6 further develops this very idea, offering in the second half a philosophical interpretation along Aristotelian lines:[56]

It is right not to omit this either, which also has been granted by the divine providence to mankind, and which we mentioned briefly also in the preceding. It is that in piety toward the divine lies our greatest happiness, not that we expect because of this some external rewards from it, but that in worship of it we attain the greatest of goods.[57]

It is an acknowledged truth that happiness for men has its culmination in contemplation. For this is the activity of the most important faculty of the soul, which is the one in accordance with the mind. For contemplation is the true knowledge of the best among beings. The best of all beings are the divine. Therefore in the knowledge of the divine is our happiness. (Cyr. *CI* 3. 17; translation by R. M. Grant, slightly modified.)

This tallies well with Aristotle, who in his *Nicomachean Ethics* maintains that perfect happiness consists in the activity of the best part of a human being, i. e. of his $\nu o\hat{v}\varsigma$, in its best possible way, i. e. in $\theta\epsilon\omega\rho\epsilon\hat{\iota}\nu$ (*EN* 10. 7–8). Since fr. 5 deals with ethics in a rather basic sense (acquisition of virtue in general, including the $\beta\acute{\iota}o\varsigma$ $\pi\rho a\kappa\tau\iota\kappa\acute{o}\varsigma$), and since the hierarchy of $\theta\epsilon\omega\rho\acute{\iota}a$ over

---

[55] Cf. also Fazzo 2000, 413–14.

[56] The observation by Sharples 2002, 13 'But . . . the mystical approach is present in Alexander potentially rather than in actuality; and the point appears at the conclusion of *On Providence*—once again, it is not developed' needs therefore some modification in the light of this fragment. Genequand 2001, 161, commenting on Alex. Aphr. *De mundo* 98–9, pp. 96/7 Genequand 'and the highest bliss which encompasses all praiseworthy things is to think that thing (sc. the First Mover), since true perfection for men resides in philosophical contemplation as has been shown elsewhere', which could well refer to *De prou.* fr. 6, similarly takes no account of our fragment.

[57] Cf. Alex. Aphr. *In Arist. An. prior.* p. 5. 20–1 Wallies $\mathring{a}\lambda\lambda\grave{a}$ $\kappa a\grave{\iota}$ $\mu\acute{\epsilon}\gamma\iota\sigma\tau o\nu$ $\tau\hat{\omega}\nu$ $\mathring{a}\nu\theta\rho\omega\pi\acute{\iota}\nu\omega\nu$ $\mathring{a}\gamma a\theta\hat{\omega}\nu$ $\mathring{\eta}$ $\theta\epsilon\omega\rho\acute{\iota}a$; id. *De prou.* interp. Arab. D18, p. 102. 1 ff. Ruland '(. . .) insoweit die Kenntnis von den (Göttern) das *höchste Gut* ist—für uns, die wir eine Kraft haben, die weiß, daß die göttlichen Himmelskörper unter allen existierenden Dingen am *besten* sind! Denn die göttliche Kraft bzw. Vorsehung für die anderen Dinge, auf die sie sich in der bekannten Art erstreckt, ist auch für den Menschen Ursache aller Güter.'

πρᾶξις is taken for granted by Alexander,[58] the conclusion seems warranted beyond reasonable doubt that fr. 5 originally preceded fr. 6 in Alexander's treatise. The latter will have served as a kind of climax to the whole exposition of the Aristotelian doctrine of providence, praising its most sublime effects.

Fr. 7 is thematically extremely close to fr. 6, so that one would like to know how it relates to it: is it simply a doublet (Alexander seems rather fond of repeating the same or similar thoughts in different places)?[59] Could Cyril himself have freely reformulated fr. 6? Or are we dealing with a reworking of the passage of the Arabic translation D18 quoted above (p. 100. 13 ff. Ruland)? We just do not know. If both fragments belonged to the same treatise, the somewhat tentative introduction in fr. 7 'But possibly one should speak the truth' would suggest, that it came before fr. 6 in the original. Grant, who did not yet know about the Arabic translations, indeed proposed that fr. 6 at its beginning referred to fr. 7.[60] I wonder, however, whether the fact that Cyril in fr. 7 gives a slightly different title—not just Περὶ τῆς προνοίας, but Περὶ τῆς καθ' ἕκαστα προνοίας—should not be taken seriously:[61] It might well be that Alexander has written two treatises on providence and that fr. 7 belongs to the second.[62]

Be that as it may, I hope that it has become clear how mutually illuminating are the Greek and the Arabic traditions in this case of philosophical 'culture in pieces'. Both Cyril's quotations and the Arabic translations, in particular D18, decisively contribute to reconstructing Alexander's *On Providence*. It seems indeed possible to recover this treatise to a surprising degree. The original wording can, of course, be retrieved mainly from Cyril. Yet, the (Syro-)Arabic version D18 has proven to be even more reliable and faithful to the original than previously thought: there are quite a substantial number of

---

[58] Cf. Alex. Aphr. *In Arist. Top.* 3. 1, p. 236. 21 ff. Wallies πάλιν εἰ ζητεῖται πότερον αἱρετώτερον θεωρία ἢ πρᾶξις, δεικνύοιτο ἂν ὅτι θεωρία τῶι εἶναι περὶ τὰ τιμιώτερα τὴν ἐνέργειαν αὐτῆι (ἡ μὲν γὰρ πρᾶξις περὶ τὰ πρακτά τε καὶ ἐφ' ἡμῖν, ἡ δὲ θεωρία περὶ τὰ θεῖα), καὶ ἐπειδὴ τῶι τιμιωτάτωι τῆς ψυχῆς γίνεται· τιμιώτατον γὰρ ὁ νοῦς τῶν τῆς ψυχῆς δυνάμεων, οὗ ἐνέργεια ἡ θεωρία.

[59] Cf. the apparatus with parallel passages to the fragments.          [60] Grant 1964, 279.

[61] A different view in Fazzo 2000, 415, 419, who, by the way, rightly corrects Migne by attributing the phrase Τούτων γὰρ οὕτως ἐχόντων . . . κείμενον still to Alexander (411).

[62] Cf. already Thillet 1979, i. 59; 2003, 59 (that 'Abd al-Laṭīf al-Baġdādī should have known this second treatise, as Thillet suggests, seems, however, rather doubtful; cf. Zonta in Fazzo and Zonta 1998, 91–2 and infra on fr. 5). In a different way, Sharples 2000, 364 reckons with two treatises on providence by Alexander, a reworking of the topic being announced, as he thinks, at the end of *Quaest.* 2. 21, 'it seems to me that a natural way to see *Quaestio* 2. 21 is as the beginning of an attempt . . . to cast the doctrines of the treatise *On Providence* into a different literary form [sc. a dialogue]. Such repackagings of material from one work in the form of another are not without parallel in the body of work attributed to Alexander, the last section of the *Mantissa* . . . looks like an attempt, whether by Alexander himself or by another, to present material fromt the treatise *On Fate* in a more positive and more systematic form' etc. It may be worth mentioning that another Arabic author, Ǧābir ibn Ḥayyān, also uses a different title ('De la Providence première', Thillet 2003, 66) in quoting a passage which is not to be found in either D15 and D18 or the Greek fragments.

passages where only thanks to a careful consideration of ʾAbū Bišr Mattā ibn Yūnus's translation are we still in a position to realize that Cyril has changed the text or omitted something, be it for ideological reasons, through misunderstanding, or from simple lack of care.[63] For the original sequence of the Greek fragments too the Arabic version D18 is of vital importance, since Cyril picks out passages from Alexander's text according to his own needs, paying no heed to the line of thought in the original. At the same time, at least two of Cyril's quotations for which there is no equivalent in the Arabic texts allow us to recognize that most probably neither of the Arabic translations covers the whole of Alexander's Περὶ προνοίας. The fragments rather indicate that the treatise will have culminated in a hymnic exaltation of the highest human activity made possible by providence: the contemplation of the divine principles of the world.

Both Orient and Occident substantially contributing to piecing together and mending a scattered tradition—this is a reassuring idea these days.[64]

## ALEXANDER OF APHRODISIAS, *DE PROVIDENTIA* EDITION OF THE GREEK FRAGMENTS WITH TRANSLATIONS[65]

*Sigla*
(*a*) Cyril. *CI*

| | |
|---|---|
| F | Scorial. *Ψ*.III.12. (gr. 467) (saec. XII exeuntis uel saec. XIII ineuntis) |
| G | Scorial. *Ω*.II.13. (gr. 530) et Haun. Fragm. 3121 (olim Kaps. 20 Exp. 5) (saec. XIV ineuntis, nunc pauca prosphonematos et libri 1 capita continens) |
| κ | Capnioneus (initio saec. XIV? codex ab Oecolampadio adhibitus, nunc amissus) |
| V | Marc. gr. 122 (1343, libros 1–5 continens) |
| M | Marc. gr. 123 (saec. XIV) |
| E | Scorial. *Ω*.III.5 (gr. 538) (saec. XV ineuntis, ut uidetur) |
| R | Vat. gr. 597 (circa 1450 scriptus) |
| N | Marc. gr. 124 (inter 1450 et 1475 scriptus) |
| P | Paris. gr. 1261 (circa 1537 scriptus, prosphonema et libros 1–3 continens) |
| C | Berol. 1444 Phill. (saec. XVI) |
| D | Matrit. 4669 (O–6) (post 1555 consutus) |
| B | Monac. gr. 65 (circa 1550 scriptus) |
| I | Vat. Palat. gr. 339 (circa 1550 scriptus, libros 1–5 continens) |
| H | Vat. Palat. gr. 18 (saec. XVI exeuntis uel saec. XVII, nunc libros 4–10 continens) |
| Q | Paris. suppl. gr. 424 (saec. XVII) |
| β | consensus codd. FME |
| ε | consensus codd. descript. CDBIHQ |

[63] Or, less likely, because he was quoting from second hand, cf. supra, n. 28.
[64] Cf. in general on the 'rôle des Arabes dans la formation de l'héritage grec' as to philosophy Badawi 1968, 7 ff.
[65] The following translations are freely adapted from Grant 1964, 277 ff.

(*b*) Alex. Aphr. *De prou.* interpp. Arabb. D15 et D18

E                     Scorial. arab. Derenbourg 798/Casiri 794 (saec. XIII)

S (C Ruland)   Constantinopolit. Millet-Carullah 1279 (1477–78)


# Fr. 1 (= Fr. 3a Grant)


Cyril. *CI* 3. 13 (625 в–с) et interp. Arab. D18, p. 6. 1–9 Ruland = p. 3. 1–8 Thillet 1979
= p. 87 Thillet 2003 = pp. 100/1 Zonta.[66]

Πείϲει δὲ ἴϲωϲ αὐτόν, μᾶλλον δὲ καὶ οὐχ ἑκόντα περιτρέψει εἰϲ τὸ εὐθὺ τῶν
ὁμοδόξων ἡ πίϲτιϲ. Ἀλέξανδροϲ τοίνυν, ἀνὴρ ἐλλόγιμοϲ, ἐν τῶι Περὶ προνοίαϲ
λόγωι φηϲὶν οὕτωϲ·

<. . .> μηδὲν γὰρ τῶν ἐν τῶι κόϲμωι γίνεϲθαι <φαϲι> χωρὶϲ προνοίαϲ.
πάντα γὰρ εἶναι μεϲτὰ τοῦ θείου καὶ διὰ πάντων διήκειν αὐτὸ τῶν ὄντων.
διὸ καὶ πάντα τὰ γινόμενα γίνεϲθαι κατὰ βούληϲιν **τῶν θεῶν** <. . .>.

[625 с] Καὶ τοῦτο μαρτυρεῖϲθαι μὲν ὑπὸ τῶν φαινομένων. ἥ τε γὰρ
**<ἀκολουθία καὶ>** τάξιϲ τῶν γινομένων φύϲει, ἀεὶ παραπληϲίωϲ ἔχουϲα,
μέγαϲ ἔλεγχοϲ τοῦ μὴ κατὰ τύχην ταῦτα γίνεϲθαι.

(. . .) For nothing in the world, **<they maintain>**, happens without providence.
Because all things [they say] are full of the divine, and it pervades all that is. Therefore
also everything that comes into being does so according to the will of the gods **<. . .>**.

[625 с] And this fact is attested by the phenomena. For the **<sequence and>** order
of things that come to be by nature, remaining nearly equal, is a great proof that these
things do not happen according to chance.

625 в πάντα . . . θεῶν] cf. Ps.-Arist. *De mundo* 6. 397ᵇ9 sqq.; iam Thales 11 A 22 D.-K.
(= Arist. *De anima* 1. 5. 411ᵃ7–8); Plat. *Leg.* 10. 899ᵇ8–9 | διὰ . . . ὄντων] cf. Alex. Aphr. *De mixt.*
3–4. 594 sqq, p. 216. 14 sqq. Bruns (= Chrys. fr. 473, *SVF* ii. 154. 6 sqq.), 10. 603–4, p. 223. 6 sqq.
Bruns, 11. 606, p. 225. 1 sqq. Bruns (= Chrys. fr. 310, *SVF* ii. 112. 29 sqq.), 12. 609, p. 227. 9–10
Bruns (= Chrys. fr. 475. *SVF* ii. 156. 15–16), etc.; etiam Diog. Laert. 7. 147 (= Chrys. fr. 1021, *SVF*
ii. 305. 15 sqq.), ut saepius | πάντα τὰ γινόμενα . . . θεῶν] cf. Alex. Aphr. *De prou.* interp. Arab.
D18, pp. 60. 1 sqq., 68. 4 sqq. Ruland; etiam Nemes. *De nat. hom.* 343 | κατὰ βούληϲιν τῶν
θεῶν] cf. etiam Chrys. fr. 914 (*SVF* ii. 265. 12)

625 с Καὶ . . . φαινομένων] cf. Arist. *De caelo* 270ᵇ4–5, *EE* 1. 6. 1216ᵇ27–8; etiam Alex. Aphr.
*De prou.* interp. Arab. D18, p. 96. 14 sqq. Ruland 'Wenn wir aber die Entstehung dessen,
was unter den Himmelskörpern liegt, auf deren wohlgeordnete und ewige Kreisbewegung
['movimenti circolari, ordinati ed eterni' Zonta] zurückführen, so stehen wir mit *empirischen*
Tatsachen in Einklang ['si accorda coi fenomeni' Zonta] — und das ist überzeugender als alles
andere!'; id. *De fato* 16, p. 35. 3–4 Thillet | Ἥ τε γὰρ . . . γίνεϲθαι] cf. Chrys. fr. 534, *SVF* ii. 170.
30 sqq.; Alex. Aphr. *De prou.* interp. Arab. D18, p. 80. 5 sqq. Ruland; id. *De fato* 22, p. 43. 7 sqq.
Thillet (= Chrys. fr. 945, *SVF* ii. 272. 38 sqq.); id. *Mant.* 25, p. 185. 1 sqq. Bruns (= Chrys. fr. 920,
*SVF* ii. 266. 9 sqq.) (supra, p. 283); etiam Ps.-Arist. *De mundo* 6. 400ᵃ21 sqq. de rerum caelestium
aeterno ordine | Ἥ τε γὰρ <ἀκολουθία καὶ> τάξιϲ] cf. etiam Alex. Aphr. *De fato* 34, p. 65. 21–2
Thillet (= Chrys. fr. 1002, *SVF* ii. 295. 23–4) (supra, p. 283)


[66] Cf. Grant 1964, 278; Fazzo 2000, 405 ff.

625 в Πείσει βκ : ἥσει V | εἰς β : πρὸς V | ἀνὴρ sqq. suppl. M¹ | λόγωι om. V | < . . . )> initium capitis om. Cyr. : 'Ansicht und Meinung anderer über Philosophie und Vorsehung ist der dieser Philosophen [sc. Leukipps, Demokrits, Epikurs] diametral entgegengesetzt' Alex. Aphr. interp. Arab. D18 | <φασι> conieci sec. Alex. Aphr. interp. Arab. D18 ('Denn sie behaupten . . .') | μεστὰ βκ Alex. Aphr. interp. Arab. D18 : μεστὰ V | αὐτὸ διήκειν transp. V | γινόμενα seq. ras. (5 fere litt.) M | τῶν θεῶν Alex. Aphr. interp. Arab. D18 ('der Götter') : τοῦ θεοῦ Cyr. | <. . .>] <ὡς φυλασσόντων τε καὶ διοικούντων ἕκαστον αὐτῶν> ex. gr. conieci sec. Alex. Aphr. interp. Arab. D18 ('insofern sie für die Dinge sorgten und ein jedes von ihnen leiteten' Ruland; 'du fait qu'ils sont les garants et les administrateurs de chacune d'elles' Thillet 1979, 2003; 'inquantoché questi ultimi sono i custodi e gli amministratori di ciascuna di esse' Zonta) (possis et <καθ' ὅσον (uel καθὸ) οὗτοι φυλάττουσί τε καὶ διοικοῦσιν ἕκαστον αὐτῶν>)

625 с <ἀκολουθία καὶ> conieci sec. Alex. Aphr. interp. Arab. D18 cod. S ('la suite et l'ordre' Thillet 1979; 2003; cf. cod. E 'Denn die *Abhängigkeit* der Naturvorgänge von einer ewigen und unveränderlichen Ord-nung' Ruland; Zonta uerbum omisit, Graeca secutus) | τῶν γινομένων τάξις transp. V | φύσει ad τῶν γινομένων referunt interp. Arab. reddentes Ruland, Thillet 1979; 2003, Fazzo 2000 : ad ἀεὶ παραπλησίως ἔχουσα refert Zonta interp. graec. codicis V reddens

# Fr. 2 (= fr. 1 Grant)

Cyril. *CI* 2. 38–9 (596 а–в) et interp. Arab. D18, p. 8. 10–10. 3 Ruland = p. 4. 13 sqq. Thillet 1979 = pp. 89–90 Thillet 2003 = pp. 102/3–104/5 Zonta.[67]

Ἀλλ' ἴσως αὐτὸς ὡς οὐκ οὖσαν ἀληθῆ παραγράψεται τὴν φωνήν—θεομαχεῖ γὰρ ἐκτόπως—παραδέξεται δὲ τοὺς οἰκείους αὐτῶι γεγονότας, κατά γε τὸ πεπλανῆσθαί φημι. γράφει τοίνυν Ἀλέξανδρος ὁ Ἀριστοτέλους μαθητὴς [596 в] ἐν τῶι Περὶ προνοίας οὕτως·

<. . .> τὸ δὲ λέγειν μὴ βούλεσθαι τοὺς θεοὺς τῶν ἐνταῦθα προνοεῖν παντελῶς ἀλλότριον θεῶν. φθον<ερ>οῦ γάρ τινος καὶ παντάπασιν ἀτόπου φύσεως τὸ τὰ βελτίω μὴ ποιεῖν δυνάμενον.

Ἐπειδὴ δὲ ἑκάτερον τούτων ἀλλότριον θεῶν <καὶ διαφέρον> <. . .>, οὔτ' ἂν ἄμφω εἴη περὶ αὐτὸ[ν] οὔτε θάτερον. λείπεται τοίνυν τὸ καὶ δύνασθαι καὶ βούλεσθαι προνοεῖν τὸ θεῖον τῶν ἐνταῦθα. εἰ δὲ βούλεταί τε καὶ δύναται, δῆλον ὡς καὶ προνοεῖ. οὐδὲν ἄρα οὐδὲ τῶν τυχόντων εὔλογον χωρὶς τῆς θείας γενέσθαι γνώμης τε καὶ βουλήσεως.

39. Ταύτης δὲ τῆς δόξης φασὶ μὲν εἶναί τινες καὶ Πλάτωνα· φανερῶς δὲ Ζήνων τε ὁ Κιττιεὺς καὶ οἱ ἀπὸ τῆς Στοᾶς πρεσβεύουσι τὸ δόγμα τοῦτο.

<. . .> But to say that the gods do not want to exert providence over things on earth is completely alien to gods. For it testifies to an envious and completely foul nature not to do what is better even if able [sc. to do it].

But since both of these [sc. sub-possibilities] are alien to gods <and at variance [with their nature]> <. . .>, neither both nor one of both [sc. sub-possibilities] would regard it [sc. the divine]. Therefore it remains that the divine is both able and willing to exert providence over things on earth. But if it is willing and able, it is obvious that it also exerts its providence. It is reasonable then that not even the slightest thing happens without the divine decision and will.

---

[67] Cf. Grant 1964, 277; Fazzo 2000, 403 ff.

**39.** Some say that also Plato holds this view. Openly Zeno of Citium and the followers of the Stoa maintain this doctrine.

**596 B** *Τὸ . . . θεῶν*] cf. ad uerborum iuncturam Alex. Aphr. *Quaest.* 2. 21, p. 68. 19 sqq. Bruns *Τὸ γὰρ . . . λέγειν . . . παντελῶς ἀλλότριον θεῶν* | *Φθον<ερ>οῦ . . . δυνάμενον*] inuidiam a natura diuina alienam esse statuunt Plat. *Phdr.* 247 A 7 *Φθόνος γὰρ ἔξω θείου χοροῦ ἵςταται,* *Ti.* 29 E 1–3, Arist. *Metaph.* 1. 2. 983ᵃ2–3 *οὔτε τὸ θεῖον φθονερὸν ἐνδέχεται εἶναι*; cf. Alex. Aphr. *In Arist. Metaph.* 1. 2, p. 17. 22 sqq. Hayduck | *Ἐπειδὴ δὲ ἑκάτερον τούτων*] cf. Alex. Aphr. *De prou.* interp. Arab. D18, p. 6. 22 sqq. Ruland (infra in app. crit. ad loc.); etiam Nemes. *De nat. hom.* 354–5 | *ἀλλότριον θεῶν*] cf. supra ad *Τὸ . . . θεῶν*
**39** *Ταύτης . . . Πλάτωνα*] Plat. *Ti.* 30 B 6 sqq. etc.; cf. Riedweg 1999, 70 n. 93 etiam Nemes. *De nat. hom.* 345 sqq. | *φανερῶς . . . τοῦτο*] cf. Zeno fr. 172. 174 sqq., *SVF* i. 44–5; Chrys. fr. 634, *SVF* ii. 192; Cic. *De nat. deor.* 2. 73 sqq. etc.

596 A *Ἀριστοτέλους*] *Ἀριστοκλέους* coni. Núñez, Zeller
596 B <. . .>] primam argumentationis partem om. Cyr. (cf. supra, p. 293) | *τοὺς θεοὺς* Alex. Aphr. interp. Arab. D18, ut uidetur ('Auch daß sie die Vorsehung für das Irdische nicht *mögen* . . . ') : *τὸν θεὸν* scr. Cyr. | *θεῶν* Alex. Aphr. interp. Arab. D18 (' . . . sei mit den Göttern ganz unvereinbar') : *θεοῦ* scr. Cyr. | *Φθον<ερ>οῦ* conieci sec. Alex. Aphr. interp. Arab. D 18 ('Denn diese [Abneigung] sei das Verhalten von jemand, der *neidisch* sei'): *φθον<ερ>ᾶς* tempt. Holford-Strevens: *Φθόνου* codd. Cyr. | *παντάπαςιν . . . δυνάμενον*] 'dessen Natur ein Höchstmaß an Verworfenheit, Verdorbenheit und Untätigkeit . . . aufweise' Alex. Aphr. interp. Arab. D18 ('probabilmente da considerarsi come un'amplificazione esegetica' Fazzo 2000, 404 n. 16) | *τούτων ἑκάτερον* transp. V | *θεῶν* Alex. Aphr. interp. Arab. D18 (cf. infra) : *θεοῦ* scr. Cyr. | *<καὶ διαφέρον>* suppleui sec. Alex. Aphr. interp. Arab. D18 ('mit dem Wesen der Götter unvereinbar sei und im Widerspruch stehe'; ad uerbum 'sich trennend von, unähnlich': U. Rudolph per litteras) | <. . .>] *<καὶ δὴ καὶ ἀμφότερα ἅμα τῶι θείωι οὐχ ὑπάρχει>* ex. gr. conicias sec. Alex. Aphr. interp. Arab. D18 ('und auch beide *zusammen* Gott nicht zukämen') (possis et < . . . τῶι θείωι οὐ προςήκει>) | *αὐτὸ[ν]* emendaui | *οὐδὲ . . . τυχόντων* om. Oec. | *γενέςθαι* β : *γίνεςθαι* V (fort. recte)
**39** *τινες εἶναι* transp. V | *καὶ* Cyr. : om. Alex. Aphr. interp. Arab. D18 | *Κιττιεὺς*] *Κιτιεὺς* Burg./Év., sed cf. Cyril. *CI* 3. 22 (636 A), codd. Athen. (Epit.) Diog. Laert. | *τὸ* om. edd. uett.

## Fr. 3 (= fr. 3b Grant)

Cyril. *CI* 3. 13 (625 c) et interp. Arab. D18, p. 34. 1–7 Ruland = pp. 17. 18–18. 5 Thillet 1979 = p. 105 Thillet 2003 = pp. 124/5–126/7 Zonta.[68]

*Καὶ μὴν καὶ ἑτέρωθι·*

*Τὴν γὰρ τῶν ἐνταῦθα cωτηρίαν τε καὶ γένεcιν καὶ κατ᾽ εἶδος ἀΐδιον διαμονὴν οὐκ ἄνευ θείας προνοίας Ἀριστοτέλης φηcὶ γενέcθαι. ἡ γὰρ ἀπό τε τοῦ ἡλίου <καὶ τῆς cελήνης> καὶ τῶν ἄλλων ἄcτρων τῶν ἡλίωι cυννόμων δύναμις κατ᾽ αὐτὸν τῆς γενέcεως τοῖς φύcει cυνεcτῶcι καὶ τῆς cωτηρίας αὐτῶν ἔχει τὴν αἰτίαν.*

For Aristotle says that the preservation of things on earth and its generation and eternal continuation in form does not happen without divine providence. For the power from the sun **<and the moon>** and the other stars which run with the sun is, according to him, the cause of generation and preservation for those things that have come into existence by nature.

[68]  Cf. Grant 1964, 278; Fazzo 2000, 407–8.

**625 c** Τὴν ... αἰτίαν] sim. Alex. Aphr. *De prou.* interp. Arab. D18, pp. 52. 1 sqq., 96. 18 sqq. Ruland; id. *Quaest.* 1. 25, p. 41. 8 sqq. Bruns; Ps.-Arist. *De mundo* 6. 398ᵇ6 sqq.; cf. etiam infra fr. 5 ad τῆς θείας φύσεως | κατ᾽ ... διαμονὴν] cf. etiam Alex. Aphr. *De prou.* interp. Arab. D18, p. 88. 14 sqq. Ruland; id. *Quaest.* 3. 5, p. 89. 20–1 Bruns ἀΐδιον ἕκαστον αὐτῶν κατ᾽ εἶδος (τούτου γὰρ αἰτία ἡ τῶν θείων περιφορά); id. *In Arist. Metaph.* 4. 5, p. 361. 24 sqq. Hayduck; id. *De mundo* 57, pp. 72/3 Genequand etc.; Arist. *GA* 2. 1. 731ᵇ35–6; id. *De an.* 2. 4. 415ᵇ3 sqq.; Plot. 2. 1. 1. 24 sqq.; Sharples 1982, 198–9; 2002, 8; Moraux 1942, 199–200; 1984, 772; Bergjan 2002, 232 sqq.; Fazzo 2002, 155 sqq.; 2007*b*: 252 sqq.

**625 c** καὶ² ἐτέρωθι usque ad 628 A παραδείσωι om. V | καὶ (sc. κατ᾽ εἶδος) κ Alex. Aphr. interp. Arab. D18 ('Entstehung und Erhaltung') : om. βB⁴I⁴Q | κατ᾽ εἶδος κB⁴I⁴Q Alex. Aphr. interp. Arab. D18 : κατειδὼς β | κατ᾽ ... διαμονὴν] 'le maintien essentiel perpétuel, qui leur appartient spécifiquement' (Thillet 1979; 2003; cf. Zonta ad loc. 'Il testo arabo aggiunge qui: "essenziale"') Alex. Aphr. interp. Arab. D 18 (deest in D15) | ἄνευ θείας] ἂν εὐθείας B⁴Q | Ἀριστοτέλης] Ἀλέξανδρος maluit Bruns 1890, 234 | γενέσθαι] γίνεσθαι B⁴Q | ἀπό τε τοῦ ἡλίου] 'Mond' add. Alex. Aphr. interp. Arab. D18 (deest in D15) | τῶν (sc. ἡλίωι συννόμων) β : τῶι B⁴I⁴Q

## Fr. 4 (= fr. 5 Grant)

Cyril. *CI* 4. 26 (704 B) et interp. Arab. D18, p. 56. 1–5 'Ruland = p. 24. 10–15 Thillet 1979 = pp. 111–12 Thillet 2003 = pp. 136/7 Zonta.[69]

**26.** Καίτοι φησὶν ὁ Ἀριστοτελικὸς Ἀλέξανδρος ἐν τῶι Περὶ προνοίας λόγωι περὶ θεοῦ·

Αὐτὸ μὲν γὰρ συνεχῶς τε καὶ ἀδιαλείπτως τὰς ἀρίστας τε καὶ μακαρίους ἐνεργείας ἐνεργεῖν αἱρεῖ λόγος, καθ᾽ ἃς **<τὸ ὑπάρχειν>** καὶ τὸ εἶναί ἐστιν αὐτῶι, γίνεσθαι δὲ τὴν τῶν ἐνταῦθα ὑπ᾽ αὐτοῦ πρόνοιαν, καθ᾽ ὅσον ἀγαθόν τέ ἐστι καὶ ἀγαθοποιόν. ἴδιον γὰρ παντὸς ἀγαθοῦ τὸ ὠφελεῖν.

For reason proves that what [the divine] itself does is continuously and uninterruptedly to perform the best and most blessed activities, in accordance with which its own **<existence>** and being is, and that its providence for the things on earth happens inasmuch as it is good and doing good. For to be of use is characteristic of everything [that is] good.

**704 B** Αὐτὸ ... αὐτῶι] cf. Alex. Aphr. *In Arist. An. prior.* 1, p. 6. 1–2 Wallies τοῖς μὲν οὖν θεοῖς συνεχής τε καὶ ἀδιάλειπτος ἡ τῆς ἀληθείας θεωρία; iam 1, p. 5. 22–3 Wallies; id. *In Arist. Metaph.* 1. 2, p. 18. 7–8 Hayduck ἐνεργεῖν μὲν γὰρ εὔλογον τὸ θεῖον, οὐκ ἄλλη δέ τις ἐνέργεια θεῶν ἀξία παρὰ τὴν τοιαύτην; Arist. *EN* 10. 8. 1178ᵇ21–2 | Αὐτὸ ... αἱρεῖ λόγος] cf. Alex. Aphr. *De mundo* 105 sqq., pp. 100/1 sqq. Genequand | <τὸ ὑπάρχειν> καὶ τὸ εἶναί] cf. Alex. Aphr. *In Arist. Metaph.* pp. 285. 19 sqq., 431. 10 sqq. Hayduck (supra, n. 46) et id. *in sens.* p. 116. 11 sqq. Wendland | καθ᾽ ὅσον ... ἀγαθοποιόν] de diuini bonitate cf. Plat. *Ti.* 29 E 1–2; Plut. *Non posse suau. uiui sec. Epic.* 1086 D; Atticus fr. 4. 82 des Pl. (= Eus. *Praep. eu.* 15. 6. 13); etiam Procl. *In Plat. Ti.* 1, p. 359. 20 sqq. Diehl ad loc.; Alex. Aphr. *De prou.* interp. Arab. D18, p. 102. 1–2 Ruland etc.; praeterea Platonis primum τύπον περὶ θεολογίας in *R.* 2. 379 B 1 sqq.; Ph. *Conf.* 180; Clem. Al. *Strom.* 1. 86. 3; etc. | Ἴδιον ... ὠφελεῖν] cf. Alex. Aphr. *In Arist. Metaph.* 1. 9, p. 130. 17–18 Hayduck τὸ ἀγαθὸν ὠφέλιμόν ἐστι τῆι αὐτοῦ φύσει; id. *In Arist. An. prior.* 1. 25, p. 271. 34 Wallies; Plat. *Men.* 87 E 2; id. *R.* 379 B 11 etc.

⁶⁹ Cf. Grant 1964, 279; Fazzo 2000, 408–9.

**704 B** Αὐτὸ (sc. τὸ θεῖον) V : αὐτῶι β : αὐτὸν edd. uett. | ἀρίστας] ἀρίστους β | μακαρίους] μακαρίας β | ἀρίστας τε καὶ μακαρίους Cyr. Alex. Aphr. interp. Arab. D15 : ʻ(daß … aus den Tätigkeiten … wesensgemäß) seine Areté und seine Eudaimonie (resultieren)ʼ Alex. Aphr. interp. Arab. D18, cf. Zonta ad loc. ʻLa versione araba rovescia qui la struttura sintattica del testo grecoʼ | ἐνεργεῖν κV : om. β | αἱρεῖ βκ (? ʻcolligimusʼ Oec.) Alex. Aphr. interp. Arab. D18 (ʻDie Lehre steht somit festʼ: Ulrich Rudolph per litteras) : ἐρεῖ V | <τὸ ὑπάρχειν> conieci sec. Alex. Aphr. interp. Arab. D18 (cf. ʻdurch die Gott existiert und durch die er ist, was er istʼ) | τὸ εἶναί … αὐτῶι om. Oec. | αὐτῶι ἐστι transp. V | δὲ om. β | τέ om. F

# Fr. 5 (= fr. 2 Grant)

Cyril. *CI* 3. 9 (621 B–C).[70] Fragmentum deest in interpp. Arabb. D18 et D15. In ultima libri parte fortasse collocatum fuerit. E prima fragmenti sententia colligi potest Alexandrum in his quae antecederent posuisse naturam homini consuluisse et de omnibus ad uitam necessariis prouidisse, sed malum (uel errorem) non omnino expellere potuisse. Quod reapse id. *De prou.* interp. Arab. D18, p. 98. 1 sqq. Ruland et D15 p. 104 sqq. Ruland adumbrat. Cf. etiam ʻAbd-al-Laṭīf al-Baġdādī *Metaph.* 8, pp. 216–17 Rosenthal (supra, n. 54).

**9.** Ἆρά coι δοκεῖ τῆς ἀληθείας ἀφαμαρτεῖν ὁ παρ᾽ ἡμῶν λόγος, ἢ ςυναγορεύςεις τοῖς coῖς ὧδέ τε ταῦτ᾽ ἔχειν καὶ αὐτὸς ἐρεῖς; εἰ δὲ δὴ δεῖν οἴεται καὶ ἑτέρων αὐτῶι πρὸς τοῦτο μαρτυριῶν, Ἀλεξάνδρου παροίςω λόγους, ἀνδρὸς γεγονότος τῶν ὅτι μάλιστα παρ᾽ αὐτοῖς ἰςχνοῦ [**621 c**] τε καὶ ἀκριβοῦς. ἔφη γὰρ οὕτως ἐν τῶι Περὶ προνοίας λόγωι·

Ἴδοι δ᾽ ἄν τις καὶ ἐπ᾽ αὐτῶν τούτων τὸ τῆς θείας φύςεως πρὸς ἡμᾶς εὐμενές. ἐπειδὴ γὰρ οὐχ οἷόν τε ἦν ἐν ἡμῖν φύςει τὰς ἀρετὰς ὑπάρχειν, δοῦςα τὴν δύναμιν, ἧς ἦν αὐτὴ κυρία, τὴν κτῆςιν αὐτῶν οὐκ ἐπ᾽ ἄλλοις τιςίν, ἀλλ᾽ ἐφ᾽ ἡμῖν αὐτοῖς ἐποιήςατο, ἵνα, ὅπερ παρ᾽ ἐκείνης ἡμῖν ἔχειν ἦν ἀδύνατον, τοῦτο δι᾽ ἑαυτῶν λαμβάνειν ὡς παρ᾽ ἐκείνης ἔχωμεν.

Εἰ μὲν οὖν ἐκ φύςεως τὰς ἀρετὰς ἔχειν ἐδυνάμεθα, οὐδεμία ἂν χώρα τῆι κακίαι κατελείπετο. ἐπειδὴ δὲ τοῦτο ἀδύνατον—μέχρι γὰρ τοῦ δεκτικοὺς ἡμᾶς εἶναι τῶν ἀρετῶν ἡ φύςις πρόειςι μόνον—ἀναγκαίως πᾶν τὸ δεκτικόν τινος, ὧι ἔςτι τι ἐναντίον, καὶ τοῦ ἐναντίου δεκτικόν ἐςτιν.

One may see in precisely these examples the favour of the divine nature against us. For since it was not possible that by nature the virtues should be in us, it gave [sc. us] the power, over which it had control, and made the acquisition of the virtues not dependent on others, but on ourselves, so that what was impossible for us to have [directly] from it, we might receive it through ourselves as if from that.

If actually we could have the virtues on the ground of nature, no room would have been left for wickedness. But since this is impossible—for nature goes only so far as to make us capable of receiving the virtues—necessarily everything capable of receiving something to which there is an opposite is capable of receiving the opposite as well.

**621 c** τῆς θείας φύςεως] cf. Alex. Aphr. *De prou.* interp. Arab. D18, p. 76. 8 sqq., 78. 13–14 Ruland, praeterea p. 88. 5–6 Ruland; id. *Mant.* 20, p. 163. 26 Bruns; id. *De fato* 27, p. 52. 5–6 Thillet

[70] Cf. Grant 1964, 277–8; Fazzo 2000, 409s. 411 ff.

et *Quaest.* 2. 3. 1, p. 48. 28 sqq. Bruns et *De mundo* 127 sqq., pp 112/3 sqq. Genequand. Natura cum astrorum ui cohaeret, cf. id. *De prou.* interp. Arab. D18, p. 102. 5 sqq. Ruland, iam p. 34. 1 sqq. (1–7 = Alex. Aphr. *De prou.* fr. 3), p. 88. 5 sqq. Ruland; id. *De mundo* passim; Ps.-Arist. *De mundo* 2. 392ᵃ31, 6. 398ᵇ19 sqq.; cf. Ruland 1976, 136, 138–9; Sharples 1992, 11 n. 53; 2001, 526–7; u. etiam supra, adnot. ad Alex. Aphr. *De prou.* fr. 3 | ἐφ᾽ ἡμῖν . . . δεκτικόν ἐστιν] cf. Arist. *EN* 2. 1. 1103ᵃ23 sqq., 3. 7. 1113ᵇ6 sqq.; Alex. Aphr. *De fato* 27, p. 51. 21 sqq. Thillet | Ἐπειδή . . . δεκτικόν ἐστιν] cf. etiam Alex. Aphr. *Mant.* 5, p. 121. 26–7 Bruns; Iust. *2 Apol.* 7. 6 | μέχρι . . . μόνον] cf. Alex. Aphr. *Eth. probl.* 29, p. 161. 20 sqq. Bruns

621 в  τε om. F | δή VME sqq. F¹ : om. edd. uett. | ἰσχνοῦ] ἰσχυροῦ ε

621 c  θείας] ἀληθείας ε | πρὸς ἡμᾶς 'abest à P.' Q¹ | ἧς . . . αὕτη κV : ἡ σὺν αὐτῆι β : ᾗ ἦν αὕτη edd. uett. | ἐκείνης] ἐκείνοις a. corr. V | ἡμῖν (sc. ἔχειν ἦν ἀδύνατον) om. M | ἀδύνατον ἦν transp. V | ἑαυτῶν p. corr. ut uidetur V | τὰς ἀρετὰς ἐκ φύσεως transp. V | Ἐπειδή β : ἐπεὶ V | γὰρ om. βk | δεκτικοὺς] δεκτικοῦ V | τῶν ἀρετῶν εἶναι transp. V | ἀναγκαίως] δὲ add. βκ(? a uerbo 'Necessario' nouam sententiam exorditur Oec.)

# Fr. 6 (= fr. 4 Grant)

Cyril. *CI* 3. 17 (628 ᴅ–629 ᴀ).[71] Fragmentum deest in interpp. Arabb. D18 et D15. In libri fine, post fr. 5, mihi collocatum fuisse uidetur.

17. Ὅτι δὲ τῆς ἀνωτάτω πασῶν εὐημερίας πρόξενον τοῖς ἑλεῖν ἀξίοις εἴη ἂν τῆς ἀκριβοῦς θεοπτίας τὸ χρῆμα, καὶ τῶν πρὸς ἡμᾶς ἑτερογνωμόνων ἐκδείξειαν ἂν οἱ λόγοι. ἔφη γὰρ πάλιν ὁ μνημονευθεὶς ἡμῖν ἀρτίως Ἀλέξανδρος·

Ἄξιον δὲ [629 ᴀ] μηδὲ ἐκεῖνο παραλιπεῖν τὸ καὶ αὐτὸ παρὰ τῆς θείας προνοίας τοῖς ἀνθρώποις δεδωρημένον, οὗ καὶ διὰ τῶν ἤδη προειρημένων ἐπ᾽ ὀλίγον ἐμνημονεύσαμεν. ἔστι δὲ τοῦτο ἐν τῆι πρὸς τὸ θεῖον εὐσεβείαι τὴν ἀκροτάτην ἡμῖν εὐδαιμονίαν κεῖσθαι, ὡς μὴ μισθοὺς ἔξωθέν τινας παρ᾽ αὐτοῦ διὰ τοῦτο περιμένειν, ἀλλ᾽ ἐν τῆι θεραπείαι τῆι πρὸς τοῦτο τοῦ μεγίστου τῶν ἀγαθῶν τυγχάνειν.

Ὁμολογεῖται μὲν οὖν τὸ εὐδαιμονεῖν τοῖς ἀνθρώποις ἔχειν τὸ κεφάλαιον ἐν θεωρίαι. τῆς γὰρ τιμιωτάτης τῶν τῆς ψυχῆς δυνάμεων, ἥτις ἐστὶν ἡ κατὰ τὸν νοῦν, ἥδε ἐνέργεια. θεωρία γάρ ἐστιν ἡ τῶν ἐν τοῖς οὖσιν ἀρίστων ἀληθὴς γνῶσις. ἄριστα δὲ τῶν ὄντων ἁπάντων τὰ θεῖα. ἐν τῆι τῶν θείων ἄρα γνώσει τὸ εὐδαιμονεῖν ἡμῖν.

It is right [629 ᴀ] not to omit this either, which also has been gifted by the divine providence to mankind, and which we mentioned briefly also in the foregoing. It is that in piety towards the divine lies our greatest happiness, not that on this account we expect some rewards externally from it, but that in worship of it we attain the greatest of goods.

It is an acknowledged truth that happiness for men has its culmination in contemplation. For this is the activity of the most important faculty of the soul, which is that in accordance with the mind. For contemplation is the true knowledge of the best among beings. The best of all beings are the divine. In the knowledge of the divine then is our happiness.

[71] Cf. Grant 1964, 278–9; Fazzo 2000, 410, 413–14.

**628 D–629 A** Ἄξιον . . . ἡμῖν] sim. fr. 7 (= fr. 6 Grant) (cf. infra).

**629 A** οὗ . . . ἐμνημονεύσαμεν] cf. Alex. Aphr. *De prou.* interp. Arab. D18, p. 98. 9 sqq. (de donis a prouidentia hominibus datis), 100. 12 sqq. Ruland (de hominum uita beata in rerum diuinarum contemplatione constituta) Ἔςτι . . . τυγχάνειν] cf. Plat. *Leg.* 4. 716 D 6 sqq. Ἔςτι . . . κεῖςθαι] cf. etiam Alex. Aphr. interp. Arab. D18, p. 100. 13 sqq. Ruland (supra, p. 289) ἀλλ᾽ . . . τυγχάνειν] cf. Alex. Aphr. *In Arist. An. prior.* 1, p. 5. 20–1 Wallies (supra, n. 57); etiam id. *De prou.* interp. Arab. D18, p. 102. 4 sqq. Ruland (supra, n. 57) τῆι θεραπείαι . . . τοῦτο] cf. etiam Diog. Laert. 7. 119 (= fr. 604, *SVF* iii. 157. 25–6) Ὁμολογεῖται . . . ἡμῖν] cf. Arist. *EN* 10. 7. 1177ª12 sqq. (cf. 1. 3. 1096ª4–5, 1. 8. 1098ᵇ9 sqq.); 10. 8. 1178ᵇ7 sqq.; etiam id. *Protr.* fr. 6 Ross = fr. 73 Gigon; Alex. Aphr. *In Arist. An. prior.* 1, p. 5. 19 sqq. Wallies, *In Arist. Metaph.* 1. 2, p. 18. 6 sqq. Hayduck ἡ δὲ τοιαύτη [sc. ἐπιστήμη, i. e. θεωρία] θειοτάτη κατά τε τὸ μάλιστα ὁμοίαν τῆι τῶν θείων ἐνεργείαι εἶναι . . . , ἀλλὰ καὶ διὰ τὸ τῶν θείων γνῶςιν εἶναι κτλ.; id. *De mundo* 98–9, p. 96/7 Genequand; Rashed 2000, 4 ff. = 2007a, 182 ff. Τῆς γὰρ . . . θεῖα] cf. etiam Alex. Aphr. *In Arist. Top.* 3. 1, p. 236. 21 sqq. Wallies (supra, n. 58) θεωρία . . . θεῖα] cf. etiam Alex. Aphr. *In Arist. An. prior.* 1, p. 3. 17 sqq. Wallies; Rashed 2000, 9 = 2007a, 187) ἄριστα . . . θεῖα] cf. Alex. Aphr. *De prou.* interp. Arab, p. 102. 6 sqq. Ruland; praeterea etiam supra ad ἀλλ᾽ . . . τυγχάνειν

**628 D** ἐκδείξειαν] ἐκδείξειεν M | ἂν om. V

**629 A** οὗ] ὃ V | οὗ . . . προειρημένων om. Migne | μὴ sqq. suppl. F¹ | τὸν om. F

# (?) fr. 7 (= fr. 6 Grant)

Cyril. *CI* 5. 9 (741 A–B).[72] Fragmentum deest in interpp. Arabb. D18 et D15. Fieri potest ut ex alio Alexandri de prouidentia libro excerptum sit.

**9.** Οὐκοῦν αὐχημάτων ἄριστον εἴη ἂν ἡ περὶ θεοῦ γνῶςις. ὀρθῶς δὲ ταῦτ᾽ ἔχειν καὶ αὐτοῖς τοῖς Ἑλλήνων λογάςι ςυνδοκεῖ. καὶ γοῦν Ἀλέξανδρος ὁ Ἀριστοτέλους ἐραςτὴς ἐν τῶι Περὶ τῆς καθ᾽ ἕκαστα προνοίας λόγωι φηςίν·

Ἴςως δὲ χρὴ τἀληθὲς εἰπεῖν· δι᾽ αὐτῆς περὶ τὸ θεῖον εὐςεβείας τὸ μέγιστον μὲν καὶ τελεώτατον ἀγαθόν, πάντως δὲ τὸ εὐδαιμόνως ζῆν. τοῦτο δὲ [**741 B**] ὂν ἐν θεωρίαι δείκνυται· ἡ δὲ θεωρία ἐν γνώςει τῶν ἀρίστων· ἄριστα δὲ ὁμολογεῖται πρὸς ἁπάντων εἶναι τὰ θεῖα. τούτων γὰρ οὕτως ἐχόντων, ἐν τῆι γνώςει τῶν θείων εἴη ἂν ἡμῖν τὸ εὐδαιμονεῖν κείμενον.

But perhaps one should speak the truth: through piety itself regarding the divine comes the greatest and most perfect good, and at all events a life in full happiness. The latter is shown to consist in contemplation. Contemplation is the knowledge of the best things; the best things are agreed by all to be the divine. Under these circumstances, being fully happy should lie in the knowledge of things divine.

**741 A–B** Ἴςως . . . κείμενον] sim. fr. 6 (= fr. 4 Grant) (cf. supra adnott. ad loc.).

**741 A** ἄριστον αὐχημάτων transp. V | ςυνδοκεῖ] δοκεῖ β | ὁ Ἀριστοτέλους μαθητὴς Ἀλέξανδρος transp. V | ἐραςτὴς βκ : μαθητὴς V | δὲ] an δ᾽ ε<ἰ> scribendum? | δι᾽ αὐτῆς] διὰ τῆς edd. uett. | καὶ βκ : om. V | ἀγαθόν] sc. ἀνθρώπῳ περιγίνεται? | πάντως βκ : πάντων V

[72] Cf. Grant 1964, 279; Fazzo 2000, 411, 413–14.

# BIBLIOGRAPHY

Badawi, A. 1968, *La Transmission de la philosophie grecque au monde arabe* (Paris).

Bergjan, S.-P. 2002, *Der fürsorgende Gott: Der Begriff der ΠΡΟΝΟΙΑ Gottes in der apologetischen Literatur der Alten Kirche* (Berlin and New York).

Brock, S. 2005, 'Du grec en syriaque: L'art de la traduction chez les Syriaques', in *Les Syriaques transmetteurs de civilisation: L'expérience du Bilâd El-Shâm à l'époque omeyyade* (Patrimoine syriaque, Actes du colloque IX; Antelias (Lebanon) and Paris), 11–34.

Bruns, L. 1890, 'Studien zu Alexander von Aphrodisias', *RhM*² 45: 223–35.

Burguière, P., and Évieux, P. (eds.) 1985, *Cyrille d'Alexandrie: Contre Julien,* i (Paris).

Chaniotis, A. 2004*a*, 'New Inscriptions from Aphrodisias (1995–2001)', *AJArch* 108: 377–416.

—— 2004*b*, 'Epigraphic Evidence for the Philosopher Alexander of Aphrodisias', *BICS* 47: 79–81.

D'Ancona, C., and Serra, G. (eds.) 2002, *Aristotele e Alessandro di Afrodisia nella tradizione araba: Atti del colloquio La ricezione araba ed ebraica della filosofia e della scienza greche (Padova, 14–15 maggio 1999)* (Padua).

Dietrich, A. 1964, 'Die arabische Version einer unbekannten Schrift des Alexander von Aphrodisias über die Differentia specifica', *Nachrichten der Akademie der Wiss. in Göttingen, Phil.-hist. Kl.,* 1964/2, 88–148.

Fazzo, S., 2000, 'La versione araba del ΠΕΡΙ ΠΡΟΝΟΙΑΣ di Alessandro di Afrodisia e i frammenti greci nel trattato *Contra Iulianum* di Cirillo Alessandrino', *Aevum,* 74/2, 299–419.

—— 2002, *Aporia e sistema: la materia, la forma, il divino nelle* Quaestiones *di Alessandro di Afrodisia* (Pisa).

—— and Wiesner, W. 1993, 'Alexander of Aphrodisias in the Kindī-Circle and in al-Kindī's cosmology', *Arabic Sciences and Philosophy,* 3, 119–53.

—— and Zonta, M. (eds.) 1998, *Alessandro di Afrodisia: La provvidenza. Questioni sulla provvidenza* (Milan).

Genequand, Ch. 2001, *Alexander of Aphrodisias on the Cosmos* (Leiden, Boston, and Cologne).

Goulet, R., and Aouad, M. 1989, 'Alexandros d'Aphrodisias', in R. Goulet (ed.), *Dictionnaire des philosophes antiques,* i (Paris), 125–9.

Grant, R. M. 1964, 'Greek Literature in the Treatise *De Trinitate* and Cyril *Contra Julianum*', *JTLSt* 15, 265–79.

Heiland, H. 1925, *Aristoclis Messenii reliquiae* (diss. Giessen).

Moraux, P. 1942, 'Appendice II: La théorie alexandriste de la providence', in id., *Alexandre d'Aphrodise exégète de la Noétique d'Aristote* (Liège), 195–202.

—— 1967*a*, 'Alexander of Aphrodisias Quaest. 2, 3', *Hermes,* 95: 159–69.

—— 1967*b*, 'Aristoteles, der Lehrer Alexanders von Aphrodisias', *Archiv für Gesch. der Philos.,* 49: 169–182.

—— 1970, *D'Aristote à Bessarion: Trois exposés sur l'histoire et la transmission de l'aristotélisme grec* (Quebec City).

Neuwirth, A. 1976, ʿ*Abd al-Laṭīf al-Baġdādī's Bearbeitung von Buch Lambda der aristotelischen Metaphysik* (Wiesbaden).

Pines, S. 1959, 'Addenda et Corrigenda (to "Un texte inconnu d'Aristote en version arabe"), *AHMA* 26, 295–99; repr. in *Studies in Arabic Versions of Greek Texts and in Mediaeval Science* (= The collected works of Shlomo Pines, 2) (Leiden, 1986), 196–200.

Rashed, M. 2000, 'Alexandre d'Aphrodise lecteur du *Protreptique*', in J. Hamesse (ed.), *Les Prologues médiévaux* (Turnhout, 2000), 1–37; repr. 2007*a*, 179–215.

——— 2004, 'Priorité de l'*ΕΙΔΟΣ* ou du *ΓΕΝΟΣ* entre Andronicos et Alexandre: Vestiges arabes et grecs inédits', *Arabic Sciences and Philosophy*, 14 (2004), 9–63; repr. 2007*a*, 29–83.

——— 2007*a*, *L'Héritage aristotélicien: Textes inédits de l'Antiquité* (Paris).

——— 2007*b*, *Essentialisme. Alexandre d'Aphrodise entre logique, physique et cosmologie* (Berlin and New York).

Regazzoni, P. 1928, 'Il "Contra Galilaeos" dell'imperatore Giuliano e il "Contra Iulianum" di San Cirillo Alessandrino', *Didaskaleion*, 6/3, 1–114.

Riedweg, C. 1990, '*TrGF* 2.624—A Euripidean Fragment', *CQ*² 40: 124–36.

——— 1999, 'Mit Stoa und Platon gegen die Christen: Philosophische Argumentations-strukturen in Julians *contra Galilaeos*', in T. Fuhrer and M. Erler (eds.), *Zur Rezeption der hellenistischen Philosophie in der spätantike Akten der 1. Tagung der Karl- und Gertrud-Abet-Stiftung vom 22.–25. September 1997 in Trier* (Stuttgart), 55–81.

——— 2000, 'Zur handschriftlichen Überlieferung der Apologie Kyrills von Alexandrien *Contra Iulianum*', *Museum Helveticum*, 57, 151–65.

——— and Oesterheld, C. 2000, 'Scritto e controscritto: per una nuova edizione di Cirillo Alessandrino *Contra Iulianum*', in *Giuliano Imperatore: Le sue idee, i suoi amici, i suoi avversari. Atti del Convegno Internazionale di Studi (Lecce, 10–12 Dicembre 1998) = Rudiae* (Ricerche sul mondo classico), 10 (2000), 415–433.

Rosenthal, F. 1965, *Das Fortleben der Antike im Islam* (Zurich and Stuttgart).

Rudolph, U. 2004, *Islamische Philosophie: Von den Anfängen bis zur Gegenwart* (Munich).

Ruland, H.-J. 1976, *Die arabischen Fassungen von zwei Schriften des Alexander von Aphrodisias: Über die Vorsehung und Über das liberum arbitrium* (Saarbrücken).

Sharples, R. W. 1982, 'Alexander of Aphrodisias on Divine Providence: Two Problems', *CQ*² 32: 198–211.

——— 1987, 'Alexander of Aphrodisias: Scholasticism and Innovation', in *ANRW* II, 36.2 (Berlin and New York), 1176–1243.

——— 1995, 'World under Management? Details, Delegation and Divine Providence, 400 B.C. A.D. 1200' (An Inaugural Lecture delivered at University College London, 1st March 1995; London, 1995).

——— 2000, 'Alexander of Aphrodisias *Quaestio* 2.21: A Question of Authenticity', *Elenchos*, 21, 361–79.

——— 2001, 'Determinism, Responsibility and Chance', in P. Moraux, *Der Aristotelis-mus bei den Griechen*, iii (Berlin and New York), 513–92.

——— 2002, 'Alexander of Aphrodisias and the End of Aristotelian theology', in T. Kobusch and M. Erler (eds), *Metaphysik und Religion: Zur Signatur des spätantiken Denkens. Akten des Internationalen Kongresses von 13.–17. März 2001 in Würzburg* (Munich and Leipzig), 1–21.

—— 2003, 'Threefold Providence: The History and Background of a Doctrine', in R. W. Sharples and A. D. R. Sheppard (eds.), *Ancient Approaches to Plato's Timaeus* (*BICS* Suppl. 78), 107–27.

—— 2005, 'Implications of the New Alexander of Aphrodisias Inscription', *BICS* 48, 47–56.

Thillet, P. 1960, 'Un traité inconnu d'Alexandre d'Aphrodise sur la Providence dans une version arabe inédite', in *L'Homme et son destin d'après les penseurs du Moyen Âge. Actes du 1er Congrès International de Philosophie médiévale, Louvain/Bruxelles 1958* (Louvain and Paris), 313–24.

—— 1979, 'Alexandre d'Aphrodise: Traité de la Providence. Version arabe d'Abû Bishr Mattâ Ibn Yûnus' (typewritten diss. Université de la Sorbonne Nouvelle Paris III).

—— (ed.) 1984, *Alexandre d'Aphrodise: Traité du Destin* (Paris).

—— 1987, 'Alexandre d'Aphrodise et la poésie', in J. Wiesner (ed.), *Aristoteles: Werk und Wirkung (Paul Moraux gewidmet)*, ii (Berlin and New York), 107–19.

—— 2003, *Alexandre d'Aphrodise: Traité de la Providence* Περὶ προνοίας. *Version arabe de Abū Bišr Mattā ibn Yūnus* (Lagrasse).

# 16

## Missing Pages: Papyrology, Genre, and the Greek Novel

### *Albert Henrichs*

What better way to pay homage to Peter Parsons than to talk about the Greek novel and the enormous impact the papyrus finds of the past hundred years have had on the chronology of the extant novelists, on our awareness of the number and nature of novels lost long before the Byzantine period, and last but not least on our understanding of the genre as a whole in all its amazing diversity, including its preoccupation with the pathetic, the macabre, and the lewd? Through his own work and example, Parsons has contributed in signal fashion to each of the core areas of the papyrological exploration of the novel. On more than one occasion he has produced editions of previously unknown novels and novelistic texts such as the narratives about Iolaos, Amenophis, and most recently Panionis.[1] As the editor of the earliest papyrus fragment of Achilles Tatius, he was able to assign a more precise date to this author.[2] At the same time, he has enhanced our appreciation of the literary and aesthetic boundaries of the genre through his exemplary interpretations of several papyrus texts conspicuously located at or near its margins.[3]

After some initial reflections on various attempts to define the Greek novel during the past three hundred years, the central part of my paper will address the chronology, authorship, and transmission of the extant novels from a strictly papyrological point of view. In the final part, I shall take the *Phoinikika* of Lollianos as a point of departure for concluding remarks on the role of intertextuality in the interpretation of papyrus fragments identified as novels.

---

[1] P.Oxy. XLII 3010, 3011, LXXI 4811.
[2] P.Oxy. LVI 3836, discussed below.
[3] The *Iolaos* fragment (P.Oxy. XLII 3010) is a case in point. Defined by its vulgar language, weird characters, and unconventional plot construction as a 'comic novel' (Parsons), the *Iolaos* shows a greater affinity to Petronius than to the extant Greek novels. Does its deviancy make it a 'fringe novel' as opposed to a 'novel proper' (on this distinction see Holzberg 2003, 13–15, 28)?

## Defining the Genre: Julian, Fabricius, and Beyond

The modern study of the Greek novel *qua* literature began in 1726 with the publication of volume six of the first comprehensive history of Greek literature, the monumental *Bibliotheca Graeca* by Johann Albert Fabricius (1668–1736). A work of vast scope and astonishing erudition, it covers all of Greek literature from Homer and Hesiod to the Church Fathers and into the Byzantine period. At the time Fabricius wrote, only three Greek novels had been published, Heliodorus, Longus, and Achilles Tatius—in that order. The publication of Xenophon of Ephesus was imminent (London 1726), but Chariton did not appear until 1750.[4] The full extent of Fabricius' lack of information is reflected in the elaborate Latin title he gave to his chapter on the novel: *De Heliodoro & aliis Scriptoribus Graecis Eroticis, editis, ineditis ac deperditis* ('On Heliodorus and other Greek writers of love stories, published, unpublished, lost').[5] This title, in combination with Fabricius' account of the limited number of novels to which he had access, raises two issues that remain fundamental today—namely, the twin problems of genre definition and canonization. Thanks to the papyri, we are infinitely better informed about the Greek novel than Fabricius was. By the same token, the papyri have also substantially deepened our sense of ignorance and loss. Amazingly, the two areas in which we continue to lack consensus or clarity are still the same as in Fabricius' day, namely how to define the genre that lies behind Fabricius' *scriptores erotici*, and what to make of the fact that compared to the five novels that managed to survive many more perished—Fabricius' *deperditi*.

Fabricius concludes his chapter with an alphabetical list of the names of some forty-five ancient writers who composed love stories which did not survive. Fragments of only two of these texts have turned up on papyrus, the *Incredible Things Beyond Thule* by Antonius Diogenes, of which Parsons has recently published two additional papyri, thus bringing the total to four, as well as fragments from two different versions of the anonymous and polymorphous Greek *Ass Tale* or *Eselsroman* that inspired Apuleius.[6] In addition, fragments of at least a dozen or, on a more optimistic count, of as many as forty novels have been identified on papyrus. Not one of them appears to coincide with any of the entries in Fabricius' list of lost novels. What little has survived of the ancient novel production is merely the proverbial tip of the iceberg. On a conservative estimate, hundreds of papyrus columns or

---

[4] See Reeve 2008, 288–95.    [5] Fabricius 1726, 768–814.
[6] Antonius Diogenes: P.Oxy. LXX 4760, 4761, in addition to P.Oxy. XLII 3012 (also edited by Peter Parsons) and PSI X 1177. *Ass Tale*: P.Lond.Lit. 194 (identified by Lenaerts 1974 as Ps.-Lucian, *Asinus* 47) and P.Oxy. LXX 4762 (discussed in the final section), from a lost ass novel.

codex leaves of prose fiction have been lost for every column or leaf that survives. These missing pages are but one example of the extreme fragmentation of Greek literary culture. The most recent collection of the Greek novels on papyrus lists single or multiple fragments of forty works.[7] More than half of them are marked with the warning label *incertum*, suggesting that most of these *fragmenta incerta* should be classified as types of prose fiction other than the novel.

For more than a century, a steady stream of papyri identified by their editors as 'novels' has come to light. Editors who recognize diminutive scraps of prose fiction on papyrus as fragments of novels seem to be guided by the heuristic principle famously applied by the late US Supreme Court Justice Potter Stewart to a more contentious case concerning the definition of pornography: 'I know it when I see it.'[8] To this day no working definition of what constitutes a Greek novel exists. The only type of ancient novel with which Fabricius was familiar was the so-called love novel. For Fabricius, these texts did not represent a uniform genre but happened to be love stories produced by different authors whom he classified as *erotici scriptores*. This term remained in use until the late 1850s, when Rudolf Hercher published his two volumes of *Erotici scriptores Graeci* for the Bibliotheca Teubneriana. The concept, if not the term, can be traced back to the emperor Julian, who in his capacity as Pontifex Maximus instructed his pagan priests not to read fiction (πλάcματα) 'in the form of history' (ἐν ἱcτορίαc εἴδει), including 'love stories' (ἐρωτικαὶ ὑποθέcειc).[9] Julian is the only pre-Byzantine man of letters who recognized erotic prose fiction as a literary entity, but he does not mention a single author by name, perhaps because he was aware that texts that fitted his description tended to be pseudonymous.

The tensions between the twin concepts of authorship and genre were addressed on an unprecedented scale by Erwin Rohde in his celebrated but wrong-headed 1876 book on the Greek novel.[10] He argued that the love

---

[7] López Martínez 1998. See Messeri 2010 for an illuminating chronological account of the modern rediscovery of lost novels on papyrus; her discussion of the papyri of Achilles Tatius virtually duplicates mine.

[8] Jacobellis v. Ohio, 378 U.S. (1964).

[9] Epist. 89b, 301b p. 169 Bidez (Jan. AD 363) ὅcα δέ ἐcτιν ἐν ἱcτορίαc εἴδει παρὰ τοῖc ἔμπροcθεν ἀπηγγελμένα πλάcματα παραιτητέον, ἐρωτικὰc ὑποθέcειc καὶ πάντα ἀπλῶc τὰ τοιαῦτα. Given that ἱcτορία can mean 'history', 'account', or 'story' in Julian, ἐν ἱcτορίαc εἴδει could refer to 'prose narratives' in general (Ruiz-Montero 2003, 34), but a specific reference to historical novels such as Chariton is more likely (below, n. 12). Bowersock 1994, 16, 111, and 123, to whom the translation 'in the form of history' is owed, suppresses the 'erotic stories' in his quotation of this passage and connects it solely with the *Acts of the Apostles* and similar historical fiction rather than the love novel, even though he treats Chariton at some length in his book. Holzberg 2001, 46 renders the decisive phrase as 'in Gestalt eines Geschichtswerkes'. Cf. Whitmarsh 2005, 607–8, who argues that the reference to 'previous generations' (παρὰ τοῖc ἔμπροcθεν) rules out the novelists; Goldhill 2008, 190 n. 17.

[10] Rohde 1914. On Rohde's chronology and its step-by-step refutation thanks to the successive finds of new papyri see Kussl 1991, 2–11 and Swain 1999b, 12–19.

novel was the creation of the Second Sophistic and that the extant novels perpetuated the Sophistic models, even though they were written later, in most cases much later, than the second century AD. Rohde's false reconstruction of the history of the Greek novel began to unravel in 1893, five years before his death, when a Berlin papyrus with substantial fragments from the *Ninos* romance was published.[11] Penned around the mid-first century AD, the Berlin copy of *Ninos* clearly predates the Second Sophistic and is the earliest specimen of the historicizing type of love story also represented by two near-contemporary novels, Chariton and *Metiochos and Parthenope*.[12] The emergence at regular intervals of papyrus copies with new subgenres of the novel has generated an ongoing debate over the proper definition of the Greek novel as prose fiction.[13] Susan Stephens has proposed a new classification of the fragmentary novels, which she assigns to three types or subgenres, the 'ideal-romantic novel' (e.g. *Metiochos and Parthenope*), the 'nationalistic novel' (*Ninos, Sesonchosis*, and the *Babyloniaka*, among others) and the 'criminal-satiric' novel (especially Lollianos and *Iolaos*).[14] This is a workable typology that accommodates the majority of known fragments, but it is unlikely to be the last word. Future discoveries may require modifications of Stephens' categories, not to mention the existence of *Mischformen*. Interpretation of the novel today is by nature a work in progress, just as the development of the genre was in antiquity.

[11] P. Berol. inv. 6926 (ed. pr. Wilcken 1893) + P. Gen. 85 (ed. pr. Wehrli 1970), second half of the 1st c. AD (Stephens and Winkler 1995, 31; Cavallo 1996, 15 and 124); Messeri 2010, 5 dates the Berlin copy of *Ninos* to the first half of the 1st c. AD. or even to the end of the Ptolemaic period. PSI XIII 1305, from another copy of *Ninos*, has also been assigned to the second half of the 1st c. AD (Cavallo 1996, 31). See the editions by Kussl 1991, 15–101; Stephens and Winkler 1995, 23–71; López Martínez 1998, 37–80. The date of the actual novel is controversial; Bowie 2002, 48–52 makes a strong case for composition in the 1st c. AD rather than the 1st c. BC.

[12] The two most comprehensive studies of the 'subcategory' of the 'historical novel' are Hägg 1987 and Dostálová 1996. On *Metiochos and Parthenope*, first published in 1895 from a Berlin papyrus of the 2nd c. AD, see Maehler 1976; Stephens and Winkler 1995, 72–100; López Martínez 1998, 121–44; Stephens 2003, 657–60; Hägg and Utas 2003 (whose edition of the fragments includes P.Mich. 3402, from a 3rd-c.-AD copy of the novel, edited by Alvares and Renner 2001); Parsons 2010, 44–9 (below, n. 53). On Chariton as a 'historical novel' see Hunter 1994. Bowie 2002, 57 concludes that the three earliest novels 'all seem likely to have been composed within a few decades'. He proposes the following dates (57): 'Chariton between A.D. 41 and 62', *Ninos* 'between A.D. 63 and ca. 75', and *Metiochos and Parthenope* very close in time to *Ninos*. If OBodl. 2175 preserves an excerpt from *Metiochos and Parthenope* (Gronewald 1977; Stephens and Winkler 1995, 93–4; López Martínez 1998, 135) and *if* Cavallo has dated the ostracon convincingly to the first decades of the 1st c. AD (ap. Stramaglia 1996, 123), this novel would have to be even earlier than Bowie suggests. See now Tilg 2010, 92–126.

[13] See esp. Swain 1999*b*; Fusillo 2003; Holzberg 2003; Reardon 2006. Goldhill 2008 excludes the novels on papyrus from his thought-provoking assessment of the genre, to the detriment of his argument.

[14] Stephens 2003. Stephens' 'nationalistic novel' is hardly more than a subcategory of the 'historical novel' (above, n. 12).

## The Chronology of the Extant Novels in the Light of the Papyri

What follows is a discussion of the chronology of the extant novels in light of the papyri. The papyrus discoveries of the past one hundred years have fundamentally altered our understanding of the chronology of the novel, both in terms of the beginnings of the genre and as regards the sequence of the extant novels. In Rohde's erroneous reconstruction of the history of the Greek novel, Achilles Tatius was placed in the middle of the fifth century, after Xenophon of Ephesus, Heliodorus, Chariton, and Longus.[15] In a series of stunning reversals, Rohde's chronology was turned on its head, and now the oldest extant copies of Chariton and Achilles Tatius are safely dated to a much earlier period. In the case of Achilles Tatius, the road from late antiquity to the reign of Antoninus Pius has been particularly long and laborious. Between 1910 and 2009, nine papyri with portions of *Leukippe and Kleitophon* were published, some short and others quite long.[16] Three of them played a crucial role in successive attempts to pin down the author's date, but in the end a single papyrus proved decisive.[17]

That papyrus was published by Peter Parsons, and its publication has brought closure to a discussion that has been going on for almost a century. Let me briefly recapitulate the most memorable moments in this convoluted saga of the dating of Achilles Tatius, which began rather inauspiciously with a missed opportunity. The individual facts are well known, but taken together they comprise a narrative that is new and worthy of the occasion. The first papyrus of Achilles Tatius (P.Oxy. VII 1014) was published in 1910 by Arthur S. Hunt under the erroneous heading 'Historical Fragment'. Assigned to the third century AD, it even found its way into Felix Jacoby's collection of the

---

[15]  Rohde 1914, 503.

[16]  For the papyri of Achilles Tatius published before 1969, see Conca 1969. The most recent list in Plepelits 2003, 391f., omits P. Duk. inv. 722 (see following note).

[17]  The following seven papyri, which represent five different copies of *Leukippe and Kleitophon*, are too late to be relevant for establishing the date of Achilles Tatius: (1) P.Berol. inv. 16971, a papyrus codex of the 3rd c., ed. as P.Schubart 30 in Schubart 1950, 59–60; cf. Poethke 2002, with pl. 1. (2–3) P.Colon. inv. 901 + P.Duk. inv. 722 (formerly P.Rob. inv. 35), early 3rd c. (Willis 1990, 75; Cavallo 1996, 1, 37) or late 3rd c. (Henrichs 1968). (4) P.Oxy. VII 1014 (P.Brux. inv. E 5977), identified by Gronewald 1976 and dated to the beginning or first half of the 3rd c. by Cavallo 1996, 16, 21 pl. 5, and 37. (5) P.Oxy. LVI 3837, 3rd c., published by Parsons in Parsons and Rea 1989, 66–9. Written in the same hand as (6) P.Oxy. X 1250 (below, nn. 20–1), but apparently not from the same papyrus roll. (7) P.Oxy. LXXIII 4948, edited by D. Obbink and Y. Trnka-Amrhein and assigned to the 3rd c., contains a very fragmentary text of Ach. Tat. 2. 37. 8–38. 4. The two papyri on which the date of Achilles Tatius depends, P.Mil. Vogl. III 124 and P.Oxy. LVI 3836, are discussed below.

fragments of the Greek historians.[18] By the time Michael Gronewald made the correct identification in 1976, the papyrus had become irrelevant for the purpose of the dating of this novel.[19] In the intervening period, the fortune of Achilles Tatius had taken a decisive turn for the better with the publication of a series of papyri that, in a quantum leap, lowered the accepted date for his novel by more than three centuries. In January of 1914, Hunt edited P.Oxy. X 1250, which contains the famous description of the invention of wine-making from the beginning of Book II of *Leukippe and Kleitophon* in three consecutive columns and in a narrative order that deviates substantially from that of the medieval manuscripts.[20] The papyrus is written in a handsome book hand, which Hunt assigned to the early fourth century. His date was instantly accepted as the new *terminus ante quem* for Achilles Tatius, who until that time had been universally dated to the fifth or even the sixth century.[21] The revised date enabled Hunt to rewrite literary history in a single sentence and without fanfare: 'The composition of the romance cannot then be put much after the year AD 300, and Achilles need not be supposed to have lived more than a generation or two later than Heliodorus, who is assigned to the latter part of the third century.'[22] As we shall see in due course, Hunt's assumption, inherited from Rohde, that Heliodorus wrote before Achilles Tatius is no longer tenable.

It is noteworthy that in a striking departure from the manuscripts and against the prevailing practice of his time, Hunt reversed the names of the heroine and hero in the title of Achilles' novel and refers to it as *Clitophon and Leucippe* instead of the attested *Leukippe and Kleitophon*. Perhaps Hunt's hierarchy of gender was different from that of Achilles Tatius or of Achilles' Byzantine readers, or Hunt may have been inadvertently influenced by one of the attested titles of Longus' novel, *Shepherd Tales about Daphnis and Chloe* (Ποιμενικὰ περὶ Δάφνιν καὶ Χλόην), conventionally quoted in abbreviated form as *Daphnis and Chloe*. Not surprisingly, the order of the two names is also reversed in the alternate title given by one of the two principal MSS of Longus, the Vaticanus Gr. 1348, which marks the closure of the work with the following colophon: 'The end of Longus' Goatherd Tales about Chloe and Daphnis' (τέλος τῶν κατὰ Χλόην καὶ Δάφνιν Λόγγου αἰπολικῶν). Attested titles of extant novels such as these and numerous references to them

---

[18] *FGrH* 105 F 8.    [19] Above, n. 17 (4).
[20] Hunt in Grenfell and Hunt 1914, 135–42, with pl. VI. See Bowersock 1994, 125–8, who connects the discovery of wine in Achilles Tatius (2. 2. 1–6) with the account of the Eucharist in the gospels.
[21] Going beyond Rohde, W. Schmid, *RE* i. 245 advocated a date in the 6th c. He recanted after the publication of P.Oxy. X 1250 and assigned Achilles Tatius to the late 3rd c. (Schmid in Schmid and Stählin 1924, 1047).
[22] Hunt in Grenfell and Hunt 1914, 135.

in Byzantine authors suggest that these titles must have been in flux since antiquity, and Hunt's lapse simply perpetuates their fluidity.[23] Unfortunately the papyri are of limited help in this regard. The titles of only two novels survive on papyrus, the *Phoinikika* of Lollianos and the *Kallirhoe* of Chariton, both of which will be discussed at a later point.

In 1989, seventy-five years after Hunt's redating of Achilles Tatius, Peter Parsons published P.Oxy. LVI 3837, another fragment from the same MS as P.Oxy. X 1250.[24] As he points out, the two papyri come from different volumes of one and the same copy of Achilles, which occupied three or four papyrus rolls. His edition of that papyrus corrects Hunt's dating and moves the papyrus from the fourth to the third century.[25] In a deliciously judicious description of the handwriting, he compares the two versions of the same hand and observes: 'The script too is very similar, although in 3837 it looks less bold and emphatic; it is a mixture of formal and informal letter-shapes, mostly bilinear, with quite heavy shading, suggesting an early Biblical Uncial gone slumming. Grenfell and Hunt assigned it to the fourth century, Schubart more plausibly to the third (PSchubart p. 60).'[26]

By this time, however, new discoveries had made the third-century date for Achilles Tatius obsolete. As early as 1938 his date was brought down even further by a fragment from a Milan papyrus codex assigned to the late second century by Achille Vogliano.[27] In 1989, the second-century date was confirmed by another Oxyrhynchos papyrus edited by Peter Parsons (P.Oxy. LVI 3836). But this is not the end of the story. In a remarkable twist of events, Guglielmo Cavallo, an eminent palaeographer, rejected Vogliano's date for the Milan codex in 1996. Instead of the late second century suggested by Vogliano, he opted for a date towards the end of the third century.[28] The photo that accompanies his article bears him out. At that point, the Milan codex ceased to matter for deciding Achilles' date. Although nobody seems to be aware of it, the universally accepted second-century date for *Leukippe and Kleitophon* now depends entirely on Peter Parsons's dating of P.Oxy. 3836. Fortunately, the hand that penned it is of an abundantly attested type— labelled 'round informal' by Parsons—that makes the second-century date indisputable. In fact Cavallo himself has followed suit and dates this papyrus more precisely to the *first* half of the second century AD—although

---

[23] For a typology of the titles of the Greek novel see the detailed study by Whitmarsh 2005, who does not, however, distinguish adequately between pre-Byzantine and Byzantine conventions of quoting or fabricating such titles.

[24] Above, n. 17 (5–6).

[25] Parsons's date has been accepted by Cavallo 1996, 16, 37 n. 61.

[26] Parsons in Parsons and Rea 1989, 66.

[27] Vogliano 1938; the papyrus was later re-edited as P.Mil.Vogl. III 124.

[28] Cavallo 1996, 16, 24 pl. 6, and 37–8 ('non anteriore al tardo secolo III').

whether such meticulous precision is ultimately sustainable remains to be seen.[29]

Before we proceed to the other novelists, let us pause for a moment to consider what the papyri tell us about the ancient editions of Achilles Tatius and the status of his text. Written in seven different hands ranging in date from the early or mid-second to the late third century, the papyri of Achilles Tatius come from two codices and six rolls, which represent seven separate editions of the novel.[30] All seven editions were produced within a time span of 150 to 200 years, namely between AD 100–50 and 300. Such a high concentration of papyrus copies in a single period would be exceptional for any genre of Greek literature other than the novel. As Cavallo has demonstrated, almost 90% of the existing papyrus copies of extant as well as lost novels cluster within the same two centuries.[31] The second and third centuries of the empire were clearly a period of unparalleled productivity and popularity for the Greek novel. After this burst of creativity, few if any new novels were written. The majority of the novels produced in this period were soon forgotten, and the history of the novel became a process of progressive elimination. There were few survivors, but Achilles Tatius was one of them.

The survival of Achilles Tatius into Byzantine times makes it all the more remarkable that so far no papyrus or parchment text of his work has emerged with a date later than the third century. Late antique and early Byzantine copies of *Leukippe and Kleitophon* obviously existed, and they may still come to light. Needless to say, they would not provide further clues regarding the date of Achilles' novel, but they might supplement our scanty knowledge of the early history of its text. As the extensive Cologne/Duke fragments from an exceptionally informative third-century papyrus roll have shown, the text of Achilles Tatius was infinitely less stable and much more in flux than its Byzantine recensions suggest.[32] The transposition of an entire narrative episode in one of the Oxyrhynchos papyri of Achilles Tatius points in the same direction.[33] Wilamowitz explained major discrepancies between the Codex Thebanus of Chariton and the codex *unicus* in Florence as the inevitable result of 'unprotected texts run wild' ('Verwilderung ungeschützter Texte').[34] It is conceivable that cases like these are not representative of the

[29] Cavallo 1996, 16, 36. Dostálová 1991, 21 mistakenly assigns P.Oxy. LVI 3836 to the 4th c. AD. If Cavallo's early dating of P.Oxy. 3836 holds, Achilles Tatius' novel must have been written 'nearer 120 than 150 CE' (Bowie 2008, 23, who does not give a reason for his proposed date).
[30] See above, nn. 16–17.
[31] Cavallo 1996, 15–16.
[32] On the Cologne/Duke papyrus see above, n. 17 (2–3).
[33] P.Oxy. X 1250 (above, at n. 20).
[34] Wilamowitz 1901, 34, quoted by Lucke 1985, 22. On the respective merits of the Codex Thebanus and Laur. Conv. Soppr. 627 see Conca 2010.

pre-Byzantine textual history of the novel and that we are dealing with a few aberrant manuscripts or recensions, with 'rogue' copies as it were.[35] But Achilles Tatius and Chariton happen to be the only extant novelists of whose work we have multiple copies on papyrus. The fact that three of these copies differ substantially from the Byzantine manuscripts suggests that textual deviation may have been endemic to a genre as fluid as the Greek novel. Martin West surely had a point when he observed a long time ago 'that copyists of this type of work ... felt themselves at liberty to change the wording as they went along'.[36] He was talking about textual discrepancies between the two principal manuscripts of Longus. The Cologne/Duke papyrus of Achilles Tatius, which deviates drastically from the manuscript tradition, amply confirms West's observation, and does so for a much earlier phase of the textual transmission than that represented by the Byzantine manuscripts.

Thanks to the papyri, Achilles Tatius has been restored to his proper period, and the earliest history of his text has been illuminated, albeit in unexpected ways that have made the task of editing him all the more difficult. Fortune has been equally kind to Chariton, whose case is more straightforward. Fragments of three papyrus rolls survive on four papyri published between 1900 and 1972. Their dates suggest that copies of his novel circulated from the early to the late second century AD and beyond.[37] This represents a signal improvement upon the chronology of Rohde, who dated Chariton between the late third and the early sixth century.[38] Though much older than Rohde thought, Chariton's novel was still copied in late antiquity, which helps to explain why it survived into the Byzantine period. While travelling in Upper Egypt in 1898, Ulrich Wilcken acquired several pages from a parchment codex, the so-called 'codex Thebanus deperditus', which he dated to the sixth or seventh century.[39] Remarkably, this codex contained a collection of prose fiction that included Chariton's *Kallirhoe* as well as another novel about Chione and her suitors. The Codex Thebanus must be seen as a precursor to

[35] Reardon 2003, 315 refers to the Codex Thebanus of Chariton (below, at n. 39) as 'a "rogue" text'.

[36] West 1973, 17.

[37] They are, in order of publication, (1) P. Fayum 1, first half of 2nd c. (Cavallo 1996, 16, 25 pl. 7, 38); (2–3) P.Oxy. VII 1019 and P.Oxy. XLI 2948, from the same 2nd/3rd c. roll. P.Oxy. 1019 is reproduced in Turner and Parsons 1987, no. 66, P.Oxy. 2948 in the *ed. pr.*; (4) P. Michael. 1, 2nd c. (Messeri 2010, 8 n. 26 refers to an image of the papyrus on the website of the Schoyen Collection: http://www.schoyencollection.com/papyri.htm#2930). On these papyri see Lucke 1985, Dostálová 1991, 14–18.

[38] Rohde 1914, 521–2, according to whom Chariton used Heliodoros (dated by him to the late 3rd c. AD) and possibly also Achilles Tatius (whom he assigned to the mid-5th c.).

[39] Wilcken 1901; Cavallo 1996, 14, 16, 38. Chione: Dostálová 1991, 15–17; Stephens and Winkler 1995, 289–301; López Martínez 1998, 287–95.

Byzantine miscellaneous manuscripts such as the thirteenth-century Codex Laurentianus Conventi Soppressi 627 in Florence that contains the text of Chariton, Xenophon of Ephesus, Longus, and Achilles Tatius, and that is our only source for Xenophon of Ephesus and for most of Chariton. But alas, all that remains of Wilcken's codex are his own transcripts, which he made while sailing down the Nile. The actual palimpsest leaves were destroyed when the ship that brought them to Germany caught fire in the dockyards of Hamburg. As so often, our knowledge of the earliest history of the Greek novel turns on missing pages.

In the case of Chariton and Achilles Tatius, the earliest papyrus copies furnish merely a *terminus ante quem* for the actual date of composition. In theory both novels could be earlier. This is where internal criteria enter into the discussion and the ground gets more slippery again. Chariton is an infinitely more likely candidate for a first-century-AD date than Achilles. The earliest extant copy of Chariton, P. Fayum 1, has been plausibly assigned to the first half of the second century by Cavallo; its first editors, including Grenfell and Hunt, had dated it more generally to the second century.[40] But the decisive piece of evidence for Chariton's date may not come from papyri, but from Roman literature. In the first of his *Satires*, Persius attacks consumers of popular literature of the light variety and ends his poem by sarcastically recommending 'Callirhoe' as an after-lunch treat (134 *post prandia Calliroen do*). If this is a reference to Chariton's novel, it was not only known and available in Neronian Rome but had, in George Goold's words, 'achieved the status of a classic.'[41] In fact it is more than likely that Persius' reference to Callirhoe preserves not only the name of Chariton's heroine but also the abbreviated title of his novel. According to the subscription in the Michaelidis papyrus of Chariton, published in 1955, the novel's title was simply *The Story of Kallirhoe* (τὰ περὶ Καλλιρόην διηγήματα), with no mention of her soulmate Chaireas.[42] A mid-first-century-AD date for Chariton thus imposes itself and reflects the consensus of the majority of scholars today.[43] Those who prefer an even earlier date, i.e. in the late Hellenistic period, must resort to stylistic arguments, which are far from conclusive.

The combined testimony of Persius and the papyri suggests that Chariton's work predates that of Achilles Tatius, even if their lifetimes may have overlapped. I am not aware of anybody who would want to place Achilles Tatius

---

[40] Above, n. 37 (1); Grenfell, Hunt, and Hogart 1900, 74–82.

[41] Goold 1995, 5; cf. Bowie 2002, 54. According to Whitmarsh 2005, 590 Persius is referring to a poetic text, not a novel. See Tilg 2010, 69–78 for a full discussion.

[42] Tilg 2010, 74–5, 214–15. On P. Michael. 1 see above, n. 37 (4).

[43] Reardon 2003, 316–17, as well as in the preface to his 2004 Teubner edition of Chariton; Bowie 2002, esp. 57 (quoted above, n. 12); Tilg 2010, 78–9.

earlier than the second century AD, the date supported by the earliest papyrus. Ewen Bowie asserted not long ago that Achilles' novel 'can hardly antedate 150 AD'.[44] But if Cavallo's early-second-century date for P.Oxy. LVI 3836 should gain universal acceptance, we shall have to contemplate the possibility that *Leukippe and Kleitophon* may have been composed in the late first century rather than the second. That is indeed hard to believe. But the final verdict is still outstanding, all the more since Cavallo's early date for the oldest papyrus of Achilles Tatius seems to have gone unnoticed. Time will tell whether it will win acceptance.

Chariton and Achilles Tatius are the two novelists who have benefited substantially from the papyri. Unfortunately the other three have not been so lucky, at least not yet. As far as I know, neither Longus nor Xenophon of Ephesos has come to light on papyrus. Both are generally believed to have been active in the mid to late second century AD. There is no hard evidence that would make such a date compelling for either author, but the case for Longus is arguably slightly stronger than that for Xenophon.[45] The date for Heliodoros is still wide open. In 1979, before the availability of the *TLG* made identification easier, Michael Gronewald recognized two passages from the *Aithiopika* on a minute and barely legible scrap from a vellum codex that had been first published as a piece of indistinguishable prose by Grenfell and Hunt.[46] With an assigned date in the sixth to seventh century,[47] the parchment is, alas, much too late to settle the controversy over the lifetime of the author, who has been dated on internal grounds either in the 230s or 240s, close to Rohde's date, or else in the second half of the fourth century. Much depends on one's assessment of converging descriptions of military siege strategies by Heliodoros, the emperor Julian, and Ephraem the Syrian.[48] The case of Heliodoros reminds us that the papyri are not a panacea for all the problems besetting the chronology of the novel. Rohde still casts his long and formidable shadow. Only a new papyrus of Heliodoros from the third century or the first half of the fourth century could bring absolute certainty.

The progress that has been made in establishing a more precise chronology for the novelists is inextricably linked to the assignment of palaeographical dates for the earliest papyrus texts containing portions of known novels or fragments of lost novels. The dating of these texts does not depend on the dubious internal criteria that led Rohde astray but on the more objective

---

[44] Bowie 2003.

[45] Dalmeyda 1926, pp. xii–xv; Weinreich 1962, 18–19; Morgan 2004, 2.

[46] Gronewald 1979 on P.Amh. II 160.

[47] Cavallo 1996, 16, 38.

[48] Bowersock 1994, 48–9, 149–55 makes the strongest possible case for a post-Julian date for Heliodoros' *Aithiopika*, 'the latest of the extant novels'. Holzberg 2001, 140–1 defends the conventional 3rd-c. date.

dating of the papyrus hands. Unfortunately dating papyri on palaeographical grounds is a more precarious business than the philological man in the street might think. Even under the best of circumstances, dates assigned to literary hands by the most experienced papyrologists have a margin of error of plus or minus twenty-five to thirty years, enough to move a papyrus from one century to the next. Most literary papyri can be dated reliably within a span of fifty years, but not necessarily within a given century. Even so, four of the five longest papyri with fragments of lost novels, including the *Iolaos* papyrus and the *Phoinikika* of Lollianos, have all been squarely dated within the second century AD by their editors.[49] I have no intention of disputing these dates, least of all the one for which I am responsible. Their combined testimony suggests that the Greek novel was particularly popular in the second century, a trend that is self-evident and widely acknowledged in the more recent histories of Greek literature.[50]

## The *Phoinikika*: Text and Context

With its scenes of human sacrifice, cannibalism, group sex, ghoulish masquerades, ghost apparitions, and male defloration, the *Phoinikika* is unrivalled among extant novels in its relentless appeal to the most visceral and vulgar instincts of its readers.[51] It is so unique that it prompted Bryan Reardon to remark in a recent article: 'We can of course always hope that the patient teasing-out of increasingly rare papyrus fragments will bring some valuable information, especially about dating; but we can scarcely hope for another *Phoenicica*.'[52] The discovery of another novel like the *Phoinikika* is perhaps more than can be expected, but we can certainly hope that another copy of the *Phoinikika* itself may come to light. Lollianos' work is one of the few novels on papyrus of which multiple copies exist.[53] Two of them are

[49] The Berlin papyrus with the principal fragments of *Metiochos and Parthenope* (above, n. 12) as well as the *Herpyllis* papyrus in Dublin (Kussl 1991, 105–40; Stephens and Winkler 1995, 158–72; López Martínez 1998, 107–20) have also been dated to the 2nd c.

[50] e.g. Lesky 1963, 919; Dihle 1989, 147, 247.

[51] On what to make of the initiation scene of the *Phoinikika* (P.Colon. inv. 3328, fr. B 1 recto) and on the ongoing debate over the status of religion in the ancient novel see most recently Henrichs 2006, Bierl 2007, Harland 2007, Harrison 2007, and Zeitlin 2008.

[52] Reardon 2006, 236–7.

[53] The two others are *Ninos* (above, n. 11) and *Kalligone* (PSI VIII 981 and P.Oxy. inv. 112/130(a); see Stephens and Winkler 1995, 267–76 and López Martínez 1998, 145–55). The two papyri with fragments of the *Eselsroman* come from two separate versions (above, n. 5). If P.Oxy. LXXI 4811 (*Panionis*) and PSI XI 1220 (*Staphylos*, see Stephens and Winkler 1995, 429–37, López Martínez 1998, 307–16) preserve fragments of the same novel, they must come from the same roll or the same copy (Messeri 2010, 17–18). The assignment of the *Panionis* and *Staphylos* fragments to *Metiochos and Parthenope* (above, n. 12) remains speculative (Parsons 2010).

Oxyrhynchos papyri penned by different hands in the third century AD. Their attribution to the *Phoinikika* is absolutely certain because they share a number of narrative features with the Cologne papyrus, our main source for the novel, and because the name of Glauketes occurs in all three papyri.[54]

Dated to the mid to late second century AD on palaeographical grounds, the Cologne papyrus codex with substantial fragments of Lollianos' *Phoinikika* happens to be the only pre-Byzantine copy of a Greek novel that preserves the author's name as well as the title of his work. In the case of all the other novels transmitted exclusively on papyrus, the names of the authors are unknown, and the titles of their works are lost. Whenever possible, modern editors identify the novels on papyrus by the names of their leading characters, for instance *Ninos, Metiochos and Parthenope, Iolaos* or *Chione*, a practice that goes back to the Byzantine period and beyond. In many cases, however, they resort to utterly fictitious titles derived from some conspicuous detail of the story. Here is a representative sampling of such fabricated titles found in German, English, and Spanish collections of these papyri: 'Absage an Eros', 'Gefunden', 'Dem Tode entronnen', 'The Love Drug', 'The Apparition', 'Inundation', 'Initiation', 'Muchacho', 'Amigo', 'Padres', 'Sueño', 'Fiesta campestre', 'Educación', 'El filósofo', and 'Cocodrilos'.[55] It is not at all clear how many of these texts qualify as novels, but the range and diversity of the narratives to which they allude are indicative of a defining feature of the Greek novel, namely its open form and protean transformability.

The struggle of editors to make up for missing titles sharpens one's appreciation of the one attested title, *Phoinikika*. *Phoenician Tales* rings a familiar bell.[56] It implies an interest in Phoenicia that is in keeping with the ubiquitous presence of the Eastern Mediterranean from Asia Minor to Egypt and beyond in the extant novels. It also reminds us that the novelists were distant heirs of Herodotos and loved to entertain their Greek readers with their constructs of non-Greek ethnic landscapes, be they Phoenician, Persian, or Ethiopian. Titles of this particular type, with their distinctive linguistic formation and ethnographical connotation, were well established by the time

---

[54] On the *Phoinikika* see most recently Casanova 2010 and Henrichs 2010, 76–80. The known copies of the *Phoinikika* are these: (1) P.Oxy. XI 1368, published as a fragment of an unknown novel by Grenfell and Hunt in 1915, was identified as belonging to the *Phoinikika* by Michael Reeve (ap. Henrichs 1970). (2) P.Colon. inv. 3328 (ed. Henrichs 1972), which preserves the title of the novel, the name of its author, and the most extensive fragments. (3) P.Oxy. LXXIII 4945, from a third copy of the *Phoinikika*, was published by Dirk Obbink in 2009; cf. Cavallo 1996, 14 n. 5. The two copies from Oxyrhynchus are rolls, whereas the Cologne copy is in codex format. For recent editions of (1) and (2) see Stephens and Winkler 1995, 314–57; López Martínez 1998, 163–208.

[55] For these fabricated titles see Zimmermann 1936; Stephens and Winkler 1995; López Martínez 1998.

[56] Henrichs 1972, 11–23.

Lollianos composed the *Phoinikika*.[57] Comparable works of prose fiction with similarly formed titles include the *Ephesiaka* of Xenophon of Ephesos, the *Lesbiaka* of Longus, the *Babyloniaka* of Iamblichus, and the *Aithiopika* of Heliodorus. Their most prominent Hellenistic ancestor, the *Milesiaka* of Aristeides, is first mentioned in Plutarch's *Life of Crassus* (32), where the work is referred to as 'licentious books' (ἀκόλαστα βιβλία). The salacious content of works like the *Milesiaka* is certainly reflected in some of the novels of the early imperial period, beginning with Petronius' *Satyricon libri*, whose title Ϲατυρικά is a clever parody of the Greek convention.[58]

Who was this Lollianos? Questions of authorship and authorial identity arise even in connection with the extant novels. With the exception of their names, the identities of novelists like Chariton and Xenophon of Ephesos remain elusive. Apart from his work, even Longus survives only as a mere name with a family connection on Lesbos. Achilles Tatius and Heliodoros do not fare much better; the scarce biographical data attached to their names are Christian fabrications. Lollianos fits this pattern of virtual anonymity all too well—in fact nothing at all is known about the author of the *Phoinikika*. Inevitably, his name invites comparison with the sophist P. Hordeonius Lollianus of Ephesos, who was the first holder of the Athenian chair of rhetoric under Hadrian or Antoninus Pius. According to an honorary epigram from Athens, he made his reputation as 'a case lawyer and expert in rhetorical declamations' (ῥητῆρα δικῶν μελέτῃϲί τε ἄριϲτον).[59] The sophist's professional persona and polished prose stand in stark contrast to the hiatus-ridden style and vulgar subject-matter of the *Phoinikika*.[60] It is thus prudent, to say the least, to distinguish the novelist from the sophist. After all, the name Lollianus/-os was common enough in the early imperial period. Christopher Jones and the late George Goold are among the few scholars who convinced themselves of the identity of the two.[61] In support of his claim, Goold refers to analogous modern cases, but he fails to mention that even the Revd Charles Dodgson, a lifelong resident of Christ Church, adopted a pseudonym when he published *Alice in Wonderland*. I am afraid Professor Lollianos might have lost his chair—an imperial appointment—had he

---

[57] Ibid. 11–12; Stephens and Winkler 1995, 318–19. Whitmarsh 2005 makes a convincing case for diachronic fluidity as far as the titles of the Greek novels are concerned. But he resorts to special pleading because the evidence is not on his side when he argues for the conceptual and generic primacy of titles derived from the names of the hero and/or heroine as opposed to 'geographical' titles of the type Φοινικικά and Αἰθιοπικά.

[58] See e.g. Whitmarsh 2005, 594. Perry 1967, 191–2 rendered the title *Satyrica* of Petronius' novel as 'A Tale from the Land of Lascivious'. The existence of a Greek *Satyrika* that inspired Petronius has been repeatedly posited, most recently by Jensson 2004.

[59] *IG* ii/iii² 4211.

[60] Henrichs 1972, 24–7.

[61] Jones 1980, 253–4; Goold 1995, 8–9.

written the *Phoinikika* and circulated the novel under his own name.[62] Still, could it be more than mere coincidence that the sophist and the novelist shared a name? Ewen Bowie suggested that the *Phoinikika* may have been deliberately attributed to the sophist and 'circulated maliciously under his name.'[63] Ironically, Bowie's suggestion would turn Rohde's thesis on its head. Far from originating in the intellectual climate of the Second Sophistic, the *Phoinikika* would have concealed its true provenance by taking cover behind the name of one of the most distinguished representatives of this movement. Sailing under a false sophistic flag would have been a real coup for the author of the *Phoinikika*. Such a scenario is not inconceivable, but it is perhaps too good to be true. While further collapsing Rohde's edifice, it nevertheless echoes the intimate link between sophists and novelists that he posited.

Finally, I present some tentative thoughts on thematic connections between one of the canonical novels and two of the new novels on papyrus. To the detriment of both, the two sets of texts are all too often studied separately, as if they belonged to two distinct traditions that existed on separate planes. In one exceptional case, however, Jones and Winkler have compared a sequence of events and a series of motifs that can be found in the *Phoinikika* as well as in Apuleius' *Metamorphoses* (4. 8, 22).[64] The convergences between the two texts have been summed up as follows by Susan Stephens: 'Events take place in a similar order in the party scenes in both texts: the bandits enter, there is feasting, mention of Lapiths and Centaurs, drinking, singing songs, dressing up in white and black costume and exiting into night for criminal purposes, followed by an attempted escape in Apuleius and possibility of escape in Lollianus.'[65] Stephens concludes that 'there are too many convergences . . . in too small a space for the pattern to be accidental.'[66]

Various explanations come to mind: Apuleius borrowed from Lollianos, Lollianos was inspired by Apuleius (a most unlikely scenario), or both used a common source. As Stephens points out, the major obstacle to postulating too close a connection between the two novels is that there is no ass transformation in the extant fragments of Lollianos. In the absence of any trace of such a metamorphosis in the preserved portions of the *Phoinikika*, I cannot

---

[62] According to Stephens and Winkler 1995, 317, the notion that novel-writing was socially reprehensible 'cannot be justified by the ancient evidence'. Yet, while there is no evidence to support my belief, more importantly I know of no evidence that would contradict it.

[63] Bowie 1985, 686 = 1999, 43.

[64] Jones 1980, 251–3; Winkler 1980, 158–9; Stephens and Winkler 1995, 322–5.

[65] Stephens 2003, 672.

[66] Stephens 2003, 672, echoing Stephens and Winkler 1995, 324. The possible occurrence of the name Myrrhine in l. 6 of the new Oxyrhynchus fragment of the *Phoinikika* (above, n. 54) would strengthen Stephens's case; a slave girl of the same name appears in *Metam.* 2. 24 (see Cioffi and Trnka-Amrhein 2010). But as Obbink points out in his edition of P.Oxy. LXXIII 4945, the sequence $] \,_{.} \iota \delta \epsilon \ \mu \upsilon \rho \rho \iota \nu \eta \varsigma \ \upsilon \delta \alpha \tau [$ can be interpreted as the proper name or as a reference to the myrtle plant or myrtle wine.

transform Androtimos into an ass, but I can and will draw attention to a new fragment from an unknown ass romance on a recently published papyrus (P.Oxy. LXX 4762; Pl. 16) that reads like a Greek version of one of the most notorious sex scenes in Apuleius.

In Book 10 of the *Metamorphoses*, a wealthy Corinthian lady lusts for the man-turned-ass Lucius and pays to have sex with him. Apuleius describes the climax of their love-making in vivid detail: 'Looking at me with ravishing eyes, she redoubled her enticing nicknames, relentless kisses, and sweet moans, till at last exclaiming, "I embrace you, I embrace you, my little dove, my sparrow", she showed through her words that all my fears were falsely grounded. She held me tight and received all of me, absolutely all of me' (*artissime namque complexa totum me prorsus, sed totum recepit*).[67] The corresponding female figure in the new papyrus seems hardly less eager, but she urges caution, falling inexplicably into iambic trimeters: 'Wow, it's thick and big as a roof-beam. Hold it, not so fast. Don't thrust it all in' (οὐ⟨ᾶ⟩, παχεῖα καὶ μεγάλη 'στιν, ὡς δοκός. / μένε, κατὰ μικρόν· μη⟨δ⟩' ὅλην ἔσω βάλῃς).'[68] In both cases, the male has the looks and measurements of a donkey. His organ is so huge that its size threatens to jeopardize the sexual encounter while adding a comic touch that mitigates the explicit reference to penetration. The similarities linking the two texts are remarkable—two ill-matched lovers going for it, the direct speech by the woman immediately before intercourse, and at the moment of physical union the complete convergence of *totum* and ὅλην. The new papyrus confirms that Apuleius used a Greek ass-novel as his source of inspiration, but if the depth of penetration is any indication, Apuleius (*totum recepit*) appears to be distinctly closer to the Lucianic *Onos* (ὅλον παρεδέξατο[69]) than to the new papyrus (μη⟨δ⟩' ὅλην ἔσω βάλῃς, in iambics!). The juxtaposition of these passages strongly suggests that P.Oxy. LXX 4762 cannot come from the lost ass romance that was the common source for the *Onos* as well as Apuleius' *Metamorphoses*.[70]

Sex looms large in the relatively small portion of the *Phoinikika* that survives—a burning desire that leads to intercourse, sex for pay, 'defloration'

---

[67] *Met.* 10. 22, in Jack Lindsay's transl. (adapted).

[68] The two prosimetric trimeters are either the work of the novelist or a quotation from an unkown comedy. On the trimeters in question and on the fluid interaction of verse and prose in certain types of prose fiction see Hunter 2010, 226–30.

[69] In his edition of P.Oxy. LXX 4762, Dirk Obbink compared Ps.-Lucian, *Onos* 51, where the donkey-narrator relates how the rich oversexed lady 'embraced me as if she were lying with a man, and lifting me/it up she received all of me/it inside' (ὥσπερ ἀνδρὶ παρακειμένη περιβάλλεταί με καὶ ἄρασα εἴσω ὅλον παρεδέξατο). This passage is crucial for an assessment of the relationship between the new papyrus, the *Onos*, and Apuleius' *Metam.* (cf. Stramaglia 2010, 178–9 and Zanetto 2010, 53–4).

[70] On this source, erroneously identified as Loukios of Patrai by Photios, see van Thiel 1971, 2–7 and Mason 1994.

(διακόρηϲιϲ) of a male by a female, and group sex.[71] But talk about sex in the *Phoinikika* is not remotely as graphic or as hilarious as in the various versions of the ass novel, including Apuleius, or for that matter in Petronius.[72] A similar restraint can be observed in the canonical Greek love novels. Descriptions or mention of intercourse can be found in all of them, but no direct reference is made to male or female genitalia, let alone to penetration.[73] Descriptions of sexual activity that border on pornography are widely believed to be one of the hallmarks of the early Roman novel. But since the publication of P.Oxy. LXX 4762, such a view is no longer tenable. A penchant for raunchy sex scenes is not what separates the Roman from the Greek novel, but a higher degree of sexual realism does seem to separate the 'comic' from the 'serious' novels, regardless of the language in which they are written.

In his comprehensive survey of the Greek novels on papyrus J. R. Morgan observed ten years ago: 'Discoveries like the "Phoinikika" of Lollianus or the so-called "Iolaos Romance" have revealed that fiction of quite a different kind existed in ancient Greece: sensational, sexually explicit, low-life, sometimes overtly comic, sometimes combining prose and verse.'[74] The papyrus discoveries of the last few decades have indeed redefined the genre of the Greek novel by redrawing its thematic and narrative boundaries. By the same token, they have also narrowed the gap, as conventionally defined in the not-so-distant past, between the 'Greek' and the 'Roman' novel.[75] On a smaller scale, they have given us new tools with which to tackle some of the perennial problems surrounding the canonical novels—their date, their pre-Byzantine text history, and their popularity as measured by the number of surviving copies. In all of this, Peter Parsons has been a major player, and a shining example for the rest of us. [76]

# BIBLIOGRAPHY

Alvares, J., and Renner, T. (eds.), 2001, 'A New Fragment of the Metiochus and Parthenope Romance?', in I. Andorlini *et al.* (eds.), *Atti del XXII Congresso Internazionale di Papirologia* (Florence), i. 35–40.

---

[71] P.Oxy. LXXIII 4945, ll. 11, 14, and 19; P.Colon. inv. 3328 (above, n. 54 (2)), fr. A 2 recto 8–14, B 1 verso 20–1.

[72] Petron. 127, cf. Sullivan 1968, 232–53 on sex in the *Satyrica*; Ps.-Lucian, *Onos* 8–10, 51; Apul. *Met.* 2. 17, 10. 21–2.

[73] Ach. Tat. 5. 27; Chariton 2. 8. 4, 4. 4. 9; Heliod. 1. 15. 8, 3. 17. 4; Longus 3. 18, 4. 40; Xen Eph. 1. 9. 9, 3. 12.

[74] Morgan 1998, 3295–6.

[75] Holzberg 2003; Barchiesi 2006; Paschalis *et al.* 2007; Henrichs 2010, 69.

[76] I am indebted to Robert Cioffi, Sarah Nolan, Dirk Obbïnk, Richard Rutherford, Yvona Trnka-Amrhein, and John Tully for their help with successive versions of this paper, which was completed more than three years before the publication of Messeri 2010.

Barchiesi, A. 2006, 'Romanzo greco, romanzo latino: problemi e prospettive della recerca attuale', in L. Graverini, W. Keulen, and A. Barchiesi (eds.), *Il romanzo antico: forme, testi, problemi* (Rome), 193–218.

Bastianini, G. and Casanova, A. (eds.), 2010, *I papiri del romanzo antico. Atti del Convegno Internazionale di Studi, Firenze, 11–12 giugno 2009*' (Florence).

Bierl, A. 2007, 'Mysterien der Liebe und die Initiation Jugendlicher: Literatur und Religion im griechischen Roman', in A. Bierl, R. Lämmle, and K. Wesselmann (eds.), *Literatur und Religion*, ii: *Wege zu einer mythisch-rituellen Poetik bei den Griechen* (Berlin and New York), 239–334.

Bowersock, G. W. 1994, *Fiction as History: Nero to Julian* (Berkeley, Los Angeles, and London).

Bowie, E. L. 1985, 'The Greek Novel', in P. E. Easterling and B. M. W. Knox (eds.), *The Cambridge Companion to Classical Literature*, i: *Greek Literature* (Cambridge), 683–99; repr. in Swain 1999*a*, 39–59.

—— 2002, 'The Chronology of the Earlier Greek Novels since B. E. Perry: Revisions and Precisions', *Ancient Narrative*, 2, 47–63.

—— 2003, 'Achilles Tatius', *OCD* 7.

—— 2008, 'Literary Milieux', in Whitmarsh 2008, 17–38.

Casanova, A. 2010, 'Ambienti e luoghi nei frammenti di Lolliano', in Bastianini and Casanova 2010, 121–37.

Cavallo, G. 1996, 'Veicoli materiali della letteratura di consumo: maniere di scrivere e maniere di leggere', in Pecere and Stramaglia 1996, 11–46; repr. in id., *Il calamo e il papiro: la scrittura greca dall'età ellenistica ai primi secoli di Bisanzio* (Florence, 2005), 213–33.

Cioffi, R. and Trnka-Amrhein, Y. (2010), 'What's in a Name? Further Similarities between Lollianos' *Phoinikika* and Apuleius' *Metamorphoses*', *ZPE* 173, 66–8.

Conca, F. 1969, 'I papiri di Achille Tazio', *RIL* 103, 649–77.

Conca, F. 2010, 'Il *Codex Thebanus* e i papiri: suggestioni sul testo di Caritone', in Bastianini and Casanova 2010, 139–52.

Dalmeyda, G. 1926, *Xénophon d'Éphèse, les Éphésiaques, ou le roman d'Habrocomès et d'Anthia* (Paris).

Dihle, A. 1989, *Die griechische und lateinische Literatur der Kaiserzeit von Augustus bis Iustinian* (München).

Dostálová, R. 1991, *Il romanzo greco e i papiri* (Prague).

—— 1996, 'La dissoluzione della storiografia: il "romanzo storico"', in Pecere and Stramaglia 1996, 169–88.

Fabricius, J. A. 1726, *Bibliothecae Graecae libri V pars altera, sive volumen sextum, quo Graeci auctores annalium, et historiae ecclesiasticae ac Byzantinae, nec non erotici scriptores recensentur* (Hamburg).

Fusillo, M. 2003, 'Modern Critical Theories and the Ancient Novel', in Schmeling 2003, 277–305.

Goldhill, S. 2008, 'Genre', in Whitmarsh 2008, 185–200.

Goold, G. 1995, *Chariton: Callirhoe* (Loeb Classical Library, Cambridge, MA, and London).

Grenfell, B. P., and Hunt, A. S. 1914, *The Oxyrhynchus Papyri*, Part X (Oxford).

—— —— and Hogart, D. G. 1900, *Fayum Towns and their Papyri* (London).

Gronewald, M. 1976, 'Ein verkannter Papyrus des Achilleus Tatios (P.Oxy. 1014 = Achilleus Tatios IV 14, 2–5)', *ZPE* 22, 14–17.

—— 1977, 'Ein neues Fragment aus dem *Metiochos-Parthenope-Roman* (Ostrakon Bodl. 2175 = Pack² 2782)', *ZPE* 24, 21–2.

—— 1979, 'Ein Fragment aus den Aithiopica des Heliodor (P. Amh. 160 = Pack² 2797)', *ZPE* 34, 19–21.

Hägg, T. 1987, '*Callirhoe* and *Parthenope*: The Beginnings of the Historical Novel', *Classical Antiquity*, 6, 184–204; repr. in Swain 1999a, 137–60.

—— and Utas, B. 2003, *The Virgin and Her Lover: Fragments of an Ancient Greek Novel and a Persian Epic Poem* (Leiden).

Harland, P. A. 2007, '"These People Are . . . Men Eaters": Banquets of the Anti-Associations and Perceptions of Minority Cultural Groups', in Z. A. Crook and P. A. Harland (eds.), *Identity and Interaction in the Ancient Mediterranean: Jews, Christians and Others. Essays in Honour of Stephen G. Wilson* (Sheffield), 56–75.

Harrison, S. 2007, 'Parallel Cults? Religion and Narrative in Apuleius' *Metamorphoses* and Some Greek Novels', in Paschalis *et al.* 2007, 204–18.

Henrichs, A. 1968, 'Achilleus Tatios, Aus Buch III (P. Colon. inv. 901)', *ZPE* 2, 211–26.

—— 1970, 'Lollianos und P.Oxy. 1368', *ZPE* 6, 42–3.

—— 1972, *Die Phoinikika des Lollianos* (Bonn).

—— 2006, 'Der antike Roman. Kerényi und die Folgen', in R. Schlesier and R. S. Martínez (eds.), *Neuhumanismus und Anthropologie des griechischen Mythos: Karl Kerényi im europäischen Kontext des 20. Jahrhunderts* (Locarno), 57–70.

—— 2010, 'Fractured Communications: Narrators, Narratives and Discourse in Greek Novels on Papyrus', in Bastianini and Casanova 2010, 65–80.

Holzberg, N. 2001, *Der antike Roman: Eine Einführung* (Düsseldorf and Zurich).

—— 2003, 'The Genre: Novels Proper and the Fringe', in Schmeling 2003, 11–28.

Hunter, R. 1994, 'History and Historicity in the Romance of Chariton', *ANRW* II 34. 2 (Berlin and New York), 1055–86.

—— 2010, 'Rhythmical Language and Poetic Citation in Greek Narrative Texts', in Bastianini and Casanova 2010, 223–43.

Jensson, G. 2004, *The Recollections of Encolpius: The Satyrica of Petronius as Milesian Fiction* (Groningen).

Jones, C. 1980, 'Apuleius' *Metamorphoses* and Lollianus' *Phoinikika*', *Phoenix*, 34, 243–54.

Kussl, R. 1991, *Papyrusfragmente griechischer Romane: Ausgewählte Untersuchungen* (Tübingen).

Lenaerts, J. 1974, 'Fragment de parchemin du *Lucius ou l'Âne*: P. Lit. Lond. 194', *CdÉ* 49, 115–20.

Lesky, A. 1963, *Geschichte der griechischen Literatur*, 2nd edn. (Bern).

López Martínez, M. P. 1998, *Fragmentos papiráceos de novela griega* (Alicante).

Lucke, C. 1985, 'Zum Charitontext auf Papyrus', *ZPE* 58, 21–33.

Maehler, H. 1976, 'Der Metiochos-Parthenope-Roman', *ZPE* 23, 1–20.

Mason, H. J. 1994, 'Greek and Latin Versions of the Ass-Story', in *ANRW* II 34. 2 (Berlin and New York), 1665–707.

Messeri, G. 2010, 'I papiri di narrativa dal 1893 ad oggi', in Bastianini and Casanova 2010, 3–22.

Morgan, J. R. 1998, 'On the Fringes of the Canon: Work on the Fragments of Ancient Greek Fiction 1936–1994', in *ANRW* II 34. 4 (Berlin and New York), 3293–390.

—— 2004, *Longus, Daphnis and Chloe, Translated with an Introduction and Commentary* (Oxford).

Parsons, P. J., and Rea, J. R. (eds.) 1989, *The Oxyrhynchus Papyri*, LVI (Oxford).

—— 2010, 'Panionis and the Culture of Culture (P.Oxy. LXXI 4881)', in Bastianini and Casanova 2010, 43–9.

Paschalis, M., Frangoulidis, S., Harrison, S. and Zimmerman, M. (eds.) 2007, *The Greek and the Roman Novel: Parallel Readings* (Groningen).

Pecere, O. and Stramaglia, A. (eds.), 1996, *La letteratura di consumo nel mondo greco-latino* (Cassino).

Perry. B. E, 1967, *The Ancient Romances: A Literary-Historical Account of their Origins* (Berkeley).

Plepelits, K. 2003, 'Achilles Tatius', in Schmeling 2003, 387–416.

Poethke, G. 2002, 'Der Achilleus-Tatios-Papyrus P. Schubart 30 identifiziert', *APF* 48, 1–5.

Reardon, B. P. 2003, 'Chariton', in Schmeling 2003, 309–35.

—— 2006, 'The Ancient Novel at the Time of Perry', in S. N. Byrne, E. P. Cueva, and J. Alvares (eds.), *Authors, Authority, and Interpreters in the Ancient Novel: Essays in Honor of Gareth L. Schmeling* (Groningen), 227–38.

Reeve, M. 2008, 'The Re-Emergence of Ancient Novels in Western Europe, 1300–1810', in Whitmarsh 2008, 282–98.

Rohde, E. 1914, *Der griechische Roman und seine Vorläufer*, 3rd edn. (Leipzig).

Ruiz-Montero, C. 2003, 'The Rise of the Greek Novel', in Schmeling 2003, 29–85.

Schmeling, G. (ed.) 2003, *The Novel in the Ancient World*, rev. edn. (Leiden and Boston).

Schmid, W., and Stählin, O. 1924, *Geschichte der griechischen Literatur*, ii. 2 (Handbuch der Altertumswissenschaft 7.2.2; Munich).

Schubart, W. 1950, 'Griechische literarische Papyri', *Berichte über die Verhandlungen der Sächsischen Akademie der Wissenschaften zu Leipzig*, Phil.-hist. Klasse 97/5 (Berlin).

Stephens, S. 2003, 'Fragments of Lost Novels', in Schmeling 2003, 655–83.

—— and Winkler, J. J. 1995, *Ancient Greek Novels: The Fragments* (Princeton).

Stramaglia, A. 1996, 'Fra "consumo" e "impegno": usi didattici della narrativa nel mondo antico', in Pecere and Stramaglia 1996, 99–166.

—— 2010, 'Le *Metamorfosi* di Apuleio tra iconografia e papiri', in Bastianini and Casanova 2010, 165–92.

Sullivan, J. P. 1968, *The 'Satyricon' of Petronius: A Literary Study* (London).

Swain, S. (ed.) 1999*a*, *Oxford Readings in the Greek Novel* (Oxford).

—— 1999*b*, 'A Century and More of the Greek Novel', in Swain 1999*a*, 3–35.

Thiel, H. van, 1971, *Der Eselsroman, Teil I: Untersuchungen* (Munich).

Tilg, S. 2010, *Chariton of Aphrodisias and the Invention of the Greek Love Novel* (Oxford and New York).

Turner, E. G., rev. Parsons, P. J. 1987, *Greek Manuscripts of the Ancient World*, 2nd edn. (*BICS* Suppl. 46, London).

Vogliano, A. 1938, 'Un papiro di Achille Tazio', *SIFC* 15, 121–30.

Wehrli, C. 1970, 'Un fragment du roman de Ninos', *ZPE* 6, 39–41.

Weinreich, O. 1962, *Der griechische Liebesroman* (Zurich).

West, M. L. 1973, *Textual Criticism and Editorial Technique* (Stuttgart).

Whitmarsh, T. 2005, 'The Greek Novel: Titles and Genre', *AJP* 126, 587–611.

—— (ed.) 2008, *The Cambridge Companion to the Greek and Roman Novel* (Cambridge).

Wilamowitz-Moellendorff, U. von, 1901, review of Grenfell, Hunt, and Hogart 1900, *GGA* 163, 30–45.

Wilcken, U. 1893, 'Ein neuer griechischer Roman', *Hermes*, 28, 161–93.

—— 1901, 'Eine neue Romanhandschrift', *APF* 1, 227–72.

Willis, W. H. 1990, 'The Robinson–Cologne Papyrus of Achilles Tatius', *GRBS* 31, 73–102.

Winkler, J. 1980, 'Lollianos and the Desperadoes', *JHS* 100, 155–81.

Zanetto, G. 2010, 'P.Oxy. LXX 4762 e il *Romanzo dell'Asino*', in Bastianini and Casanova 2010, 51–63.

Zeitlin, F. 2008, 'Religion', in Whitmarsh 2008, 91–108.

Zimmermann, F. 1936, *Griechische Roman-Papyri und verwandte Texte* (Heidelberg).

# Bibliography of Peter Parsons

## Books

*The Oxyrhynchus Papyri* XLII (London, 1973).

*Supplementum Hellenisticum* (Berlin and New York, 1983) (with Hugh Lloyd-Jones).

E. G. Turner, *Greek Manuscripts of the Ancient World*, revised and expanded edn. (London, 1987).

*City of the Sharp-Nosed Fish* (London, 2007); translated as: *Dějiny ukryté v písku* [History Hidden in the Sand] (Prague, 2008); *ΟΞΥΡΥΓΧΟΣ Η Πόλη που ἔφερε το ὄνομα ενός ψαριού* (Athens, 2008); *Die Stadt des scharfnasen Fisches* (Munich, 2009); *La Cité du poisson au nez pointu* (Paris, 2009); *La ciudad del pez elefante* (Barcelona, 2009).

## Contributions to *The Oxyrhynchus Papyri*

### XXXI (1966)

2555, 2557  Horoscopes.

2558  Edict of Clodius Culcianus.

2559  Letter of Arrius Eudaemon.

2563  Petition to Epistrategus.

2567  Registration of Druggist's Stock.

2568  Acknowledgement for Return of Boat.

2572–6  Orders to Arrest.

2577  Order from Strategus.

2580  Account of Pitch.

2582  Sale of Slave.

2583  Division of Inherited Property.

2585  Lease of Fallow Land.

2586  Contract of Apprenticeship.

2588–91  Sitologus Documents.

2592  Invitation.

2593  Letter of Apollonia.

2594  Letter of Remonstrance.

2595  Letter of Horigenes.

2601  Letter of Copres.

2602  Letter of Agathos.

## XXXIII (1968)

2662  Plato, *Meno.*
2663  Plato, *Cratylus.*
2664  Proclamation of Rationalis and Procurator.
2669  Report of Anachoresis.
2670  Shipper's Receipt.
2671  Census Return.
2672  Petition of Aphynchis.
2676  Lease of Land.
2677  Formula of Deposit.
2679  Letter from Onesimus.
2682  Letter from Ammonis.

## XXXIV (1968)

2683  Gospel of Matthew.
2684  Epistle of Jude.
2720  Sale of House.
2723  Sale of Vineyard.
2725  Letter of Adrastus.
2730  Letter of Horion.
2731  Letter of Maximus.

## XLII  (1973)

2999  Hesiod, *Eoiai* or *Megalai Eoiai.*
3000  Eratosthenes, *Hermes.*
3001  Homeric Verses.
3002  Ethopoea.
3003  Homeric Narratives.
3004  Gnomology.
3005  Gnomology.
3006  Gnomology.
3007  Ethical Questions.
3008  Prose about Dualism.
3009  *Epistula Philippi* (Dem. xviii 221).
3010  Narrative about Iolaus.
3011  Narrative about Amenophis.
3012  Romance (Antonius Diogenes?).
3013  Argument of a *Tereus*?
3014  Gnomon of the Idios Logos.
3015  Extracts from Court Records.
3016  Judicial Proceedings.
3017  Edict of Prefect.
3018  Privileges of Paeanistae.

3019  Decision of Severus.
3020  Letter of Augustus and Proceedings of Embassy.
3021  *Acta Alexandrinorum.*
3022  Letter of Trajan to Alexandria.
3023  Proceedings before an Emperor.
3024  Letter of Prefect.
3025  Letter of Epistrategus.
3026  Official Correspondence.
3027  Official Letter.
3028  Official Correspondence.
3029  Letter to Strategi.
3030  Official Letter of Royal Scribe.
3031  Official Letter of *Procurator Alexandreae.*
3032  Publication of Official Letters.
3033  Petition to Prefect.
3034  Sworn Declaration.
3035  Order to Arrest.
3036–45  Receipts for *Epikephalaion.*
3046  Return of Uninundated and Artificially Irrigated Land.
3047  Declaration of Uninundated and Artificially Irrigated Land.
3048  Proclamation of Iuridicus and Registration of Corn.
3049  Deposit of Grain.
3050  Proclamation and Official Letters.
3051  Receipt for Arrears of Rent.
3052  Itinerary.
3053  Registration of Sale of Slave.
3054  Registration of Sale of Slave.
3055–6  Orders to Supply.
3057  Letter of Ammonius to Apollonius.
3058  Letter of Flavius to Morus.
3059  Letter of Didyme to Apollonius.
3060  Letter of Ptolemaeus to Horis.
3061  Letter of Heraclas to Archelaus.
3062  Letter of Sarapion to Archelaus.
3063  Letter of Diogenes to Apollogenes.
3064  Letter of Theagenes and Panechotes.
3065  Letter of Arius to Agrippina and Cornelius.
3066  Letter of Apollonius to Sarapammon.
3067  Letter of Achillion to Hieracapollon.
3068  Note about Amulet.
3069  Letter of Aquila to Sarapion.
3070  Indecent Proposal.
3071  Edict of Prefect.
3072  Day-book of Strategus.
3073  Day-book of Strategus.
3074  Day-book of Strategus.
3075  Formulary for Opening of Will.

3076  Petition to Ti. Claudius Herennianus.
3077  Census Return.
3078  Oracle Question.
3079  List of Ships.
3080  Order for Supplies.
3081  Account of Jars.
3082  Letter of Agathus to Phanias.
3083  Letter of Aur. Sarapiacus to Dioscorus.
3084  Letter of Heraclius to Themistocles.
3085  Letter of Hermias to Sarapion.
3086  Letter of Nemesianus to Colluthus.
3087  Letter of Pataris to Nunechium.

## XLIX (1982)

3454  List of Prosodiai.

## L (1983)

3522  LXX Job.
3525  Gospel of Mary.
3529  Passion of St Dioscorus.
3530  Euripides, *Aegeus? Theseus?*
3537  Hexameter Verse: Ethopoea and Encomium.
3545–9, 3551 Theocritus.

## LII (1984)

3656  Philosophical Biography.
3680–2  Plato, *Theaetetus.*

## LIV (1987)

3723  Elegy (with J. M. Bremer).
3724  List of Epigrams.
3725–6  Epigrams.

## LVI (1989)

3831  Homer Oracle.
3836–7  Achilles Tatius.
3840  Aristophanes, *Thesmophoriazusae.*
3851  Nicander.

## LIX (1992)

3965  Simonides, *Elegies.*

## LX (1994)

4018–19  Menander, *Dyscolos.*
4020–3  Menander, *Epitrepontes*: Hypothesis (with E. G. Turner).
4024  Menander, *Leucadia*?
4025  Menander, *Misoumenos*?
4026  Menander(?), *Progamon.*

## LXII (1995)

4302  New Comedy (with C. F. L. Austin and E. W. Handley).
4303  New Comedy, ?Menander (with P. G. McC. Brown).

## LXIV (1997)

4412  New Comedy (with P. G. McC. Brown).
4424  Apollonius Rhodius (with M. Richter).
4426  Commentary on Aratus, *Phaenomena* (with R. Dilcher).
4427  Callimachus, *Aetia* III (with M. Richter).
4429  Lycophron, *Alexandra* (with K. Bühler).

## LXVI (1999)

4501  Epigram (Nicarchus II?).
4502  Epigrams (Nicarchus II?).

## LXVIII (2003)

4643  Menander, *Hymnis*? (with C. F. L. Austin).
4644  Comedy (or Satyr Play?) (with C. F. L. Austin).
4657  Hesiod, *Theogonia.*
4669  Writing exercise.
4670  Notice.
4671  Tabula Ansata.

## LXX (2006)

4760  Antonius Diogenes.
4761  Novel (Antonius Diogenes?).

## LXXI (2007)

4808  On Hellenistic Historians (with A. G. Beresford and M. P. Pobjoy).
4809  On Hellenistic Monarchs.
4811  Novel ('*Panionis*').

## Articles

'Return of Sheep and Goats', 'Greek Supplement to Demotic Deed of Sale', *Corpus Papyrorum Judaicarum*, iii (Cambridge, MA, 1964), 57–61; 'Application to Strategus', ibid. 79–81; 'Letter from Cosmas', ibid. 94–5.
'Philippus Arabs and Egypt', *JRS* 57 (1967), 134–41.
'A Proclamation of Vaballathus?', *CdE* 42 (1967), 397–401.
'*ΧΑΡΤΑΡΙΑ*', *PP* 121 (1968), 1–4.
'Three Documents from Trinity College, Dublin', *CdE* 44 (1969), 313–24.
'New Readings', *BASP* 6 (1969), 44.
'M. Aurelius Zeno Januarius', in D. Samuel (ed.), *Proceedings of the Twelfth International Congress of Papyrology, Ann Arbor, Michigan, 12–17 August 1968* (Toronto, 1970), 389–97.
'A School-Book from the Sayce Collection', *ZPE* 6 (1970), 133–49.
'The Wells of Hibis', *JEA* 57 (1971), 165–80.
'A Greek Satyricon?', *BICS* 18 (1971), 53–68 with plate VII.
'Ulpius Serenianus', *CdE* 49 (1974), 135–57.
'Papyrology in the United Kingdom', *Stud. Pap.* 15 (1976), 95–102.
'Petitions and a Letter: The Grammarian's Complaint', in A. E. Hanson (ed.), *Collectanea Papyrologica: Texts Published in Honor of H. C. Youtie* (Bonn, 1976), 409–46.
'The Oyster', *ZPE* 24 (1977), 1–12.
'Callimachus: Victoria Berenices', *ZPE* 25 (1977), 1–50.
'The Lille "Stesichorus"', *ZPE* 26 (1977), 7–36.
(with H. Lloyd-Jones) 'Iterum de "Catabasi Orphica"', *Kyklos: Griechisches und. Byzantinisches, Rudolf Keydell zum neunzigsten Geburtstag* (Berlin and New York, 1978), 88–100.
'The Burial of Philip II?', *AJAH* 4 (1979), 97–101.
(with R. D. Anderson and R. G. M. Nisbet) 'Elegiacs by Gallus from Qaṣr Ibrîm', *JRS* 69 (1979), 125–55.
'The Earliest Christian Letter?', *Misc. Pap.* (1980), 289.
'Latin Papyri', in A. C. de la Mare and B. C. Barker–Benfield (eds.), *Manuscripts at Oxford: An Exhibition in Memory of Richard William Hunt* (Oxford, 1980), 2–8.
'Background: The Papyrus Letter', *Didactica classica Gandensia*, 20 (1980), 3–19.
(with I. H. M. Hendriks and K. A. Worp) 'Papyri from the Groningen Collection I: Encomium Alexandreae', *ZPE* 41 (1981), 71–83.
(with P. J. Sijpesteijn and K. A. Worp) 'Hesiod, Catalogue', *Papyri: Greek and Egyptian, Edited by Various Hands in Honour of Eric Gardner Turner on the Occasion of his Seventieth Birthday* (London, 1981), 1–20.
'Facts from Fragments', *G&R* 29 (1982), 184–95.

'Latin Letter', *Festschrift zum 100jährigen Bestehen der Papyrussammlung der Österreichischen Nationalbibliothek, Papyrus Erzherzog Rainer* (Vienna, 1983), 483–9.

(with R. G. M. Nisbet and G. O. Hutchinson) 'Alcestis in Barcelona', *ZPE* 52 (1983), 31–6.

'Recent Papyrus Finds: Greek Poetry', *Actes du VII<sup>e</sup> Congrès de la Fédération Internationale des Études Classiques, 1979* (Budapest, 1984), ii. 517–31.

'Eine neugefundene griechische Liebeselegie', *MH* 45 (1988), 65–74.

'Papyrology: Future Perspectives', *Bulletin of the Council of University Classical Departments*, 18 (1989), 43–6.

'The Scripts and their Date' in E. Tov, *The Greek Minor Prophets Scroll from Nahal Hever: 8 Hev XII gr* (Oxford, 1990), 19–26.

(with O. Murray *et al.*) 'A "Stork–Vase" from Mola di Monte Gelato', *PBSR* 59 (1991), 177–95.

'The Palaeography and Date of the Greek Manuscripts', in P. W. Skehan *et al.*, *Qumran Cave 4.IV, Palaeo–Hebrew and Greek Biblical Manuscripts* (Oxford, 1992), 7–13.

'Poesia ellenistica: testi e contesti', *Aevum* 5 (1992), 9–19.

'Identities in Diversity', in A. W. Bulloch *et al.* (eds.), *Images and Ideologies: Self-Definition in the Hellenistic World* (Berkeley, Los Angeles, and London, 1993), 152–70.

'Die Kahlköpfe', in A. Griffiths and F. Carey, *German Printmaking in the Age of Goethe* (London, 1994), 97.

'Summing Up', in A. Bülow-Jacobsen (ed.), *Proceedings of the XX International Congress of Papyrologists (Copenhagen: 23–29 August, 1992)* (Copenhagen, 1994), 118–23.

'ΦΙΛΕΛΛΗΝ', *MH* 53 (1996), 106–15.

'Callimachus (3)', 'Forgeries, Literary 1. Greek', 'Libraries', 'Lobon', 'Simonides', 'Stesichorus', 'Stichometry', 'Xanthus (1)' in *OCD*.

'These Fragments We Have Shored against Our Ruin', in D. Boedeker and D. Sider (eds.), *The New Simonides* (Baltimore, 2001), 55–64.

'Rhetorical Handbook', in T. Gagos and R. S. Bagnall (eds.), *Essays and Texts in Honor of J. David Thomas* (Oakville, CT, 2001), 153–66.

'Callimachus and the Hellenistic Epigram', in F. Montanari and L. Lehnus (eds.), *Callimaque. Entretiens sur l'Antiquité classique XLVIII* (Vandœuvres-Geneva, 2002), 99–136 (and 137–41).

'New Texts and Old Theories', in T. P. Wiseman (ed.), *Classics in Progress: Essays on Ancient Greece and Rome* (Oxford, 2002), 39–57.

'Copyists of Oxyrhynchus', in A. K. Bowman, R. A. Coles, N. Gonis, D. Obbink, and P. J. Parsons (eds.), *Oxyrhynchus: A City and its Texts* (Egypt Exploration Society; London, 2007), 262–70.

'Homeric Glossary', in A. J. B. Sirks and K. A. Worp assisted by R. S. Bagnall and R. P. Salomons (eds.), *Studies in Memory of Piet Sijpesteijn = American Studies in Papyrology*, 40 (2007) 4–9.

'P. Artemid.: A Papyrologist's View', in K. Brodersen and J. Elsner (eds.), *Images and Texts on the Artemidorus Papyrus* (Historia Einzelschriften, 214; Stuttgart, 2009), 31–7.

'P.Köln XI 431: A Further Note', *ZPE* 171 (2009), 15–16.

'The Artemidorus Papyrus in Papyrological Context', in C. Gallazzi, B. Kramer, S. Settis with A. Soldati (eds.), *Intorno al Papiro di Artemidoro*, I. *Contesto culturale, lingua, stile e tradizione: atti del colloquio del 15 novembre, 2008* (Milan, 2009), 19–28.

'*Panionis* and the Culture of Culture (P.Oxy. 4811*)*', in G. Bastianini and A. Casanova (eds.), *I papiri del romanzo greco* (Florence, 2010), 43–9.

'Callimachus and his Koinai', in S. A. Stephens and B. Acosta–Hughes (eds.), *The Brill Companion to Callimachus* (2011) (forthcoming).

# Reviews

J. IJsewijn, *De sacerdotibus sacerdotiisque Alexandri Magni et Lagidarum eponymis* (Brussels, 1961), in *JHS* 84 (1964), 187–8.

P. Sattler, *Studien aus dem Gebiet der alten Geschichte* (Wiesbaden, 1962), in *CR²* 13 (1963), 324–5.

G. Arrighetti (ed.), *Satiro:* Vita di Euripide (Pisa, 1964), in *CR²* 16 (1966), 179–80.

B. R. Rees, *Papyri from Hermopolis and other Documents of the Byzantine Period* (London, 1964), in *JHS* 86 (1966), 218–19.

I. Cazzaniga et al., *Papiri della Università degli Studi di Milano* (P. Mil. Vogliano), III (Milano/Varese, 1965), in *Gnomon* 38 (1966), 672–5.

E. G. Turner, *Greek Papyri. An Introduction* (Oxford, 1968), in *AntJ* 49 (1969), 150–1.

J. W. B. Barns and H. Zilliacus (eds.), *The Antinoopolis Papyri. Part III* (London, 1967), in *CR²* 20 (1970), 86–7.

G. Cavallo, *Ricerche sulla maiuscola biblica* (Florence, 1967), in *Gnomon*, 42 (1970), 375–80.

E. Boswinkel and P. J. Sijpesteijn, *Greek Papyri, Ostraca and Mummy Labels* (Amsterdam, 1968), in *Gnomon*, 42 (1970), 733–4.

E. Kiessling, *Wörterbuch der griechischen Papyrusurkunden, mit Einschluß der griechischen Inschriften, Aufschriften, Ostraka, Mumienschilder usw. aus Ägypten. Supplement 1 (1940–1966), 1. Lieferung; 2. Lieferung* (Amsterdam, 1969), in *Gnomon*, 43 (1971), 407–8.

*Atti dell'XI Congresso Internazionale di Papirologia. Milano, 2–8 settembre 1965* (Milan, 1966), in *JEA* 57 (1971), 231–2.

*Studien zur Papyrologie und antiken Wirtschaftsgeschichte Friedrich Oertel zum achtzigsten Geburtstag gewidmet* (Bonn, 1964), in *JEA* 57 (1971), 232–3.

R. A. Coles, *Reports of Proceedings in Papyri* (Brussels, 1966), T. Reekmans, *La.sitométrie dans les Archives de Zénon* (Brussels, 1966); P. Vidal–Naquet, *Le Bordereau d'ensemencement dans l'Égypte ptolémaïque* (Brussels, 1967); G. Poethke, *Epimerismos: Betrachtungen zur Zwangspacht in Ägypten während der Prinzipatszeit* (Brussels, 1969); and J. Schwartz, *Papyri variae Alexandrinae et Gissenses* (Brussels, 1969), in *JEA* 57 (1971), 233–4.

S. Sauneron, *Le Papyrus magique illustré de Brooklyn* (New York, 1970), in *CR²* 23 (1973), 96–7.

B. E. Donovan, *Euripides Papyri I: Texts from Oxyrhynchus* (New Haven and Toronto, 1969), in *JEA* 59 (1973), 271–2.

G. M. Browne, *Documentary Papyri from the Michigan Collection* (Michigan Papyri, Volume X), (Toronto, 1970), in *JEA* 59 (1973), 272.

D. Samuel (ed.), *Proceedings of the Twelfth International Congress of Papyrology, Ann Arbor, Michigan, 12–17 August 1968* (Toronto, 1970), in *JEA* 59 (1973), 272–3.

A. E. Samuel, W. K. Hastings, A. K. Bowman, and R. S. Bagnall, *Death and Taxes: Ostraka in the Royal Ontario Museum* I (Toronto, 1971), in *JEA* 59 (1973), 273–4.

E. Husselman, *Papyri from Karanis: 3rd Series* (Cleveland, OH, 1971), in *CR²* 24 (1974), 147–8.

E. Kiessling, *Wörterbuch der griechischen Papyrusurkunden, mit Einschluß der griechischen Inschriften, Aufschriften, Ostraka, Mumienschilder usw. aus Ägypten, IV. Band, 4. Lieferung* (Marburg, 1971), in *Gnomon*, 46 (1974), 85.

I. M. Hamdi, Ἡ ἑλληνορωμαϊκὴ παιδεία ἐν Αἰγύπτῳ ἀπὸ τοῦ Α΄ ἕως τοῦ Δ΄ αἰῶνος κατὰ τοὺς παπύρους (Athens, 1972), in *JEA* 61 (1975), 301.

O. Montevecchi, *La papirologia* (Torino, 1973), in *JEA* 62 (1976), 200–1.

A. Blanchard, *Sigles et abréviations dans les papyrus documentaires grecs* (London, 1974), in *JHS* 96 (1976), 265–6.

G. Foti Talamanca, *Ricerche sul processo nell'Egitto greco–romano. I. L'organizzazione del 'conventus' del 'praefectus Aegypti'* (Milan, 1974), and *II. L'introduzione del giudizio* (Milan, 1979), in *JRS* 70 (1980), 236–7.

G. Mastromarco, *Il pubblico di Eronda* (Padua, 1979), in *CR²* 31 (1981), 110.

E. Boswinkel, P. W. Pestman, and H.-A. Rupprecht, *Berichtigungsliste der griechischen Papyrusurkunden aus Ägypten, sechster Band* (Leiden, 1976), in *CR²* 31 (1981), 145.

'Old Flames', review of J. N. Adams, *The Latin Sexual Vocabulary* (London, 1982); *Ovid: The Erotic Poems*, tr. P. Green (Harmondsworth, 1982); M. Lefkowitz with M. Fant, *Women's Life in Greece and Rome* (Baltimore, MD, 1982); and M. Lefkowitz, *Heroines and Hysterics* (London, 1981), in *London Review of Books*, 5/1 (20 January 1983), 15.

C. H. Roberts, *Manuscript, Society and Belief in Early Christian Egypt* (London, 1979) and C. H. Roberts and T. C. Skeat, *The Birth of the Codex* (London, 1983), in *JRS* 74 (1984), 254–5.

'Roman Wall Blues', review of A. K. Bowman and J. D. Thomas, *Vindolanda: The Latin Writing-Tablets* (London, 1984); R. Wilken, *The Christians as the Romans Saw them* (New Haven, CT, 1984); W. Meeks, *The First Urban Christians: The Social World of the Apostle Paul* (New Haven, CT, 1983); and N. Lewis, *Life in Egypt under Roman Rule* (Oxford, 1983), in *London Review of Books*, 6/9 (17 May 1984), 10–11.

G. M. Parássoglou, *The Archive of Aurelius Sakaon: Papers of an Egyptian Farmer in the Last Century of Theadelphia* (Bonn, 1978), in *JEA* 71 (1985), 209–10.

R. S. Bagnall, *The Florida Ostraka (O. Florida), Documents from the Roman Army in Upper Egypt* (Durham, NC, 1976), in *JEA* 71 (1985), 210–11.

R. S. Bagnall, G. M. Browne, A. E. Hanson, and L. Koenen (eds.), *Proceedings of the Sixteenth International Congress of Papyrology, New York, 24–31 July, 1980* (Chico, CA, 1981), in *JEA* 71 (1985), [Reviews Supplement] 64.

J. A. L. Lee, *A Lexical Study of the Septuagint Version of the Pentateuch* (Chico, CA, 1983), in *CR²* 36 (1986), 326–7.

G. Tibiletti, *Le lettere private nei papiri greci del III e IV secolo d.C. Tra paganesimo e cristianesimo* (Milan, 1979), in *CR²* 36 (1986), 353–4.

H. D. Betz (ed.), *The Greek Magical Papyri in Translation: including the demotic spells. Volume One: Texts* (Chicago, 1986), in *Times Literary Supplement*, no. 1295 (21 November 1986), 1316.

C. H. Roberts and T. C. Skeat, *The Birth of the Codex* (London, 1983), in *CR*² 37 (1987), 82–4.

G. Grimm, H. Heinen, and E. Winter (eds.), *Das römisch–byzantinische Ägypten. Akten des internationalen Symposions 26.–30. September, 1978 in Trier* (Mainz am Rhein, 1983), in *CR*² 37 (1987), 85–7.

G. Cavallo, *Libri, scritture, scribi a Ercolano* (Napoli, 1983), in *CR*² 39 (1989), 358–60.

'Learned Pursuits', review of L. Holford–Strevens, *Aulus Gellius* (London, 1988) in *London Review of Books*, 11/7 (30 March 1989), 22–3.

'Writing it down', review of R. Thomas, *Oral Tradition and Written Record in Classical Athens* (Cambridge, 1989), in *London Review of Books*, 11/16 (31 August 1989), 6.

'Book ends', review of L. Canfora, *The Vanished Library*, tr. M. Ryle (London, 1989), in *Times Literary Supplement*, no. 4536 (9 March 1990), 249.

'Paper play', review of T. Harrison, *The Trackers of Oxyrhynchus* (London, 1990), in *Times Literary Supplement*, no. 4540 (6 April 1990), 374.

'How do Babylonians Boil Eggs?', review of S. Stephens and J. Winkler (eds.), *Ancient Greek Novels: The Fragments* (Princeton, 1995), in *London Review of Books*, 18/8 (18 April 1996), 23–4.

'Allusions in Alexandria: Trying to Piece Together Theocritus' Urban Poetry', review of J. B. Burton, *Theocritus's Urban Mimes* (Berkeley, 1955), and R. Hunter, *Theocritus and the Archaeology of Greek Poetry* (Cambridge, 1996), in *Times Literary Supplement*, no. 4892 (3 January 1997), 13.

'Eels Tomorrow, but Sprats Today', review of J. Davidson, *Courtesans and Fishcakes: The Consuming Passions of Classical Athens* (London, 1997), in *London Review of Books*, 19/18 (18 September 1997), 6–7.

'Valete Romani!', review of S. Young, *Farewell Britannia: A Family Saga of Roman Britain* (London, 2007), in *Literary Review*, no. 344 (June 2007), 36–7.

'Pay Attention', review of A. Harker, *Loyalty and Dissidence in Roman Egypt: The Case of the Acta Alexandrinorum* (Cambridge, 2008), in *Times Literary Supplement*, no. 5537 (15 May 2009), 10.

# Memorials

'Stefan Weinstock' in *Gnomon*, 46 (1974), 217–20 (biographical memoir).

(with E. G. Turner), 'Herbert Chayyim Youtie' (obituary), *APF* 28 (1982), 99–100.

'Sir Eric Turner' (obituary), *JEA* 70 (1984), 128–9.

'Eric Gardner Turner' (obituary), *S&C* 9 (1985), 337–40.

'Eric Gardner Turner' (biographical memoir), *Proceedings of the British Academy*, 73 (1987), 685–704.

(with D. A. F. M. Russell), 'Colin Henderson Roberts (1909–1990),' (biographical memoir), *PBA* 84 (1993), 479–83.

'Professor Colin Austin', *The Times* (14 September 2010).

'Hugh Lloyd-Jones', *Christ Church 2009* (Oxford 2010), 98–100.

## Occasional pieces

'Cornelius Gallus', *London Review of Books*, 2/2 (7 February 1980), 9–10.
'Antigone in Middle Age', *London Review of Books*, 3/15 (21 August–3 September 1980), 13–14.
'The Oldest Roman Book Ever Found', *Omnibus*, 1 (1981), 1–4.
'Papyri and Greek Literature', *Bulletin of the Council of University Classical Departments*, 10 (1981), 7–8.
'*Quid minutius hypostigma*', Oratio Bodleiana, 1981.
'Ancient Greek Romances', *London Review of Books*, 3/15 (20 August–2 September 1981), 13–14.
'First Catch Your Text: Latin Manuscripts Old and New', *Omnibus*, 7 (March 1984), 21–3.
'Oxyrhynchus: Waste-Paper City', *Omnibus*, 19 (March 1990), 1–4.
'500 Years of Greek Teaching', *Oxford Magazine* (Trinity Term, Week 4, 1992), 5–8.
'A Wealth of Garbage: 100 Years of Tracking the Buried Treasures of Oxyrhynchus', *Times Literary Supplement*, no. 4965 (29 May 1998), 3–4.
'One Foot in the Quad', *Christ Church Matters*, 11 (Trinity Term 2003), 5.
'The Study of Ancient Tongues: Gaisford and Liddell', in C. Butler (ed.), *Christ Church, Oxford: A Portrait of the House* (London, 2006), 104–6.
'Forging Ahead: Has Simonides Struck Again?', *Times Literary Supplement*, no. 5473 (22 February 2008), 14

# Index Nominum et Rerum*

* This index is selective. References in the main text have been listed more fully than those in footnotes, authors more often than mythical or historical characters in their works. For the most part the names of modern scholars are not included unless there is direct quotation or some discussion of their views (this rule has been somewhat relaxed in the case of the honorand). For ancient authors, see also the Index locorum potiorum.

# Index Locorum Potiorum